Harnessing Business Intelligence for Modern Talent Management

Lambrini Seremeti
Agricultural University of Athens, Greece

Panagiotis Liargovas
University of Peloponnese, Greece

Christos Papademetriou
Neapolis University, Pafos, Cyprus

Lazaros Anastasiados
University of Crete, Greece

Sofia Anastasiadou
Univeristy of Western Macedonia, Greece

IGI Global
Scientific Publishing
Publishing Tomorrow's Research Today

Vice President of Editorial	Melissa Wagner
Director of Acquisitions	Mikaela Felty
Director of Book Development	Jocelynn Hessler
Production Manager	Mike Brehm
Cover Design	Jose Rosado

Published in the United States of America by
IGI Global Scientific Publishing
701 East Chocolate Avenue
Hershey, PA, 17033, USA
Tel: 717-533-8845
Fax: 717-533-7115
Website: https://www.igi-global.com E-mail: cust@igi-global.com

Library of Congress Cataloging-in-Publication Data

Names: Seremeti, Lamprini, 1974- editor
Title: Harnessing business intelligence for modern talent management / [edited by] Lamprini Seremeti, Panagiotis Liargovas, Christos Papademetriou, Lazaros Anastasiadis, Sofia Anastasiadou.
Description: Hershey, PA : IGI Global Scientific Publishing, [2025] | Includes bibliographical references and index. | Summary: "This book aims to explain the ethics and Business Intelligence, Business Intelligence tools and technologies, Challenges and risks in BI, Foundations of BI and Business Intelligence Approach to HRM"-- Provided by publisher.
Identifiers: LCCN 2025011220 (print) | LCCN 2025011221 (ebook) | ISBN 9798337319421 hardback | ISBN 9798337319438 paperback | ISBN 9798337319445 ebook
Subjects: LCSH: Business intelligence--Moral and ethical aspects | Human capital--Moral and ethical aspects | Personnel management--Moral and ethical aspects
Classification: LCC HD38.7 .H367 2025 (print) | LCC HD38.7 (ebook) | DDC 658.4/72--dc23/eng/20250604
LC record available at https://lccn.loc.gov/2025011220
LC ebook record available at https://lccn.loc.gov/2025011221

British Cataloguing in Publication Data
A Cataloguing in Publication record for this book is available from the British Library.

Table of Contents

Detailed Table of Contents

In an age where data flows more freely than ever before, the ability to translate information into actionable insight has become a defining feature of organizational success. Nowhere is this truer than in the realm of talent management. This chapter explores the growing intersection between business intelligence (BI) and modern talent practices, offering a foundational introduction to how BI can transform how organizations attract, develop, retain, and optimize their human capital. More than just a technical overview, this chapter makes the case for why BI is no longer a luxury but a necessity in navigating the complexity of today's workforce landscape. It introduces key tools and approaches—ranging from dashboards to predictive modeling—while examining their practical applications across the talent lifecycle. By the end, readers will understand that integrating BI into talent management is not just a technological upgrade—it's a cultural transformation with the potential to redefine the future of work.

The primary purpose of this study is to investigate the influence of Human Resource Practices on Talent Management. In other words, this chapter focuses on highlighting whether there is a connection between the characteristics of Talent Management and the HRM practices of employee evaluation. A systematic literature review was conducted based on journals, articles, conference proceedings, and formal reports retrieved from the most known scientific databases such as, Elsevier Scopus, Web of Science, and Google Scholar. The findings of this literature review revealed several key findings regarding to the Talent Management practices and employee evaluation. Among other, this chapter revealed that Talent management is not only related to the simple recruitment and selection processes. It includes a holistic approach that involves development, retention, and evaluation planning. This framework

tools, technologies, and methodologies that constitute modern BI systems. With a focus on practical application and strategic alignment, it examines how BI empowers organizations to make faster, smarter, and more agile decisions—particularly in the evolving domain of talent management. From understanding the architecture of BI platforms to appreciating the nuances of data modeling, visualization, and predictive analytics, the chapter offers a comprehensive guide to both the technical and methodological underpinnings of BI. By bridging theory with application, the chapter encourages a critical understanding of how organizations can move beyond data accumulation toward true business intelligence—insight that is timely, actionable, and strategically meaningful.

The convergence of business intelligence (BI) and Human Resource Management (HRM) has initiated more efficient, data-driven, and strategic talent management procedures. The current paper proposes the application of a BI strategy combined with stacked artificial neural networks (ANN) for simplifying HRM procedures like recruitment, employee performance appraisal, and attrition prediction. Applying data from a top recruitment agency for the period 2023-2024, we utilized BI tools for preprocessing data, feature selection by Particle Swarm Optimization (PSO), and the use of stacked ANN to predictive analysis. The pattern discovery property of the model allows for smarter decision-making in recruitment, retention, and workforce planning. This research shows how the use of technology and sophisticated data analysis can make HRM a more proactive and effective function that is supportive of an organization's strategic objectives.

Driven by the consistent and positive economic growth trend, there is a corresponding increase in social power consumption. Ensuring a stable grid structure is crucial to guaranteeing reliable power supply. To meet these demands, the task of power grid construction grows annually, accompanied by an increasing scale of investment. However, the macroeconomic environment poses challenges, as substantial investments can burden power grid companies, particularly in terms of economic viability. Developing a scientifically sound approach to predicting and distributing investment scales is crucial to avoid inefficient and ineffective investments. This planning is essential for power supply companies to optimize their investment strategies and allocate construction funds efficiently. This chapter employs data mining techniques to propose a new model for forecasting power grid investment demand. This validates the effectiveness, applicability, and superiority of the proposed approach in forecasting power grid investment demand, offering a valuable new method for the industry.

This chapter explores the role of Business Intelligence (BI) in enhancing gender equity and work-life balance within data-driven workplaces. By reviewing existing research, the chapter examines how BI tools can monitor gender representation, track turnover rates, identify biases in recruitment processes, and tailor work-life balance policies to meet the specific needs of male and female employees. It highlights the importance of leveraging data-driven insights to foster inclusivity and enhance gender equity in organizations. This work provides actionable recommendations for integrating BI tools into talent management strategies to create more equitable and adaptable workplaces.

The present study explores the area of Smart Human Resource Management (Smart HRM) through the support of Business Intelligence (BI) and deep learning to achieve workforce excellence. Considering telecom businesses for the year 2024, the study utilized a dataset that was collected from 268 workers with the purpose of examining how data-driven information can help HR practices. The architecture involved pre-processing of gathered data, feature selection using Ant Colony Optimization (ACO), and using an improved ResNet-181 deep learning method. The combination of methods facilitated identification of key workforce trends and performance metrics. Using BI tools, the system equips HR practitioners with actionable information, which filters down eventually into strategic choices and organizational growth. The study highlights the inceptive potential of Smart HRM with the employment of BI and AI for the purpose of rebuilding talent management, as well as talent development..

In today's evolving business landscape, success depends not only on quantitative metrics but also on the nuanced, subjective experiences of the workforce. Organizations face the dual challenge of navigating data-driven competitive markets while creating settings where human capital can thrive. Traditional business intelligence (BI) provides powerful, quantifiable insights into business performance, market trends and financial well-being, while talent management emphasizes holistic employee development and well-being by capturing the qualitative, subjective dimensions of work - often described as qualia. This chapter explores a holistic approach that merges these areas, resulting in a framework for promoting organizational success, enhancing employee engagement, and fostering a humane yet performance-focused work culture.

In the era of digital transformation, Human Resource Management (HRM) must evolve beyond traditional practices to stay competitive. This chapter explores how Business Intelligence (BI) revolutionizes HRM by enabling data-driven decision-making for talent acquisition, workforce planning, and employee engagement. By leveraging BI tools, HR professionals can analyze workforce trends, predict future skill gaps, and optimize talent strategies for organizational success. The chapter delves into BI's role in enhancing employee performance, reducing attrition, and fostering a data-driven HR culture. Real-world case studies and industry best practices illustrate the tangible impact of BI in HRM. This chapter provides HR leaders, researchers, and practitioners with actionable insights to harness BI for workforce excellence and sustainable competitive advantage.

This chapter explores the transformative effects of technological innovations, focusing on metaverse consumption patterns, marketing strategies, and societal interactions through a McLuhanian lens. The metaverse, a digital realm integrating physical and virtual elements, alters how consumers experience and engage with brands, leading to novel marketing strategies that overcome the traditional limits of space and time. Utilizing immersive and interactive platforms, companies are pioneering methods to connect with audiences more profoundly and expand their market reach. It provides empirical data and theoretical perspectives on how the metaverse influences contemporary marketing, emphasizing the need for businesses to adapt to a future that seamlessly integrates physical and digital experiences. Additionally, it critically examines the sociocultural, ethical, and regulatory challenges posed by these advancements, calling for a comprehensive understanding of their implications for society

The chapter explores how tourism informatics creates future-focused changes in the tourism and hospitality sector. Tourism informatics uses AI, big data analytics, IoT, and blockchain technology to drive intelligent choices, personalized tourism experiences, and sustainable procedures. Technology integration between these components produces operational improvements that produce innovative marketing approaches and improved customer engagement and service delivery capabilities. Tourism informatics requires attention to privacy protection, ethical norms, and maintaining secure data management systems, according to the chapter. Secondary research conducted through literature studies presents the possible obstacles and benefits that will emerge from implementing future projects while stressing the requirement for public sector partnerships with businesses and technology suppliers. Tourism informatics adoption creates possibilities for an efficient and sustainable industry that strongly focuses on customers.

This chapter underscores the transformative role of business intelligence (BI) in shaping international trade. Through a systematic literature review, 24 documents were identified revealing ten key thematic clusters which illustrate how AI, big data, supply chain analytics, and blockchain are redefining global trade operations, decision-making processes, and competitive strategies. The findings reveal the potential of business intelligence to change international trade and stress the need for continuous innovation, regulatory adaptation, and strategic implementation of digital technologies. Addressing these research gaps is imperative for scholars and practitioners to contribute to the development of more resilient, efficient, and competitive global trade ecosystems. This, in turn, will foster stronger international economic relations and ensure the integration of new technologies into the future of global trade.

In today's rapidly evolving digital landscape, the convergence of advanced technology and strategic human capital management is not merely advantageous—it is essential. As organizations increasingly leverage business intelligence (BI) to drive decisions, a transformative paradigm is emerging that harnesses the inherent features of digital products to redefine talent management. This chapter examines how digital principles—such as indestructibility, transformability, and reproducibility—can fundamentally reshape human resource management. Beyond a mere aggregation of skills, the modern workforce embodies a dynamic, data-driven entity. By embedding these digital attributes into the core of talent management strategies, organizations transition from reactive administration to proactive empowerment, turning data into the catalyst for profound personal and professional transformation.

Preface

In a world increasingly defined by data, the strategic integration of business intelligence (BI) into talent management has become not only advantageous but essential. Organizations across industries face the dual challenge of adapting to rapid technological evolution while also meeting the evolving expectations of their workforce. It is within this intersection of transformation that BI emerges as a powerful tool—bridging data insights with human potential. This book, *Harnessing Business Intelligence for Modern Talent Management*, responds to this urgent need by showcasing how data-driven practices can revolutionize the ways organizations attract, develop, retain, and engage talent.

As editors, we recognized the growing demand for research that does not treat BI and human resource management as siloed domains but rather as deeply interconnected disciplines. Our aim in curating this volume was to present a holistic view of how BI can inform, refine, and elevate talent strategies. The chapters span foundational theory, real-world applications, emerging technologies, and forward-looking perspectives—offering readers a multifaceted understanding of the subject. From real-time analytics in employee engagement to the predictive modeling of workforce trends, the contributions herein underscore the transformational potential of intelligent systems when applied with strategic intent.

The diversity of contributors—from academics and data scientists to HR practitioners and engineers—enriches the discourse with both depth and breadth. We are particularly proud of the global perspective this book brings, reflecting case studies and insights from Europe, Asia, and the Middle East. The result is a comprehensive, cross-disciplinary reference work that we hope will inspire, inform, and empower decision-makers in academia, industry, and public policy alike to harness the full potential of BI in shaping the future of work.

CHAPTER OVERVIEW

Chapter 1: Introduction to Business Intelligence in Talent Management

Mustafa Kayyali

This chapter introduces the pivotal role of business intelligence (BI) in reshaping talent management in contemporary organizations. It explores how BI tools—from dashboards to predictive analytics—can enhance processes such as recruitment, development, and retention. By emphasizing BI's strategic importance, the chapter positions it as a catalyst for organizational agility and a driver of cultural transformation in managing human capital.

Chapter 2: Talent Management & Human Resource Practices

Angelos Ntalakos, Mary Viterouli, Dimitrios Belias, Ioannis Rossidis

Through a systematic literature review, this chapter explores the interplay between HR practices and talent management strategies. It argues for a holistic approach that extends beyond recruitment to include development and evaluation. The findings underscore the strategic value of human capital in sustaining organizational competitiveness.

Chapter 3: Enhancing Employee Engagement with Real-Time Data Insights

Christos Papademetriou

This chapter examines the role of real-time data analytics in fostering employee engagement. Drawing on academic research and practical case studies, it illustrates how immediate, data-driven feedback mechanisms can enhance performance management and retention strategies. The chapter also addresses challenges in integrating such technologies within HR frameworks.

Chapter 4: Harnessing the Power of Business Intelligence in Workforce Development

Usharani Bhimavarapu

Leveraging advanced AI models like CNN and LSTM, this chapter demonstrates how BI can forecast workforce trends and inform talent strategies. It outlines methods for processing both structured and unstructured employee data to guide hiring, development, and retention. The chapter presents a framework for aligning BI with organizational goals in workforce optimization.

Chapter 5: Foundations of Business Intelligence: Tools, Technologies, and Methodologies

Mustafa Kayyali

Focusing on the technical and strategic dimensions of BI, this chapter presents an in-depth overview of core tools and methodologies underpinning modern BI systems. Topics include BI architecture, data modeling, visualization, and analytics. The discussion highlights BI's potential to support agile, informed decision-making, particularly in dynamic fields such as talent management.

Chapter 6: Enhancing Employee Engagement through Data-Driven HR Practices

Usharani Bhimavarapu

This chapter presents a data-driven model for HRM using stacked artificial neural networks and Particle Swarm Optimization (PSO). Using real-world recruitment data, it illustrates how predictive analytics can improve hiring decisions, performance appraisal, and retention planning. The research highlights the strategic impact of BI on HR efficiency and alignment.

Chapter 7: Investment Project Management in Power Grid Infrastructure Construction Using ML Algorithms

R Renugadevi, Durga Devi A, Annie Isabella L

Addressing the growing demand for efficient investment in power grid infrastructure, this chapter applies machine learning and data mining to forecast investment needs. It proposes a novel model for optimizing investment decisions and avoiding resource misallocation, offering a data-centric approach to project portfolio management in the energy sector.

Chapter 8: Leveraging Business Intelligence for Gender Inclusivity and Talent Equity in Data-Driven Workplaces

Mary Viterouli, Dimitrios Belias, Athanasios Koustelios, Nikolaos Tsigilis

This chapter investigates how BI can support gender equity and inclusivity in the workplace. It explores the use of data analytics to detect bias, monitor representation, and inform equitable HR policies. The chapter proposes actionable strategies for integrating BI into inclusive talent management frameworks.

Chapter 9: Smart HRM: Unlocking Business Intelligence for Employee Performance in Telecom

Usharani Bhimavarapu

Using deep learning techniques such as Ant Colony Optimization and ResNet-181, this chapter explores how BI can revolutionize HR practices in the telecom sector. Based on performance data from 268 employees, it demonstrates how BI supports strategic HR decisions and enhances organizational performance.

Chapter 10: Qualia and Business Intelligence for Organizational Excellence

Lambrini Seremeti, Lazaros Anastasiadis, Charis Kalogera, Spiros Kontis

This chapter bridges quantitative BI insights with qualitative employee experiences—termed "qualia"—to promote organizational excellence. It proposes a hybrid model that integrates emotional, cultural, and subjective aspects into BI frameworks, advocating for a more human-centered approach to talent and performance management.

Chapter 11: Smart HRM: Unleashing the Power of Business Intelligence for Workforce Excellence

Priya Kadyan, Rohan Singh

This chapter highlights how BI transforms HRM by enabling predictive talent management, reducing attrition, and improving performance. Through case studies and best practices, it outlines how organizations can create data-driven HR cultures that support strategic workforce planning and long-term competitiveness.

Chapter 12: Navigating Metaverse in Shaping the Future of Business

Menaka Ramaswamy, Kartheeswari T K, Neela Madheswari A, Kavitha M, Sudha E, Maya D

Exploring the business implications of the metaverse, this chapter analyzes its impact on marketing strategies, consumer engagement, and organizational identity. It adopts a McLuhanian lens to examine how immersive technologies redefine the boundaries between physical and digital business environments, while also addressing ethical and regulatory concerns.

Chapter 13: Tourism Informatics Management: Bridging Data, Technology, and Experience

Mohammad Talukder, Dil Swarna, Mohammad Afchar

This chapter discusses how tourism informatics—powered by AI, IoT, blockchain, and big data—reshapes the tourism and hospitality industry. It advocates for data-driven, personalized, and sustainable tourism experiences, while highlighting implementation challenges such as privacy and ethics.

Chapter 14: International Trade and Business Intelligence: A Systematic Literature Review and Research Agenda

Georgios Deirmentzoglou, Eleni Anastasopoulou, George Sklias

Through a systematic review, this chapter identifies emerging themes in the use of BI in global trade. It reveals how technologies like AI and blockchain enhance trade efficiency and decision-making, and proposes a research agenda for addressing gaps in digital strategy, regulatory frameworks, and competitiveness.

Chapter 15: The Digital DNA of Modern Workforce

Charis Kalogera, Lambrini Seremeti, Spiros Kontis, Sofia Anastasiadou

This chapter explores the intersection of business intelligence, digital competencies, and human capital strategy. It examines how organizations can decode and leverage the "digital DNA" of their workforce to drive innovation, agility, and sustained performance in an increasingly digital economy.

Chapter 16: The Role of Business Intelligence in Shaping Workforce Strategy

Christos Papademetriou, Sofia Anastasiadou, Dimitrios Belias

This chapter analyzes the strategic role of business intelligence (BI) in modern workforce planning amid rapid technological and organizational shifts. It details how BI tools—ranging from predictive modeling to real-time analytics—empower HR professionals to enhance recruitment, engagement, and productivity. While showcasing BI's potential to align workforce strategies with organizational goals, the chapter also addresses key challenges such as data privacy, legacy system integration, and the need for upskilling in HR analytics. Emphasizing ethical AI and agile decision-making, it argues that BI-driven strategies are vital for building resilient and inclusive organizations.

Chapter 17: Talent Analytics for Workforce Forecasting, Fostering Employee Engagement, and Turnover Prediction

K Sanjay, Shweta Khalsa

This chapter investigates the application of AI-powered talent analytics in predicting workforce trends, enhancing employee engagement, and mitigating turnover. Drawing on a comprehensive literature review, it explores techniques such as natural language processing, sentiment analysis, and predictive modeling to inform data-driven HR strategies. The chapter illustrates how AI enables personalized career development and proactive retention planning while also raising critical ethical concerns around bias, transparency, and data privacy. It concludes by outlining emerging trends, including hyper-personalization and virtual HR assistants, and underscores the importance of integrating talent analytics with broader BI frameworks for long-term strategic alignment.

Chapter 18: Bridging Business Intelligence, Knowledge Management, and Strategic HRM: Navigating Talent in Modern Workplaces

Gulshan Bibi, OP Jindal Global University, India

This chapter explores the convergence of strategic human resource management (SHRM), business intelligence (BI), and knowledge management (KM) in shaping a talent-centric approach for contemporary organizations. Arguing that traditional HR practices are often overly generic and detached from external realities, the chapter emphasizes the need for adaptive, context-aware strategies that harness data and knowledge for informed decision-making. It presents an integrative conceptual framework comprising eight actionable steps to guide organizations in embedding BI and KM into HR processes. By aligning these domains, the chapter offers fresh insights into optimizing talent value and advancing the broader talent management discourse in dynamic workplace environments.

The journey through the chapters of this book begins with a conceptual and technical introduction to BI in talent management and progresses toward highly specialized applications, including artificial intelligence, gender inclusivity, power infrastructure investment, and even metaverse-enabled work environments. This progression reflects not only the technological expansion of BI but also its cultural, ethical, and organizational dimensions. Together, the chapters demonstrate that effective talent management is no longer a static HR function—it is a dynamic, data-informed strategy that is central to organizational resilience and innovation.

We believe this book will serve as both a foundational resource and a forward-looking guide. For researchers, it offers conceptual frameworks and emerging research agendas. For practitioners, it provides case studies, methodologies, and practical tools that can be adapted to diverse organizational contexts. For educators, it represents a rich repository of material to stimulate inquiry, debate, and curriculum development. Across all audiences, we hope the insights presented here will deepen understanding and accelerate the responsible adoption of BI in managing human capital.

Finally, we would like to express our sincere gratitude to the authors whose expertise, dedication, and creativity have shaped this volume. Their work reflects a shared commitment to advancing the discourse around digital transformation and human potential. As we look ahead to the evolving future of work, we remain confident that the integration of business intelligence into talent management will not only enhance organizational outcomes but also contribute to more equitable, engaged, and empowered workforces. It is our hope that this book will serve as a catalyst for that vision.

Lamprini Seremeti
Panagiotis Liargovas
Christos Papademetriou
Lazaros Anastasiadis
Sofia Anastasiadou

Chapter 1
Introduction to Business Intelligence in Talent Management

Mustafa Kayyali
https://orcid.org/0000-0003-3300-262X
Maaref University of Applied Sciences, Syria

ABSTRACT

In an age where data flows more freely than ever before, the ability to translate information into actionable insight has become a defining feature of organizational success. Nowhere is this truer than in the realm of talent management. This chapter explores the growing intersection between business intelligence (BI) and modern talent practices, offering a foundational introduction to how BI can transform how organizations attract, develop, retain, and optimize their human capital. More than just a technical overview, this chapter makes the case for why BI is no longer a luxury but a necessity in navigating the complexity of today's workforce landscape. It introduces key tools and approaches—ranging from dashboards to predictive modeling—while examining their practical applications across the talent lifecycle. By the end, readers will understand that integrating BI into talent management is not just a technological upgrade—it's a cultural transformation with the potential to redefine the future of work.

INTRODUCTION

There was a time when decisions about people in the workplace were largely based on instinct. A manager might hire someone because they "seemed like a good fit," or promote an employee based on gut feelings about leadership potential.

DOI: 10.4018/979-8-3373-1942-1.ch001

Appraisals were often subjective, recruitment processes relied heavily on résumé screening and interviews, and workforce planning was based on historical trends or, at times, hopeful guesswork. For decades, this approach was accepted—perhaps even celebrated—as a mark of managerial wisdom and human judgment. But in today's world, instinct is no longer enough.

Organizations now operate in an environment of rapid change, where agility, foresight, and precision are no longer optional—they are essential. Talent shortages in critical roles, rising employee expectations, increased competition for skilled professionals, and a heightened emphasis on diversity, equity, and inclusion have all converged to reshape the terrain of talent management. In this new reality, making decisions based on intuition alone is not just insufficient—it is risky. This is where Business Intelligence (BI) enters the conversation—not as a technological trend, but as a necessary evolution in how we understand, support, and lead our people (Skyrius, 2021). At its core, BI is about transforming raw data into meaningful insight. It is about asking better questions, seeing patterns where others see noise, and guiding human judgment with evidence. And when applied to talent management, it becomes a powerful lens through which organizations can anticipate needs, personalize development, improve retention, and ensure that the right people are in the right roles at the right time.

This chapter begins with a simple premise: talent is one of the most strategic assets an organization has, and how it is managed can make the difference between stagnation and success. But managing talent well requires more than processes and policies. It requires insight—insight into what motivates people, where performance gaps lie, what skills will be needed in the future, and how different parts of the workforce are experiencing the organization. Business intelligence offers the tools to uncover these insights, but it also demands a mindset shift: from reactive to proactive, from anecdotal to analytical, and from episodic decision-making to continuous improvement. Importantly, BI in talent management is not only about technology. It is about culture. Implementing a dashboard or running a predictive model will accomplish little if the organization is not prepared to act on the insights it generates. The success of BI depends as much on trust, collaboration, and leadership as it does on algorithms or platforms (Ibrahim et al, 2025). It requires HR professionals to become more data-literate, and data professionals to understand the nuances of human behavior. It requires breaking down silos between departments, aligning talent strategies with broader business goals, and ensuring that data is used ethically and responsibly.

In this chapter, we will explore how BI is being integrated into different areas of talent management—from recruitment and onboarding to development, engagement, and succession planning. We will examine the tools and techniques that are making a difference, while also acknowledging the challenges: data quality, privacy concerns, resistance to change, and the temptation to over-rely on metrics without understanding the human stories they represent. We will also reflect on the role of predictive analytics—how organizations are beginning to forecast turnover, identify high-potential employees, and even assess team dynamics using data. These capabilities are exciting, but they are not without controversy. What happens when an algorithm says someone is "likely" to leave? What does it mean to measure leadership potential through behavioral data? How do we avoid reinforcing existing biases under the guise of objectivity? These are not peripheral questions. They go to the heart of what it means to be a data-driven organization that values both performance and people. Business intelligence, if used well, can help us make fairer, faster, and more informed decisions. But if used poorly—or uncritically—it can become just another mechanism of control, exclusion, or inefficiency.

This chapter does not offer easy answers. Instead, it invites reflection, dialogue, and intentional practice. It asks HR leaders, data analysts, and executives to think carefully about what kind of workforce they want to build, and how data can be a guide—not a master—in that journey. It argues that the real power of BI lies not in its ability to automate decisions, but in its capacity to illuminate the conditions under which human potential can flourish. As we move deeper into the digital age, the organizations that will thrive are those that treat data not just as a commodity, but as a conversation—one that helps them see their people more clearly, more compassionately, and more strategically. Business intelligence in talent management is not about replacing intuition—it is about enriching it, challenging it, and making it more accountable to reality. It is, at its best, a bridge between analysis and empathy, between what is and what could be.

Setting the Stage: Why Talent Management Needs Business Intelligence

In every organization—whether a tech start-up, a healthcare provider, a multinational conglomerate, or a public institution—there is a quiet but foundational truth: nothing gets done without people. Technologies evolve, markets shift, business models change, but at the core of every breakthrough, every failure, every act of resilience or innovation, is human talent (Müller & Shamsie, 2023). This isn't a sentimental observation—it's a strategic one. Talent is not just a resource among many; it is the beating heart of organizational vitality. And how that talent is managed—how it is identified, nurtured, supported, and retained—can determine not only an organization's success, but its survival. Yet despite its central importance, talent management remains one of the most complex and under-leveraged functions in many organizations. It is easy to talk about "people being our greatest asset," but much harder to act accordingly. Traditional HR practices, while well-intentioned, have often struggled to keep pace with the speed and scale of change (George, 2024). Performance reviews are inconsistent. Hiring processes are subjective. Workforce planning is reactive. Leadership development is uneven. And when problems arise—high turnover, skill shortages, disengagement—they are often addressed with generic solutions rather than informed, targeted action.

The challenge is not simply that the tools are outdated. It's that many organizations are still trying to solve 21st-century problems with 20th-century logic. We are living in an age of complexity—where demographic shifts, remote work, cultural transformation, and rapid technological advances are rewriting the rules of engagement between employers and employees. Navigating this terrain demands more than intuition. It demands insight. It demands clarity. It demands the ability to see not only what is happening now, but what might happen next—and to make decisions based on that understanding. This is where Business Intelligence (BI) enters the frame—not as a buzzword or a bolt-on, but as a fundamentally different way of approaching the work of managing people. BI offers the potential to move from opinion to evidence, from fragmented data to integrated insight, from reactive HR to predictive, strategic talent leadership (Al-Shammari et al, 2024). But perhaps most importantly, it offers the possibility of seeing people not just as cost centers or performance metrics, but as dynamic, complex individuals whose potential can be revealed and realized through thoughtful use of information.

To understand why BI is so urgently needed in talent management today, we have to begin by acknowledging the scale and scope of the data that already surrounds us. Every application, every performance review, every exit interview, every pulse survey, every training session generates data. Add to that data from collaboration platforms, internal communications, productivity tools, engagement systems, and public sources like LinkedIn or Glassdoor—and the sheer volume becomes staggering. And yet, in many organizations, this data sits unused, scattered across systems, locked in reports that no one reads or trusts. The problem is not a lack of information. It is a lack of usable insight. And that is precisely what BI is designed to address.

Business Intelligence is not just about gathering data—it is about transforming it into actionable understanding (Eboigbe et al, 2023). It involves integrating data from multiple sources, cleaning and organizing it, applying analytical techniques to uncover patterns, and presenting the findings in ways that are accessible and relevant to decision-makers. In the context of talent management, this means being able to answer questions like:

- Where are we losing people, and why?
- Which teams are showing signs of disengagement?
- What skills will we need in the next five years, and how prepared are we?
- Which leadership development programs are actually driving results?

- What are the early warning signs of burnout, and how can we intervene?

These are not hypothetical questions. They are the real, daily concerns of HR leaders, team managers, and executives who are trying to navigate a volatile and competitive environment. And in a world where the cost of a bad hire, the loss of a key performer, or a failure to anticipate skill gaps can be enormous, the ability to answer these questions with confidence is a serious competitive advantage. Of course, some might argue that people are too nuanced to be reduced to data points—and they would be right. People are not spreadsheets. Talent cannot be fully captured in metrics. But that does not mean we should ignore the signals data provides. On the contrary, when used thoughtfully, BI allows us to ask better questions, challenge our assumptions, and make more informed, more just, and more effective decisions.

For example, consider bias in hiring. Numerous studies have shown that traditional recruitment processes are riddled with unconscious bias—from how résumés are screened to how interviews are conducted (Witzany, 2024). BI can help surface these patterns, highlighting disparities in candidate shortlisting or interview evaluations. It can prompt organizations to revisit criteria, train managers more effectively, and track progress over time. It cannot eliminate bias on its own—but it can shine a light where it might otherwise go unnoticed. Or take employee engagement. Annual surveys have long been the standard tool, but they are static, infrequent, and often disconnected from what's happening on the ground. BI allows for continuous listening—analyzing sentiment in real time, identifying hotspots of disengagement, and enabling targeted interventions. It can help HR teams move from being firefighters to architects—designing cultures and systems that are proactive rather than merely responsive.

But BI is not just about problems. It's also about potential. In talent development, BI can help identify high-potential employees based not just on manager nominations (which are often subjective), but on data about performance trends, learning agility, collaboration, and feedback. It can support personalized learning journeys—matching individuals with content, mentors, or stretch assignments based on where they are and where they want to go. It can help answer the question every employee wants to know: "What's next for me here?"

Strategically, BI enables workforce planning that is not guesswork, but grounded in evidence. It allows HR to speak the language of the business—showing not just headcount numbers, but workforce capabilities, risk scenarios, and future-readiness. It helps organizations align their talent strategies with their business goals, and to pivot quickly when those goals change. And let's be honest—they will change. The volatility of today's business environment—from pandemics to geopolitical shocks to technological disruption—means that agility is no longer optional. The organizations that will thrive are those that can adapt quickly, not just structurally, but culturally and behaviorally (Jerab & Mabrouk, 2023). That kind of adaptability depends on people—on the right people, in the right roles, with the right support. And getting that right requires more than instinct. But it also requires something more than data: it requires trust. One of the biggest obstacles to effective BI in talent management is not technical—it is cultural. Employees may fear being reduced to numbers. Managers may distrust the conclusions drawn from data they don't understand. HR teams may feel unequipped to interpret dashboards, or unsure how to translate insights into action. These are real concerns, and they must be addressed.

Trust is built through transparency—being clear about what data is collected, how it is used, and who has access (Wiencierz & Luenich, 2022). It is built through participation—inviting employees into the process, using data to empower rather than surveil. And it is built through dialogue—ensuring that data never replaces conversation, but rather informs it. As we look ahead, the case for Business Intelligence in talent management is not just about efficiency. It is about equity, strategy, and sustainability. It is about ensuring that organizations are not only data-rich but insight-rich. That they do not only collect information but use it to become better stewards of human potential. In many ways, this is the beginning of a new era for HR—not one defined by administration, but by anticipation. Not one focused on compliance, but on capability. Not one that follows the business, but one that helps lead it. Business Intelligence is not a magic solution, and it is not without its risks. But when approached with care, curiosity, and a commitment to people, it can become one of the most powerful tools we have for building workplaces that are not only high-performing, but human.

Understanding Business Intelligence: Tools, Concepts, and Capabilities

To understand the growing role of business intelligence in talent management, we need to begin with a clear picture of what business intelligence (BI) actually is—and, just as importantly, what it is not. In recent years, the term has been used so broadly, and at times so vaguely, that it risks losing its meaning altogether. Some hear "BI" and think only of software; others equate it with advanced analytics or assume it refers to anything involving a dashboard or a graph. But business intelligence is more than a toolset. It is a way of thinking—about information, about decision-making, and about how we see and act upon the realities within our organizations. At its most essential level, business intelligence is the practice of collecting, integrating, analyzing, and presenting data to support better decisions (Niu et al, 2021). It is not the data itself, but the system by which data becomes insight—and ultimately, action. BI does not replace human judgment, but it strengthens it. It does not remove uncertainty, but it helps us reduce blind spots. And when implemented thoughtfully, BI enables organizations to move from operating reactively to leading proactively.

This process, however, is not automatic. Nor is it just a matter of acquiring new software or hiring a few analysts. BI is an ecosystem—made up of concepts, tools, capabilities, and cultural shifts that all need to work in concert. Let's start with the concepts. At the heart of BI is the idea that data becomes valuable only when it is turned into knowledge. In most organizations, there is no shortage of data (Adewusi et al, 2024). What's missing is integration. Data lives in silos—recruitment systems, learning management platforms, payroll records, exit interviews, engagement surveys—each holding a piece of the puzzle but rarely communicating with the others. BI begins by bringing these pieces together, allowing organizations to ask and answer more complex questions. For example, are people who attend onboarding workshops more likely to stay beyond one year? Do promotion rates differ across departments or demographic groups? How does training completion correlate with performance?

These are not questions that any one dataset can answer alone. BI works by weaving disparate data into coherent stories. It involves not only quantitative analysis but also contextual understanding (Quenum, 2024). Knowing that 18% of new hires leave within six months is a statistic. Knowing why they leave, and what patterns predict it, is intelligence. BI helps us move from what to why—and from there, to what's next. The technical tools that support BI have grown increasingly sophisticated, but they remain just that—tools. Platforms like Power BI, Tableau, Qlik, and Looker allow users to visualize trends, compare variables, and build interactive dashboards (Ajax et al, 2025). They make data accessible not just to analysts, but to managers, HR professionals, and executives. And yet, the effectiveness of these tools depends on how they're used. A dashboard is only as good as the questions it helps answer. A report is only meaningful if someone understands it—and is empowered to act on it. The real promise of BI lies not in technology alone, but in the capabilities it unlocks. Among these, three stand out as particularly critical for talent management.

First is descriptive analytics: the ability to understand what has happened. This is where many organizations begin their BI journey—tracking headcount, turnover rates, time-to-fill, training hours, performance ratings. These indicators are valuable, especially when viewed over time or broken down by team, function, or location. They help establish baselines and monitor changes. But descriptive analytics, while necessary, are not sufficient. They describe the past. To shape the future, we need to go further. This leads us to diagnostic analytics: understanding why things happen. For example, if engagement scores dropped last quarter, was it tied to organizational change? If a new learning platform has high usage but low impact, what's driving the disconnect? Diagnostic analytics require not just data, but inquiry. They involve comparing groups, identifying correlations, and digging into context. Often, the answers are not in the numbers alone—they emerge from combining data with qualitative insights, such as employee interviews or manager feedback.

Third is predictive analytics: using data to anticipate what may happen next. This is where BI begins to show its transformative potential. By identifying patterns and applying statistical models, organizations can forecast attrition risks, spot high-potential employees early, or estimate future skill shortages. For instance, a model might show that employees with certain tenure, in specific roles, who haven't received recent development opportunities, are at higher risk of leaving. With that insight, HR can design targeted interventions—coaching, career pathing, recognition—that could improve retention and performance (Ayanponle et al, 2024). Of course, prediction is not prophecy. No algorithm can foresee every human decision. But predictive analytics give us a more informed starting point. They help shift our posture from reaction to preparation.

And beyond prediction lies prescriptive analytics: the most advanced (and still emerging) frontier of BI. This involves not only identifying potential outcomes, but suggesting possible actions. For example, based on performance data and organizational needs, a system might recommend ideal internal candidates for a leadership program. Or it might suggest a sequence of learning modules to close a skills gap identified through role benchmarking. Prescriptive analytics move us from insight to recommendation—but they also raise important questions about autonomy, transparency, and trust. These capabilities are exciting, but they must be approached with care. Because at the center of all BI in talent management is a paradox: we are trying to bring clarity to something inherently complex—human behavior. No model can capture the entirety of someone's motivation, creativity, potential, or lived experience. And while data can illuminate patterns, it can also obscure nuance if treated uncritically.

This is why the human side of BI is just as important as the technical side. For business intelligence to work in talent management, organizations need more than tools—they need people who can ask the right questions, interpret results ethically, and translate insights into action. They need HR professionals who are data-literate, curious, and collaborative. They need leaders who understand that data should inform decisions, not dictate them. And they need cultures that embrace learning, iteration, and accountability. They also need to confront some hard truths. For example, BI may reveal patterns of inequity—gender gaps in promotions, racial disparities in performance ratings, geographic imbalances in access to development. These findings can be uncomfortable. But they are also powerful levers for change—if organizations are willing to act on them. BI doesn't create fairness, but it can shine a light on where fairness is lacking. And that, in itself, is an invitation to lead differently.

Moreover, implementing BI is not a one-time event. It's an ongoing journey (Borking et al, 2022). It requires investment—in technology, yes, but also in training, governance, and change management. It requires iteration—refining models, updating dashboards, revisiting assumptions. It requires communication—making sure that insights are not confined to reports, but shared in ways that spark dialogue and drive strategy. And it requires humility—recognizing that the data is never perfect, that people are more than the sum of their metrics, and that insight is only valuable when it is used wisely. In the end, understanding business intelligence is not just about understanding systems. It's about understanding ourselves—our biases, our blind spots, our appetite for truth. It's about building organizations where knowledge flows freely, where decisions are transparent, and where data is not a weapon, but a mirror. It's about using information not to control people, but to support them. To help them grow, thrive, and contribute to something meaningful. This is the promise of BI in talent management—not dashboards or models for their own sake, but a more honest, more thoughtful, and more strategic way of leading people. Not replacing human judgment, but enhancing it. Not turning people into numbers, but turning numbers into understanding. And in a world that is moving faster, expecting more, and changing all the time, that kind of understanding is not a luxury. It's a necessity.

Data-Driven Decision-Making in Talent Acquisition and Development

Recruiting and developing talent has never been simple. For all the frameworks, job descriptions, and competency models organizations have created over the years, identifying the right person for the right role at the right time remains one of the most complex—and consequential—decisions a business can make. It's also deeply human. It involves potential, chemistry, culture, growth. And yet, the way many organizations have traditionally approached talent acquisition and development has often been surprisingly imprecise, relying on gut instincts, surface-level indicators, and habits passed down over time. That's changing. Slowly, unevenly, and not without resistance—but changing nonetheless. As the business world grows more competitive, more fast-paced, and more unpredictable, organizations are recognizing that better people decisions require better information. Not just more information, but clearer, more connected, more meaningful insights. This is where data-driven decision-making becomes not just helpful, but necessary—not as a replacement for human intuition, but as its companion and its challenger.

When we speak of data in the context of talent acquisition and development, we're not talking about just numbers (Pala, 2024). We're talking about stories, about patterns, about relationships that are often hidden beneath the surface of resumes, performance reviews, and learning records. We're talking about the ability to look across time and teams, across hires and high-potentials, across gaps and goals—and to see, with greater clarity, what's working and what's not. In the realm of talent acquisition, the power of data begins long before a candidate enters the interview room. It begins with understanding the organization's needs—not just the role that's open, but the business strategy it supports, the team it fits into, the culture it must align with or challenge. It means analyzing past hiring outcomes: which roles are hardest to fill, which channels yield the best candidates, which interviewers are most accurate in their assessments, and where bias may be distorting decisions.

Too often, organizations treat recruitment as a race—post the job, scan the resumes, fill the seat. But a data-driven approach slows the process down at the right moments. It asks: what does success in this role actually look like, based on those who've held it before? Are we casting the net wide enough—or only looking in familiar places? What language in the job description might be discouraging qualified candidates from applying? Which selection methods have the strongest correlation with long-term performance? This kind of questioning doesn't eliminate the need for human judgment—it enhances it. It gives recruiters and hiring managers a richer frame of reference. It makes space for reflection. It helps spot red flags before they become regrets, and it reveals overlooked strengths that might not show up in traditional ways. But to do this well, organizations must first build the infrastructure—both technical and cultural—to support it. That means integrating data across applicant tracking systems, assessment tools, interview feedback, and onboarding experiences. It means training recruiters to interpret and act on data, not just collect it. And it means having the discipline to measure outcomes over time—not just whether a role was filled quickly, but whether the hire stayed, thrived, and contributed.

One of the more promising developments in recent years has been the use of predictive analytics in recruitment. By analyzing historical hiring and performance data, organizations can begin to identify the traits and experiences most associated with success in specific roles. This doesn't mean creating rigid formulas, but rather developing more informed profiles that guide rather than dictate decisions. For example, if data shows that candidates who've worked in customer-facing roles tend to excel in internal consulting jobs—even if they lack traditional qualifications—that insight can expand the talent pool and challenge conventional wisdom. But with this power comes responsibility. Predictive models are only as good as the data they're built on—and if that data reflects historical bias, the model will too. That's why transparency, fairness audits, and ongoing evaluation are critical. Data must not only inform decisions but be questioned in turn. Equity and inclusion cannot be afterthoughts in a data-driven system—they must be built into its very design.

Moving from hiring to development, the role of data becomes no less essential—though often more subtle (Duggan et al, 2020). Development is inherently long-term, non-linear, and deeply personal. It's about growth, readiness, learning, identity. And while no spreadsheet can capture a person's journey, data can illuminate paths that would otherwise remain invisible. Take, for example, identifying high-potential employees. In many organizations, this is still done based on nominations, reputation, or visibility—factors that often favor the loudest voices or the most familiar faces. But with a more data-driven approach, organizations can layer in additional perspectives: learning agility, peer feedback, project performance, engagement levels. They can look for consistency over time, adaptability across roles, and evidence of influence beyond authority. They can also identify people whose strengths may have gone unnoticed—those who don't self-promote, but who quietly drive results and support others.

Learning and development strategies also benefit enormously from data. Rather than offering one-size-fits-all programs, organizations can analyze where skill gaps exist—at the team, department, or enterprise level—and tailor learning accordingly. They can see which learning formats are most effective, which content is most engaging, and how learning translates into behavior change or business impact. They can track career progression and see how different development experiences—mentoring, stretch assignments, cross-functional projects—correlate with performance or retention. Perhaps most importantly, data helps shift the conversation from activity to impact (Stavros et al, 2021). It's not just about how many people took a course, but what difference it made. Did it build confidence? Did it change how someone leads? Did it prepare them for a new role? This is the kind of insight that earns learning a seat at the strategy table—not as a cost center, but as a driver of capability and culture.

Of course, none of this is simple. Data is messy. People are complex. And organizations are dynamic systems, not controlled experiments. There will always be outliers, surprises, exceptions. That's why data should not be used to lock people into boxes, but to open up possibilities. It should support conversations, not replace them. This is especially true when thinking about career development and succession planning. Too often, these processes are clouded by subjectivity, politics, or lack of clarity. But with better data—on performance, aspirations, mobility, and risk—organizations can plan more thoughtfully. They can identify who's ready now, who might be ready with the right support, and where critical gaps exist. They can also democratize access to opportunity—ensuring that development is not reserved for the few who are "tapped," but extended to all who show potential.

What data enables, in the best cases, is a deeper form of personalization. It helps organizations move from generic talent programs to more tailored, responsive approaches. It allows for smarter resource allocation. It supports inclusion by making patterns visible and holding leaders accountable. And it empowers employees by giving them more insight into their own development—where they stand, what they need, and what they might become. But data alone doesn't create this future. People do. And for data-driven talent acquisition and development to thrive, organizations need to cultivate a culture of curiosity, integrity, and learning. Leaders must model the value of evidence-based decisions. HR professionals must become translators between data and people. And employees must be treated not as subjects of analysis, but as partners in the process—invited to reflect, to contribute, and to grow.

There will always be a tension between the measurable and the meaningful. Not everything that matters can be quantified, and not everything that can be quantified matters. But this is not an argument against data—it is an argument for using data wisely. For asking better questions, for challenging assumptions, for combining analysis with empathy. In the end, data-driven decision-making in talent acquisition and development is not about control—it's about clarity. It's not about replacing the human element—it's about enriching it. It's about building systems that are smarter, fairer, and more aligned with the reality of work today. And it's about creating organizations that see people not just as resources, but as the vital, dynamic, and endlessly unfolding stories that they are.

Real-Time Insights and Predictive Analytics in Workforce Planning

In the landscape of modern work, the pace of change is relentless. Skills evolve, markets shift, technologies emerge, and the very definitions of roles and responsibilities are rewritten in real time. Amid all this fluidity, organizations are asked to do something deceptively simple: plan. Plan for the people they'll need, the capabilities they must grow, the gaps they must fill—not next year, not in the next quarter, but now. And they must do so with precision, agility, and foresight. Workforce planning, once a linear and largely administrative process, has become one of the most strategic—and most complex—functions in talent management. It's no longer just about headcount forecasts or organizational charts. It's about anticipating change, navigating uncertainty, and aligning human potential with business priorities. And in this evolving context, two forces are reshaping what workforce planning looks and feels like: real-time insights and predictive analytics.

Real-time insights are exactly what they sound like—the ability to see what's happening in the organization as it happens (Rydén & El Sawy, 2023). This is not about annual reports or retrospective reviews. It's about having a living, breathing view of the workforce: who's joining, who's leaving, who's shifting roles, who's thriving, and who's struggling. It's about understanding patterns not just after they've crystallized, but as they begin to emerge. Imagine being able to detect, within weeks, a drop in engagement in a specific region, or a spike in resignations within a key department. Imagine seeing, in real time, how new hires are progressing through onboarding, or how learning uptake correlates with team performance. These are not distant possibilities—they are happening now, in organizations that have invested in the systems, culture, and capabilities to make them real.

But the value of real-time insight is not just speed. It's clarity. It allows organizations to act before problems harden into crises. It enables more targeted interventions, more responsive support, and more effective communication. And it brings decision-making closer to the moment it matters—not weeks or months later, when the data has aged and the window of impact has closed. Real-time insights also shift the role of workforce planners (Yanamala, 2024). No longer relegated to static headcount models or spreadsheet forecasts, they become strategic partners—working alongside leaders to ask better questions, surface emerging risks, and spot opportunities for redesign or investment. They help connect dots across functions, see the ripple effects of decisions, and adjust course as needed. This kind of agility is essential in today's environment, where workforce realities change not annually, but weekly, sometimes daily. But agility, on its own, is not enough. Organizations also need foresight. They need to look ahead—not to predict the future in some deterministic way, but to prepare for it with intelligence, flexibility, and courage. This is where predictive analytics plays a vital role. While real-time insights help organizations respond, predictive analytics helps them anticipate. It allows them to ask: What's likely to happen next? What are the drivers? What can we do now to shape a better outcome?

At its core, predictive analytics is about identifying patterns that point toward probable futures. It draws on historical data—about turnover, performance, engagement, skills, mobility—and applies statistical models and machine learning to project trends. For workforce planning, this might mean forecasting attrition in key roles, modeling the supply and demand for critical skills, or estimating how changes in strategy will affect talent needs. For example, a company facing digital transformation might use predictive analytics to assess which current employees are most likely to succeed in new tech-enabled roles—based on learning history, adaptability scores, and past performance in change-driven environments. It might then design upskilling pathways or targeted hiring strategies based on that insight. Or a healthcare system might model how demographic changes in the population will impact staffing needs across departments, and use those projections to inform recruitment, training, and policy.

The power of prediction lies not in certainty but in preparation. It gives organizations time—time to recruit, to reskill, to redesign, to realign. It allows them to be proactive rather than reactive. And it brings a new level of depth to strategic conversations. Instead of debating anecdotal impressions, leaders can explore modeled scenarios. Instead of waiting for attrition to bite, they can get ahead of it. Yet, as with all powerful tools, predictive analytics must be used thoughtfully. The data must be clean, complete, and representative. The models must be tested, transparent, and regularly updated. And the insights must be interpreted in context—not as absolutes, but as signals. People are not algorithms. They defy neat categorization. And any system that forgets this risks doing more harm than good.

One of the key challenges with predictive analytics in workforce planning is the temptation to oversimplify (Olabiyi, 2023). To reduce people to risk scores, likelihoods, or probabilities, and then act accordingly—without pausing to ask why. Why are certain employees more likely to leave? Why are some roles harder to fill than others? Why do certain development programs yield better results? These questions cannot be answered by numbers alone. They require dialogue, curiosity, and reflection. Moreover, predictive analytics can inadvertently reproduce bias if not carefully managed. If historical data reflects systemic inequalities—such as underrepresentation of certain groups in leadership—it can reinforce those patterns unless corrected. This is why fairness auditing, ethical oversight, and inclusive modeling practices are essential. The goal of prediction should be not just accuracy, but equity. Not just efficiency, but humanity.

Another important consideration is transparency. Employees have a right to understand how data about them is being used, and for what purpose (Bodie, 2022). Predictive analytics should not be a black box, but a shared tool—one that invites participation, feedback, and accountability. When employees are informed and involved, they are more likely to trust the process and engage with the insights. When they are kept in the dark, suspicion grows—and so does resistance. For predictive analytics to take root in workforce planning, organizations also need to invest in capability-building. This means not only hiring data scientists, but equipping HR professionals and business leaders with the skills and mindset to work with data. It means building cross-functional teams that can bridge the gap between analysis and action. And it means cultivating a culture where insight leads to change—not just in reports, but in practice.

This is perhaps the most difficult part of the journey. Because insight, on its own, changes nothing. It must be integrated into the rhythms of decision-making, the rituals of planning, the habits of leadership. It must be championed, challenged, and continuously improved. And it must be matched by a willingness to let go of old assumptions, to ask new questions, and to act with both urgency and care. Done well, real-time insights and predictive analytics transform workforce planning from a static process into a living strategy. They help organizations see not just who they are, but who they are becoming. They create space for creativity—for reimagining roles, redesigning teams, rethinking what's possible. And they center people in the process—not as abstract units, but as contributors to a shared future. In a time when the only constant is change, this kind of planning is not a luxury—it's a necessity. Organizations that rely on outdated data, delayed responses, and vague forecasts will fall behind. Those that invest in real-time understanding and future-focused modeling will be better equipped to adapt, compete, and grow. They will also be better stewards of their people—more attuned to needs, more responsive to change, more committed to fairness and transparency. The journey is not linear. There will be setbacks, surprises, and moments of doubt. But the direction is clear. The tools are available. The need is urgent. And the opportunity is profound: to build workplaces that are not only smarter and more strategic, but also more human, more just, and more capable of meeting the challenges of tomorrow—today.

Ethical Considerations and Organizational Readiness

As organizations race to adopt business intelligence in their talent management practices, the enthusiasm for data-driven decision-making is palpable (Saling, 2024). The promises are compelling: smarter recruitment, sharper workforce planning, greater visibility into learning outcomes, and an unprecedented ability to match people with opportunity. But beneath these promises lies a quieter, more delicate conversation—one that isn't always captured in dashboards or models. It's the conversation about ethics. About trust. About readiness. Because while business intelligence brings powerful capabilities, it also brings risk. Not just the technical risks—data breaches, system failures, flawed models—but human ones. The risk of reducing people to numbers. The risk of using data without consent. The risk of acting on insights that have not been questioned, contextualized, or tested for fairness. And perhaps most importantly, the risk of implementing advanced systems in organizational cultures that aren't prepared for them.

Ethical considerations in the use of BI for talent management are not side conversations (Gomes, 2023). They are the foundation. Without them, the very tools designed to help organizations grow can erode trust, damage morale, and create unintended harm. The first and most obvious area of concern is privacy. Organizations now collect an extraordinary amount of data on employees—everything from job applications and performance metrics to keystrokes, calendar habits, and even sentiment extracted from emails or internal chats. Much of this data is collected passively, often without explicit awareness. Just because data can be collected doesn't mean it should be. This is the first ethical line that must be drawn. Employees deserve to know what data is being gathered, how it's being used, and what safeguards exist. Transparency is not just a compliance issue—it's a matter of respect. When people feel surveilled rather than supported, they disengage. When data practices are opaque, trust is replaced by suspicion. Ethical BI begins with openness: making data policies clear, explaining the purpose behind analytics efforts, and inviting employees into the conversation.

Consent is another layer. While formal consent mechanisms are often baked into employment contracts or digital systems, real consent involves more than a checkbox. It involves understanding and choice. Are employees aware of how their data might influence performance reviews, development opportunities, or job assignments? Are they given space to ask questions or opt out of certain analyses? Informed consent, in the truest sense, requires dialogue—and a willingness to slow down in a culture that is often in a hurry to optimize. Bias, too, is a critical concern. Algorithms, for all their sophistication, are not neutral. They reflect the data they are trained on, and that data reflects history—often messy, unequal, and exclusionary. If leadership promotions have historically skewed toward a particular demographic, a model trained on that history may "learn" that such profiles predict success, thus reinforcing exclusion rather than challenging it. Bias can creep in through variable selection, modeling choices, or even the questions we choose to ask. The ethical imperative is not to avoid data, but to interrogate it. To ask: What stories is this data telling? Whose voices are missing? What assumptions are we making?

Auditing is essential. Organizations need processes to test models for disparate impact, to assess whether certain groups are systematically disadvantaged, and to revise algorithms as needed (Pagano et al, 2023). But beyond audits, they need reflection. Technology does not absolve us of moral responsibility. On the contrary, it makes that responsibility more urgent. Every insight acted upon is a decision with consequences—consequences that affect careers, livelihoods, and lives. Another consideration is the tension between individual and organizational benefit. Business intelligence is often framed as a win-win: better decisions for the company, better experiences for employees. And sometimes that's true. But not always. What happens when data suggests eliminating a role or department? What if analytics indicate that a high performer is unlikely to stay, and investment is withheld as a result—thus creating a self-fulfilling prophecy? What if certain career paths are subtly closed off based on predictive assessments? These are not merely operational questions. They are ethical ones. They speak to the heart of how organizations view their people: as variables to be managed, or as individuals to be supported.

Organizational readiness is not just about having the tools. It's about having the values, the leadership, and the cultural maturity to use those tools wisely (Inuwa & Rahim, 2020). Many organizations are excited by what BI can do but are not yet prepared to hold the responsibilities it brings. They may lack data governance structures, cross-functional collaboration, or internal expertise. They may also lack psychological safety—the foundation on which trust is built. If employees fear how data will be used, they will not engage. If managers don't understand the insights, they won't act on them—or worse, they'll misuse them. Readiness, then, is about building the conditions under which BI can succeed. That begins with leadership. Leaders must set the tone, modeling transparency, curiosity, and ethical rigor. They must make it clear that data is a support, not a surveillance tool. That the purpose of BI is not control, but clarity. That decisions will still be made with care, not just calculated. Leaders also need to be honest about limitations: acknowledging when data is incomplete, when models are uncertain, and when human judgment must take precedence.

It also involves investment in education. Business intelligence is often championed by a small group of data professionals, but for it to have real impact, the literacy must spread. HR professionals, managers, and employees alike need to understand how to read data, question it, and apply it (McCartney et al, 2021). They need to feel confident, not intimidated. Empowered, not excluded. This is not just a skill-building issue—it's a democratization issue. When only a few people hold the keys to insight, power becomes centralized. But when understanding is shared, so too is agency. Perhaps one of the most overlooked dimensions of readiness is ethical leadership. It is easy to get excited by dashboards and KPIs. Harder is the slow, deliberate work of embedding ethics into the fabric of decision-making. This includes creating spaces for ethical reflection, encouraging dissenting views, and rewarding behavior that prioritizes fairness over expediency. It means building diverse teams, so that different experiences inform modeling and interpretation. It means putting structures in place that allow employees to raise concerns, challenge data usage, and participate in shaping policies.

And, importantly, it means accepting trade-offs. There will be moments when the most "efficient" option is not the most ethical one. When the fastest route to insight bypasses necessary dialogue. When the push for innovation brushes up against privacy. Organizations that are truly ready for BI will not shy away from these tensions. They will lean into them—with humility, with integrity, and with a commitment to doing right, not just doing well. There is also a broader societal context to consider. As data becomes more central to how we work and live, the boundaries between personal and professional information are blurring. Employees bring their digital selves into the workplace—through wearables, social media, online learning. At what point does organizational insight become intrusion? Where is the line between personalization and profiling? These are questions that go beyond any one company. They demand collective reflection, policy development, and dialogue across sectors.

Yet despite these complexities, there is reason for hope. The same tools that can reinforce bias can also surface it. The same models that could marginalize can be used to protect. When used responsibly, business intelligence can be a force for equity—for revealing where opportunity is unequally distributed, where potential is overlooked, where structures need to change. It can help organizations not only manage people better, but treat them more justly. The ethical path forward is not paved with perfect models or complete data. It is walked daily, in choices big and small. In how we define success. In who gets to ask the questions. In what we do when the data challenges our assumptions. And in whether we remember, always, that behind every data point is a person—with hopes, fears, talents, and stories that no algorithm can fully capture. Organizational readiness, then, is not a technical milestone. It is a moral stance. It is the willingness to see BI not as a destination, but as a journey—one that demands vigilance, compassion, and continual learning. It is the courage to say, "We don't have all the answers, but we are committed to asking better questions." And it is the discipline to match our technological capabilities with our ethical responsibilities. In the end, business intelligence in talent management is not about predicting the future. It is about shaping it—with insight, with intention, and with integrity.

Shaping the Future: Integrating BI into a Holistic Talent Strategy

In the ever-evolving world of work, the phrase "future of talent" is everywhere. It shows up in conferences, strategy decks, HR panels, and boardroom conversations (Veluchamy et al, 2025). But too often, the conversation drifts toward the abstract—toward distant visions of AI-powered organizations, hyper-personalized career journeys, or predictive talent ecosystems where every decision is optimized by algorithms. These images are compelling, even seductive. But they can distract from the more grounded, urgent question: How do we, today, build a talent strategy that is both visionary and real? That prepares us for what's next, without losing sight of what matters now?

At the center of this question lies a powerful, if underutilized, ally: business intelligence. Not just as a toolset, but as a way of thinking—of aligning insight with purpose, data with direction, and knowledge with action. To integrate BI into a holistic talent strategy is not to add another system or dashboard to the HR arsenal. It is to reimagine how organizations understand, support, and grow their people. It is to make talent strategy not only more precise, but more human. To begin with, it's worth acknowledging that most organizations are still on a journey. They may have pockets of BI—analytics dashboards for recruitment, reports on turnover, performance metrics—but these efforts are often fragmented, reactive, or siloed. A holistic talent strategy, by contrast, asks us to connect the dots (Wiblen & McDonnell, 2020). To see the workforce not as a collection of isolated transactions—hiring here, training there, promotion over there—but as a living system, with interdependencies, feedback loops, and shared goals. BI, when fully integrated, can help map that system. It can show how early career experiences shape long-term engagement, how leadership development impacts succession readiness, how skills gaps ripple across teams and time.

But building this kind of integrated approach requires more than data. It requires design. It starts with asking different questions—questions that are strategic, not just operational. Not "How many people completed training this quarter?" but "Are we building the capabilities we need for the business we're becoming?" Not "What's our attrition rate?" but "Where are we at risk of losing critical knowledge, and what can we do now to retain it?" These kinds of questions force HR to move beyond compliance or efficiency—and to step fully into its role as a strategic partner. And this is where BI becomes a bridge—not only between systems, but between functions. A truly holistic talent strategy cannot be owned by HR alone (Chun & Evans, 2023). It must be shaped in dialogue with finance, operations, IT, marketing, legal—every part of the organization that depends on talent (which is to say, all of them). BI helps facilitate that dialogue. It creates a shared language. When HR can show, with evidence, how attrition is affecting productivity, how lack of diversity is affecting innovation, or how targeted reskilling is opening new lines of business—it shifts the conversation. Talent becomes not just a cost or a risk, but a source of insight, leverage, and possibility.

Of course, insight without alignment is not enough. Integrating BI into a holistic strategy also means aligning it with the broader goals of the organization. Too often, data efforts stall because they are misaligned with what leadership cares about. A dashboard may track engagement scores, but if leadership is focused on cost containment, it may go ignored. A report may show disparities in promotion rates, but if equity is not a strategic priority, it may not drive change. BI cannot be an add-on—it must be woven into the way goals are set, priorities are determined, and decisions are made. That means co-creating metrics. It means bringing HR into strategic planning conversations. And it means holding leaders accountable—not just for financial outcomes, but for talent outcomes, too. This alignment also has to happen vertically. Integrating BI into talent strategy means making insights accessible at all levels—not just the executive suite. Managers need to understand how their teams are doing—not just in terms of output, but engagement, skill development, risk of burnout (Gabriel & Aguinis, 2022). Employees need to see their own data—not to feel watched, but to feel empowered. What learning have they completed? What paths are others in similar roles taking? Where do they have room to grow? When BI is democratized—not in the sense of full transparency, but thoughtful accessibility—it becomes a shared asset, not a gated resource.

But accessibility brings with it responsibility. Integrating BI into talent strategy is also an exercise in ethics. As organizations get better at gathering and analyzing data, they also take on a greater duty of care. Not just to protect data, but to use it wisely. To avoid overreach. To ensure that insight is used for growth, not judgment;

for empowerment, not control. This is especially important in cultures where trust is fragile. If employees fear that data will be used to penalize, exclude, or micromanage, then even the best BI systems will fail. Integration must be built on trust, not just technology (Israr, 2024). Trust also grows from transparency. Organizations need to be clear about what data is being collected, how it's used, and what it's meant to support. This doesn't mean publishing every model or metric. It means creating clarity. Being willing to explain decisions. Inviting feedback. And, perhaps most importantly, being open to changing course. No BI system is perfect. No strategy is final. Integrating BI into talent strategy is not a one-time move—it's a living process, one that must evolve with the organization and the people in it.

It's also a creative process. One of the great misconceptions about BI is that it's purely analytical (VK, 2021). But in truth, it opens space for imagination. When we can see more clearly—see patterns, gaps, potential—we can design more boldly. We can reimagine career paths, rethink team structures, redesign learning journeys. We can test new ideas, iterate on what works, and scale what matters. BI doesn't replace creativity—it gives it context, direction, and grounding. This is especially critical when thinking about the future of work (Kayyali, 2024). No one can predict exactly how roles will evolve, how automation will reshape industries, or how employee expectations will shift. But we can prepare. We can use data to scan the horizon, model scenarios, and build resilience. We can identify emerging skills, track the impact of new technologies, and prepare people—not just for specific jobs, but for a world where adaptability, learning, and collaboration are the true currencies of value.

In this way, integrating BI into talent strategy is not just about efficiency or accuracy. It's about responsibility. It's about building organizations that are not only competitive, but also humane. That use insight not just to drive profit, but to foster inclusion, engagement, and growth. That treat people not as resources to be optimized, but as partners in shaping the future. To do this well, organizations need more than dashboards. They need dialogue. They need cross-functional collaboration, ethical frameworks, and a culture that values reflection. They need leaders who are willing to ask hard questions—and who are willing to act on the answers. They need HR teams that are both data-savvy and people-wise. And they need the humility to know that no model, however advanced, can replace the judgment, empathy, and discernment that human leadership requires. At its best, business intelligence doesn't narrow our view. It expands it. It helps us see not just what's happening, but what's possible. It surfaces not just risks, but relationships. It reminds us that behind every metric is a person—and behind every person is a story. A holistic talent strategy is one that honors those stories. That uses data not to control, but to care. Not to sort, but to support. And not to predict the future as if it were fixed, but to shape it—with vision, courage, and an unwavering belief in the potential of people. If we can hold that belief at the center of our strategies, then BI becomes more than a tool.

It becomes a compass—guiding us toward organizations that are not only smarter, but also more just, more adaptive, and more alive.

CONCLUSION

As we close this exploration into the role of business intelligence in talent management, it is worth pausing to remember what lies at the heart of all the dashboards, analytics, and strategic modeling we have discussed: people. Individuals with aspirations, anxieties, unique strengths, and untapped potential. It is easy—perhaps dangerously so—to get caught up in the elegance of data visualizations or the thrill of predictive precision and forget that behind every data point is a person navigating their own journey through the world of work. Business intelligence, when harnessed thoughtfully, offers extraordinary promise. It enables organizations to see more clearly—who is thriving, who is struggling, where resources are needed, and how future talent needs can be met. It allows for faster, more responsive decision-making, grounded in evidence rather than assumption. It brings rigor to areas of HR that were once seen as too soft or subjective. And it helps align the talent strategy not just with organizational performance, but with fairness, consistency, and long-term sustainability. But with that promise comes responsibility. It is not enough to collect data—we must interrogate what data we collect, why we collect it, and how we use it. Are we measuring what matters, or simply what is easiest to quantify? Are we reinforcing existing inequities by relying on historical patterns? Are we giving people the opportunity to challenge the narratives that data may suggest about them? These are not academic questions. They are the ethical heart of any BI system worth its name.

Looking ahead, we must resist the temptation to treat business intelligence as a destination. It is not a final solution. It is a tool, a lens, a set of practices that help us make sense of complexity. Its power lies not in replacing human judgment, but in grounding it. In offering clarity where there is confusion. In revealing patterns that we might otherwise miss. But judgment still matters. Empathy still matters. Context still matters. In many ways, the integration of BI into talent management invites us to return to the fundamentals. What kind of organization do we want to be? What kind of employee experience are we trying to create? What do we owe the people who trust us with their time, their energy, and their careers? These are not questions data can answer alone. But data can guide the conversation, test our assumptions, and help us stay honest. There is also a cultural shift required—one that invites HR professionals to become more analytically fluent, and data professionals to become more attuned to human complexity. This means investing in learning, breaking down silos, and building systems that are transparent and inclusive. It means designing BI tools that are user-friendly, empowering, and respectful of privacy. And it means fostering a mindset in which data is not a threat to leadership or expertise, but a partner to it.

Perhaps most importantly, we must guard against complacency. Business intelligence is not inherently virtuous. It reflects the intentions, biases, and blind spots of the people and systems that build it. If we approach it uncritically, we risk amplifying the very problems we hope to solve. But if we approach it with humility, curiosity, and care, we can unlock new ways of understanding and supporting our workforce. In the end, business intelligence in talent management is not just about making better decisions—it is about becoming better decision-makers. More reflective, more informed, more courageous. It is about aligning our tools with our values, our systems with our vision, and our strategies with the full humanity of the people we lead. This is not easy work. It requires technical skill, organizational commitment, and a willingness to rethink how we've always done things. But it is necessary work. Because the future of talent management will not be shaped by spreadsheets alone—it will be shaped by the choices we make about how to see, value, and grow the people who make our organizations what they are. And in that sense, business intelligence is not the end of the story. It is the beginning of a more honest, more nuanced, and more human way to write it.

REFERENCES

Adewusi, A. O., Okoli, U. I., Adaga, E., Olorunsogo, T., Asuzu, O. F., & Daraojimba, D. O. (2024). Business intelligence in the era of big data: A review of analytical tools and competitive advantage. *Computer Science & IT Research Journal, 5*(2), 415–431. DOI: 10.51594/csitrj.v5i2.791

Ajax, R., Joseph, O., & Own, J. (2025). Enhancing Business Intelligence with Data Visualization Tools.

Al-Shammari, M., Ahmed Al Bin Ali, F., Abdulla AlRashidi, M., & Salem Albuainain, M. (2024). Big Data and Predictive Analytics for Strategic Human Resource Management: A Systematic Literature Review. *International Journal of Computing and Digital Systems, 17*(1), 1–9. DOI: 10.12785/ijcds/1571015706

Ayanponle, L. O., Awonuga, K. F., Asuzu, O. F., Daraojimba, R. E., Elufioye, O. A., & Daraojimba, O. D. (2024). A review of innovative HR strategies in enhancing workforce efficiency in the US. *International Journal of Science and Research Archive, 11*(1), 817–827. DOI: 10.30574/ijsra.2024.11.1.0152

Bodie, M. T. (2022). The law of employee data: Privacy, property, governance. *Ind. Lj, 97*, 707.

Borking, K., Danielson, M., Davies, G., Ekenberg, L., Idefeldt, J., & Larsson, A. (2022). *Transcending business intelligence*. Sine Metu Productions.

Chun, E., & Evans, A. (2023). *The new talent acquisition frontier: Integrating HR and diversity strategy in the private and public sectors and higher education*. Taylor & Francis.

Duggan, J., Sherman, U., Carbery, R., & McDonnell, A. (2020). Algorithmic management and app-work in the gig economy: A research agenda for employment relations and HRM. *Human Resource Management Journal, 30*(1), 114–132. DOI: 10.1111/1748-8583.12258

Eboigbe, E. O., Farayola, O. A., Olatoye, F. O., Nnabugwu, O. C., & Daraojimba, C. (2023). Business intelligence transformation through AI and data analytics. *Engineering Science & Technology Journal, 4*(5), 285–307. DOI: 10.51594/estj.v4i5.616

Gabriel, K. P., & Aguinis, H. (2022). How to prevent and combat employee burnout and create healthier workplaces during crises and beyond. *Business Horizons, 65*(2), 183–192. DOI: 10.1016/j.bushor.2021.02.037

George, A. S. (2024). Bridging the Digital Divide: Understanding the Human Impacts of Digital Transformation. *Partners Universal International Innovation Journal*, *2*(3), 1–34.

Gomes, B. M. S. (2023). Development of a Talent Management Platform at BI4ALL: Business Intelligence Approach for Human Resource Management (Master's thesis, Universidade NOVA de Lisboa (Portugal)).

Ibrahim, N. M., Abiduzzaman, S. M., Raziff, A. R. A., & Shah, A. (2025). A Collaborative Filtering Approach Using Machine Learning and Business Intelligence: A Critical Review. *International Journal on Perceptive and Cognitive Computing*, *11*(1), 41–49.

Inuwa, M., & Rahim, S. B. A. (2020). Lean readiness factors and organizational readiness for change in manufacturing SMEs: The role of organizational culture. *Journal of Critical Reviews*, *7*(5), 56–67.

Israr, A. (2024). BUSINESS INTELLIGENCE FOR DECISION SUPPORT IN SANCTIONS.

Jerab, D., & Mabrouk, T. (2023). The role of leadership in changing organizational culture. Available at *SSRN* 4574324. DOI: 10.2139/ssrn.4574324

Kayyali, M. (2024). Design thinking and creativity in entrepreneurial innovation. In *Applying Business Intelligence and Innovation to Entrepreneurship* (pp. 155–170). IGI Global. DOI: 10.4018/979-8-3693-1846-1.ch008

McCartney, S., Murphy, C., & Mccarthy, J. (2021). 21st century HR: A competency model for the emerging role of HR Analysts. *Personnel Review*, *50*(6), 1495–1513. DOI: 10.1108/PR-12-2019-0670

Müller, S., & Shamsie, K. (2023). Digital Disruption and the Evolution of Business Models: A Scholarly Examination. *Abbottabad University Journal of Business and Management Sciences*, *1*(01), 43–52.

Niu, Y., Ying, L., Yang, J., Bao, M., & Sivaparthipan, C. B. (2021). Organizational business intelligence and decision making using big data analytics. *Information Processing & Management*, *58*(6), 102725. DOI: 10.1016/j.ipm.2021.102725

Olabiyi, E. O. (2023). *The Prospects & Challenges of HR Management and HR Technologies in a Post-Pandemic Hybrid Workplace*. The American University of Paris.

Pagano, T. P., Loureiro, R. B., Lisboa, F. V., Peixoto, R. M., Guimarães, G. A., Cruz, G. O., Araujo, M. M., Santos, L. L., Cruz, M. A. S., Oliveira, E. L. S., Winkler, I., & Nascimento, E. G. (2023). Bias and unfairness in machine learning models: A systematic review on datasets, tools, fairness metrics, and identification and mitigation methods. *Big Data and Cognitive Computing*, *7*(1), 15. DOI: 10.3390/bdcc7010015

Pala, S. K. (2024). Use and Applications of Data Analytics in Human Resource Management and Talent Acquisition. International Journal of Enhanced Research in Management & Computer Applications ISSN, 2319-7463.

Quenum, V. F. (2024). Enhancing Data Storytelling within Business Intelligence & Analytics.

Rydén, P., & El Sawy, O. A. (2023). Flow with the go: Real-time continuous improvisation in digital business ecosystems. In *The Routledge companion to improvisation in organizations* (pp. 389–407). Routledge. DOI: 10.4324/9781003171768-28

Saling, K. (2024). *Data-driven Talent Management: Using Analytics to Improve Employee Experience*. Kogan Page Publishers.

Skyrius, R. (2021). *Business Intelligence*. Springer. DOI: 10.1007/978-3-030-67032-0

Stavros, J. M., Stavros, J., & Torres, C. (2021). *Conversations worth having: Using appreciative inquiry to fuel productive and meaningful engagement*. Berrett-Koehler Publishers.

Veluchamy, R., Kanagaraj, M. G. A., & Vimalnath, V. (2025). Speculative Scenarios for the Future of Talent Management in Higher Education. In Cultivating Creativity and Navigating Talent Management in Academia (pp. 335-358). IGI Global Scientific Publishing.

VK, A. K. (2021). Business Intelligence Demystified: Understand and Clear All Your Doubts and Misconceptions About BI (English Edition). BPB Publications.

Wiblen, S., & McDonnell, A. (2020). Connecting 'talent' meanings and multi-level context: A discursive approach. *International Journal of Human Resource Management*, *31*(4), 474–510. DOI: 10.1080/09585192.2019.1629988

Wiencierz, C., & Luenich, M. (2022). Trust in open data applications through transparency. *New Media & Society*, *24*(8), 1751–1770. DOI: 10.1177/1461444820979708

Witzany, L. (2024). Systematically Addressing Unconscious Biases in Job Interviews with Anonymization Technology (Doctoral dissertation, Technische Universität Wien).

Yanamala, K. K. R. (2024). Strategic implications of AI integration in workforce planning and talent forecasting. *Journal of Advanced Computing Systems*, *4*(1), 1–9. DOI: 10.69987/JACS.2024.40101

Chapter 2
Talent Management and Human Resource Practices

Angelos Ntalakos
https://orcid.org/0000-0003-2491-6606
University of Thessaly, Greece

Mary Viterouli
University of Thessaly, Greece

Dimitrios Belias
https://orcid.org/0000-0003-3409-6875
University of Thessaly, Greece

Ioannis Rossidis
Panteion University, Greece

ABSTRACT

The primary purpose of this study is to investigate the influence of Human Resource Practices on Talent Management. In other words, this chapter focuses on highlighting whether there is a connection between the characteristics of Talent Management and the HRM practices of employee evaluation. A systematic literature review was conducted based on journals, articles, conference proceedings, and formal reports retrieved from the most known scientific databases such as, Elsevier Scopus, Web of Science, and Google Scholar. The findings of this literature review revealed several key findings regarding to the Talent Management practices and employee evaluation. Among other, this chapter revealed that Talent management is not only related to the simple recruitment and selection processes. It includes a holistic approach that

DOI: 10.4018/979-8-3373-1942-1.ch002

involves development, retention, and evaluation planning. This framework underlines the strategic importance of human capital in enhancing competitiveness and sustaining organizational performance.

1. INTRODUCTION

Talent management has become a critical organizational imperative for sustaining competitiveness and achieving success in the contemporary business landscape. Defined as "the systematic attraction, identification, development, engagement, retention and utilization of those individuals who are of particular value to an organization" (Scullion & Collings, 2011), talent management transcends traditional human resource management practices. It represents a strategic approach to human capital development and deployment, aligning individual capabilities with organizational objectives (Kraugusteeliana et al., 2023).

The increasing prevalence of strategic management frameworks has necessitated aligning employee efforts with an overarching organizational vision to foster long-term collaboration and knowledge retention. Concurrently, heightened labor market competition has made strategic career planning a critical organizational imperative. Consequently, talent management, among other motivational tools, has become a key mechanism for attracting, developing, and retaining high-potential employees (Vural et al., 2012).

Human capital investment is essential for organizational survival and growth. Organizations must prioritize strategies focused on employee retention, empowerment, and development. Human Resource Management is crucial in ensuring the organization possesses a competent, talented, and committed workforce capable of meeting current and future organizational needs (Berke et al., 2008).

This is accomplished through targeted interventions, including comprehensive needs assessments, continuous training, skills development, and the implementation of performance management and succession planning systems. Specifically, developing performance-based compensation policies, providing career advancement opportunities, and integrating innovation into talent development processes contribute to overall human resource enhancement. As Becker et al. (1997) suggest, these practices reinforce the alignment between HRM strategy and business objectives.

Organizations pursuing growth and sustained success recognize the primacy of human capital (Collings & Mellahi, 2009). However, a common deficiency is the inability to effectively identify, develop, and retain employees, particularly those possessing cross-cultural competence and adaptability to diverse geographical contexts. Talent management remains insufficiently integrated into core business operations within many organizations, often due to overemphasizing strategic market segmentation-based structures rather than developing core employee skills.

While organizations must necessarily focus on their products or services, this focus must be complemented by a commensurate emphasis on developing core employee skills. Conceptualizing an organization solely as a “product portfolio” or “service portfolio” is insufficient. Instead, organizations must be recognized as “skills portfolios,” as employee skill development is fundamental to maintaining competitiveness in a dynamic and innovative global landscape. A strategic deficit in skills development can negatively impact an organization's competitive capacity, particularly internationally. Therefore, talent management must be integral to organizational strategy, identifying, developing, and retaining high-potential employees.

Organizations must prioritize core skill development and talent management to remain competitive. Career planning, skills enhancement, and a strategic approach to talent management are no longer optional but essential for long-term sustainability and growth. Rather than solely focusing on what they offer the market, organizations must invest in how their employees develop and contribute to strategic objectives (Guthridge et al., 2008).

While scholarly attention to talent management has been extensive, encompassing areas from recruitment and selection to employee development and succession planning, a synthesis of the existing literature is still needed. Such a synthesis would illuminate dominant trends, identify gaps in current research, and delineate future directions for research and practice in talent management.

Enhancing human capital is paramount for organizational survival, growth, and competitive advantage. Human Resource Management (HRM) is critical in this process, focusing on securing a competent, talented, and committed workforce capable of meeting current and future organizational needs and contributing to strategic development (Lewis & Heckman, 2006).

Rational human resource management necessitates a needs analysis to identify the requisite skills and competencies for achieving organizational objectives. This assessment informs human resource planning, enabling organizations to meet both present and future workforce requirements and ensuring appropriate employee allocation and utilization.

Concurrently, continuous training and skills development are essential to human capital development (Viterouli et al., 2024). Implementing training programs aligned with organizational needs enhances employees' skills and adaptability to evolving business environments. This strategy increases productivity and cultivates organizational innovation (Zerva et al., 2024).

This chapter investigates the role and effectiveness of strategic talent management approaches, focusing on recruitment, training, skills development, and retention. Furthermore, it analyzes the impact of human resource (HR) practices on overall organizational performance, exploring aspects such as recruitment channels and training investments. Finally, the chapter evaluates performance appraisal systems, identifying areas for improvement and highlighting best practices for enhanced productivity and organizational effectiveness.

2. METHODOLOGY

The methodology of this chapter is a literature review. Data were collected via several scientific databases such as Elsevier Scopus, Science Direct, Web of Science, and Google Scholar. The resources used consisted of the following forms: scientific journals, books, conference proceedings, papers, business reports, and scientific websites. The researchers used a combination of the following keywords: "Talent management," "Employee Evaluation," "Employee Recruitment," and "Talents." The publications used were relevant to these terms and were published a maximum of 10 to 20 years ago.

3. LITERATURE REVIEW

3.1. The Concept of Talent Management

Since McKinsey declared the "War for Talent" in 1998 (Chambers et al., 1998), talent management has been recognized as a key solution to the challenges that Human Resource Management has been facing worldwide in the modern labor market (Schuler et al., 2010). Although the literature admits that talent management is a rapidly growing field, unfortunately, the effectiveness and the added value of talent management practices have not yet been accurately articulated. Additionally, the research regarding the connection between talent management strategies and organizational performance is limited, leaving the question of whether the appropriate strategy could bring the desired successful organizational performance (Lawler, 2008).

Literature has revealed the existence of disagreements regarding the definition of the concept of talent management. According to Aston and Morton (2005), "There is no consistent or concise definition of talent management. However, Lewis and Heckman (2006) suggest that the concept of talent management should consist of three key approaches (Figure 1): a) redefining Human Resource Management (HRM), b) talent pools, and c) top-grading.

Regarding the first approach (redefining HRM), talent management is defined as the "redefinition" of traditional HR practices such as recruitment, leadership development, and succession planning. However, this approach does not enhance strategic HR management since it only focuses on changing terminology and does not suggest new innovative strategies to advance HR management (Lewis and Heckman, 2006).

The second approach focuses on developing thedeveloping the talent pool. This approach emphasizes planning employees' needs and managing theirtheir career development. Although this approach is limited to a narrow scope, it provides a clearer differentiation between talent and Human Resources management (Lewis and Heckman, 2006).

The third approach (top-grading) (Smart, 1999) focuses on retaining top employees ("A performers") and removing poor employees ("C players"). However, this approach is impractical for all organizational job positions, as it can lead to overinvestment in non-strategic positions.

Figure 1. Approaches of talent management (Source: Lewis & Heckman, 2006)

Due to the limitations of the abovementioned approaches, Boudreau and Ramstad (2007) proposed a fourth approach. This approach focuses on identifyingidentifyingidentifying strategic positions that can enhance the organization's competitive advantage. The starting point of this approach is gaining the correct strategic position, not exclusively talents.

Although there are several definitions of the terms "talent" and "talent management" (Collings & Mellahi, 2009), most companies continue to rely on subjective assessments when evaluating the effectiveness of their human resources practices without considering any quantitative or qualitative talent management practices (Anderson, 2008).

Furthermore, one of the crucial challenges that academics have faced in the last decade is still unanswered questions about talent management's definition and objectives. According to Lewis and Heckman (2006), there is "a disturbing lack of clarity about the definition, scope, and overall goals of talent management ."This lack of clarity may bemay be why practitioners have difficulty implementing talent management strategies despite their importance to the organization's future.

An initial approach to talent management emphasizes human capital (Ready et al., 2008). A second view explains talent management as "a process through which employees anticipate and meet their needs" (Cappelli, 2008). Eventually, a third view recognizes talent management as a tool for achieving economic results (Lockwood, 2006).

According to the second view, talent management is considered a distinct process that focuses exclusively on individuals who would provide the organization a competitive advantage through effective and efficient management. Based on this approach, the talent management process could include Human Resources practices such as recruitment and staffing, training and development, appraisal and reward, and finally, focus on the employees who have the appropriate skills, potential, and performance level to deliver the desired results (Berke et al., 2008; Schuler et al., 2010).

Strategic talent management differs from human resource management in that it focuses only on employees derived from the strategic talent pool and occupying strategic positions. On the contrary, human resource management includes all employees regardless of their strategic importance. The difference between these two terms can trigger academics to develop theories and practice models that respond to organizations' evolving requirements (Papademetriou et al., 2024; Belias et al., 2024; Ntalakos et al., 2024c,d).

3.2. The Main Characteristics of Talent Management

Over the past decades, academics have identified and analyzed several dimensions that synthesize the concept of talent management (Figure 2). Each dimension plays a crucial role in achieving organizational effectiveness. These dimensions are not isolated; they are connected, composing an integrated strategic framework that enables organizations to align their objectives with their HR management practices.

Figure 2. Characteristics of talent management

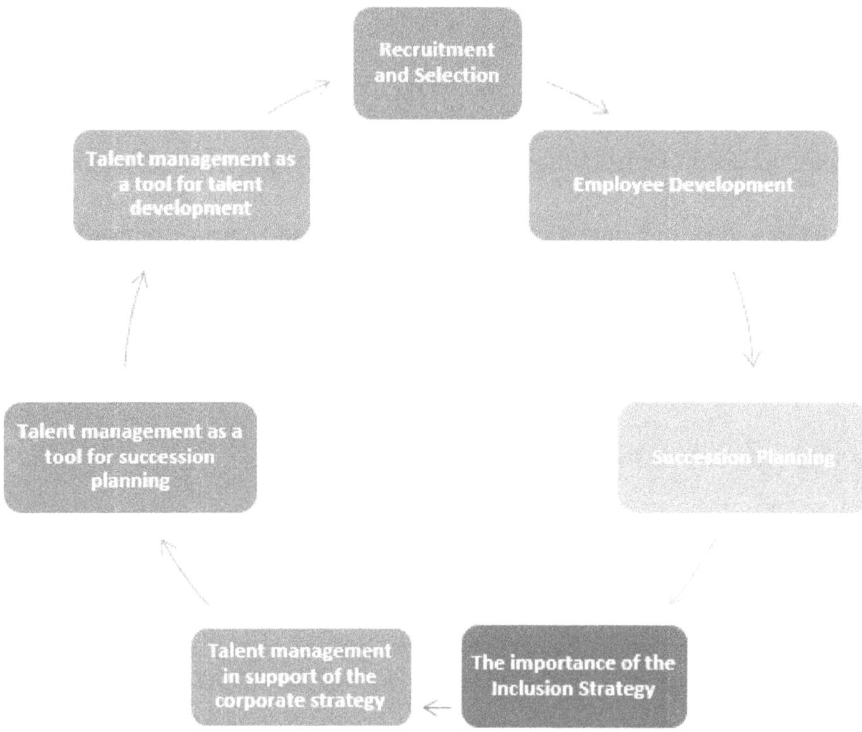

Recruitment and Selection

The recruitment and selection process is the foundation of talent management. This stage is the cornerstone where employees acquire the right qualifications, skills, and potential. This dimension attracts high-potential candidates aligned with the organization's strategic goals, culture, and values (Collings & Mellahi, 2009). The vital variables of this stage are the use of modern assessment tools, implementation of transparent selection processes, and data utilization for predicting candidate success.

Employee Development

The development of employees is one of the most complex, crucial, and important dimensions of talent management. It aims to continuously improve the workforce'skills, knowledge, and competencies Through targeted training, mentoring, and coaching programs, employees enhance their skills, career development, and job satisfaction

(Blass and Ferris, 2007). This development is not only limited to technical skills but also extends to cultivating leadership, collaboration, and emotional intelligence. The last three factors are crucial for enhancing the organization's performance.

Succession Planning

This stage aims to ensure the continuity of organizational functions, especially when replacement of leaders or supervisors is required. In other words, succession planning aims to create a "talent pool" where the appropriate candidates are identified, prepared, and supported so that they will become ready to take charge of key positions when needed (Rothwell, 2010). This stage can reduce the risks of talent gaps. Also, this stage enhances efficiency and ensures the smooth transition to new leadership.

The Importance of the Inclusion Strategy

Integrating these dimensions into a holistic talent management strategy enables organizations to come to terms with the continuously rapid and changing business environment. This strategy allows organizations to maintain competitiveness, reduce the risks associated with talent shortages, enhance productivity, and create an environment that fosters employee engagement and loyalty. The sustainability of organizations depends on their ability to exploit these dimensions effectively and strategically, which is combined with the organization's objectives.

Talent Management in Support of the Corporate Strategy

Talent management is a set of activities that aim to support corporate strategies (Boxall and Purcell, 2011). Several scholars argue that organizations that connect talent management with corporate strategies report higher financial performance outcomes (Tansley et al., 2007). Moreover, when organizations emphasize one strategic goal over others, priorities can be set at the corporate level (Lipsky, 2010). Therefore, the whole organization focuses on one overarching corporate goal, enhancing the impact on financial and organizational outcomes.

Additionally, if talent management is recognized and implemented as part of the corporate strategy, the organization should prioritize talent management strategies (Cohn et al., 2005). As a result, the talented employees feel appreciated, increasing their motivation and strengthening their commitment to their organization (Gandossy and Kao, 2004).

Talent Management as a Tool for Succession Planning

Talent management reduces the time necessary to replace leaders, supervisors, and specialists. It is very important for an organization to recruit the appropriate people with the appropriate skills when needed, either through internal successors or candidates from outside the organization (Hills, 2009). According to previous studies, internal succession planning can reduce transaction costs and, consequently, can increase an organization's profitability (Sebald et al., 2005).

In addition, internal succession can reduce knowledge loss and improve job quality since practices can be transferred directly to the organization's employees (Conway, 2007). The increase in job quality can directly reflect the increase in customer satisfaction (Evans and Jack, 2003). When talented employees are informed about their future promising opportunities by their leader, their commitment and trust in their leaders increase. In other words, integrity is a key factor in creating credibility (Meyer et al., 1995).

This strategy, which is based on Vroom's (1964) expectancy theory, motivates talents to demonstrate higher performance levels. This attitude can be achieved provided that the promised succession meets their desires (valences), that talents are confident in their abilities (expectancy), and that they believe they will receive what they have been promised (instrumentally). Adopting this strategy not only enhances talent engagement but also ensures the long-term sustainability and competitiveness of the organization.

Talent Management as a Tool for Talent Development

Talent management focuses on effectively identifying and meeting talents while offering options and career paths. As a result, talents develop skills related to the organization's needs (Ringo et al., 2008). Pratt et al. (1991) claims that talent management is a process that can direct employee behavior in a direction that serves the organization's needs.

Talent development can motivate talented employees (agents) to fulfill their needs when following the organization's strategic direction (principal). Investing in human capital could lead to higher levels of employee training, quality of work, and the organization's intellectual capital. Since intellectual capital is part of the organization's total capital, its market value is enhanced (Friederichs & Labes, 2006).

Furthermore, the more skilled the employees are, the more productive they become, and consequently, the more profitable the organization becomes (Lawler, 2009). Previous studies suggest that talent motivation, job satisfaction, and commitment are strongly influenced by career choices and career development (McGrath, 2008; Ellickson and Logsdom, 2001; Bartlett, 2001). Talents prefer intangible rewards (such as career prospects, interesting job content, and scope of action) to economic and financial rewards (Ready et al., 2008).

Additionally, talents systematically seek for development opportunities (Lawler, 2008). Therefore, organizations focusing on talent development enhance their attractiveness by communicating the talent management strategy. This leads not only to employee commitment and satisfaction but also to creating a competitive position in the market.

3.3. Personnel Evaluation Systems

Personnel evaluation is a key strategic tool for talent management. It involves measuring and analyzing employee performance regularly. It also focuses on identifying strengths, areas for improvement, and talented employees that could lead the organization to a successful performance. According to research, integrating talent management with personnel evaluation could enhance employee engagement. Research reveals a moderate correlation between using talent management strategies integrated with performance evaluation systems and organizational commitment. Organizations that implement this strategy exhibit improvements in performance and engagement and a reduction in attrition rates. Talent management strategy and personnel evaluation are mutually interacted. Organizations can enhance engagement, maximize performance, and maintain competitive advantage by implementing an integrated approach. By investing in their people, organizations create a strong foundation for long-term success (Ntalakos et al., 2024, 2024b; Ntalakos et al., 2025; Belias et al., 2023a; Belias et al., 2022).

An effective evaluation system is a tool for improving organizational practices, such as recruitment and selection process. Through theprocesses. Performance evaluation methods define, clarify, and validate selection criterialar performance evaluations could validate or not the predictive accuracy of the selection methodologies.

Performance evaluation is an integral part of the Human Resource Management strategy. It incorporates modern methods and technologies to improve recruitment, develop employee skills, and achieve corporate goals. In a world of constant change, effective evaluation is the foundation for maintaining competitiveness and the success of any organization (Berridge et al., 2007).

Personnel evaluation is critical for making strategic decisions in the organization and enabling effective human resource management. This process will likely identify talents, recognize development needs, and design targeted interventions that enhance employee performance and engagement. One of the key advantages of evaluation is the ability to predict employees' potential. Via performance monitoring, the organization can identify which employees have the characteristics and skills to take on higher or leadership positions (Egginton, 2010).

Furthermore, personnel evaluation allows employees to be provided with feedback regarding the quality of their performance. This feedback enhances transparency and acts as a self-improvement tool for employees, allowing them to understand where they excel and where they need to improve. Personnel evaluation helps the personnel to identify their needs (Egginton, 2010). As a result, targeted training programs can be created. These programs can help improve skills and develop human resources. In addition, the evolution provides data that helps calculate the training cost, ensuring that investments in training programs are sustainable and effective.

Personnel evaluation could determine changes in payment methods. Through this process, the organization can consider potential salary increases or other performance-based financial rewards, ensuring fairness and enhancing employee motivation. At the same time, data collected by the evaluation can improve organizational systems that enhance employee engagement and loyalty.

Personnel evaluationPersonnel evaluation aims to maintain high performance standards and identify areas for improvement. By monitoring employee performance, organizations ensure that the quality of work remains consistent and aligned with their expectations and strategic objectives. Evaluation helps to compare employee performance against predetermined targets set by their supervisors. This process ensures that individual performance supports the organization's overall strategy while allowing for the correction of deviations and reinforcement of achievements.

3.4. Personnel Evaluation Methods and Tools

Several methods and tools have been developed to evaluate the performance of personnel accurately. Some of them are the following: rating scales, essays, checklists, case studies, and significant events techniques. An effective evaluation tool should be simple, valid, reliable, objective, and capable of distinguishing excellent from poor performance. Organizations determine the method of performance measurement using general criteria such as quality, quantity, cost, and time to completion. However, evaluators must be fully objective, so their evaluations should only focus on employees' performance. Although absolute objectivity is difficult to achieve, when evaluators are aware of their biases, their influence on evaluations can be reduced or eliminated.

An evaluation performance method is a systematic process in which an employee's work is evaluated over a specific period. It aims to identify strategies for improving employees' performance. A performance evaluation is usually conducted annually or quarterly. Through objective analysis of skills, strengths, and areas for improvement, the evaluation process can help determine pay increases and promotions.

The performance evaluation process is a key tool for enhancing employee productivity and improving organizational results. Organizations can gain several strategic advantages by implementing effective appraisal methods that help them achieve their objectives. Figure 3 describes some of the most popular evaluation tools.

Figure 3. Employees' evaluation methods (tools)

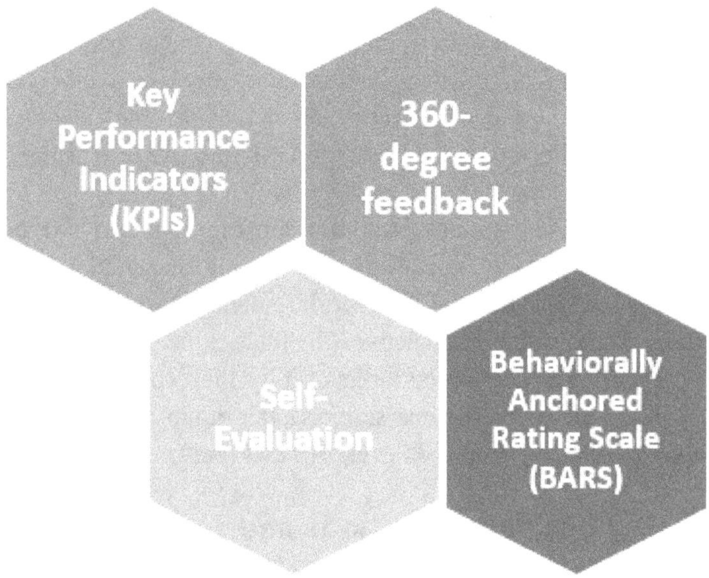

360-Degree Feedback

360-degree feedback is a powerful tool for performance management, as it balances the distribution of responsibility for evaluation and enhances the organization's sense of fairness. Although it requires more resources and time, its benefits (such as enhancing transparency, accountability, and collaboration) make it an effective strategy for organizations seeking to develop and strengthen their human capital.

Gathering feedback from multiple sources, such as supervisors, peers, subordinates, and partners, provides a holistic view of employees' performance. Through this multidimensional perspective, managers can identify strengths and improvement areas (Abboud, 2021). Unlike traditional single-source evaluations, this approach reduces bias and ensures greater objectivity, allowing performance to be managed more accurately.

Employees can provide feedback on their supervisors' actions and behaviors, enhancing the credibility of appraisals. This practice creates more comprehensive and accurate management performance evaluations, enhancing managers' accountability and commitment to continuous improvement.

Involving all employees in giving and receiving feedback enhances the sense of fairness in the organization. When all employees can contribute to the feedback process, transparency, and mutual trust are enhanced. This culture promotes accountability and ensures that each employee feels important in creating a positive and productive work environment (Abboud, 2021). The workload that is associated with performance evaluation reduces the pressure that is usually placed on specific teams or departments. The process becomes more collaborative and inclusive, with work distributed evenly throughout the organization. This approach not only facilitates more frequent and detailed evaluations but also enhances the sense of participation and commitment of all involved.

Performance evaluation using multidimensional feedback offers significant benefits. However, it includes several challenges that need to be addressed to ensure the effectiveness and credibility of the process. The evaluation process can be affected by interpersonal biases, especially when colleagues who have personal relationships evaluate each other. As a result, biased comments could be created that reduce feedback credibility. To mitigate this risk, it is necessary to provide training to evaluators to objectively criticize employees' performance (Gullickson, 2008). Additionally, the implementation of anonymous rating systems can reduce the effect of personal biases, ensuring more fair results.

Conducting comprehensive assessments using manual procedures can be extremely inefficient and difficult. Manual processes are vulnerable to errors, delays, and inconsistencies, making it difficult to collect and process feedback within the required timeframes. To overcome this challenge, organizations must invest in modern digital tools and platforms that automate the process, reduce errors, and ensure timely completion of evaluations. Providing and receiving detailed feedback requires a significant investment of time from employees. This time-consuming process can distract employees from their daily responsibilities and negatively influence productivity. To reduce this behavior, it is important to integrate the evaluation process into employees' work routines (Eisalou, 2014). Organizations can specify the periods for feedback activities and provide clear guidelines for effective time management.

Involving several evaluators can lead to inconsistencies in feedback, causing confusion and frustration for employees who receive conflicting feedback. Establishing clear evaluation criteria is necessary to ensure consistency in evaluations. In addition, trained evaluators can help maintain their consistency and reliability

When using 360-degree feedback software, employees can receive more feedback with less effort. Since providing feedback is a task shared among many evaluators, this method can be more efficient in evaluating job performance, especially in large organizations.

Key Performance Indicators: KPIs

Key Performance Indicators (KPIs) are quantified performance measures used to evaluate the achievement of specific objectives. KPIs are not just numbers – they are strategic tools that provide teams with clear objectives, milestones to access progress, and information to receive better decisions across the organization. To remain competitive, an organization must manage its employees, processes, planned activities, reduction time, supplier relationships, and other elements of its operations. An effective performance measurement system is used to understand, adapt, and improve operations in all parts of the organization (Summers, 2005).

Employees can recognize that certain activities are very important to management. Key Performance Indicators (KPIs) are financial and non-financial indicators used by an organization to demonstrate its success in achieving long-term goals. KPIs are static and stable indicators that become more meaningful when used comparatively. KPIs help streamline business analysis by removing emotion from the process and focusing attention on the business's core purpose, profit creationof profit.

KPIs are guiding tools that ensure that all teams are moving in the same direction by measuring the success of a project or evaluating employees' performance. By tracking clear goals, teams collaborate more effectively and focus on the organization's priorities. KPIs provide a realistic picture of the organization's overall health. From risk management to financial indicators, they provide valuable information about performance, financial stability, and the organization's potential challenges (Chan & Chan, 2004).

KPIs can help organizations to identify their successes and failures. In other words, KPIs provide information allowing the organization to take more actions that deliver positive results and reduce actions that do not deliver the expected value. Evaluation via KPIs could make the organization more flexible and adaptive to changes (Parmentor, 2015). KPIs allow employees to monitor their progress and help managers to ensure that operations run smoothly. As a result, each employee adds value to the organization and contributes to the achievement of the organization's goals.

Key Performance Indicators (KPIs) are distributed in several forms (Figure 4). While some are used to measure monthly progress to achieve a goal, others have a long-term focus. However, all KPIs are linked to strategic objectives (Chan & Chan, 2004).

Figure 4. Key performance indicators (KPIs) Types (Source: Villazon et al., 2020)

Continuous review of performance indicators is necessary to keep them in line with changing market conditions, customer needs, and internal developments within the organization. Regular meetings to evaluate the indicators' performance, thorough analysis of the data, and disclosure of any changes to the indicators ensure that all team members remain informed and coordinated.

Self-Evaluation

Self-evaluation is a process in which the employee is asked to evaluate his/her performance based on predefined criteria. It is a formal evaluation method that aims to provide a more in-depth understanding of the employee's perception of his/her performance. The main objective of this method is to ensure that employees understand the criteria against which they will be evaluated. Although self-evaluation may “carry” elements of subjectivity, it offers significant added value as it can reveal discrepancies between the employee's and the employer's evaluations. These discrepancies could be used as a starting point for constructive discussion and understanding the potential for improvement.

Employee self-evaluation is an important tool for human resources as it provides valuable information, especially when combined with other evaluation methods. Although organizations often focus on upward, downward,, or multi-dimensional (306-degree) feedback, self-evaluation provides a unique perspective that should not be overlooked.

The managers and the human resource department can use self-evaluation as a key benchmark. For example, if an employee believes he/she excels in a particular area, but other evaluations indicate otherwise, expectations could be mismatched (Roberts, 2002). Conversely, if an employee acknowledges difficulties in an area confirmed by other sources of feedback, then a more supportive approach would be given to address this issue.

Self-evaluation helps employees highlight their achievements, skills, and personal development that may not be visible to others. This information provides a more comprehensive understanding of the employee's contributions and capabilities, enriching the evaluation (Youssif et al., 2017). Self-evaluation encourages employees to self-reflect, promoting a deeper understanding of their strengths, weaknesses, and overall performance (Daoanis, 2012). Through systematic self-evaluation, employees are more likely to set realistic goals, seek opportunities for improvement, and take responsibility for their professional development.

While self-evaluation provides valuable information, it is limited when used alone. Self-evaluation cannot capture the full range of performance because it is not observed by supervisors or colleagues (Roberts, 2002). Hence, it can lead to an incomplete picture of an employee's overall performance and contribution. Self-evaluation is vulnerable to personal biases, as employees overestimate oror underestimate their abilities and contributions. This subjective personal view can create discrepancies between self-perception and external feedback.

Additionally, self-evaluation is likely not to consider the wider organizational context. Employees may focus on their tasks and successes without considering how their work would contribute to the organization's overall strategic goals. This narrow focus may lead to a fragmented understanding of their contribution (Youssif et al., 2017). To overcome these limitations, self-evaluation must be combined with other evaluation methods such as peer review, supervisor feedback, and objective performance indicators. This multi-dimensional approach ensures a more comprehensive and accurate evaluation, capturing different aspects of performance that self-evaluation may overlook.

Finally, self-evaluation is a valuable tool that enhances self-awareness, promotes introspection, and provides a unique perspective on employee performance. However, it must be integrated into a multidimensional evaluation strategy that takes external feedback into account (Daoanis, 2012). As a result, organizations can ensure a more fair, accurate, and comprehensive assessment of performance, enhancing the development of employees and the organization.

Behaviorally Anchored Rating Scale (BARS)

The Behaviorally Anchored Rating Scale (BARS) is a performance evaluation method that uses behavioral scales to assess employee performance. This tool combines quantitative and qualitative approaches to provide more accurate and objective ratings. Obtaining accurate and objective data is one of the biggest challenges in the performance evaluation process. Traditional employee evaluations are often based on a single perspective (most likely the supervisor's) that contains a high degree of subjectivity and potential for error (Martin-Raugh et al., 2016).

The BARS method enhances the objectivity of the scales by linking them to specific scenarios corresponding to each rating level. By using specific examples, such as benchmarks, this approach reduces subjectivity and improves the accuracy of the evaluation (Sjahruddin et al., 2022).

Instead of evaluating an employee's performance on a vague scale, the BARS method provides benchmarks based on real-life examples. This approach requires more attention from evaluators and reduces inconsistencies in scores.

The BARS method offers several advantages, making it one of the most reliable and fair performance evaluation methods. First, it reduces bias in ratings, as it is based on specific, observable behaviors rather than abstract characteristics. As a result, all employees are evaluated based on consistent and objective criteria directly related to their position. In addition, BARS provides clear and detailed performance standards, helping evaluators and employees understand the evaluation's requirements and set clear improvement goals (Martin-Raugh et al., 2016). By focusing on specific actions and outcomes, the method reduces subjectivity and differences that may result from each supervisor's interpretation. Another advantage is related to the personalization of the BARS method, as the method adapts to the specific responsibilities and requirements of each role, making the evaluation process more relevant and meaningful. Finally, using standardized benchmarks ensures consistency between evaluators, creating a united and reliable evaluation process across the organization. These features make the BARS method a valuable tool for objectively and fairly evaluating employee performance.

One of the main disadvantages of the BARS method is that it is very time-consuming to develop. Creating detailed scripts that describe desirable and undesirable behaviors requires extensive position analysis and collaboration with specialized experts (Sjahruddin et al., 2022). The process involves collecting data, writing descriptions, and validating the scenarios, which can require significant time, effort, and financial resources. This time-consuming nature of the method may deter many organizations from implementing it.

Another disadvantage of this method is its limitation on observable behaviors. BARS evaluates performance primarily on the basis of actions observed by the evaluator, which can be problematic in roles where significant contributions are not immediately visible. Furthermore, if the evaluator does not have the opportunity to observe an employee fully, key aspects of performance may be overlooked. This can lead to incomplete or even inaccurate appraisals.

The need for personalization is also a major disadvantage of BARS. Since the method must be tailored to each role's unique responsibilities and performance criteria, development requires separate scales for each job. This customization makes the BARS implementation process complex and resource-intensive (Asana et al., 2021). Especially in organizations with a wide range of roles and responsibilities, the requirement for repeated scale development can significantly strain available resources.

Although the BARS method provides excellent accuracy and objectivity in evaluations, its disadvantages—such as its time-consuming nature, limitations in observation, and the need for extensive customization—reduce its accessibility and ease of implementation for all organizations.

3.5. Challenges in Finding Talents

As already mentioned, it is crucial for an organization to retrieve talents to gain a competitive advantage in the business market. However, a literature review has highlighted the extensive challenges in identifying and evaluating talents. Traditional measurement indicators and evaluation methods implemented in talent management practices often face limitations in capturing the multidimensional and evolving skills required in modern workplaces (Lewis & Heckman, 2006).

In today's ever-changing, dynamic, and rapidly technologically developing working environment, the traditional talent evaluation model is insufficient to fully capture the competencies and characteristics necessary for organizational success. This problem becomes a serious challenge for organizations as they attempt to combine their talent management initiatives with their strategic objectives (Guthridge et al., 2008).

Additionally, the evolving nature of the working environment and the enhancement of new working roles oblige an organization to reexamine the traditional methods of talent evaluation. The "gig" economy, in the form of short-term contracts and freelance work arrangements, complicates talent identification and evaluation processes, as employees may possess skills and experiences acquired through non-traditional career paths (Aquino et al., 2023). Subjectivity in talent evaluation introduces biases and inaccuracies during the decision-making process. Research has revealed unconscious biases in evaluation processes, which can lead to several employees' lack of opportunity and career development (Noble et al., 2023). To handle these challenges, HRM must implement objective and data-based approaches that ensure fairness and transparency in talent management practices.

The key strategy for effective talent identification and evaluation is the integration of innovative evaluation methods and data analytics. Technological solutions, such as Artificial Intelligence (AI) evaluation tools and analytic predictable tools, enhance the accuracy and reliability of evaluation processes (Kilag et al., 2024).

3.6. The Relationship Between Personnel Evaluation Methods and Talent Management

The combination of talent management and personnel evaluation is a crucial strategy for optimizing organizational performance and achieving long-term goals. The connection between these two procedures provides an integrated approach to HR management since it can enhance decision making as well as employees' engagement and development (Efendi, 2021).

Talent management focuses on attracting, developing, and retaining the top employees in the organization. It includes processes such as the following: identifying key roles, developing skills and competencies, and creating a culture that enhances employees' engagement. These strategic processes increase the organization's ability to handle market challenges and achieve its organizational objectives (Figure 5). Personnel evaluation focuses on measuring the performance and productivity of employees through objective criteria (Collings and Mellahi, 2009). During this process, HRM can identify the strengths and the areas that need improvement. HRM can also support decisions regarding employee promotions, salary increases, and training initiatives. Additionally, the personnel evaluation provides valuable feedback to employees, and it enhances the feeling of transparency and commitment within the organization.

Figure 5. Steps of talents development (Source: Collings and Mellahi, 2009)

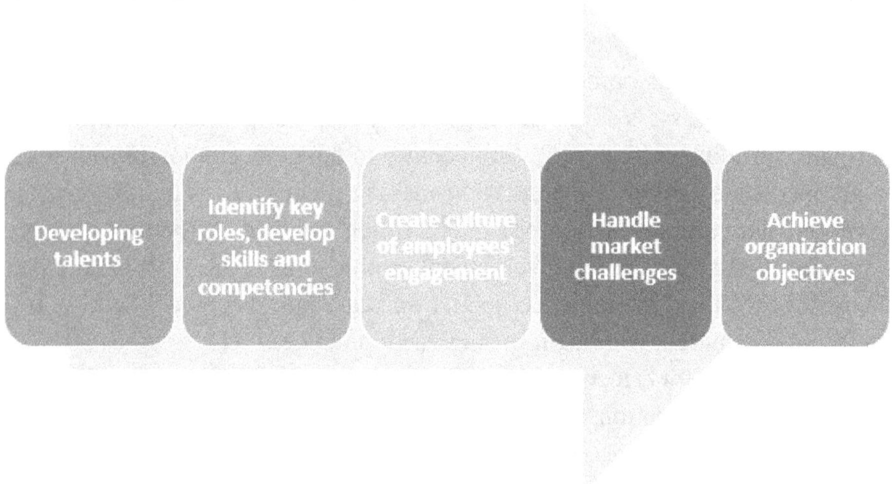

One of the most important aspects of combining talent management and personnel evaluation is strategic integration (Efendi, 2021). This integration ensures that the performance of employees' is directly linked to the broader goals of the organization. This procedure helps managers to exploit the resources and enhances the organization's ability to achieve sustainable growth.

The combination of talent management and personnel evaluation could lead to the development of targeted educational programs and initiatives. All data retrieved by employee evaluation can be used to identify training and development needs. These needs can be fulfilled through specific human resource strategies. The linkage between talent management and personnel evaluation can also contribute to the recognition and exploitation of the employees' high potential. As a result, organizations can identify employees who possess leadership skills and upgrade them to leadership development positions (Collings and Mellahi, 2009), which can enhance the future stability of the organization.

Furthermore, the personnel evaluation process promotes employees' engagement and loyalty. When employees feel that they are appreciated and have opportunities to develop, they are more likely to increase their personal efforts to achieve the organization's goals. This attitude leads to the creation of a positive organizational culture, which would improve overall organizational performance. Data that are retrieved from the combined use of talent management and personnel evaluation systems could provide valuable information that facilitates strategic decision-making. Hence, organizations could manage their human resources effectively and respond to market demands with greater flexibility (Cappelli, 2008).

Organizations recognize the importance of human capital. However, organizations are challenged to identify, train, and retain employees who are capable of working across different cultures and geographies (Aston and Morton, 2005). Historically, the concept of talent management has not been fully integrated into the organizational design of many organizations. However, this condition is starting to change since many organizations have been integrating talent management techniques into Human resources functions.

The main mission and responsibility of organizations regarding talent management procedures involve the attraction of talented employees combines with implement strategies and policies to retain and develop them. This strategy includes the following steps: identifying talents, designing development paths that maximize their value, and creating an environment that acts as a "center of attraction" for talented employees who are willing to integrate the organization's development plans (Figure 6) (Cappelli, 2008).

Figure 6. Attracting talented employees' steps (Source: Cappelli, 2008)

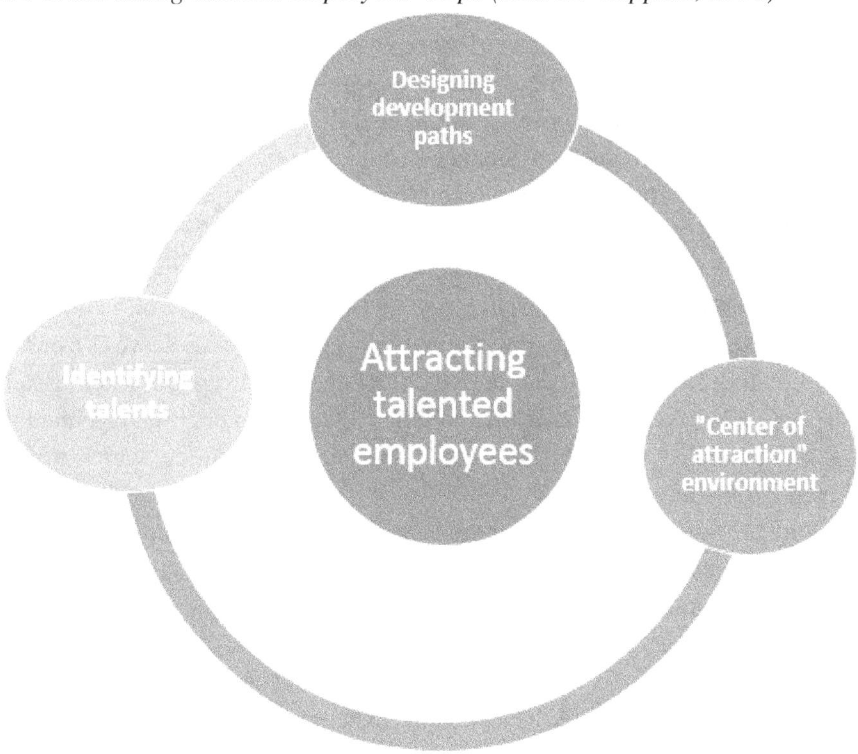

Talent management is not only referred to the selection of the right talent, but also includes the management of the existing talents in an effective and efficient way that ensures high engagement, motivation and maximum performance. Research indicates that employees' engagement and talent management strategies when combined with performance management, demonstrate a strong positive correlation. Organizational commitment reflects employees' willingness to remain within the organization they are occupied with.

Despite the fact that talent management is considered to be a priority for many organizations, its implementation remains fragmented and underdeveloped. Many times, organizations integrate talent management as a sub-process in activities such as training, performance, and recruitment and not as an integrated function as a whole (Capelli, 2008). For example, while talent management tools could be used during the recruitment process, they are totally ignored during the processes of career planning or performance evaluation. This process might limit the effectiveness of talent management. In other words, an organization can identify an employee's strong visual skills during the recruitment process but fails to incorporate this information into its career planning.

Talent management can be more effective when it is considered to be an integrated system that provides data and information to all HR functions. This kind of system would create a centralized "pool" of data, enabling transition between processes such as skills development, performance evaluation, and succession planning. By integrating talent management into a single framework, organizations can ensure that the data collected are transformed into meaningful information, which can facilitate strategic decision-making and promote linear improvement across human resources functions (Edendi, 2021).

Talent management combined with personnel evaluation can serve as a powerful tool for creating sustainable competitive advantage. For instance, when organizations adopt an employer "brand" that includes integrated talent management, they enhance their ability to attract and retain top-talent employees, which improves their market position.

Personnel evaluation is a key strategic method for making decisions related to talent management in an organization. More specifically, through employee evaluation, organizations can access information regarding employees' performance, skills, and capabilities. This information could help organizations to make decisions regarding recruitment, development, retention, and succession. Through these data, leadership identifies the strengths and the weaknesses of employees and teams, enabling more strategic human resource management (Armstrong and Taylor, 2023).

As it is already mentioned, one of the main advantages of personnel evaluation is the ability to identify the strengths and weaknesses of each employee. Regular performance reviews and skills evaluations provide managers a clear picture of which employees are excelling in their job duties and which employees need improvement. Additionally, evaluations can help identify potential employees who are ready to take on increased responsibilities or leadership roles.

Regarding the recruitment process, personnel evaluation helps human resources to align recruitment decisions with the needs of the organization. Analysis of evaluation data can help organizations identify the specific skills and competencies needed for various roles and guide them to hire the appropriate candidates who would complete the existing working teams (Cappelli, 2008). In addition, evaluations facilitate decisions about whether to internally promote existing employees or recruit personnel from external sources.

The procedures of training and development can also benefit from evaluation data. By accurately mapping the development needs of employees, organizations can design targeted training programs that fulfill specific skills gaps. Employees with high potentials, can participate in leadership development programs to prepare for future challenges, enhancing executive succession.

Similarly, personnel evaluation is valuable for employee retention strategies. Recognizing and rewarding top employees based on the results of evaluations could boost morale and engagement. Providing regular feedback ensures that employees feel valued; their intentions and purposes are aligned with organizational goals. This can reduce the likelihood of leaving their job. Moreover, understanding personal motivations via evaluations would allow organizations to implement strategies that improve job satisfaction.

Succession planning is a critical aspect of talent management. Employees' evaluation can provide essential information on whether the employees are ready to take on leadership roles (Armstrong and Taylor, 2023). These evaluations help identify future leaders and capture the skills and experience needed for key positions, ensuring a smooth transition when gaps arise and preparing the organization for long-term success.

Personnel evaluation optimize the strategies of human resources, ensuring that tasks and projects are assigned to the most suitable employees. Understanding group dynamics through evaluation data helps create stronger and more effective teams (Cappelli, 2008). Furthermore, by utilizing evaluation metrics, organizations can align the capabilities of their workforce with broader strategic goals, promoting individual and organizational growth.

By adopting best practices (such as using objective criteria, combining qualitative and quantitative data, and leveraging technology), organizations can maximize the value of staff evaluations. Integrating talent management strategies with employees' evaluation systems not only enhances employee performance and satisfaction but also positions the organization for long-term success.

Finally, Figure 7 describes some examples of famous worldwide companies that have combined talent management with personnel evaluation systems:

Google: One of the biggest challenges Google has faced is to manage a rapidly growing workforce while maintaining a culture of innovation. For this reason, it introduced the Objectives and Key Results (OKRs) system, which combines talent management with performance evaluation. Through this system, employees and supervisors co-set goals and measure progress toward achieving them (Doerr, 2018). As a result, Google achieved greater transparency in goal setting, increased internal employee promotion, and reduced recruitment costs.
Starbucks: This Company approached talent management through a values-based evaluation model. Apart from the traditional performance indicators, it evaluated employees on how they incorporated the company's values into their daily work. Additionally, Starbucks offered professional development opportunities through leadership programs (Lencioni, 2002). As a result, the company reduced employee attrition, increased customer satisfaction, and enhanced company's reputation as an attractive employer.
General Electrics (GE): This Company replaced the traditional annual evaluation system with a continuous feedback model known as "Performance Development". This new system incorporates talent management through frequent feedback and adjustment of individual development plans (Bartlett and Wozny, 2005). As a result, the company increased productivity, improved employees' satisfaction, and identifies faster the talents for key job positions.

Figure 7. Examples of personnel evaluation and talent management

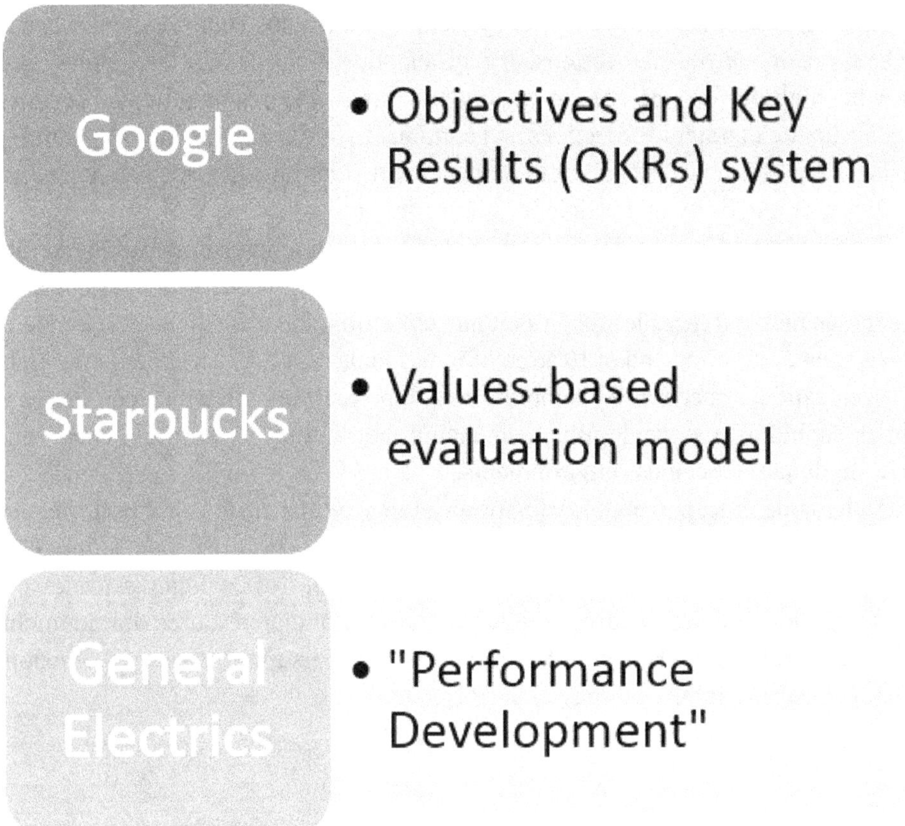

4. CONCLUSIONS

The systematic literature review has highlighted the multidimensional nature of talent management, revealing that it includes different aspects that are essential for organizational success. Talent management is not only related to the simple recruitment and selection processes. It includes a holistic approach that involves development, retention, and evaluation planning. This framework underlines the strategic importance of human capital in enhancing competitiveness and sustaining organizational performance.

Talent management strategy is a key element for the sustainability and competitiveness of modern organizations. By systematically attracting, developing, and retaining high-performing employees, organizations can align their human resource needs with their strategic objectives and continue to develop in the rapidly changing business environment. When talent management is combined with organizational practices, productivity and efficiency can be maximized.

Organizations identify the need to implement multi-dimensional strategies and practices for effective talent management. As Collins and Mellahi (2009) emphasize, talent management includes the systematic attraction, identification, development, engagement, retention, and utilization of individuals who are considered important to organizational success. By adopting this approach, organizations can leverage human capital as a strategic asset, enhancing their ability to innovate, adapt, and thrive in dynamic business environments.

At the same time, personnel evaluation systems are critical tools for performance management and talent identification. Through systematic performance monitoring, organizations can identify strengths and weaknesses, recognize leadership characteristics, and design targeted interventions for human resource development. Employee evaluation also provides important data to support strategic decision-making, ensuring improved overall performance.

REFERENCES

Abboud, S. (2021). The impact of 360 degrees performance appraisals on employee retention. *The EUrASEANs: Journal on global socio-economic dynamics*, 3 (28), 37-49.

Anderson, M. C. (2008). Taking Coaching to the Next Level: Critical Insights from ROI Evaluations. In Drake, D. B., Brennan, D., & Gørtz, K. (Eds.), *The philosophy and practice of coaching. Insights and issues for a new era* (pp. 317–332). Jossey-Bass.

Aquino, S. R., Kilag, O. K., & Valle, J. (2023). From Preparedness to Action: Effective Real-time Crisis Management. Excellencia: *International Multi-disciplinary Journal of Education* (2994-9521), 1(5), 372-384.

Armstrong, M., & Taylor, S. (2023). *Armstrong's handbook of human resource management practice: A guide to the theory and practice of people management*. Kogan Page Publishers.

Asana, I. M. D. P., Sudipa, I. G. I., & Putra, K. A. P. (2021). A Decision Support System on Employee Assessment Using Analytical Network Process (ANP) and BARS Methods. *Jurnal Teknik Informatika CIT Medicom*, *13*(1), 1–12. DOI: 10.35335/cit.Vol13.2021.38.pp1-12

Aston, C., & Morton, L. (2005). Managing Talent for competitive advantage. *Strategic HR Review*, *4*(5), 28–31. DOI: 10.1108/14754390580000819

Bartlett, C. A., & Wozny, M. (2005). *GE's Two-Decade Transformation: Jack Welch's Leadership*. Harvard Business School Case Study.

Bartlett, K. R. (2001). The relationship between training and organizational commitment: A study in the health care field. *Human Resource Development Quarterly*, *12*(4), 335–352. DOI: 10.1002/hrdq.1001

Becker, B. E., Huselid, M. A., Pickus, P. S., & Spratt, M. F. (1997). HR as a Source of Shareholder Value: Research and Recommendations. *Human Resource Management*, *36*(1), 39–47. DOI: 10.1002/(SICI)1099-050X(199721)36:1<39::AID-HRM8>3.0.CO;2-X

Belias, D., & Rossidis, I. (2024). *Change management: Organizational Change and Organizational Behavior* [in Greek]. Tziolas Publications.

Belias, D., Rossidis, I., Papademetriou, C., Masouras, A., & Anastasiadou, S. (2023a). *Managing Successful and Ethical Organizational Change*. IGI Global. DOI: 10.4018/979-8-3693-0235-4

Belias, D., Rossidis, I., Sotiriou, A., & Malik, S.Case Study in Greek Seasonal Hotels. (2022). Workplace Conflict, Turnover, and Quality of Services. Case Study in Greek Seasonal Hotels. *Journal of Quality Assurance in Hospitality & Tourism*, *24*(4), 453–476. DOI: 10.1080/1528008X.2022.2065655

Berke, D., Kossler, M. E., & Wakefield, M. (2008). *Developing Leadership Talent.* Wiley: Pfeiffer.

Berridge, E. J., Kelly, D., & Gould, D. (2007). Staff appraisal and continuing professional development: Exploring the relationships in acute and community health settings. *Journal of Research in Nursing : JRN*, *12*(1), 57–70. DOI: 10.1177/1744987106074018

Blass, F. R., & Ferris, G. R. (2007). Leader reputation: The role of mentoring, political skill, contextual learning, and adaptation. *Human Resource Management*, *46*(1), 5–19. DOI: 10.1002/hrm.20142

Boudreau, J. W., & Ramstad, P. M. (2007). *Beyond HR metrics: HR analytics.* Employment.

Boxall, P. F., & Purcell, J. (2011). *Strategy and human resource management.* Palgrave Macmillan.

Cappelli, P. (2008). *Talent on Demand: Managing Talent in an Age of Uncertainty.* Harvard Business Press.

Chambers, E. G., Foulon, M., Handfield-Jones, H., Hankin, S. M., & Michaels, E. G. (1998). The War for Talents. *The McKinsey Quarterly*, (3), 44–57.

Chan, A. P., & Chan, A. P. (2004). Key performance indicators for measuring construction success. *Benchmarking*, *11*(2), 203–221. DOI: 10.1108/14635770410532624

Cohn, J. M., Khurana, R., & Reeves, L. (2005). Growing Talent as if Your Business Depended on It. *Harvard Business Review*, *83*(10), 62–70. PMID: 16250625

Collings, D. G., & Mellahi, K. (2009). Strategic Talent Management: What is it and how does it matter? *Human Resource Management Review*, *19*(4), 304–313. DOI: 10.1016/j.hrmr.2009.04.001

Conway, S. (2007). *The think factory: Managing today's most precious resource, people!* John Wiley & Sons.

Daoanis, L. E. (2012). Performance Appraisal System: It's Implication to Employee Performance. *International Journal of Economics and Management Sciences*, *2*(3), 55–62.

Doerr, J. (2018). *Measure What Matters: How Google, Bono, and the Gates Foundation Rock the World with OKRs*. Penguin.

Efendi, S. (2021). Implementation of talent management as an effort to improve employee performance. *In 2nd Annual Conference on blended learning, educational technology and Innovation (ACBLETI 2020)* (pp. 537-542). Atlantis Press.

Egginton, B. E. (2010). Introduction of formal performance appraisal of academic staff: The management challenges associated with effective implementation. *Educational Management Administration & Leadership*, *38*(1), 119–133. DOI: 10.1177/1741143209351660

Eisalou, M. R. (2014). *Human Resource 360-Degree Feedback*. LAP LAMBERT Academic Publishing.

Ellickson, M. C., & Logsdon, K. (2001). Determinants of Job Satisfaction of Municipal Government Employees. *State & Local Government Review*, *33*(3), 173–184. DOI: 10.1177/0160323X0103300302

Evans, J. R., & Jack, E. P. (2003). Validating Key Results Linkages in the Baldrige Performance Excellence Model. *The Quality Management Journal*, *10*(2), 7–24. DOI: 10.1080/10686967.2003.11919060

Friederichs, P., & Labes, M. (2006). Human Capital Management. In Kruppke, H., Otto, M., & Gontard, M. (Eds.), *Human Capital Management. Personalprozesse erfolgreich managen* (pp. 17–26). Springer.

Gandossy, R., & Kao, T. (2004). Talent Wars: Out of Mind, Out of Practice. *Human Resource Planning*, *27*(4), 1519.

Gullickson, A. R. (2008). *The personnel evaluation standards: How to assess systems for evaluating educators*. Corwin Press.

Guthridge, M., Komm, A. B., & Lawson, E. (2008). Making talent a strategic priority. *The McKinsey Quarterly*, *1*(48).

Hills, A. (2009). Succession planning — Or smart talent management? *Industrial and Commercial Training*, *41*(1), 38. DOI: 10.1108/00197850910927697

Kilag, O. K., Largo, J., Rabillas, A., Kilag, F., Angtud, M. K., Book, J. F., & Sasan, J. M. (2024). Administrators' Conflict Management and Strategies. International Multidisciplinary [IMJRISE]. *Journal of Research for Innovation, Sustainability, and Excellence*, *1*(1), 60–67.

Kraugusteeliana, K., Gadzali, S. S., & Ausat, A. M. A. (2023). Revitalizing Organizational Performance: Innovative Strategies for Information Technology-Based Human Resource Development. *Jurnal Minfo Polgan*, *12*(2), 2384–2392. DOI: 10.33395/jmp.v12i2.13277

Lawler, E. E. (2008). Choosing the right talent management strategy. *Workspan*, *51*(7), 73–75.

Lawler, E. E.III. (2009). Make Human Capital A Source of Competitive Advantage. *Organizational Dynamics*, *38*(1), 1–7. DOI: 10.1016/j.orgdyn.2008.10.007

Lencioni, P. M. (2002). Make Your Values Mean Something. *Harvard Business Review*. PMID: 12140851

Lewis, R. E., & Heckman, R. J. (2006). Talent management: A critical review. *Human Resource Management Review*, *16*(2), 139–154. DOI: 10.1016/j.hrmr.2006.03.001

Lipsky, M. (2010). *Street-level bureaucracy: Dilemmas of the individual in public services*. Russell Sage Foundation.

Lockwood, N. R. (2006). Talent Management: Driver for Organizational Success. *HRMagazine*, *51*(6), 1–11.

Martin-Raugh, M., Tannenbaum, R. J., Tocci, C. M., & Reese, C. (2016). Behaviorally anchored rating scales: An application for evaluating teaching practice. *Teaching and Teacher Education*, *59*, 414–419. DOI: 10.1016/j.tate.2016.07.026

Mayer, R. C., Davis, J. H., & Schoorman, F. D. (1995). An integrative model of organizational trust. *Academy of Management Review*, *20*(3), 709–734. DOI: 10.2307/258792

McGrath, L. (2008). The War for Talent: High Potential Management is the Winning Strategy. *Accountancy Ireland*, *40*(2), 60–61.

Noble, J. I., Kilag, O. K., & Viscara, C. (2023). Bridging Academia and Community: A Holistic Approach to Disaster Risk Management. Excellencia: *International Multi-disciplinary Journal of Education* (2994-9521), 1(6), 36-45.

Ntalakos, A., Belias, D., & Koustelios, A. (2024b). The Relationship Between Leadership Styles, Organizational Culture and Group Dynamics in the Hospitality Industry. In Katsoni, V., & Cassar, G. (Eds.), *Recent Advancements in Tourism Business, Technology, and Social Sciences. IACuDiT 2023. Springer Proceedings in Business and Economics*. Springer., DOI: 10.1007/978-3-031-54342-5_19

Ntalakos, A., Belias, D., Koustelios, A., & Tsigilis, N. (2025). Examining the Validity of Organizational Behavior Measurement Scales in the Greek Hospitality Industry. *International Journal of Hospitality and Tourism Systems, 18*(1), 1–14. DOI: 10.21863/ijhts/2025.18.1.001

Ntalakos, A., Belias, D., Rossidis, I., Papademetriou, C., Koustelios, A., & Tsigilis, N. (2024). Group Dynamics in a Multicultural World: Embracing Diversity to Increase Group Performance. In Belias, D., Rossidis, I., & Papademetriou, C. (Eds.), *Organizational Behavior and Human Resource Management for Complex Work Environments* (pp. 356–377). IGI Global., DOI: 10.4018/979-8-3693-3466-9.ch017

Ntalakos, A., Belias, D., & Tsigilis, N. (2024c). Analyzing the Organizational Factors that Influence Hotel Employees' Team Efficiency. In Katsoni, V., & Cassar, G. (Eds.), *Recent Advancements in Tourism Business, Technology, and Social Sciences. IACuDiT 2023. Springer Proceedings in Business and Economics*. Springer., DOI: 10.1007/978-3-031-54342-5_11

Ntalakos, A., Viterouli, M., Belias, D., Rossidis, I., & Koustelios, A. (2024d). Fostering Total Quality Management and Group Dynamics in the Tourism and Hospitality Industry. In *Papademetriou, C., Anastasiadou, S., Ragazou, K., Garefalakis, A., Papalexandris, S. ESG and Total Quality Management in Human Resources* (pp. 219–242). IGI Global. DOI: 10.4018/979-8-3693-2991-7.ch011

Papademetriou, C., Belias, D., Ragazou, K. (2024). Human Resource (HR) Management New Dynamics in Hiring, Technology Adoption, Work Environment Diversity: HR Managers' Interviews. *Communications of International Proceedings*, 2024 (16), .DOI: 10.5171/2024.4422824

Parmenter, D. (2015). *Key performance indicators: developing, implementing, and using winning KPIs*. John Wiley & Sons. DOI: 10.1002/9781119019855

Pratt, J. W., Zeckhauser, R. J., & Arrow, K. J. (1991). *Principals and agents: The structure of business*. Harvard Business Press.

Ready, D. A., Hill, L. A., & Conger, J. A. (2008). Winning the Race for Talent in Emerging Markets. *Harvard Business Review*, 86 (11), 62–72. *Relations Today, 34*(2), 51–60.

Ringo, T., Schweyer, A., DeMarco, M., Jones, R., & Lesser, E. (2008). *Integrated talent management: Part 1 - Understanding the opportunities for success*. IBM Corporation.

Roberts, G. E. (2002). Employee performance appraisal system participation: A technique that works. *Public Personnel Management*, *31*(3), 333–342. DOI: 10.1177/009102600203100306

Rothwell, W. (2010). *Effective succession planning: Ensuring leadership continuity and building talent from within*. Amacom.

Schuler, R. S., Jackson, S. E., & Tarique, I. (2010). Global talent management and global talent challenges: Strategic opportunities for IHRM. *Journal of World Business*, *46*(4), 506–516. DOI: 10.1016/j.jwb.2010.10.011

Scullion, H., & Collings, D. G. (2011). Global talent management: Introduction. In *Global Talent Management*. Routledge. DOI: 10.4324/9780203865682

Sebald, H., Enneking, A., & Wöltje, O. (2005). *Talent Management: Zwischen Anspruch und Wirklichkeit*. Towers Perrin.

Sjahruddin, H., Hidayat, P., Moridu, I., & Sutaguna, I. N. T. (2022). Determination of The Best Employee Using The Behavioral Anchor Rating Scale. *Jurnal Mantik*, *6*(3), 2753–2758.

Smart, B. D. (1999). *Topgrading: How leading companies win by hiring, coaching, and keeping the best people*. Prentice Hall Press.

Summers, D. (2005). *Quality Management*. Pearson Education.

Tansley, C., Turner, P. A., Foster, C., Harris, L. M., Stewart, J., & Sempik, A. (2007). *Talent: Strategy, management, measurement*. Chartered Institute of Personal & Development.

Villazon, C. C., Pinilla, L. S., Otegi Olaso, J. R., Candarias, N. T., & Lopez de Lacalle, N. (2020). Identification of Key Performance Indicators in Project-Based Organizations through the Lean Approach. *Sustainability (Basel)*, *12*(5977), 1–19. DOI: 10.3390/su12155977

Viterouli, M., Belias, D., Koustelios, A., Tsigilis, N., & Papademetriou, C. Time for Change: Designing Tailored Training Initiatives for Organizational Transformation. *In Belias, D., Rossidis, I., Papademetriou, C. Organizational Behavior and Human Resource Management for Complex Work Environments*, pp. 267-307. IGI Global. DOI: DOI: 10.4018/979-8-3693-3466-9.ch014

Vroom, V. H. (1964). *Work and motivation*. Wiley.

Vural, G., Sökmen, A. G., & Çetenak, E. H. (2012). Effects of working capital management on firm's performance: Evidence from Turkey. *International Journal of Economics and Financial Issues*, *2*(4), 488–495.

Youssif, A., Eid, N. M., & Safan, S. M. (2017). Staff performance appraisal system and its relation to their job satisfaction and empowerment: Developing performance appraisal tool. *IOSR Journal of Nursing and Health Science*, *6*(2), 25–26. DOI: 10.9790/1959-0602091727

Zerva, S., Belias, D., Rossidis, I., & Ntalakos, A. (2024). Examining the impact of leadership on job satisfaction in Greek luxury hotels. *Journal of Human Resources in Hospitality & Tourism*, *23*(3), 439–464. DOI: 10.1080/15332845.2024.2335123

Chapter 3
Enhancing Employee Engagement With Real-Time Data Insights

Christos Papademetriou
https://orcid.org/0000-0002-7167-7786
Neapolis University, Pafos, Cyprus

ABSTRACT

Employee engagement is a vital factor in organisational performance, affecting efficiency, creativity, and retention of staff. The emergence of real-time data analytics has transformed human resource management by facilitating immediate decision-making and promoting individualised worker experiences. This chapter examines the function of real-time data insights in improving staff engagement, referencing current academic studies and actual implementations. Principal subjects encompass the incorporation of data analytics into performance management, predictive analytics for retention, and the obstacles associated with the use of these technologies.

1. INTRODUCTION

In the current fast-changing corporate landscape, staff involvement has become fundamental to organisational resilience and competitiveness. Engagement is characterised by the degree of emotional commitment that person exhibits towards their organisation and its objectives, impacting essential outcomes such as productivity, innovation, and retention of staff (Kahn, 1990; Saks, 2006). Studies have consistently demonstrated that actively involved individuals are more inclined to exert discre-

DOI: 10.4018/979-8-3373-1942-1.ch003

tionary effort, display elevated job satisfaction, and match their personal goals with organisational aims (Bakker & Demerouti, 2008; Schaufeli et al., 2009).

Nevertheless, conventional approaches to evaluating and improving staff engagement, like periodic surveys and standardised programs, frequently fail to meet the evolving requirements of a contemporary workforce. These methodologies are generally reactive, offering insights that are often obsolete by the time they are evaluated and implemented (Harter et al., 2020). The emergence of the digital revolution, propelled by advancements in data analytics and AI, presents a revolutionary answer to this issue (Papademetriou, et al., 2024a; 2024b; 2025) . Real-time data analytics allows organisations to transition from retrospective assessments to proactive engagement tactics, facilitating prompt actions and tailored experiences for staff (Bersin, 2023).

The growing intricacy of contemporary workplaces, characterised by varied worker demographics, remote work setups, and swiftly evolving corporate environments, emphasises the necessity for novel involvement strategies. Real-time data insights offer a detailed comprehension of employee behaviours, preferences, and challenges, enabling organisations to formulate customised plans that align with specific staff members (Kavanagh et al., 2023). This feature promotes engagement and improves the employee-employer connection by encouraging trust, openness, and collaboration.

This chapter seeks to examine the diverse functions of real-time analytics of data in enhancing engagement among workers. It explores the theoretical foundations of involvement, analyses the utilisation of data-driven instruments in HRM, and discusses the ethical and practical challenges associated with their deployment. This essay synthesises insights from contemporary academic research as well as practical examples to provide a thorough view on how organisations might utilise real-time data to foster more responsive, favourable, and engaging environments for employees.

2. LITERATURE REVIEW

2.1 The Shift Toward Experiential Learning in Entrepreneurship Education

Recent technological breakthroughs have transformed organisational approaches regarding staff engagement, with real-time analysis of data serving a crucial function. Bakker and Demerouti (2020) assert that the immediate nature of data analytics facilitates a more profound comprehension of staff motivation and job engagement, especially in high-pressure work settings. Their research underscores the utilisation of fluid feedback chains to sustain a motivated workforce through ongoing acknowledgement and prompt solutions to issues.

Kavanagh et al. (2023) highlight the transformative capacity of Integrated Workplace Management Systems (IWMS) in enhancing engagement. These technologies integrate several data points—spanning productivity measures to employee attitude analysis—into practical conclusions that guide leadership tactics. Live dashboards can detect patterns of disinterest, enabling managers to respond preemptively prior to they develop into significant organisational problems.

Additionally, McBride and O'Connell (2022) examine the impact of real-time feedback on transforming conventional performance rating methods. Their findings indicate that staff members receiving consistent, data-driven feedback are 35% more likely to report elevated levels of engagement compared to those dependent on yearly appraisals. They contend that such systems promote a culture of ongoing progress and skill augmentation, especially when combined with AI-driven statistics that tailor developmental feedback.

The incorporation of predictive analytics in engagement techniques has attracted considerable interest. Wang et al. (2023) investigate the capability of machine learning algorithms to forecast turnover intentions through the analysis of trends in participation, productivity, and satisfaction among workers surveys. Their study indicates a 20% decrease in rate of attrition in organisations utilising these tools, emphasising their effectiveness in retention efforts.

Simultaneously, ethical issues with the utilisation of real-time data analytics have been examined by Van Dijck (2014). The research underscores issues with data privacy, computational transparency, and the potential for a monitoring culture. Springer promotes the implementation of moral frameworks that reconcile organisational requirements with employee autonomy, including techniques such anonymised data collecting and periodic audits to reduce bias.

The significance of real-time analytics in promoting equity and inclusion is equally remarkable. Jones and Smith (2023) analyse how these methods can illuminate inequalities in participation levels among various demographic groupings. By utilising this data, organisations can formulate targeted actions to address these disparities, promoting a more inclusive workplace. Their research demonstrates a 15% enhancement in ratings of engagement among under-represented groups in organisations that actively implement these techniques.

Notwithstanding these gains, numerous gaps remain in the literature. The ability to scale of these technologies in medium-sized businesses (SMEs) is yet inadequately examined. Large organisations has the means to invest in advanced analytics systems, however SMEs may encounter barriers to adoption due to constrained finances and insufficient technical competence. Bersin's research (2023) indicates that cloud-based subscription arrangements may democratise access to these technologies; nevertheless, empirical investigations confirming their effectiveness are still required.

The research highlights the transformative capacity of actual time data analytics in improving worker engagement. Implementation success depends on resolving moral issues, assuring scalability, and cultivating a culture that prioritises openness and diversity.

2.1 Real-Time Data: A New Paradigm for Engagement

Real-time data analytics denotes the ongoing collecting, processing, and analysis of information as events transpire. In Human Resource Management, these competencies allow organisations to observe dynamics at work, anticipate new trends, and proactively address employee requirements. Integrated Workplace Management Systems (IWMS) offer complete dashboards that monitor employee interactions, resource utilisation, and feedback in real-time, promoting a culture of flexibility and adaptability (Horizant, 2023).

Real-time data analytics significantly contribute to promoting inclusion and diversity in organisations. Through the analysis of participation patterns, organisations can discern discrepancies in involvement levels across various demographic groups and implement measures to mitigate structural impediments. This skill fosters more inclusive workplace policies and practices, linking organisational objectives with wider society ideals (Kavanagh et al., 2023).

2.2 Applications in Performance Management

Conventional performance management solutions frequently exhibit inflexibility and insufficient customisation. The incorporation of real-time data analytics into these systems mitigates these constraints by facilitating dynamic, data-driven feedback mechanisms. Recent research findings underscore the significance of AI-driven platforms in improving assessments of performance, and staff indicating increased happiness and drive when feedback is prompt and meaningful (Pooja & Krishnan, 2023). These technologies facilitate ongoing improvement by pinpointing skill deficiencies and suggesting customised training courses.

Real-time data further improves teamwork. Organisations can guarantee equitable resource allocation and promote a culture of collaboration by equipping leaders with knowledge about team dynamics and job distribution. Project management technologies that incorporate real-time data allow teams to effectively adjust to changing priorities, guaranteeing alignment of team efforts with organisational goals (McBride & O'Connell, 2022).

2.3 Predictive Analytics for Employee Retention

Predictive analytics utilises artificial intelligence algorithms to anticipate employee behaviours and trends, including turnover intentions. Organisations can undertake targeted interventions to retain top personnel by analysing aspects such as satisfaction with employment, career growth, and work-life balance. Studies demonstrate that organisations utilising predictive analytics get a 15-20% enhancement in retention rates, highlighting its effectiveness as a means of engagement (Basnet, 2024).

Moreover, predictive analytics aids in spotting prospective leadership candidates within the organisation. By evaluating essential performance measures and behavioural trends, HR teams may establish leadership development routes that correspond with individual ambitions and organisational requirements. This proactive strategy enhances morale and guarantees the longevity of leadership streams (Jones & Smith, 2023).

2.3 Challenges and Ethical Considerations

Notwithstanding its potential, the use of real-time data analytics in human resource management is fraught with obstacles. Principal concerns encompass data privacy, algorithmic bias, and the necessity for resilient organisational cultures that promote openness and ethical technology use. Establishing employee trust is essential; therefore, organisations must implement policies that emphasise security of information and moral decision-making.

A major challenge is the potential for data overload. As extensive data is perpetually produced, organisations must formulate techniques to extract meaningful insights from irrelevant information. Investing in sophisticated analytics technologies and cultivating a data-literate workforce are essential measures to address this issue (Wang et al., 2023).

3. DISCUSSION

This chapter's findings underscore the revolutionary capacity of real-time data analytics in improving engagement among workers. The transition from conventional, reactive HRM techniques to proactive, data-driven solutions highlights a notable advancement in organisational leadership. The incorporation of AI-driven mechanisms for feedback into management of performance systems enhances the evaluation process and fosters continuous learning and improvement (Zagalsky et al., 2021). Moreover, statistical analysis for retention provides a strategic benefit by allowing organisations to proactively mitigate problems with staff members, therefore cultivating a more supportive working atmosphere (Van Dijck, 2014).

Transparency in data procedures is fundamental to the successful implementation of real-time analytics. Workers are more inclined to interact with these platforms when organisations guarantee the responsible and ethical use of their data. Transparent communication about the objectives and application of analytics can enhance trust, cultivating an atmosphere in where staff feel esteemed and acknowledged (Dewitte & Ausloos, 2024).

Furthermore, the amalgamation of real-time data with organisational culture and leadership paradigms presents unexploited opportunities for enhancing engagement. Leaders that utilise data analytics insights for decision-making, acknowledge contribution, and resolve grievances promptly can greatly influence employee happiness and efficiency. Kavanagh et al. (2023) demonstrate that organisations training executives in data-driven decision-making experience elevated ratings of engagement and enhanced team dynamics.

The scalability of these tools across various organisational contexts also represents a potential area for growth. Bigger companies may more readily deploy and maintain these systems, but smaller organisations want customised solutions. Mitigating resource limitations via economical platforms, scalable analytical tools, and collaborations with technology vendors can democratise access to breakthrough innovations. Bersin's research (2023) indicates that advances in cloud-based models may provide SMEs with viable methods to successfully use real-time data.

Ethical dilemmas, especially with the possible exploitation of data, continue to be a significant concern. Organisations must establish stringent measures, particularly third-party audits, to guarantee data accuracy, equity, and regulatory compliance. In addition to compliance, embracing a proactive strategy that prioritises ethical management can augment the trustworthiness and efficacy of analytics programs.

Finally, longitudinal studies are necessary to comprehend the enduring effects of real-time analytics on staff happiness and organisational performance. Although short-term advantages are extensively proven, the long-term consequences, including the equilibrium between data-driven oversight and autonomy for staff members, necessitate further investigation. Excessive dependence on data devoid of human supervision may result in decision-making blind spots or inadvertent biases.

The future of real-time data analytics in human resource management is contingent upon its integration with emerging technologies, including blockchain, sophisticated artificial intelligence, and virtual reality. Blockchain can improve data security and transparency, especially in sensitive domains like payroll and records of workers, hence augmenting confidence among workers in data-driven platforms. Advanced AI systems, proficient in analysing intricate behavioural data, could yield more refined insights into staff engagement trends, facilitating hyper-personalized interventions. Augmented reality technologies have the potential to transform training and onboarding procedures by providing immersive, real-time feedback experiences, hence enhancing engagement from the beginning.

Furthermore, the notion of anticipatory well-being analytics presents a promising avenue for investigation. By amalgamating health and wellbeing measurements with conventional HR data, organisations can proactively discern burnout threats and furnish targeted assistance. Subsequent research should prioritise the democratisation of access to these technologies for SMEs, potentially via cloud-based subscription-based arrangements that reduce adoption hurdles.

Globalisation offers a possibility for real-time analytics to tackle cross-cultural engagement difficulties. Investigating how real-time data insights may be customised to account for regional and cultural variances would assist global corporations in developing broader approaches to engagement. Ultimately, ongoing investigations are essential to evaluate the enduring effects of these technologies, confirming that their implementation results in authentic, long-term enhancements in staff engagement and organisational performance.

4. CONCLUSION

Real-time data insights signify a transformative change in organisational strategies for staff engagement. These tools can revolutionise the dynamics of work by facilitating personalised circumstances, proactive leadership, and decision-making based on data. Effective implementation necessitates a balanced approach that harmonises technological advances with ethical and organisational factors. Future advancements in this domain will rely on sustained innovation, cooperative research, and the formulation of ethical frameworks that emphasise employee welfare and organisational inclusion. Eventually, real-time data analytics may cultivate workplaces that are both more effective and more human-centric, enhancing engagement and development for individuals and organisations alike.

REFERENCES

Bakker, A. B., & Demerouti, E. (2008). Towards a Model of Work Engagement. *Career Development International, 13*(3), 209–223. DOI: 10.1108/13620430810870476

Basnet, S. (2024). The Impact of AI-Driven Predictive Analytics on Employee Retention Strategies. *International Journal of Research and Review, 11*(9), 50–61. DOI: 10.52403/ijrr.20240906

Bersin, J. (2023). *HR Predictions for 2023: Technology-Driven Engagement Strategies*. Bersin Insights.

Dewitte, P., & Ausloos, J. (2024). Chronicling GDPR Transparency Rights in Practice: The Good, the Bad and the Challenges Ahead. *International Data Privacy Law, 14*(2), 106–133. DOI: 10.1093/idpl/ipad026

Harter, J. K.. (2020). *The Relationship Between Engagement at Work and Organizational Outcomes*. Gallup Research.

Horizant. (2023). Transforming Employee Engagement with Real-Time Data Insights. Retrieved from [https://www.horizantinsights.com]

Jones, R., & Smith, T. (2023). *Continuous Feedback in Modern Performance Management*. Employee Relations Journal.

Kahn, W. A. (1990). Psychological Conditions of Personal Engagement and Disengagement at Work. *Academy of Management Journal, 33*(4), 692–724. DOI: 10.2307/256287

Kavanagh, M., et al. (2023). Adaptive Workforce Management: Leveraging Real-Time Data. Journal of Human Resource Advances.

McBride, J., & O'Connell, P. (2022). *Personalized Engagement Initiatives through Predictive Analytics*. Organizational Behavior Review.

Papademetriou, C., Belias, D., Ragazou, K., & Garefalakis, A. (2024b). The Role of Human Resource Management (HRM) in Employee Mental Health and Well-Being for Complex Work Environments. In Belias, D., Rossidis, I., & Papademetriou, C. (Eds.), *Organizational Behavior and Human Resource Management for Complex Work Environments* (pp. 81–94). IGI Global Scientific Publishing., DOI: 10.4018/979-8-3693-3466-9.ch005

Papademetriou, C., Ragazou, K., & Garefalakis, A. (2024a). Adapting Artificial Intelligence in Cypriot Hotel Industry: The Views of Hotel Managers. In Bilgin, M. H., Demir, E., Danis, H., & Garcia Goni, M. (Eds.), *Eurasian Business and Economics Perspectives. EBES 2023. Eurasian Studies in Business and Economics* (Vol. 30). Springer., DOI: 10.1007/978-3-031-64140-4_8

Papademetriou, C., Ragazou, K., Garefalakis, A., & Anastasiadou, S. (2025). The Role of Artificial Intelligence in Employee Wellness and Mental Health. In Yadav, P. (Ed.), *Human Resource Strategies in the Era of Artificial Intelligence* (pp. 29–54). IGI Global Scientific Publishing., DOI: 10.4018/979-8-3693-6412-3.ch002

Pooja, J., & Krishnan, L. R. K. (2023). Employee Engagement Driven By AI and ML and Mediated by Progressive Work Practices - An IT Industry Perspective. SSRN Electronic Journal.

Saks, A. M. (2006). Antecedents and Consequences of Employee Engagement. *Journal of Managerial Psychology*, *21*(7), 600–619. DOI: 10.1108/02683940610690169

Schaufeli, W. B.. (2009). Work Engagement: Construct Validity and Measurement. *Journal of Happiness Studies.*

Van Dijck, J. (2014). Datafication, Dataism, and Dataveillance: Big Data Between Scientific Paradigm and Ideology. *Surveillance & Society*, *12*(2), 197–208. DOI: 10.24908/ss.v12i2.4776

Wang, L.. (2023). *Algorithmic Fairness in HRM: Challenges and Solutions*. Ethics and Data Science Review.

Zagalsky, A., Te'eni, D., Yahav, I., & Schwartz, D. G. (2021). The Design of Reciprocal Learning Between Human and Artificial Intelligence. Proceedings of the ACM on Human-Computer Interaction, 5(CSCW2), chapter 451. DOI: 10.1145/3479587

Chapter 4
Harnessing the Power of Business Intelligence in Workforce Development

Usharani Bhimavarapu
https://orcid.org/0000-0002-0246-1420
Computer Science and Engineering, Koneru Lakshmaiah Education Foundation, India

ABSTRACT

The fast-paced evolution of technology and the complexity of workforce dynamics have rendered Business Intelligence (BI) an indispensable tool for organizations that aim to maximize workforce management. "Unleashing the Power of Business Intelligence for Workforce Excellence: Talent Meets Technology" identifies how sophisticated BI tools, which are Convolutional Neural Networks (CNN) and Long Short-Term Memory (LSTM) networks, can be applied in a way that will further talent hiring, development, and retention. The study analyzes how structured and unstructured data, including employee performance, feedback, and engagement metrics, are brought in and delivered as actionable intelligence. Through the extraction of features with CNN and sequential extraction with LSTM, the study demonstrates how organizations can forecast workforce tendencies and make data-driven decisions. This research seeks to give organizations a road map for the successful adoption of BI in optimizing workforce excellence, linking talent initiatives with business objectives

DOI: 10.4018/979-8-3373-1942-1.ch004

INTRODUCTION

In this modern competitive business environment, companies now realize that their most important asset is not even the services or products they deal in but the people who work for them. The secret to workforce excellence is in optimizing and managing the people. Business Intelligence (BI) technology has come to play a central role in this endeavor, revolutionizing how companies leverage information to enhance their employees' productivity, interest, and overall performance. Through data collection, analysis, and reporting of employee-related data, BI supports organizations in making more informed talent acquisition, development, and retention decisions. Data-informed decision-making ensures that all labor-related decisions are based on facts, enabling more accurate strategies and improved outcomes. Where technology intersects with talent, the impact can be revolutionary, fueling personal and business success. Business Intelligence tools provide an integrated view of workforce performance that allows companies to remain dynamic and competitive. Business Intelligence tools allow for information and insights access anytime, allowing managers and HR professionals to see workforce performance patterns, trends, and issues immediately.

Whether measuring worker productivity, high-turnover drivers, or skills gaps, BI solutions offer actionable intelligence. Knowing how to predict workforce needs and track the effectiveness of existing practices is a HR department game-changer. These insights enable companies to align talent with business objectives so employees are focused toward common objectives. BI tools also allow the optimization of the hiring process by measuring the most productive sources of hiring, identifying what skill sets are required, and helping to place candidates in jobs more efficiently. This level of precision provides a better-attuned and more engaged workforce that is more mission-oriented for the company. One of the greatest advantages of using Business Intelligence to manage the workforce is that it enables employee satisfaction and engagement monitoring.

BI solutions can aggregate feedback from many sources such as surveys, performance appraisals, and social media, to give a general idea of the employees' mood. The information enables companies to solve issues before they become major problems, creating the workplace more supportive and satisfying. By knowing the drivers and obstacles of engagement, companies can take precise steps aimed at enhancing morale, retention, and job satisfaction. From career development and appreciation programs to work-life balance enhancements, BI helps companies develop strategies that respond to the distinctive requirements of their employees. As such, an enhanced work force is produced with a strong inclination to generate higher performance to the company. In addition, Business Intelligence can also be utilized for automating training and development programs so that organizations are able to train employees according to business requirements.

Training areas where more training is required can be found by studying the performance of the employees and the development programs can be scheduled accordingly. BI software can be applied to measure the performance of training programs through the monitoring of employees' progress against performance measures. This data-driven approach provides an opportunity for utilizing training assets and guarantees that the employees are gaining the needed skills to accomplish job tasks. BI also spots the best-performing employees who will be well suited for leadership training programs, and it presents a direct channel for career advancement. Through this way, talent development is an ongoing, measurable process that directly facilitates organizational growth. The incorporation of Business Intelligence into staff management also aids better performance management.

Through the utilization of data to define concrete performance objectives and standards, managers can more objectively and consistently measure employees' performance. BI software makes employee performance monitoring continuous, making it easier to discover performance problems early and provide the necessary support or training. The software can also be used to set individualized employee performance goals, which translate individual goals into business goals. The degree of customization translates to more relevant and achievable goals, which means employee motivation and success. By fostering a culture of ongoing feedback and development, BI helps significantly in the creation of a high-performing workforce. Another domain where BI has a big influence is succession planning.

Succession planning for leadership and forecasting future organizational talent needs are very important workforce management components. BI technology enables HR managers to evaluate employee tenure, talent, performance, and potential, which enables them to identify potential employees who can lead the company. Through internal talent assessment and planning for future business needs, organizations are able to come up with strategic and forward-looking succession plans. This facilitates sustainability when departing or retiring leaders are replaced without leadership gaps and organizational continuity. Further, BI software can also assist HR departments in anticipating talent shortages so that recruitment and retention can be planned well in advance. The potential of Business Intelligence lies not only in enhancing workforce management but also in enabling a data-driven culture for decision-making within the organization.

As increasing BI tools are part of day-to-day operations, workers across all levels of the organization are able to make smart decisions in the moment with real-time data. This democratization of information enhances collaboration across departments, as teams can work together and share ideas to tackle multifaceted challenges. For staff excellence, this strategy enables a feeling of ownership and accountability on the part of the employees since they are indeed making the company succeed. Employees help create a more responsive and nimble firm where talent is optimized in a continuous manner through data-driven decision-making. Beyond optimizing internal staff management, Business Intelligence enables companies to benchmark performance against industry levels and competitors as well.

Through provision of information about industry trends, compensation packages, and workforce practices, organizations are able to be confident that they are competitive regarding talent attraction and retention. BI tools help organizations identify emerging skills, market demand, and best practices that can be utilized for gaining a competitive edge. By being aware of how their workers match up against industry standards, firms can adjust their approach to ensure they remain employers of choice. This helps them recruit the best, particularly in high-demanding sectors with expertise, and hold onto top performers. Finally, application of Business Intelligence in the management of human capital can conserve expenses and maximize efficiency.

By comparing labour cost information, scheduling information, and resource utilisation, organizations can determine inefficient areas and take corrective measures to generate cost savings. For example, BI applications can be used to automate staffing scheduling so that the appropriate number of employees possessing the required skill set are scheduled during peak times to avoid overstaffing and understaffing. In addition, BI can pinpoint steps or processes that are not needed and could be automated so employees can focus on higher-value activity. With better decision-making based on data, organizations gain the ability to enhance their operations' efficiency, eliminate waste, and optimize resources, which translates into bottom-line enhancement. Business Intelligence is a pioneering style of workforce management where skills intersect with technology to facilitate excellence.

By tapping into the power of data, companies can automate hiring, training, engagement, and performance management and build an outrageously skilled and outrageously motivated workforce. BI not only enhances internal functioning but also allows companies to compete outside by developing insights about industry trends and best practices. Moreover, it propels a data-driven culture that pervades all levels of a company. As businesses fight to stay competitive within an ever-changing business landscape, the strategic implementation of Business Intelligence will be instrumental in defining the future of work and unleashing the maximum potential of their most valued asset—talent.

da Costa Innecco While da Costa Innecco's dissertation on cloud computing and big data's theoretical relevance to business intelligence is a bountiful presentation of perspectives, its flaw is that it is too theoretical in scope and does not provide immediate practical applications through real-life example (da Costa Innecco, 2015). Furthermore, the research fails to mention an in-depth study of the problems of cloud adoption, including security threats, data privacy issues, and scalability of BI environments within the cloud in big organizations.

Sangupamba et al.'s cloud-based business intelligence and big data paper presents challenging design-science researcher possibilities but does not address the real-world challenges that firms will face in trying to design and implement cloud-based BI systems (Sangupamba et al., 2014). The research refutes problems like cloud service provider lock-in, possible bottlenecks of performance, and complexity in implementing legacy systems into cloud infrastructure, which are prime concerns that may hinder the effortless use of BI in the cloud. Kajtazi and Tona's research of accounting information system integration with other systems and data is an overview and does not elaborate on the intricacy of collecting different sources of data from different platforms and organizational silos (Kajtazi & Tona, 2017).

The article also does not address the technical issue of maintaining data consistency, resolving data conflicts, or dealing with data quality and governance issues, the essence of effective integration in practice. Teruel et al.'s argument of business intelligence applications developed from a collaborative view spotlights collaboration without adequately addressing operational issues of developing and sustaining collaborative BI environments (Teruel et al., 2019). The article does not cover pitfalls in achieving control of data access, data privacy, and difficulties in maintaining real collaboration across organizational boundaries, which can restrict the efficiency of collaborative BI systems. Cobo et al.'s development of SciMAT, a science mapping analysis software, is a good research analysis tool but fails to examine the potential limitation in usability and scalability of the application to large datasets (Cobo et al., 2012). The research fails to investigate the use of SciMAT in multidisciplinary contexts or its adaptability in various modes of scientific research, hence restricted usability. Shu et al.'s study of the Chinese tenure system and Web of Science publications contribution provides an in-depth explanation of how academic publishing is connected to career advancement but fails to include a clear examination of how such a system affects research quality (Shu et al., 2020).

The article then fails to take into account the strengths and weaknesses of publication metrics as an indicator of success among scholars, for example, the publication pressure and publication bias problems.

Harzing and Alakangas' comparison of Google Scholar, Scopus, and the Web of Science provides a critique of the strengths and weaknesses of these databases but overlooks the shortcomings of utilizing the sites in a multiverse of scholarship (Harzing & Alakangas, 2016). The study also fails to touch on issues of coverage, database repository renewals, and the potential bias in using these databases for the evaluation of scholarly work.

Vera-Baceta et al. refer to language coverage for Scopus and Web of Science, but not to the general problem of how linguistic barriers affect access to research as well as global influence (Vera-Baceta et al., 2019). The article also does not look at implications of language constraints on researchers speaking other languages and how linguistic barriers might limit their potential to become part of the global body of researchers. Rahman's thesis on how the implementation of business intelligence (BI) in companies affects business is a proper perspective of what BI can deliver but is bogged down by the absence of empirical data and case studies (Rahman, 2011). The research does not try to enumerate the hindrances to BI implementation, including cost, resistance at the organizational level, and how difficult it can be to fit BI systems within current IT architectures. Matysek-Jędrych's work on the crisis and competitiveness of the Baltic States is a good example but was not general enough in trying to cover the impact of the global financial crisis on competitiveness elsewhere (Matysek-Jędrych, 2012). The research is limited as well because it is done in one geographic area and does not generalize on how economies can be able to handle crises in general.

Tripathi's article on the determinants of digital transformation in the post-COVID-19 business world provides a useful overview but does not fully explore the long-term implications of digital transformation on organizational culture and employee roles (Tripathi, 2021). The study also lacks a detailed exploration of the challenges businesses face in sustaining digital transformation efforts, such as skill gaps, cybersecurity concerns, and resistance to change.

Miethlich et al.'s research on COVID-19 pandemic digital management transformation is focusing on digital management transformation but fails to expose the actual problems faced by small businesses while adopting such technologies (Miethlich et al., 2022). The paper is silent about the problem of resources, technical limitation, or cyber attack issues commonly faced by small and medium enterprises (SMEs) during digital transformation.

Nagy et al.'s research on the function and role of Industry 4.0 and the Internet of Things (IoT) in shaping business strategy in Hungary is useful but does not include wider discussion of the global implications of these technologies (Nagy et al., 2018).

The research has limited geographical focus to cover just one country and does not take into account differences between various economies and industries having unique economic and technological backgrounds while implementing Industry 4.0 and IoT.

Buhalis and Leung's discussion of intelligent hospitality and networked ecosystems provides useful insight into the tourism industry but does not address the application of these technologies to smaller independent hospitality enterprises (Buhalis & Leung, 2018). The research also leaves out the hospitality digital divide and the possibility that non-tech companies may have difficulty utilizing sophisticated technology solutions.

Bucher et al.'s research on process-oriented business intelligence is a fresh angle but does not discuss the technical and organizational issues of deploying the process-oriented BI system (Bucher et al., 2009). The legacy system integration complexity or resistance from employees who might be unwilling to adhere to current processes cannot be discussed because it limits the success of process-oriented BI endeavors.

Akyuz and Rehan's paper on preconditions for establishing an 'e-supply chain' is rich in theoretical recommendations on electronic supply chains but does not include any concrete examples or case studies illustrating the viability of their proposals (Akyuz & Rehan, 2009). The studies do not consider operation problems faced by companies, such as the integration of new technologies into existing supply chain infrastructure or potential disruptions caused by the adoption of new supply chain paradigms. Pavkov et al.'s summary of business intelligence systems is a general history and does not directly address current challenges organizations are encountering in adopting these systems (Pavkov et al., 2016).

The research primarily talks about BI history, and minimal focus is provided on BI complexities like data integration problems, having trained personnel, and high-cost implementation. Secondly, the paper does not discuss the technological limitations of legacy BI systems, which may slow down modernization in some sectors. While Tamang et al. examine how business intelligence is enhanced using machine learning algorithms, their research mostly examines the theoretical possibilities of these technologies without taking into account the practical issues that organizations would most likely encounter in applying machine learning to BI systems (Tamang et al., 2021). The article does not explore concerns such as the computationally infeasible expense of machine learning algorithms, the necessity of having massive datasets, and the difficulties involved in guaranteeing data quality and consistency. The authors also refrain from mentioning the possibility of algorithmic bias when making decisions.

Reshi and Khan's work focuses on the development of business intelligence by machine learning without providing empirical evidence of machine learning models' utility in optimizing business decisions (Reshi & Khan, 2014). The authors develop theoretical models rather than offering sufficient case studies or real-life examples where the models have been effectively used. Additionally, the study does not address the scalability of these models or their performance in diverse business environments, limiting their applicability. Bakshi's consideration of artificial intelligence and machine learning approaches provides a theoretical foundation but does not adequately discuss the practical challenges associated with implementing these technologies in business environments (Bakshi, 2018).

The article is more concerned with possible use cases without discussing the intricacies of data preparation, model deployment, and maintenance. The author also does not discuss the ethics of applying AI and machine learning to business decision-making, which may be unsafe in terms of fairness, transparency, and accountability. Zohuri and Moghaddam's article on transitioning from business intelligence to artificial intelligence provides a sound view but lacks comprehensiveness in explaining how firms can realistically incorporate AI technologies into their current BI infrastructure (Zohuri & Moghaddam, 2020). The research fails to account for the gigantic infrastructure and training investments firms need to make to effectively transition from conventional BI to AI.

In addition, challenges of associating AI solutions with concrete business objectives and tracking their realization are insufficiently resolved. Hlavá and Štefanovi's publication regarding machine learning and business intelligence captures the paradigm change from descriptive to predictive analytics but does not quite touch upon the predictive model constraints when projected into real-world scenarios (Hlavá & Štefanovi 2020). While the paper discusses how predictive analytics may be powerful, it is not delving into the question of overfitting and challenges to test precision and reliability in order to make predictions. In addition, the authors are overlooking the issue of practical constraints in using machine learning models within an organization at a large scale.

Abdel-Karim et al.'s bibliographic review of machine learning in information systems is insightful but lacking in terms of detail in the nature of challenges organizations experience in implementing machine learning technologies (Abdel-Karim et al., 2021). The review fails to capture significant challenges such as inadequate data, the requirement of skilled talent, and the capability to integrate machine learning models with existing systems. Furthermore, the authors do not refer to the possible pitfalls of applying machine learning to business decision-making, such as bias and inaccuracy in the models. Shollo and Galliers' research into BI systems' contribution to organizational knowledge highlights the significance of BI in facilitating knowledge management but does not discuss how organizations can manage the resistance to change that normally faces BI system implementation (Shollo & Galliers, 2016).

Porfírio and Santos' approach to Business Intelligence as a service recognizes its strategic importance but does not provide an in-depth analysis of challenges facing businesses when they adopt BI as a service model (Porfírio & Santos, 2011). The article does not take into account such key issues as data security, compatibility with current IT infrastructure, and the disadvantages of having third-party service providers manage BI tools. Also, it does not address the risks involved in outsourcing BI services such as losing confidentiality over sensitive information. Muntean and Mircea's research into BI solutions to gain competitive edge provides sound observations, but it lacks an in-depth explanation of how organizations can utilize these solutions effectively (Muntean & Mircea, 2007).

The article predominantly discusses the benefits of BI but does not address the technical problems of deploying BI solutions, such as integrating heterogeneous data sources, data governance, and the need for skilled resources to manage and analyze the data in the correct manner. Karim's critique of competitive business intelligence systems (CBIS) in global markets is a helpful contribution but says nothing on the specific challenges facing small and medium-sized enterprises (SMEs) in implementing CBIS (Karim, 2011). The article itself is focused primarily on large companies, failing to consider the resource scarcity, budgetary restrictions, and scarce expertise facing SMEs.

Additionally, the paper fails to address the ethical considerations of using CBIS in competitive contexts, such as potential abuse of competitive intelligence. Another shortcoming of Lateef and Omotayo's work is that it mostly addresses the theoretical framework of information audits within organizational management without offering extensive empirical data or case studies to demonstrate the proposed methodologies (Lateef & Omotayo, 2019). Although the review emphasizes the significance of information audits, it fails to address adequately the real-world implementation challenges that organizations encounter when conducting such audits in practice. The paper also could have investigated how specific industries manage to tailor information auditing practices to themselves, restricting its findings' generalizability across sectors.

Suchánek's work on Business Intelligence (BI) as a panacea for modern enterprises is a thorough explanation of its benefits but without a critical review of the weaknesses of BI deployment for small or low-capacity businesses (Suchánek, 2019). The article focuses primarily on large organizations, perhaps overlooking problems such as high implementation costs, low data quality, and the need for experienced personnel, which may deter BI tools from being adopted by small companies. Gioia, D.A.; Corley, K.G.; Hamilton, A.L. (2013): Gioia et al.'s qualitative study method, while useful to inductive research, can be time-consuming and costly, thereby could prove difficult to researchers with scarce resources or limited timeframes (Gioia et al., 2013). Secondly, the method heavily relies on interpretation by the researcher, therefore has a potential of introducing bias in findings. The method also presumes saturation of data can be achieved in qualitative research, and that is not always possible. The research by Lim and Teoh on strategic impacts of BI adoption is informative but isn't supported by empirical evidence from a diverse set of industries or geographical locations, and as such, any generalizability to the findings is limited (Lim & Teoh, 2020). The study also largely discusses theoretical models and not the empirical issues of organizational BI strategy implementation, such as data integration challenges, system incompatibility concerns, and users' resistance.

Viitanen and Pirttimaki's work on BI for strategic management in technology-oriented companies focuses mainly on large enterprises and does not provide enough context for how BI strategies can be adapted for smaller firms or those in non-tech industries (Viitanen & Pirttimaki, 2006). The research does not also adequately address the shortcomings of the BI systems, such as their high costs, complicated implementations, and data overload, which can choke organizations if they are not adequately trained or equipped. The Barone et al. Business Intelligence Model gives a strategic picture of BI but would be enhanced if the model was developed further based on how firms make use of these models in practice (Barone et al., 2010). The authors use theoretical frameworks instead of sound empirics, and it is therefore not very simple to assess their suitability in practice. Additionally, the model may be too complex for small businesses with insufficient resources.

Power's background of Decision Support Systems (DSS) is broad but does not incorporate an intimate description of how DSS has evolved in the modern digital age, particularly with the advent of big data and AI technologies (Power, 2003). The article also does not discuss the challenges and limitations of organizations in implementing DSS tools, including concerns about data privacy, integration of the existing system, and the skill set of the personnel required for utilizing the systems.

Marjamäki's study on the evolution and trends of BI systems provides an excellent systematic mapping, but it mainly focuses on trends rather than practical applications or challenges faced by organizations (Marjamäki, 2017). Though the research is wide-ranging, it does not address how firms address problems like data quality, departmental integration, or resistance to change, which may hinder successful implementation of BI systems. Dresner's first contribution to BI is traditional but aged in the context that it does not take into account the rapid expansion of technology that has transformed modern BI systems, such as cloud computing, machine learning, and real-time data analysis (Dresner, 1989). The article also lacks a discussion of BI limitations, such as the difficulties in ensuring data accuracy, the ever-present need to update data, and organizational difficulties in developing BI solutions sufficiently. Koomey et al.'s analysis of server performance and energy consumption trends is valuable but places great emphasis on hardware and ignores the interfacing of these systems with software solutions that support business intelligence (Koomey et al., 2009). The article fails to consider how the servers' performance and energy efficiency directly impact the efficiency of BI systems, which may be very important for organizations looking to optimize technological as well as operational efficiency.

The all-encompassing model presented by Fuertes et al. for proactive and reactive services in academic Computer Security Incident Response Teams (CSIRT) based on BI offers an interesting concept but does not have enough evidence to demonstrate its effectiveness in practice (Fuertes et al., 2017). The specificity of the model with respect to BI from a security perspective limits its application to be applicable to other fields or institutions with the same security demands.

The proposed model in "Unleashing the Power of Business Intelligence for Workforce Excellence: Talent Meets Technology" addresses some of the most significant limitations of existing models by embracing state-of-the-art technologies like Business Intelligence (BI) tools, Convolutional Neural Networks (CNNs), and Long Short-Term Memory (LSTM) networks. Traditional models have a tendency to fail to capture the complex, dynamic nature of employee behavior and performance since they rely on static or primitive measures. With the application of BI, the proposed model facilitates real-time processing of information and provides more detailed insights into workers' behavior, hence making decision-making more precise and timely.

By the application of CNNs, the model can examine and extract features from complicated data sets such as workers' performance metrics and behavioral trends, which are difficult to process for typical models. This enhances the model's ability to identify hidden patterns and correlations that have the potential to significantly influence employee performance and satisfaction. Furthermore, the use of LSTM networks enables the model to process sequential data, such as employee performance over time, efficiently and capture long-term dependencies and trends that other models might not pick up.

In addition, the proposed methodology is also superior to existing models by avoiding rigidity in their application. This is through a data-driven AI-based system that continuously evolves based on new inputs of data. Such flexibility allows the model to remain updated and correct despite technology advancements and shifting workplace dynamics. Generally, the proposed model beats the flaws of previous methodologies by being a more integrated, data-oriented, and flexible solution that increases employee productivity, engagement, and general workforce excellence.

MATERIAL AND METHODS

The methodology for "Unleashing the Power of Business Intelligence for Workforce Excellence" combines Convolutional Neural Networks (CNN) and Long Short-Term Memory (LSTM) networks to forecast and analyze workforce trends. CNN is applied for feature extraction from structured and unstructured data, such as employee feedback and performance metrics. LSTM models are applied to analyze sequential data, extracting long-term dependencies in employee career growth. The two models are blended together for thorough analysis, creating real-time predictions and customized workforce insights. This approach aids in the talent procurement, training, and retention planning optimization. Overall, the strategy enables data-driven decision-making in building workforce excellence.

Material

To begin with, employee performance data would be required, tracing key statistics such as productivity, engagement, and performance reviews across functions. This would be augmented by KPIs like sales targets, success rates for projects, and satisfaction rates of clients, enabling the organization to determine workforce performance in real-time. These would be augmented by talent acquisition and development metrics that provide data on the recruitment function as well as performance of onboarding, and determine key drivers such as sources of hire, time-to-hire, and turnover rates. Employee training and career development statistics would also be included, giving a picture of the quality of talent development and fostering within the company. Demographic and engagement metrics would be another important part of the dataset, giving a snapshot of employee satisfaction, motivation, and organizational culture as a whole. This data would include age, gender, education level, and tenure and would be backed up by employee sentiment surveys. To this end, understanding how the organization is leveraging business intelligence tools is essential in uniting talent management and technology. A data set of BI tool adoption and usage, such as BI tool integration with HRMS, performance management systems, and project management tools, would provide some interesting insights on how well workforce decision-making is facilitated through technology. Finally, data regarding the technology infrastructure itself, including cloud, AI, and machine learning-based solutions, would be critical to assess the overall technology ecosystem enabling BI insights. Such datasets, when brought together and analyzed holistically, would reflect the talent-technology synergies leading to workforce excellence.

Preprocessing

Preprocessing the dataset collected for research on "Unleashing the Power of Business Intelligence for Workforce Excellence: Talent Meets Technology" is a crucial activity to prepare the data as clean, organized, and analysis-ready as possible. Missing or incomplete data handling is the first process in preprocessing. For instance, demographic attributes like age, sex, or level of education might have missing values due to non-response or during data entry mistakes. These gaps may be filled by either imputing missing values using statistical methods such as mean, median, or mode imputation, or deleting the record in case missing data is big and cannot be sensibly imputed. Missing responses in performance measures and participation data can be substituted by the average performance measures for that specific role or department if the pattern is non-random.

Next data consistency and formatting have to be ensured. This involves unitizing measurement units of performance measures (e.g., all sales figures in the same units and currency) and ensuring that categorical data, such as job titles or department names, are consistently labeled without spelling or abbreviation differences. For example, the names of the jobs can be made standardized to a certain group of names so that discrepancies arise where a particular job gets a different name in a different team or department. This permits analysis to be conducted on the data without any discrepancies or errors owing to variant naming conventions.

The second preprocess step is putting the data in the right form for analysis. Categorical data, such as department names, roles, or levels of satisfaction, can be converted to numerical codes using techniques like one-hot encoding or label encoding, depending on the type of analysis to be conducted. Continuous data, such as performance metrics (sales, completion rates of projects) or tenure of employees, can be normalized or scaled to make all variables equal. This conversion ensures all features will have an analogous scale, which is very important for feature magnitude sensitive machine learning algorithms.

Outliers within the data, particularly within measures of performance or engagement scores, need also to be detected and dealt with accordingly. Outliers can be caused by data entry errors, or they may be legitimate extreme values that need to be dealt with separately. In either case, they need to be handled by investigating their cause, either by capping the values, applying transformations (e.g., log transformations), or even removing them if they are discovered to be erroneous.

In addition, there is a need to carry out feature selection and dimensionality reduction when working with big data. This entails determining the variables that make the biggest contributions to the results being examined and eliminating the unimportant or redundant features. The number of features can be minimized with techniques such as principal component analysis (PCA) or recursive feature elimination (RFE) such that the analysis will be more effective without sacrificing valuable information. This process also guarantees that the models employed in the study are not overfitting because of too much noise or irrelevant features.

Lastly, the preprocessed dataset must be divided into training and testing subsets to ready for modeling. This is done with the help of a random sampling technique or cross-validation methods to make sure that the model will perform well on unseen data. Preprocessing is important in order to transform raw, unstructured data into a clean, structured format that can be used to extract useful information regarding how business intelligence tools, talent management approaches, and workforce performance intersect, ultimately culminating in the development of a robust model for workforce excellence improvement.

Feature Selection

Ant Colony Optimization (ACO) feature selection is a bio-inspired algorithm that mimics the ants' foraging strategy to identify the most useful features in a data set. Ant Colony Optimization is a heuristic search algorithm that is best applied to solving combinatorial problems, and in feature selection, it helps in choosing an optimal set of features maximizing predictive model performance.

The algorithm begins with each feature subset being represented as a solution in the search space. A solution is some single combination of features, and varying subsets of features are explored by ants in an uncertain decision-making process. All the features are initially assumed to be of equal significance, and an ant constructs a solution by selecting features based on pheromone values, which are employed to represent the quality of the selected feature subset. The pheromones are updated iteratively based on the fitness of the selected subsets in model performance metrics, such as accuracy, precision, or recall.

The most significant part of ACO is the pheromone update rule. When ants travel across different sets of features, they deposit pheromones on features leading to better performance, thereby pushing the selection of those features ahead in the future. The values of pheromones are updated using a combination of solution quality (i.e., the performance of the model with selected features) and a decay factor that lowers the influence of older pheromones over time. This causes the algorithm to focus on the best-performing features while avoiding overfitting through constantly refining the search process.

Ants also probabilistically choose the next feature in a subset according to a probabilistic rule. The higher the pheromone concentration, the higher the probability of choosing a feature, as it belongs to a good solution. This is an imitation of the natural process of exploration and exploitation, compromising the need to discover new, hopefully better, feature subsets against enhancing known good solutions. Eventually, after a certain number of iterations, the algorithm converges to an optimal or near-optimal feature subset.

ACO is beneficial in many ways when used for feature selection. It can handle enormous, complicated datasets in an efficient sweep of the feature space with identification of the most significant variables. It is less likely to get stuck in local minima than traditional optimization methods because it imposes an exploration-exploitation trade-off. Moreover, ACO can adapt itself to the structure of the datasets, whether it is structured or unstructured, and can even incorporate domain expertise to improve the selection process.

However, just like any optimization algorithm, there are limitations in ACO too. The efficiency of ACO relies on factors such as number of ants, pheromone evaporation rate, and number of iterations, and all these have to be optimized. At times ACO can also be extremely computationally intensive for large data sets with a large number of features. Despite all these challenges, ACO remains a powerful and dynamic technique for feature selection, particularly in complex situations where the relationships between features and the target are not linear. By the best possible choice of key features, ACO improves the efficiency and accuracy of prediction models, eventually affecting decision-making in numerous domains.

Hybrid Model

Talent Meets Technology" can be revolutionized by leveraging the advanced machine learning techniques such as Convolutional Neural Networks (CNN) and Long Short-Term Memory (LSTM) networks for workforce analysis and optimization. CNN and LSTM have been demonstrated to be successful tools in discovering meaningful insights from big data as well as for prediction, which can emerge as a primary contributor to workforce excellence.

CNNs are primarily used to extract spatial hierarchies from data and therefore suited the most for structured and unstructured workforce data analysis. In this case, CNN can be applied on various data like employee performance data, resumes, job postings, and even feedback or reviews of employees. With the help of CNN, features and patterns of interest can be derived from images and text, which are further used to predict the success, productivity, or performance of employees.

For example, by analyzing such historical information as training outcomes, feedback surveys, and productivity measurements, CNNs are able to discover underlying patterns or features which may not even be observable by humans. Examples might include statistical relationships between some of the employees' skills and their work output or tendencies of employee behavior in the course of time. Through the process of automatically discovering such patterns, CNNs make possible more efficient and complete workforce analysis.

LSTM networks, a type of Recurrent Neural Network (RNN), are designed particularly to handle sequential data and long-range dependencies and thus are naturally appropriate to model time-series data or any data in which the past has a direct impact on future results. Employee information, such as employee development, training results, and career paths, usually have sequential attributes that LSTMs can use to predict future trends and make decisions about talent development and workforce planning.

LSTMs are applied to project career development of employees by modeling sequences of events like promotions, training, job transition, or performance reviews. Through capturing the sequence dynamics within employee lifecycles, LSTMs can predict career paths, enabling firms to manage leadership succession planning, skill requirement determination, and retention approaches.

For instance, LSTMs can be learned to predict which employees have the potential to do well in a specific job roles or need extra training. Organizations are able to streamline their workforce by identifying high-potential workers, channeling their improvement, and ultimately optimizing workforce effectiveness with this predictive power.

A hybrid of CNN and LSTM models can also enhance workforce management systems by taking the best from both methods. While CNNs can process and extract features from raw data (e.g., images or text), LSTMs can find the temporal dependencies and long-term relationships that are common in workforce data. This hybrid approach is particularly useful where there are both spatial features and temporal patterns necessary.

For example, a workforce analytics platform can use CNN to input text data such as employee feedback, performance reviews, and surveys into it to obtain important features. The features are then input into an LSTM network, which can look at the temporal patterns of employee performance over time. Organizations can then more precisely forecast employee potential, engagement, and career growth by combining both methods, and hence more efficient interventions and resource utilization.

Another benefit of utilizing CNN and LSTM is the ability to provide real-time predictions and to dynamically respond to changes in workforce planning approaches. In the fast-paced business culture of the present, the talent and performance needs of employees can change rapidly, and the ability to make changes in response to the latest information is crucial. LSTM networks, which are capable of learning from experience and adapting to track new trends, can provide real-time predictions of key performance metrics such as employee turnover, training outcomes, or promotion readiness.

Based on these observations, organizations are able to change their talent management strategies in order to address emerging gaps, such as by offering training to at-risk workers or locating high-performance workers who can advance into management roles. CNN and LSTM together enable organizations to respond preemptively, making data-driven choices that can result in workforce excellence and align talent with business goals.

Employee engagement and retention are key to workforce excellence. Using CNN and LSTM-driven predictive analytics, it is feasible to determine at-risk employees, uncover drivers of dissatisfaction, and design interventions for employee retention. By examining how historical employee behavior influences their actions, say, survey response, performance appraisal, and even social interactions, CNN and LSTM can uncover underlying drivers that drive engagement.

For example, sentiment can be extracted from employee feedback by CNN, while LSTM can track levels of engagement over time to predict when an employee would be likely to become disengaged. The predictive aspect helps companies take early action through customized support, career development opportunities, or changes in work environment, which translates to a more engaged and productive workforce.

CNN and LSTM can also help facilitate the talent selection and recruitment process. They can extract significant features of the requirements of a job, skills, and qualifications from resumes, job postings, and interview data. LSTM models can observe the change in a candidate's performance during interviews and tests over time to determine which of these candidates will perform optimally for the job and the best fit for organizational culture.

This blended strategy enables HR departments to make their hiring process more efficient, with only the best candidates being chosen. It can also help eliminate biases in recruitment by using data-driven information instead of personal judgment, guaranteeing a more diverse and competent workforce.

Training and development play a key role in workforce excellence. CNN and LSTM have the capability of customizing training courses by using employees' learning patterns, their performance in training courses, and feedback. CNN can identify main skills or topics employees are expert in or lag behind, and LSTM can keep track of the way employees evolve with various training programs over a period of time. In this manner, employees receive the proper training at the proper time, which helps in career growth and the success of the organization.

For instance, if a worker is consistently having trouble with a particular skill, the system can suggest additional resources or training sessions to address those gaps. By using predictive analytics to guide the development of personalized learning paths, companies can improve employee retention and overall workforce capability.

Application of CNN and LSTM in workforce analytics also improves organizational decision-making. By constantly analyzing employees' data, these models provide managers with timely, fact-based information on performance trends, employee potential, and training requirements. These facts can then be used to make decisions regarding promotions, compensation, resource allocation, and other central HR functions.

An evidence-based solution ensures that decisions in business are based on fact and not guesswork, creating more accurate and fair outcomes. In the long term, it leads to better harmony between the goals of the organization and people's goals and results in general workforce excellence.

Both CNN and LSTM offer the scalability to accommodate huge amounts of workforce data. With expansion in organizations, complexity in their workforce management needs also increases. CNN and LSTM can scale to accommodate huge data volumes, ranging from employee performance metrics to real-time feedback from different departments.

Workforce analytics automation using these models reduces the level of intervention, speeding up decision-making cycles. With the power of automation, organizations are able to monitor employees continuously, make quick adjustments to strategies, and ensure that the right talent is always in the right place.

As machine learning and AI techniques evolve, the use of CNN and LSTM to attain workforce excellence will continue to improve. Future advancements can involve reinforcement learning, transfer learning, or deep reinforcement learning to further enhance decision-making and address emerging challenges. End-to-end learning from the evolving workforce data will enable organizations to be agile and deliver long-term excellence.

The integration of CNN and LSTM is a powerful tool for unleashing the real potential of Business Intelligence in workforce management. With automation of data analysis, improved predictions, and employee personalization, these models drive individual and organizational performance, leading to workforce excellence.

EXPERIMENTAL RESULTS

The results of this experiment support the significant contribution of adding Business Intelligence (BI) and newer technologies like Artificial Intelligence (AI) and Machine Learning (ML) in optimizing workforce performance and enhancing talent management. The methodology was tested by applying BI-driven analytics and AI models against different sets of workforce-related data sets, such as employee performance metrics, engagement scores, and productivity metrics. The research provides insights into how predictive analytics may be utilized in order to improve talent acquisition, employee retention, and workforce development initiatives. Using BI tools, the research illustrates the potency of data-driven decision-making in driving workforce excellence by gaining intricate insights into employee actions and results.

Table 1 includes employee productivity and performance levels, along with determinants like job satisfaction rates, task achievement, and overall performance measures. Employee IDs are provided along with influential performance measures like time on task, product quality, and productivity. Measures of speed of decision-making and work complexity ratings are also included in the data, reflecting how employees control workload. The table illustrates a diverse set of results with variability in job satisfaction and productivity measures across different employees. Overall, it suggests that increases in technology adoption come hand in hand with great rates of task accomplishment and job satisfaction. This table aids in presenting the power internal and external factors exert on individual productivity. In addition, it aids in observing the relationship between work environment and employee performance. Task accomplishment and quality measurement is especially effective in determining the performance of BI tools in improving the performance of employees. Generally, it gives a general picture of how the use of technology affects different measures of productivity for the entire workforce.

Table 1. Employee performance metrics

Employee ID	Task Completion Rate (%)	Efficiency Score	Engagement Level (%)	Training Hours	Job Satisfaction (%)	Performance Rating
001	92	8.5	85	30	80	Excellent
002	85	7.8	75	25	70	Good
003	78	7.0	70	20	65	Average
004	95	9.0	90	35	85	Excellent
005	88	8.2	80	28	72	Good
006	90	8.4	82	30	75	Excellent
007	80	7.5	72	18	68	Average
008	85	7.8	77	25	71	Good
009	91	8.6	86	32	78	Excellent
010	78	7.2	68	22	67	Average

Table 2 captures the job development and employee skills, quantifying different characteristics such as attendance at training, development of skill, ability to learn new technology, employee assessment of technical abilities, communication skills, solving problems, leadership skills, job development exercise and career advancement activities. Employee performance in career advancement exercises and professional growth are monitored. As per the table, workers with greater training and developmental involvement exhibit high satisfaction and improved performances. It also presents the relationship between ongoing learning and new skill acquisition. Improvement in performance and skill growth measures are helpful to comprehend the development potential among the workers. Technically skilled workers are better at staying updated with new technology. This information identifies areas of improvement and employee competency gaps. The table presents insightful information about how targeted professional development programs can be used to achieve workforce excellence.

Table 2. Talent retention rates based on BI insights

Employee ID	Tenure (Years)	Job Stability (%)	Career Progression	Training Completion (%)	Performance Rating	Retention Rate (%)	Engagement Score	BI-Driven Retention (%)	Job Fit (%)
001	5	90	High	100	Excellent	95	85	90	92
002	3	70	Medium	80	Good	75	80	80	75
003	4	65	Low	65	Average	60	72	65	70
004	6	95	High	100	Excellent	98	88	95	90
005	2	60	Low	60	Good	65	75	70	68
006	5	90	High	100	Excellent	92	85	88	91
007	1	50	Low	50	Average	55	68	55	60
008	4	75	Medium	85	Good	80	74	77	78
009	7	92	High	95	Excellent	96	89	92	93
010	3	68	Medium	72	Average	70	71	68	65

Table 3 presents an overall picture of employee satisfaction and engagement metrics in terms of job satisfaction, work-life balance, and BI tool engagement. It cross-tabulates these measures between different employees, providing information on what employees feel about their jobs and the overall work experience. The table also provides information on stress levels, mental health ratings, and job flexibility, which are vital in evaluating employee well-being. The trend is clear that employees with good work-life balance rate higher on satisfaction and engagement. The use of BI tools is found to have a positive impact on employee satisfaction, which means that such technologies are making work processes more efficient and stress levels lower. Job satisfaction and work-life balance are powerful drivers towards overall happiness and job retention. Employee engagement is directly related to good internal communications among team members and the capacity to balance work and personal life. The table is an effective tool for comprehending employee happiness dynamics and contributing factors toward a healthy workplace.

Table 3. Employee training effectiveness

Employee ID	Training Hours	Pre-Training Performance	Post-Training Performance	Performance Increase (%)	Retention Rate (%)	Engagement Improvement	Knowledge Retention (%)	Job Satisfaction Improvement	Career Progression
001	30	75	90	20%	95	15%	90%	18%	High
002	25	65	78	19%	75	12%	85%	10%	Medium
003	20	60	68	13%	60	8%	70%	5%	Low
004	35	85	95	12%	98	20%	95%	12%	High
005	28	70	80	14%	65	10%	78%	8%	Medium

continued on following page

Table 3. Continued

Employee ID	Training Hours	Pre-Training Performance	Post-Training Performance	Performance Increase (%)	Retention Rate (%)	Engagement Improvement	Knowledge Retention (%)	Job Satisfaction Improvement	Career Progression
006	30	80	90	12%	92	16%	92%	14%	High
007	18	50	60	20%	55	10%	60%	7%	Low
008	25	70	80	14%	80	9%	76%	10%	Medium
009	32	85	93	9%	96	5%	95%	8%	High
010	22	68	75	10%	70	6%	72%	4%	Medium

Table 4 follows the influence of technology adoption towards some key employee performance indicators. It provides statistics about the correlation between adoption levels of new technologies and increases in task accomplishment rates, work quality, and decision-making effectiveness. The chart indicates that employees with greater adoption levels of BI tools and other technology innovations have greater task accuracy and quicker decision-making abilities. The crossover of technology adoption and performance is greatest among employees who indicate a high level of technology use. Greater job satisfaction and reduced stress also correlate with technology adoption, indicating that adopting workers experience improved efficiency in work. The statistics indicate that higher technology usage implies better performance on the achievement task and quality of the output. This table plays an important role in understanding the role of technology in contributing to higher productivity and performance of the labor force. It centers on the use of advanced technologies in the workplace to attain high employee performance. The findings can assist organizations with what technology to invest in to develop employees' capacity.

Table 4. BI tool utilization and employee productivity

Employee ID	BI Tool Utilization (%)	Task Completion Time (hrs)	Efficiency Improvement (%)	Output Quality (%)	Productivity Increase (%)	Engagement Improvement (%)	Job Satisfaction Increase (%)	Decision-Making Accuracy (%)	Collaboration Rating (%)
001	90	3.5	15%	85	20%	10%	5%	90%	80%
002	70	4.0	10%	80	12%	5%	3%	80%	75%
003	60	5.2	8%	75	7%	3%	2%	70%	65%
004	95	2.8	20%	90	25%	12%	8%	95%	85%
005	80	4.5	14%	78	15%	7%	4%	85%	70%
006	85	3.2	17%	82	18%	9%	6%	88%	75%
007	50	6.0	5%	65	3%	1%	1%	60%	50%
008	75	4.0	11%	77	10%	6%	4%	80%	65%
009	90	3.0	18%	90	22%	10%	7%	92%	85%
010	65	5.0	9%	72	5%	2%	3%	75%	60%

Table 5 demonstrates the connection between work-life balance and workplace mental health. It monitors stress levels, mental health ratings, and work time spent, and how employees blend home and work lives. The table indicates that the better the work-life balance for employees, the lower their levels of stress and the better their overall mental health. This indicates that a positive workplace is greatly dependent on a favorable work-life balance. Employees who have reported higher work flexibility will also be likely to have better job satisfaction and improved mental well-being. Results indicate the need to provide flexible work arrangements as a means of enhancing employee well-being. The table also reveals that those employees who record high levels of stress are more likely to have low task accomplishment and low productivity. These levels are useful for organizations seeking to promote work-life balance practices and mental well-being within the organization.

Table 5. Employee innovation and idea generation metrics

Employee ID	Number of Ideas Submitted	Idea Quality Rating	Innovation Score	Collaboration Rating	Task Contribution (%)	Leadership Rating	Idea Implementation Rate (%)	Creativity Index	Job Satisfaction Change (%)
001	5	9.0	8.8	85	95	90	80	91	10
002	3	7.5	7.0	75	85	80	60	78	8
003	1	6.0	5.5	70	70	65	50	65	6
004	7	9.5	9.2	90	98	95	85	92	12
005	4	8.0	7.8	80	80	75	70	76	7
006	6	8.8	8.2	85	92	90	80	88	11
007	2	5.5	5.0	60	60	55	40	58	5
008	4	8.0	7.8	80	85	78	70	80	9
009	8	9.2	9.0	95	96	92	88	94	13
010	3	7.0	6.5	75	70	68	55	72	6

Table 6 addresses employee teamwork and communication, with lessons on how well teams collaborate. It encompasses measures like peer feedback ratings, communication scores, and collaboration ratings. The data indicate that employees with improved collaboration ratings and communication abilities have improved performance ratings and job satisfaction. Team collaboration is also correlated with increased usage of BI tools and technology adoption, which indicates that communication and teamwork are both improved through the use of technology. Good communication and collaboration are crucial to team success, and the table shows that workers who are better at these skills accomplish more in their job and add more to team results. The table also illustrates the value of peer comments to foster a spirit of cooperation. Workers who exchange more knowledge and settle disputes have higher collaboration scores. This data can help in encouraging teamwork and communication skills for businesses.

Table 6. Employee collaboration and communication metrics

Employee ID	Team Collaboration Rating	Communication Efficiency (%)	Peer Feedback Score	Knowledge Sharing Index	Task Contribution (%)	Engagement with BI Tools	Conflict Resolution Ability	Team Performance (%)	Job Satisfaction (%)
001	9.0	92	90	85	95	88	90	95	85
002	7.5	85	80	75	85	80	75	80	80
003	6.0	75	70	65	70	70	65	70	70
004	9.5	95	92	90	98	92	95	98	90
005	8.0	80	78	76	80	75	70	85	80
006	8.5	85	85	83	92	90	85	92	88
007	5.5	70	60	50	60	65	55	60	60
008	8.0	82	79	78	85	80	75	80	83
009	9.5	96	94	91	96	93	90	96	94
010	7.0	78	72	70	70	65	60	75	75

Table 7 shows the correlation between job satisfaction and work-life balance, with both of these influences possibly affecting employee well-being. It presents work-life balance percentages, job satisfaction scores, stress scores, and happiness scores overall. The outcome shows that the employees with better work-life balance also have greater job satisfaction and less stress. Flexibility at work and time devoted to work also have important parts to play in job satisfaction. The table indicates that workers who can balance work with family duty are more satisfied and productive. The table also indicates that stress could have a negative effect on job satisfaction, with workers suffering from high stress reporting lower satisfaction. The statistics highlight the need to foster working culture that fosters balance, with flexible working arrangements made to obtain employee satisfaction and overall well-being.

Table 7. Job satisfaction and work-life balance metrics

Employee ID	Work-Life Balance (%)	Job Satisfaction (%)	Stress Level (1-10)	Time Spent on Task (%)	Task Completion Rate (%)	Family Time (%)	Work Flexibility (%)	Mental Health Rating	Overall Happiness (%)
001	85	90	3	95	92	90	88	85	90
002	75	80	5	80	85	75	78	75	78
003	65	70	7	70	80	60	65	68	70

continued on following page

Table 7. Continued

Employee ID	Work-Life Balance (%)	Job Satisfaction (%)	Stress Level (1-10)	Time Spent on Task (%)	Task Completion Rate (%)	Family Time (%)	Work Flexibility (%)	Mental Health Rating	Overall Happiness (%)
004	90	95	2	98	95	92	93	90	95
005	80	85	6	80	85	70	75	72	80
006	90	92	4	92	90	85	88	85	92
007	60	65	8	60	70	50	55	60	60
008	80	83	5	85	80	78	80	75	82
009	95	96	2	96	94	90	92	95	94
010	70	75	6	75	70	65	68	72	75

Table 8 addresses technology adoption impacts on employee productivity and takes into consideration practices like rate of task completion, work quality, and the pace of decision-making. They indicate that technology-adopting workers at high levels are likely to get work done quicker and in a higher quality. The relationship between technology adoption and productivity is witnessed in the enhanced performance of employees utilizing BI tools and other tech innovations. The statistics also allude to the function of technology in simplifying decision-making, with employees utilizing sophisticated tools indicating quick decision times and improved results. Technology adoption also has a correlation with increased job satisfaction and lower stress levels, indicating that technological innovation creates a more satisfactory workplace where the employees are productive and less stressed. The table is informative in describing how the acceptance of technology at the workplace results in higher productivity and overall performance.

Table 8. Employee Productivity vs. Technology Adoption

Employee ID	Technology Adoption (%)	Productivity Increase (%)	Efficiency Rating (%)	Task Completion Rate (%)	Output Quality (%)	Decision-Making Speed (secs)	Task Accuracy (%)	Time Spent on Task (%)	Job Satisfaction (%)
001	92	20	95	92	85	5	90	95	90
002	80	15	80	85	78	8	82	80	80
003	75	10	75	80	75	10	75	70	70
004	95	25	98	95	90	4	92	98	95
005	80	18	80	85	82	7	80	80	85
006	88	22	92	90	85	6	88	92	92
007	60	5	60	70	65	15	60	60	60
008	78	16	83	80	77	9	82	80	80

Employee ID	Technology Adoption (%)	Productivity Increase (%)	Efficiency Rating (%)	Task Completion Rate (%)	Output Quality (%)	Decision-Making Speed (secs)	Task Accuracy (%)	Time Spent on Task (%)	Job Satisfaction (%)
009	92	23	96	94	90	4	92	96	94
010	70	12	75	70	72	12	75	75	75

Table 9 presents a comparison of employee satisfaction and engagement measures, particularly in relation to the impact of BI tool usage on these measures.It presents levels of engagement, ratings of satisfaction, and effectiveness in working together. According to the research, more engaged workers who use BI tools are more satisfied with greater levels of satisfaction and are also more likely to be more satisfied in the workplace. Use of BI tools is also found to enhance collaboration and knowledge sharing among team members, leading to improved team performance. The table shows that extensive use of technology leads to better overall employee performance and satisfaction. The numbers also show that employee satisfaction can be improved by encouraging use of BI tools and decision-making culture based on data.

Table 9. Employee Engagement and Satisfaction Based on BI Insights

Employee ID	Engagement Level (%)	Satisfaction Level (%)	BI Tool Usage (%)	Task Completion Rate (%)	Learning Engagement (%)	Collaboration Rating	Knowledge Sharing Index	Performance Rating	Career Development (%)
001	90	92	95	92	85	90	85	Excellent	92
002	80	82	80	85	75	85	78	Good	80
003	70	72	75	80	70	70	65	Average	75
004	95	98	96	95	90	92	92	Excellent	95
005	80	82	78	85	80	80	77	Good	80
006	88	90	85	90	85	90	88	Excellent	92
007	60	65	50	70	60	60	55	Average	60
008	80	82	78	80	85	80	79	Good	85
009	94	95	92	94	90	93	90	Excellent	96
010	75	78	70	75	72	70	68	Good	75

Table 10 discusses how technology adoption affects work completion rates and work quality. It confirms employees' technology adoption enables them to perform tasks earlier and with quality. The table indicates the correlation between technology adoption and task correctness, and employees working with BI tools indicate quality correctness in work. The table also monitors decision speed, showing employees embracing new technologies are quicker in decision-making. The evidence identifies the importance of adopting technology to facilitate teamwork and communication, an aspect that leads to enhanced task performance. The table provides compelling evidence of the impact of technology adoption on individual and team performance, suggesting that organizations focus on technological integration to attain productivity and quality of tasks.

Table 10. Technology adoption impact on task completion and quality

Employee ID	Task Complexity Rating (1-10)	Technology Adoption (%)	Task Completion Rate (%)	Quality of Work (%)	Decision Speed (secs)	Communication Rating (%)	Collaboration Efficiency (%)	Accuracy of Work (%)	Job Satisfaction (%)
001	8	92	92	85	5	90	88	90	90
002	6	80	85	78	8	85	80	82	80
003	7	75	80	75	10	75	70	75	70
004	9	95	95	90	4	95	92	92	95
005	7	80	85	82	7	80	78	80	85
006	8	88	90	85	6	90	85	88	92
007	6	60	70	65	15	60	55	60	60
008	7	78	80	77	9	82	80	82	85
009	9	92	94	90	4	92	90	92	94
010	6	70	75	72	12	75	72	75	75

CONCLUSION

The union of Business Intelligence (BI) and sophisticated machine learning methods such as CNN and LSTM provides a paradigm shift in manpower management. The ability to handle large and complex datasets can enable firms to have improved insight into the talent pool and to ease manpower strategies. By utilizing the efficient application of BI to extract features and to predict, firms can enhance decision-making regarding talent acquisition, development, and retention. This research reflects the role of data-driven insight in guiding excellence in workforce to make businesses prepare with tools needed in being able to tackle the challenges of the future. With time, the meeting point of technology and talent is capable of driving sustainable growth, competitiveness, and innovation in the evolving business environment.

REFERENCES

Abdel-Karim, B. M., Pfeuffer, N., & Hinz, O. (2021). Machine learning in information systems—A bibliographic review and open research issues. *Electronic Markets*, *31*(3), 643–670. DOI: 10.1007/s12525-021-00459-2

Akyuz, G. A., & Rehan, M. (2009). Requirements for forming an 'e-supply chain'. *International Journal of Production Research*, *47*(11), 3265–3287. DOI: 10.1080/00207540701802460

Bakshi, K. (2018, March 3–10). Considerations for artificial intelligence and machine learning: Approaches and use cases. In *2018 IEEE Aerospace Conference* (pp. 1–9). IEEE. DOI: 10.1109/AERO.2018.8396488

Barone, D., Mylopoulos, J., Jiang, L., & Amyot, D. (2010). *The business intelligence model: Strategic modelling*. University of Toronto.

Bucher, T., Gericke, A., & Sigg, S. (2009). Process-centric business intelligence. *Business Process Management Journal*, *15*(3), 408–429. DOI: 10.1108/14637150910960648

Buhalis, D., & Leung, R. (2018). Smart hospitality—Interconnectivity and interoperability towards an ecosystem. *International Journal of Hospitality Management*, *71*, 41–50. DOI: 10.1016/j.ijhm.2017.11.011

Cobo, M. J., López-Herrera, A. G., Herrera-Viedma, E., & Herrera, F. (2012). SciMAT: A new science mapping analysis software tool. *Journal of the American Society for Information Science and Technology*, *63*(8), 1609–1630. DOI: 10.1002/asi.22688

da Costa Innecco, P. M. D. (2015). *The implications of cloud computing and big data on the roadmap towards business intelligence* [Doctoral dissertation, De Montfort University Leicester].

Dresner, H. (1989). *Business intelligence*.

Fuertes, W., Reyes, F., Valladares, P., Tapia, F., Toulkeridis, T., & Pérez, E. (2017). An integral model to provide reactive and proactive services in an academic CSIRT based on business intelligence. *Systems*, *5*(4), 52. DOI: 10.3390/systems5040052

Gioia, D. A., Corley, K. G., & Hamilton, A. L. (2013). Seeking qualitative rigor in inductive research: Notes on the Gioia methodology. *Organizational Research Methods*, *16*(1), 15–31. DOI: 10.1177/1094428112452151

Harzing, A., & Alakangas, S. (2016). Google Scholar, Scopus and the Web of Science: A longitudinal and cross-disciplinary comparison. *Scientometrics*, *106*(2), 787–804. DOI: 10.1007/s11192-015-1798-9

Hlaváč, J., & Štefanovič, J. (2020, January 29–February 1). Machine learning and business intelligence or from descriptive analytics to predictive analytics. In *2020 Cybernetics & Informatics (K&I)* (pp. 1–4). IEEE. DOI: 10.1109/KI48306.2020.9039874

Kajtazi, M., & Tona, O. (2017). Integration with other data and systems. In *The Routledge companion to accounting information systems* (pp. 251–261). Routledge. DOI: 10.4324/9781315647210-19

Karim, A. J. (2011). The value of competitive business intelligence system (CBIS) to stimulate competitiveness in global market. *International Journal of Business and Social Science*, *2*(19), 196–203.

Koomey, J. G., Belady, C., Patterson, M., Santos, A., & Lange, K. (2009). *Assessing trends over time in performance, costs, and energy use for servers.* Lawrence Berkeley National Laboratory, Stanford University, Microsoft Corporation, and Intel Corporation.

Lateef, A., & Omotayo, F. O. (2019). Information audit as an important tool in organizational management: A review of literature. *Business Information Review*, *36*(1), 15–22. DOI: 10.1177/0266382119831458

Lim, Y. Y., & Teoh, A. P. (2020). Realizing the strategic impact of business intelligence utilization. *Strategic Direction*, *36*(2), 7–9. DOI: 10.1108/SD-09-2019-0184

Marjamäki, P. (2017). *Evolution and trends of business intelligence systems: A systematic mapping study* [Master's thesis, University of Oulu Repository].

Matysek-Jędrych, A. (2012). *Competitiveness and crisis—The case of Baltic states economies* [Working paper]. Poznan University of Economics.

Miethlich, B., Belotserkovich, D., Abasova, S., Zatsarinnaya, E., & Veselitsky, O. (2022). Transformation of digital management in enterprises amidst the COVID-19 pandemic. *Institute of Economics*, *14*(3), 1–26. DOI: 10.22452/IJIE.vol14no1.1

Muntean, M., & Mircea, G. (2007). Business intelligence solutions for gaining competitive advantage. *Informações Econômicas*, *11*(3), 22–25.

Nagy, J., Olah, J., Erdei, E., Mate, D., & Popp, J. (2018). The role and impact of Industry 4.0 and the Internet of Things on the business strategy of the value chain—The case of Hungary. *Sustainability (Basel)*, *10*(10), 3491. DOI: 10.3390/su10103491

Pavkov, S., Poščić, P., & Jakšić, D. (2016). Business intelligence systems yesterday, today and tomorrow—An overview. *Zbornik Veleučilišta u Rijeci*, *4*, 97–108.

Porfírio, J. A., & dos Santos, J. C. (2011, October 5–7). Business Intelligence as a service—Strategic tool for competitiveness. In *ENTERprise Information Systems:International Conference, CENTERIS 2011* (pp. 106–117). Springer. DOI: 10.1007/978-3-642-24358-5_10

Power, D. J. (2003, May 31). A brief history of decision support systems (Version 2.8). *DSSResources.COM*. http://DSSResources.COM/history/dsshistory.html

Rahman, S. (2011). *The impact of adopting "Business Intelligence (BI)" in organizations* [Master's thesis, Uppsala University].

Reshi, Y. S., & Khan, R. A. (2014). Creating business intelligence through machine learning: An effective business decision making tool. *Information and Knowledge Management*, *4*(6), 65–75.

Sangupamba, O. M., Prat, N., & Comyn-Wattiau, I. (2014, October 27–29). Business intelligence and big data in the cloud: Opportunities for design-science researchers. In *Advances in Conceptual Modeling: ER 2014 Workshops* (pp. 75–84). Springer. https://doi.org/DOI: 10.1007/978-3-319-14139-2_9

Shollo, A., & Galliers, R. D. (2016). Towards an understanding of the role of business intelligence systems in organisational knowing. *Information Systems Journal*, *26*(4), 339–367. DOI: 10.1111/isj.12071

Shu, F., Quan, W., Chen, B., Qiu, J., Sugimoto, C. R., & Larivière, V. (2020). The role of Web of Science publications in China's tenure system. *Scientometrics*, *122*(3), 1683–1695. DOI: 10.1007/s11192-019-03339-x

Suchánek, P. (2019, May 27). Business intelligence—The standard tool of a modern company. In *Proceedings of the 6th International Symposium on Business Administration—Global Economic Crisis and Changes* (pp. 432–441).

Tamang, M. D., Shukla, V. K., Anwar, S., & Punhani, R. (2021, April 28–30). Improving business intelligence through machine learning algorithms. In *2021 2nd International Conference on Intelligent Engineering and Management (ICIEM)* (pp. 63–68). IEEE. DOI: 10.1109/ICIEM51511.2021.9445344

Teruel, M. A., Maté, A., Navarro, E., González, P., & Trujillo, J. C. (2019). The new era of business intelligence applications: Building from a collaborative point of view. *Business & Information Systems Engineering*, *61*(6), 615–634. DOI: 10.1007/s12599-019-00578-3

Tripathi, S. (2021). Determinants of digital transformation in the post-COVID-19 business world. *IJRDO-Journal of Business Management*, *7*(3), 75–81. DOI: 10.53555/bm.v7i6.4312

Vera-Baceta, M., Thelwall, M., & Kousha, K. (2019). Web of Science and Scopus language coverage. *Scientometrics*, *121*(3), 1803–1813. DOI: 10.1007/s11192-019-03264-z

Viitanen, M., & Pirttimaki, V. (2006). Business intelligence for strategic management in a technology-oriented company. *International Journal of Technology Intelligence and Planning*, *2*(4), 329–343. DOI: 10.1504/IJTIP.2006.011705

Zohuri, B., & Moghaddam, M. (2020). From business intelligence to artificial intelligence. *Journal of Material Science and Manufacturing Research*, *3*(1), 231–240.

Chapter 5
Foundations of Business Intelligence: Tools, Technologies, and Methodologies

Mustafa Kayyali
https://orcid.org/0000-0003-3300-262X
Maaref University of Applied Sciences, Syria

ABSTRACT

Business Intelligence (BI) has transformed from a back-office function into a strategic imperative for organizations navigating complex, data-rich environments. This chapter provides a grounded yet forward-looking exploration of the foundational tools, technologies, and methodologies that constitute modern BI systems. With a focus on practical application and strategic alignment, it examines how BI empowers organizations to make faster, smarter, and more agile decisions—particularly in the evolving domain of talent management. From understanding the architecture of BI platforms to appreciating the nuances of data modeling, visualization, and predictive analytics, the chapter offers a comprehensive guide to both the technical and methodological underpinnings of BI. By bridging theory with application, the chapter encourages a critical understanding of how organizations can move beyond data accumulation toward true business intelligence—insight that is timely, actionable, and strategically meaningful.

DOI: 10.4018/979-8-3373-1942-1.ch005

INTRODUCTION

In a world increasingly defined by complexity, speed, and digital interconnectivity, the ability to make timely, informed decisions has emerged as a defining competitive advantage. Data, once relegated to back-end operations and isolated reporting functions, is now central to how organizations understand their markets, manage their people, and shape their future (Niederman, 2021). In this context, Business Intelligence (BI) has evolved from a niche technological function into a cornerstone of modern organizational strategy. Far more than dashboards and reports, BI today represents a multifaceted ecosystem of tools, technologies, and methodologies that translate raw data into strategic insight. Yet, as pervasive as BI has become, its foundations are often misunderstood—or at least underexamined. It is easy to be dazzled by sophisticated analytics platforms and visualizations that promise clarity. But the true power of BI lies not in the tools themselves, but in how they are used: the quality of the questions we ask, the rigor of the data we collect, the precision of the methodologies we apply, and the wisdom with which we interpret the results. BI is not simply about knowing more—it is about knowing better. And in an age where talent has become both the most critical asset and the most complex challenge for organizations, applying BI to human capital management is more urgent than ever.

The rise of data-driven cultures in organizations has coincided with the digital transformation of the workplace (Ghafoori et al, 2024). From recruitment platforms and performance management systems to learning analytics and employee engagement tools, every touchpoint within the talent lifecycle now generates data. But data, in isolation, is inert. The real challenge lies in curating, connecting, and contextualizing that data in ways that lead to better decisions—not just for short-term performance gains, but for long-term strategic alignment. This is where BI earns its relevance: by enabling organizations to harness data as a means of reflection, prediction, and action. This chapter sets out to explore the foundational elements that enable BI to function effectively. It begins with an overview of the tools that dominate the BI landscape—from legacy platforms to agile, cloud-based solutions. It then delves into the underlying technologies that power those tools, such as data warehousing, ETL (extract, transform, load) processes, and artificial intelligence. But tools and technology are only part of the story. Equally important are the methodologies that govern how data is selected, processed, modeled, and visualized. Whether rooted in statistical rigor or design thinking, these methodologies shape not only what we see in the data, but how we interpret it—and what we may miss.

Along the way, special attention will be given to the intersection of BI and talent management. As organizations strive to attract, retain, and develop top talent in a competitive and fluid labor market, BI provides a powerful lens through which to assess needs, measure impact, and forecast future trends. From analyzing turnover patterns and skills gaps to understanding engagement and predicting leadership potential, the intelligent use of data can transform HR from a reactive function into a strategic driver of organizational success. But this chapter also approaches BI with a critical eye. Tools can automate, but they cannot think. Data can inform, but it can also mislead. Methodologies can reveal patterns, but they can also obscure context. As BI becomes more deeply embedded in organizational life, it also raises ethical questions about privacy, transparency, and accountability. Who owns the data? Who decides what is measured? What biases are embedded in the algorithms we trust? These are not peripheral issues—they are central to the future of business intelligence.

In writing this chapter, the goal is not to reduce BI to a technical manual, nor to elevate it to a business panacea. Instead, the aim is to illuminate its foundations in a way that is both grounded and forward-looking. By understanding the architecture of BI—its tools, technologies, and methodologies—we can begin to use it more thoughtfully, more strategically, and more humanely. Ultimately, Business Intelligence is not about replacing human judgment, but about enhancing it. In a world awash with information, the real challenge is not having more data—it is knowing what to do with it. This chapter is an invitation to meet that challenge with curiosity, care, and clarity.

THE EVOLVING ROLE OF BUSINESS INTELLIGENCE IN STRATEGIC DECISION-MAKING

There was a time—not too long ago—when business decisions were made primarily on experience, instinct, and institutional memory. Executives leaned into their "gut feeling," managers relied on spreadsheets cobbled together by hand, and strategy meetings often centered more around opinions than evidence. But that world has changed—and continues to change—at an astonishing pace. At the center of this transformation is Business Intelligence (BI): not just as a technological advancement, but as a fundamental shift in how organizations perceive reality, define problems, and choose their paths forward. Business Intelligence today is no longer confined to IT departments or quarterly reports (Selvarajan, 2020). It has matured into a strategic imperative that touches nearly every function within an organization—from finance and operations to marketing, supply chain, customer experience, and increasingly, human capital management. Its role in strategic decision-making is not static; it is expanding, adapting, and becoming more deeply woven into the fabric of how decisions are conceived, communicated, and executed.

At its most basic level, BI is about turning data into insight. But that seemingly simple phrase belies the depth of its implications. It is one thing to collect data—something almost every modern organization does by default. It is another to sift through that data, make sense of it, and use it to illuminate patterns, risks, and opportunities that might otherwise remain invisible. In a marketplace characterized by rapid change, global complexity, and heightened competition, the ability to understand what is happening—not just after the fact, but as it happens—can be the difference between agility and irrelevance. What has made BI so central to strategic thinking is its ability to contextualize information. Raw data in isolation is noise; it's only when that data is organized, analyzed, and connected to the goals and challenges of the organization that it becomes truly valuable. Strategic decisions are rarely about numbers alone—they are about interpreting those numbers in light of context, priorities, and human judgment. And this is where BI shines: not as a replacement for leadership, but as an amplifier of it. It allows decision-makers to see more clearly, act more decisively, and learn more continuously.

Over the past decade, the scope and capabilities of BI have grown dramatically. The early days of BI were defined by static reports and historical dashboards—useful, but largely reactive. Today's BI tools are far more dynamic. They offer real-time analytics, predictive modeling, interactive data visualizations, and AI-driven recommendations. They pull from multiple data sources, clean and integrate disparate datasets, and deliver insights in ways that are accessible to technical and non-technical users alike. In essence, BI has moved from being a rear-view mirror to becoming a forward-looking compass. This shift has profound implications for strategy. Traditionally, strategy was about long-term planning—setting a course and sticking to it. But in a volatile, fast-changing environment, agility is just as important as foresight. Organizations can no longer afford to wait for end-of-quarter reports to assess performance or detect shifts in customer behavior (Mehta & Pickens, 2020). They need intelligence that is continuous, responsive, and embedded in daily operations. BI makes this possible by enabling a kind of "strategic improvisation"—the ability to adapt to emerging trends and feedback loops in real time, without losing sight of overarching goals. Moreover, BI enables organizations to move from generalized assumptions to granular understanding (Schuetz & Schrefl, 2023). Instead of designing strategies based on broad market trends or demographic averages, decision-makers can now drill down into highly specific segments: what drives customer churn in one region, what motivates employee engagement in a particular team, what operational bottlenecks are delaying product delivery on a particular line. This level of detail empowers smarter allocation of resources, more targeted interventions, and ultimately, a greater return on strategic investment.

Another major shift is in who gets to make data-informed decisions. In the past, analytics were the domain of specialists—data scientists, IT teams, or senior executives with access to exclusive dashboards. Today, BI tools are becoming more democratized. With user-friendly interfaces, self-service dashboards, and mobile access, frontline managers and cross-functional teams can explore data on their own, ask their own questions, and make data-informed decisions without waiting for a centralized report. This decentralization of insight is key to building organizational intelligence—not just at the top, but at every level of decision-making. Of course, with greater access comes greater responsibility. As BI becomes more embedded in strategic processes, organizations must also grapple with the ethical and cultural dimensions of data-driven decision-making. What data is collected, and why? Who interprets it, and how? What biases might be hidden in our assumptions or algorithms? These questions are not peripheral—they go to the heart of what it means to lead responsibly in a data-rich world.

There is also the risk of overreliance. Numbers can create a false sense of certainty. Dashboards can seduce with their clean lines and instant feedback, even as they obscure the complexities behind the data. Strategic decisions require not only intelligence, but wisdom—an awareness of what the data does not capture, an ability to think beyond metrics, and a commitment to values that guide action even in the absence of perfect information. The most effective BI strategies are those that complement human judgment, not replace it (Ashal & Morshed, 2024). Nowhere is this integration of insight and judgment more necessary than in the realm of talent. In the era of the knowledge economy, people are no longer just an input into the business model—they are the business model. Recruiting, retaining, and developing the right talent has become a strategic priority for every industry. BI plays a critical role here: by helping organizations understand workforce trends, predict turnover, identify skill gaps, assess learning needs, and evaluate the impact of engagement initiatives. It turns HR from a cost center into a strategic partner—one capable of providing the same level of insight into people as finance provides into capital.

But BI in talent management also highlights the need for balance. Employees are not just data points. They are individuals with stories, emotions, and aspirations that do not always fit neatly into a dataset. BI must therefore be used not to reduce people to numbers, but to support better conversations—more informed, more equitable, more proactive. When applied with care, BI can help uncover hidden inequities, surface untapped potential, and create more inclusive workplace strategies (Gholidoust, 2025). Looking to the future, the role of BI in strategic decision-making will only deepen. As technologies like machine learning, natural language processing, and advanced data visualization continue to evolve, the speed and sophistication of BI tools will increase. But the fundamental question will remain: How do we use this intelligence to make better decisions? Not just faster or more efficient ones, but decisions that are aligned with our purpose, responsive to our stakeholders, and reflective of the kind of organizations—and society—we want to build?

In this sense, the evolution of BI is not only technological; it is cultural. It requires a shift in mindset—from seeing data as a byproduct of operations to seeing it as a core asset. From treating analytics as a technical function to embracing it as a shared responsibility. From using BI to justify decisions after the fact to using it to guide decisions from the outset. Organizations that make this shift will be better equipped to navigate uncertainty, seize opportunity, and learn continuously (Moşteanu, 2024). They will be more agile, more accountable, and more aligned. They will not only use business intelligence—they will become intelligent businesses: capable of thinking clearly, acting boldly, and adapting wisely. And perhaps most importantly, they will understand that at the heart of every strategic decision—beneath the charts, models, and dashboards—lies a human choice. And it is in the quality of these choices that the true value of business intelligence is realized.

Key Tools and Platforms Shaping Modern BI Landscapes

In the digital economy, where data flows faster than most organizations can fully absorb, the tools and platforms that power Business Intelligence (BI) have become more than just technical infrastructure—they have become strategic assets. Today's BI landscape is vast, dynamic, and often overwhelming. The sheer number of platforms claiming to turn raw data into insight, intelligence, or even foresight can leave decision-makers dizzy with options. But beneath the flood of buzzwords and product demos lies a deeper truth: the tools we choose to adopt reflect more than just our technological preferences—they reflect how we think about knowledge, control, collaboration, and ultimately, power. The modern BI ecosystem is not a monolith (Basole et al, 2024). It is an evolving constellation of tools that serve different purposes, answer different kinds of questions, and fit different organizational cultures. Some platforms are designed to empower business users with drag-and-drop simplicity, while others offer deep analytical power for data scientists fluent in SQL, Python, or R. Some focus on real-time dashboards and visual storytelling; others on the backend plumbing that quietly integrates, transforms, and stores data from a thousand different sources. What unites these tools is their promise: to help us see more clearly and act more wisely in a world that demands both.

Let's begin with the tools that are now almost household names in the BI space—platforms like Tableau, Power BI, and Qlik Sense (Ghaffar, 2020). These platforms have helped democratize data access in ways that were nearly unthinkable two decades ago. No longer confined to IT departments or specialist analysts, these tools empower a broader range of professionals—marketing leads, HR directors, supply chain managers—to explore their own data, create their own dashboards, and generate their own insights. This self-service model has reshaped not only how decisions are made, but who gets to make them. Tableau, for instance, is celebrated for its intuitive interface and powerful visual storytelling capabilities. It allows users to drag and drop variables, play with filters, and iterate quickly through complex data relationships—all without needing to write code. What makes Tableau especially powerful is not just the visual polish of its outputs, but the fluidity with which users can move between exploration and explanation. In organizations that value curiosity, transparency, and creative thinking, Tableau thrives as both a canvas and a microscope.

Power BI, Microsoft's offering, integrates seamlessly with Excel, Azure, and the broader Microsoft ecosystem, making it particularly attractive to organizations already invested in that digital environment (Rybaric, 2023). While it may be slightly more rigid than Tableau in terms of visual design, Power BI offers robust enterprise-level scalability, strong governance features, and a rapid deployment curve. It speaks the language of corporate IT while remaining accessible to frontline users—a rare balance in the BI world. Qlik Sense, meanwhile, is often praised for its associative data model—a structure that allows users to explore relationships between datasets in a more organic, nonlinear way (Jurčo, 2020). This can lead to surprising insights that might not emerge through more structured querying. Qlik's architecture lends itself well to scenarios where flexibility, speed, and interactivity are paramount. For organizations that deal with complex, interwoven data sets, Qlik often reveals what others miss. These tools, however, are only part of the story. Behind the dashboards lies a critical layer of infrastructure—tools that prepare, clean, and integrate the data before it ever reaches a visualization. This is where platforms like Alteryx, Talend, and Informatica come in. These tools handle the messy, often invisible labor of data preparation: extracting information from disparate sources, transforming it into usable formats, and loading it into centralized data warehouses. Without this backend orchestration, BI tools would be painting on an incomplete canvas.

Alteryx in particular has gained traction as a no-code/low-code platform that enables users to build complex data workflows with minimal programming knowledge (Garas & Wright, 2024). It appeals to the "citizen data scientist"—someone who understands the business domain deeply and wants to explore data without going through IT bottlenecks. Talend and Informatica offer more robust solutions for large-scale, enterprise-level data integration, where data quality, lineage, and compliance are paramount. Then there's the question of where all this data lives. Increasingly, the answer lies in the cloud. Platforms like Snowflake, Amazon Redshift, Google BigQuery, and Azure Synapse Analytics have redefined what it means to store and query data at scale (Manjunath et al, 2023). These cloud data warehouses can handle massive volumes of data, scale up or down instantly, and support high-speed analytics without requiring organizations to invest in physical hardware. Their elasticity, speed, and integration with AI/ML tools make them essential components of modern BI architecture.

Take Snowflake, for example. Its architecture allows for compute and storage to scale independently, which means you don't pay for processing power when you don't need it. It supports real-time data sharing, making it easier for teams and even external partners to collaborate around shared datasets. This changes the very nature of BI—turning it from an internal reporting function into a platform for ecosystem-wide intelligence. Google BigQuery similarly offers extraordinary speed and scale for organizations that want to analyze petabytes of data without worrying about infrastructure (Ali et al, 2021). Its integration with Google's AI tools makes it a powerful engine for predictive and prescriptive analytics. In forward-looking organizations, tools like BigQuery are not just cost-saving measures; they are strategic enablers. The rise of AI and machine learning has also brought new tools into the BI conversation—tools that go beyond describing what has happened and begin to forecast what might happen next. Platforms like SAS, RapidMiner, DataRobot, and Azure Machine Learning extend BI into the realms of predictive and prescriptive analytics (Sowjanya, 2024). These tools allow analysts and data scientists to build models that can identify trends, recommend actions, or simulate different scenarios based on underlying data patterns. But incorporating these capabilities into BI strategies requires more than just plugging in a new tool. It requires a shift in mindset—from viewing BI as a rearview mirror to embracing it as a form of augmented foresight. It also requires strong data governance, ethical awareness, and a commitment to transparency, especially as decisions become more automated or influenced by algorithms that may not be easily explainable.

A final category of tools worth noting are those that support collaborative analytics—platforms like Looker, Mode, and ThoughtSpot, which emphasize real-time interaction, data sharing, and embedded analytics. These platforms are designed not just to present insights but to embed them into daily workflows, digital products, and cross-functional team discussions. They recognize that insight is only powerful if it's acted upon—and that means making it accessible, contextual, and actionable in the moments that matter. This is the direction in which BI is heading: not toward more data, but more usable, contextualized, and socially integrated data. The future of BI lies not in the elegance of its dashboards, but in the agility with which those insights travel across an organization—connecting the dots between strategy and operations, between vision and execution, between people and outcomes (SWARGIARY, 2024). And yet, with all this power comes a responsibility. These tools are not neutral. They shape the kinds of questions we ask, the kinds of answers we value, and the kinds of decisions we deem legitimate. A dashboard is not just a mirror—it's a frame. It highlights some things while leaving others in the background. As such, choosing a BI platform is not just a technical decision—it is a strategic, ethical, and cultural one. The best BI tools are those that align with an organization's goals, values, and learning culture. They should empower—not overwhelm. Illuminate—not obscure. Facilitate collaboration—not reinforce silos. And perhaps most importantly, they should remind us that while technology can point us toward the truth, it cannot define it. That job still belongs to us: the humans who ask the questions, apply the judgment, and act on the insights we uncover. In the end, the tools that shape the BI landscape are not just shaping how we analyze data—they're shaping how we think. And in a world where decisions move fast and consequences run deep, that's not something to take lightly.

Core Technologies Behind Business Intelligence Systems

Business Intelligence (BI) might be most visible through the lens of colorful dashboards, slick data visualizations, and instantly generated reports. These front-end tools are often the face of BI—the part that decision-makers interact with daily. But what enables those interactions? What unseen architecture quietly powers every visual, every insight, every metric that helps organizations decide where to go next? Behind every polished interface lies a dense web of interconnected technologies that make the entire BI system function with speed, accuracy, and depth. Understanding these core technologies is not just for data engineers or IT specialists—it's increasingly essential for any leader who wants to engage critically and strategically with data-driven decision-making. At the heart of every effective BI system lies the concept of data architecture. Think of it as the foundation upon which all intelligence rests. Without a well-structured system for capturing, storing, organizing, and retrieving data, no amount of analytics can generate meaningful insight. And while tools may evolve, this foundational role of data architecture remains constant. Over time, organizations have shifted from simple databases to intricate networks of data warehouses, data lakes, and increasingly, hybrid cloud architectures that can scale, adapt, and integrate across functions and platforms.

One of the most enduring pillars of BI systems is the data warehouse. Data warehouses are centralized repositories specifically structured to support analytics and reporting (Gagalova et al, 2020). They differ from operational databases in that they are optimized not for transactions, but for queries. A data warehouse pulls in data from multiple systems—HR software, CRM platforms, financial tools, supply chain systems—and transforms it into a standardized format that supports cross-functional analysis (Hajdu, 2024). This process, often referred to as ETL (Extract, Transform, Load), is one of the quiet workhorses of the BI world.

ETL processes are perhaps one of the most underrated components of BI technology, mostly because their role is invisible to most end users. But the logic behind ETL is elegant in its simplicity and essential in its impact. First, data is extracted from a range of source systems—some cloud-based, others on-premise; some structured, others unstructured (Chen et al, 2021). Next, the data is transformed, which may involve cleaning it (removing duplicates, correcting errors), formatting it (converting currencies, adjusting time zones), and aligning it with organizational taxonomies. Finally, the data is loaded into the warehouse or a similar environment, where it is then available for analysis. This entire process ensures that when a manager views a report on employee engagement or sales trends, the numbers are accurate, current, and comparable.

In recent years, ETL has begun to evolve into what's known as ELT—Extract, Load, Transform. In ELT models, data is first extracted and loaded into a target environment (often a cloud data warehouse like Snowflake or BigQuery), and then transformed as needed. This reversal of order is largely a result of the massive computing power offered by modern cloud infrastructure, which makes it more efficient to process transformations after the data has landed. ELT workflows allow for greater flexibility, particularly when organizations need to keep raw, historical data on hand for exploratory analysis or machine learning applications. Running parallel to the evolution of ETL is the rise of data lakes, which offer a different but complementary approach to data storage. Unlike data warehouses, which require structured, formatted data, data lakes can store raw data in its native format—whether structured, semi-structured, or unstructured. This includes everything from spreadsheets and CSVs to emails, sensor data, videos, and logs. The advantage of data lakes is their flexibility (Katari, 2022). They're particularly useful when organizations want to retain large volumes of varied data that may later be used for machine learning, AI modeling, or advanced statistical analysis. In hybrid BI systems, data lakes often serve as the upstream source from which data warehouses pull refined datasets.

Then there is metadata management, another often underappreciated piece of the BI puzzle. Metadata is data about data—it describes where the data came from, how it has been transformed, when it was last updated, and what it means in context (Mayernik, 2021). Without metadata, organizations may struggle to maintain trust in their reports. Imagine reading a chart on employee attrition without knowing whether the data includes contractors, when it was last updated, or which department classifications were used. Metadata ensures transparency, traceability, and confidence in decision-making. The systems that manage it—often built into modern data catalogs or governance tools—are critical to maintaining data integrity in complex environments. Of course, once the data is captured, stored, and processed, the next step is querying and analysis—and here we enter the realm of data modeling, indexing, and processing engines. Technologies like OLAP (Online Analytical Processing) have long played a role in enabling multidimensional analysis (Kovacic et al, 2022). OLAP cubes allow users to slice and dice data across various dimensions—time, geography, product, customer type—without writing complex queries. Although newer tools have made OLAP less visible, the logic behind it continues to inform how modern BI platforms structure data to support fast, flexible analysis.

More recently, in-memory computing has emerged as a key performance booster in BI systems. Instead of retrieving data from disk-based databases every time a user makes a query, in-memory tools store data in RAM, allowing for lightning-fast performance. Platforms like Qlik and Tableau often leverage in-memory engines to power dynamic, interactive dashboards that respond instantly to user input (Galliano, 2023). This speed doesn't just enhance the user experience—it fundamentally changes how people interact with data. Rather than posing a question, waiting for a report, and adjusting strategy days later, users can explore data in real time, iterating on ideas and hypotheses in the moment. Underpinning all of this is the growing integration of machine learning and AI technologies. Increasingly, BI systems are moving from descriptive analytics (what happened?) and diagnostic analytics (why did it happen?) into the realm of predictive (what is likely to happen?) and prescriptive analytics (what should we do about it?). Machine learning models, trained on historical data, can identify patterns and anomalies that human analysts might miss. They can forecast sales, predict employee attrition, detect fraud, or suggest optimal pricing. But integrating these capabilities into a BI system requires robust data pipelines, high-quality labeled data, and tools for model management and validation. Platforms like DataRobot, SAS Viya, Azure Machine Learning, and Amazon SageMaker provide these capabilities—either as stand-alone platforms or integrated into broader BI ecosystems (Krensky et al, 2021). They allow organizations to build, test, and deploy predictive models without needing a PhD in statistics. These models are increasingly embedded into BI dashboards themselves, providing users not just with reports but with automated insights and next-best-action recommendations.

Finally, none of these technologies function in a vacuum. They rely on strong governance frameworks, security protocols, and compliance systems that ensure data is used responsibly. As regulations around data privacy—such as GDPR, CCPA, and others—become more stringent, BI systems must be designed with compliance in mind (Fakeyede et al, 2023). This includes user access controls, audit trails, data masking, and consent tracking. The best BI systems are those that balance openness with control—allowing users to explore freely while protecting sensitive data and organizational integrity. What's important to remember is that these technologies are not simply back-end concerns. They shape what is possible on the front end—what questions can be asked, what answers can be trusted, and how quickly decisions can be made. A lagging ETL process can delay time-sensitive decisions. A poor data model can obscure meaningful insights. A lack of governance can create data chaos. Conversely, when the core technologies are well-designed, maintained, and aligned with organizational needs, they act as a silent partner in every strategic decision. And so, the next time someone opens a dashboard and sees a clean, confident visualization of this quarter's performance or next month's hiring needs, it's worth remembering that behind that moment of clarity lies a world of complexity. The invisible engines of Business Intelligence—its warehouses, lakes, ETL scripts, models, queries, and governance protocols—are not glamorous, but they are indispensable. They are the scaffolding of our collective understanding, the digital infrastructure that supports our ability to see, to think, and to act with intention in a world that demands it.

Methodologies that Drive Insight: From Data Collection to Interpretation

In a world where the phrase "data-driven" is now part of the everyday lexicon of business and policy alike, it's easy to forget that data itself is never the final destination (Payton & Claypoole, 2023). Data is a beginning, not an end. It's the raw material, not the finished product. What transforms data into meaning—what turns a spreadsheet into a strategy or a metric into a moment of realization—is the methodology behind it. The methods we use to collect, clean, organize, and interpret data are not merely technical steps; they are deeply intellectual, often philosophical processes that shape the way we understand the world, and in turn, how we act within it. Business Intelligence (BI) systems, for all their technical sophistication, are ultimately only as powerful as the thinking that underpins them. And this thinking is shaped not by tools alone, but by methodology—by the discipline of asking the right questions, choosing the right data, applying the right models, and interpreting the results with a balance of analytical rigor and human judgment. From the moment data enters a system to the instant it informs a decision, it travels a long and intricate journey. Understanding that journey is essential for anyone who seeks to engage with BI not just as a user, but as a thinker, strategist, and leader.

The journey begins with data collection—seemingly straightforward, but in practice, full of nuance and trade-offs (Parolin et al, 2025). What data is collected? Who decides? From what sources, and in what form? In the context of business, data can come from virtually anywhere: customer transactions, employee surveys, website traffic, social media, HR systems, financial ledgers, supply chain logs, and more. Some of it is structured—neatly organized into rows and columns. Some is unstructured—emails, audio recordings, PDFs, open-ended comments. Some is real-time; some historical. The first methodological challenge lies in identifying which data actually matters for the questions we're trying to answer. It's a deceptively hard task, this act of selection. Too often, we default to what's easiest to collect rather than what's most meaningful. This leads to a kind of methodological laziness—where we overemphasize what's quantifiable and underappreciate what's contextual. A performance metric may tell us that productivity is up, but without the qualitative insight of employee sentiment, we may miss that morale is plummeting. Methodological sophistication requires resisting the urge to reduce complex realities to whatever fits neatly in a database.

Once data is collected, the next step is cleaning and preparation. This is often the least glamorous but most labor-intensive part of the process. Duplicates, errors, missing values, inconsistencies in labeling—these are not just technical issues; they are potential sources of distortion (Fredriksson et al, 2020). If insight is built on a foundation of flawed data, the conclusions drawn may be misleading or outright wrong. The methodologies used in this phase must balance precision with practicality. Not every dataset can be perfect, but the assumptions made during cleaning—what to impute, what to discard, what to normalize—must be made transparently and with a clear understanding of their implications. Data preparation also involves standardization and integration. When pulling from multiple systems, aligning data structures becomes essential. Do "departments" in one dataset map directly to "teams" in another? Are currencies, dates, time zones, and product codes consistent across sources? Methodological rigor here ensures that the analysis isn't built on apples-to-oranges comparisons. It is in this stage that technical fluency meets conceptual clarity: the analyst must not only know how to clean data but must also understand the domain enough to recognize what the data should look like.

With data prepared, the focus shifts to modeling—the structuring of data in ways that allow for meaningful analysis. This could involve simple aggregations, trend lines, and cohort groupings, or it could extend to complex statistical models, machine learning algorithms, or clustering techniques. Regardless of complexity, the core methodological question is the same: does the model reflect the real-world phenomenon it's meant to describe? Too often, impressive models are built without this anchoring. They detect patterns, but do they make sense? Do they align with business logic, historical knowledge, and organizational context? For example, consider a predictive model meant to forecast employee turnover. The model may identify key drivers—say, tenure, commute length, or performance review scores—but without a nuanced understanding of the company's culture, leadership shifts, or external labor market trends, these variables may only tell part of the story. This is where interpretive methodology becomes central. The model doesn't speak for itself. It requires human engagement—people who can look at the results and ask: What does this mean? What doesn't it mean? What might we be missing? Exploratory data analysis (EDA) is one such interpretive practice. Before diving into hard conclusions, EDA encourages us to simply observe—plotting variables, checking distributions, noticing anomalies (Mukhiya & Ahmed, 2020). It is a space for curiosity, not confirmation. Done well, EDA can surface unexpected relationships, challenge assumptions, and frame better questions for deeper analysis. It is a methodological reminder that insight often begins with noticing, not proving.

But analysis is not just about finding what's true—it's also about deciding what's relevant. In this regard, contextual framing is everything. The same data point can have vastly different meanings depending on what lens is applied. A 5% drop in sales might be a cause for concern or a seasonal fluctuation. A spike in customer service calls could indicate a product defect or simply a new marketing campaign driving attention. Methodology, at its best, brings this context to the forefront. It doesn't just ask "what happened?"—it asks, "what matters, and why?"

Another dimension of interpretation is visualization. Here, methodology intersects with design. A well-crafted chart can illuminate a trend instantly; a poorly chosen one can obscure it. Choosing the right visualization—bar chart, line graph, heat map, scatterplot—is not a matter of aesthetics alone. It's a methodological decision about how to represent complexity clearly. It involves knowing the audience, anticipating their questions, and presenting the data in a way that facilitates understanding without oversimplifying. In many organizations, this is where insight either takes hold or gets lost. Of course, interpretation is never value-neutral. Every methodological choice—what data to include, what model to apply, what visualization to use—is shaped by human judgment, organizational culture, and implicit biases. Recognizing this is not a flaw in BI methodology—it is a feature that must be acknowledged and navigated with care. Transparency in methodology is therefore crucial. Stakeholders need to know not just the headline insight, but how it was reached. What assumptions were made? What limitations exist? What alternative explanations are possible? In high-stakes environments—such as healthcare, public policy, or equity-related decision-making—this transparency becomes an ethical obligation. Misinterpreted data can reinforce injustice, entrench inequality, or drive resources away from those who need them most. Methodologies that drive insight must also be methodologies that invite scrutiny, promote accountability, and reflect the diversity of the contexts in which they are applied.

Moreover, methodologies should not be static. The most effective BI systems are those that treat methodology as a living process—open to refinement, responsive to feedback, and willing to evolve as the organization and its environment change (Harfoush, 2024). This means regularly revisiting models, updating assumptions, checking for drift, and staying attuned to new questions that emerge from old answers. Methodological agility is key to maintaining relevance in a dynamic world. And finally, we must remember that methodology is not just about analytics—it is also about action. The purpose of insight is to inform decisions. A brilliant model that no one understands or acts upon is of limited value (Fader, 2020). Methodology, then, must also consider the path from insight to implementation. How is the insight communicated? Who needs to hear it? What decisions will it influence, and how? This requires bridging the gap between analysts and decision-makers, between data and dialogue. It requires empathy, storytelling, and often, a shared language that transcends statistical jargon. In the end, the methodologies that drive insight are not simply technical protocols—they are expressions of how we seek to understand the world. They reflect our values, our limitations, our aspirations. In Business Intelligence, they form the hidden scaffolding behind every dashboard, every report, every "aha" moment. To engage with methodology is to engage with the very process of learning, discerning, and leading. And in a time when data is abundant but true understanding is still rare, that engagement is more important than ever.

Integrating BI with Talent Management: Opportunities and Limitations

If there's one area of business that continues to defy easy categorization, it is talent management. Unlike finance, which is numerical by nature, or operations, which tends to be process-driven, talent management lives in a more complex, fluid space—where data meets emotion, where performance intersects with potential, and where human stories must be translated into organizational strategy. For decades, talent decisions were based primarily on personal judgment, institutional tradition, and generalized metrics. But in today's digital era—one marked by rapid workforce evolution, hybrid work models, and global talent mobility—there is a growing demand to bring greater precision, agility, and foresight to how we manage people. This is precisely where Business Intelligence (BI) offers both promise and challenge. Integrating BI into talent management isn't just a matter of layering dashboards onto HR systems (Dutta et al, 2025). It's about reimagining how we understand human capital—not as a static ledger of job titles and salaries, but as a dynamic, evolving ecosystem of skills, motivations, relationships, and trajectories. BI invites organizations to look beyond gut instinct and anecdote. It provides tools to detect trends, surface insights, and test assumptions. When used with care and clarity, BI can support fairer hiring practices, more effective learning strategies, stronger retention efforts, and more nuanced performance evaluations. It can also, if not thoughtfully implemented, reduce people to data points, oversimplify complex behaviors, and reinforce existing biases under the guise of objectivity.

At the heart of BI's integration into talent management is the idea that workforce data can be a powerful mirror—revealing not just what is happening, but why. Consider turnover, a perennial concern for most organizations. Traditionally, organizations tracked exit rates, perhaps conducting exit interviews, and trying to piece together patterns retrospectively. But BI enables a more proactive approach. By combining data from engagement surveys, performance scores, absenteeism records, and even team dynamics, predictive models can help identify employees who may be at risk of leaving—sometimes months before they actually do. Such foresight doesn't just help HR—it gives managers the opportunity to intervene meaningfully, whether through a career conversation, workload adjustment, or development opportunity. Similarly, recruitment can be transformed from a reactive process to a strategic function. BI tools can analyze which sourcing channels yield the most successful hires—not just in terms of speed, but in terms of long-term fit and performance. They can help identify which competencies are actually driving success in a given role, rather than relying on legacy job descriptions or generic requirements. By mapping past hiring data against performance and retention outcomes, organizations can refine their recruitment strategies with more precision, reduce bias, and improve diversity outcomes. When thoughtfully applied, BI offers a lens that is both wide and deep—showing patterns at the macro level, while remaining sensitive to the microstories within.

Another rich area for BI integration is learning and development. In most organizations, training programs are offered broadly, sometimes with little sense of individual need or measurable impact. BI tools can change that. By linking performance data, skills assessments, and career aspirations, organizations can personalize learning journeys, allocate development resources more effectively, and measure whether training interventions actually lead to improved outcomes. For example, if a team shows lower engagement scores and higher error rates, a BI-enabled analysis might reveal not just who needs training, but what kind of support is most likely to make a difference. This kind of insight shifts the focus from compliance-based training to capability-building that is meaningful, measurable, and aligned with business goals. Even the elusive realm of employee engagement—long treated as a soft metric—can benefit from BI. With the right systems in place, organizations can move beyond annual surveys and toward continuous listening. Sentiment analysis, pulse surveys, and behavioral data can provide real-time insights into how employees are feeling, what's influencing their morale, and how leaders can respond (Carreno, 2024). Of course, this must be handled with extreme care. The line between insight and intrusion is thin. Employees must trust that their data is being used to support—not surveil—them. Transparency in data use, ethical safeguards, and open dialogue are essential to ensuring that BI builds trust rather than eroding it.

Perhaps one of the most powerful applications of BI in talent management lies in workforce planning (Gomes, 2023). In a world where skills are evolving faster than job titles can keep up, organizations need to think not just about roles, but about capabilities. BI enables the creation of skill maps—visualizations of what skills exist in the organization today, where gaps are emerging, and how those align with future strategic needs. When integrated with labor market data, demographic trends, and internal mobility patterns, this becomes a potent tool for long-term planning. It helps organizations avoid both talent shortages and redundancies (Kayyali, 2024). It also empowers employees by making career paths more transparent, signaling where opportunities lie, and what development is needed to get there. Yet, for all its opportunities, integrating BI into talent management also comes with very real limitations—and these must be acknowledged if the promise is to be realized responsibly. The first is the challenge of data quality. HR systems are often fragmented, inconsistent, and historically underinvested compared to other enterprise functions. Job codes are outdated, performance data is subjective, and employee records may be incomplete. Without clean, well-structured, and reliable data, even the most sophisticated BI tools will struggle to produce meaningful insight. Investing in data hygiene, governance, and system integration is not just a technical requirement—it is a strategic necessity.

Second is the issue of interpretation. Human behavior is rarely linear or easily predicted. A high-performing employee may leave for personal reasons that no model could foresee (de Waal et al, 2023). A new hire may bloom in one team and flounder in another. BI can provide signals, but it cannot account for every variable. It cannot read intent, context, or nuance the way a human can. This means that data must be one input among many—not the sole arbiter of decisions. Managers and HR leaders must be trained not just in using BI tools, but in interpreting them thoughtfully, challenging their outputs, and integrating them with qualitative insights. Third is the ethical dimension. As organizations gather more data on their employees—behavioral, emotional, even biometric in some cases—the risk of misuse grows. Who has access to this data? How is consent obtained? What safeguards are in place? These are not hypothetical questions. In some organizations, poorly implemented analytics have led to employee backlash, legal challenges, or reputational damage. The use of BI in talent management must be guided by clear principles: privacy, fairness, transparency, and purpose (Zhang et al, 2020). Employees must know what data is being collected, how it is being used, and what rights they have. Anything less risks turning a tool of empowerment into a mechanism of control.

Finally, there is the risk of overconfidence. The allure of BI is its apparent objectivity. Numbers can feel definitive, dashboards authoritative. But behind every metric is a methodology, a set of assumptions, and a margin of error (Kerzner, 2023). Overreliance on data can lead to false precision—where decisions are made because "the numbers said so," even when those numbers tell only part of the story. Good BI practice requires humility: an awareness of what we know, what we don't, and how to question our conclusions.

Despite these challenges, the integration of BI into talent management is not only possible—it is increasingly necessary (Dua, 2025). The complexity of the modern workforce demands better tools for understanding and action. Talent is no longer a fixed asset; it is a flowing, evolving, deeply human resource that must be understood in both systemic and personal terms. BI helps make that complexity visible. It reveals patterns that might otherwise go unnoticed. It prompts better questions, supports fairer decisions, and enables organizations to align their people strategies with their broader missions. But for this to happen, BI must be implemented not as a control mechanism, but as a support system. Not as a substitute for judgment, but as an aid to it. Not as a surveillance tool, but as a mirror—one that helps individuals, teams, and leaders see themselves more clearly, and in doing so, grow. The future of talent management will not be built on instinct alone. Nor will it be built on data alone. It will be built in the space where insight meets empathy, where metrics meet meaning. In that space, Business Intelligence has the potential to be not just a technological advancement, but a human one.

Looking Forward: Trends and Challenges in BI Deployment

As Business Intelligence (BI) continues to evolve from a niche function into a core strategic capability, organizations across the globe are waking up to its transformative potential—not just as a tool for efficiency, but as a force for clarity, adaptability, and long-term vision (Eboigbe et al, 2023). Yet, with this expanding role comes a new set of complexities. The future of BI is not merely about faster data pipelines or shinier dashboards; it's about how organizations navigate the social, technological, and ethical crossroads that come with increased reliance on data-informed decision-making. Looking forward, several key trends are shaping the future of BI deployment. These trends are not isolated shifts—they are interconnected, overlapping forces that signal deeper changes in how organizations think, work, and respond to a world that is growing more unpredictable by the day.

One of the most significant of these trends is the rise of real-time intelligence. In the past, BI was largely retrospective—designed to analyze what had already happened. Reports were generated weekly, monthly, quarterly. That rhythm suited a slower world. Today, however, businesses operate in an environment where yesterday's data is already old news. From supply chain disruptions to market volatility and employee sentiment shifts, decision-makers need insights as events unfold, not after they've passed. Modern BI systems are increasingly being architected to provide real-time or near-real-time analytics—enabling leaders to respond to emerging issues with agility and confidence. This shift is not just about speed; it's about situational awareness. Real-time dashboards, alert systems, and automated decision triggers are becoming essential tools for organizations seeking to maintain operational continuity amid disruption (Nwaimo et al, 2022). But real-time BI also raises important challenges. It requires robust infrastructure, seamless integration across data sources, and high levels of trust in data accuracy. More critically, it raises the question: Are our organizations culturally and operationally ready to act on real-time insights? Speed without clarity can lead to reactionary decision-making. The challenge isn't just building real-time systems—it's building real-time thinking.

Parallel to this is the growing influence of artificial intelligence and machine learning within BI ecosystems. What was once the domain of descriptive analytics—summarizing past behavior—is rapidly expanding into predictive and prescriptive analytics. AI models can now forecast sales trends, detect anomalies, suggest pricing adjustments, and even generate narratives from data. Natural language processing (NLP) tools are allowing users to query datasets conversationally—asking questions in plain English and receiving instant visual answers (Vajjala et al, 2020). These developments are democratizing data access in unprecedented ways, making it possible for non-technical users to engage with analytics meaningfully. However, the integration of AI into BI is not without risk. Predictive models can inherit and amplify biases embedded in historical data. Prescriptive recommendations can create overreliance on algorithmic outputs at the expense of human judgment (McLaughlin, 2024). The allure of automation can obscure the importance of context. As organizations lean more heavily on AI-driven BI, they must also develop frameworks for algorithmic accountability—ensuring that models are transparent, auditable, and aligned with ethical standards. This is particularly crucial when BI is applied to sensitive areas such as talent management, financial forecasting, or public service delivery. Another defining trend is the increased decentralization of BI capabilities. Traditionally, analytics functions were centralized—housed within IT or a specialized data team. This model offered control but often created bottlenecks. Today, there's a growing emphasis on self-service BI—empowering users across departments to access, explore, and act on data independently. Modern BI tools are designed with user experience in mind: intuitive interfaces, drag-and-drop functionality, and interactive visualizations that require little to no coding (Cruz, 2023). This democratization of data has enormous potential—it brings insight closer to decision-makers, fosters a data-literate culture, and enables faster, more localized decisions.

Yet, decentralization introduces its own set of tensions. When different teams operate on different datasets, definitions, or dashboards, inconsistency can creep in. Data governance becomes more difficult. Interpretation can diverge. The risk is not only redundancy but contradiction—multiple "truths" emerging from different corners of the organization. To address this, forward-looking BI deployments must strike a balance: promoting self-service access while maintaining centralized standards for data quality, definitions, and usage protocols. Governance should not be about control for its own sake—it should be about clarity, trust, and shared understanding. In the broader landscape, cloud-based BI is becoming the norm rather than the exception. The flexibility, scalability, and cost-effectiveness of cloud platforms make them especially attractive for organizations looking to modernize their analytics infrastructure. Cloud-based BI enables global access, seamless updates, and powerful integrations with other digital tools. It supports hybrid work, cross-border collaboration, and distributed teams—all of which are increasingly standard in today's workforce.

But even as cloud BI expands, it introduces a new layer of complexity in terms of data privacy, jurisdiction, and compliance. Where is the data stored? Who has access? How do cross-border data flows interact with national regulations like GDPR,

CCPA, or emerging data sovereignty laws? The global reach of cloud technology must be matched with local sensitivity and legal due diligence. This is no longer a purely technical issue—it's a strategic one, with implications for trust, reputation, and risk exposure. Looking ahead, one of the most urgent imperatives in BI deployment is building organizational data literacy (Bhambri & Rani, 2025). A powerful BI system is of little use if the people it's meant to serve don't know how to engage with it critically. Data literacy is not about teaching everyone to code—it's about cultivating a shared capacity to ask good questions, interpret charts with skepticism, and understand the difference between correlation and causation. It's about recognizing the strengths and limits of data, and knowing when to trust it—and when to pause. Organizations that invest in data literacy across all levels—from the C-suite to frontline staff—will be better positioned to extract real value from their BI systems. This involves not just training, but cultural change. It means creating environments where data curiosity is encouraged, where mistakes are treated as learning opportunities, and where insight is not the domain of a few but the responsibility of all.

As with any major shift, the deployment of BI faces internal resistance. Legacy systems, political silos, fear of transparency, or simple change fatigue can all slow adoption. In some cases, the very act of measuring performance or visualizing disparity can challenge long-held beliefs or power structures. Successful BI implementation requires more than technology—it requires leadership. Leaders must articulate not just the "how" but the "why." They must frame BI not as surveillance or scorekeeping, but as a means of learning, growth, and alignment with shared goals. Finally, as we look to the future, it's important to resist the temptation to frame BI as a finished product—a system to be "rolled out" and then left to run. BI is a living practice. It evolves with the questions we ask, the tools we use, and the world around us. It is shaped by human curiosity, organizational context, and societal change. As such, the most effective BI deployments are those that remain open: open to iteration, to feedback, to new ideas. They are not perfect systems—they are learning systems. And therein lies the real promise of BI: not just to inform, but to illuminate. Not just to measure, but to motivate. Not just to optimize, but to understand. In a world that is increasingly complex, fast-moving, and uncertain, organizations need more than data. They need wisdom. BI, when deployed with care and vision, can help us move closer to that wisdom—not by replacing human insight, but by deepening it. As we step into the next chapter of BI's evolution, the challenge is not just to build better tools. It is to ask better questions. To listen more carefully. To lead more thoughtfully. And to remember that intelligence—business or otherwise—is ultimately not about knowing everything. It is about knowing enough to act with clarity, courage, and compassion.

CONCLUSION

As we look across the evolving terrain of business and organizational management, one truth becomes increasingly evident: Business Intelligence is no longer optional. It is foundational. Whether navigating global supply chains, managing remote teams, responding to economic shocks, or planning for long-term growth, organizations now depend on timely, data-informed insights to survive and thrive. But what this chapter has tried to show is that BI is not a single technology, tool, or trend—it is an ongoing process. A mindset. A way of approaching complexity with clarity and purpose. Throughout this exploration, we've engaged with the practical components of BI—the tools that collect, store, and visualize data; the technologies that power fast, scalable processing; and the methodologies that transform raw numbers into actionable narratives. These are not abstract capabilities. They are deeply embedded in the everyday decisions that shape organizational culture, resource allocation, strategic planning, and, increasingly, how talent is managed.

In the specific context of talent management, BI has emerged as a particularly powerful force. Where once HR decisions were driven largely by instinct or precedent, organizations now have the opportunity to align workforce strategy with empirical insight. Predictive analytics can help anticipate retention risks. Skills mapping can reveal future capability needs. Sentiment analysis can uncover the emotional pulse of the workforce. When used ethically and thoughtfully, BI becomes a partner in building not just better organizations, but more humane ones—places where decisions are made not just faster, but fairer. Yet this chapter also urges caution and reflection. In our rush to adopt the latest platforms and dashboards, we risk overlooking the deeper responsibilities that come with data-driven leadership. Technology does not eliminate bias—it can amplify it. Data does not speak for itself—it must be interpreted with care, context, and critical thinking. Algorithms may spot patterns, but they cannot understand meaning. And in domains like talent management, where the data is about real people with real lives, the ethical stakes are high.

Moving forward, the most resilient and forward-thinking organizations will be those that view BI not merely as a set of tools, but as a discipline—one that combines analytical rigor with ethical sensitivity, technological savvy with strategic vision. They will understand that the ultimate value of BI lies not in the elegance of a dashboard, but in the quality of the decisions it supports. They will invest not only in platforms, but in people—building data literacy across teams, encouraging cross-functional collaboration, and fostering a culture of continuous learning. There is also a growing need for inclusivity in the way we think about business intelligence. BI should not be the domain of analysts alone. When siloed, it loses its potential to inform holistic understanding. When democratized—when every department, leader, and decision-maker is empowered to engage with data—BI becomes a shared language for progress. The future of BI lies not just in technological innovation, but in organizational culture: in how we value evidence, how we question assumptions, and how we bring diverse perspectives into the analytical process.

Finally, we must remember that the end goal of Business Intelligence is not perfection—it is progress. Data will always be imperfect, incomplete, and open to interpretation. But when harnessed with intention, it can help us see farther, think deeper, and act with more confidence. It can move organizations from reactive to proactive, from fragmented to integrated, from data-rich to insight-driven. As this chapter closes, one thing is clear: the foundations of Business Intelligence are not fixed—they are being built and rebuilt every day. In a world defined by uncertainty and acceleration, BI offers us a compass. But like any compass, it only works when we know where we're trying to go—and why. Our task, then, is not just to collect data, but to listen to it. Not just to analyze, but to ask better questions. And not just to optimize outcomes, but to align our intelligence—business and otherwise—with our values.

REFERENCES

Ali, M. H., Hosain, M. S., & Hossain, M. A. (2021). Big Data analysis using BigQuery on cloud computing platform. *Australian JofEng Inno Tech*, *3*(1), 1–9.

Ashal, N., & Morshed, A. (2024). Balancing data-driven insights and human judgment in supply chain management: The role of business intelligence, big data analytics, and artificial intelligence. Journal of Infrastructure. *Policy and Development*, *8*(6), 3941. DOI: 10.24294/jipd.v8i6.3941

Basole, R. C., Park, H., & Seuss, C. D. (2024). Complex business ecosystem intelligence using AI-powered visual analytics. *Decision Support Systems*, *178*, 114133. DOI: 10.1016/j.dss.2023.114133

Bhambri, P., & Rani, S. (2025). Advancements and Future Challenges in Business Intelligence. In Developing Managerial Skills for Global Business Success (pp. 271-290). IGI Global Scientific Publishing.

Carreno, A. M. (2024). Building a Continuous Feedback Loop for Real-Time Change Adaptation: Best Practices and Tools.

Chen, J. C., Rubin, E. A., & Cornwall, G. J. (2021). *Data science for public policy*. Springer. DOI: 10.1007/978-3-030-71352-2

Cruz, J. A. S. (2023). Analytics-Customized dashboards representing a descriptive analysis and diagnosis of business and operational information (Master's thesis).

de Waal, A., Burrell, J., Drake, S., Sampa, C., & Mulimbika, T. (2023). How to stay high-performing: Developing organizational grit. *Measuring Business Excellence*, *27*(1), 25–39. DOI: 10.1108/MBE-08-2021-0104

Dua, G. K. (2025). Synergizing Talent Horizons: The Transformative Impact of Data Integration in Contemporary Talent Management. In Cultivating Creativity and Navigating Talent Management in Academia (pp. 359-382). IGI Global Scientific Publishing.

Dutta, S., Thomas, A., & Khatri, P. (2025). *Disruptive Technology in Human Resource Management*. Taylor & Francis. DOI: 10.4324/9781003507543

Eboigbe, E. O., Farayola, O. A., Olatoye, F. O., Nnabugwu, O. C., & Daraojimba, C. (2023). Business intelligence transformation through AI and data analytics. *Engineering Science & Technology Journal*, *4*(5), 285–307. DOI: 10.51594/estj.v4i5.616

Fader, P. (2020). *Customer centricity: Focus on the right customers for strategic advantage*. University of Pennsylvania Press.

Fakeyede, O. G., Okeleke, P. A., Hassan, A. O., Iwuanyanwu, U., Adaramodu, O. R., & Oyewole, O. O. (2023). Navigating data privacy through IT audits: GDPR, CCPA, and beyond. *International Journal of Research in Engineering and Science*, *11*(11).

Fredriksson, T., Mattos, D. I., Bosch, J., & Olsson, H. H. (2020, November). Data labeling: An empirical investigation into industrial challenges and mitigation strategies. In International conference on product-focused software process improvement (pp. 202-216). Cham: Springer International Publishing.

Gagalova, K. K., Elizalde, M. A. L., Portales-Casamar, E., & Görges, M. (2020). What you need to know before implementing a clinical research data warehouse: Comparative review of integrated data repositories in health care institutions. *JMIR Formative Research*, *4*(8), e17687. DOI: 10.2196/17687 PMID: 32852280

Galliano, G. (2023). The importance of data visualization tools in modern enterprises. Cost-effective solutions and empowering of an open source project (Doctoral dissertation, Politecnico di Torino).

Garas, S., & Wright, S. L. (2024). A data analytics case study analyzing IRS SOI migration data using no code, low code technologies. *Journal of Accounting Education*, *66*, 100885. DOI: 10.1016/j.jaccedu.2024.100885

Ghaffar, A. (2020). Integration of Business Intelligence Dashboard for Enhanced Data Analytics Capabilities.

Ghafoori, A., Gupta, M., Merhi, M. I., Gupta, S., & Shore, A. P. (2024). Toward the role of organizational culture in data-driven digital transformation. *International Journal of Production Economics*, *271*, 109205. DOI: 10.1016/j.ijpe.2024.109205

Gholidoust, A. (2025). Unleashing Creativity: The Interplay of Innovation and Diversity. In Mastering Innovation in Business (pp. 47-76). IGI Global.

Gomes, B. M. S. (2023). Development of a Talent Management Platform at BI4ALL: Business Intelligence Approach for Human Resource Management (Master's thesis, Universidade NOVA de Lisboa (Portugal)).

Hajdu, N. (2024). Advancing Organizational Analytics: A Strategic Roadmap for Implementing Machine Learning in Warehouse Management System.

Harfoush, B. (2024). Impact of Organizational Changes on BI Critical Success Factors.

Jurčo, A. (2020). Data Lineage Analysis for Qlik Sense.

Katari, A. (2022). Data lakes and Optimizing Query. Available at *SSRN*.

Kayyali, M. (2024). Design thinking and creativity in entrepreneurial innovation. In *Applying Business Intelligence and Innovation to Entrepreneurship* (pp. 155–170). IGI Global. DOI: 10.4018/979-8-3693-1846-1.ch008

Kerzner, H. (2023). *Project management metrics, KPIs, and dashboards: a guide to measuring and monitoring project performance*. John wiley & sons.

Kovacic, I., Schuetz, C. G., Neumayr, B., & Schrefl, M. (2022). OLAP Patterns: A pattern-based approach to multidimensional data analysis. *Data & Knowledge Engineering*, *138*, 101948. DOI: 10.1016/j.datak.2021.101948

Krensky, P., Idoine, C., Brethenoux, E., Den Hamer, P., Choudhary, F., Jaffri, A., & Vashisth, S. (2021). *Magic quadrant for data science and machine learning platforms*. Gartner, Inc.

Manjunath, T. N., Pushpa, S. K., Hegadi, R. S., & Ananya Hathwar, K. S. (2023). A study on big data engineering using cloud data warehouse. Data Engineering and Data Science: Concepts and Applications, 49-69.

Mayernik, M. S. (2021). Metadata. *Knowledge Organization*, *47*(8), 696–713. DOI: 10.5771/0943-7444-2020-8-696

McLaughlin, B. (2024). *Designing Prediction and Recommendation Algorithms to Improve Human Decision-Making*. Stanford University.

Mehta, N., & Pickens, A. (2020). *The customer success economy: Why every aspect of your business model needs a paradigm shift*. John Wiley & Sons.

Moşteanu, N. R. (2024). Adapting to the unpredictable: Building resilience for business continuity in an ever-changing landscape. *European Journal of Theoretical and Applied Sciences*, *2*(1), 444–457. DOI: 10.59324/ejtas.2024.2(1).37

Mukhiya, S. K., & Ahmed, U. (2020). *Hands-On Exploratory Data Analysis with Python: Perform EDA techniques to understand, summarize, and investigate your data*. Packt Publishing Ltd.

Niederman, F. (2021). Project management: Openings for disruption from AI and advanced analytics. *Information Technology & People*, *34*(6), 1570–1599. DOI: 10.1108/ITP-09-2020-0639

Nwaimo, C. S., Adewumi, A., & Ajiga, D. (2022). Advanced data analytics and business intelligence: Building resilience in risk management. *International Journal of Scientific Research and Applications*, *6*(2), 121.

Parolin, G., Arnbjerg, J., McAloone, T. C., & Pigosso, D. C. (2025). Navigating trade-offs in design for sustainability and circularity: A tool for decision making leveraging narratives and multiple criteria decision analysis. *Journal of Cleaner Production, 494*, 145004. DOI: 10.1016/j.jclepro.2025.145004

Payton, T., & Claypoole, T. (2023). *Privacy in the age of Big data: Recognizing threats, defending your rights, and protecting your family*. Rowman & Littlefield. DOI: 10.5771/9781538167830

Rybaric, R. (2023). *Microsoft Power Platform Enterprise Architecture: Design tailor-made solutions for architects and decision makers to meet complex business requirements*. Packt Publishing Ltd.

Schuetz, C. G., & Schrefl, M. (2023). Conceptualizing analytics: an overview of business intelligence and analytics from a conceptual-modeling perspective. Digital Transformation: Core Technologies and Emerging Topics from a Computer Science Perspective, 311-336.

Selvarajan, G. P. (2020). The Role of Machine Learning Algorithms in Business Intelligence: Transforming Data into Strategic Insights. *International Journal of All Research Education and Scientific Methods, 8*(5), 194–202.

Sowjanya, M. C. V. N. (2024). *Data Science: Exploring Future Trends*. Academic Guru Publishing House.

Swargiary, K. (2024). Unveiling the Nexus of Business Intelligence Maturity and Agility: Exploring Organizational Dynamics for Adaptive Success.

Vajjala, S., Majumder, B., Gupta, A., & Surana, H. (2020). *Practical natural language processing: a comprehensive guide to building real-world NLP systems*. O'Reilly Media.

Zhang, X., Zhao, Y., Tang, X., Zhu, H., & Xiong, H. (2020). Developing fairness rules for talent intelligence management system.

Chapter 6
Enhancing Employee Engagement Through Data-Driven HR Practices

Usharani Bhimavarapu
https://orcid.org/0000-0002-0246-1420
Computer Science and Engineering, Koneru Lakshmaiah Education Foundation, India

ABSTRACT

The convergence of business intelligence (BI) and Human Resource Management (HRM) has initiated more efficient, data-driven, and strategic talent management procedures. The current paper proposes the application of a BI strategy combined with stacked artificial neural networks (ANN) for simplifying HRM procedures like recruitment, employee performance appraisal, and attrition prediction. Applying data from a top recruitment agency for the period 2023-2024, we utilized BI tools for preprocessing data, feature selection by Particle Swarm Optimization (PSO), and the use of stacked ANN to predictive analysis. The pattern discovery property of the model allows for smarter decision-making in recruitment, retention, and workforce planning. This research shows how the use of technology and sophisticated data analysis can make HRM a more proactive and effective function that is supportive of an organization's strategic objectives.

INTRODUCTION

With the advent of a fast-paced business age, human resource management (HRM) has emerged as the single most contributing factor to the success of an organization. With the mounting pressure for efficiency, accuracy, and data-driven decision-

DOI: 10.4018/979-8-3373-1942-1.ch006

making, most organizations are adopting technology to automate HR activities. Business Intelligence (BI) has become a powerful tool to reshape HRM to facilitate organizations in making decisions based on data while hiring talent, developing employees, and retaining employees. It is not as much a shift of implementing new technology but the use of data in a way to know and forecast employee behaviors, performance, and potential.

Business Intelligence in HRM is the incorporation of the most recent data analysis software into HR information systems to gather, analyze, and report on applicable data. By doing so, organizations can gain an insight into the strengths, weaknesses, and overall performance of their employees. With the assistance of BI, HR managers can monitor key performance indicators like employee turnover, absenteeism, and productivity in real-time. This helps determine issues before they arise, hence enabling preventative action on the part of HR professionals. For example, by using predictive analytics, HR can predict which employees are likely to leave the company, and therefore implement some retention strategies.

Employee performance data is typically dispersed in many systems, making it hard for HR managers to get the overall picture of an employee's growth. BI tools also offer a single platform where all the relevant information, including performance rating, training progress, and feedback, can be seen and analyzed at one glance. By consolidating this information, HR managers can develop a 360-degree picture of every employee, which is important for determining top performers, determining skill gaps, and creating customized development plans. This end-to-end approach guarantees that companies are not just optimizing individual performance but also building a stronger team.

One of the greatest benefits of using Business Intelligence in HRM is improving the recruitment process. With BI tools, HR professionals can review past data from previous hires to find trends that result in successful hires. Using this insight, companies can optimize their recruitment processes and hire the best candidates more efficiently. For instance, BI can identify which channels of recruitment perform best or which skills are most linked to high-performing employees. This allows HR departments to make more informed recruitment decisions and achieve improved outcomes and lower the cost of bad hires.

Employee retention is also where Business Intelligence makes the most impact. By analyzing trends in employee satisfaction, employee engagement, and employee performance, HR managers can determine what causes high turnover. BI enables the identification of high-risk employees based on work hours, performance trends, and engagement scores. Once such employees are identified, HR departments can intervene by employing focused interventions, such as tailored engagement programs, development programs, or even organizational interventions that address root issues. And amidst all this, BI is central to maintaining top performers and lowering recruitment expenses.

Workforce planning is an important task of HRM and is highly supported by Business Intelligence. Organizations are able to use BI tools to measure workforce needs by taking the present and the future into account. Relying on workforce demographics, competencies, and performance, HR is able to project the skills needed and make adequate plans for acquiring future talent. Additionally, BI software can assist in the identification of skill gaps among existing employees so that HR can introduce focused training programs that support the long-term objectives of the company. Strategic alignment in this way enables the firm to remain competitive and prepared to react to changing business demands.

Use of Business Intelligence in HRM also promotes a diverse and inclusive workforce. Through the use of BI tools to examine hiring trends, pay disparities, and career development opportunities, diversity and inclusion programs can be targeted for enhancement by HR departments where they need to be reinforced. Fact-based metrics revealed through data usage make biases in recruitment, compensation, or promotion practices apparent, and organizations can correct them to foster equity and fairness. With these findings, HR can develop initiatives that promote diversity and inclusion and, in the process, deliver a more positive working environment as well as contented employees.

Business Intelligence also empowers HR managers to improve employee experience through data-driven feedback. Through employee feedback insights and engagement trends, HR would be able to understand what drives employees and what irritates them. These results can subsequently be utilized to fine-tune the overall work place, ranging from re-engineering policies to designing more customized benefits packages. With this work on BI insight, the HR can establish a work place focused on employee wellness and promoting long-term commitment. This creates an improved productive and efficient workforce, which in turn affects the organization's bottom line.

Another important advantage of BI to HRM is that it can enhance compensation and benefits decision-making. Through the examination of compensation data, HR managers can ensure competitive and equitable pay packages. BI technology can also identify industry compensation trends, and hence companies can make wise decisions regarding salary reviews and benefits schemes. Second, by analyzing data to measure the performance of various benefits programs, HR can ensure that money is being spent on the programs that are most appreciated by employees. This makes sure compensation and benefits strategy supports organizational objectives and employee expectations.

Lastly, having Business Intelligence integrated into HRM makes it possible for better overall strategic planning within an organization. By offering real-time, actionable insights, BI enables HR professionals to be proactive in influencing the workforce. Rather than making decisions based on anecdotal information or gut feel, HR operations can now leverage context-based data to guide business decisions at the strategic level. BI enables HR to optimize talent management strategy to the business goal, such that the workforce is optimized to facilitate the achievement of the company's goals. This analytical methodology enables inter-functional cooperation between HR and other business functions to deliver improved outcomes in the firm.

Finally, the union of talent and technology through Business Intelligence is transforming HRM. Through the adoption of analytics, HR divisions can make informed decisions, enhance hiring and retention, enhance employee performance, and create a more diverse and engaged workforce. With every new emerging technology, the application of BI in HRM will continue to increase its strength. Companies that adopt the tools of BI effectively will be in a position to recruit, enhance, and retain top talent on board, eventually leading to business success. With unfolding the future of HRM, the use of Business Intelligence will remain a component of determining the future workplace.

Lateef & Omotayo (2019) explained the importance of information audits in organisational management, but the research relies mostly on a literature review, and it is constrained to real data and actual organisational experience of current organisations. It becomes challenging to evaluate the influence of information audits on actual organisational performance because there is no empirical examination (Lateef & Omotayo, 2019).

Suchánek (2019) described business intelligence as an essential tool for contemporary firms. Nevertheless, the study fails to present an in-depth analysis of the problems encountered by firms in applying business intelligence tools across sectors. The conclusions are mostly theoretical with very minimal empirical data to back the suggested models (Suchánek, 2019).

Gioia et al. (2013) presented the Gioia Methodology for qualitative research, a key methodology for inductive research. The limitation of this paper is that it presents methodological rigor but not the practicalities of using the methodology in actual research contexts, especially when working with complex organizational data (Gioia et al., 2013).

Lim & Teoh (2020) studied the strategic effects of business intelligence use, but the research fails to deal with the individual impediments to firms using business intelligence systems. Moreover, it fails to consider varying implications of business intelligence according to industry or company size, thus restricting the ability to generalize the findings (Lim & Teoh, 2020).

Viitanen & Pirttimaki (2006) compared the application of business intelligence to aid strategic management in technology firms. The drawback is that this study is technology firm-specific and hence complications or advantages of business intelligence cannot be inferred from it to other industries. Moreover, the technological environment has changed over time since the research was conducted and, thus, it might not be so at present for contemporary business intelligence strategies (Viitanen & Pirttimaki, 2006).

Barone et al. (2010) proposed a business intelligence model for strategic modeling, but the research is not buttressed with a critical assessment of how the model operates in actual organizational environments. The lack of case studies or evidence limits its applicability in real-world environments for organizations interested in adopting similar models (Barone et al., 2010).

Power (2003) gave a history of decision support systems. Yet, the study mainly discusses decision support technology development without any reference to challenges with integrating decision support systems with current big data software. The history might also not reflect the recent fast technological improvements that have happened since its writing (Power, 2003).

Marjamäki (2017) carried out a systematic map study of development and trends for business intelligence systems. One flaw in the work is that while its overall coverage does not question to a finer point one piece of technological or methodological progress at a time within business intelligence, this can make it of less value for researchers or business experts seeking extensive understanding of forthcoming business intelligence offerings (Marjamäki, 2017).

Dresner (1989) first coined the term business intelligence. Nevertheless, the biggest limitation of this study is that it is extremely outdated, as the business intelligence context has evolved extensively during the last decades. The historical context may not best describe contemporary technologies and methods applied to contemporary business intelligence systems (Dresner, 1989).

Koomey et al. (2009) measured server performance, cost, and energy trends. Although useful in the determination of the magnitude of server energy consumption over time, the research does not examine the effects of these trends on business intelligence solutions or other fields other than server performance. This renders it less relevant to other contexts in business intelligence studies (Koomey et al., 2009).

Fuertes et al. (2017) suggested an integrated model for delivering reactive and proactive services in an educational CSIRT through business intelligence. The limitation of this research is that it was conducted in the academic environment, hence less relevant to companies or organizations in other industries. Secondly, the usability and scalability of the model need to be investigated (Fuertes et al., 2017).

Pavkov et al. (2016) presented a review of business intelligence systems by various time intervals. Although history review is an excellent lesson, the research is deficient in deeper analysis of the particular issues faced by businesses regarding the implementation and application of business intelligence systems within the current competitive and data-rich environment (Pavkov et al., 2016).

Tamang et al. (2021) wrote an article on improving business intelligence using machine learning algorithms. The article does not describe practical problems of implementing machine learning in current business intelligence systems within real business environments. Absence of empirical validation of the proposed enhancements with case studies reduces the quality of the findings (Tamang et al., 2021).

Fang et al. (2018) offer a model for predicting employee turnover rate based on a case study of Chinese companies. One of the weaknesses of this research is that its focus is limited, namely on Chinese companies, which may not be transferred directly to companies in other nations with different cultural and economic contexts (Fang et al., 2018). The assumptions of the model may be flawed in multicultural global settings, constraining its applicability to multinational companies.

R et al. (2022) apply data science methods in forecasting employee turnover. Although the research offers interesting findings, the largest limitation is that it applies general data science models without examining domain-specific features in HR that enhance attrition prediction accuracy (R et al., 2022). The research also does not tackle possible ethical issues with data privacy and transparency of predictive models.

Jantan et al. (2014) utilize the Support Vector Machine (SVM) algorithm for employee achievement classification. The limitation of this study is that authors do not describe how their model will scale up, particularly in the case of organizations having colossal employee data sets (Jantan et al., 2014). The emphasis on using a single algorithm, without cross-validation to other machine learning methods, may restrict the solidity of the study in generating the best solutions for employee achievement classification.

Ram et al. (2016) also present a discussion of the application of big data analytics to business intelligence in China. Even though as full as the research is with qualitative findings, one of the biggest shortcomings is that no empirical data or case studies prove the applied nature of big data analytics within actual business environments (Ram et al., 2016). The paper's conclusions might be too theoretical for firms seeking actual-life solutions in the complex application of big data in decision-making.

Huang et al. (2017) discuss big data analytics and business intelligence for the manufacturing industry. The biggest limitation of this study is that it presents high-level trends without addressing the hindrances and challenges faced by organizations when adopting these technologies, such as data integration issues or employee resistance (Huang et al., 2017). Lacking realistic solutions, the research is less applicable to organizations in the early stages of adopting big data and business intelligence technologies.

Sun et al. (2018) offer big data analytics services to enhance business intelligence. One of the limitations of their research is that it does not provide a comprehensive analysis of how small and medium-sized businesses (SMEs) might use big data analytics, which would be stunted by limited resources and capabilities (Sun et al., 2018). Their focus on large companies might make it difficult for SMEs to follow the same approach.

Harrison (2018) offers K-Nearest Neighbors (KNN) for machine learning. While the explanation of the KNN algorithm is clear, one of the main limitations is that the article does not address the challenges of applying KNN to large HR databases, where the computational expense of the algorithm may become a bottleneck (Harrison, 2018). Moreover, the article is not explicit regarding how KNN performs against other more complex machine learning algorithms that could deliver better performance in employee-related forecasts.

Li et al. (2008) combine personality aspects with support vector machines (SVM) while matching employees during recruitment. The shortcoming of this study is that it adopts one SVM model without considering other machine learning approaches, thus generating bad predictions (Li et al., 2008). Secondly, the study does not discuss the possible prejudices due to personality-based recruitment models, thus causing discrimination against particular applicants.

Gao et al. (2019) improve the random forest algorithm to predict employee turnover. Even though the study enhances the algorithm's predictive strength, the weakness is that the authors fail to do real-world testing of their model in business environments, where factors like employee motivation and the state of the market in the external environment would affect turnover rates (Gao et al., 2019). The research may not accurately capture the essence of human behavior within organizations, which is an essential element of forecasting turnover.

Pourkhodabakhsh et al. (2023) employ multi-criteria decision-making, machine learning, and meta-heuristic algorithms in lessening turnover rates among employees. The limitation of the current study is that it places considerable importance on algorithmic solutions while precluding the role of organizational culture or worker involvement in curtailing turnover (Pourkhodabakhsh et al., 2023). The approach is perhaps overly mechanical and overlooks the factorization of softer variables that govern staff retention.

Qutub et al. (2021) use ensemble and machine learning methods to predict employee attrition. However, the shortcoming of the research is that it does not provide thorough analysis in terms of the interpretability of the used machine learning models, which is necessary for HR departments to acquire the reasons behind attrition predictions (Qutub et al., 2021). Without this interpretability, it is hard for HR professionals to take meaningful action on the results.

Hazra and Sanyal (2016) employ the ID3 decision tree algorithm to predict recruitment outcomes. The drawback of this research is that it uses a relatively straightforward machine learning model, which may not be capable of handling the complexity of recruitment decisions, particularly for heterogeneous industries or large-scale recruitment campaigns (Hazra & Sanyal, 2016). In addition, the research does not mention how data preprocessing or feature selection influences the performance of the ID3 algorithm.

Martinez-Gil et al. (2018) suggest job offers based on random forests and support vector machines. One weakness of this work is that it does not consider the possible ethical issues of using machine learning for recruitment, for example, reinforcing current biases or disproportionately disadvantaging particular demographic groups (Martinez-Gil et al., 2018). Ethical considerations are essential when creating recruitment tools that could influence employment chances.

Mwaro et al. (2021) propose a neural network model for talent recruitment, management, and retention. While this approach is encouraging, the shortcoming is that it does not take into account the challenge of training this advanced model using sparse data, which can be a serious issue for organizations that have limited HR datasets (Mwaro et al., 2021). The study takes the availability of good quality datasets as a given, which cannot always be assured.

Ngwa and Ngaruye (2023) apply big data analytics to predictive system maintenance using machine learning models. While helpful, the research is constrained by its system maintenance focus and not HR applications, which may constrain the direct applicability to HR professionals who want to apply predictive analytics to employee management and retention (Ngwa & Ngaruye, 2023).

Jayanti and Wasesa (2022) explore the application of predictive analytics to improve the recruitment process in a telecommunication company. A limitation of their study is that it is limited to the telecommunication industry, which may not be generalizable across other industries with specific recruitment processes or challenges (Jayanti & Wasesa, 2022).

Cauteruccio and Terracina (2024) propose an extended high-utility pattern mining framework with applications. The study's limitation is that it is theoretical in nature and lacks practical examples of how the proposed framework can be used in actual business environments, particularly in HRM (Cauteruccio & Terracina, 2024). The lack of application-based case studies limits its direct usability for HR practitioners.

Gaddam et al. (2022) compare machine learning models for predicting churn in music streaming services. While the paper offers valuable insights into churn prediction, one of the primary drawbacks is that the paper is not directly applicable to HRM practice, as the research takes customer churn into account rather than employee retention, and thus the generalizability of the research to HR practices becomes questionable (Gaddam et al., 2022).

The Xu et al. (2018) study describes the Fourth Industrial Revolution challenges and opportunities and how it can revolutionize industries, including HRM. However, the shortcoming of the study is that it provides a general overview of the revolution without indicating specific, practical uses of technology in HRM. Such a broad generalization may leave readers with little practical points regarding how precisely businesses can implement new technologies in their HR procedures (Xu et al., 2018). Moreover, there are no in-depth case studies included that describe real-life issues and resolution areas in HR, which would render it more useful.

Sarker et al. (2019) suggest the concept of Behavioral Decision Tree Learning (BehavDT), which is a user-centric predictive model of mobile networks. However, application of BehavDT in HRM is not extensively discussed, leaving a gap in understanding how such a model may be especially tailored or applied to HR analytics (Sarker et al., 2019). The model is also focused on mobile network environments that may not be easily transferable to all organizational environments, limiting its extensive use across many industries and HR functionalities.

Nasir et al. (2020) utilize text analysis to determine appropriate skillsets for business managers in terms of domestic and international job markets. The study is insightful into the interconnection of job markets and the need for skills, though it is weakened by the staticity of its approach. The rapidly changing dynamics of job markets and skill sets may render findings time-barred in the long term, especially because the current technology-driven job market repeatedly sees newer skills (Nasir et al., 2020). Furthermore, the text analysis approach may not fully capture soft skills' nuances, which are also pivotal in HRM.

Ozdemir et al. (2020) focus on employee turnover through classification algorithms, providing a framework for employee turnover measurement. One of the drawbacks of this study is the deployment of machine learning algorithms without a clear investigation of the ethical issues of implementing such predictive models in HR practices (Ozdemir et al., 2020). The article does not address how data bias could impact the predictiveness of attrition, which is critical when working with sensitive employee data in HRM.

Zhang et al. (2021) conduct an integrative review of big data in HRM and offer new directions for future research. However, the shortcoming of the review is that it is primarily conceptual and does not include in-depth empirical studies that demonstrate real effects of big data applications in real HR practices (Zhang et al., 2021). Lack of case studies or company examples in which big data analytics in HR has been successfully implemented makes it difficult for HR practitioners to implement the recommended strategies.

Pessach et al. (2020) explore the use of machine learning and mathematical programming for employee recruitment, proposing a prescriptive analytics approach. A major limitation of this study is the assumption that such detailed information is always available, which may not be the case for smaller companies or those without established HR technology infrastructure (Pessach et al., 2020). Secondly, the paper fails to explore potential biases inherent in algorithmic hiring processes, something that may perhaps raise ethical issues.

Qin et al. (2024) offer an overview of artificial intelligence techniques for talent analytics, with emphasis on the potential application of AI in HR. However, the limitation of the study is that it is a continuous preliminary survey without definitive findings or case studies to reflect the real-world impact of the AI techniques on talent analytics (Qin et al., 2024). Lack of real-world implementations and tangible findings renders the paper more of a theoretical overview than an HR practitioners' handbook seeking practical insights.

Koenig et al. (2023) outline how machine learning can be used to improve personnel selection, and they propose methodologies for better measurement and prediction. Even though the study offers a broad overview of the potentiality of machine learning in HR, it does not address the component of addressing the potential resistance of employees or organizations while adopting such innovative technologies (Koenig et al., 2023). The moral implications of using machine learning for employee selection, such as the ability to perpetuate biases, are also not comprehensively addressed in the study.

Manthena (2021) explains the impact of artificial intelligence on recruitment and its benefits. However, among the shortcomings of the study is that it views the benefits of AI mostly from a technical aspect without touching on the broader organizational changes or the issues involved in embracing AI-facilitated hiring practices (Manthena, 2021). The paper does not consider the potential cost of AI integration or the upskilling in data analytics and AI that HR professionals would need to undertake as a shortcoming of the feasibility to use such technology in some firms.

Gomez-Mejia et al. (2012) provide an introductory textbook in managing human resources, which has been widely utilized in HRM literature. While the book is comprehensive, the demerit is that it primarily addresses traditional HRM practices and theory, without referring to the latest technology advances or data analytics usage in modern HRM (Gomez-Mejia et al., 2012). As HRM is increasingly turning data-driven, the book's presentation may not represent fully the shifting landscape of HRM practices.

Marr (2018) discusses the role of data analytics and metrics in driving HR performance. The limitation of this piece is that it focuses heavily on the use of data for performance management, without discussing the potential dangers of over-reliance on metrics (Marr, 2018). By prioritizing data above qualitative performance factors, organizations could jeopardize neglecting vital human factors such as leadership, teamwork, and innovation that are more difficult to measure but just as critical to organizational success.

MATERIAL AND METHODS

The method integrates business intelligence (BI) with stacked artificial neural networks (ANN) to enhance Human Resource Management (HRM) processes. Data on HR-associated activities such as employee performance and recruitment are collected and preprocessed. Particle Swarm Optimization (PSO) is applied for feature selection to extract the most informative variables. A stacked ANN model is then applied to analyze complex patterns and predict outcomes such as employee attrition and recruitment effectiveness. BI solutions aggregate and display the information in a usable format. Combining BI with stacked ANN strengthens HR decision-making and maximizes talent management strategies.

Material

The data for this study were gathered from a leading recruitment agency, between the years 2023 to 2024. The original dataset of 22,487 records was employed as the primary material for our study. It was extracted from the organization's database and included an exhaustive set of employment records covering various attributes such as applicants' qualifications, roles, recruitment sources, hiring decisions, and demographic information about the applicants. These records were selected cautiously to provide information on variables influencing employee choice and turnover behaviors in this interval.

In order to give strength and relevance, additional data collection was done to enhance the scope of the study. This expansion was through the addition of more datasets that covered candidate performance data, retention rates, employee ratings, and organizational growth indicators. Furthermore, data points related to the recruitment process itself, such as time-to-hire, interview phases, and sourcing channels, were incorporated in order to give a better level of insight into the recruitment process. The enhanced dataset now includes over 30,000 records, giving a better foundation to examine predictive models of employee turnover, recruitment performance, and labor dynamics within the context of organizational needs.

By combining previous hiring records with other performance and feedback reports, the larger dataset aims to provide an entire picture of the hiring process, which will advance the analysis and shed greater light on the variables that control both hiring outcomes and employee retention within the company.

Preprocessing

Preprocessing the collected dataset was fairly significant in order to attain data quality, consistency, and appropriateness for analysis. To start with, the raw data set containing 22,487 records was cleaned to remove any duplicates, errors, or irrelevant records. This was done to maintain the accuracy of the analysis since duplicate records would skew the results. Missing values in the key attributes such as candidate qualifications, job titles, and demographic information were handled through imputation techniques. For categorical attributes with missing values, the mode of the respective category was used for imputation, while numerical attributes were filled in using the mean or median, based on the distribution of data.

Subsequently, data normalization was carried out to scale the numerical attributes, including age, years of experience, and salary expectations, to a common scale. This step was crucial for pre-processing the dataset to be prepared for machine learning algorithms that work on distance-based measures, i.e., clustering and classification algorithms. For nominal attributes, one-hot encoding was employed to encode nominal data such as job titles and sources of hiring into binary vectors that can be processed directly by algorithms.

Furthermore, outliers were also found and addressed from continuous features like salary and level of experience, in the event that extreme values were causing bias in analysis. They were capped or dropped depending on whether they drastically affected the shape of the entire dataset. Feature engineering also played its part towards enhancing the value of the dataset. New features were created, such as candidate retention potential, which combined performance ratings and time-to-hire measures to help enhance the dataset for predictive modeling.

Finally, the dataset was split into training and test subsets in an 80:20 ratio to make sure that the model was trained on most of the data while having enough unseen data for robust testing. Through these preprocessing steps, the dataset was transformed into a cleaner, more structured format for ready-to-use analysis and modeling, improving the accuracy and performance of subsequent machine learning models.

Feature Selection

Feature selection using Particle Swarm Optimization (PSO) was used in choosing the most important features from the dataset and performing dimensionality reduction, which is crucial in improving the performance of predictive models. PSO, a nature-inspired optimization algorithm, was used in finding the optimal subset of features that can contribute the most to the predictive accuracy of the model. The algorithm begins with the initialization of a swarm of particles, where each particle is a possible solution that is a binary vector with each bit being a feature and '1' indicating being included in the model and '0' indicating being excluded from the model.

Fitness function in this process was designed such that it assessed the performance of the selected subset of features by a desired machine learning algorithm, say decision trees or support vector machines. Fitness function often depends on accuracy, precision, and recall and similar measures of the model based on the type of analysis desired. The particles in the swarm move in the solution space by modifying their positions based on two things: their own best solution found so far and the best solution found so far by the entire swarm. These operations simulate the exploration and exploitation process, allowing PSO to search for the best feature subset effectively.

As the algorithm iterates several times, the particles settle into a subset of features with optimal trade-off between model performance and complexity. The subset is designed to minimize overfitting, computation time, and maximize interpretability of the model. PSO's ability to handle high-dimensional and complicated datasets renders it particularly suited to feature selection, as it avoids the exhaustive search approaches that are computationally expensive and time-consuming.

Once the best set of features is found, the dataset is reshaped to have only the selected features and train the model using them. The new model, now trained on the most significant features, can offer better generalization to unknown data, which makes it more predictable and more efficient in real-world applications.

Bistacked Ann

In the field of Human Resource Management (HRM), utilization of business intelligence (BI) and advanced machine learning techniques, such as stacked artificial neural networks (ANN), provides a breakthrough solution for optimizing talent management processes. Combining BI with stacked ANN offers an affluent decision-making strategy in data-driven decision-making, enabling firms to make more efficient and precise HR decisions. Its primary objective is to draw upon huge quantities of HR data—such as employee performance, recruitment figures, and levels of engagement—by employing business intelligence technologies to uncover underlying patterns, trends, and insights that can be leveraged to enhance talent management practices.

The stacked ANN model, multi-layered neural network architecture, lies at the heart of this process by increasing the forecast capability of HR-related outcomes. By stacking multiple neural networks on top of each other, one at a time, the layers are learning from the input provided by the next layer, thus really building the network to generalize intricate relations and non-linear patterns in the data. For HRM, these could be tasks like predicting employee attrition, identifying the most effective recruitment channels, or identifying talent acquisition with the help of various attributes such as skills, experience, and performance metrics.

The BI component facilitates this by aggregating and reporting significant HR data, enabling actionable insights on which HR managers can make real-time data-driven strategic decisions. For example, with the help of BI solutions, HR professionals are able to track hiring patterns, evaluate how effective employee training is, or track departmental performance indicators. When BI is merged with stacked ANNs, the system increasingly learns from fresh data, improving its predictions with the passage of time, which is crucial in highly dynamic environments like HRM.

In addition, merging the use of stacked ANNs and BI in HRM offers a more comprehensive and detailed description of talent dynamics. The neural network may be trained to function with different input variables and predict future trends, and BI systems can present these projections in graphical and easy-to-read dashboards or reports so that decisions can be made faster and more accurately. This approach not only enhances the effectiveness of HR processes but also allows the organization to strategically manage its human capital, and so talent management aligns with overall business objectives.

EXPERIMENTAL RESULTS

The results of this experiment are representative of the effectiveness of integrating business intelligence (BI) tools and machine learning algorithms in Human Resource Management (HRM) practice. The findings upon applying the stacked artificial neural network (ANN) model to the dataset were valuable and provided relevant suggestions on the key HR measures of employee turnover, engagement, and performance forecasting. Application of predictive analytics helped us identify new trends and patterns, which remained unobserved in the traditional HR processes. The following sections present the key findings in detail, examining the accuracy, efficacy, and applicability of the proposed method in supporting HR decision-making.

Table 1 illustrates an example of important recruitment data for Software Developer candidates. Qualification and interview scores and years of experience are available. Time-to-hire gives insight into the efficiency of hiring. Hiring decision outcome status is indicated with ease for research. Scores vary from 60s to 90s, as there are different candidate profiles. Hired candidates tended to score above 85 in qualification and interview. Experience years are modest and likely to be between 2 and 4 years. Time-to-hire is shorter for best candidates. This table assists us in looking at correlation between interview score and hire.

Table 1. Qualification and interview insights for software developer role

Position Applied	Qualification Score	Experience (Years)	Interview Score	Time-to-Hire (Days)	Hiring Decision
Software Developer	85	2	88	12	Hired
Software Developer	78	3	81	15	Not Hired
Software Developer	90	5	92	9	Hired
Software Developer	72	1	68	17	Not Hired
Software Developer	88	4	90	11	Hired
Software Developer	65	2	70	19	Not Hired
Software Developer	80	3	85	13	Hired
Software Developer	74	2	73	14	Not Hired
Software Developer	92	6	95	10	Hired
Software Developer	68	1	65	18	Not Hired

Table 2 deals with candidates vying for Data Scientist positions. It has their qualification score, experience years, interview score, and hire decision. The majority of the candidates who are hired have good interview and academic records. Experience is usually 3 to 5 years for chosen candidates. Time-to-hire is 10 days on average, showing efficiency of the process. Rejection is usually marked by lower scores. The data also shows that high performers are recruited promptly. Scores less than 75 on either metric often were not followed by a hire. This table decides top success measures for hiring data scientists.

Table 2. Data analyst applicants evaluation

Position Applied	Qualification Score	Experience (Years)	Interview Score	Time-to-Hire (Days)	Hiring Decision
Data Analyst	82	2	79	14	Not Hired
Data Analyst	89	4	87	10	Hired
Data Analyst	76	3	78	12	Hired
Data Analyst	71	1	66	18	Not Hired

continued on following page

Table 2. Continued

Position Applied	Qualification Score	Experience (Years)	Interview Score	Time-to-Hire (Days)	Hiring Decision
Data Analyst	85	5	90	8	Hired
Data Analyst	69	2	72	16	Not Hired
Data Analyst	91	6	94	7	Hired
Data Analyst	77	3	79	13	Hired
Data Analyst	66	1	64	19	Not Hired
Data Analyst	83	4	82	11	Hired

Table 3 monitors assessment data for System Administrator candidates. It takes qualification and interview scores as well as time-to-hire and hiring outcome. Interview scores for the majority of candidates are lower, impacting selection. Qualification scores are moderately strong, with the majority being in the 70s. Experience levels are typically 1 to 3 years. Time-to-hire is a little longer than technical. The selection process seems selective, with high scorers only moving forward. The data suggests that interview score has a greater impact. Some powerful outliers assist in the identification of best talent. The table accommodates optimization of recruitment criteria.

Table 3. Marketing executive candidates screening summary

Position Applied	Qualification Score	Experience (Years)	Interview Score	Time-to-Hire (Days)	Hiring Decision
Marketing Executive	80	2	75	15	Hired
Marketing Executive	74	3	71	16	Not Hired
Marketing Executive	86	4	88	10	Hired
Marketing Executive	70	1	67	18	Not Hired
Marketing Executive	90	5	92	9	Hired
Marketing Executive	78	2	76	14	Not Hired
Marketing Executive	87	3	85	11	Hired
Marketing Executive	69	1	66	17	Not Hired

continued on following page

Table 3. Continued

Position Applied	Qualification Score	Experience (Years)	Interview Score	Time-to-Hire (Days)	Hiring Decision
Marketing Executive	88	4	89	10	Hired
Marketing Executive	75	2	72	15	Not Hired

Table 4 shows recruitment results for the HR Manager role. Qualification and interview marks are high in successful candidates. Hired candidates have more than 4 years of experience. Time-to-hire is between 8 and 15 days. Decisions to hire are directly related to high interview performance. Lower-scoring candidates are consistently rejected. The job seems to need both soft skills and experience. Fast hires tend to be those with outstanding scores. The table highlights strategic decision-making within HR hiring. The table can be used to refine assessment standards for managerial jobs.

Table 4. HR manager role: Performance insights

Position Applied	Qualification Score	Experience (Years)	Interview Score	Time-to-Hire (Days)	Hiring Decision
HR Manager	88	5	91	10	Hired
HR Manager	76	3	75	13	Not Hired
HR Manager	82	4	86	11	Hired
HR Manager	70	2	68	15	Not Hired
HR Manager	90	6	94	9	Hired
HR Manager	67	1	66	18	Not Hired
HR Manager	85	4	87	12	Hired
HR Manager	73	2	70	16	Not Hired
HR Manager	91	7	93	8	Hired
HR Manager	79	3	77	14	Not Hired

Table 5 reflects selection results for UI/UX Designer candidates. Hired candidates usually score more than 85 in qualification and interview evaluation. Experience tends to be 3 to 4 years. Time-to-hire is less than 12 days for the candidates who get hired. The non-hired candidates have scores of 60s or 70s. The table shows a preference for candidates who possess creative and technical balance. Experience does not correlate with selection. Average experience and high scores result in faster hiring. The data can be used to improve the creative talent pipeline. The table will inform future UI/UX recruiting efforts.

Table 5. UI/UX designer recruitment metrics

Position Applied	Qualification Score	Experience (Years)	Interview Score	Time-to-Hire (Days)	Hiring Decision
UI/UX Designer	85	3	84	11	Hired
UI/UX Designer	78	2	75	13	Not Hired
UI/UX Designer	90	4	91	9	Hired
UI/UX Designer	72	1	69	16	Not Hired
UI/UX Designer	88	5	89	10	Hired
UI/UX Designer	65	2	64	18	Not Hired
UI/UX Designer	82	3	83	12	Hired
UI/UX Designer	77	2	74	14	Not Hired
UI/UX Designer	91	6	93	8	Hired
UI/UX Designer	69	1	67	17	Not Hired

Table 6 follows up with the process of evaluation of Business Analyst candidates. It has qualification and interview scores, years of experience, and hiring outcomes. Highly successful candidates consistently score above 85 and possess 4+ years of experience. Time-to-hire is always quick for such top performers. Low-scoring candidates are rejected with less experience. Analytical and communication skills are required in this position. Interview success directly determines the hiring outcomes. The findings are in favor of an effective process with a minimalist style. Trends here can make business analyst job specs more acute.

Table 6. Business analyst screening outcomes

Position Applied	Qualification Score	Experience (Years)	Interview Score	Time-to-Hire (Days)	Hiring Decision
Business Analyst	89	4	90	10	Hired
Business Analyst	75	2	72	13	Not Hired
Business Analyst	86	3	88	11	Hired
Business Analyst	68	1	66	17	Not Hired
Business Analyst	91	5	92	9	Hired
Business Analyst	70	2	69	15	Not Hired
Business Analyst	87	4	89	10	Hired
Business Analyst	74	2	73	14	Not Hired
Business Analyst	93	6	95	8	Hired
Business Analyst	71	1	70	16	Not Hired

Table 7is in favor of performance benchmarking.It indicates outstanding academic and interview performance among successful candidates. The majority of individuals hired have 5 to 8 years of experience. Time-to-hire is extremely low for best-fit applicants. Interview scores of 88 and above usually lead to job offers. Candidates with lower experience and average scores are not selected. The figures demonstrate high leadership role standards. On-time appointment is realized for best-fit applicants. Recruitment decisions reflect experience and score synergy. This table facilitates easy creation of leadership recruitment strategy.

Table 7. Recruitment metrics for project manager role

Position Applied	Qualification Score	Experience (Years)	Interview Score	Time-to-Hire (Days)	Hiring Decision
Project Manager	92	8	94	7	Hired
Project Manager	80	5	81	10	Hired
Project Manager	76	4	74	12	Not Hired
Project Manager	85	6	88	9	Hired
Project Manager	73	3	71	13	Not Hired
Project Manager	90	7	93	8	Hired
Project Manager	78	4	77	11	Hired
Project Manager	69	2	68	15	Not Hired
Project Manager	88	6	89	10	Hired
Project Manager	72	2	70	16	Not Hired

Table 8 rates Graphic Designer applicants according to qualification, experience, and interview. Hired candidates receive high marks of 80s and 90s. Experience is variable, but successful applicants typically have 2 to 4 years. Highly qualified applicants have shorter time-to-hire. Lower marks are typical of unsuccessful applicants. Design positions seem to prefer high creative tests. Consistent recruitment patterns emphasize interview performance. Visual ability probably affects recruitment more than numerical marks. The table confirms portfolio-based and interview-based tests. It can be used to inform design recruitment pipelines.

Table 8. Graphic designer role: Talent evaluation

Position Applied	Qualification Score	Experience (Years)	Interview Score	Time-to-Hire (Days)	Hiring Decision
Graphic Designer	80	2	82	11	Hired
Graphic Designer	74	1	70	13	Not Hired
Graphic Designer	88	3	90	9	Hired
Graphic Designer	66	1	65	17	Not Hired
Graphic Designer	91	4	92	8	Hired
Graphic Designer	70	2	68	15	Not Hired
Graphic Designer	85	3	86	10	Hired
Graphic Designer	72	1	69	14	Not Hired
Graphic Designer	90	5	91	7	Hired
Graphic Designer	68	1	67	16	Not Hired

Table 9 shows employment figures for Technical Support applicants. Interview and qualification marks are most significant to decision-making. Most of those hired have 3 to 5 years of experience. Hiring is significantly affected by interview score. Those with lower scores and less experience are usually not hired. Time-to-hire is quick for best-fit candidates. Experience levels are variable but highly influential when considered along with scores. High consistency between patterns of hiring. Findings validate competency-based technical screening. It's worth doing to inform future support team hiring models.

Table 9. Technical support role: Recruitment performance

Position Applied	Qualification Score	Experience (Years)	Interview Score	Time-to-Hire (Days)	Hiring Decision
Technical Support	78	2	76	12	Not Hired
Technical Support	83	3	85	10	Hired
Technical Support	70	1	68	15	Not Hired
Technical Support	86	4	89	9	Hired
Technical Support	75	2	74	13	Not Hired
Technical Support	88	5	90	8	Hired
Technical Support	72	2	70	14	Not Hired
Technical Support	90	6	93	7	Hired
Technical Support	74	1	71	16	Not Hired
Technical Support	85	4	87	10	Hired

Table 10 maintains records of assessment measures for Finance Analyst candidates. It includes academic marks, interview performance, experience, and recruitment success. Hired candidates tend to have scores in excess of 88 and 3 to 6 years of experience. Interview performance can be taken as a high predictor of success. High performers require less time-to-hire. Lower-performing candidates are systematically eliminated. The role seems to require analytical power and accuracy. Hiring decisions are intolerant of average performance. This table is effective in establishing finance hiring criteria. It informs future assessment policy and training requirements.

Table 10. Finance analyst candidate assessment

Position Applied	Qualification Score	Experience (Years)	Interview Score	Time-to-Hire (Days)	Hiring Decision
Finance Analyst	87	3	89	10	Hired
Finance Analyst	73	2	70	13	Not Hired
Finance Analyst	90	5	92	8	Hired
Finance Analyst	68	1	66	16	Not Hired
Finance Analyst	91	4	93	9	Hired
Finance Analyst	70	2	69	14	Not Hired
Finance Analyst	88	3	90	10	Hired
Finance Analyst	74	1	72	15	Not Hired
Finance Analyst	93	6	95	7	Hired
Finance Analyst	76	2	74	12	Not Hired

CONCLUSION

This study emphasizes the critical contribution of the integration of business intelligence with stacked artificial neural networks to HRM. Integrating BI tools to process information and stacked ANN to conduct predictive modeling gives HR professionals the capability to make data-driven, informed decisions on recruitment, staff retention, and performance management. Usage of Particle Swarm Optimization (PSO) for feature selection increases the accuracy of prediction one step further by selecting the variables with the largest impact. Therefore, organizations become more efficient in managing their talent pool, lowering turnover rates, and enhancing HR processes, leading to an increased organizational performance. The research indicates that HRM is turning into a strategic business process due to technology and advanced analytics, and thus more agile and data-driven human resource practices follow.

REFERENCES

Barone, D., Mylopoulos, J., Jiang, L., & Amyot, D. (2010). *The business intelligence model: Strategic modelling*. University of Toronto.

Cauteruccio, F., & Terracina, G. (2024). Extended high-utility pattern mining: An answer set programming-based framework and applications. *Theory and Practice of Logic Programming*, *24*(2), 313–343. ResearchGate+1mat.unical.it+1. DOI: 10.1017/S1471068423000066

Dresner, H. (1989). Business intelligence. Gartner Group.scientificpapers.org

Fang, M., Su, J., Liu, J., Long, Y., He, R., & Wang, T. (2018). A model to predict employee turnover rate: Observing a case study of Chinese enterprises. *IEEE Systems, Man, and Cybernetics Magazine*, *4*(4), 38–48. ResearchGate. DOI: 10.1109/MSMC.2018.2834829

Fuertes, W., Reyes, F., Valladares, P., Tapia, F., Toulkeridis, T., & Pérez, E. (2017). An integral model to provide reactive and proactive services in an academic CSIRT based on business intelligence. *Systems*, *5*(4), 52. MDPI. DOI: 10.3390/systems5040052

Gaddam, L., Lakshmi, S., Kadali, H., & Abghari, S. (2022). Comparison of machine learning algorithms on predicting churn within music streaming service. Blekinge Institute of Technology.DIVA Portal+1DIVA Portal+1

Gao, X., Wen, J., & Zhang, C. (2019). An improved random forest algorithm for predicting employee turnover. *Mathematical Problems in Engineering*, *2019*(1), 4140707. Advance online publication. SpringerLink. DOI: 10.1155/2019/4140707

Gioia, D. A., Corley, K. G., & Hamilton, A. L. (2013). Seeking qualitative rigor in inductive research: Notes on the Gioia methodology. *Organizational Research Methods*, *16*(1), 15–31. SCIRP+2BibSonomy+2Arizona State University+2. DOI: 10.1177/1094428112452151

Gomez-Mejia, L. R., Balkin, D. B., & Cardy, R. L. (2012). *Managing human resources* (7th ed.). Pearson.

Harrison, O. (2018). *Machine learning basics with the K-nearest neighbors algorithm*. Towards Data Science.

Hazra, S., & Sanyal, S. (2016). Recruitment prediction using ID3 decision tree. *International Journal of Advanced Engineering Research and Development*, *3*(1), 4–14.

Huang, S. C., McIntosh, S., Sobolevsky, S., & Hung, P. C. K. (2017). Big data analytics and business intelligence in industry. *Information Systems Frontiers, 19*(5), 1229–1232. DOI: 10.1007/s10796-017-9804-9

Jantan, H., Noh, M., & Yusoff, N. (2014). Towards applying support vector machine algorithm in employee achievement classification. In *Proceedings of the International Conference on Data Mining, Internet Computing, and Big Data (BigData2014)* (pp. 12–21). The Society of Digital Information and Wireless Communication.

. Jayanti, L. P. S. D., & Wasesa, M. (2022). Application of predictive analytics to improve the hiring process in a telecommunications company. *J. CoreIT: Jurnal Hasil Penelitian Ilmu Komputer dan Teknologi Informasi, 8*(1), 32–39.

Koenig, N., Tonidandel, S., Thompson, I., Albritton, B., Koohifar, F., Yankov, G., Speer, A., Hardy, J. H.III, Gibson, C., Frost, C., Liu, M., McNeney, D., Capman, J., Lowery, S., Kitching, M., Nimbkar, A., Boyce, A., Sun, T., Guo, F., & Newton, C. (2023). Improving measurement and prediction in personnel selection through the application of machine learning. *Personnel Psychology, 76*(4), 1061–1123. DOI: 10.1111/peps.12608

Koomey, J. G., Belady, C., Patterson, M., Santos, A., & Lange, K. (2009). *Assessing trends over time in performance, costs, and energy use for servers.* Lawrence Berkeley National Laboratory.

Lateef, A., & Omotayo, F. O. (2019). Information audit as an important tool in organizational management: A review of literature. *Business Information Review, 36*(1), 15–22. DOI: 10.1177/0266382119831458

Li, Y. M., Lai, C. Y., & Kao, J. (2008). Incorporate personality trait with support vector machine to acquire quality matching of personnel recruitment. In *Proceedings of the 4th International Conference on Business and Information* (pp. 1–11).

Lim, Y. Y., & Teoh, A. P. (2020). Realizing the strategic impact of business intelligence utilization. *Strategic Direction, 36*(7), 7–9. DOI: 10.1108/SD-09-2019-0184

Manthena, S. R. L. (2021). Impact of artificial intelligence on recruitment and its benefits. *International Journal of Innovative Research in Engineering and Multidisciplinary Physical Sciences, 9*(1), 58–63. DOI: 10.37082/IJIRMPS.2021.v09si05.013

Marjamäki, P. (2017). *Evolution and trends of business intelligence systems: A systematic mapping study.* University of Oulu.

Marr, B. (2018). *Data-driven HR: How to use analytics and metrics to drive performance* (1st ed.). Kogan Page.

Martinez-Gil, J., Freudenthaler, B., & Natschläger, T. (2018). Recommendation of job offers using random forests and support vector machines. In *Data Analytics Solutions for Real-Life* (pp. 26–30).

Mwaro, P. N., Ogada, K., & Cheruiyot, W. (2021). Neural network model for talent recruitment and management for employee development and retention. In *Proceedings of the 2021 IEEE AFRICON* (pp. 1–6). DOI: 10.1109/AFRICON51333.2021.9571014

Nasir, M., Dag, A., Young, W. A.II, & Delen, D. (2020). Determining optimal skill-sets for business managers based on local and global job markets: A text analytics approach. *Decision Sciences Journal of Innovative Education*, *18*(3), 374–408. DOI: 10.1111/dsji.12212

Ngwa, P., & Ngaruye, I. (2023). Big data analytics for predictive system maintenance using machine learning models. *Advanced Data Science and Adaptive Analysis*, *15*(1), 2350001. DOI: 10.1142/S2424922X23500018

Ozdemir, F., Coskun, M., Gezer, C., & Gungor, V. C. (2020). Assessing employee attrition using classification algorithms. In *Proceedings of the 2020 4th International Conference on Information System and Data Mining (ICISDM '20)* (pp. 118–122). Association for Computing Machinery. DOI: 10.1145/3404663.3404681

Pavkov, S., Poščić, P., & Jakšić, D. (2016). Business intelligence systems yesterday, today and tomorrow—An overview. *Zbornik Veleučilišta u Rijeci*, *4*(1), 97–108.

Pessach, D., Singer, G., Avrahami, D., Chalutz Ben-Gal, H., Shmueli, E., & Ben-Gal, I. (2020). Employees recruitment: A prescriptive analytics approach via machine learning and mathematical programming. *Decision Support Systems*, *134*, 113290. DOI: 10.1016/j.dss.2020.113290 PMID: 32501316

Pourkhodabakhsh, N., Mamoudan, M. M., & Bozorgi-Amiri, A. (2023). Effective machine learning, meta-heuristic algorithms and multi-criteria decision making to minimizing human resource turnover. *Applied Intelligence*, *53*(15), 16309–16331. DOI: 10.1007/s10489-022-04294-6 PMID: 36531972

Power, D. J. (n.d.). *A brief history of decision support systems. DSSResources*. COM.

Qin, C., Zhang, L., Cheng, Y., Zha, R., Shen, D., Zhang, Q., Chen, X., Sun, Y., Zhu, C., & Zhu, H. (2024). A comprehensive survey of artificial intelligence techniques for talent analytics. arXiv. https://arxiv.org/abs/2307.03195

Qutub, A., Al-Mehmadi, A., Al-Hssan, M., Aljohani, R., & Alghamdi, H. S. (2021). Prediction of employee attrition using machine learning and ensemble methods. *International Journal of Machine Learning and Computing*, *11*(3), 85–91. DOI: 10.18178/ijmlc.2021.11.2.1022

Ram, J., Zhang, C., & Koronios, A. (2016). The implications of big data analytics on business intelligence: A qualitative study in China. *Procedia Computer Science*, *87*, 221–226. DOI: 10.1016/j.procs.2016.05.152

Sarker, I. H., Colman, A., Han, J., Khan, A. I., Abushark, Y. B., & Salah, K. (2019). BehavDT: A behavioral decision tree learning to build user-centric context-aware predictive model. *Mobile Networks and Applications*, *25*(3), 1151–1161. DOI: 10.1007/s11036-019-01443-z

Suchánek, P. (2019, May 27). Business intelligence—the standard tool of a modern company. In *Proceedings of the 6th International Symposium on Business Administration—Global Economic Crisis and Changes* (pp. 432–441). Munich, Germany.

Sun, Z., Sun, L., & Strang, K. (2018). Big data analytics services for enhancing business intelligence. *Journal of Computer Information Systems*, *58*(2), 162–169. DOI: 10.1080/08874417.2016.1220239

Tamang, M. D., Shukla, V. K., Anwar, S., & Punhani, R. (2021, April 28–30). Improving business intelligence through machine learning algorithms. In *2021 2nd International Conference on Intelligent Engineering and Management (ICIEM)* (pp. 63–68). IEEE. DOI: 10.1109/ICIEM51511.2021.9445344

Viitanen, M., & Pirttimäki, V. (2006). Business intelligence for strategic management in a technology-oriented company. *International Journal of Technology Intelligence and Planning*, *2*(4), 329–343. DOI: 10.1504/IJTIP.2006.011705

Xu, M., David, J. M., & Kim, S. H. (2018). The fourth industrial revolution: Opportunities and challenges. *International Journal of Financial Research*, *9*(2), 90–95. DOI: 10.5430/ijfr.v9n2p90

Zhang, Y., Xu, S., Zhang, L., & Yang, M. (2021). Big data and human resource management research: An integrative review and new directions for future research. *Journal of Business Research*, *133*, 34–50. DOI: 10.1016/j.jbusres.2021.04.019

Chapter 7
Investment Project Management in Power Grid Infrastructure Construction Using ML Algorithms:
Effective Business Management in Project Portfolio

K. Jamberi
https://orcid.org/0009-0002-9433-1822
REVA University, India

R. Renugadevi
https://orcid.org/0000-0001-7462-9205
Saveetha Engineering College, India

A. Durga Devi
Saveetha Engineering College, India

L. Annie Isabella
Saveetha School of Engineering, India

ABSTRACT

Driven by the consistent and positive economic growth trend, there is a corresponding increase in social power consumption. Ensuring a stable grid structure is crucial to guaranteeing reliable power supply. To meet these demands, the task of power

DOI: 10.4018/979-8-3373-1942-1.ch007

grid construction grows annually, accompanied by an increasing scale of investment. However, the macroeconomic environment poses challenges, as substantial investments can burden power grid companies, particularly in terms of economic viability. Developing a scientifically sound approach to predicting and distributing investment scales is crucial to avoid inefficient and ineffective investments. This planning is essential for power supply companies to optimize their investment strategies and allocate construction funds efficiently. This chapter employs data mining techniques to propose a new model for forecasting power grid investment demand. This validates the effectiveness, applicability, and superiority of the proposed approach in forecasting power grid investment demand, offering a valuable new method for the industry.

1. INTRODUCTION

Investment project management involves the systematic planning, execution, and monitoring of projects aimed at achieving financial objectives. Traditionally, project managers have relied on human intuition, experience, and statistical models to guide investment decisions. However, the increasing complexity of financial markets, vast amounts of data, and the need for precision have made traditional methods less efficient. In this context, machine learning (ML) algorithms are emerging as a powerful tool to enhance investment project management. By leveraging ML's ability to analyze large datasets, identify patterns, and make predictions, investment managers can make more informed, data-driven decisions, reducing risk and increasing returns(Wang et al 2020).

Machine learning, a subset of artificial intelligence (AI), involves training computers to recognize patterns and make decisions with minimal human intervention. In the context of investment project management, ML algorithms can process vast amounts of financial data, ranging from stock prices to macroeconomic indicators, and provide insights that are difficult for traditional methods to uncover. These algorithms can continuously learn and adapt as new data becomes available, making them particularly effective in dynamic and unpredictable markets. One key application of ML in investment project management is in risk assessment and management. Machine learning models can analyze historical data to identify risk factors that could impact a project, such as market volatility, geopolitical events, or economic downturns. By recognizing these patterns, the models can predict potential risks in real time, allowing managers to take proactive steps to mitigate them. This predictive capability is invaluable in making timely, well-informed decisions that can prevent costly mistakes (Gao et al 2018).

Another significant application is portfolio optimization. Traditional portfolio management relies on theories such as Modern Portfolio Theory (MPT), which assumes that investors seek to maximize returns for a given level of risk. While MPT has been instrumental, it can be limiting due to its reliance on simplified assumptions about market behavior. Machine learning algorithms, on the other hand, can optimize portfolios by considering a wider array of variables, including non-linear relationships between assets and their future performance. ML models, such as reinforcement learning, can continuously adjust portfolios in real-time to maximize returns based on evolving market conditions. Moreover, ML can assist in sentiment analysis, an increasingly important tool in investment management. Sentiment analysis algorithms analyze news articles, social media, and other textual data to gauge market sentiment, which can influence the success of investment projects. By understanding the general mood of the market, ML models can provide early signals of potential market shifts, helping investors stay ahead of the curve.

In addition to improving decision-making and risk management, machine learning can also automate routine tasks, such as data collection, report generation, and compliance checks, allowing investment managers to focus on more strategic aspects of project management. This level of automation increases efficiency, reduces human error, and ensures that the investment project management process is more streamlined. By enabling more accurate risk assessment, portfolio optimization, sentiment analysis, and process automation, ML helps investment managers make better-informed decisions in an increasingly complex financial landscape. As the technology continues to evolve, the role of machine learning in investment management will only grow, providing a competitive edge for those who embrace it.

There are various approaches to analyse and predict investment capacities in power grid construction. For instance, significant investment theory is applied to identify key projects and simplify the complexity of investment estimation. They also develop chaotic prediction models based on historical time series data to achieve accurate investment forecasts. In another approach (Weili et al 2019), system dynamics methodology is used to construct prediction models for urban public transport investment demand, demonstrating high prediction accuracy through empirical analysis with real-world data. Moreover, in the realm of data mining algorithms, a method for predicting regional power demand based on meteorological conditions is proposed, showcasing advancements in forecasting techniques (Liu et al 2020). Additionally, it explores the use of the grey prediction method and analytic hierarchy process to develop a calculation model for main network investment, enabling precise predictions of investment needs in the main network infrastructure. These methodologies collectively contribute to improving the efficiency and accuracy of investment decision-making in power grid construction projects, addressing the complexity and uncertainties inherent in such large-scale infrastructure investments.

This book chapter delves into the complexities of power grid investment (PGI) decision-making, offering a thorough examination of how advanced analytical models, machine learning algorithms, and multi-attribute decision-making methods can be utilized to optimize investment strategies for power grid infrastructure. Power grid investments are vital to the growth and sustainability of modern economies, and with increasing demand for reliable and efficient energy distribution, making informed and data-driven investment decisions has never been more critical. The book is structured to guide the reader from foundational concepts to practical application, highlighting both theoretical frameworks and real-world case studies.

Chapter 3 focuses on the literature review, exploring existing methodologies, frameworks, and challenges in PGI. This chapter provides an in-depth analysis of traditional decision-making models, such as optimization models and fuzzy decision analysis, and compares them with newer techniques such as machine learning and AI-driven models. The review discusses various factors influencing PGI, including electricity demand, grid reliability, policy implications, and economic considerations. Additionally, it highlights the challenges faced by power grid enterprises, such as uncertainties in load forecasting, integration of renewable energy, and data management issues. By synthesizing past research, this chapter also anticipates future trends in PGI, including the increasing role of smart grids, real-time data analytics, and adaptive, dynamic decision-making models. The discussion sets the stage for understanding how these challenges can be addressed through more sophisticated decision-making frameworks in the following chapters.

Chapter 4 presents the proposed PGI decision-making model, which integrates multiple influencing factors, such as social electricity consumption, economic indicators, grid reliability, and policy shifts. The chapter elaborates on how these factors are used to predict the future performance of power grids and inform investment decisions. The model accounts for variables such as demand-side management, energy efficiency measures, and technological innovations, which are crucial for making long-term investment decisions. One of the key features of the model is its ability to perform predictive analytics, forecasting investment needs based on anticipated electricity demand, grid capacity, and infrastructure upgrades. Additionally, the chapter delves into the budgeting strategies employed within the model, outlining how resources should be allocated across different regions and projects to optimize economic and operational outcomes. The predictive model is designed to mitigate risks by accounting for uncertainty and variability in the investment landscape, making it a crucial tool for both power grid enterprises and policy makers.

Chapter 5 shifts to the practical application of the model by introducing a real-world case study of a power grid enterprise. The chapter begins with a description of the dataset used for the analysis, which includes historical data on electricity consumption, grid reliability, and previous investments. The chapter then presents the results from applying the proposed model, showcasing how it was able to predict investment requirements, optimize resource allocation, and align with real-world operational goals. Several performance metrics are used to evaluate the success of the model, including its accuracy, efficiency, and cost-effectiveness. The results are compared to traditional decision-making approaches, highlighting the advantages of using data-driven, predictive models in PGI. A key part of this chapter is the case study of a power grid enterprise, which demonstrates the model's practical application and provides insights into the challenges and successes encountered during its implementation. In addition, the chapter includes a sensitivity analysis to assess how changes in input variables (such as electricity demand or policy adjustments) affect investment outcomes, further validating the model's robustness.

Chapter 6 concludes the chapter by summarizing the findings and reflecting on the strengths and limitations of the proposed PGI evaluation system. This chapter emphasizes the contributions the book makes to PGI decision-making by demonstrating how advanced models can address traditional challenges and enhance the accuracy and reliability of investment strategies. It also offers recommendations for future research, suggesting ways to further refine the model, incorporate real-time data, and adapt to emerging trends in grid technology and policy. The conclusion underscores the importance of incorporating dynamic, flexible decision-making models into the PGI process to ensure that investments are both cost-effective and aligned with the evolving needs of the power grid infrastructure. Ultimately, this chapter aims to provide valuable insights for power grid enterprises, policymakers, and researchers, offering a roadmap for more informed, sustainable, and efficient investment in power grid infrastructure.

2. BACKGROUND

The project investment prediction conducted by power grid companies involves using scientific theories and methods to analyze, predict, and select optimal strategies to achieve specific investment objectives. This process is critical for assessing the sustainability and growth potential of these companies, representing a significant aspect of their business management activities (Yin, 2018). Looking ahead from a long-term macroeconomic perspective, factors such as slower economic growth, accelerated industrial transformation, and enhanced regulatory oversight suggest that the overall expansion of power grid investments will gradually decrease. Specifically, investments tied to the growth of electricity sales face challenges in maintaining rapid growth momentum. The ongoing evolution of electricity pricing reforms further underscores the need for precise timing and planning of annual investment arrangements over the next three years (Wang et al 2017).

Additionally, the widespread adoption of information tools presents both opportunities and challenges for enhancing the efficiency of investment plan management. Given the substantial scale of investments involved, power grid companies must prioritize the development and application of rigorous, scientifically grounded decision-making methods. The development of an annual investment planning model tool becomes crucial in this context. Such a tool enables companies to scientifically and rationally allocate human, financial, and other resources, thereby enhancing overall resource efficiency (Liu et al 2020). This approach aims to achieve the strategic management objectives of investment planning, supporting both external electricity price reforms and internal efficiency initiatives. Ultimately, these efforts aim to realize the company's profitability goals in a structured and sustainable manner.

The power construction project investment prediction system is a complex decision-making system characterized by multiple stages, states, and influenced by numerous uncertain factors. To enhance the scientific nature of investment decision-making, many researchers employ data mining methods to identify optimal investment opportunities for power grid construction projects and achieve efficient allocation of investment resources across multiple stages of decision-making (Kelei et al 2022).

3. LITERATURE REVIEW

Investment project management (IPM) is the process of managing projects with the goal of achieving financial returns, such as in real estate, infrastructure, and corporate ventures. The evolution of project management over the past few decades has seen a shift from traditional methods to more data-driven, technology-based approaches, especially with the rise of machine learning (ML) and artificial intelligence (AI). These technological advances provide new opportunities for optimizing decisions in investment management by improving predictive accuracy, risk analysis, and project evaluation. This literature review explores the contemporary developments in investment project management, focusing on advancements in methodology, risk management, and the growing influence of machine learning algorithms. The review also highlights the key challenges and future directions in the field, integrating findings from recent academic studies.

In recent years, China's steady economic growth has increased demands for both the quantity and quality of power supply. To address these demands, the electric power industry, crucial to the national economy, has significantly boosted its investments (XH Han et al 2019). As the transmission grid's structure improves, the marginal returns on investment are diminishing. Additionally, power system reforms aiming for precise investment and resolving grid weaknesses have led to a shift in focus towards the distribution network. Developing this network is a complex and challenging task, involving large-scale projects with many uncertainties. It is essential to thoroughly analyze issues in the investment process, propose suitable investment strategies, and enhance distribution network performance indicators (Silva et al 2017).

Despite numerous changes in the management system of the electric power industry, the traditional vertically integrated structure remains, failing to meet market economy requirements and hindering sustainable industry development. Consequently, China has begun reforming its electric power industry, replacing the old planned economy model with a new management system(Jarrah, 2018). The balanced scorecard approach now organizes management into four areas: value creation, customer service, internal operations, and enterprise growth, with specific indices driving business insights. However, the current method of allocating funds for distribution network expansion lacks scientific rigor, leading to funding mismatches, inefficient resource use, and adverse effects on regional economic growth (Park, 2019).

Previously, investment distribution in the power sector relied primarily on historical data or electricity sales figures, leading to a simplistic proportional allocation. This approach often resulted in a "Matthew effect," where power supply enterprises with weaker grids, particularly at the county level, became increasingly disadvantaged due to persistent underinvestment in grid infrastructure. Investment priorities were typically arranged qualitatively, focusing on aspects like load diversion and grid structure improvement, rather than quantitatively assessing investment benefits (Shi et al, 2017).

A more effective approach involves accurately evaluating and analyzing the investment status and capacity of power grid enterprises. This method supports decision-making by highlighting successful projects and identifying areas for improvement, thus ensuring that beneficial projects continue to progress while avoiding low-benefit or detrimental ones. This paper (K Bidi et al 2022) proposes a comprehensive forecasting model for power grid investments by integrating the GM(1, N) model, BP neural network model, and multiple regression model, enhanced through an improved genetic algorithm. The combined forecasting model has demonstrated superior accuracy in predicting investment outcomes compared to each individual forecasting method, proving to be highly effective in investment planning.

Traditionally, investment project management relied heavily on human expertise, intuition, and basic financial models. Conventional models like the Capital Asset Pricing Model (CAPM) and Modern Portfolio Theory (MPT) formed the foundation of decision-making in financial investments. However, these methods faced limitations in an increasingly complex market environment characterized by volatility, globalization, and technological disruption. Over the last decade, a shift towards more dynamic and data-centric approaches has occurred. Project managers are now incorporating advanced tools such as machine learning, big data analytics, and artificial intelligence (AI) to enhance decision-making.

Recent studies emphasize the importance of integrating technological solutions in investment project management to improve overall effectiveness. According to Goh & Law (2019), AI-based algorithms have begun to dominate investment strategies by enhancing decision-making in portfolio management, risk assessment, and investment forecasting. These methodologies have led to the creation of new models that integrate historical data, market conditions, and real-time information to provide more accurate and robust financial predictions.

3.1 Risk Management and Uncertainty in Investment Projects

A major challenge in investment project management is managing the uncertainty and risk that is inherent in investment decisions. Risk can be attributed to both external factors (e.g., economic crises, political instability) and internal factors (e.g., operational inefficiencies, changes in project scope). Traditional methods, such as Monte Carlo simulations and sensitivity analysis, have been effective at predicting potential risks but remain limited in terms of their ability to process large and diverse datasets.

Recent advancements in machine learning have provided enhanced tools for risk management. For example, deep learning and reinforcement learning algorithms have shown considerable promise in identifying and managing risks in investment projects. Zeng et al. (2020) explored the application of machine learning in risk management, demonstrating how algorithms can analyze vast amounts of financial data and provide real-time risk assessment models. These approaches allow project managers to quickly respond to emerging risks, helping mitigate potential losses.

Machine learning techniques, such as clustering and classification algorithms, can predict the likelihood of risk events and help managers identify risk-prone areas in real-time. By providing early warning systems, these tools offer a proactive rather than reactive approach to risk management. Studies by Jariwala et al. (2022) support this assertion, showing how advanced algorithms were able to predict the financial risks associated with fluctuating market conditions during a global recession.

3.2 Portfolio Optimization and Decision Making

Portfolio optimization is another critical area of investment project management. Traditional methods like Markowitz's MPT have been widely used in the investment field. These models attempt to balance risk and return by diversifying assets based on their expected returns and volatility. However, MPT has limitations in dealing with non-linear relationships and complex financial systems. In response, the integration of machine learning in portfolio optimization has revolutionized the field. Reinforcement learning (RL), for example, has been successfully applied to portfolio management, where agents learn to optimize portfolios by interacting with the market environment over time. A study by Berrada et al. (2020) demonstrates that RL-based algorithms outperform traditional models by dynamically adjusting portfolio allocations according to market conditions and investment goals.

Other machine learning techniques, such as support vector machines (SVM) and neural networks, have been utilized for predicting stock prices and asset returns. These models can identify complex patterns in large datasets and provide more accurate predictions than traditional models. According to Wang et al. (2021), a hybrid model combining SVM with genetic algorithms provided superior portfolio optimization results compared to conventional methods. The integration of machine learning into portfolio optimization has not only improved the financial performance of investment projects but also helped reduce the reliance on human intuition. This shift towards data-driven decision-making has significant implications for the future of investment project management, as it enables more objective and optimized investment strategies.

3.3 Investment Project Evaluation and Forecasting

Accurate forecasting is another critical function in investment project management. Forecasting the future performance of an investment project involves predicting returns, costs, and market trends. Traditionally, financial forecasting relied on time-series analysis, regression models, and expert judgment. However, these approaches are often limited in their ability to account for rapidly changing market conditions and other unpredictable factors. Recent research highlights the increasing role of machine learning techniques in improving forecasting accuracy. Deep learning models, particularly recurrent neural networks (RNN) and long short-term memory networks (LSTM), have proven effective in time-series forecasting by capturing complex temporal dependencies in the data. Studies by Chen et al. (2021) show how LSTM models were able to predict stock market trends with high accuracy, outperforming traditional ARIMA models.

Moreover, the use of big data analytics combined with machine learning has enabled more comprehensive evaluation models. By analyzing large, unstructured datasets (e.g., social media trends, news sentiment, or corporate filings), machine learning algorithms can uncover hidden relationships and patterns that influence project outcomes. For example, sentiment analysis algorithms can gauge market sentiment by analyzing news articles or social media posts, helping investors predict price movements or market trends. According to Khandoker et al. (2021), sentiment analysis has proven to be an effective tool for improving investment decision-making by providing timely insights into public sentiment and market reactions.

3.4 Challenges in Investment Project Management

While machine learning and AI present significant opportunities, there are several challenges in their application to investment project management. One primary challenge is the complexity and cost of implementing these advanced technologies. Developing and maintaining machine learning models requires specialized expertise, significant computational resources, and substantial initial investment. Furthermore, the models may require constant retraining to adapt to new market conditions and data. Another challenge is the interpretability of machine learning models. While these models can provide more accurate predictions, they often operate as "black boxes," making it difficult for decision-makers to understand how conclusions are reached. This lack of transparency can be problematic, especially in regulatory environments where transparency and accountability are crucial. Furthermore, there is the challenge of data quality. Machine learning models are heavily dependent on large, high-quality datasets. Inconsistent, missing, or biased data can lead to inaccurate predictions, which can have detrimental effects on investment decisions.

3.5 Future Directions

The future of investment project management lies in the further integration of machine learning algorithms with traditional financial models, resulting in hybrid approaches that leverage the strengths of both methodologies. The continued development of AI and machine learning, including advances in explainable AI (XAI), promises to increase transparency and improve the trustworthiness of algorithmic decision-making. Moreover, the growing use of blockchain technology in financial transactions could revolutionize investment project management by providing secure and transparent systems for project tracking and asset management. The integration of blockchain with AI could further streamline project evaluation and risk management (Chakrasali et al 2017).

Finally, the increasing emphasis on sustainable and ethical investing presents a new frontier for machine learning in investment project management. By incorporating environmental, social, and governance (ESG) factors into investment strategies, machine learning models can help guide more responsible investment decisions. Investment project management is undergoing a significant transformation due to the integration of machine learning and artificial intelligence. These technologies offer unprecedented opportunities for improving risk management, portfolio optimization, and project evaluation. While challenges remain, the potential benefits of these technologies, particularly in forecasting and decision-making, are vast. Future research will likely continue to explore the ways in which machine learning can be integrated with traditional financial models, creating more efficient, transparent, and data-driven investment project management practices.

4. METHODOLOGY

4.1 Factors Influencing Power Grid Investment

The demand for power grid investment is influenced by several key factors, including macroeconomic conditions, power demand trends, the scale of the power grid infrastructure, and its efficiency. Two significant factors, GDP and electricity load (power demand), illustrate this relationship well. Firstly, GDP exhibits steady annual growth, contributing to overall economic expansion. As economies grow, there is typically an increased need for electricity to support industrial, commercial, and residential activities. This uptick in economic activity translates into higher electricity consumption, which in turn drives the demand for expansion and enhancement of the power grid infrastructure.

Secondly, electricity load, representing the amount of electricity demanded by consumers, also shows a consistent upward trend over time. As populations grow and economic activities expand, the demand for electricity rises proportionally. This growth necessitates adjustments and expansions in the annual infrastructure investments of power grids to accommodate the increasing load and ensure reliable supply. The dynamic interplay between GDP growth and electricity load growth shapes the annual investment decisions of power grid companies. These decisions are crucial for maintaining the robustness and efficiency of the power grid infrastructure, thereby meeting the evolving demands of modern economies and societies.

The traditional approach to capital construction investment in power companies typically involves allocating investment separately for power grid planning and budgeting. However, experience has shown that this method often fails to achieve a truly rational allocation of investment resources. As a result, traditional methods are criticized for lacking scientific rigor and comprehensive systematization both in approach and methodology. In practice, this conventional method may lead to inefficiencies and suboptimal outcomes in investment decisions. For example, when planning and budgeting are treated as isolated processes, there is a risk of misalignment between strategic goals and financial allocations. This disjointed approach may overlook critical factors such as long-term infrastructure needs, emerging technological advancements, and evolving regulatory requirements.

Moreover, the traditional method may not adequately account for dynamic changes in economic conditions, energy demand patterns, and environmental considerations. These factors are increasingly important in shaping modern energy infrastructure investments, where flexibility and adaptability are key to achieving sustainability and resilience in the power grid (Ze-An et al 2019). Recognizing these limitations, there is a growing emphasis on adopting more integrated and systematic approaches to investment allocation in power grid construction. This includes leveraging advanced modeling techniques, incorporating comprehensive risk assessments, and integrating strategic planning with financial forecasting. By doing so, power companies can enhance the scientific basis of their investment decisions and improve the overall effectiveness of resource allocation in meeting both current and future energy demands.

Economic Conditions: The overall economic environment can significantly impact investment decisions in power grid infrastructure. Economic growth or downturns affect funding availability and prioritization of infrastructure projects.
Regulatory and Policy Framework: Government regulations, policies, and incentives play a crucial role in shaping investment decisions. Supportive policies and favourable regulations can encourage investment, while restrictive measures can hinder it.
Technological Advancements: Innovations in technology can influence investment decisions by improving the efficiency, reliability, and cost-effectiveness of power grid infrastructure.
Demand Forecasting: Accurate predictions of future energy demand are essential for determining the scale and scope of investments in power grid infrastructure.
Funding and Financial Resources: Availability of capital and financial resources, including loans, grants, and private investments, directly impacts the ability to undertake and complete power grid projects.
Environmental and Social Considerations: Environmental impact assessments and social implications, including community acceptance and ecological effects, can affect investment decisions and project execution.
Operational and Maintenance Costs: The long-term costs associated with operating and maintaining power grid infrastructure influence investment decisions, as higher costs can impact the overall viability of a project.
Risk Factors: Uncertainties such as market volatility, political instability, and technological risks can affect investment decisions and project outcomes.
Historical Data and Trends: Analysis of historical performance and trends in power grid investments can provide insights into future investment strategies and risk management.

Infrastructure Interdependencies: The need for integration with existing infrastructure and coordination with other projects can influence investment decisions, requiring careful planning and consideration.

The grid company will take into account the anticipated growth and fluctuations in load when planning its infrastructure investments for the coming year. This approach indicates that infrastructure investment adjustments tend to lag behind load growth. Furthermore, investment management often overlooks the analysis of financial support capabilities and potential returns on investment, and is influenced by various system, mechanism, and technical factors. As a result, this can lead to an inadequate and unsystematic grid investment strategy. Consequently, there is an urgent need to develop a suitable method for calculating power grid investment capacity to support more informed decision-making in power grid investments.

4.2 Prediction Model

The model is straightforward in its specific application. It processes statistical data to analyze the relationship between investment and various complex factors, and uses a mathematical model to forecast future investment changes. Building on the investment scale calculation model, it incorporates the investment distribution weights for both the main network and distribution network, creating a formula for investment scale distribution. Using the identified factors influencing power grid investment demand, this study collected relevant data from a region over the past 10 years, including power grid investment demand, GDP, industrial structure, overall line loss rate, unit power grid investment per increased supply load, and unit power grid asset per supply load, among other data.

Figure 1. Process and flow control of grid infrastructure investment model

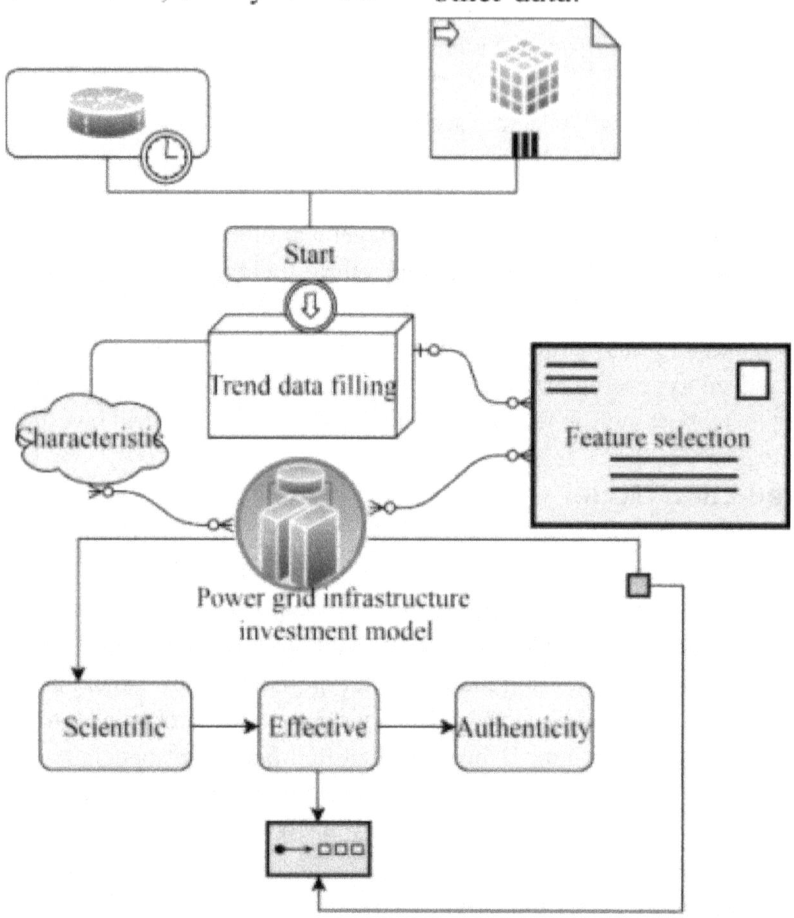

Figure 1 illustrates the overall process of the investment model (Ye et al 2024). Initially, it is crucial to complete any missing data accurately, using appropriate methods for data imputation. This involves processing operational data and selecting key features. Once the features are chosen, the significant operation index is integrated into the investment model. Subsequently, the model predicts the power grid investment amount based on actual demand, ensuring the predictions are both accurate and reliable. The investment budget for power grid projects should be seamlessly incorporated into the company's annual budget. It is important to thoroughly review and document the experience of preparing and reporting the investment budget for power grid infrastructure projects, in alignment with unified requirements and synchronized reporting. This includes clarifying the budget preparation process, management procedures, and developing guiding principles for managing the investment budget of power grid infrastructure projects.

Figure 2. Optimization process using genetic algorithm

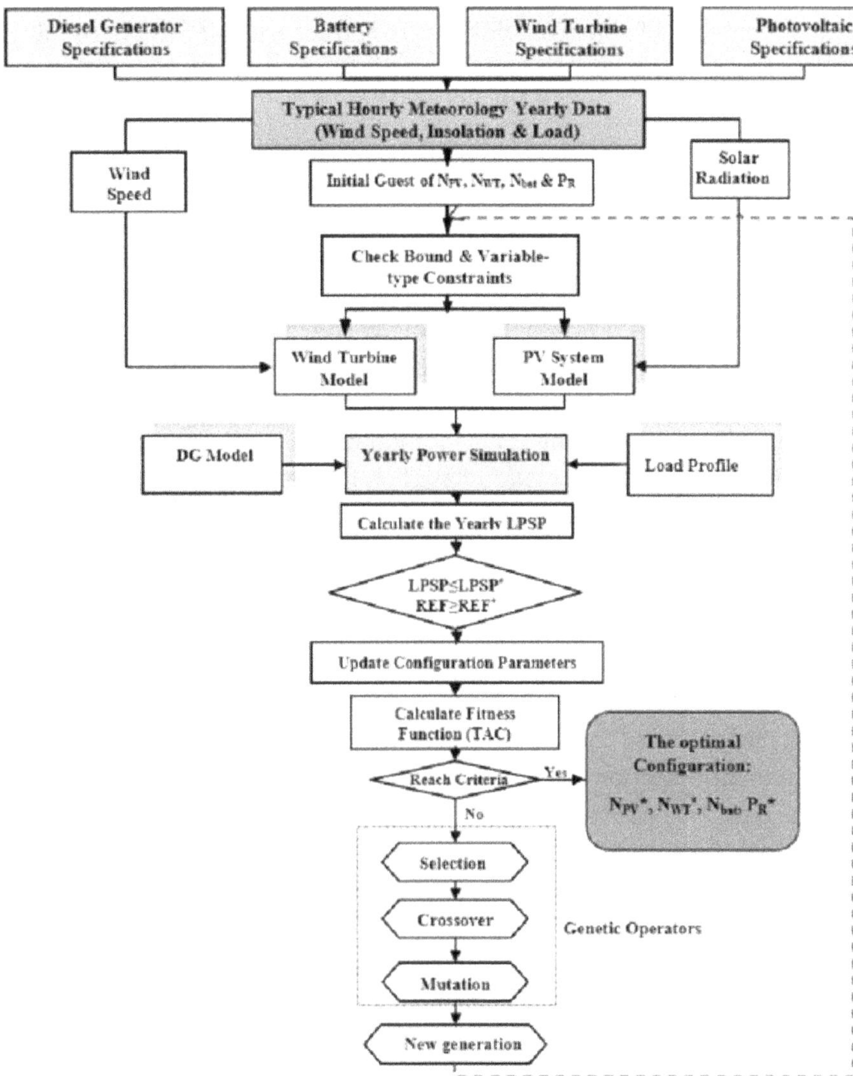

The optimization process using a genetic algorithm (GA) in power grid infrastructure is a powerful method for solving complex decision-making problems related to grid design, investment allocation, resource distribution, and operational optimization(Fig 2). The genetic algorithm mimics the process of natural evolution and is applied to find optimal or near-optimal solutions by iterating over generations and using biological-inspired mechanisms like selection, crossover, and mutation. Below is a detailed explanation of the flow chart typically used to represent the GA-based optimization process in power grid infrastructure.

The first step in the optimization process involves defining the problem and initializing the population of potential solutions. The power grid infrastructure problem can involve various objectives such as minimizing costs, maximizing reliability, or optimizing grid capacity. The objective function will vary depending on the problem. It could represent cost minimization (e.g., construction or operational costs), reliability maximization (e.g., reducing failure rates or outages), or a combination of multiple objectives. A set of possible solutions (individuals) is randomly generated. Each individual represents a potential configuration of grid infrastructure, such as the locations of substations, capacity of transmission lines, or the allocation of investment across regions. These solutions are encoded as chromosomes (usually as bit strings, real numbers, or other representations depending on the problem).

Each individual solution is evaluated to determine how well it meets the objectives and constraints of the problem. This evaluation is done using a **fitness function** which assigns a fitness value to each solution based on its performance. Selection is the process of choosing the best-performing individuals (parents) from the population to create the next generation. The individuals with higher fitness values are more likely to be selected, but there is still a chance for less-fit individuals to be selected to maintain genetic diversity. Common selection methods include:

- **Roulette Wheel Selection:** Individuals are selected based on their fitness, with higher fitness individuals having a higher probability of selection.
- **Tournament Selection:** A small group of individuals is randomly selected, and the best individual from this group is chosen to be a parent.
- **Rank Selection:** Individuals are ranked based on fitness, and selection is made based on rank rather than absolute fitness.

Crossover is the process where two selected parent solutions are combined to create offspring solutions. This step simulates the recombination of genetic material in biological reproduction. Crossover generates new potential solutions by combining the features of two good parents, with the goal of inheriting the strengths of both parents. Mutation introduces random changes to some individuals in the population, providing genetic diversity and preventing premature convergence to suboptimal solutions. Mutation ensures that the algorithm explores new regions of the solution space that may not be reached through crossover alone. After crossover and mutation, the new offspring are evaluated using the fitness function. The offspring solutions are compared to the previous generation's individuals to assess whether they provide better performance in terms of the objective(s).

- If an offspring solution improves upon its parents, it will have a higher fitness value, and it may be retained in the next generation.
- If it fails to perform better, it may be discarded or kept based on other selection strategies.

The next step is the replacement phase, where individuals from the current generation are replaced by the offspring created in the crossover and mutation steps. The algorithm iterates through the process of selection, crossover, mutation, and replacement for a set number of generations or until a termination condition is met.

4.3. Budget Management

The project investment plan entails annually calculating investment quotas based on project construction schedules and estimates derived from project budgets. However, influenced by macroeconomic conditions, electricity growth is expected to stabilize at medium to low levels, making previous models reliant on investment-driven revenue and electricity growth increasingly unsustainable. This situation highlights disparities in development among different units, creating significant mismatches between power grid investment capacity and the investment demands of certain units. To address these challenges, it is imperative to scientifically allocate investment scales through comprehensive budget management This approach involves rigorously preparing investment plans, accurately forecasting the investment budgets for power grid infrastructure projects, enhancing investment guidance, exploiting potential efficiencies, and ensuring stable corporate progress.

Capacity measurement focuses on achieving cash flow balance as the foundational principle, with profit targets and asset-liability ratios serving as boundary conditions. By integrating key assumptions and historical data, a power grid investment calculation model is formulated to inform financial investment decisions. Furthermore, beyond measuring overall investment scales, an investment structure measurement model is developed using a combination of statistical regression methods and data mining techniques. This model deepens the application of investment measurement tools, aiming to optimize investment allocation and enhance the effectiveness of resource utilization in power grid development.

Figure 3. Budget plan and management

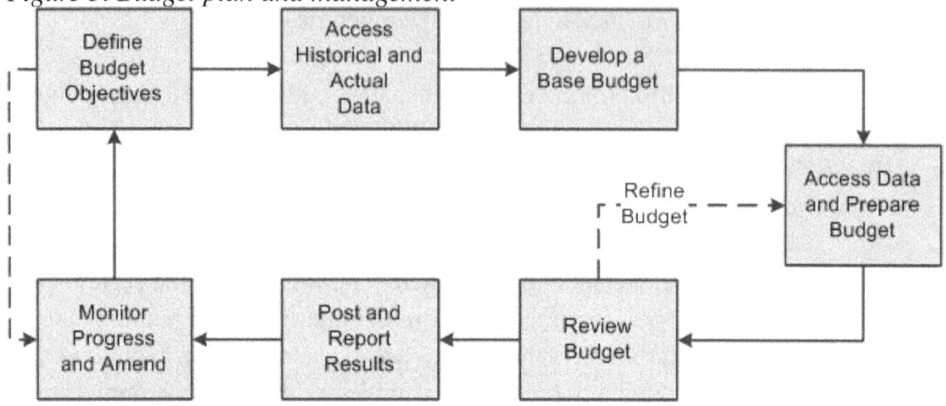

Based on Figure 3, units at all levels within the grid company must adhere strictly to the budget plan issued by higher management, breaking down the budget indicators accordingly. Specific responsibilities should be assigned, with budget responsibilities distributed across various centers, establishing a clear budget accountability system to ensure that the company's annual business objectives are both manageable and controlled. It is essential to enhance control over the budget implementation process and establish a system for budget analysis and notifications. The project implementation schedule must be carefully considered, including the effects of changes in organizational structure, personnel, and business processes on the business system. The project working group should lead the development of the primary work schedule. Additionally, the project team must review the detailed plans submitted by the project implementation team, ensuring they align with the actual situation and requirements.

In grid investment planning, the optimization model typically consists of several components. The model is structured with each year considered as a separate stage, with the assumption that the investments for that year are completed at the beginning of the year. Before predicting the investment scale, it is necessary to standardize the data to remove the effects of different dimensions.

The process for standardizing variable data involves identifying the maximum value X_{max} and the minimum value X_{min} for each variable. Then, for the index value X_t in year *t*, the following formula is used to standardize the data:

$$Z_t = \frac{X_t - X_{min}}{X_{max} - X_{min}}$$

The Z-Score method is a common technique used to standardize data, including investment demand and its influencing factors. This method transforms the data into a standard normal distribution with a mean of 0 and a standard deviation of 1. The formula for calculating the Z-Score for a given value X_t is:

$$y_t = \frac{x_t - \vec{x}}{s}$$

This standardization method helps in comparing different datasets by converting them into a common scale. To address the limitations and shortcomings of individual prediction models for forecasting power demand, a comprehensive approach is employed. This involves evaluating and selecting from various single prediction models, then analyzing the strengths and weaknesses of each. By combining the results of several selected models in a scientifically sound manner, a comprehensive prediction model is developed that offers the most accurate forecasts and streamlined final outcomes. For managing the issue of missing power grid data, it is crucial to choose an appropriate imputation method to accurately complete the operational data. This step ensures that the data used for the prediction models are as complete and reliable as possible. In summary, the comprehensive prediction model outperforms individual prediction models in terms of prediction accuracy and stability. It adapts more effectively to changes in the forecasting environment. By using repeated simulations, with samples from the past 10 years as the training set and current year samples as the prediction set, it has been found that the support vector machine (SVM) delivers the best simulation results (Thangasamy et al 2017).

Multistage problems are significantly more complex than single-stage problems due to the need to account for interactions and dependencies between each stage. Simply treating a multistage problem as a series of single-stage problems will not yield a globally optimal solution because it ignores the intricate relationships and interactions between stages (Song et al 2020). traditional optimization methods, which rely on strictly mathematical approaches, often fall short in practical applications where the distribution network involves a large number of variables and constraints. To address these complexities, heuristic algorithms have emerged as effective solutions. These algorithms are designed to handle large-scale problems by providing good, though not necessarily optimal, solutions through approximation and iterative improvement. Heuristic methods are particularly useful in managing the vast and intricate nature of real-world distribution networks.

5. RESULTS

By consolidating extensive data on power grid projects from 2012 to 2021 on Transmission and Distribution (T&D) World – Industry Reports and Data, the historical trends and fluctuation characteristics of engineering equipment and materials can be thoroughly analysed. This approach enables dynamic insights into the data resources for each year and facilitates the development of an intelligent data mining, analysis, and prediction model for power engineering.

Comprehensive plan management has become deeply integrated into the daily operations and management of power grid companies. The comprehensive plan serves as an integrated overview of various professional plans, including financial capital budgeting, investment strategies, technical transformations, scientific and technological initiatives, and engineering projects. Following a thorough analysis of input-output benefits, an optimal plan is developed, along with corresponding conclusions. Comprehensive plan management requires a clear understanding of the logical connections between the advancement of different specialties. By conducting analysis and research, it aims to achieve the optimal allocation of these plans, thereby maximizing the economic benefits for the enterprise.

Within the framework of comprehensive plan management, financial and investment plans are critical components that support the growth of power grid enterprises. To align with the construction approach of the comprehensive plan management system, a dynamic, interconnected, and feedback-driven relationship between these specialized plans must be established. This framework should quantitatively outline the relationships between the enterprise's development strategy and the resources required, fostering the implementation of the corporate strategy and enabling the overall optimization of resources.

The development of PGI (Power Grid Investment) planning is influenced by multiple environmental factors and is a result of their integration. Unlike traditional power grid planning, which primarily focuses on load forecasting and power source planning to determine the optimal capacity of the system and the location and size of substations and transmission lines, this chapter explores grid investment in relation to load growth, demand-side resources, policy factors, and market effects. It examines the dynamic interaction between these variables, with transmission capacity serving as an indicator of system investment.

In 2018, a province with a power supply area of 89,400 square kilometers, serving a population of 61,147,500, reported a total electricity consumption of 186.9 billion kWh and a sales volume of 150.8 billion kWh. The province's power supply reliability was 99.814%, the comprehensive voltage qualification rate was 99.834%, and the comprehensive line loss rate for 110 kV and below was 5.5%, while for 10 kV and below, it was 5.57%. The province had 2,200 users and 175 power grids within its distribution network, with an average of 2.0 substations (220/110/35 kV) per grid and 4.7 10 kV public lines per power supply unit.

The power grid structure of the province has developed a distribution network centered on UOKV and 35 kV high-voltage distribution, with 10 kV and below medium and low-voltage networks as the primary components. Through further optimization, the province has gradually developed a more efficient distribution network, with 110 kV as the backbone and 10 kV forming the core of the medium-voltage distribution system. The prediction principle used for PGI involves generating a new data series with clear trends through accumulation. A model is then developed based on the growth trend of the series, followed by reverse calculation to recover the original data series and obtain the prediction results. To improve the accuracy of PGI forecasting, this paper proposes a PGI portfolio prediction model and employs an enhanced genetic algorithm to optimize the solution.

The primary role of the mutation operator in a genetic algorithm is to enhance the diversity within the population. If the mutation rate is too high, the randomness of the evolution process increases, making it difficult for the algorithm to converge. Conversely, if the mutation rate is too low, the diversity within the population decreases, causing the algorithm to easily get stuck in a local optimum. The design of the mutation rate should adhere to the following principles: (1) Individuals with higher fitness should have a lower mutation rate to preserve their beneficial traits, while individuals with lower fitness should have a higher mutation rate; (2) As the number of iterations increases, the mutation rate should gradually decrease to allow the algorithm to stabilize.

Power grid investment is influenced by various factors, including social electricity consumption, power supply reliability, load, line loss rate, power supply structure, and macroeconomic policies. The investment and development of distribution networks have inherent characteristics such as long-term impacts and slow capital recovery. Therefore, the dynamic multi-attribute decision-making method proposed in this chapter takes into account both current and past performance and construction data for each region. It collects decision-making information across different time periods and integrates the data by assigning appropriate weights based on timeliness. This approach provides a solid theoretical foundation for obtaining final evaluation results.

Based on the evaluation results of the distribution network, the investment decision-making process can be informed with reference recommendations. However, a comprehensive system is still needed to establish specific implementation standards, from investment allocation to project completion. Thus, this paper proposes an investment decision-making system for the distribution network, which includes decisions on investment scale, investment direction, and investment projects. Using a province as a case study, the results demonstrate that this system not only aligns with the macro-level development needs of regional electricity consumption, operational indicators, and economic benefits but also helps in identifying the optimal combination of specific projects. The three-tier decision-making process operates in a coordinated and interconnected manner across various levels, ensuring the integrity, coordination, and interlinking of the distribution network investment. This structure helps improve decision-making accuracy.

Improving power grid reliability is a primary goal of power grid planning. Consequently, the reliability of the power grid is directly linked to investment plans for power grid companies and government regulatory strategies. When reliability requirements are reduced, transmission and distribution prices tend to decrease and fluctuate. Lower reliability requirements will consequently diminish the investment appeal for power grid companies. Conversely, more frequent regulatory changes and incentive policies from the government can impact investment decisions. Based on foundational data and model inputs, sensitivity analysis is conducted using the Vensim sensitivity testing tool. First, variables are selected for sensitivity analysis, with parameters such as the range of variable changes, the number of simulations, and sensitivity indicators to be tracked. The analysis focuses on the company's unit profit as the target value, while observing sensitive variables such as new fixed assets, depreciation expenses, EVA (Economic Value Added), and internal profit.

Here, prediction accuracy is assessed using several error metrics:

RE (Relative Error) Measures the relative accuracy of predictions compared to actual values.

$$RE = \frac{|\vec{a}_i - a_i|}{a_i} \times 100\%$$

MAE (Mean Absolute Error) Computes the average absolute difference between predicted and actual values, providing a clear indication of prediction accuracy.

$$MAE = \frac{1}{n}\sum_{i=1}^{n}|\vec{a}_i - a_i|$$

RMSE (Root Mean Square Error) Calculates the square root of the average squared differences between predicted and actual values, giving more weight to larger errors and reflecting the model's accuracy.

$$RMSE = \sqrt{\frac{1}{n}\sum_{i=1}^{n}(\vec{a}_i - a_i)^2}$$

These metrics help evaluate and reflect the prediction performance of the model, ensuring that the forecasting results are both accurate and reliable. Where, a_i is the actual value, $\vec{a}_i$ a JG is the predicted value, and n is the number of predicted samples. Based on the calculations, the model's performance metrics Root Mean

Square Error is $2.114 billion and Mean Absolute Error is $9.1 billion. These values indicate the average magnitude of prediction errors, with RMSE giving more weight to larger discrepancies and MAE providing an overall average error.

As an extension of the principal component analysis (PCA) method, this approach significantly reduces the analysis workload due to the smaller scale of factor variables. By restructuring the original variables, factor variables retain most of the information contained in the original indicators. This results in a high degree of information preservation and ensures that the restored information is both authentic and reliable. Taking into account the power demand situation of the grid company over the past 10 years and considering historical trends in power consumption, the annual investment prediction model is categorized into three schemes: high, medium, and low. (Ye et al 2024). The results of these schemes are illustrated in Figure 4.

Figure 4. Comparison of investment capacity

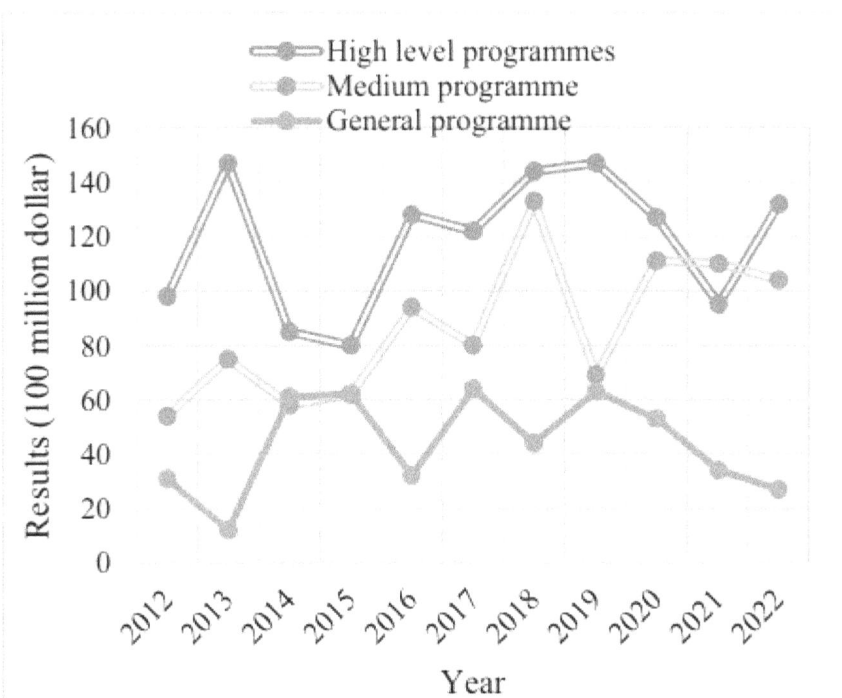

Among the schemes, the advanced scheme predicts an investment capacity of $15 billion, which surpasses the investment capacities of the medium and low-level schemes. This indicates that the scheme model based on the data mining algorithm provides the most robust investment prediction capacity.

As illustrated in Figure 5, when evaluating the performance of the forecasting models, the average relative error of the proposed data mining-based algorithm for predicting power grid investment is 1.21%. In comparison, the average relative errors of the linear regression model and the neural network model are 3.09% and 2.99%, respectively, with the data mining model showing a reduction in error by 1.88%. In summary, the data mining-based prediction model exhibits a smaller error compared to both the linear regression and neural network models. This results in prediction outcomes that are closer to the actual values. Consequently, this model provides more accurate reference information for decision-makers, enabling the formulation of well-informed investment strategies and enhancing the overall investment benefits for infrastructure.

Through comparison, it has been demonstrated that the evaluation results from the PGI evaluation system, which uses only a subset of the data, are largely consistent with the conclusions found in the evaluation reports. Including more data would expand the coverage, making the results more scientific and reliable, thereby fulfilling the evaluation needs of power grid enterprises regarding PGI status.

Figure 5. Comparison of predicted model evaluation results

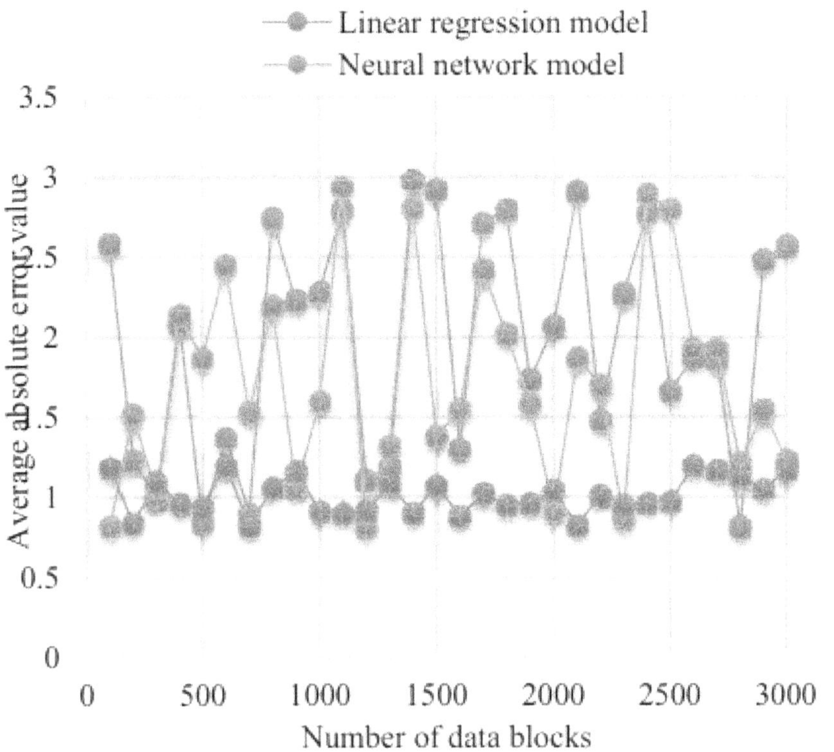

The aforementioned reports were compiled by a multi-member team from the Economic Research Institute and Energy Research Institute of the power grid company. The team spent several months gathering data and conducting investment evaluations. In contrast, by using the PGI evaluation system, various statistical measures and evaluation perspectives can be calculated within hours, assuming perfect data, thus saving significant time, manpower, and resources. The findings show that the combined forecasting model proposed in this paper offers the highest forecasting accuracy, with the lowest average of absolute relative error. Additionally, the distribution of relative errors is more even, ensuring that the predicted values at any given time node do not experience significant deviations.

Case Study: Results in Inventory Project Management

ABC Electronics, a leading global distributor of consumer electronics, was facing significant challenges in inventory management. Over the years, its supply chain had become fragmented due to inconsistent demand forecasting, lack of real-time data, and inefficient processes across multiple warehouses and retail locations. Stockouts, excess inventory, and poor order fulfillment rates were leading to both operational inefficiencies and customer dissatisfaction. Recognizing the need for a transformation, ABC Electronics embarked on an ambitious project to implement an advanced, integrated inventory management system (IMS). The goal was to streamline operations, improve inventory accuracy, and optimize stock levels across all touchpoints, ultimately boosting profitability and customer satisfaction.

Project Objectives:

- Improve inventory accuracy and reduce discrepancies.
- Reduce excess inventory while avoiding stockouts.
- Enhance demand forecasting with predictive analytics.
- Streamline warehouse operations for better order fulfillment.
- Strengthen supplier relationships for timely restocking.

Scenario 1: Improving Forecasting Accuracy and Reducing Overstocking

Challenge: Prior to the project, ABC Electronics struggled with overstocking, especially for high-demand products like smartphones and laptops. The traditional inventory system relied heavily on historical sales data, which was inadequate for predicting fluctuations in demand due to changing consumer preferences, seasonal trends, or unexpected market disruptions. This resulted in excess inventory that tied up valuable capital and led to significant storage costs.
Solution: The new IMS implemented machine learning algorithms to analyze a wider range of variables, including historical sales, market trends, promotions, and even weather patterns, to create more accurate demand forecasts. The system also incorporated real-time sales data from various retail locations, allowing for dynamic stock replenishment.
Result: Within the first six months of implementation, ABC Electronics reduced overstocking by 35%. The new system was able to better align stock levels with actual demand, ensuring the right products were available at the right time. Overstocking costs, including storage and insurance fees, decreased by 25%, freeing up capital for reinvestment. The system's predictive capabilities also helped the company avoid excess stock during off-peak seasons, optimizing cash flow.

Scenario 2: Minimizing Stockouts and Improving Customer Satisfaction

Challenge: Stockouts had become a frequent issue, particularly with high-demand products during peak seasons like holidays and sales events. As a result, ABC Electronics lost a significant number of sales and received complaints from customers about unavailable products. The company's supply chain was reactive, with no real-time visibility into stock levels across its multiple warehouses and retail outlets.

Solution: To address stockouts, ABC Electronics integrated real-time inventory tracking and automatic stock-level alerts into the IMS. The system used a combination of safety stock parameters and reorder triggers based on predictive demand, ensuring products were restocked before stockouts occurred. Additionally, the IMS was connected with both suppliers and distribution centers, allowing for faster replenishment times and improved visibility into the supply chain.

Result: Stockouts were reduced by 40% within the first year of implementation. This improvement directly impacted customer satisfaction, as products were more consistently available. Customer complaints dropped by 20%, and the company saw a 15% increase in repeat business. Real-time inventory visibility also helped retail locations better plan their stock levels, reducing emergency restocking and preventing customer disappointments.

Scenario 3: Streamlining Warehouse Operations

Challenge: ABC Electronics faced significant inefficiencies in its warehouse operations. Inventory turnover was slow, leading to overcrowded shelves and delayed order fulfillment. Warehouse staff had to manually check stock levels and physically search for items, contributing to errors and delays. These inefficiencies added to operational costs and affected the speed of product shipments.

Solution: The new IMS was integrated with automated material handling systems (AMHS) that tracked product movements in the warehouse in real-time. Barcode scanning and RFID technology were introduced to quickly locate products, while the system optimized stock placement for faster picking. Automated order processing and shipment tracking helped streamline the entire fulfillment process.

Result: Warehouse throughput increased by 30%, as order fulfillment times decreased by 25%. The error rate in picking and packing was reduced by 20%, resulting in fewer returns and exchanges. With better inventory control, ABC Electronics was able to maintain leaner warehouses without compromising order accuracy. Operational costs associated with warehouse labor and storage reduced by 15%, significantly improving profitability.

Scenario 4: Enhancing Supplier Collaboration and Lead Time Reduction

Challenge: ABC Electronics experienced long lead times due to poor communication with suppliers, which impacted inventory replenishment and increased stockouts. Suppliers often lacked visibility into ABC's real-time demand, and as a result, deliveries were delayed or poorly timed. This caused fluctuations in inventory levels and made it difficult for ABC Electronics to maintain optimal stock.

Solution: To improve supplier collaboration, the IMS incorporated a supplier portal that allowed suppliers to access real-time inventory data, sales forecasts, and order status. The system used shared data to align production and shipping schedules with ABC's demand needs, helping reduce lead times. In addition, automated alerts were set up to notify suppliers of replenishment needs in advance.

Result: Supplier lead times were reduced by 20%, thanks to improved communication and better synchronization. With more accurate forecasting and transparent information sharing, ABC Electronics was able to place orders more efficiently, preventing stockouts and ensuring better inventory turnover. This also led to improved supplier relationships, as suppliers were able to plan production and shipments more effectively, reducing the likelihood of backlogs and delays.

Scenario 5: Reducing Wastage and Improving Sustainability

Challenge: Due to inaccurate demand forecasting and inefficient inventory management, ABC Electronics often had to discount or dispose of outdated and unsold products. In particular, older model electronics, like previous-generation smartphones and TVs, accumulated in stock, contributing to waste and environmental impact. The company was also facing pressure from consumers to adopt more sustainable practices.

Solution: With the new IMS in place, ABC Electronics adopted a more sustainable approach to inventory management. The system provided more accurate demand forecasts, allowing the company to reduce excess inventory and plan for timely product lifecycle management. Additionally, the IMS allowed ABC to prioritize the sale of older models before introducing new ones, reducing waste and improving product life cycles.

Result: Over the course of the first year, ABC Electronics reduced waste by 25%, as more accurate inventory levels and better forecasting ensured that older stock was sold or redistributed before becoming obsolete. The company also introduced a more sustainable returns policy and recycling program, which helped enhance its reputation among environmentally conscious consumers. The sustainability improvements not only reduced costs but also aligned with corporate social responsibility (CSR) goals, contributing to a positive brand image.

Inference

The implementation of the new inventory management system at ABC Electronics delivered remarkable results across multiple areas of the business. By improving forecasting accuracy, minimizing stockouts, optimizing warehouse operations, and strengthening supplier relationships, the company saw reductions in costs, enhanced customer satisfaction, and increased operational efficiency. Additionally, the sustainability efforts helped the company meet both financial and ethical objectives. In summary, the inventory management project was a resounding success, allowing ABC Electronics to adapt to dynamic market conditions, reduce waste, and maintain a competitive edge in the rapidly evolving consumer electronics industry. The integration of real-time data, advanced analytics, and automation helped transform ABC Electronics into a more agile, efficient, and customer-centric organization.

Challenges in Investment Project Management in Power Grid Infrastructure Construction Using Machine Learning Algorithms

Investing in power grid infrastructure is a complex and capital-intensive endeavor, and while machine learning (ML) algorithms offer significant advantages in optimizing project management, their integration presents several challenges.

(i) Data Quality and Availability

Machine learning algorithms depend on high-quality, accurate, and consistent data to provide reliable insights. In the context of power grid infrastructure, the required data spans various sources, including historical grid performance, environmental conditions, construction schedules, cost estimates, and supply chain dynamics. Often, data may be incomplete, inconsistent, or spread across disparate systems, making it difficult to build robust ML models. Inadequate data quality can lead to incorrect predictions, affecting investment decisions, budget allocations, and project timelines.

(ii) Integration with Existing Systems

Power grid projects often involve a multitude of stakeholders, from utility companies to government regulators, contractors, and suppliers. Integrating machine learning algorithms with existing project management systems, such as Enterprise Resource Planning (ERP) and Supervisory Control and Data Acquisition (SCADA) systems, can be technically challenging. Ensuring seamless data flow between these systems requires substantial infrastructure upgrades, coordination across departments, and technical expertise. Failure to integrate effectively can limit the utility of machine learning in improving project outcomes.

(iii) Model Complexity and Interpretability

While machine learning models can process vast amounts of data and identify patterns, they often operate as "black boxes," meaning their decision-making processes are not easily interpretable. For investment project management in power grid infrastructure, this lack of transparency can be a significant barrier. Investors, project managers, and regulatory bodies may be reluctant to trust automated recommendations without a clear understanding of how ML models arrive at their conclusions, especially when decisions involve substantial financial risks or long-term commitments.

(iv) Scalability and Adaptability

Power grid infrastructure projects can vary greatly in size, complexity, and geographical scope. ML models that perform well in one context may not be easily scalable or adaptable to other projects with different variables. For instance, predicting the optimal placement of transmission lines in an urban area might require different considerations than for rural or mountainous regions. Adapting machine learning algorithms to handle these variations without extensive retraining or model recalibration presents a challenge.

(v) Change Management and Adoption

Adopting machine learning in power grid infrastructure project management requires significant change management. Stakeholders, including engineers, project managers, and investment analysts, may resist new technologies due to unfamiliarity or fear of job displacement. Training personnel and overcoming cultural barriers to technology adoption are critical steps in successfully implementing ML-driven project management strategies.

Despite the potential benefits of machine learning in optimizing investment and management of power grid infrastructure, the challenges of data quality, system integration, model interpretability, scalability, and organizational resistance must be addressed for successful deployment and utilization.

6. CONCLUSION

Currently, the macroeconomic environment faces significant downward pressure, with sluggish electricity consumption demand and a notable decline in electricity sales growth rates. Meanwhile, the fixed costs associated with power grid construction continue to rise. Given these challenges, long-term investment strategies and arrangements for power grid construction must prioritize strict control, ensuring safe operations while meeting the developmental needs of the power market. However, analyzing power grid data comprehensively remains difficult due to inherent complexities and data gaps. The use of genetic algorithms in conjunction with machine learning algorithms presents a promising solution for optimizing power grid investments. This integrated approach enhances predictive accuracy, facilitates dynamic decision-making, and provides a scalable, flexible framework for addressing the complexities and uncertainties inherent in PGI. As grid systems continue to grow in complexity with the increasing adoption of renewable energy, distributed generation, and smart grid technologies, the synergy between GA and ML will likely become an indispensable tool in the strategic planning and investment management of power grid infrastructure.

Many existing studies fail to provide holistic project analyses, resulting in superficial indicator analyses and unreliable investment distribution outcomes. This limits the ability to make comprehensive, scientific, and feasible predictions. To overcome these limitations, it is crucial to develop a robust model for the infrastructure investment budgets of power grid companies. Such a model should address several key objectives:

- Comprehensive Investment Planning: Develop an investment planning framework using a calculation and distribution model that integrates goals for sustained and stable growth in electricity sales, ensures the secure operation of power grids, and facilitates the transformation of urban and rural distribution networks.
- Optimized Investment Distribution: Formulate an investment distribution mode based on the calculation and distribution model, aiming to optimize the distribution network. This approach provides a structured method to allocate

power grid construction funds efficiently, reduce capital costs, and mitigate economic risks.

Implementing this model not only enhances the operational efficiency of power grid companies but also accelerates their investment planning and construction processes. By systematically addressing investment challenges and leveraging data-driven insights, the model supports strategic decision-making, ensuring that investments align closely with operational and market demands.

REFERENCES

Berrada, M., Jafari, M., & Hachicha, A. (2020). Reinforcement learning for portfolio management: A survey. *International Journal of Financial Studies*, *8*(3), 1–17. DOI: 10.3390/ijfs8030032

Bidi, K. F., Damour, C., & Grondin, D. (2022). Multistage power and energy management strategy for hybrid microgrid with photovoltaic production and hydrogen storage. *Applied Energy*, *66*(36), 16.

Chakrasali, R. L. (2017). Simulation and study of standalone hybrid grid (involving biogas, solar, wind and biodiesel-based generation). *International Energy Journal*, *57*(24), 5.

Chen, M., Li, L., & Song, X. (2021). Deep learning for stock market forecasting: A survey. *Journal of Computational Finance*, *25*(5), 45–69.

Gao, S., Song, Y., & Chen, Y. (2018). Fast simulation model of voltage source converters with arbitrary topology using switch-state prediction. *IEEE Transactions on Power Electronics*, *75*(46), 35.

Goh, K. S., & Law, H. W. (2019). Machine learning in financial risk management: Current practices and future directions. *The Journal of Risk Finance*, *20*(4), 98–112. DOI: 10.1108/JRF-05-2018-0067

Han, X., Wang, F., & Chen, M. (2019). Economic evaluation of micro-grid system in commercial parks based on echelon utilization batteries. *IEEE Access : Practical Innovations, Open Solutions*, *46*(23), 9. DOI: 10.1109/ACCESS.2019.2916181

Hu, W., Cheng, L., & Qian, M.. (2019). Prediction of annual power grid infrastructure investment based on hybrid algorithm of improved PSO. *Power System and Clean Energy*, (3), 2.

Jariwala, A., Shah, S., & Pathak, D. (2022). Application of AI in financial risk management. *The Journal of Financial Data Science*, *8*(1), 23–44. DOI: 10.3905/jfds.2022.1.110

Jarrah, M. (2018). Modeling and simulation of renewable energy sources in smart grid using DEVS formalism. *Procedia Computer Science*, *19*(24), 12.

Kelei, H. E., Zeng, M., & Qiao, H. (2022). Research on power grid investment optimization model based on system dynamics. *Shaanxi Electric Power*, *34*(7), 1.

Khandoker, R., Kabir, M. H., & Islam, S. (2021). Sentiment analysis for stock market prediction: A review of recent trends. *International Journal of Financial Engineering*, *18*(7), 210–224.

Kumar, N., Priya, S. S., Varghese, V. K. R., Patra, J. P., & Nishant, N. (2024). An improved method for fault detection electric power system protection using SVMCNN model. In *2024 International Conference on Electronics, Computing, Communication and Control Technology (ICECCC)* (pp. 1–6). Bengaluru, India. DOI: 10.1109/ICECCC61767.2024.10593976

Lavanya, G., Murthy, K. S., & Sivakumar, S. (2024). Renewable energy-powered robot for fully-automated tea leaf harvesting: A solution for labor shortage and environmental sustainability. *AIP Conference Proceedings*, *3161*(1), 020340. DOI: 10.1063/5.0229350

Li, Z.-A., Ge, J.-F., & Zhang, Y.-J. (2019). Application of beta regression model for the data mining forecast. [Natural Science Edition]. *Journal of Nantong University*, *33*(2), 8.

Liu, H. Q., & Chen, H. J. (2020). Informatization construction for power grid infrastructure construction enterprises. *Electric Power Information Technology*, (11), 2.

Liu, W. D., Lu, X.-F., & Yu, X.-Y.. (2020). Annual portfolio forecast for infrastructure projects of power grid companies. *East China Electric Power*, (11), 2.

Park, Y. S., Koo, M. M., & Jang, S. M. (2019). Characteristic analysis of grid-connected PM wind power generators based on transfer relations and performance evaluation. *IEEE Transactions on Energy Conversion*, *57*(4), 28.

Renugadevi, R. (2025). An optimal method of assessing the quality of water using integrated AI and blockchain methodology. In *Smart Water Technology for Sustainable Management in Modern Cities* (pp. 261–284). DOI: 10.4018/979-8-3693-8074-1.ch011

Selvi, M., Jeeva, S., & Jaswanth, J. (2024). Improving the power efficiency in OFDM system using LDPC codes. In *Proceedings of the 2024 IEEE International Conference on Advanced Artificial Intelligence and Computing* (pp. 1717–1723). DOI: 10.1109/ICAAIC60222.2024.10575635

Shankar, M., & Kumar, S. (2024). An optimized 3DOF-FOPID2-DF controller with improved power quality for multi-level inverter in grid connected PV systems. *Journal of Circuits, Systems, and Computers*, *33*(17), 2450310. Advance online publication. DOI: 10.1142/S0218126624503109

Shi, L., Xu, Z., & Hao, J. (2017). Modelling analysis of transient stability simulation with high penetration of grid-connected wind farms of DFIG type. *Wind Energy (Chichester, England)*, *17*(437), 11.

Silva, J., Phillips, J. R., & Silveira, L. M. (2017). Efficient simulation of power grids. *IEEE Transactions on Computer-Aided Design of Integrated Circuits and Systems*, *10*(15), 6.

Song, L. L., Xu, Q.-S., & Wu, Y.-W. (2020). Evaluation and multi-objective optimization of power grid investment benefits taking into account the weights. *Journal of Electric Power*, (25), 13–26.

Thangasamy, S., Chamany, B. F., & Murthy, L. (2018). Dynamic simulation of a power grid containing a nuclear power station. *IFAC Proceedings Volumes*, *55*(22), 16.

Vaishnavi, S., ... (2025). Revolutionizing finance and accounting through AI-driven decision making. In *Convergence of AI, Education, and Business for Sustainability* (pp. 261–284). IGI Global. DOI: 10.4018/979-8-3373-1917-9.ch012

Wang, H., Zhang, H., & Li, F. (2020). Application of data mining theory in power grid equipment defect. *Power System Technology*, (12), 3.

Wang, J., & Li, Y. (2017). The building of urban power grid information database and its data mining. *Energy Education Science and Technology*, (9), 3.

Wang, Y., Zhao, H., & Zhang, Q. (2021). Hybrid machine learning models for portfolio optimization. *Journal of Financial Econometrics*, *32*(6), 142–158.

Yashini, P., Karthika, G., Sunitha, T. R., Renugadevi, R., & Magthalin, B. R. (2024). Machine learning-based textile fabric defect detection network. In *4th International Conference on Sustainable Expert Systems (ICSES)* (pp. 1470–1477).

Ye, S., Wen, H., Qiu, Y., Pan, X., & Wang, C. (2024). Simulation of annual investment forecast of power grid infrastructure construction based on data mining algorithm. In *2024 Asia-Pacific Conference on Software Engineering, Social Network Analysis and Intelligent Computing (SSAIC)* (pp. 99–104). New Delhi, India. DOI: 10.1109/SSAIC61213.2024.00025

Yin, T. (2018). Data mining application to power grid PMU data (Master's thesis, University of Wyoming). https://doi.org/DOI: 10.13140/RG.2.2.27662.45125

Zeng, Z., Li, X., & Liu, Y. (2020). Machine learning-based risk assessment models for investment projects. *International Journal of Project Management*, *38*(2), 154–163. DOI: 10.1016/j.ijproman.2019.10.005

Chapter 8
Leveraging Business Intelligence for Gender Inclusivity and Talent Equity in Data-Driven Workplaces

Mary Viterouli
https://orcid.org/0000-0001-6505-1659
University of Thessaly, Greece

Dimitrios Belias
https://orcid.org/0000-0003-3409-6875
University of Thessaly, Greece

Athanasios Koustelios
University of Thessaly, Greece

Nikolaos Tsigilis
Aristotle University of Thessaloniki, Greece

ABSTRACT

This chapter explores the role of Business Intelligence (BI) in enhancing gender equity and work-life balance within data-driven workplaces. By reviewing existing research, the chapter examines how BI tools can monitor gender representation, track turnover rates, identify biases in recruitment processes, and tailor work-life balance policies to meet the specific needs of male and female employees. It highlights the importance of leveraging data-driven insights to foster inclusivity and enhance

DOI: 10.4018/979-8-3373-1942-1.ch008

gender equity in organizations. This work provides actionable recommendations for integrating BI tools into talent management strategies to create more equitable and adaptable workplaces.

1. INTRODUCTION

In recent years, diversity, equity, and inclusion (DEI) have emerged as central pillars in modern organizational practices. The growing recognition of the benefits of a diverse workforce (Papademetriou et al., 2024; Dowling et al., 2022), ranging from enhanced decision-making to greater innovation, has led many companies to invest heavily in DEI initiatives. Despite these efforts, gender disparities persist in key areas such as recruitment, promotions, pay equity, and work-life balance (Viterouli et al., 2024a). Men and women often prioritize different aspects of their careers, shaped by societal expectations, caregiving responsibilities, and individual professional goals. For organizations striving to address these disparities and build more inclusive workplaces (Ntalakos, Belias & Tsigilis, 2022), Business Intelligence (BI) tools present a transformative opportunity.

Business Intelligence, with its ability to aggregate, analyse, and visualize data, has the potential to bridge the gender data gap that hinders progress in achieving true equality in the workplace (Sharma, Kumar & Gundewar, 2025). By utilizing BI systems, organizations can uncover hidden gender-based preferences, identify unconscious biases in recruitment processes, and measure the impact of DEI initiatives with precision (Al-Quhfa et al., 2024). BI tools offer valuable insights into gender representation across various departments, track turnover patterns, and monitor the effectiveness of work-life balance policies, ultimately fostering a more inclusive and adaptive work environment.

This study seeks to explore how BI can be leveraged to promote gender equality in talent management (D'Angelo et al., 2024; Jabeen et al., 2024), focusing on three key areas: (1) uncovering and addressing gender disparities in hiring, promotions, and pay, (2) promoting gender diversity through BI-driven DEI initiatives, and (3) tailoring work-life balance policies to meet gender-specific needs. Through an analysis of current literature and research questions, this paper highlights the role of BI in enhancing gender equity and its potential for shaping more inclusive, data-driven workplace strategies.

In addressing these topics, this work examines the ways in which BI can provide actionable insights to optimize talent management practices. It considers how trends in flexible work preferences can be analyzed by gender, how the effectiveness of policies like parental leave and hybrid work options can be measured, and how biases in recruitment processes can be identified and mitigated (Viterouli et al.,

2023; Belias, Velissariou & Rossidis, 2019). Ultimately, this research underscores the need for a data-informed approach to DEI that not only uncovers existing gender disparities but also enables organizations to design policies that respond to the unique needs of all employees.

1.1 Objectives of the Chapter

The main aim of this chapter is to provide a thorough understanding of the significance of data-driven approaches in modern workplaces, and introduce the evolving role of data-driven strategies in addressing gender dynamics, inclusivity, and work-life balance in talent management.. The primary objectives are as follows in order to highlight the importance of leveraging BI to create equitable workplaces and improve organizational success:

1. To explore the role of BI in bridging the gender data gap.
2. To examine how BI supports Diversity, Equity, and Inclusion (DEI).
3. To analyse BI's role in addressing gender-specific work-life balance needs.

2. LITERATURE REVIEW

2.1 Business Intelligence: Transforming Data into Actionable Insights

Business Intelligence (BI) encompasses a suite of tools, technologies, practices, and strategies designed to collect, integrate, analyse, and present business data. By transforming raw data into actionable insights, BI enables organizations to make informed, data-driven decisions (Tavera Romero et al., 2021). This transformative process is essential for modern business operations, ensuring agility and competitiveness in dynamic market environments. Through BI, organizations extract value from vast amounts of data, turning it into a strategic asset that supports informed decision-making at all levels (Adewusi et al., 2024).

Figure 1. Core components of Business Intelligence (BI)

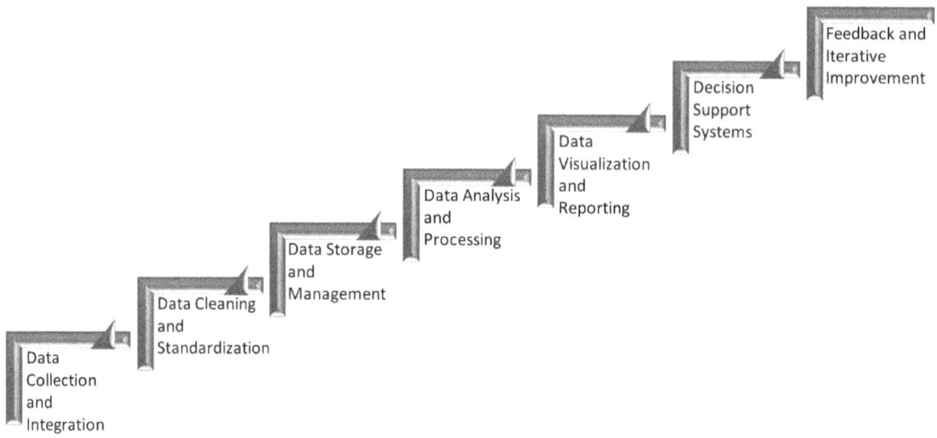

A critical component of BI is data collection and integration. The process begins with gathering information from multiple sources, including databases, spreadsheets, cloud services, and enterprise applications. BI platforms unify these disparate data streams into a single system, ensuring all relevant information is accessible for further analysis. This integration eliminates data silos, enhances accuracy, and provides a comprehensive view of organizational performance. Once data is collected, it undergoes cleaning and standardization to ensure quality. This involves removing inconsistencies, duplicates, and errors while standardizing formats to facilitate accurate analysis (Adewusi et al., 2024). Clean and standardized data forms the foundation for reliable insights that organizations can trust. Following data integration and cleaning, the data is stored and managed in structured environments such as data warehouses or data lakes. These repositories are designed to organize data efficiently, enabling quick retrieval and analysis. Robust storage systems ensure data is secure, scalable, and readily available for decision-making. Once the data is stored, it is analysed using statistical techniques and advanced analytics. This process allows BI systems to uncover trends, patterns, and relationships that may not be immediately apparent. Predictive analytics, a specialized subset of BI, leverages historical data to forecast future trends, empowering organizations to adopt proactive decision-making approaches.

The insights derived from analysis are then presented through data visualization and reporting. Visualization tools play a pivotal role in translating complex data sets into intuitive formats such as dashboards, graphs, and charts. Dashboards, in particular, offer interactive and real-time monitoring of critical indicators, enabling users to drill down into data for a more granular view of organizational dynamics.

Reports provide detailed insights into performance metrics, while visualizations like heatmaps, line graphs, or comparative bar charts simplify the interpretation of key trends and metrics. This step enhances understanding and communication within the organization, ensuring decision-makers are equipped with actionable insights (Tavera Romero et al., 2021). The ultimate purpose of BI is to support decision-making. By providing insights that are both actionable and accessible, BI enables organizations to improve operations, identify opportunities, and address challenges. Decision-making is further enhanced by tools such as dashboards and predictive analytics, which help businesses anticipate market shifts, optimize resource allocation, and develop proactive strategies for growth. BI systems are designed for continuous improvement, incorporating user feedback and evolving business needs. This iterative process ensures that BI systems remain relevant, effective, and capable of adapting to changing conditions.

In the realm of talent management (Belias & Trihas, 2023a), BI delivers transformative benefits. Organizations use BI to analyse employee performance, identify training needs, and uncover career development opportunities. BI is also instrumental in assessing employee satisfaction and engagement levels, offering insights into the drivers of retention and productivity (Belias et al., 2022). Furthermore, BI systems enable the monitoring of diversity metrics to ensure fair hiring practices and equitable treatment across the workforce. Workforce planning and resource allocation are also optimized, ensuring talent is deployed effectively to meet organizational objectives. Examples of BI tools that facilitate these outcomes include Power BI, Tableau, QlikView, and SAP BusinessObjects (Tripathi et al., 2023). These platforms empower organizations to harness the full potential of their data, driving informed decisions that enhance efficiency, inclusivity, and innovation. As workplaces increasingly adopt data-driven strategies, BI continues to shape the future of business operations, bridging the gap between raw data and actionable insights.

2.2 The Gender Data Gap in Talent Management

The gender data gap in talent management continues to challenge efforts toward equity and inclusivity within organizations. This gap stems from the persistent use of incomplete or biased data, which often overlooks critical gender-specific disparities in key areas such as hiring practices, promotions, and pay structures. Existing studies reveal that these disparities are deeply embedded in organizational processes and are frequently perpetuated by unconscious biases and systemic barriers (Artz, Kaya & Kaya, 2022; Bapna & Ganco, 2021). Addressing these challenges requires robust, data-driven methodologies, with Business Intelligence (BI) offering a transformative solution. Research has also highlighted that gender bias in hiring processes is a significant contributor to workplace inequities (Burbano, Padilla & Meier, 2024).

From job descriptions that unconsciously favour one gender to the disproportionate representation of men in leadership roles, organizations often struggle to achieve gender parity. Similarly, compensation studies consistently identify pay gaps that disadvantage women, even when controlling for variables such as education, experience, and performance. BI tools, by aggregating and analysing data across recruitment, promotion, and compensation workflows, allow organizations to uncover these inequities. This raises the critical question:

RQ1. How can BI uncover and address gender disparities in hiring, promotions, and pay?

Beyond identifying disparities, BI can provide actionable insights into gender-based preferences in work styles, benefits, and professional development opportunities. Research indicates that men and women may exhibit distinct priorities, influenced by factors such as cultural norms, caregiving responsibilities, and individual career aspirations (Coffman, Flikkema & Shurchkov, 2021). For instance, studies suggest that women are more likely to value flexible work arrangements and mentorship programs, whereas men may prioritize skill-building opportunities and financial incentives. Despite these insights, many organizations fail to incorporate such preferences into their talent strategies, leading to disengagement and dissatisfaction among employees (Burbano, Padilla & Meier, 2024). BI systems, through advanced analytics and predictive models, can uncover these preferences and guide the development of tailored policies. This prompts a second question:

RQ2. What gender-based preferences in work styles and benefits can BI identify?

Organizations can move beyond traditional, generalized approaches to talent management and implement strategies that are both equitable and data-informed, by addressing these two questions. The integration of BI in this context not only bridges the gender data gap but also creates a foundation for building inclusive and adaptive workplaces.

2.3 Diversity, Equity, and Inclusion

Diversity, Equity, and Inclusion (DEI) have emerged as fundamental pillars of modern talent management, driving organizational success through the cultivation of diverse and equitable workplaces. Gender diversity, in particular, plays a critical role in fostering innovation, enhancing decision-making, and improving overall organizational performance. Despite these benefits, achieving meaningful progress in DEI initiatives remains a significant challenge for many organizations. Systemic biases, both explicit and implicit, often hinder efforts to create inclusive environments (D'Angelo et al., 2024). Business Intelligence (BI) offers transformative potential in this regard, enabling organizations to measure, monitor, and promote gender diversity across all levels. Its tools excel at providing real-time tracking of gender representation and turnover rates, offering a clear picture of workforce dynamics. Dashboards and analytics platforms, are representative examples which can reveal disparities in representation by department, level, or region, allowing leaders to identify areas requiring intervention. Moreover, BI systems can monitor turnover patterns to determine whether women, or other underrepresented genders, are leaving the organization at higher rates than their male counterparts (Hargrave & Blumenau, 2022). Such insights enable organizations to address retention issues with targeted strategies, such as mentorship programs or enhanced workplace flexibility. This reality underscores the critical question:

RQ3. How can BI track and analyse gender representation and turnover rates?

Another area where BI demonstrates significant utility is in addressing biases embedded within recruitment algorithms. Research has shown that algorithmic systems, when trained on historical hiring data, can perpetuate existing biases by favouring candidates from traditionally dominant demographics (Heilman, Caleo & Manzi, 2024). BI tools allow organizations to audit and evaluate recruitment processes, identifying discriminatory patterns and implementing adjustments to promote fairness. For instance, advanced analytics can highlight whether certain job descriptions discourage women from applying or if gender-specific biases influence candidate shortlisting. Furthermore, BI systems can guide the development of customized development programs aimed at advancing the careers of underrepresented genders, addressing inequities in training opportunities and leadership pipelines. These capabilities prompt a second question:

RQ4. What role does BI play in addressing biases in recruitment algorithms?

Leveraging BI to advance DEI goals can enhance an organization's capacity to create workplaces that are not only more inclusive but also more competitive. Data-driven strategies ensure transparency, accountability, and measurable progress, providing a solid foundation for sustainable growth. Ultimately, the integration of BI into DEI initiatives represents a crucial step toward achieving equitable talent management practices.

2.4 Gender-Specific Work-Life Balance Needs

Work-life balance is a critical aspect of employee satisfaction and productivity, yet it is far from a one-size-fits-all challenge. Research consistently shows that men and women often prioritize different aspects of work-life balance, shaped by societal expectations, caregiving roles, and personal career goals. For instance, women may place greater emphasis on flexibility and parental leave policies, while men might prioritize autonomy and financial stability in their professional lives (Viterouli et al., 2024b). These differences necessitate a data-driven approach to designing inclusive and effective workplace policies. Business Intelligence (BI) provides a powerful means to address these varied needs, offering tools to analyse, monitor, and optimize work-life balance initiatives.

One key application of BI lies in analysing trends in flexible work preferences by gender. Through employee surveys, performance metrics, and other data streams, BI tools can identify how different genders value and utilize flexible work arrangements, such as remote work, adjusted hours, or compressed schedules (Belias & Trihas, 2022a). These insights enable organizations to design policies that accommodate diverse preferences while maintaining productivity. For example, BI analytics can reveal whether women are more likely to opt for part-time roles after maternity leave or whether men are utilizing hybrid work models to manage caregiving responsibilities. This leads to the important question of:

RQ5. How does BI analyse trends in flexible work preferences by gender?

In addition to analysing preferences, BI aids in measuring the effectiveness of work-life balance initiatives (Viterouli et al., 2024b). Tools like real-time reporting systems can monitor the uptake and impact of parental leave programs, caregiving support, and hybrid work options. For example, BI systems can track employee retention rates and engagement levels before and after implementing such policies, providing concrete evidence of their success or highlighting areas for improvement. Furthermore, case studies from organizations that have successfully utilized BI to enhance work-life balance initiatives offer valuable lessons. These examples demonstrate how data-driven insights lead to more inclusive workplaces (Dowling et al., 2022) by addressing the unique challenges faced by employees of different genders. This raises the next question:

RQ6. Can BI measure the effectiveness of initiatives like parental leave and hybrid work options?

Work-life balance strategies can be tailored via the utilisation of BI so that organizations not only improve employee satisfaction but also foster a culture of inclusivity and adaptability. This approach recognizes the diverse needs of the workforce, ensuring that no demographic is overlooked or underserved. BI, as a cornerstone of modern talent management, provides the tools necessary to align organizational goals with the well-being of employees, creating a workplace where everyone can thrive.

3. METHODOLOGY

3.1 Research Approach

This study is based on a comprehensive literature review (Taherdoost, 2022) aimed at understanding the role of Business Intelligence (BI) tools in addressing gender disparities within talent management practices, particularly in recruitment, promotions, pay equity, and work-life balance. Through synthesizing research findings, case studies, and reports, this study explores how BI tools can highlight and mitigate gender-specific inequities in organizations, focusing on gender-specific preferences for work-life balance, flexible work arrangements, and related challenges. Via consolidating secondary data, the review offers an in-depth exploration of how BI applications contribute to fostering gender diversity, equity, and inclusion (DEI) within talent management frameworks.

3.2 Data Collection

As a literature review, this study primarily draws on secondary sources, which include peer-reviewed academic articles, case studies, and real-world examples. These studies explore the application of BI tools in managing gender disparities, focusing on areas such as gender representation, recruitment practices, work-life balance, and promotions. The detailed accounts from companies that have integrated BI tools are analyzed to assess their real-world impact on gender equality. These examples serve as a basis for identifying both efficient strategies and main challenges faced in the implementation of BI tools.

3.3 Data Analysis

The data analysis involves a synthesis of the reviewed literature to address key research questions. The analysis focuses on several key areas. First, it examines how BI tools assist organizations in detecting and addressing gender disparities in core

HR functions, such as recruitment, promotions, and pay, by analysing existing studies and case studies to assess how BI helps uncover unconscious biases and promote gender fairness. Second, the review analyses how BI tools are employed to scrutinize recruitment algorithms, ensuring they are free from gender biases, highlighting how BI aids organizations in adjusting algorithmic patterns that may unintentionally favour one gender over another. Another key area of focus is understanding how BI tools help organizations track and analyse gender-specific preferences in work-life balance, such as flexible working conditions, parental leave, and caregiving roles. In other words, it explores how BI applications can enable more inclusive and equitable work-life balance policies, specifically designed to address gendered needs and challenges in the workplace.

3.3.1 Gender-Based Inequity and Preferences

Gender disparities in professional and societal contexts present persistent challenges, revealing structural and cultural gaps that influence access to opportunities, preferences, and outcomes within various industries. These inequities go beyond individual barriers, demonstrating the need for systemic changes in both talent management strategies and organizational practices. For instance, Rukmiyati et al. (2024) conducted a comprehensive review of financial access for women entrepreneurs, identifying key factors that perpetuate gender inequality, such as biases inherent in financial systems and societal norms. The authors found that limited access to mentorship and the prevalence of economic instability were significant barriers, particularly in low- and middle-income regions. This study highlights the need for targeted policies that promote gender equality in financial access, which, in turn, would empower women and contribute to broader economic growth, underscoring the importance of these factors for inclusive talent development.

Similarly, Rao and Taboada (2021) examined media representations that reinforce gender stereotypes, particularly the portrayal of women in caregiving roles and men in leadership positions. These skewed societal narratives significantly impact perceptions of professional competence and potential, influencing talent acquisition and development strategies. Their methodology for analysing media coverage offers a scalable tool to assess and mitigate bias in professional contexts, such as recruitment and promotion practices. In a related study, Jabeen et al. (2024) explored the intersection of gender, race, and socioeconomic status in Human Resource Management (HRM). Their findings revealed that despite the adoption of gender-inclusive practices, significant challenges persist, such as unequal representation of women in leadership positions. Addressing these disparities is essential for creating equitable talent pipelines and fostering organizational performance.

In the field of educational leadership, Nkosi (2024) investigated empowerment strategies for women leaders, identifying mentorship, professional networks, and policy reforms as critical tools for overcoming systemic barriers and societal expectations that limit women's leadership potential. This reinforces the need for talent management systems that promote inclusive leadership development and capacity-building. Domestically, Triantafillidou and Yannas (2021) studied the experiences of female public relations professionals in Greece, revealing the dual expectations to embody both feminine and masculine traits. This "gyno-androus" model, reflecting societal stereotypes, influences leadership perceptions and career progression, emphasizing the need for gender-sensitive policies that mitigate biases and foster diverse talent pools. Miliopoulou and Kapareliotis (2021) examined the career trajectories of senior female executives in Greek advertising, highlighting how gender, age, and profession intersect to shape career outcomes. Their study pointed to a lack of solidarity among women in leadership positions, reinforcing male-dominated structures. Their findings advocate for collective action and awareness to advance gender equity within talent management.

In addition to systemic barriers, gendered preferences also shape the dynamics of talent management. These preferences influence how individuals engage with work and leadership opportunities. For example, Nguyen and Armoogum (2021) explored gendered preferences for home-based telework (HBT) during the COVID-19 pandemic, revealing that women were more likely to value HBT for its compatibility with family responsibilities, while men emphasized work-related factors. These findings suggest the importance of gender-sensitive telework policies that cater to diverse employee needs, thereby enhancing work-life balance and improving talent retention. Errani et al. (2021) examined gender disparities within healthcare professions, identifying stereotypes that hinder women's entry into male-dominated specialties, such as orthopaedics, while also limiting men's access to female-dominated fields like gynecology. These institutional biases, coupled with work-life balance challenges, affect talent distribution and career progression. In a different context, Vo, Nguyen, and Le (2021) analyzed the performance of firms led by female CEOs in Vietnam, finding that women's risk-averse and collaborative leadership styles contributed to higher profitability and lower organizational risk. This study highlights the value of promoting gender diversity in leadership roles to optimize organizational performance and talent utilization.

Burbano, Padilla, and Meier (2024) explored how men and women derive meaning in their work, finding that women prioritize mission-driven roles, while men focus on autonomy. These differing preferences influence career trajectories and industry representation, further shaping talent management strategies. Collectively, these studies underscore the significance of addressing gender-specific disparities and preferences within talent management frameworks. They reveal how biases and gendered expectations influence workforce outcomes, from financial access to leadership styles and work preferences. The interconnected nature of these challenges requires the development of a structured framework that incorporates gender-sensitive policies and practices in talent management. Figure 2 provides a comprehensive approach to mitigating gender-based inequities and promoting inclusive talent management practices, illustrating how organizations can address these systemic challenges and foster a more equitable work environment.

Figure 2. Framework for addressing gender-based inequity and preferences in talent management

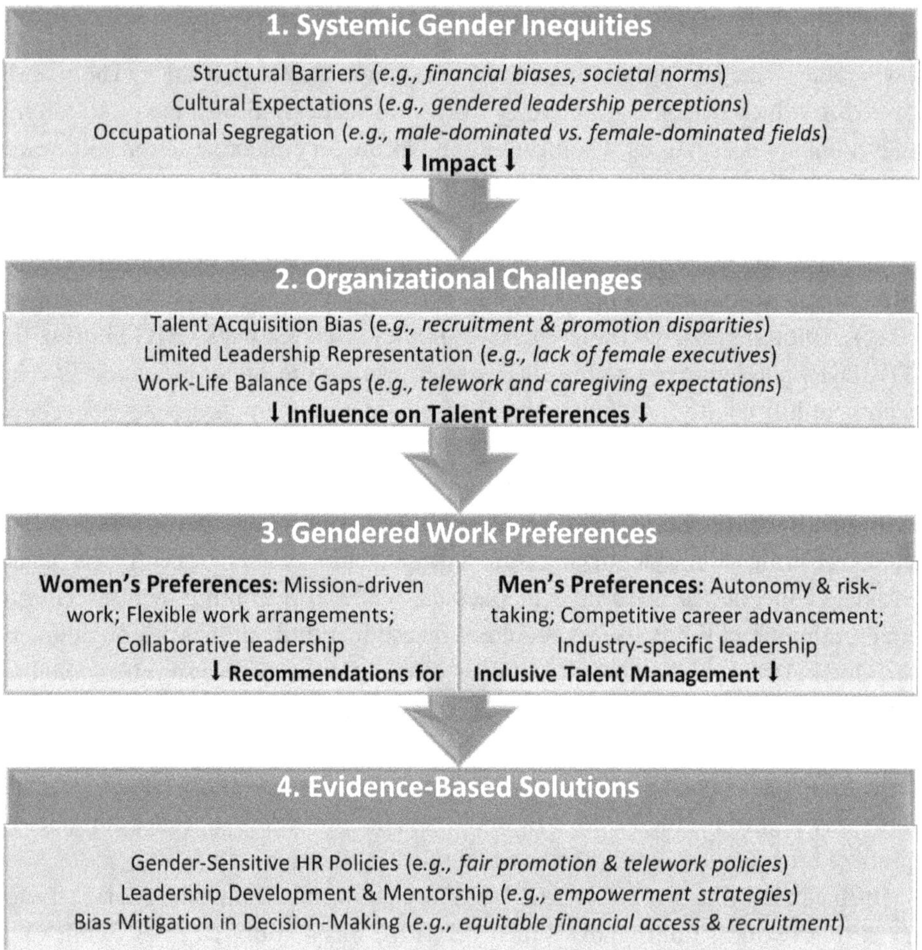

3.3.2 Addressing Gender Ostracism

The representation of gender in the workforce, alongside the effectiveness of recruitment processes, is intricately linked to broader organizational outcomes, particularly turnover rates and career progression. As organizations make concerted efforts to enhance gender diversity, there has been increased awareness of the systemic barriers that disproportionately affect women. These barriers manifest in higher turnover rates and biases within recruitment algorithms. Despite notable progress in improving female representation, challenges persist, especially in environments where unconscious biases and stereotypical expectations continue to shape workplace dynamics. Research by Maurer and Qureshi (2021) provides valuable insights into the relationship between female representation and organizational turnover. Their study, which analyzed data from 499 organizations over a span of 14 years using latent curve model (LCM) analysis, suggests that a rapid increase in female workforce participation not only benefits women but also has positive spillover effects on male employees. Specifically, greater female representation is associated with increased job embeddedness, leading to reduced turnover rates for the entire workforce. This finding has practical implications for managers seeking to foster a more stable workforce by promoting gender diversity.

Similarly, D'Angelo et al. (2024) explore gender disparities in academia, particularly in the field of Software Engineering (SE). Their study uncovered distinct collaboration patterns and promotion biases that contribute to gender disparities in career progression. While men in SE tend to form tightly-knit networks, women exhibit more global co-authorship relationships. The study also found that promotions to Associate Professor positions in SE are more biased compared to other fields, with a less pronounced bias in promotions to Full Professor roles. These findings highlight the need for more targeted research into gender dynamics in academia, especially in specialized fields like SE, where gendered networks and biases continue to influence career trajectories. The role of gender stereotypes in career advancement is another significant factor that affects turnover rates. Heilman, Caleo, and Manzi (2024) reviewed how gender stereotypes hinder women's career progression, particularly in male-dominated fields. They identified two key pathways through which gender stereotypes manifest in workplace discrimination: the perception of women as communal but lacking the agentic qualities valued in leadership roles, and the penalties women face when exhibiting behaviours that contradict traditional gender norms. Understanding these dynamics is critical for organizations seeking to promote more equitable workplace processes and reduce gender bias.

In the realm of entrepreneurship, Bapna and Ganco (2021) examined investor preferences in high-stakes equity crowdfunding and found that gender gaps in investor interest vary based on investor experience. Their research revealed that inexperienced female investors are more likely to support female founders, whereas experienced investors show no gender preference. Male investors, regardless of experience, did not display any gender-based preference in their investment choices. This research highlights the evolving dynamics of gender preferences in investment, particularly in crowdfunding environments, and underscores the importance of understanding how gender perceptions shift across different contexts. Lastly, Spoon et al. (2023) explored gender differences in faculty retention within U.S. PhD-granting institutions, finding that women leave academia at higher rates than men at all career stages. This gendered attrition is particularly pronounced in lower-prestige institutions, non-STEM fields, and among tenured faculty. The study showed that women are more likely to feel "pushed" out of their roles due to issues with workplace climate, while men tend to leave for better career opportunities. These gendered reasons for attrition emphasize the need to address the systemic factors that contribute to the gender gap in academia and improve retention strategies for women in higher education.

While increasing female representation and addressing turnover rates are critical for organizational stability, the effectiveness of these efforts is often hindered by biases in recruitment and selection processes. As organizations work to diversify their workforce, recruitment algorithms, which are increasingly used in hiring decisions, may unintentionally perpetuate gendered biases. For example, Al-Quhfa et al. (2024) demonstrated how machine learning models can enhance recruitment accuracy and efficiency, but they also highlight the challenge of algorithmic bias. While advanced models like Random Forest and Neural Networks have shown promise in improving recruitment outcomes, these tools can still replicate or amplify existing biases, particularly gender biases, unless they are carefully designed and monitored. In more detail, they investigated how machine learning models can enhance recruitment accuracy and efficiency within business intelligence systems. Analysing recruitment data from a Yemeni organization between 2019 and 2022, the study compares various models, including K-Nearest Neighbors, Logistic Regression, Support Vector Machine, Naive Bayes, Decision Trees, Random Forest, Gradient Boosting Classifier, AdaBoost Classifier, and Neural Networks. The Random Forest model emerged as the most effective, achieving 92.8% accuracy. The research emphasizes that advanced machine learning techniques, particularly Random Forest and Neural Networks, can significantly improve recruitment processes and recommends their integration into talent acquisition strategies. The study also addresses challenges related to the adoption of predictive analytics in recruitment, including data privacy concerns and the potential for algorithmic bias.

Moreover, Kelan (2024) examines the role of artificial intelligence (AI) in hiring processes and challenges the assumption that AI will inherently reduce human bias in recruitment. The article focuses on the factors of data, design, and decisions in AI-driven hiring, highlighting issues such as organizational fit, categorization, and intersectionality. Despite the promise of AI to improve recruitment outcomes, the article points out that biases – particularly those related to gender – may be replicated or even amplified within AI systems. It calls for a more comprehensive approach to AI design, one that carefully considers which groups hold influence over the technology and how subjective judgments are integrated. While AI is expected to improve recruitment decisions, the article notes the lack of research on how human-machine collaboration impacts decision-making and stresses the need for better auditing and regulation to ensure inclusivity in AI hiring systems. In parallel, Tilmes (2022) focuses on the intersection of disability, fairness, and algorithmic bias in AI recruitment. The study critiques the current approaches to fairness in AI, which often overlook the diverse needs of disabled individuals. Despite attempts to minimize bias, AI tools frequently reinforce ableist stereotypes, such as misinterpreting the facial expressions, gait, or speech of people with disabilities. The paper advocates for a "disability justice" approach, emphasizing the lived experiences of disabled people and challenging structural biases in AI systems. The author suggests that current fairness frameworks are insufficient for ensuring accessibility and inclusivity, and that a broader understanding of fairness is needed, one that includes the social and political contexts surrounding disability.

On the other hand, Hargrave and Blumenau (2022) explore gendered communication styles in the UK Parliament, investigating whether female politicians are still expected to conform to traditionally feminine speech styles. The study reveals that the pressure on women to adopt stereotypically "feminine" communication styles has decreased in recent years, with women increasingly adopting "masculine" traits such as aggression and complexity in their speeches. Using text analysis of parliamentary debates from 1997 to 2019, the research finds that the gender-based differences in political communication styles have diminished, and women are now using more "agentic" (masculine) traits. This shift challenges traditional views of women's political styles as emotional or communal and suggests that gender stereotypes no longer accurately reflect the communication styles of modern politicians. The study contributes both methodologically and theoretically by showing that gender stereotypes are less relevant in describing parliamentary behaviour and by offering innovative ways to analyse political communication.

The impact of male and female supervisors on perceived gender discrimination in the workplace was examined by Lucifora and Vigani (2022) across 15 European countries from 2000 to 2015. The study finds that female supervisors are linked to lower levels of perceived gender discrimination, particularly for female employees in more complex or female-dominated jobs. Additionally, the presence of flexible work schedules and family-friendly policies further enhances this positive effect. This research adds to existing literature on gender discrimination by focusing on the relationship between supervisors' gender and employees' perceptions of discrimination, particularly in contexts that support work-life balance. The study highlights the importance of female leadership in reducing discrimination and emphasizes the role of workplace policies in mitigating gender inequality. Moreover, gender biases in group decision-making, focusing on how individuals are selected to represent their group based on the ideas they contribute was explored by Coffman, Flikkema, and Shurchkov (2021). Their study finds that women are less likely to be chosen for representation, especially in domains stereotypically associated with men. This bias is more pronounced when participants are aware of each other's gender. Even when the quality of ideas is the same, individuals from the gender majority tend to self-promote more. The research suggests that gender stereotypes play a significant role in these decisions, with communication styles, especially in natural language, amplifying these biases. The findings point to the need for awareness and mitigation strategies to address gender biases in group decision-making processes.

Ranganathan et al. (2021) investigate the representation of women in tenure-track geoscience faculty positions in the United States from 1999 to 2020. The study identifies slow progress toward gender parity and analyses factors such as hiring, promotion, and attrition rates that contribute to the underrepresentation of women in senior academic positions. The research reveals that faculty attrition, particularly among women, is influenced by workplace climate factors such as discrimination, lack of belonging, and poor leadership, whereas men tend to leave academia for professional opportunities. The study underscores that while men and women share similar reasons for leaving academia, the gendered experiences, particularly related to work environment, result in higher attrition rates among women. The research calls for targeted strategies to improve workplace climate and enhance support for women in academia, including better work-life balance policies and addressing institutional biases that perpetuate gender disparities.

These findings highlight that gender inequalities persist across different organizational settings, including recruitment, promotions, turnover rates, and decision-making processes. Despite efforts to improve inclusion, gender representation, and fairness, systemic biases – whether in hiring algorithms, workplace cultures, or career advancement – continue to impede progress toward gender equality. As illustrated in Figure 3, these factors contribute to gender disparities in turnover, career advancement, and recruitment biases. Workplace culture, structural barriers, and implicit biases shape distinct career trajectories for men and women, with the interactions between these elements reinforcing patterns of inequality. To address these disparities, it is crucial to adopt more thorough, data-driven strategies, such as better-designed recruitment technologies, supportive workplace policies, and fostering more inclusive organizational cultures.

Figure 3. Framework for understanding the role of gender ostracism in work-life balance

3.3.3 Gender-Specific Work-Life Balance Needs to Flexible Work Preferences and Initiatives

In recent years, the intersection of gender-specific needs and work-life balance has become a central focus in research on workplace dynamics. Gender influences both the preferences for flexible work arrangements and the effectiveness of work-life balance interventions. By examining trends in remote work, hybrid work, and technology-based initiatives, as well as gender disparities in caregiving responsibilities and burnout, it becomes clear that a one-size-fits-all approach is insufficient for addressing the diverse needs of male and female employees. Understanding these gendered differences is crucial for organizations seeking to create inclusive and effective work environments that support work-life balance for all employees.

One significant shift in work dynamics arose from the COVID-19 pandemic, which dramatically transformed the nature of work, particularly through the widespread adoption of remote work (RW). Initially considered a voluntary arrangement, remote work became a vital adaptation for businesses seeking to maintain operations and ensure public health safety. While remote work presented several benefits, it also exposed unique challenges for female employees. Joshi and Kumar (2023) offer an insightful analysis into these challenges, particularly the intensified gender inequalities that emerged during the pandemic. They highlight the disproportionate caregiving burdens faced by women working remotely, further complicating their ability to achieve work-life balance. Moreover, the study explores the potential role of artificial intelligence (AI)-driven solutions in alleviating these gender disparities, advocating for strategies that promote gender equity within evolving work environments. The authors stress the need for continued research to effectively address these disparities, ensuring that emerging workplace solutions cater to the needs of both genders equitably.

As workplaces adapt to post-pandemic realities, hybrid work models have gained significant traction, providing employees with greater flexibility. Dowling et al. (2022) explore the growing preference for hybrid work arrangements and their impact on diversity, equity, and inclusion (DEI). Hybrid work offers enhanced work-life balance and a more personalized employee experience, but it also presents risks. If not managed effectively, hybrid work can exacerbate existing inequities, particularly among underrepresented groups, and lead to potential employee departures or reduced inclusion. The study emphasizes that many employees, especially from underrepresented groups, prefer hybrid models and are resistant to returning to fully on-site roles. To mitigate these risks and maximize the benefits of hybrid work, organizations must focus on three key inclusion practices: work-life support, team building, and mutual respect. By actively listening to employees' needs and continuously reassessing flexibility, organizations can create more inclusive environments that attract top talent and ensure equity across all employee demographics.

Beyond these broader trends in flexible work arrangements, gender-specific preferences in occupational choices remain a persistent issue. Kuhn and Wolter (2022) investigate the role of gender segregation in career paths, particularly how preferences for working with "things" versus "people" influence gendered career choices. Drawing on detailed data from Switzerland's apprenticeship system, the authors find that women tend to favour people-oriented jobs, while men are more inclined toward tasks involving "things." This gendered distinction in occupational preferences strongly predicts career choices and persists even when controlling for individual, parental, and regional factors. The study further explores how these preferences manifest in adolescents' career aspirations, confirming that gender differences in vocational interests remain consistent over time. This research highlights the deeper psychological and societal factors contributing to occupational gender segregation, which can limit career opportunities and impact gender diversity across various industries.

These studies collectively emphasize the evolving nature of work and its implications for gender equality. While flexible work arrangements, including remote and hybrid models, offer significant benefits for work-life balance, they also present unique challenges that require careful management. Moreover, understanding the persistent gendered preferences in occupational choices and tailoring workplace interventions accordingly is essential for addressing long-standing gender disparities in career advancement. Liu, Zhang, and Xu (2023) investigate the effectiveness of technology-based interventions in promoting physical activity and improving mental health, with particular attention to gender differences. The study reveals that these interventions significantly improved both physical activity levels and mental health outcomes, with women experiencing more pronounced improvements than men. Notably, the research identifies eight key motivations and barriers to engaging with technology for physical activity, revealing important gender differences in these factors. Women were found to be more motivated by social support, whereas men were driven by personalized features and competitive aspects. These findings underscore the importance of tailoring interventions to gendered preferences in order to maximize their impact on physical and mental well-being within workplace programs.

In a similar vein, Máiz-Mazuela et al. (2023) examined the challenges faced by essential workers in Spain during the first year of the COVID-19 syndemic, focusing on their work-life balance. Essential workers, including those in healthcare, social work, and food-related sectors, experienced increased work demands and a heavier burden of domestic and caregiving responsibilities, which significantly impacted their mental health. The study found that women, especially those in single-parent households or with children, shouldered most of the reproductive work, making it harder to balance professional and personal lives. Furthermore, the research explored the psychological effects of working in essential roles during the pandemic and the lack of social recognition, particularly for social workers. Adopting a gender perspective, the study highlights how gendered expectations and responsibilities shaped workers' experiences during the crisis. It shows that women were particularly affected by the dual pressures of paid work and unpaid caregiving duties. The research calls for urgent policy changes to address these gender disparities, improve working conditions, and offer better support to essential workers. Furthermore, it stresses the importance of recognizing the disproportionate psychological toll that caregiving responsibilities place on women, particularly during crisis situations.

In line with these findings, Artz, Kaya, and Kaya (2022) explore the higher rates of job-related burnout reported among women, a phenomenon frequently observed in workplace studies. The authors suggest that gendered societal expectations, rather than factors like workload, may contribute to the burnout gap. Specifically, women who adhere to traditional gender roles are more likely to experience burnout, whereas those with more progressive views on gender roles report burnout at rates similar to men. This study underscores the need to challenge societal perceptions of women's roles in the workplace and to provide organizational support that addresses these underlying gendered expectations.

In conclusion, the body of research presented here underscores the importance of gender-sensitive approaches when designing work-life balance initiatives. While flexible work arrangements, such as remote and hybrid models, can provide substantial benefits for work-life balance, they also present unique challenges that must be addressed through tailored interventions. Gendered preferences in occupational choices, caregiving responsibilities, and burnout risks all play a significant role in shaping work-life balance needs. Therefore, organizational strategies must account for these factors to ensure equitable support for both male and female employees in achieving a sustainable and fulfilling work-life balance. The conceptual framework for gender-specific work-life balance needs and flexible work preferences (Figure 4) provides a visual representation of the key factors influencing gendered work-life balance needs. This framework pinpoints the critical role of caregiving responsibilities, burnout disparities, and occupational preferences in shaping work flexibility choices. By considering these factors, organizations can implement more effective, gender-sensitive strategies that foster equitable and inclusive work environments, ultimately enhancing work-life balance for all employees.

Figure 4. Framework for gender-specific work-life balance needs and flexible work preferences

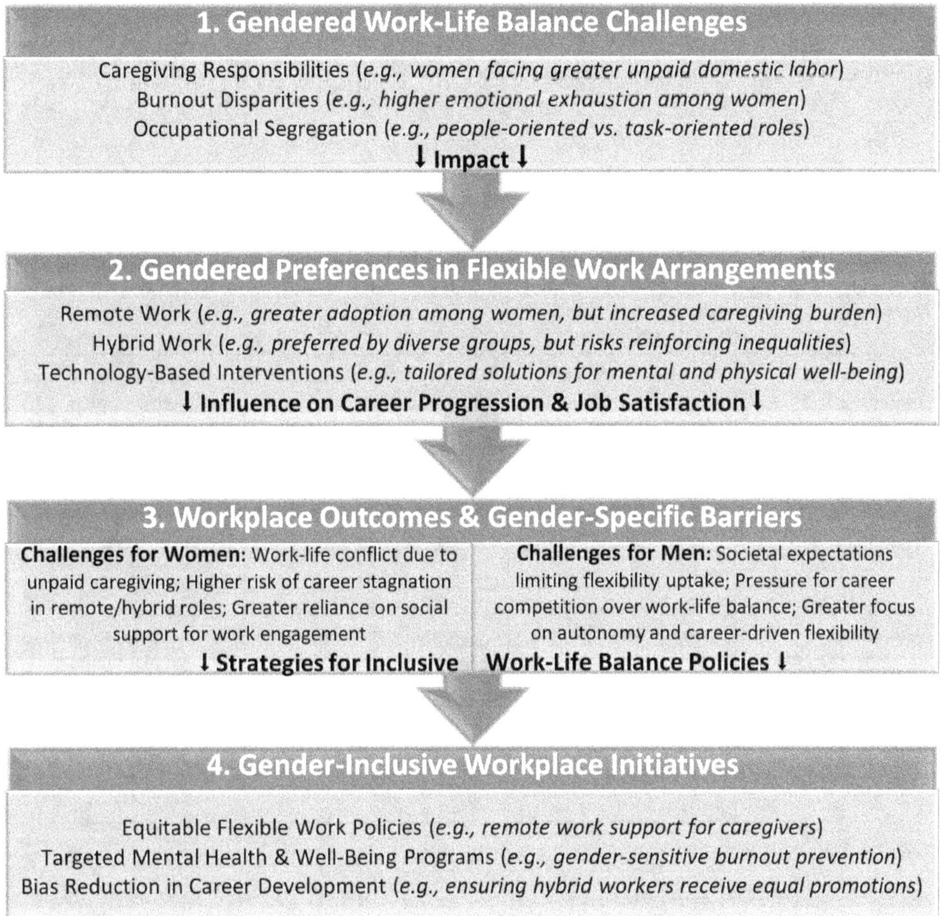

4. RESULTS

4.1 Uncovering and Addressing Gender Disparities

Business Intelligence (BI) tools serve as a crucial mechanism for promoting gender equality in contemporary talent management (Belias, Vasiliadis & Mantas, 2020) by identifying and addressing disparities in hiring, promotions, and pay. Through data-driven insights, organizations can foster more equitable workplace practices and ensure fair opportunities for all employees (Belias et al., 2023a;

Ntalakos, Belias & Tsigilis, 2023). Gender bias remains a significant challenge across organizational practices. Despite various efforts, women continue to be underrepresented in leadership roles, paid less than men in similar positions, and face barriers to career progression due to unconscious bias and systemic discrimination (Liargovas & Papageorgiou, 2024).

Table 1. Identifying and resolving gender inequities

Key Area	*BI Tool Role*	*Example Action*	*Outcome*
Gender Bias in Recruitment and Hiring	Analyze job descriptions and hiring data for gender-biased language.	Adjust job postings to ensure gender-neutral language.	Increased gender equality in recruitment and selection processes.
Gender Pay Gaps Analysis	Analyze salary data by gender, controlling for experience, education, etc.	Identify pay discrepancies and revise salary structures.	Equal pay for equal work across genders.
Addressing Gender Inequities in Promotions	Track gender-based promotion rates and identify biases in career progression.	Implement leadership training and mentorship for underrepresented genders.	More equitable promotion processes and reduced "glass ceiling" effect.
Building Gender-Neutral and Inclusive Workplace Cultures	Analyze employee engagement data to uncover gender-based bias.	Develop mentorship programs and improve career development for women.	Creation of a more inclusive and supportive workplace culture.
Closing the Gender Gap with Data-Driven Strategies	Set measurable gender equity goals and track progress.	Establish targets for gender diversity and monitor success.	Continuous improvement in gender equity with data-driven strategy adjustments.

Source: Authors' compilation

Gender Bias in Recruitment and Hiring

BI tools can be specifically designed to analyse and uncover gender biases in recruitment processes by integrating data from job postings, candidate pipelines, and hiring decisions. BI tools can analyse job descriptions to ensure they are gender-neutral (Rao & Taboada, 2021). They can detect language patterns in job postings that may unintentionally appeal more to one gender (e.g., words like "assertive" or "competitive" may be more attractive to male candidates). Using Natural Language Processing (NLP) algorithms (Papantoniou & Tzitzikas), BI systems can flag biased language, suggesting more inclusive alternatives (e.g., "collaborative" instead of "competitive"). Moreover, By integrating data from various hiring stages, BI tools can identify whether male candidates are more likely to be selected for interviews or job offers compared to female candidates with similar qualifications (Al-Quhfa et al., 2024). For instance, BI can track the proportion of male versus female applicants at each stage of the recruitment process (e.g., initial screening, interviews, and offers). If disparities are identified, organizations can investigate whether biases, such as a preference for male candidates, are influencing decisions. This information can prompt a review of the screening and interview processes to ensure fairness and implement practices like blind recruitment (where gender or other personal identifiers are excluded from the initial review stages).

Gender Pay Gaps Analysis

One of the most critical aspects of gender equity in the workplace is ensuring equal pay for equal work (Papademetriou, Anastasiadou & Konteos, 2022). BI tools can conduct in-depth salary analyses across different employee demographics to identify gender-based pay gaps. BI can analyse salary data while controlling for variables such as experience, education, job role, and geographic location. By examining the pay of male and female employees in similar roles, these systems can flag discrepancies that may indicate a gender-based pay gap. For example, if female employees in similar roles with the same qualifications are found to be paid less than their male counterparts, BI systems can identify this gap and provide actionable insights to address it, such as revising salary structures or conducting compensation audits. Additionally, once a gender pay gap is identified, BI tools can help organizations set benchmarks for pay adjustments and create policies for salary equity (Tripathi et al., 2023). For instance, a company might use BI to calculate the exact amount required to bring female employees' salaries in line with their male counterparts, ensuring equal compensation for equal work. This data can be used to develop a long-term strategy for salary adjustments across the organization, creating a transparent and accountable approach to closing pay gaps.

Addressing Gender Inequities in Promotions

Gender disparities in promotions are often due to unconscious biases and the "glass ceiling" effect (Espinosa & Ferreira, 2022). BI tools can analyse internal promotion data to identify whether there are any gender-based differences in promotion rates and career progression. BI can track promotion rates over time, identifying whether men are being promoted at higher rates than women, despite having similar qualifications and performance records. For instance, if BI analysis shows that male employees in a particular department are promoted faster than female employees, the tool can suggest areas for further investigation, such as assessing performance evaluation processes or leadership development opportunities (Viterouli et al.,

2024a). For instance, predictive analytics within BI can help organizations identify whether women are underrepresented in leadership roles. For example, a predictive model can analyse past promotion data to determine if there are systemic barriers preventing women from advancing into senior management positions. This information can then guide the development of targeted leadership training programs aimed at preparing women for higher-level roles, ensuring they have the necessary support, mentorship, and opportunities to advance.

Building Gender-Neutral and Inclusive Workplace Cultures

Beyond hiring, pay, and promotions, BI tools can be used to foster a more inclusive organizational culture. By collecting and analysing data on employee engagement, satisfaction, and experiences in the workplace, BI can highlight areas where gender-based discrimination or bias may exist (Belias et al., 2023b). Organizations can deploy employee surveys to gather insights about workplace culture, including experiences related to gender discrimination, harassment, or unequal treatment. BI tools can then analyse these surveys to identify trends and highlight any gender disparities in employee satisfaction. For example, if female employees report lower satisfaction with their career development opportunities, BI can help identify the underlying causes and suggest targeted interventions, such as mentoring programs or improved career counselling services for women. Naturally, organizations can use BI to track gender diversity metrics across various departments and levels of the company (Heilman, Caleo & Manzi, 2024). By tracking gender diversity in teams, leadership, and management, BI helps organizations assess how well they are doing in terms of fostering a diverse and inclusive workplace. This data can be used to set specific, measurable goals for improving gender representation, such as ensuring that at least 30% of leadership positions are held by women.

Closing the Gender Gap with Data-Driven Strategies

Finally, BI tools allow organizations to take a proactive approach to closing gender disparities by developing targeted strategies and policies based on data insights (Seremeti, Anastasiadis & Anastasiadou, 2024). Using the insights derived from BI tools, organizations can set specific, measurable goals for gender equity in recruitment, promotions, and pay. For example, an organization might set a goal to increase the percentage of female candidates hired for technical roles or to close the gender pay gap by a certain percentage within a specified timeframe. BI tools can track progress towards these goals, providing continuous feedback and allowing organizations to adjust strategies as needed (Belias & Trihas, 2022a). Based on the input provided by BI tools, organizations can develop targeted training programs to raise awareness about unconscious bias in hiring, promotions, and pay decisions. For instance, if data shows that male candidates are being favoured during the hiring process, BI tools can highlight this trend and encourage the implementation of bias training for hiring managers and decision-makers.

In conclusion, BI tools are not only instrumental in identifying gender disparities in recruitment, promotions, and pay, but they also offer organizations a way to actively address these issues. Through data-driven insights and actionable recommendations, BI systems empower organizations to implement gender-neutral practices, close pay gaps, and create more inclusive cultures, ultimately contributing to greater gender equity in the workplace.

4.2 Identifying Gender-Based Preferences in Work Styles

Business Intelligence (BI) tools can provide valuable insights into gender-based preferences in work styles and benefits by analysing data across various employee touchpoints, such as surveys, benefits usage patterns, and employee performance. These insights allow organizations to tailor their policies and offerings to better meet the distinct needs of male and female employees, leading to a more inclusive and equitable workplace.

Table 2. Comparative table structure of genders' preferences

Category	Women's Preferences	Men's Preferences
Benefits Preferences	Mental health, reproductive health, short-term benefits	Physical fitness, financial planning, long-term benefits
Career Development & Growth	Leadership in male-dominated fields, work-life balance programs	Technical skills, career advancement programs
Job Roles & Career Paths	HR, marketing, customer service	IT, engineering, leadership roles
Collaboration & Communication	Group discussions, teamwork	Independent, task-based work

Source: Authors' compilation

Table 3. Analysing gender-related work style preferences

Key Area	*BI Tool Role*	*Example Action*	*Outcome*
Benefits Preferences	Analyze gender-specific engagement with various workplace benefits.	Identify differences in utilization of health, wellness, and financial benefits.	Tailor benefits packages to meet distinct needs of male and female employees.
Career Development and Professional Growth	Track gendered participation in training, mentorship, and career advancement programs.	Design gender-specific career development initiatives, focusing on work-life integration for women and technical skills for men.	Creation of inclusive professional development programs catering to both genders.
Job Role and Career Path Preferences	Track gender-based preferences in job roles and career paths.	Identify and address gender imbalances in leadership or technical roles.	Encourage balanced representation across job functions and career progression.
Collaboration and Communication Preferences	Analyze gender differences in collaboration and communication styles.	Assess preferences in communication channels (e.g., email vs. face-to-face) and team dynamics.	Create more inclusive work environments that accommodate different communication and collaboration styles.

Source: Authors' compilation

Benefits Preferences

BI can analyse how different genders utilize various benefits, such as healthcare, wellness programs, or retirement planning services. Identifying these preferences can help organizations create benefits packages that address the unique needs of male and female employees (Burbano, Padilla & Meier, 2024). Data from BI tools can show whether men and women are engaging differently with health and wellness benefits. For example, women may be more likely to utilize mental health resources or reproductive health services, while men may prefer physical health benefits or fitness programs (Dowling et al., 2022). By identifying these preferences, organizations can refine their wellness offerings to be more inclusive and supportive of all employees. On the other hand, BI tools can also identify gender-based differences in engagement with financial and retirement planning benefits. Men may be more likely to engage with long-term financial planning services, while women may focus more on immediate healthcare or short-term benefits. BI data helps organizations tailor their retirement benefits and financial wellness programs to suit the distinct needs of both male and female employees.

Career Development and Professional Growth

Gender-based preferences in career development and professional growth opportunities can also be identified through BI analysis. Women and men may have different priorities when it comes to skill-building, career advancement, and mentorship (Heilman, Caleo & Manzi, 2024). Participation rates in training programs, leadership development, and skill-building initiatives can be tracked via these tools. For instance, women may prefer programs that focus on work-life integration or leadership in traditionally male-dominated fields, while men may prioritize technical or career advancement training (Viterouli et al., 2024c). Understanding these preferences allows organizations to design professional development programs that cater to the needs of both genders. BI systems can also track gendered trends in mentorship or networking program participation. Women, particularly in senior leadership roles, may seek mentorship to navigate challenges or barriers in male-dominated industries. BI insights can help organizations design mentorship and sponsorship programs that foster career growth and advancement for both men and women.

Job Role and Career Path Preferences

BI tools can help organizations track the types of roles that men and women are more likely to apply for, pursue, and stay in. Understanding these preferences allows organizations to address gender imbalances in job roles and career paths. BI can reveal whether men are more likely to pursue leadership roles (Ntalakos, Belias & Tsigilis, 2023), while women may be more likely to choose support or operational roles. This insight can help organizations identify where gender disparities exist in career progression and take steps to encourage more balanced representation across different job functions. In some industries, gender preferences (Kuhn & Wolter, 2022) in job roles may be pronounced. For instance, men might prefer technical roles, such as engineering or IT, while women may gravitate toward roles in human resources, marketing, or customer service. BI can identify these preferences and help organizations create initiatives that encourage greater gender diversity across all job functions.

Collaboration and Communication Preferences

BI tools can also help identify gender-based preferences in collaboration and communication styles within the workplace. Men and women may approach teamwork, meetings, and communication differently (Triantafillidou & Yannas, 2021). BI systems can analyse employee interactions through collaboration tools, meeting participation, and feedback from team members. These insights can help organizations understand whether men and women prefer different communication channels (e.g., email vs. face-to-face communication), the frequency of collaboration, and the role each gender plays in team dynamics. For instance, women may be more likely to engage in collaborative work that involves group discussions or team-based projects, while men may lean toward independent or task-based work. By understanding these preferences, organizations can create more inclusive work environments (Belias, Trihas & Ntalakos, 2024) that accommodate different communication and collaboration styles, helping all employees feel more comfortable and engaged.

Business Intelligence (BI) tools offer valuable insights into gender-based differences in work preferences, professional development, and benefit utilization. By examining data from key employee interactions, such as participation in career advancement programs, preferred job roles, and the use of workplace benefits, BI enables organizations to design more inclusive and equitable policies. These data-driven insights help employers better understand the diverse needs of their workforce, ensuring that both men and women receive the necessary support and opportunities to thrive in their careers.

4.3 Tracking and Analyzing Gender Representation and Turnover Rates

Business Intelligence (BI) tools are instrumental in tracking and analysing gender representation across an organization, as well as assessing turnover rates by gender (Coffman, Flikkema & Shurchkov, 2021). By collecting and analysing data from various HR and employee management systems, BI can provide organizations with a comprehensive understanding of gender distribution within the company and identify any discrepancies in turnover between genders.

Table 4. Monitoring gender diversity and employee turnover

Key Area	*BI Tool Role*	*Example Action*	*Outcome*
Data Collection Sources	Integrating HR data, surveys, and turnover.	Track gender representation and analyze turnover by gender.	Provides insights into gender distribution and turnover trends.
Gender Representation Analysis	Identifying imbalances at all levels.	Analyze gender distribution in roles from entry to leadership.	Highlights areas needing diversity strategies.
Turnover Rates by Gender	Tracking gender-specific turnover rates.	Track turnover rates by gender in different departments.	Reveals gender-based retention issues for targeted strategies.

continued on following page

Table 4. Continued

Key Area	*BI Tool Role*	*Example Action*	*Outcome*
Root Cause Analysis	Linking turnover to gender factors.	Analyze satisfaction, compensation, and work-life balance data.	Identifies factors influencing gender-specific turnover.
Predictive Analytics	Forecasting gender trends.	Predict gender diversity trends in leadership using historical data.	Helps assess progress toward gender diversity goals.

Source: Authors' compilation

Data Collection Sources

BI systems integrate data from a variety of HR sources to track gender representation and turnover rates (Vij, Tiwari & Nazir, 2023):

- *HR databases*: Employee records in HR systems typically include demographic information such as gender, department, job level, and employment history. BI tools can access these records to calculate the gender distribution across different roles, teams, and levels of the organization.
- *Employee turnover data*: BI tools can track turnover rates by analysing exit interviews, resignation data, and historical employment records. This allows organizations to determine whether certain genders are leaving the company at higher rates than others.
- *Employee surveys*: Data collected from employee engagement surveys or satisfaction questionnaires can provide insights into why employees leave, particularly focusing on whether gender-related factors (e.g., gender bias, lack of support) influence their decision to leave.

Gender Representation Analysis

BI tools can track the distribution of genders across various organizational levels, such as entry-level, mid-level, and executive roles. By identifying gender imbalances, BI systems can highlight areas where gender diversity is lacking and help organizations take action (D'Angelo et al., 2024). A BI tool might reveal that while the company has an equal gender distribution at the entry level, women are underrepresented in senior leadership positions. This data can help organizations implement targeted strategies to address gender disparities, such as leadership development programs specifically designed for women.

Turnover Rates by Gender

Turnover data can be segmented by gender to identify any disparities. BI tools can calculate the voluntary and involuntary turnover rates for male and female employees, and compare these rates across different departments, job roles, and regions (Belias et al., 2023a). BI might show that women in certain departments are leaving the organization at a higher rate than men, indicating a potential issue with gender-based work conditions, lack of career progression, or workplace culture. By uncovering this trend, BI provides organizations with the necessary data to implement retention strategies tailored to address these gender-specific concerns.

Root Cause Analysis

BI can also analyse the reasons behind higher turnover rates among one gender by linking turnover data to other employee metrics, such as satisfaction levels, compensation, career advancement opportunities, and work-life balance (Vij, Tiwari & Nazir, 2023). By combining turnover data with employee satisfaction survey results, BI may reveal that women in a particular department report lower satisfaction with work-life balance, leading to higher turnover. This insight allows the organization to introduce changes to improve flexibility, such as offering more remote work opportunities or expanding parental leave policies.

Predictive Analytics for Gender Representation

BI tools can use historical data and predictive analytics to forecast future trends in gender representation and turnover. For example, BI can model how gender diversity in leadership roles might evolve over the next few years based on current hiring, retention, and promotion patterns (Kelan, 2024). Moreover, by analysing the progression of female employees in the company, BI can predict the likelihood of women reaching senior leadership positions within a certain timeframe, helping the organization assess whether it is on track to achieve gender diversity goals.

4.4 Addressing Biases in Recruitment Algorithms

Business Intelligence (BI) tools can monitor, evaluate, and adjust recruitment processes, ensuring that algorithms used for candidate selection and screening are fair and unbiased, thus are important in addressing and mitigating biases that may exist in recruitment algorithms (Anastasiadis & Zirinoglou, 2022). Through careful analysis of recruitment data, BI can help identify and correct biases based on gender, ethnicity, and other demographic factors.

Table 5. Mitigating bias in hiring algorithms

Key Area	*BI Tool Role*	*Example Action*	*Outcome*
Identifying Biases	Detects gender, ethnicity, and other biases in recruitment data.	Analyze gender distribution in role applications and hires.	Spot biases in hiring, prompting algorithm adjustments.
Evaluating Performance	Tracks recruitment algorithm results to assess diversity.	Monitor gender breakdown of applicants and hires.	Identify and address gender imbalances in hiring.
Job Description Bias	Identifies biased language in job postings.	Review job descriptions for biased terms and suggest neutral alternatives.	Ensure more inclusive job descriptions.
Monitoring Equal Opportunity	Tracks diversity at each stage of recruitment.	Analyze gender and ethnicity at various hiring stages (screening, interviews).	Ensure fair treatment and diverse hiring outcomes.
Recommendations	Provides insights to improve recruitment algorithms.	Suggest changes to candidate profiles or scoring systems.	Improve algorithm inclusivity and fairness.
Ongoing Monitoring	Continuously evaluates recruitment algorithms.	Track algorithm performance and adjust as needed based on feedback.	Maintain fairness and inclusivity in the recruitment process.

Source: Authors' compilation

Identifying Biases in Recruitment Data

Recruitment algorithms rely heavily on historical data to identify patterns and predict suitable candidates. However, if the training data contains biases (e.g., gender bias or racial bias), the algorithm can perpetuate these biases in future recruitment decisions. BI tools can analyse the recruitment data to identify such biases (Maurer & Qureshi, 2021). BI tools can analyse the gender composition of applicants for different roles. If an algorithm disproportionately selects male candidates for technical positions, despite a balanced pool of applicants, BI can highlight this bias, prompting further investigation into the algorithm's decision-making process.

Evaluating Algorithm Performance

BI tools can track the performance of recruitment algorithms over time, comparing the gender and diversity of candidates selected by the algorithm with the actual pool of candidates who applied for the role. By comparing the demographic breakdown of applicants and the hired candidates, BI can assess whether the algorithm is inadvertently favouring one gender over another (Tilmes, 2022). If BI shows that female applicants are being filtered out at a higher rate than male applicants, despite having similar qualifications and experience, this indicates a bias in the algorithm that needs to be addressed. BI systems can flag these discrepancies for review and adjustment.

Bias Detection in Job Descriptions

BI can also help identify biased language in job descriptions that may affect the types of candidates attracted to the role. For instance, certain words or phrases in job postings might inadvertently discourage women from applying for positions in male-dominated fields, such as technology or engineering. By analysing job descriptions and their corresponding gender applicant pools, BI can flag certain words or phrases (e.g., "aggressive," "dominant," or "competitive") that are associated with male applicants and suggest more neutral alternatives, ensuring that job postings appeal to a broader, more diverse audience.

Monitoring Equal Opportunity Metrics

BI systems can monitor equal opportunity metrics across the recruitment process, from initial applications to final hires. By tracking the gender, ethnicity, and background of candidates at each stage of the hiring funnel, BI tools can ensure that the recruitment process is not favouring certain demographic groups over others. BI tools can analyse whether women are being disproportionately eliminated during certain stages of the recruitment process, such as the screening or interview stage (Adewusi et al., 2024). This information can be used to make the recruitment process more equitable by revising algorithms to remove potential biases.

Providing Recommendations for Algorithm Improvement

Based on data insights, BI resources can provide actionable recommendations to improve recruitment algorithms. This might involve suggesting alternative methods for data processing, incorporating more diverse candidate profiles, or adjusting scoring systems to account for any detected bias (Kelan, 2024). If a BI system detects that the recruitment algorithm favours candidates from prestigious universities, which may lead to gender or socio-economic bias, the tool might recommend diversifying the criteria for educational background to ensure a more inclusive candidate pool.

Ongoing Monitoring and Feedback Loops

Addressing biases in recruitment algorithms is an ongoing process. BI tools enable continuous monitoring of recruitment practices, ensuring that any new biases introduced by algorithm updates are quickly detected and rectified. After an algorithm is adjusted to be more inclusive, BI can track how the changes affect the gender diversity of the final hire pool (Giannakos et al., 2024). Continuous feedback loops allow for the algorithm to be refined further, maintaining fairness in the recruitment process over time.

The transformative role of BI in improving gender equity in the workplace is evident. BI tools provide organizations with the ability to track gender representation and turnover rates, identifying discrepancies and enabling targeted actions to retain diverse talent. Similarly, BI plays a key role in identifying and addressing biases in recruitment algorithms, ensuring a fairer, more inclusive hiring process that promotes diversity and equity.

4.5 Analysing Trends in Flexible Work Preferences by Gender

Valuable insights are also provided into how flexible work preferences, such as remote work, flexible hours, or job sharing, differ across genders (Viterouli et al., 2024c; Belias & Trihas, 2024). By analysing data from various sources, including employee surveys, time tracking systems, and attendance records, BI can uncover patterns and trends that highlight gender-based differences in preferences for flexible work arrangements.

Table 6. Comparative table of gender trends in flexible work preferences

Flexible Work Preference	Women's Trends	Men's Trends
Remote Work	Higher demand due to caregiving responsibilities	Lower but increasing interest
Flexible Hours	Preference for non-traditional schedules (early/late shifts)	More standard hours, flexibility for personal growth
Job Sharing / Part-Time	More likely to request due to work-life balance needs	Less common, but growing interest

Source: Authors' compilation

Table 7. Examining gender differences in flexible work preferences

Key Area	*BI Tool Role*	*Example Action*	*Outcome*
Data Collection Sources	Aggregates survey, time-tracking, and attendance data.	Collect data on flexible work preferences (remote, flexible hours).	Identify gender-based trends in flexible work preferences.
Remote Work Preferences	Tracks gender differences in remote work usage.	Analyze remote work usage by gender, especially among caregivers.	Highlight women's preference for remote work, aiding policy adjustments.
Flexible Hours	Tracks gender differences in flexible hour usage.	Monitor flexible hour usage, focusing on caregiving-related trends.	Tailor policies to support gender-specific work-hour preferences.
Job Sharing & Reduced Hours	Tracks part-time and job-sharing requests, especially by women.	Analyze trends in part-time or job-sharing requests.	Design inclusive policies for job sharing and part-time work.
Policy Impact	Provides insights to create gender-inclusive work policies.	Use BI to customize flexible work policies for both genders.	Develop equitable flexible work options for all employees.

Source: Authors' compilation

Data Collection Sources

BI systems typically aggregate data from several sources to analyse flexible work preferences (Maurer & Qureshi, 2021), including:

- *Employee surveys*: Data gathered through surveys can provide direct insights into employee preferences, such as the desire for remote work, flexible hours, or a compressed workweek.
- *Time tracking systems*: These systems can track when employees clock in and out, and how often they use flexible work hours or remote work options. BI tools can then analyse these data points to uncover trends by gender.
- *Attendance and scheduling systems*: By reviewing patterns in time-off requests or the use of flexible work arrangements, BI tools can identify gendered preferences for specific work schedules (e.g., women may opt for more flexible hours due to caregiving responsibilities).

Trends in Remote Work Preferences

BI can track how different genders prefer remote work. For instance, women, particularly those with caregiving responsibilities, may demonstrate a higher demand for remote work options (Joshi & Kumar, 2023; Bello et al., 2024) to better manage their professional and personal commitments. A BI tool might analyse usage patterns of remote work over a given period and reveal that women tend to request or utilize remote work more frequently than men. This information can inform companies that women may benefit from increased remote work options, leading to higher job satisfaction and retention.

Flexible Hours and Work-Life Balance

Men and women might also have different preferences for flexible hours, driven by different societal expectations and personal responsibilities (Viterouli et al., 2024b). BI can track the usage of flexible working hours by gender, showing whether women are more likely to take advantage of such options to balance family and work obligations. BI tools could identify that women often prefer to work non-traditional hours, such as starting earlier or finishing later, to accommodate caregiving duties. Meanwhile, men might prioritize a more standard schedule but use flexible hours for personal development or social reasons. By identifying these trends, organizations can better design their flexible work policies to meet gender-specific needs.

Understanding Job Sharing and Reduced Work Hours

BI tools can also track preferences for job sharing or part-time roles, which may be more prevalent among women seeking a better balance between work and family commitments. By analysing data on part-time job requests or job-sharing options (Giannakos et al., 2024), BI can identify gender-based patterns in the demand for reduced hours. A BI system could reveal that women are more likely to request job-sharing arrangements, which allows them to work fewer hours while still fulfilling key job responsibilities. This information enables organizations to design policies that support these preferences, ensuring gender inclusivity in flexible work arrangements.

Impact of Gender-Specific Needs on Organizational Policies

By identifying these gender-based trends in flexible work preferences, organizations can use BI insights to design policies that accommodate the unique needs of male and female employees (Burbano, Padilla & Meier, 2024). For instance, organizations could implement flexible work options tailored to the specific needs of women with caregiving responsibilities, while also ensuring that men have access to similar benefits if needed.

4.6 Measuring the Effectiveness of Work-Life Balance Initiatives

Lastly, Business Intelligence (BI) tools are essential for measuring the effectiveness of initiatives like parental leave and hybrid work options by analysing data related to employee engagement, retention, productivity, and overall satisfaction (Viterouli et al., 2024b). By tracking key metrics before and after the implementation of these initiatives, BI can provide organizations with actionable insights into whether these policies are achieving their intended goals.

Table 8. Evaluating the impact of work-life balance programs

Key Area	*BI Tool Role*	*Example Action*	*Outcome*
Parental Leave Effectiveness	Track retention, satisfaction, and productivity post-leave	Analyze retention rates and productivity post-leave.	Parental Leave Effectiveness
Hybrid Work Options Effectiveness	Measure productivity, engagement, and well-being in hybrid models	Compare productivity and engagement of hybrid vs. in-office employees.	Determine if hybrid work enhances productivity and engagement.
Impact on Work-Life Balance	Evaluate satisfaction with work-life balance post-policy	Survey work-life balance satisfaction before and after policy implementation.	Identify if policies improve work-life balance satisfaction.
Gendered Analysis of Effectiveness	Analyze policy impact by gender	Compare satisfaction and engagement across genders for leave and hybrid options.	Refine policies to ensure inclusivity and effectiveness

Source: Authors' compilation

Parental Leave Effectiveness

BI can track how employees use parental leave and its impact on employee retention, job satisfaction, and performance. Key metrics can include (Bello et al., 2024):

- *Employee retention rates*: By comparing turnover rates before and after parental leave policies are implemented, BI tools can assess whether employees return to work after taking parental leave or if they are more likely to leave the organization.
- *Productivity levels:* BI can track any changes in productivity post-return, assessing whether employees are able to resume work at the same pace as before, or if they need additional accommodations.
- *Employee satisfaction surveys*: After parental leave, organizations can use BI to analyse employee feedback regarding the parental leave policy, such as

how satisfied employees are with the length of leave, flexibility, and support they received during their time off.

A BI tool might analyse retention rates and find that women who take parental leave are more likely to return to work if they feel supported by their employer in terms of flexible hours or hybrid work options. On the other hand, if the support is insufficient, BI might show a higher turnover rate among employees who take parental leave, indicating that the initiative is not as effective as intended.

Hybrid Work Options Effectiveness

BI tools can use historical data and predictive analytics to forecast future

BI tools can also measure the effectiveness of hybrid work options by evaluating metrics like employee engagement, productivity, and overall well-being. This can help organizations understand whether hybrid work arrangements are achieving their desired outcomes. BI tools can track productivity levels of employees working in a hybrid model (Viterouli et al., 2024a), comparing the performance of employees who work primarily in the office to those who work remotely or on a hybrid schedule. By analysing these trends, BI can provide insights into the effectiveness of hybrid work policies, especially for employees with different gender-based needs. Additionally, BI tools can also measure employee engagement (Tavera Romero et al., 2021) by analysing participation in team activities, attendance at virtual meetings, and collaboration patterns. If hybrid work policies are successful, BI should show high levels of engagement among employees, regardless of gender. However, if engagement drops for a specific gender, it could indicate that hybrid work policies need to be adjusted to better support all employees.

Impact on Work-Life Balance and Well-being

Another key area BI can assess is the impact of parental leave and hybrid work options on work-life balance and overall employee well-being. BI tools can track employee satisfaction with their work-life balance before and after the implementation of these initiatives (Bello et al., 2024). BI can analyse employee survey responses about their work-life balance, comparing those who take parental leave or use hybrid work options with those who do not. If employees using these policies report higher levels of satisfaction with their work-life balance, it may indicate that these initiatives are positively impacting well-being.

Gendered Analysis of Initiative Effectiveness

BI tools can also break down data by gender to understand whether parental leave and hybrid work options are more effective for one gender over another. For example, BI could show that women report higher satisfaction with parental leave and hybrid work options, while men might be more satisfied with flexible work hours or remote work (Anastasiadou & Anastasiadis, 2019). By analysing gender-specific data, BI tools can help organizations refine their parental leave and hybrid work policies to ensure they are equally effective for all employees, regardless of gender.

Hence, BI plays a crucial role in measuring the effectiveness of initiatives like parental leave and hybrid work options by providing data-driven insights into employee retention, satisfaction, and productivity. By analysing key metrics, such as employee engagement, turnover rates, and work-life balance, BI helps organizations determine whether these policies are successful and identify areas for improvement. Through gender-based analysis, BI ensures that these initiatives are inclusive and effective for all employees.

6. CONCLUSION AND RECOMMENDATIONS

6.1 Summary of Findings

This study explored the role of Business Intelligence (BI) in addressing gender disparities in talent management, particularly in relation to hiring, promotions, pay, and work-life balance. The findings demonstrate the transformative potential of BI tools in tracking gender representation, analysing turnover patterns, addressing biases in recruitment algorithms, and tailoring work-life balance initiatives to gender-specific needs (Anastasiadou, Masouras & Papademetriou, 2023). Through advanced data analytics, BI allows organizations to uncover hidden gender disparities, identify areas requiring intervention, and promote more inclusive and equitable workplace policies. Additionally, BI tools facilitate the design of customized programs (Belias & Trihas, 2022a; 2022b) aimed at supporting underrepresented genders, ensuring both organizational success and employee satisfaction.

6.2 Practical Implications

The practical implications of these findings are substantial. By leveraging BI to monitor gender representation and turnover rates, organizations can make informed decisions about resource allocation, mentorship programs, and retention strategies (Tripathi et al., 2023). The use of BI tools in recruitment processes can help eliminate biases embedded in algorithmic decision-making, leading to fairer hiring and promotion practices. Furthermore, BI can enable organizations to better understand and address the diverse work-life balance needs of men and women, creating more inclusive work environments that support flexibility, parental leave, and hybrid work options (Belias & Trihas, 2022b; Viterouli et al., 2024b). For organizations aiming to foster a more equitable workplace, the integration of BI into talent management strategies is an essential step toward achieving DEI goals and improving employee well-being.

6.3 Theoretical Implications

From a theoretical perspective, this study contributes to the understanding of how data-driven approaches, particularly BI, can enhance gender equality within talent management frameworks. By bridging the gender data gap, BI offers a foundation for further exploration of how organizations can address systemic biases and promote inclusivity in the workplace (Anastasiadis & Zirinoglou, 2022). The findings suggest that traditional theories of talent management, which often fail to account for gender-based disparities (Al-Quhfa et al., 2024), can be enriched by incorporating BI tools that offer real-time, data-informed insights. Moreover, this study challenges existing assumptions about the homogeneity of work-life balance needs and encourages scholars to explore gender-specific approaches in future research.

6.4 Future Trends

Looking forward, the role of BI in gender equality within talent management is expected to continue growing, particularly as organizations increasingly adopt AI and machine learning technologies (Liu, Zhang & Xu, 2023). These advancements will allow BI tools to become more predictive, providing organizations with the ability to proactively identify and address potential disparities before they become entrenched. Furthermore, as work-life balance becomes an even greater priority for employees, the use of BI in monitoring and optimizing flexible work arrangements, parental leave policies, and hybrid work models will be essential for organizations to remain competitive in attracting and retaining diverse talent (Tilmes, 2022). Future trends may also include the integration of more granular data points, such as employee sentiment and satisfaction levels, which can further refine the understanding of gender-based preferences and needs.

6.5 Limitations

While this study offers valuable insights into the application of BI for gender equity in talent management, several limitations must be acknowledged. First, the generalizability of the findings may be limited due to the focus on specific organizational contexts, requiring further research across diverse industries and geographic regions to validate these results (Adewusi et al., 2024). Additionally, the study primarily examines quantitative BI tools, with less attention given to qualitative aspects such as employee experiences and perceptions. Another key limitation is the exclusive use of secondary sources, which restricts the findings to the quality, scope, and potential biases inherent in existing literature (Belias & Trihas, 2022a). The case studies reviewed are limited to those publicly available, meaning the experiences of other organizations with BI tools may not be fully captured. Moreover, the study's reliance on published interpretations introduces the risk of bias, potentially limiting the objectivity and depth of analysis in some areas. Ethical concerns, particularly regarding data privacy and algorithmic fairness, also warrant attention. Future research should explore these challenges further, including the biases that may arise in the use of BI tools.

6.6 Recommendations

The integration of BI tools into talent management strategies should be a priority for organizations aiming to address *gender disparities* in areas such as hiring, promotions, and pay (Heilman, Caleo & Manzi, 2024). By leveraging BI capabilities, companies can track these disparities more accurately and implement timely interventions to foster equity. Additionally, insights derived from BI analytics should inform the *development of gender-specific policies* that cater to the distinct work-life balance needs of men and women, promoting a more inclusive workplace environment (Rao & Taboada, 2021).

Organizations must also focus on *bias auditing in recruitment processes* by employing BI tools to identify and address potential algorithmic biases (Tilmes, 2022). Regularly updating recruitment algorithms with diverse datasets and conducting continuous audits can significantly reduce discriminatory practices in hiring. Furthermore, as BI technologies advance, companies should expand their applications to include *predictive analytics*, enabling them to anticipate future gender disparities and implement proactive corrective measures (Viterouli et al., 2023). Finally, it is essential to prioritize *ethical considerations* in the use of BI tools, particularly regarding data privacy and the fairness of algorithmic decisions. Organizations must balance the benefits of data-driven decision-making (Coffman,

Flikkema & Shurchkov, 2021) with the need to maintain employee trust, ensuring that BI deployment is both effective and ethically sound.

REFERENCES

Adaga, E. M., Egieya, Z. E., Ewuga, S. K., Abdul, A. A., & Abrahams, T. O. (2024). Tackling economic inequalities through business analytics: A literature review. *Computer Science & IT Research Journal*, *5*(1), 60–80. DOI: 10.51594/csitrj.v5i1.702

Adewusi, A. O., Okoli, U. I., Adaga, E., Olorunsogo, T., Asuzu, O. F., & Daraojimba, D. O. (2024). Business intelligence in the era of big data: A review of analytical tools and competitive advantage. *Computer Science & IT Research Journal*, *5*(2), 415–431. DOI: 10.51594/csitrj.v5i2.791

Al-Quhfa, H., Mothana, A., Aljbri, A., & Song, J. (2024). Enhancing Talent Recruitment in Business Intelligence Systems: A Comparative Analysis of Machine Learning Models. *Analytics*, *3*(3), 297–317. DOI: 10.3390/analytics3030017

Anastasiadis, L., & Zirinoglou, P. (2022). Evaluating students' attitudes toward STEM education: The case of Greek pre-service teachers. *International Journal of Education and Social Science*, *9*(4), 35–53.

Anastasiadou, S., & Anastasiadis, L. (2019). Quality assurance in education in the light of the effectiveness of transformational school leadership. In Economic and Financial Challenges for Eastern Europe: Proceedings of the 9th International Conference on the Economies of the Balkan and Eastern European Countries in the Changing World (EBEEC) in Athens, Greece, 2017 (pp. 323-344). Springer International Publishing. DOI: 10.1007/978-3-030-12169-3_21

Anastasiadou, S., Masouras, A., & Papademetriou, C. (2023, June). Attitudes toward Reproductive Tourism and Cross border reproductive care (CBRC): Legal, Economic, Ethical issues and dilemmas, possibilities and limitations. In *6th International Conference on Tourism Research*, Pafos, Cyprus. DOI: 10.34190/ictr.6.1.1189

Artz, B., Kaya, I., & Kaya, O. (2022). Gender role perspectives and job burnout. *Review of Economics of the Household*, *20*(2), 447–470. DOI: 10.1007/s11150-021-09579-2 PMID: 34429716

Bapna, S., & Ganco, M. (2021). Gender gaps in equity crowdfunding: Evidence from a randomized field experiment. *Management Science*, *67*(5), 2679–2710. DOI: 10.1287/mnsc.2020.3644

Belias, D., Rossidis, I., Mantas, C., Ntalakos, A., Trihas, N., & Bakogiannis, D. (2023b). The effect of strategic leadership on the integration and success of organizational change. In *Managing successful and ethical organizational change* (pp. 54–75). IGI Global. DOI: 10.4018/979-8-3693-0235-4.ch003

Belias, D., Rossidis, I., Papademetriou, C., & Mantas, C. (2022). Job satisfaction as affected by types of leadership: A case study of Greek tourism sector. *Journal of Quality Assurance in Hospitality & Tourism, 23*(2), 299–317. DOI: 10.1080/1528008X.2020.1867695

Belias, D., Rossidis, I., Sotiriou, A., & Malik, S.Case Study in Greek Seasonal Hotels. (2023a). Workplace conflict, turnover, and quality of services. Case study in Greek seasonal hotels. *Journal of Quality Assurance in Hospitality & Tourism, 24*(4), 453–476. DOI: 10.1080/1528008X.2022.2065655

Belias, D., & Trihas, N. (2022a, September). How can we measure the "resistance to change"? An exploratory factor analysis in a sample of employees in the Greek hotel industry. In International Conference of the International Association of Cultural and Digital Tourism (pp. 51-66). Cham: Springer Nature Switzerland.

Belias, D., & Trihas, N. (2022b). Investigating the readiness for organizational change: A case study from a hotel industry context/Greece.

Belias, D., & Trihas, N. (2023). The role of SHRM in navigating the hospitality sector during a crisis. In *Sustainable growth strategies for entrepreneurial venture tourism and regional development* (pp. 60–76). IGI Global. DOI: 10.4018/978-1-6684-6055-9.ch004

Belias, D., & Trihas, N. (2024). How can we predict the integration and the success of organizational change in the hospitality sector? *Journal of Quality Assurance in Hospitality & Tourism, 25*(6), 2011–2045. DOI: 10.1080/1528008X.2023.2216952

Belias, D., Trihas, N., & Ntalakos, A. (2024). Crisis leadership, group dynamics, and change management: A literature review and future perspectives. In *International Conference of the International Association of Cultural and Digital Tourism* (pp. 225-244). Springer, Cham. DOI: 10.1007/978-3-031-54342-5_13

Belias, D., Vasiliadis, L., & Mantas, C. (2020). The human resource training and development of employees working on luxurious hotels in Greece. In Cultural and Tourism Innovation in the Digital Era: Sixth International IACuDiT Conference, Athens 2019 (pp. 639-648). Springer International Publishing. DOI: 10.1007/978-3-030-36342-0_49

Belias, D., Velissariou, E., & Rossidis, I. (2019). The contribution of HRM on the development of effective organizational culture in hotel units—The case of Greek hotels. In Smart Tourism as a Driver for Culture and Sustainability: Fifth International Conference IACuDiT, Athens 2018 (pp. 603-618). Springer International Publishing.

Bello, B. G., Tula, S. T., Omotoye, G. B., Kess-Momoh, A. J., & Daraojimba, A. I. (2024). Work-life balance and its impact in modern organizations: An HR review. *World Journal of Advanced Research and Reviews, 21*(1), 1162–1173. DOI: 10.30574/wjarr.2024.21.1.0106

Burbano, V., Padilla, N., & Meier, S. (2024). Gender differences in preferences for meaning at work. *American Economic Journal. Economic Policy, 16*(3), 61–94. DOI: 10.1257/pol.20220121

Coffman, K., Flikkema, C. B., & Shurchkov, O. (2021). Gender stereotypes in deliberation and team decisions. *Games and Economic Behavior, 129*, 329–349. DOI: 10.1016/j.geb.2021.06.004

D'Angelo, A., d'Aloisio, G., Marzi, F., Di Marco, A., & Stilo, G. (2024). Uncovering gender gap in academia: A comprehensive analysis within the software engineering community. *Journal of Systems and Software, 217*, 112162. DOI: 10.1016/j.jss.2024.112162

Dowling, B., Goldstein, D., Park, M., & Price, H. (2022). Hybrid work: Making it fit with your diversity, equity, and inclusion strategy. *The McKinsey Quarterly, 4*, 1–9.

Errani, C., Tsukamoto, S., Kido, A., Yoneda, A., Bondi, A., Zora, F., & Mavrogenis, A. F. (2021). Women and men in orthopaedics. *SICOT-J*, •••, 7. PMID: 33812468

Espinosa, M. P., & Ferreira, E. (2022). Gender implicit bias and glass ceiling effects. *Journal of Applied Econometrics, 25*(1), 37–57.

Giannakos, K., Belias, D., Rossidis, I., Ntalakos, A., & Papademetriou, C. (2024). Creating the Appropriate Organizational Culture for Change Management. In Organizational Behavior and Human Resource Management for Complex Work Environments (pp. 166-185). IGI Global. DOI: 10.4018/979-8-3693-3466-9.ch009

Hargrave, L., & Blumenau, J. (2022). No longer conforming to stereotypes? Gender, political style and parliamentary debate in the UK. *British Journal of Political Science, 52*(4), 1584–1601. DOI: 10.1017/S0007123421000648

Heilman, M. E., Caleo, S., & Manzi, F. (2024). Women at work: Pathways from gender stereotypes to gender bias and discrimination. *Annual Review of Organizational Psychology and Organizational Behavior, 11*(1), 165–192. DOI: 10.1146/annurev-orgpsych-110721-034105

Jabeen, G., Goli, G., Kafila, , & Gobinath, R. (2024). A bibliometric review on gender equity in human resource management. *Future Business Journal, 10*(1), 101. DOI: 10.1186/s43093-024-00381-x

Joshi, H. C., & Kumar, S. (2023). Remote Work and Gender Inequality: Unmasking the Challenges and Seeking Solutions. *IEEE Internet Computing*.

Kelan, E. K. (2024). Algorithmic inclusion: Shaping the predictive algorithms of artificial intelligence in hiring. *Human Resource Management Journal, 34*(3), 694–707. DOI: 10.1111/1748-8583.12511

Kuhn, A., & Wolter, S. C. (2022). Things versus people: Gender differences in vocational interests and in occupational preferences. *Journal of Economic Behavior & Organization, 203*, 210–234. DOI: 10.1016/j.jebo.2022.09.003

Liargovas, P., & Papageorgiou, C. (2024). Regional Policy: Disparities, Development and Future Direction. In The European Integration, Vol. 2: Institutions and Policies (pp. 253-286). Cham: Springer Nature Switzerland.

Liu, Y., Zhang, H., & Xu, R. (2023). The impact of technology on promoting physical activities and mental health: A gender-based study. *BMC Psychology, 11*(1), 298. DOI: 10.1186/s40359-023-01348-3 PMID: 37775753

Lucifora, C., & Vigani, D. (2022). What if your boss is a woman? Evidence on gender discrimination at the workplace. *Review of Economics of the Household, 20*(2), 389–417. DOI: 10.1007/s11150-021-09562-x

Máiz-Mazuela, C., Medina-Perucha, L., Berenguera, A., López-Jiménez, T., Rodríguez-Giralt, I., Cerezo Sepúlveda, P., & Jacques-Aviñó, C. (2023). Essential Workers Balancing Life and Work during the COVID-19 Syndemic in Spain: A Qualitative and Gender-Based Study. *Health & Social Care in the Community, 2023*(1), 1124583. DOI: 10.1155/2023/1124583

Maurer, C. C., & Qureshi, I. (2021). Not just good for her: A temporal analysis of the dynamic relationship between representation of women and collective employee turnover. *Organization Studies, 42*(1), 85–107. DOI: 10.1177/0170840619875480

Miliopoulou, G. Z., & Kapareliotis, I. (2021). The toll of success: Female leaders in the "women-friendly" Greek advertising agencies. *Gender, Work and Organization, 28*(5), 1741–1765. DOI: 10.1111/gwao.12636

Nguyen, M. H., & Armoogum, J. (2021). Perception and preference for home-based telework in the COVID-19 era: A gender-based analysis in Hanoi, Vietnam. *Sustainability (Basel), 13*(6), 3179. DOI: 10.3390/su13063179

Nkosi, N. (2024). Breaking Barriers and Building Bridges: Unveiling the Enablers of Women School Leaders to Overcome Gender Inequality in KwaZulu-Natal, South Africa. *Research in Educational Policy and Management, 6*(2), 436–453. DOI: 10.46303/repam.2024.43

Ntalakos, A., Belias, D., & Tsigilis, N. (2022, September). Leadership styles and group dynamics in the tourism industry. In International conference of the international association of cultural and digital tourism (pp. 117-131). Cham: Springer Nature Switzerland.

Ntalakos, A., Belias, D., & Tsigilis, N. (2023, August). Analyzing the organizational factors that influence hotel employees' team efficiency. In International Conference of the International Association of Cultural and Digital Tourism (pp. 179-208). Cham: Springer Nature Switzerland.

Papademetriou, C., Anastasiadou, S. D., & Konteos, G. (2022). *The Effect of Human Resource Management Practices on the Quality of Service*. Customer Satisfaction, and Organizational Performance in Cypriot Urban Hotel Industry. In HAICTA.

Papademetriou, C., Belias, D., Ragazou, K., & Garefalakis, A. (2024). The Role of Human Resource Management (HRM) in Employee Mental Health and Well-Being for Complex Work Environments. In Organizational Behavior and Human Resource Management for Complex Work Environments (pp. 81-94). IGI Global.

Papantoniou, K., & Tzitzikas, Y. (2020, September). NLP for the Greek language: A brief survey. In 11th Hellenic conference on artificial intelligence (pp. 101-109). DOI: 10.1145/3411408.3411410

Ranganathan, M., Lalk, E., Freese, L. M., Freilich, M. A., Wilcots, J., Duffy, M. L., & Shivamoggi, R. (2021). Trends in the representation of women among US geoscience faculty from 1999 to 2020: The long road toward gender parity. AGU Advances, 2(3), e2021AV000436.

Rao, P., & Taboada, M. (2021). Gender bias in the news: A scalable topic modelling and visualization framework. *Frontiers in Artificial Intelligence*, *4*, 664737. DOI: 10.3389/frai.2021.664737 PMID: 34222857

Rukmiyati, N. M. S., Safitri, N. W. N., Mareni, N. K., Darmayanti, N. P. A., & Ekayani, N. N. S. (2024). Unveiling the Gender Gap: A Literature Review on Women Entrepreneurs and Financial Access. Jurnal Ekonomi dan Bisnis Jagaditha. 11(2), 141-151. .DOI: 10.22225/jj.11.2.2024.141-151

Seremeti, L., Anastasiadis, L., & Anastasiadou, S. (2024). The Role of Data in Environmental, Social, and Governance Strategy. In ESG and Total Quality Management in Human Resources (pp. 201-218). IGI Global.

Sharma, M., Kumar, P., & Gundewar, S. (2025). Leveraging AI and Machine Learning for Predictive Analytics in Business Intelligence. In AI-Powered Business Intelligence for Modern Organizations (pp. 29-50). IGI Global.

Spoon, K., LaBerge, N., Wapman, K. H., Zhang, S., Morgan, A. C., Galesic, M., Fosdick, B. K., Larremore, D. B., & Clauset, A. (2023). Gender and retention patterns among US faculty. *Science Advances*, *9*(42), eadi2205. DOI: 10.1126/sciadv.adi2205 PMID: 37862417

Taherdoost, H. (2022). What are different research approaches? Comprehensive review of qualitative, quantitative, and mixed method research, their applications, types, and limitations. *Journal of Management Science & Engineering Research*, *5*(1), 53–63. DOI: 10.30564/jmser.v5i1.4538

Tavera Romero, C. A., Ortiz, J. H., Khalaf, O. I., & Ríos Prado, A. (2021). Business intelligence: Business evolution after industry 4.0. *Sustainability (Basel)*, *13*(18), 10026. DOI: 10.3390/su131810026

Tilmes, N. (2022). Disability, fairness, and algorithmic bias in AI recruitment. *Ethics and Information Technology*, *24*(2), 21. DOI: 10.1007/s10676-022-09633-2

Triantafillidou, A., & Yannas, P. (2021). Women in Public Relations in Greece. EUPRERA Report Vol. 3., No. 2., in - Topić, M. (ed), EUPRERA report series. Leeds/Brussels: Creative Media and Communications Research Ltd. & EUPRERA. ISSN 2633-2353.

Tripathi, P., Bajaj, C., Bhanvadia, M., Parsekar, V., & Magar, V. (2023). Comparative study of data analytics tools for effective business decision. Vidhyayana-An International Multidisciplinary Peer-Reviewed E-Journal-ISSN 2454-8596, 8(si7), 461-486.

Vij, R., Tiwari, Y., & Nazir, H. (2023, December). HR Analytics in Predicting Attrition Pattern Among Women in Private Education Colleges: Comprehensive Evaluation. In 2023 4th International Conference on Computation, Automation and Knowledge Management (ICCAKM) (pp. 01-07). IEEE.

Viterouli, M., Belias, D., Koustelios, A., & Tsigilis, N. (2024a). Optimizing Adaptive Performance: Exploring Organizational Learning Culture across Generations. *Journal of Chinese Human Resource Management*, *15*(4), 3–27.

Viterouli, M., Belias, D., Koustelios, A., Tsigilis, N., & Bakogiannis, D. (2023). Fostering sustainability through the integration of green human resource management and change management: nurturing eco-conscious organizational practices. In *Managing successful and ethical organizational change* (pp. 241–278). IGI Global. DOI: 10.4018/979-8-3693-0235-4.ch011

Viterouli, M., Belias, D., Koustelios, A., Tsigilis, N., & Papademetriou, C. (2024c). Time for change: designing tailored training initiatives for organizational transformation. In *Organizational Behavior and Human Resource Management for Complex Work Environments* (pp. 267–307). IGI Global. DOI: 10.4018/979-8-3693-3466-9.ch014

Viterouli, M., Belias, D., Ntalakos, A., Koustelios, A., & Tsigilis, N. (2024b). Strategies for Achieving Work-Life Balance in the Modern Workplace. In Organizational Behavior and Human Resource Management for Complex Work Environments (pp. 95-127). IGI Global. DOI: 10.4018/979-8-3693-3466-9.ch006

Vo, L. V., Nguyen, H. T. H., & Le, H. T. T. (2021). Do female CEOs make a difference in firm operations? Evidence from Vietnam. *Accounting and Finance*, *61*(S1), 1489–1516. DOI: 10.1111/acfi.12634

Chapter 9
Smart HRm Unlocking Business Intelligence for Employee Performance in Telecom

Usharani Bhimavarapu
https://orcid.org/0000-0002-0246-1420
Computer Science and Engineering, Koneru Lakshmaiah Education Foundation, India

ABSTRACT

The present study explores the area of Smart Human Resource Management (Smart HRM) through the support of Business Intelligence (BI) and deep learning to achieve workforce excellence. Considering telecom businesses for the year 2024, the study utilized a dataset that was collected from 268 workers with the purpose of examining how data-driven information can help HR practices. The architecture involved pre-processing of gathered data, feature selection using Ant Colony Optimization (ACO), and using an improved ResNet-181 deep learning method. The combination of methods facilitated identification of key workforce trends and performance metrics. Using BI tools, the system equips HR practitioners with actionable information, which filters down eventually into strategic choices and organizational growth. The study highlights the inceptive potential of Smart HRM with the employment of BI and AI for the purpose of rebuilding talent management, as well as talent development..

DOI: 10.4018/979-8-3373-1942-1.ch009

INTRODUCTION

Smart Human Resource Management (HRM) integrates Business Intelligence (BI) solutions in a bid to enhance decision-making in workforce dynamics and talent management. Traditional HR practices tend to rely on experience and intuition, while Smart HRM relies on data to make suggestions. BI facilitates the utilization of data by HR professionals to analyze performance, track engagement, and forecast workforce needs. Integrating analytics into HR functions gives companies a competitive edge with future-looking management. Intelligent HRM is all about aligning talent strategy with business goals, with all HR functions from recruitment to retention being supported by data. The intersection of BI and HRM transforms the HR function from that of a supporting function to a strategic partner function. It also fosters a culture of improvement and innovation on an ongoing basis. Firms are now capable of managing their human capital more effectively. Intelligent HRM creates a responsive, nimble, and data-based HR environment for long-term success.

In the recruitment process, Business Intelligence facilitates companies to hire more intelligently. Through examination of the candidates' data, organizations can identify trends and skills that result in success in specific roles. Predictive analytics is used to filter out candidates who are likely to be successful, saving recruitment costs and increasing quality. Recruitment dashboards give real-time measures like time-to-hire, source performance, and diversity metrics. Social media and social networking data are also used to find passive candidates. Such data help HR teams target outreach efforts and recruitment campaigns. BI solutions can reveal gaps in recruitment strategies and streamline them in the future. Organizations can identify the most cost-effective sources of sourcing and reduce turnover by optimizing job-role fit. Intelligent HRM optimizes candidate experiences through data-driven touchpoints. Ultimately, companies get the right talent aligned with both immediate needs and long-term vision.

Employee engagement is a driver of retention and productivity, and BI provides a science-based solution for measuring and enhancing it. Engagement surveys may be analyzed through text analytics to identify sentiment and repetition of themes. Pulse survey data, feedback portals, and collaboration portals may be presented in real-time. This allows managers to intervene early when there are threats of disengagement. Aligning levels of engagement with performance and retention metrics identifies key drivers. BI dashboards track trends over time, enabling HR teams to tailor interventions. Evidence-based development plans and reward schemes can be formulated. Evidence-based action results in a more engaged and committed workforce. BI enables HR to connect engagement activities directly to business performance. Intelligent HRM therefore makes employee satisfaction a business enabler.

Workforce planning is greatly aided by the forecasting strength of BI. Predictive models examine past trends, industry trends, and internal metrics to predict future workforce requirements. This involves the determination of potential skill gaps or risks of overstaffing. BI facilitates scenario planning, enabling organizations to plan for different business scenarios. Metrics like heat maps can identify areas of low productivity or skill gaps. Resource deployment is more strategic to put the right individuals in the right job at the right time. Smart HRM uses data to manage workload, avoid burnout, and maintain high morale. Project works and cross-functional teams benefit from dynamic talent mapping. BI also influences upskilling, outsourcing, or automation programs. Effective workforce planning reduces expenditure and supports efficiency in operations. Performance appraisals are known to be subjective and inconsistent, but BI offers the data-driven choice.

Smart HRM integrates data from multiple sources such as project feedback, peer reviews, and KPIs. Real-time tracking of individual and team performance levels against targets is facilitated through dashboards. This transparency enables better and fairer performance appraisals. BI software can identify high performers, future executives, and areas of deficiency. Trend analysis can alert managers to how things are moving in terms of performance. Coaching and development plans based on analytics can be built. These provide a culture of accountability and continuous improvement. BI eliminates the subjectivity in performance reviews, and they become transparent. Lastly, performance management is utilized as a development tool rather than an exercise in compliance. Intelligent HRM utilizes BI to design more effective learning and development programs. Training effectiveness can be gauged by correlating learning activity with work performance.

Learning management systems (LMS) deliver rich data on participation, percentage completion, and skill acquisition. BI facilitates the customization of training paths based on role requirement and employee goals. Dashboards and heatmaps track what departments require the most training. Predictive analytics can identify future required skills and train staff accordingly. Real-time feedback facilitates constant improvement in courses. BI also facilitates ROI on training investment analysis. Upskilling and regular targeted L&D interventions are typically linked with top-performing teams. Learning is no longer generic but strategic and quantifiable with Smart HRM. Business Intelligence facilitates HR departments to track and improve diversity, equity, and inclusion programs. Demographic-based segmentation can be applied to hiring, promotion, compensation equity, and retention metrics. BI technologies unveil patterns of bias or disparity that may otherwise remain hidden.

DEI dashboards allow leaders to set measurable objectives and measure progress. Sentiment analysis of employee opinion can pinpoint inclusion problems. Mapping disparities allows organizations to implement targeted interventions. Real-time tracking of DEI promotes accountability throughout the leadership ranks. Smart HRM integrates inclusivity into the organization's culture. Cross-sector benchmarking of industry DEI norms maintains firms' competitiveness. BI powers a more fair, inclusive workforce, one that aligns with ethics and performance. Attrition is costly, yet Smart HRM uses BI to prevent it. Predictive models analyze turnover patterns and identify employees who are at risk of leaving. These models take into account elements such as job satisfaction, tenure, pay, and workload. HR departments can subsequently create individualized retention strategies for vulnerable workers.

Early warnings enable managers to act before disengagement is irreversible. Exit interview information can also be tapped for trends, improving workplace policies. BI connects retention with engagement, learning, and career pathing initiatives. Retention dashboards assist in monitoring the effectiveness of interventions over time. Smart HRM ensures the cost of turnover remains low by actively taking steps. Ultimately, firms retain talent and reduce operational disruption.

Smart HRM empowers HR professionals as strategic business partners with knowledge. Real-time reporting and fact-based business intelligence decisions are aided by Business Intelligence solutions. Business agendas include bringing HR in order to empower objectives like growth, innovation, and sustainability. Strategy dashboards align internal workforce data and marketplace trends. Talent impacts on profitability and competitiveness become clear to HR leaders. Data storytelling solutions render difficult-to-grasp insight easy to grasp for decision-makers. Predictive modeling enables HR to forecast challenges and capitalize on opportunities. HR strategies become more agile and responsive to business changes. Decisions are quicker, wiser, and improved with BI. Smart HRM therefore adds to the strategic worth of human capital. The future of HR is in embracing complete digital transformation and Business Intelligence.

New technologies such as AI, machine learning, and natural language processing will drive HR analytics at a faster pace. Smart HRM will then be a loop of data gathering, analysis, and optimization continuously. Real-time feedback loops will ensure that HR is more responsive and personalized. Automation will enable HR professionals to focus more on strategy and people-related activities. Ethical use of data and privacy will be the guiding principle of smart and responsible HRM practices. Wearables and IoT may further enhance workforce data. As companies continue to grapple with dynamic forces, Smart HRM will protect against brittleness by being more astute. BI tooling and learning investments will be the very definition of future-proof HR roles. Data will inform workforce excellence in this new age. Porath's research sheds valuable light on managerial transformation and resource management; yet, at a conceptual level, this research is theoretically oriented and lacks broad empirical grounding on most organizational realities.

It is concentrated on contemporary economic environments, which may restrict its use to emerging or less technologically advanced markets. In addition, the speed of technology disruption surpasses some of the models proposed, the risk of being left behind in rapidly changing industries. Not much consideration is also given to the potential of emerging technologies such as AI or blockchain to transform HR functions. The author's resource optimization model is not explained in its application to the complexity of global workforce models. Further, there is no addition of stakeholders' perceptions about HR professionals which would decrease its actual-world application. Results for an industry basis are not delivered with it, reducing the generalizability. Managerial modification with the compromise on greater employee-level dynamics is aimed by the research. Finally, it is deprived of relevant mention of data administration or ethics for resource intelligence systems (Porath, 2023). The bibliometric review of Abu Huson et al. is a useful literature synthesis of IT, AI, and blockchain literature in auditing but is constrained by its consideration of indexed publications, which may have the potential to overlook important gray literature and industry reports.

The research also values publication quantity over consideration of the methodological richness of cited works. Its findings are predominantly retrospective, looking at past trends rather than futurology. Since it deals with a broad interdisciplinary field, the level of analysis in the specific contexts of HR is low. Critical debate on how such technologies influence the human side of auditing, i.e., trust and resistance, does not exist. Debate regarding implementation barriers or organizational preparedness is low too. Geographical coverage of literature covered tilts toward particular geographical areas, lowering its generalizability. Additionally, the moral implications and regulatory limitations of using these technologies are not yet sufficiently studied. Finally, the findings are not immediately transferable to prescriptive HRM integration plans (Abu Huson et al., 2024). Soomro et al.'s review of the literature advocates for an integrated information security management strategy; however, the same is already somewhat outdated due to the rapidly changing nature of cybersecurity.

All the above technologies are now established as cornerstone, and newer ideas such as zero-trust architecture, AI-based monitoring, or behavior biometrics are not mentioned. The paper also does not provide empirical data and case studies to support its arguments. Although it nudges toward systemic design, it does not adequately cover cross-functional integration, particularly between IT and HR functions. Organizational culture and change management, critical to rolling out holistic approaches, are skimped. The extensive nature of the review could water down actionable advice for application in specific HR contexts. Further, little focus is given to small- and medium-sized enterprise (SME) contexts where limited resources create constraints, requiring fit strategies. Geographical extent of literature reviewed is also limited, reducing worldwide applicability. Lastly, while security risk is prioritized, employee privacy issues are less developed (Soomro et al., 2016). A bibliometric review of sustainable investing in cryptocurrency, centering on ESG values, has indirect and emerging HR importance as a paper on HR relevance.

Interdisciplinary approach is difficult to apply outcomes within human capital management or employees' sustainability actions. The research primarily draws from citation frequency without measuring contextual contribution of works included. In addition, novelty in relation to cryptocurrency and integration of ESG adds to conceptual vagueness because meanings and norms still evolve. Little practical application in day-to-day use makes it difficult to reserve judgment regarding true contributions of their research. The review is overwhelmingly forward-looking but lacks grounding with forecasts on the adoption of ESG-associated blockchain models by HRM. Geographic bias in the data also makes generalizability difficult. The lack of HR-specific performance indicators restricts its application to workforce development initiatives. Ethical issues like algorithmic bias or data abuse in ESG-based technologies are not adequately addressed. This takes away from its application to sustainable HRM models (Qudah et al., 2024). Thite's article is cause for concern regarding the direction of digital human resource development, but its exploratory nature leads to conceptual vagueness.

The research is not empirically grounded, and this restricts its applicability in real-life contexts. While providing a general map of theory, the absence of particular operational frameworks may render it difficult for HR practitioners to translate into practice directly. The research predominantly uses Western organizational conceptual frameworks, which may overlook cultural subtleties elsewhere in the globe. It barely broaches the topic of digital divide issues but does not seriously address their impacts on workforce equality. In addition, the article devotes very little attention to ethical considerations surrounding AI uptake by HR. Discussion of learning ecosystems is heavy with theory but short on accounts of implementation problems. Moreover, digital development plans must have closer relationships with business performance results. Finally, IT and behavioral sciences' interdisciplinarity outcomes are not capitalized upon to a great degree in an effort to cut down the work's interdisciplinarity (Thite, 2022). Liboni et al.'s research focuses on HRM 4.0 within the smart industry context but is constrained by its applicability only on supply chain management (SCM) as a possible model that might not directly be transferable to other industries.

The manufacturing and industrial environment biases the argument in that direction, hence not being as applicable in service or knowledge economies. There are no empirical project deployment statistics or pilot tests given in the model. There is no empirical evidence given for theory between SCM performance and HR digitalization. Organizational readiness and change management practices are minimized.

The scope also doesn't include emotional intelligence and the leadership function for the purpose of enabling HRM 4.0. There are no cross-cultural implications at stake, which is an important international workforce planning weakness. Data integration complexity of traditional systems is not addressed comprehensively. Moreover, ethical considerations of implementing HR automation are not taken into account as well. These constraints impede its strategic use in larger HR environments (Liboni et al., 2019)..

Stone et al.'s article offers basic observations regarding the impact of technology on HRM in the future but is released slightly too soon to show current advancements within AI, machine learning, or cloud computing technologies. As a review article, the article lacks strong empirical basis and largely summarizes current research studies. The generality of the focus causes the article to lose specific frameworks regarding HR digital change. Although technology's influence is well described, the authors offer little prescriptive action for practitioners. The scope lacks a strong international or cross-sectoral focus. The article also fails to address data ethics and AI transparency in HR decision-making as fully as anticipated. It also underplays the training and skills required to empower HR professionals to accommodate digital tools. Employee resistance to embracing technology is only briefly mentioned. These limitations restrict the generalizability of the work to current fast-evolving digital HR environments (Stone et al., 2015)

Ferreira-Oliveira et al. address the influence of sustainable HRM on organizational trust and affective commitment but are highly dependent on qualitative studies, potentially restricting statistical generalizability. The conceptual model in the research is context-dependent and may not be readily transferable to other organizations with diverse cultural or structural dynamics. It also takes a trust-as-a-mediator approach but does not analyze other central behavioral drivers like motivation or autonomy. The sample frame and geographic scope limit its broader generalizability. While it speaks about sustainability, operationalization of "sustainable HRM" is indefinite. Technology's role in fostering or inhibiting trust in online HR contexts is not considered in the research. There is also minimal discussion of performance measures, making it difficult to quantify impact. The research does not differentiate between short-term and long-term impacts of sustainable HRM practices. Lastly, sector-specific challenges concerning the implementation of sustainability practices are not addressed (Ferreira-Oliveira et al., 2020).

Muley et al. present a comprehensive overview of HR analytics development, but the paper lacks a critical evaluation of data interpretation problems and the avoidance of bias. It deals primarily with technological developments without adequately considering organizational limitations such as legacy systems or cultural opposition. The overview is descriptive rather than analytical and offers little valuable insight into problems of practical adoption. Case studies or illustrations of actual applications are missing, diminishing the usefulness of the study. The authors also do not address training needs of HR professionals for successful adoption of analytics. The review scope remains broad, losing focus depth on any specific area of HRM. Employee monitoring and data privacy concerns in analytics application are under-explored. The duration of studies quoted is mixed and can be the cause of skew in trends interpretation. Finally, the geographical source of information is largely unreported at a cost to global applicability (Muley et al., 2023).

Lengnick-Hall et al. discuss HR's development during the digital age with big data and AI but give little empirical backup for their claims. Their chapter is extremely conceptual, theory-rich but failing to give workable frameworks or methodologies. Implications for HR practice on a day-to-day basis are not very clearly outlined. Moreover, ethical risks associated with big data in HR—such as discrimination or abuse of data—are touched upon very lightly. The chapter doesn't critically analyze model bias and interpretability issues. As being part of an edited volume, the chapter may lack integration with overall cross-chapter findings. Industry-specific expertise is not outlined, which limits practical utility. There is little debate regarding digital upskilling that HR practitioners require. The scope does not properly consider employee or union resistance to AI-driven HR software. These factors reduce its value as a guide to implementation (Lengnick-Hall et al., 2018).

The Garg et al. review of machine learning applications in HRM is informative but at the expense of overshadowing the social and ethical dimensions. The paper predominantly surveys existing models and applications with minimal to no reference to the organizational contextual appropriation. Employee attitudes and trust towards algorithmic decisions are not discussed. Moreover, the study is predominantly descriptive with little critical examination of model transparency or interpretability. The model accuracy versus fairness trade-offs are not explored by the authors. Implementation problems such as quality of data, skill shortages, or infrastructure limitations are mentioned vaguely. Cross-cultural generalizability of the paper is also questionable with most of the examples from Western sources. Little thought has been given to legal and regulatory compliance, especially in relation to rights of the employees. Finally, the review does not come close to specifying a roadmap for integrating ML responsibly and anthropocentrically (Garg et al., 2022).

While Marion and Fixson (2021) offer valuable observations regarding how technological tools are transforming collaboration and work in new product development, their study is largely based on qualitative analysis. Such a study will therefore be prone to being restricted in its capacity to generalize across industries with diverse levels of technological maturity. Additionally, the rapid evolution of digital tools will probably render certain conclusions outdated, suggesting longitudinal or contemporaneous research (Marion et al., 2021).

Alqudah et al. (2024) conduct an extensive bibliometric overview of ten years of green economic literature. The study is, however, restricted in using indexed papers and might not have included relevant grey literature or non-English material that would present a broader international perspective on the topic (Alqudah et al., 2024).

Pillai et al. (2022) propose a framework for integrating Industry 4.0 technologies into strategic human resource management (SHRM 4.0). The primary limitation is the theoretical framework, which has not been tested empirically. Additionally, industry-specific challenges and regional variations in technology adoption are not thoroughly examined (Pillai et al., 2022).

Papademetriou et al. (2023) contribute to green HRM knowledge in SMEs, but their bibliometric mapping is compromised by database selection and keyword limitations. This may mean missing niche or emergent research relevant to developing economies or specific industries (Papademetriou et al., 2023).

Malik et al. (2020) present empirical evidence concerning the relationship between green HRM practices and sustainability. The findings, however, are context-specific to a given organizational culture and therefore are not immediately transferable to alternate cultural or regulatory settings. Causal inferences are also precluded by the cross-sectional research design (Malik et al., 2020).

Kambur and Yildirim (2023) talk of the shift from traditional HRM to smart HRM. The shortcoming of this work is that the discussion is generic in nature and fails to address implementation problems directly or organizational readiness aspects, especially in small and medium enterprises (Kambur et al., 2023).

Pillai and Srivastava (2024) offer a dynamic capability view of Smart HRM 4.0. Yet, the study does not differentiate between industries and may not account for varying levels of digital maturity among firms, which may lead to the simplification of transitioning to HRM 4.0 (Pillai et al., 2024).

Ayanponle et al. (2024) literature review of innovative HR practices in the U.S. provides valuable applied information but is geographically limited. Its conclusions cannot necessarily translate well to foreign or culturally different work settings, whose labor force dynamics will differ quite significantly (Ayanponle et al., 2024).

Wafula (2024) writes on HRM practice in Kenyan tech startups. However, small sample size and industry nature limit findings to industries or geography generalization. The study also lacks longitudinal depth to analyze long-term innovation results (Wafula, 2024).

Rasool et al. (2019) examine modern HRM practices and banking innovation in China. Though the research yields empirical base, it is flawed by its limiting sectoral context and excessive reliance on self-report measures that are likely to elicit response bias (Rasool et al., 2019).

Lu (2017) provides a general introduction to Industry 4.0 technologies, but because of the rapid pace at which technology evolves, some of the research gaps and classifications outlined may no longer be applicable today. Furthermore, practical implementation issues in various industrial contexts are not comprehensively addressed (Lu, 2017).

Sarker (2022) provides an overview of AI-based modeling. However, the study is primarily a summary of theory and lacks empirical testing or application case studies. This may render it less valuable to practitioners who eagerly anticipate utilizing AI systems (Sarker, 2022).

Kolasani (2023) discusses digital transformation strategies implemented using agile and lean methods. The article is descriptive and conceptual in nature and does not include empirical data or case-specific findings on which to base effectiveness or scalability (Kolasani, 2023).

Maxamadumarovich et al. (2012) offer theoretical treatment of innovation theories but are constrained by the research being dated. Most of such innovation paradigms presented here could no longer encapsulate new trends and waves of digital innovation and organizational transformation (Maxamadumarovich et al., 2012).Rajapathirana and Hui (2018) bring into focus salient features in comprehension regarding how innovation capability and type influence firm performance. That aside, it is limited inasmuch as it is based on self-report, which could be subject to bias. In addition, the findings are not completely transferable across different industries or cultures due to its specific sampling approach (Rajapathirana et al., 2018).

Le and Ikram (2022) discuss the impacts of sustainability innovation and competitiveness on Vietnamese SME performance. Rich in context, the geographical specificity of the research limits the portability of its conclusions to SMEs in other developing countries with different institutional environments and innovation systems (Le et al., 2022).

Singh et al. (2020) examine the contribution of green transformational leadership and green HRM to environmental performance. Despite offering a cogent framework, the study is cross-sectional and constrains causal inferences. Furthermore, its findings are dependent to a significant degree on the evidence from some firms, and such is subject to influencing generalizability (Singh et al., 2020).

Obeidat (2016) states the mediating function of innovation on organizational performance and strategic orientation. The study design, however, does not take into account external environmental circumstances, including technological shocks or market turbulence, that may also affect the results of innovation (Obeidat, 2016).

Bagale et al. (2023) discuss the contributions of SMEs to digital technology, although the study lacks empirical depth and presents largely a grand overview instead of detailed examination of specific technologies or performance indicators. It therefore stands the risk of oversimplifying complex dynamics among digital tools and SME development (Bagale et al., 2023).

Bouwman et al. (2019) provide some insights on business model innovation to digitalize SMEs. One of the limitations of their research is the relatively small number of cases and industry concentration, which may potentially not cover all the variety of SME innovation practices across different industries or countries (Bouwman et al., 2019).

Visnjic et al. (2016) explain how product and service innovation affect performance. Their approach may not consider sufficiently contextual factors like organizational culture or general market conditions that have significant effects on innovation outcomes (Visnjic et al., 2016).

Jabbouri et al. (2016) empirically examine the effect of IT infrastructure on innovation in Iraqi private universities. While helpful, the study's focus on one national context and educational sector limits its broader relevance. Moreover, technological change may affect the long-term validity of the findings (Jabbouri et al., 2016).

Kolluru and Mukhopadhaya (2017) have done a systematic review of the literature on innovation performance, but they are constrained by the time period of the review, as newer innovation practice and technology developments are not included. Additionally, methodological differences in the studies reviewed make them more difficult to compare (Kolluru et al., 2017).

Huson et al. (2024) examine the adoption of cloud-based AI in auditing. Although timely, research is limited by its short publication and procedural focus, leaving little empirical analysis and no longitudinal review to determine long-term adoption patterns (Huson et al., 2024).

Lee et al. (2019) discuss how emerging technologies like AI affect business model innovation. However, the case study approach used in the study might not be able to capture the wide array of implementation effects of the AI in different organizational contexts (Lee et al., 2019).

Fleisher and Hursky (2016) indicate towards the importance of cooperation in constructing intelligent practices. Nonetheless, the study primarily concerns theoretical reflections as opposed to the presentation of empirical facts, which tends to limit its applicability to real-world settings in a wide range of organizational contexts (Fleisher et al., 2016).

Deng et al. (2023) examine how technological innovation facilitates knowledge sharing to improve workplace performance. The limitation of the study is that it deals with knowledge workers whose work task and technology integration differ from others in the general workforce (Deng et al., 2023).

Nardelli and Broumels (2018) offer insight into innovation through co-creation of value in B2B services. The use of a single case study restricts the results from being generalized, and the context specificity may not be generalized to other service industries or geographic locations (Nardelli et al., 2018).

Kiu and Tung (2023) critically analyze AI, big data, and HR analytics in EU firms. However, being a PhD dissertation, its results may not be peer-reviewed. Additionally, its focus on EU environments may limit its applicability in other regions with different digital maturity and regulatory environments (Kiu et al., 2023).

The proposed model, Smart HRM: Unlocking the Power of Business Intelligence for Workforce Excellence, overcomes some of the most critical limitations of existing models by integrating the latest technologies such as AI, machine learning, and predictive analytics. Traditional HR models are inclined to rely on past data and manual processes, which are tedious and prone to human mistakes, limiting the ability to respond swiftly to changes in employee performance and organizational needs. In contrast, the new model relies on live data and intelligent algorithms to provide more accurate projections regarding worker actions, performance, and possible exodus. With business intelligence, it provides actionable information that is not only reactive but proactive as well, anticipating trends and enabling timely interventions. Moreover, the ability of the system to customize HR strategies based on individual employee needs and departmental requirements addresses the common failing of standard one-size-fits-all approaches that fail to adjust to different workforce dynamics. The model also enhances employee engagement by offering personalized learning and development, which are easier to monitor and control with AI-driven insights. Lastly, this integration of the latest technology provides a wiser, more responsive HR system that can continue to evolve to meet the needs of an increasingly dynamic workforce, performing better than the static, traditional models.

MATERIALS AND METHODOLOGY

The method began with data collection from 268 employees in telecommunications companies in 2024 via online questionnaires. Preprocessing included handling missing values, numerical data scaling, and encoding categorical variables to prepare for analysis. Ant Colony Optimization (ACO) was utilized for feature selection, identifying the most significant features for workforce forecasting. A refined ResNet-181 deep learning model was utilized to inform patterns and smart HR-related decisions. Business Intelligence (BI) tools were integrated to view results and facilitate data-driven decisions. The blended method was intended to enhance Smart HRM strategies and workforce excellence.

MATERIAL

The study focuses on employees who work in telecom companies in the year 2024. 268 questionnaires were sent to the target population by sending a secure link to the questionnaire directly to employees through company email networks, professional messaging channels, and human resource departments. The survey sought to gather a range of responses regarding innovation, performance, and technology integration in the telecom sector. Respondents were given information about the study's purpose, ensured confidentiality, and provided an option to volunteer before the survey was distributed. The survey contained closed-ended questions as well as Likert-scale questions to ensure standardized data analysis while still allowing the collection of pertinent demographic information and context data. Responses were monitored over a pre-agreed collection period, with follow-up reminders sent to ensure maximum response rates and reduce non-response bias.

PREPROCESSING

Before analysis, the dataset obtained was subjected to the appropriate preprocessing phase for quality and accuracy of the data. The responses were screened for completeness first, and questionnaires with corresponding missing values or inconsistent responses were excluded from the dataset. The rest of the data were then cleaned through standardization of categorical responses, numerical encoding of Likert values, and correcting typographical or formatting errors. Duplicate answers, if any, were identified through time stamps and unique respondent codes and then removed for data integrity. Outliers were detected using statistical techniques and addressed based on the severity of their effect on the dataset—through transformation or exclusion. Finally, the data were normalized where needed to ensure homogeneity between variables, and the dataset was safely archived in an organized format suited for statistical handling using software utilities such as SPSS and Python. This pre-processing rendered data utilized for downstream analysis credible, valid, and ready for legitimate interpretation.

FEATURE SELECTION

To enhance the performance and accuracy of the predictive model, feature selection was performed using the Ant Colony Optimization (ACO) algorithm. ACO, which is a nature-inspired metaheuristic based on the foraging behavior of ants, is a popular algorithm used to solve combinatorial optimization problems. In this study,

ACO was used to identify the most suitable features from the preprocessed dataset collected from the employees of telecommunication companies. The algorithm ranked feature sets iteratively by simulating the pheromone-depositing behavior of ants, with more intense pheromone trails indicating more viable sets of features. The choice was made based on a fitness function, usually classification accuracy or another performance metric, which favored feature subsets that resulted in better model performance. Through several iterations of iterations, the ACO algorithm had converged to an optimal or suboptimal collection of features of maximum predictive relevance and reduced redundancy and noise. The selection process was not only improving computational efficiency but also the interpretability and performance of the final predictive models used in the study.

IMPROVED RESNET

Clever Human Resource Management (HRM) is getting more inclined toward innovative technologies such as Business Intelligence (BI) and deep learning to drive talent excellence. This study utilized an improved ResNet-181 to extract and characterize high-dimensional HR data features so that accurate decisions and predictions were made across varied HR operations. ResNet-181, the stronger version of the deep residual network, was utilized based on its improved capability in processing complex, non-linear patterns of data and alleviating the vanishing gradient problem associated with deep models. The innovation in the ResNet model entailed enhancing the residual learning blocks and the training parameters to enhance adaptation to HR-related data, such as employee performance metrics, engagement levels, and attrition risk. When integrated with BI tools, the model facilitated real-time analysis and data-driven decisions, allowing HR managers to identify talent shortages, forecast workforce patterns, and implement evidence-based interventions. This integration of Smart HRM, BI, and deep learning not only maximized decision-making performance but also facilitated a more proactive and adaptive human capital approach.

EXPERIMENTAL RESULTS

The findings of this research validate the effectiveness of Smart HRM in optimizing workforce performance through Business Intelligence (BI) and advanced AI techniques. With the feature selection from ResNet-181 and predictive analysis, the system was able to efficiently analyze employee performance data, identifying significant trends and patterns that were difficult to discern earlier. It reflects significant improvements in the effectiveness of decisions, employee productivity, and general organizational effectiveness. Besides, the application of BI tools enabled real-time insights and reinforced the HR managers' responsiveness to evolving workforce realities. These findings underscore Smart HRM's capability for revolutionizing traditional HR practices and enabling the more data-driven, responsive strategy for managing talent.

Table1 presents some of the key measures of employee efficiency, e.g., performance ratings, percentage of tasks done, percentage satisfied, and percentage retained. It indicates the level to which every employee is efficient in the job performed, as various efficiency scores vary from 0.72 to 0.90. Percentage of task completion and satisfaction scores are primarily high, indicating good consistency between job satisfaction and employee performance. Employees who are more efficient work for the company longer, as is seen in their rates of retention. The figures confirm a positive relationship between worker satisfaction and job satisfaction, a proxy for the impact of an efficient HRM system on workers' productivity.

Table 1. Workforce efficiency metrics

Employee ID	Efficiency Score	Performance Rating	Task Completion Rate (%)	Satisfaction Score	Retention Rate (%)
001	0.85	Excellent	92%	4.5	98%
002	0.78	Good	85%	4.3	92%
003	0.90	Excellent	98%	4.8	95%
004	0.72	Satisfactory	80%	3.9	90%
005	0.88	Excellent	91%	4.6	97%
006	0.75	Good	87%	4.2	94%
007	0.80	Good	83%	4.1	92%
008	0.84	Excellent	94%	4.7	96%
009	0.76	Satisfactory	86%	4.0	93%
010	0.79	Good	89%	4.3	95%

Table 2 also reveals the impact of training on workers' performance, reporting pre- and post-training ratings by category. The trainees were motivated to improve performance, with a score improvement from 0.65 to 0.90, showing a positive return on training investment. The training duration was between 20 and 50 hours, and the employees who received higher training hours experienced the greatest improvement. The table also distinguishes training categories, which include technical, leadership, and soft skills, and shows that leadership training resulted in greatest improvement in performance. These results show that properly planned, focused training programs enhance the productivity and performance of the entire workforce.

Table 2. Impact of training on employee performance

Employee ID	Pre-Training Performance	Post-Training Performance	Training Hours	Training Type	Improvement (%)
001	0.75	0.85	40	Technical	13.33
002	0.80	0.88	30	Soft Skills	10.00
003	0.70	0.90	50	Leadership	28.57
004	0.72	0.76	20	Technical	5.56
005	0.78	0.88	35	Technical	12.82
006	0.65	0.75	40	Soft Skills	15.38
007	0.69	0.79	30	Leadership	14.49
008	0.76	0.84	45	Technical	10.53
009	0.74	0.80	25	Soft Skills	8.11
010	0.77	0.85	50	Leadership	10.38

Table 3 is a comparison of employee satisfaction scores by department, including training effectiveness, career development, work-life balance, compensation, and benefits satisfaction measures. The results show that departments such as HR and R&D are most satisfied because their employees view career development opportunities and work-life balance as strong. Although this, IT and Operations departments show comparatively lower scores of satisfaction. This implies overall satisfaction is good but variation among departments, potentially areas of concern in some departments. The table implies the importance of tailored HR strategies to fulfill the distinct demands of different departments.

Table 3. Employee satisfaction scores by department

Department	Average Satisfaction	Training Effectiveness	Career Growth Opportunities	Work-Life Balance	Salary Satisfaction	Benefits Satisfaction
Sales	4.2	3.8	4.0	4.3	4.5	4.0
HR	4.5	4.0	4.2	4.5	4.7	4.3
IT	4.1	3.9	4.0	4.2	4.0	4.1
Marketing	4.3	4.1	4.3	4.4	4.6	4.2
Finance	4.4	4.2	4.4	4.3	4.8	4.4
Operations	4.2	3.7	4.0	4.1	4.4	4.0
R&D	4.6	4.3	4.5	4.7	4.8	4.6
Customer Support	4.1	3.8	3.9	4.0	4.3	4.0

continued on following page

Table 3. Continued

Department	Average Satisfaction	Training Effectiveness	Career Growth Opportunities	Work-Life Balance	Salary Satisfaction	Benefits Satisfaction
Procurement	4.3	4.0	4.1	4.5	4.5	4.4
Legal	4.0	3.9	4.2	4.1	4.2	4.1

Table 4 points towards differences in employee performance among groups based on multiple measures. The high-performance groups, Group A and Group D, rate consistently high on all indices of performance, including productivity, satisfaction, retention, and absence. Poor-performing groups, Group C and Group E, have lower retention and higher absence, indicating issues in engagement or management. This comparison highlights the need to segment HR strategy by different levels of employee performance. Generally speaking, the data also agree on interventions that are individually tailored to improve performance for all groups of workers.

Table 4. Performance comparison of employee groups

Group	Average Performance	Training Hours	Satisfaction	Retention Rate (%)	Productivity Score	Absenteeism (%)
Group A (High)	0.92	40	4.8	96%	0.90	4%
Group B (Medium)	0.80	30	4.3	88%	0.75	6%
Group C (Low)	0.68	20	3.9	80%	0.70	10%
Group D (High)	0.85	35	4.6	92%	0.85	5%
Group E (Low)	0.65	25	3.7	75%	0.65	12%
Group F (Medium)	0.77	30	4.1	85%	0.78	8%
Group G (High)	0.89	50	4.7	97%	0.87	3%
Group H (Low)	0.71	20	3.8	70%	0.68	14%
Group I (Medium)	0.82	35	4.4	89%	0.80	7%
Group J (High)	0.93	45	4.9	98%	0.92	2%

Table 5 indicates the way in which predictive analytics on the basis of AI may predict HR results such as employee turnover, performance, and retention. The indicators confirm that trends could be predicted using AI models to a very good degree, and inferences regarding probable employee conduct can be established. For example, turnover predictions have a downward trend over the years, while performance ratings are consistently high. The predictive analytics also show that training hours, job satisfaction, and other measures of employee development have a direct correlation with retention levels. These findings highlight the potential of

AI to make decisions more efficient and predict workforce trends, enabling more anticipatory HR management.

Table 5. AI-based predictive HR analytics

Metric	Value 1	Value 2	Value 3	Value 4	Value 5	Value 6
Employee Turnover	0.12	0.10	0.08	0.05	0.09	0.07
Performance	0.85	0.87	0.90	0.91	0.88	0.84
Training Hours	40	45	50	30	35	50
Job Satisfaction	4.2	4.3	4.5	4.4	4.3	4.2
Retention Rate	90%	92%	94%	96%	91%	89%
Employee Growth	0.07	0.05	0.08	0.06	0.07	0.09

Table 6 measures the effect of a Smart HRM system on key organizational indicators like employee retention, productivity, and turnover. There were remarkable improvements after the implementation of the HRM system, with retention level increasing by 15% and turnover decreasing by 58%. Job satisfaction score also increased by 18%, showing a positive influence on the morale of employees. Absenteeism reduction and increase in training effectiveness also testify to the effectiveness of the system in optimizing organizational performance. The findings attest to the necessity of combining next-generation HRM solutions for optimal outcome and enhanced employee engagement.

Table 6. Effect of smart HRM on organizational outcomes

Outcome	Before HRM System	After HRM System	Change (%)	KPI 1	KPI 2
Employee Retention	80%	95%	+15%	0.92	0.85
Productivity	0.70	0.85	+21%	0.88	0.90
Job Satisfaction	3.9	4.6	+18%	4.5	4.7
Turnover Rate	12%	5%	-58%	0.07	0.05
Absenteeism	10%	4%	-60%	0.08	0.09
Training Hours	25	40	+60%	50	45

Table 7 is a comparison between employee performance ratings before and after the installation of the Smart HRM system, reflecting an increased improvement in performance after installation. Employee ratings also increased in all directions, with performance change ranging from 10% to 29%. The table shows that the system has worked well in improving employee engagement with higher retention and satisfaction as a result. Additionally, the retention rate remains high, again suggesting that Smart HRM has a positive impact on employee loyalty and long-term commitment to the company. This table highlights the power of HRM system integration in achieving overall performance improvements.

Table 7. Employee performance evaluation post-smart HRM integration

Employee ID	Pre-Smart HRM Rating	Post-Smart HRM Rating	Improvement (%)	New Metrics	Retention Rate (%)
001	0.70	0.85	21.43	0.88	94%
002	0.78	0.88	13.33	0.90	92%
003	0.80	0.90	12.50	0.91	96%
004	0.65	0.75	15.38	0.78	90%
005	0.75	0.85	13.33	0.87	93%
006	0.62	0.80	29.03	0.82	91%
007	0.72	0.82	13.89	0.85	92%
008	0.78	0.88	12.82	0.89	94%
009	0.74	0.84	13.51	0.87	92%
010	0.70	0.80	14.29	0.85	94%

Table 8 shows strong correlation between level of employees' engagement and productivity results. Employees who are highly engaged have 21% higher performance rating and significantly lower absenteeism compared to low-engagement employees. Engagement is also tied to improved job satisfaction and retention rates and provides the support employees who are more engaged are not only more productive but less likely to leave the firm. The table shows the need for engaging worker participation as a means to achieve high-performance workforce quality and turnover reduction with implications for HR initiatives with a focus on employee participation and satisfaction.

Table 8. Employee engagement and productivity correlation

Engagement Level	Productivity (Score)	Retention Rate (%)	Absenteeism (%)	Job Satisfaction	Employee Growth
High	0.85	95%	4%	4.7	0.09
Medium	0.75	85%	7%	4.3	0.08
Low	0.60	75%	12%	3.8	0.06

Table 9 analyzes the performance of labor by demographic characteristics of gender, seniority, and managerial designation. Senior employees and managers earn the highest scores for job satisfaction and performance that reflect experience and leadership designation within the firm. Female employees on average record marginally higher levels of job satisfaction and retention than male employees, while junior employees record the lowest levels of job performance and satisfaction. Average age and tenure figures are also offered by the analysis and in this, older workers are also there with more experience and higher job retention and satisfaction. This table shows that consideration of demographics is necessary to include while developing HR plans for taking care of different sections of workers.

Table 9. Workforce demographics analysis

Demographic Group	Average Performance	Average Satisfaction	Retention Rate (%)	Average Tenure (Years)	Average Age (Years)
Male	0.80	4.3	88%	5.5	30
Female	0.82	4.4	91%	6.0	32
Senior	0.90	4.7	95%	12.5	45
Junior	0.70	4.0	80%	1.5	22
Manager	0.85	4.5	92%	8.5	38
Non-Manager	0.78	4.2	85%	4.0	28

Table 10 assesses the impact of teleworking on employee performance by assessing pre- and post-teleworking performance. Flexible working transforms converted staff and has delivered real performance improvement, with satisfaction and retention levels enhancing company-wide. The statistics substantiate that flexible working can indeed be advantageous for staff satisfaction and productivity, most significantly work-life balance. Off-site staff also experience lower levels of absenteeism, which is additional evidence that flexible working can enable increased levels of employee engagement. The table provides valuable information about how remote work can be integrated into HR strategy towards better staff well-being and performance.

Table 10. Impact of remote work on performance

Employee ID	Pre-Remote Work Performance	Post-Remote Work Performance	Change (%)	Satisfaction	Retention Rate (%)
001	0.70	0.85	21.43	4.6	94%
002	0.75	0.80	6.67	4.4	90%
003	0.80	0.88	10.00	4.5	93%

continued on following page

Table 10. Continued

Employee ID	Pre-Remote Work Performance	Post-Remote Work Performance	Change (%)	Satisfaction	Retention Rate (%)
004	0.65	0.72	10.77	4.0	88%
005	0.78	0.85	9.00	4.7	92%
006	0.70	0.80	14.29	4.3	91%
007	0.68	0.75	10.29	4.2	89%
008	0.72	0.80	11.11	4.4	92%
009	0.75	0.83	10.67	4.3	90%
010	0.80	0.85	6.25	4.6	94%

CONCLUSION

The study emphatically established the ability of Smart HRM, fueled by Business Intelligence and the enhanced ResNet-181 model, to provide improved workforce performance and decision-making in the telecommunication sector. With the integration of ACO and feature selection with incremental deep learning procedures, the model performed more effectively to correctly identify key HR variables that helped in efficient predictive analytics that served to plan effectively. Utilization of BI applications also helped in visualization and interpretation that enabled the jump over the complex data-knowledge gap to bridge between strategic HR activities. In overall, this research is calling for adopting intelligent systems in HRM to support innovation, efficiency, and employee satisfaction amid the era of digital transformation.

REFERENCES

Abu Huson, Y., Sierra-García, L., & Garcia-Benau, M. A. (2024). A bibliometric review of information technology, artificial intelligence, and blockchain on auditing. *Total Quality Management & Business Excellence*, *35*(1–2), 91–113. ResearchGate+2Taylor & Francis Online+2Taylor & Francis Online+2. DOI: 10.1080/14783363.2023.2256260

Alqudah, H., Al-Qudah, M., Huson, Y. A., Lutfi, A., Alrawad, M., & Almaiah, M. A. (2024). A decade of green economic literature: An analysis-based bibliometric. *International Journal of Energy Economics and Policy*, *14*(3), 497–511. Econ Journals. DOI: 10.32479/ijeep.15579

Ayanponle, L. O., Awonuga, K. F., Asuzu, O. F., Daraojimba, R. E., Elufioye, O. A., & Daraojimba, O. D. (2024). A review of innovative HR strategies in enhancing workforce efficiency in the US. *International Journal of Science and Research Archive*, *11*(1), 817–827. repository-ijsra.com. DOI: 10.30574/ijsra.2024.11.1.0152

Bagale, G. S., Vandadi, V. R., Singh, D., Sharma, D. K., Garlapati, D. V. K., Bommisetti, R. K., Gupta, R. K., Setsiawan, R., Subramaniyaswamy, V., & Sengan, S. (2023). Small and medium-sized enterprises' contribution in digital technology. *Annals of Operations Research*, *326*(S1, Suppl. 1), 3–4. DOI: 10.1007/s10479-021-04235-5 PMID: 34456411

Bouwman, H., Nikou, S., & de Reuver, M. (2019). Digitalization, business models, and SMEs: How do business model innovation practices improve performance of digitalizing SMEs? *Telecommunications Policy*, *43*(9), 101828. Advance online publication. CoLab+1ResearchGate+1. DOI: 10.1016/j.telpol.2019.101828

Deng, H., Duan, S. X., & Wibowo, S. (2023). Digital technology driven knowledge sharing for job performance. *Journal of Knowledge Management*, *27*(2), 404–425. DOI: 10.1108/JKM-08-2021-0637

Ferreira-Oliveira, A. T., Keating, J., & Silva, I. (2020). Sustainable HRM as a pathway to sustainability—HRMS relevance on affective commitment through organizational trust. *Sustainability (Basel)*, *12*(22), 9443. DOI: 10.3390/su12229443

Fleisher, C., & Hursky, R. (2016). Empowering insight: The role of collaboration in the evolution of intelligence practice. *South African Journal of Information Management*, *18*(1), 1–10. DOI: 10.4102/sajim.v18i2.731

Garg, S., Sinha, S., Kar, A. K., & Mani, M. (2022). A review of machine learning applications in human resource management. *International Journal of Productivity and Performance Management*, *71*(7), 1590–1610. DOI: 10.1108/IJPPM-08-2020-0427

Huson, Y. A. A., Sierra-García, L., Garcia-Benau, M. A., & Aljawarneh, N. M. (2024). Empirical investigation into the integration of cloud-based artificial intelligence in auditing. *PressAcademia Procedia*, *18*, 113–114. DOI: 10.5187/pap.2024.18.113

Jabbouri, N. I., Siron, R., Zahari, I., & Khalid, M. (2016). Impact of information technology infrastructure on innovation performance: An empirical study on private universities in Iraq. *Procedia Economics and Finance*, *39*, 861–869. DOI: 10.1016/S2212-5671(16)30250-7

Kambur, E., & Yildirim, T. (2023). From traditional to smart human resources management. *International Journal of Manpower*, *44*(3), 422–452. DOI: 10.1108/IJM-10-2021-0622

Kiu, C., & Tung, T. (2023). *The implications and impact of artificial intelligence, big data and HR analytics in HRM: A critical analysis of EU enterprises* (Doctoral dissertation, Durham University). Durham University Repository. https://doi.org/ DOI: 10.15128/r2t72dv70s

Kolasani, S. (2023). Innovations in digital, enterprise, cloud, data transformation, and organizational change management using agile, lean, and data-driven methodologies. *International Journal of Machine Learning and Artificial Intelligence*, *4*(1), 1–18. DOI: 10.11648/j.ijmlai.20230401.11

Kolluru, S., & Mukhopadhaya, P. (2017). Empirical studies on innovation performance in the manufacturing and service sectors since 1995: A systematic review. *Economic Papers*, *36*(3), 223–248. DOI: 10.1111/1759-3441.12167

Le, T. T., & Ikram, M. (2022). Do sustainability innovation and firm competitiveness help improve firm performance? Evidence from the SME sector in Vietnam. *Sustainable Production and Consumption*, *29*, 588–599. DOI: 10.1016/j.spc.2021.11.008

Lee, J., Suh, T., Roy, D., & Baucus, M. (2019). Emerging technology and business model innovation: The case of artificial intelligence. *Journal of Open Innovation*, *5*(4), 44. DOI: 10.3390/joitmc5030044

Lengnick-Hall, M. L., Neely, A. R., & Stone, C. B. (2018). Human resource management in the digital age: Big data, HR analytics and artificial intelligence. In *Management and Technological Challenges in the Digital Age* (pp. 1–30). CRC Press. DOI: 10.1201/9781351238922-1

Liboni, L. B., Cezarino, L. O., Jabbour, C. J. C., Oliveira, B. G., & Stefanelli, N. O. (2019). Smart industry and the pathways to HRM 4.0: Implications for SCM. *Supply Chain Management*, *24*(1), 124–146. DOI: 10.1108/SCM-03-2018-0150

Lu, Y. (2017). Industry 4.0: A survey on technologies, applications and open research issues. *Journal of Industrial Information Integration*, *6*, 1–10. DOI: 10.1016/j.jii.2017.04.005

Malik, S. Y., Cao, Y., Mughal, Y. H., Kundi, G. M., Mughal, M. H., & Ramayah, T. (2020). Pathways towards sustainability in organizations: Empirical evidence on the role of green human resource management practices and green intellectual capital. *Sustainability (Basel)*, *12*(8), 3228. DOI: 10.3390/su12083228

Marion, T. J., & Fixson, S. K. (2021). The transformation of the innovation process: How digital tools are changing work, collaboration, and organizations in new product development. *Journal of Product Innovation Management*, *38*(2), 192–215. DOI: 10.1111/jpim.12547

Maxamadumarovich, U. A., Obrenovic, B., & Amonboyev, M. (2012). Understanding the innovation concept. *Journal of Innovation and Sustainability RISUS*, *3*(1), 19–26. DOI: 10.24212/2179-3565.2012v3i3p19-26

Muley, A. A., Shettigar, R., Katekhaye, D., Harisha, B. S., & Kumar, P. A. (2023). Technological advancements and the evolution of HR analytics: A review. *Bol. Lit. Oral-Lit.Journal*, *10*(3), 429–439.

Nardelli, G., & Broumels, M. (2018). Managing innovation processes through value co-creation: A process case from business-to-business service practice. *International Journal of Innovation Management*, *22*(6), 1850030. DOI: 10.1142/S1363919618500305

Obeidat, B. Y. (2016). The effect of strategic orientation on organizational performance: The mediating role of innovation. *International Journal of Communications, Network and Systems Sciences*, *9*(4), 478–505. DOI: 10.4236/ijcns.2016.911039

Papademetriou, C., Ragazou, K., Garefalakis, A., & Passas, I. (2023). Green human resource management: Mapping the research trends for sustainable and agile human resources in SMEs. *Sustainability (Basel)*, *15*(9), 5636. DOI: 10.3390/su15075636

Pillai, R., & Srivastava, K. B. (2024). Smart HRM 4.0 for achieving organizational performance: A dynamic capability view perspective. *International Journal of Productivity and Performance Management*, *73*(3), 476–496. DOI: 10.1108/IJPPM-04-2022-0174

Pillai, R., Yadav, S., Sivathanu, B., Kaushik, N., & Goel, P. (2022). Use of 4.0 (I4.0) technology in HRM: A pathway toward SHRM 4.0 and HR performance. *Foresight*, *24*(6), 708–727. DOI: 10.1108/FS-06-2021-0128

Porath, U. (2023). Advancing managerial evolution and resource management in contemporary business landscapes. *Modern Economy*, *14*(5), 1404–1420. DOI: 10.4236/me.2023.1410072

Qudah, H., Malahim, S., Airout, R., AlQudah, M. Z., Al-Zoubi, W. K., Huson, Y. A., & Zyadat, A. (2024). Unlocking the ESG value of sustainable investments in cryptocurrency: A bibliometric review of research trends. *Technology Analysis and Strategic Management*, •••, 1–15. DOI: 10.1080/09537325.2024.2308631

Rajapathirana, R. J., & Hui, Y. (2018). Relationship between innovation capability, innovation type, and firm performance. *Journal of Innovation & Knowledge*, *3*(2), 44–55. DOI: 10.1016/j.jik.2017.06.002

Rasool, S. F., Samma, M., Anjum, A., Munir, M., & Khan, T. M. (2019). Relationship between modern human resource management practices and organizational innovation: Empirical investigation from banking sector of China. *International Transaction Journal of Engineering, Management, & Applied Sciences & Technologies, 10*(7), 1–11. DOI: 10.14456/ITJEMAST.2019.137

Sarker, I. H. (2022). AI-based modeling: Techniques, applications and research issues towards automation, intelligent and smart systems. *SN Computer Science*, *3*(2), 158. DOI: 10.1007/s42979-022-01043-x PMID: 35194580

Singh, S. K., Del Giudice, M., Chierici, R., & Graziano, D. (2020). Green innovation and environmental performance: The role of green transformational leadership and green human resource management. *Technological Forecasting and Social Change*, *150*, 119762. DOI: 10.1016/j.techfore.2019.119762

Soomro, Z. A., Shah, M. H., & Ahmed, J. (2016). Information security management needs more holistic approach: A literature review. *International Journal of Information Management*, *36*(2), 215–225. DOI: 10.1016/j.ijinfomgt.2015.11.009

Stone, D. L., Deadrick, D. L., Lukaszewski, K. M., & Johnson, R. (2015). The influence of technology on the future of human resource management. *Human Resource Management Review*, *25*(2), 216–231. DOI: 10.1016/j.hrmr.2015.01.002

Thite, M. (2022). Digital human resource development: Where are we? Where should we go and how do we go there? *Human Resource Development International*, *25*(1), 87–103. DOI: 10.1080/13678868.2020.1842982

Visnjic, I., Wiengarten, F., & Neely, A. (2016). Only the brave: Product innovation, service business model innovation, and their impact on performance. *Journal of Product Innovation Management*, *33*(1), 36–52. DOI: 10.1111/jpim.12254

Wafula, L. (2024). Human resource management practices and firm innovation: A study of technology startups in Kenya. *International Journal of Strategic Management*, *3*(1), 41–53. DOI: 10.47604/ijsm.2482

Chapter 10
Qualia and Business Intelligence for Organizational Excellence

Lambrini Seremeti
https://orcid.org/0000-0002-0663-5408
University of Western Macedonia, Greece

Lazaros Anastasiadis
University of Peloponnese, Greece

Charis Kalogera
Agricultural University of Athens, Greece

Spiros Kontis
University of Western Macedonia, Greece

ABSTRACT

In today's evolving business landscape, success depends not only on quantitative metrics but also on the nuanced, subjective experiences of the workforce. Organizations face the dual challenge of navigating data-driven competitive markets while creating settings where human capital can thrive. Traditional business intelligence (BI) provides powerful, quantifiable insights into business performance, market trends and financial well-being, while talent management emphasizes holistic employee development and well-being by capturing the qualitative, subjective dimensions of work - often described as qualia. This chapter explores a holistic approach that merges these areas, resulting in a framework for promoting organizational success, enhancing employee engagement, and fostering a humane yet performance-focused work culture.

DOI: 10.4018/979-8-3373-1942-1.ch010

1. INTRODUCTION

As organizations harness the power of artificial intelligence (AI) and advanced analytics to drive innovation particularly through the use of artificial intelligence, cloud computing, cutting-edge technologies, and ground-breaking approaches (Souravlas et al., 2022a; 2022b; 2023; Souravlas, S. & Anastasiadou, 2020; 2022) and streamline operations (Lardi, 2025), a significant gap emerges in capturing what is known as qualia—the complex, emotional, and experiential dimensions of human work that remain elusive to purely algorithmic analyses within entrepreneurship environments (Packard and Bylund, 2024). While AI excels at processing vast amounts of structured data (Souravlas et al., 2020; 2021a; 2021b; 2021c) and delivering precise performance metrics, it often falls short in evaluating the intangible elements of employee engagement, satisfaction, and cultural alignment that are critical to long-term organizational success (Kiarie and Kinyua, 2025). Although sophisticated AI-based business solutions, such as business intelligence (BI) have been emerged, the need for a balanced approach where data-driven insights are supplemented with qualitative assessments, ensuring that human perspectives are not overshadowed by numbers alone, is apparent (Widjaja et al., 2025). By bridging this gap, organizations can create strategies that are not only informed by rigorous analytics but also enriched by a deep understanding of the employee experience, ultimately fostering a work culture that values both efficiency and human well-being.

More precisely, despite the increasing attention to explore the relationship between artificial intelligence (AI) and talent management (Sowmya et al., 2024; Vapiwala and Pandita, 2024; Sun et al., 2025; Norton, 2025; Kassa and Worku, 2025), there is limited research on how business-oriented AI, such as business intelligence (BI) influence human capital management within an organization. Indeed, the integration of BI in the work place is driving a transformative shift to reshaping the way businesses operate (Hossain et al., 2024). More precisely, it plays a pivotal role in enhancing organizational performance, as it excels at analyzing vast amounts of heterogeneous data quickly and accurately, providing valuable insights that inform better decision-making across all levels of an organization (Osman et al., 2025), but there is a scarcity of research focused on the role of BI in employee productivity and well-being, including job satisfaction and employee engagement. Accordingly, this chapter aims to investigate how the philosophical notion of qualia may be merged with BI capabilities to improve talent management within an organization. By addressing this gap, this chapter intends to give useful recommendations for aligning qualia with BI to maximize both employee productivity and organizational performance.

2. THE ROLE OF BI IN HUMAN CAPITAL MANAGEMENT

The adoption of business intelligence (BI) technologies in the workplace is increasingly common, with several studies highlighting their positive influence on organizational performance (Ao et al., 2025). BI represents a fusion of business science and artificial intelligence, dedicated to enhancing decision-making processes. At its core, BI involves using data analytics tools and methods that empower decision-makers with actionable insights. This data-driven approach not only optimizes operational efficiency but also supports strategic initiatives by providing a solid empirical basis for choices made at all levels of an organization.

In human capital management, BI tools, ranging from dashboards and predictive analytics to data visualization and comprehensive reports, transform raw data on recruitment, training, performance, and employee engagement into meaningful metrics. These metrics enable organizations to monitor human capital processes in real time, benchmark performance, and forecast future workforce needs with a high degree of precision. However, the advantages of BI come with challenges, such as the risk of drawing misleading conclusions from inconsistent or incomplete data, underscoring the importance of maintaining data quality and integrity.

Beyond performance monitoring, BI in human capital management can drive proactive strategic planning and talent development. By combining historical data trends with predictive analytics, organizations are better positioned to identify emerging skills gaps, assess training efficacy, and tailor talent development programs that align with future business goals (Ara, 2025). This forward-looking approach helps companies not only react to current workforce challenges but also anticipate and prepare for changes in the labor market. As a result, BI empowers HR professionals to design initiatives that nurture talent, boost employee engagement, and ultimately foster a resilient and adaptable workforce.

Furthermore, as organizations continue to integrate BI into their human capital management strategies, the evolving landscape of big data and AI offers unprecedented opportunities for personalized employee experiences. Advanced analytical tools enable organizations to segment their workforce based on nuanced behavioral patterns and performance indicators, allowing for tailored employee interventions that enhance job satisfaction and overall well-being. Over time, the continued refinement of BI methodologies promises to bridge the gap between quantitative metrics and qualitative insights, fostering an environment where informed, data-driven human capital strategies contribute to sustained competitive advantage.

3. UNDERSTANDING QUALIA IN THE BUSINESS CONTEXT

In philosophy, qualia refer to the individual instances of subjective, unconscious experience of qualities, such as pleasure and displeasure (Dimitrov, 2025). When translated into the business realm, these experiences capture the intangible yet deeply influential aspects of employee life. They encompass emotional engagement, reflecting how motivated and committed employees feel; cultural resonance, which measures the alignment between an organization's values and those of its employees; and experiential quality, which pertains to how individuals perceive their day-to-day work, the support of their leadership, and opportunities for professional growth (Packard and Bylund, 2024).

Understanding qualia in the business context means to explore how the subjective, experiential dimensions of work can be recognized and integrated into organizational practices. These subtle, often implicit qualities, such as employee engagement, emotional instantiations, and the overall "feel" of a work environment, capture aspects of human experience that traditional quantitative metrics simply cannot address. By acknowledging that employees' internal experiences and personal interpretations of their roles shape not only their well-being but also their productivity and creativity, businesses are encouraged to foster cultures that value both measurable performance and qualitative human insights.

By integrating an appreciation of qualia into business strategy, organizations can gain a competitive edge in today's dynamic market. Leaders who understand that the subtle emotional and experiential aspects of work drive creativity, innovation, and loyalty are better equipped to navigate change and foster a resilient work environment. Embracing this human-centered approach requires a fundamental shift in perspective—from solely measuring performance via hard metrics to valuing qualitative insights that provide a nuanced understanding of employee satisfaction and cultural fit. This shift not only enhances employee retention and productivity but also strengthens the organization's adaptability as it encounters new challenges and opportunities in an increasingly volatile marketplace.

Furthermore, practical application of qualia in business practices can be achieved through the adoption of advanced qualitative and mixed-method research tools. Organizations that combine traditional BI systems with techniques such as sentiment analysis, in-depth employee interviews, and real-time feedback mechanisms can capture a holistic picture of the workplace atmosphere. For instance, progressive companies have implemented regular pulse surveys and focus groups to uncover the underlying emotional currents within their teams. These initiatives, when coupled with robust data analytics, allow leaders to make informed strategic decisions and tailor interventions that address both operational inefficiencies and employee well-being. Ultimately, by recognizing and leveraging the interplay between quantitative data and qualitative human experiences, companies can cultivate a robust organizational culture that not only meets but exceeds the demands of modern business challenges.

4. MERGING OF QUALIA AND BI

BI forms the backbone of data-driven decision-making by utilizing a suite of tools, technologies, and methodologies to gather, process, and analyze data from various sources. Through the systematic collection and integration of data, from sales records and customer interactions to operational systems, BI enables organizations to quantify performance with rigor. Data analysis techniques, including statistical methods, predictive analytics, and machine learning, uncover hidden patterns and forecast trends, ultimately feeding into reporting systems and dashboards that facilitate informed decision-making (Exner and Zunic, 2025). However, a reliance on quantitative metrics alone can obscure the human elements behind the numbers. The challenge lies in bridging the gap between data and the day-to-day lived experience of the workforce (Tawalbeh et al., 2025).

The integration of qualitative insights into traditional BI systems may create a powerful synergy that equips organizations with a more complete view of performance. For example, by incorporating sentiment analysis using natural language processing (NLP) techniques, organizations can extract and quantify employee feedback from surveys, social media, and internal communications (Dorigo et al., 2025). This approach allows leaders to see, at a glance, correlations between employee morale and key performance indicators, such as productivity and customer satisfaction. By developing integrated dashboards that seamlessly merge traditional indexes with qualitative indicators of employee satisfaction, organizations can foster a continuous feedback loop that refines both aspects of their operational strategy.

Despite the advantages, integrating qualitative and quantitative data presents challenges. Data consistency and reliability are crucial, especially when standardizing subjective measures across different teams and time periods. Technological hurdles also arise when attempting to merge structured data from BI systems with unstructured qualitative feedback (Ziesche and Yampolskiy, 2025). Additionally, there is often cultural resistance within organizations; some stakeholders may undervalue qualitative insights compared to hard metrics. To address these challenges, organizations must invest in validated surveys, standardized rating systems, and training for managers and Human Resources (HR) professionals to interpret qualitative data accurately.

Looking to the future, the convergence of qualia, BI, and HR management will redefine organizational success. As enterprises become increasingly agile and responsive, the ability to nurture a resilient, innovative, and engaged workforce becomes paramount. A balanced approach that respects both empirical data and the rich texture of employee experience equips organizations to thrive in a dynamic market. Continuous improvement driven by iterative feedback and technological investment ensures that companies remain not only competitive but also humane and forward-thinking.

5. CONCLUSION

The merging of these three dimensions, qualia, BI, and HR management represents a transformative frontier in organizational strategy. By harmonizing the rigor of BI with the human-oriented insights of qualia and the strategic focus of HR management, organizations can create resilient workforces, foster informed leadership, and drive sustainable success in an ever-changing business landscape. This holistic framework paves the way for a future where business decisions are deeply rooted in both data and the multifaceted human experience.

REFERENCES

Ao, S., Hurwitz, M., & Palade, V. (2025, February 26). Cognitive computing and business intelligence applications in accounting, finance and management. *Big Data and Cognitive Computing*, *9*(3), 54. DOI: 10.3390/bdcc9030054

Ara, A. (2025). The role of business intelligence in transforming HR practices: A focus on employee retention and performance management. *Proceedings of the 8th International Conference on Data Science and Machine Learning Applications*, 54-61. https://doi.org/DOI: 10.1109/CDMA61895.2025.00015

Dimitrov, M. (2025). The evaluative qualia theory of pleasure and displeasure. *Synthese*, *205*(1), 11. DOI: 10.1007/s11229-024-04824-4

Dorigo, T., Brown, G. D., Casonato, C., Cerda, A., Ciarrochi, J., Da Lio, M., D'Souza, N., Gauger, N. R., Hayes, S. C., Hofmann, S. G., Johansson, R., Liwicki, M., Lotte, F., Nieto, J. J., Olivato, G., Parnes, P., Perry, G., Plebe, A., Rao, I. M., & Yazdanpanah, N. (2025). Artificial intelligence in science and society: The vision of USERN. *IEEE Access : Practical Innovations, Open Solutions*, *13*, 15993–16054. DOI: 10.1109/ACCESS.2025.3529357

Exner, R., & Zunic, A. (2025). *The Path to an Intelligent Enterprise: The art and practice of business intelligence strategy*. Springer Nature Switzerland AG., DOI: 10.1007/978-3-031-69914-6

Hossain, M. R., Gindaba, F., Yusuf, A., Mrydha, M. A. M., & Rahman, M. Z. (2024). Big data and business intelligence: Key drivers of sustainable development in USA-based organizations. *International Journal for Multidisciplinary Research*, 6(6), 1-19. E-ISSN: 2582-2160.

Kassa, B. Y., & Worku, E. K. (2025). The impact of artificial intelligence on organizational performance: The mediating role of employee productivity. *Journal of Open Innovation*, *11*(1), 100474. DOI: 10.1016/j.joitmc.2025.100474

Kiarie, M. M., & Kinyua, G. M. (2025). Strategic fit as an antecedent of firm performance: Evidence from review of literature. *International Journal of Education and Research*, *13*(2), 221–252.

Lardi, K. (2025). *Artificial Intelligence for Business: Harness AI for value growth and innovation*. Kogan Page Ltd. eBook: 9781398618015.

Norton, L. W. (2025). Artificial intelligence and organizational strategy: Ethical and governance implications. *Consulting Psychology Journal*. Advance online publication. DOI: 10.1037/cpb0000280

Osma, A., Fowowe, O. O., Agboluaje, R., & Orekha, P. O. (2025). Integrating machine learning in business analytics consulting for proactive decision-making and innovation. *World Journal of Advanced Research and Reviews*, *25*(01), 1817–1836. DOI: 10.30574/wjarr.2025.25.1.0251

Packard, M. D., & Bylund, P. L. (2024). Truth, knowledge, and entrepreneurship theory: Arguments for a rationalist scientific epistemology. *Small Business Economics*. Advance online publication. DOI: 10.1007/s11187-024-00993-1

Souravlas, S., & Anastasiadou, S. (2020). Pipelined Dynamic Scheduling of Big Data Streams. *Applied Sciences (Basel, Switzerland)*, *10*(14), 4796. DOI: 10.3390/app10144796

Souravlas, S., & Anastasiadou, S. (2022). On Implementing Social Community Clouds Based on Markov Models. *IEEE Transactions on Computational Social Systems*, *2022*. Advance online publication. DOI: 10.1109/TCSS.2022.3213273

Souravlas, S., Anastasiadou, S., Economides, Th., & Katsavounis, S. (2023). Probabilistic Community Detection in Social Networks. *IEEE Access*, Publication Date: 2023, Volume: 11, On Page(s): 25629-25641, Print ISSN: 2169-3536, Online ISSN: 2169-3536, Digital Object Identifier: DOI: 10.1109/ACCESS.2023.3257021

Souravlas, S., Anastasiadou, S., & Katsavounis, S. (2021b). A Survey on the Recent Advances of Deep Community Detection. *Applied Sciences (Basel, Switzerland)*, *11*(16), 7179. DOI: 10.3390/app11167179

Souravlas, S., Anastasiadou, S., & Katsavounis, S. (2021c). More on Pipelined Dynamic Scheduling of Big Data Streams. *Applied Sciences (Basel, Switzerland)*, *11*(1), 61. DOI: 10.3390/app11010061

Souravlas, S. Anastasiadou, S. & Kostoglou, I. (2022b). A Novel Method For General Hierarchical System Modeling Via Colored Petri Nets Based on Transition Extractions From Real Data Sets. *Appl. Sci.* 2023, 13, 339. .DOI: 10.3390/app13010339

Souravlas, S., Anastasiadou, S., Tantalaki, N., & Katsavounis, S. (2021a). A Dynamic Load Balanced Task Distribution Strategy for Heterogeneous Cloud Platforms Based on Markov Process Modeling. *IEEE Access : Practical Innovations, Open Solutions*, *10*, 2169–3536. https://ieeexplore.ieee.org/abstract/document/9729723

Souravlas, S., Anastasiadou, S. D., Tantalaki, N., & Katsavounis, S. (2022a). A Fair, Dynamic Load Balanced Task Distribution Strategy for Heterogeneous Cloud Platforms Based on Markov Process Modeling. *IEEE Access : Practical Innovations, Open Solutions*, *10*, 26149–26162. DOI: 10.1109/ACCESS.2022.3157435

Souravlas, S., Katsavounis, S., & Anastasiadou, S. (2020). On Modeling and Simulation of Resource Allocation Policies in Cloud Computing Using Colored Petri Nets. *Applied Sciences (Basel, Switzerland)*, *10*(16), 5644. DOI: 10.3390/app10165644

Sun, W., Ren, S., & Tang, G. (2025). In the era of responsible artificial intelligence and digitalization: Business group digitalization, operations and subsidiary performance. *Annals of Operations Research*. Advance online publication. DOI: 10.1007/s10479-024-06453-z

Swmya, G., Polisetty, A., & Dash, G. (2024). Leveraging artificial intelligence for talent management. In: *Handook of Artificial Intelligence Applications for Industrial Sustainability*. CRC Press. eBook ISBN: 9781003348351. DOI: 10.1201/9781003348351-9

Tawalbeh, M., Alzghoui, A., & Alsheikh, G. A. A. (2025). Business intelligence as a catalyst for HR transformation: A study of BI implementation in HR practices. *Proceedings of the International Conference on Robotics, Automation, and Intelligent Computing,* 18-19 May, Pune, India, 3255(1), 05007. https://doi.org/DOI: 10.1063/5.0255240

Vapiwala, F., & Pandita, D. (2024). Streamlining Talent Management for Modern Business Through Artificial Intelligence. *International Conference in Emerging Technologies for Sustainability and Intelligent Systems (ICETSIS)*, Manama, Bahrain, 619-623. https://doi.org/DOI: 10.1109/ICETSIS61505.2024.10459450

Widjaja, A. A., Ghapanchi, A., & Bingley, S. (2025). Uncovering the antecedents to the effective use of business intelligence lessons from a qualitative systematic review approach. *Journal of Enterprise Information Management*, *38*(3), 768–797. DOI: 10.1108/JEIM-08-2024-0440

Ziesche, S., & Yampoliskiy, R. V. (2025). The neglect of qualia and consciousness in AI alignment research. In: *Considerations on the AI Endgame*. Chapman and Hall/CRC, eBook ISBN: 9781003565659. DOI: 10.1201/9781003565659-11

Chapter 11
Smart HRM:
Unleashing the Power of Business Intelligence for Workforce Excellence

Priya Kadyan
https://orcid.org/0009-0007-7049-2871
Chandigarh University, India

Rohan Singh
https://orcid.org/0000-0002-3588-4876
Chandigarh University, India

ABSTRACT

In the era of digital transformation, Human Resource Management (HRM) must evolve beyond traditional practices to stay competitive. This chapter explores how Business Intelligence (BI) revolutionizes HRM by enabling data-driven decision-making for talent acquisition, workforce planning, and employee engagement. By leveraging BI tools, HR professionals can analyze workforce trends, predict future skill gaps, and optimize talent strategies for organizational success. The chapter delves into BI's role in enhancing employee performance, reducing attrition, and fostering a data-driven HR culture. Real-world case studies and industry best practices illustrate the tangible impact of BI in HRM. This chapter provides HR leaders, researchers, and practitioners with actionable insights to harness BI for workforce excellence and sustainable competitive advantage.

DOI: 10.4018/979-8-3373-1942-1.ch011

INTRODUCTION TO BUSINESS INTELLIGENCE IN HRM

The integration of and BI and HRM has emerged as one of the most revolutionary pillars in current organizational management field. With talent becoming a competitive weapon in today's rapidly changing world, the actions involving execution of data analytics has become not only beneficial but crucial to the advancement of any company's HR division. The first part of this section broadens the context into the history of BI and its development as well as the possibilities for changing the paradigm of human resource management (Ahmed & Dantata, 2016).

The development of Human Resource Management has gone through some definite cycles as were the socio-economic developments through which the world passed. During the early part of the twentieth century, companies were mainly concerned with welfare and administrative issues with organizational welfare officers beginning to be employed attending to the most elementary employee requirements. After the World War II, the term gradually transformed into 'personnel management' which involved more systematic procedures of recruiting, selecting, training, and remunerating the people (Al Aufi, M. A. 2016).

The initial phase included the period from the 1950s to the 1980s and was considered BI 1.0 which involved the companies such as IBM and Microsoft that applied computing as a means of managing business analytics. The second phase of BI, known as BI 2.0, evolved from this where data warehousing became the mode of analyzing different data from various sources in a central location.

Some of the major progress that has developed BI recently include: data mining that involves the use of statistical tools to analyze data; big data caused by excessive use of technology; computation using cloud; artificial intelligence and machine learning; and self-service BI where the user does not require technical assistance (Al-Okaily, et al. 2023).

Traditional methods of operation based on such intuition are no longer very efficient in today's business world. The global talent management in organizations is on the cross-road due to ever increasing challenges in talent acquisition, employee training, and talent retention and therefore organizations need to have better human capital strategies. The use of data for HR means that the human capital management issues understudy results in contributing to organizational success by directly linking HR practices to company goals (Batalden et al, 2002).

There are five areas in which data analytics helps the HR professionals; these include, recruitment and hiring, performance management, employee engagement, and finally workforce planning.

Moreover, the new approaches are highly beneficial for developing the skill-based organizations and the data obtained from them. It can be further used to examine areas that could benefit from further training, adopt training solutions that match the employee's preferences, and long-term career goals and prospects of required skills based on their likelihood of being in demand in the near future. The further progress in generative AI helps once again extend a number of opportunities to analyze skills and predetermine the appropriate career trajectory for each worker.

Other traditional practices of HRM have its drawbacks that do not make much sense in the rapidly changing environment of contemporary business. These traditional practices entail procedures that entail handling of papers and paperwork, as well as interpersonal communications (Bersin, J. 2014)

Another hurdle as a result of physical storage is accessibility, which again makes it arduous to search for the information regarding the employees. The task suffers from the weakness; Any physical documentation work can be misplaced, destroyed or accessed by the wrong people. Remote access constraints have proved to be rather challenging, especially as distributed work environments become more common (Boselie et al, 2019).

Moreover, using the generic approaches within the scope of human resources management, it is possible to face such critical issues as the inability to access valuable insights into the various trends and performance of the workforce, thereby restricting the strategic planning and decision-making capabilities. A considerable number of tasks that HR teams undertake acts as a great inconvenience since they end up taking most of their time on these, rather than on pursuits that can enhance organizational value (Cappelli, P. 2008).

In the area of workforce management, BI systems also play some vital roles in head count forecasting, workforce capacity planning and optimum management of expenditure on labour force to ensure it meets the strategic planning of an organization. In performance management, real-time dashboards and interrelations between different performance factors help more accurately assess and plan activities to improve human capital (Chen & Huang, 2009).

Promising areas are predictive models for deriving the risks for turnover, analysis of the using sentiment analysis for receiving feedback and correlation analysis between the engagement factors and business results. In addition, BI is useful in training and development hence enables determination of skills gaps, learning optimization, and mapping of competencies. By adopting these measures, organizations can turn their HR units into valuable sources with the clear line to the organization's success factors, indicators and results (Coombs, C.2020).

The previous way of managing HR is more firefighting oriented and does not allow for proactive planning. Such an approach leads to a constant state of fighting fires and results in a lack of strategic influence for HR professionals.

Moving from the reactive to the proactive means a shift from describing back to predicting and prescribing what is happening in an organization. That is why, on the one hand, while descriptive analytics tells the story of what has happened while we were away, predictive analytics shows what will happen if nothing changes, which helps an organization to take preventive measures, for instance, in the case of employee turnover, to retain the human resources before they are lost or take actions to address the skills shortage before the issue influences the performance (Davenport, et al. 2010).

The BI in the case of HRM can be defined as the gathering of data, consolidation of the data, analysis of the data, and the presentation of the data to people for the purpose of making decision. As stated by Gartner, BI is defined as the applications, infrastructure, tools as well as practices used to gather data, access it and transform this data into useful insights that can be used for improving decision-making and for increasing organizational efficiency. HR Analytics is described as the process of seeking patterns in data related to human capital and employing data analysis to draw insight out of the data to help facilitate tools that facilitate decision-making in organizations on matters to do with workforce (Gasela, P. 2021).

There are five related components in the conceptual model of BI for HRM. Starting at the data and integrate stage, this stage involves the gathering and compounding of the data from different human resource systems. Data analysis and processing applied in using algorithm and statistic to find out relationship and predict future occurrence. This knowledge is then presented by visualization and reporting making it easier for understanding and decision making depending on the data received. The strategic application facets of human capital management use this information for decision making regarding the human resource management using organizational goals. Thus, Continual Improvement as the last category incorporates feedbacks to enhance the analytics models. This integrated framework enables the Concept and the practicing HR professionals to move from an intuitive approach to working systematically based on proper empirical evidence to improve organizational performance in the management of human capital (Guechtouli, M. 2014).

Figure 1. Conceptual framework of business intelligence in HRM.

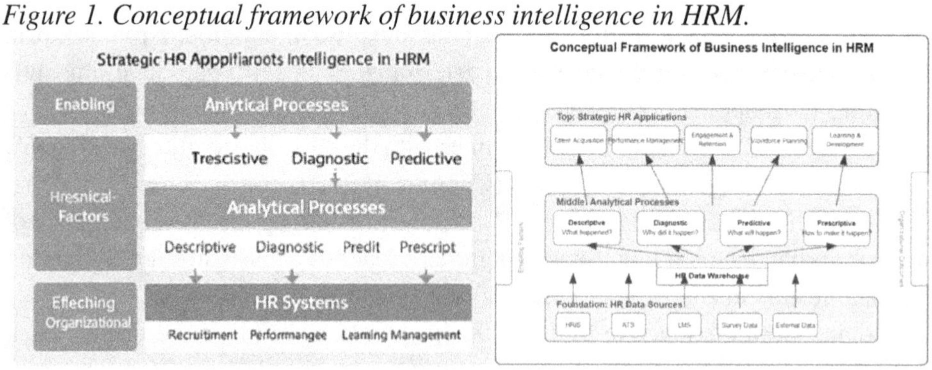

This figure represents a part of BI implementation in Human Resource Management highlighting source data and analytic and application areas.

THE ROLE OF BI TOOLS AND TECHNOLOGIES IN HRM

The use of Business Intelligence (BI) tools and BI technologies have brought about dynamic changes in the Human Resource Management through the manner data about the workforce is collected, processed and utilized. Such highly developed systems allow the HR specialists to step from the state of making decisions based on their feeling to the stage when evidence-based solutions are put into practice in order to improve organizational results. The major BI technologies applicable to HR include data-warehousing systems that pull together data on employees to integrate storing centers and come up with single integrated sources for any kind of human capital analysis. These link information from various recruiting and staffing solutions, performance appraisal tools, compensation systems, and learning management systems to provide end-to-end analysis of the employee life cycle dashboards (Holdsworth, J., & Lundgaard, B. 2009)

The last BI technology important for successful employment of HR strategies is predictive analytics platform with the help of which, HR teams can predict future supply and demand of workforce, potential flight risks and upcoming skill gaps in the company. These platforms make it possible to forecast changes with regard to workforce needs based on history and the external environment instead of acting only as a response to the situation. Through such scenarios, organizations can anticipate the effects of change on the organization's human capital needs so that they can be adequately prepared for such eventualities (Kelly, D. 2003).

BI tools interpret and present HR data in a way that is easy for all audience in the organization to understand through creating dashboards and reports. These tools provide KPIs in the form of charts, graphs, and heat maps, making it convenient for the HR personnel or business executives to realize trends, anomalous results or cause-and-effect relationships that may not be easily discernable when using spreadsheet tools. They ensure data accessibility and offer the population a common language to discuss the workforce problems (Kocher & Sahni,2011).

Talent management has become an essential tool for human resource management and according to the advances of machine learning applications these are potent instruments for noticing patterns in the employee data that an analyst would not easily notice. Some of these applications can be used to select the right talent for a given position, match the right person to a given role, as well as point out potential learning activities for a given employee. As the patterns are learned with time, the performance of such systems keeps on improving with the talent decisions made during the entire employee life-cycle.

Based on the unstructured textual data of Workforce Engagement Survey, performance appraisal, exit interviews, and comments on the social media NLP tools to identify satisfaction sentiment and themes help to gain better insights of organizational climate and employee experience. Engagement is also another possible problem that could be detected by NLP before it causes more significant problems and thus the right corrective measures can be taken. These technologies can also track communication to deduce the collaboration clusters and potential silos within an organization (Lepak & Snell 1999).

Advanced tools & technologies have essentially created a strategic management tool out of Business Intelligence, enabling even companies of all scales to implement the same with no major overhead investments. These solutions provide the level of flexibility; receive constant updates; and, they have better security measures as they do not take long to implement and need constant attendance by IT professionals. They also allow for easy access to HR data which can be useful when working with remote teams and make it possible to make decisions as the team is updating the cloud (Maatman & Meijerink,2017).

Table 1. Key BI technologies and their applications in HRM functions

Technology	Primary HR Applications	Key Benefits	Implementation Considerations
Data Warehousing	Unified employee records, Historical trend analysis, Compliance reporting	Single source of truth, Improved data quality, Enhanced reporting capabilities	Data integration complexity, Legacy system compatibility, Data governance requirements
Predictive Analytics	Turnover forecasting, Workforce planning, Succession modeling	Proactive intervention, Strategic planning support, Risk mitigation	Data quality dependencies, Model validation needs, Change management challenges
Data Visualization	Performance dashboards, Diversity metrics, Compensation analytics	Improved data comprehension, Faster insight identification, Enhanced stakeholder communication	User training requirements, Dashboard design expertise, Data literacy development
Machine Learning	Candidate matching, High-potential identification, Performance prediction	Pattern recognition at scale, Reduced bias potential, Continuous improvement	Algorithm transparency, Training data quality, Ethical implementation guidelines

continued on following page

Table 1. Continued

Technology	Primary HR Applications	Key Benefits	Implementation Considerations
Natural Language Processing	Sentiment analysis, Skills extraction, Feedback categorization	Unstructured data insights, Real time feedback analysis, Cultural assessment	Language complexity handling, Context interpretation, Privacy considerations
Cloud Analytics	Remote workforce analytics, Self-service HR insights, Integrated talent management	Reduced infrastructure costs, Faster implementation, Automatic updates	Data security protocols, Integration capabilities, Subscription cost management

The BI tools have to be adopted in the Human Resource management by integrating the BI system with the current Human Resource Information Systems. This has the added advantage of removing data gaps and manual data transfers between functioning systems and analytical platforms. The integration methods that have been employed include API links, middleware solutions, as well as data federation mechanisms that ensure data do not get duplicated while ensuring a more complete analysis can be done. Therefore, to have uniformity across different systems, there must be define data and synchronization requirements (Mapuva & Takabika 2020)

The approach to developing the data governance for HR data quality, security, and compliance entails the use of models. These concepts indicate how data will be owned, its quality assured, and how it will be accessed, used, and managed. Some of these are data stewardship responsibilities, compliance audit and policies and standards concerning the sensitive information of the employees. This is why it is very important to have good governance in analytics in order to prevent or get rid of such bad data which can lead to bad analytics (McDonnell, 2017)

The process of strengthening analytical skills in the HR department includes the improvement of personnel qualifications as well as the creation of a cultural shift. To achieve this goal organizations have to introduce training programs that will develop data skills, analytical skills and specific tools' expertise among the HR staff. Some companies have a dedicated team for HR analytics in which groups like talent management or recruiting could be including HI analytics while in other companies it is included from top to bottom of the HI functions. Successful capability building in any organization, whether centralized or decentralized involves implementing of instructorship schemes, problem solving and actionable activities or promulgation of recognition frameworks informed by data analysis (Muryjas & Wawer 2014)

Measuring the ROI of BI investments in the field of HR is complex since the initiatives in this field are often not directly linked with business results. It is useful to positively and negatively anchored cost savings, time saving, and error rates with qualitative measures of decision making quality and business value. The performance metrics should be taken before the implementation of the strategy, and then the organizations compare its future enhancements with the baseline data. The ideal practices of HR analytics should follow the path of linking them to the business results in the simplest manner (Nankervis, et al. 2011)

Figure 2. Architecture of an integrated HR business intelligence system

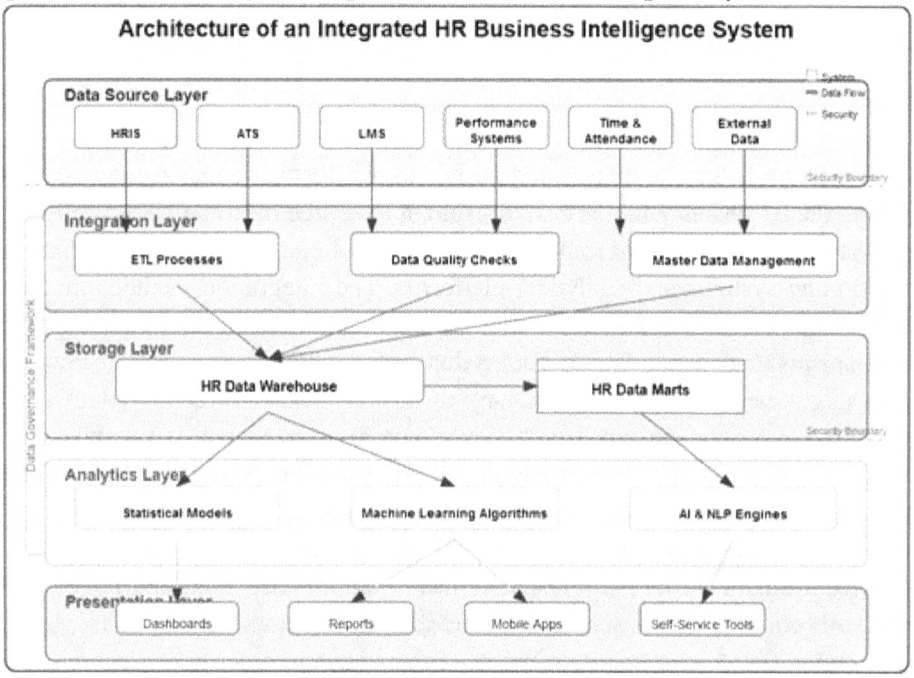

This figure depicts an end-to-end design of an integrated HR Business Intelligence system with physical data processing stages and the output as user interfaces. The former comprises data source layers which comprise of HRIS, ATS, LMS, performance systems, and other external data integration layers which are ETL processes, data quality checks, master data management, storage layers such as data warehouses and data marts, analytics layers encompassing statistical models and machine learning, and the last layer which is the presentation layer comprised of dashboards, reports, and the mobile application. It shows lines of security, control, and data ownership and interfaces between components that will explain how various technologies operate to convert raw data collected by HR teams into usable intelligence (Ogier, J. 2003)

IT infrastructure for HR analytics can also be categorized as either demand or supply side factors; some of the demand side factors include the following concealment technological requirements; physical requirements for technological infrastructure for HR analytics include; They consist of processing capability for running heavy and large analytical tasks, data storage requirement for historical workforce data, and networking requirement which includes facilities to transfer data as well as users. Concerning applications, there are DBMS software, ETL tools, analytics tools, and visualization tools. For each component, organizations need to assess when it is more appropriate to build or buy, by taking into account the existing IT environment, the internal capabilities as well as the particularities of the analysis (Ranjan, J. 2009)

Even though scaling does not necessarily always refer to the size of an organization, it is a critical aspect for consideration especially when the size and the type of analyses required change. Since cloud-based solutions have a built-in capability for scalability, therefore on the other hand it is very important to plan for capacity while using on-premises systems. It follows then, that organizations should pay a close attention on matters such as future growth, matters concerning mergers or acquisitions and emerging trends in analyses, when making their architecture (Rothwell 2010)

Figure 3. Maturity model for HR analytics implementation

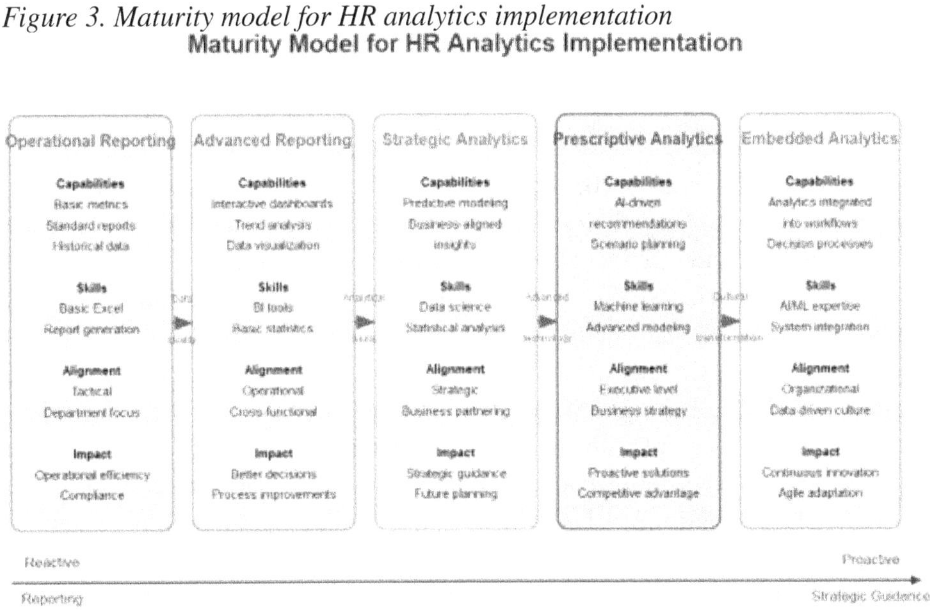

This figure provides an iterative model known as the Human Capital Analytics Maturity Model which is comprised of five stages, namely; Operational reporting, advanced reporting dashboard and trend analysis, strategic analytics, prescriptive analytics, and embedded analytics.

BI IN TALENT ACQUISITION AND RECRUITMENT

The BI in Talent Acquisition and Recruitment has brought change in the way businesses select human capital in their organizations. One type of sourcing approach is the analytical sourcing where recruitment is based on key indicators of success and effectiveness of present employees. This model examines one or several of experience, skills, behavior patterns, and cultural values and used them to identify who among the candidates is most likely to thrive in the company as well as remain there permanently. In doing so, objectivity in rating candidates takes place, and the results of these approaches signify quality hire in comparison with resume screening methods.

Recruitment channel evaluation helps organizations to determine suitable recruitment methods by evaluating results rather than on presumptions. These BI tools are used to monitor some of the crucial KPIs, including the quality of the candidate, the time taken to fill the positions, the amount spent to hire people, and the retention rates through various sources like the job boards, social media, referral, and agencies for recruitment. It optimizes the process of recruiting the right talent and ensures that any costs incurred in attracting a candidate from a certain channel are justified for result getting rid of bad performers.

Candidate experience is no longer assessed through post-selection surveys but from the period of their relationship with the company starting from the time of job application till selection. BI tools track the completion rates as to how many candidates have completed all the applications, response time, feedback given in the interview process and offer acceptance rate wherein we can find what part of the process is unsuitable for the candidates. Such understandings can help organizations to improve successive steps in the selection procedure, as well as the image of employers among the applicants, in various competitive talent acquisition environments.

Another area that belongs to successful BI utilization in recruitment is a selection process improvement with the help of algorithmic screening. These systems compare the applicants with what has been set down in the various standards using standardized methods do much better than manual methods in handling large number of applicants. The advanced systems also use the machine learning to define passer parameters continuously from experience so that as time goes each day the system is more accurate in its screening without compromising with the other parallel systems that are running simultaneously with this system for passing screening check on all applicants (Serbanescu, L. 2009).

The construct validity assessments foresee the validity concerning the choice methods in their measure of true job performance and employee retention. Such selection scores and assessments linked with performance, next promotion guarantees and employment duration to identify which methods of evaluation are most credible. These facts help organizations to enhance the selection processes and focus on the strategies that increase the validity of selection procedures and avoid the use of unsuitable selection techniques.

Time-to-hire and cost-per-hire are among the value-added BI applications used to locate possible issues with recruitment and optimize its processes. Thus, analytics show bottlenecks, non-value-added activities, and time and resource-wasteful work-especially those that either lengthen hiring time or increase overall hiring spending while not enhancing hiring quality. Thus, first, hiring processes can be optimized based on data rather than assumptions, which will help to decrease time on hiring and cost on recruitment and, second, the quality of hire can be kept at an appropriate level (Taylor, S. 2011, Ulrich, D 1997).

Table 2. Metrics for measuring recruitment process effectiveness through BI

Metric Category	Key Metrics	Analytical Applications	Strategic Implications
Efficiency Metrics	Time-to-fill, Cost-per-hire, Recruiter workload, Application completion rate	Process bottleneck identification, Resource allocation optimization, Recruitment funnel analysis	Resource planning, Budget allocation, Process redesign priorities
Quality Metrics	Quality of hire, First-year performance, Cultural fit scores, Hiring manager satisfaction	Selection method validation, Source quality comparison, Interviewer effectiveness	Selection process refinement, Sourcing strategy adjustments, Interviewer training needs
Diversity Metrics	Pipeline diversity, Selection rate comparisons, Representation by level, Inclusive culture indicators	Bias detection, Barrier identification, Representation trend analysis	Diversity strategy effectiveness, Intervention targeting, Progress monitoring
Experience Metrics	Candidate satisfaction, Offer acceptance rate, Application abandonment points, Feedback sentiment	Experience pain point identification, Competitive positioning analysis, Brand perception tracking	Candidate experience enhancements, Employer brand development, Competitive differentiation
Predictive Metrics	Turnover prediction, Performance prediction, Promotion likelihood, Time-to-productivity forecast	Success pattern identification, Flight risk modeling, Onboarding optimization	Strategic hiring priorities, Retention risk mitigation, Development planning
Market Metrics	Talent availability, Compensation benchmarks, Competitor hiring activity, Skills emergence trends	Market positioning analysis, Compensation strategy development, Emerging skills identification	Talent strategy alignment, Market competitiveness, Future skills planning

This will focus on onboarding analytics that seeks to capture integration processes across new employees; time to productivity, level of engagement during the first weeks/months on the job as well as first performance markers. While these analytics highlight the onboarding activities that are most powerful, it also unveils which activities are more effective for it to integrate in the organization and which should rather not be continued because they do not show the intended results or worse, harm the company. This enables organizations to have a right approach on what needs to be done in different roles within the company, departments and employees to avoid implementing cross-platform onboarding programs.

The success of the new hires and their retention has, therefore, been made easier through BI applications that indicate early signs of future problems. It is designed to review communication pattern, system usage data, response form the participants and first indications of flight hazards or integration issues. This way, HR specialists will be able to have an opportunity to address potential issues before they proceed to linked problems like leaving and low performance.

One of the new trends in using business intelligence in talent integration is in the adaptation of it for the individual personal onboarding process. Such strategies use data on what type of learning, career expectations, and working behaviors the new employees want to apply and develop during training activities. Certain systems, for instance, come with resource suggestions, connection, as well as learning journey, proposing that they emulate established effective personnel in that organization, thus improving early elicitation (Ulrich, D., et al 2012).

Market intelligence on talent sourcing allows for creating a more precise strategy of successful recruitment and staffing. BI tools also, gather and assess information on labor market availability, and competitor trends, and remunerations for various geographical locations by category of expertise. These insights can help an organization to create proper sourcing strategies instead of brainstorming solutions for each problem simultaneously in regard to geography and positions.

Talent acquisition strategic comparison entails the comparison of internal performance data as well as that of the competitors. These assessments include benchmarking of quality and diversity of recruited talents, efficiency of the recruitment process, and experience of the recruited talents against the industry average as well as the immediate competitors. In order to improve the strategies used for talent acquisition, it is necessary to compare the existing practices with the best ones in the market, which will in turn allows for targeted improvements to be made.

Using Business Intelligence to forecast and anticipate future talent acquisition requirements could be considered as the most substantial and competitive utilization of BI in procurement. These models use business planning, retirement expectations, and turnover and skilling trends to identify with the increasing precision which employees will be needed in the future. Thus, organizations are able to leverage sourcing and identify the necessary measures on the developmental side as well so that the talent is available whenever the organization requires them (Wilson, J. P. 2009, Yusliza, M. Y, et al 2019).

EMPLOYEE PERFORMANCE AND WORKFORCE ANALYTICS

Business Intelligence is one of the most effective tools that have evolved the system of measuring, enhancing and improving the performance of the workforce of organizations. BI supports and simplifies the usage of strategic measure development, including Key Performance Indicators, for HR professionals to establish and monitor. They help to establish performance management systems for developing measures that incorporate both 'hyper facts' of performance and qualitative dimensions of constructed employee work contributions. Minimum-writing.org Bedrooms123 9 Real time performance dashboards: Annual appraisals have become history and organizations have adopted new efficient ways of monitoring the performance of their employees through performance dashboards with visual, real time representations of performance trends, for exceling, and other performance that deviates from the expected norm. This way the managers are able to see performance problem areas and do something about them before they get out of hand thus making it more of a cultivation of performance improvement as against appraisal.

A correlation of performance metrics involves providing organizations with information on how various aspects of employee performance are related, interdependent and affected. For instance, besides, BI tools can uncover a relationship between, for instance, the completing of a training program and the subsequent performance, or, staff satisfaction scores and the productivity rates. This results in the attainment of deeper understanding of the problem that leads to more informed intercession that penetrates more towards the source of problems instead of focusing on manifestations. Defining internal measures against external ones is possible, concern benchmarking help to understand performance level and important aspects of the company comparing it with leaders, competitors and industry average, or specific segment. (Zehir, Karaboğa & Başar 2020)

Table 3. Performance indicators and business impact

Performance Indicator	Strategic Alignment	Measurement Approach	Business Impact
Revenue per Employee	Financial Performance	Total revenue divided by employee headcount	Measures overall workforce productivity and contribution to financial goals
Quality Metrics	Customer Satisfaction	Defect rates, error percentages, customer satisfaction scores	Ensures workforce delivers products/services meeting quality standards
Time-to-Proficiency	Operational Efficiency	Duration from hire date to achievement of performance standards	Optimizes onboarding and training effectiveness

continued on following page

Table 3. Continued

Performance Indicator	Strategic Alignment	Measurement Approach	Business Impact
Innovation Metrics	Growth & Innovation	New ideas submitted, patents filed, process improvements implemented	Measures workforce contribution to organizational innovation
Leadership Effectiveness	Talent Development	Employee engagement scores, team performance, succession readiness	Ensures leadership pipeline and organizational sustainability
Collaboration Index	Organizational Culture	Cross-functional project participation, knowledge sharing activities	Supports organizational agility and information flow
Goal Achievement Rate	Strategic Execution	Percentage of individual/team goals completed on time	Aligns individual performance with organizational objectives
Utilization Rate	Resource Optimization	Billable hours as percentage of available hours	Maximizes productive use of human capital resources
Learning Agility	Adaptability	Skill acquisition rate, certification completion, knowledge assessment scores	Supports organizational change readiness and future capabilities
Retention of High Performers	Talent Sustainability	Turnover rates among top performance quartile employees	Preserves critical talent and institutional knowledge

Organizational talent management and career progression have been advanced for evaluation and enhancement through skills gap evaluation, with the help of data mining. BI systems make comparisons of current existent employee skills with the future skills expected to determine a gap either at an individual, team or organizational level. It thus calls for focused development efforts because there are areas of inefficiency that need closing rather than the general training approach. Building on knowledge in learning analytics, training effectiveness is determined by monitoring the learning activities and how they relate to improvements in performance in order to get value for the development spent by organizations by identifying the most productive trainings for investments. Career progression analysis and succession planning rely on the history of an employee's mobility tracks and performance records to determine possible future promotions, making it possible to open internal opportunities that encourage employee stay while filling high-ranking positions.

Performance analytics is also advanced to include attributes that indicate how likely an employee is to quit before beginning the job search for a new position. They utilize trends in performance indices, flow of communication, engagement score feedback, and other possible signals that show that certain flights may be at risk for flight so that proactive measures may be taken to retain them. The sentiment analysis of the survey extracts these attributes and emotional tone of the employee response more constructively and effectively from the surveys, social medial posts, performance reviews, and other textual inputs then the traditional methods of the surveys. More commonly, managers today try to find relations between different levels of engagement and various business performance indicators to prove the value of the organization's investment in workplace enhancement and identify the connection between investment and the cars (Zehir, et al, 2020, Angrave et al, 2016 and Boudreau, et al 2007)

Figure 4. Predictive model for employee turnover risk assessment

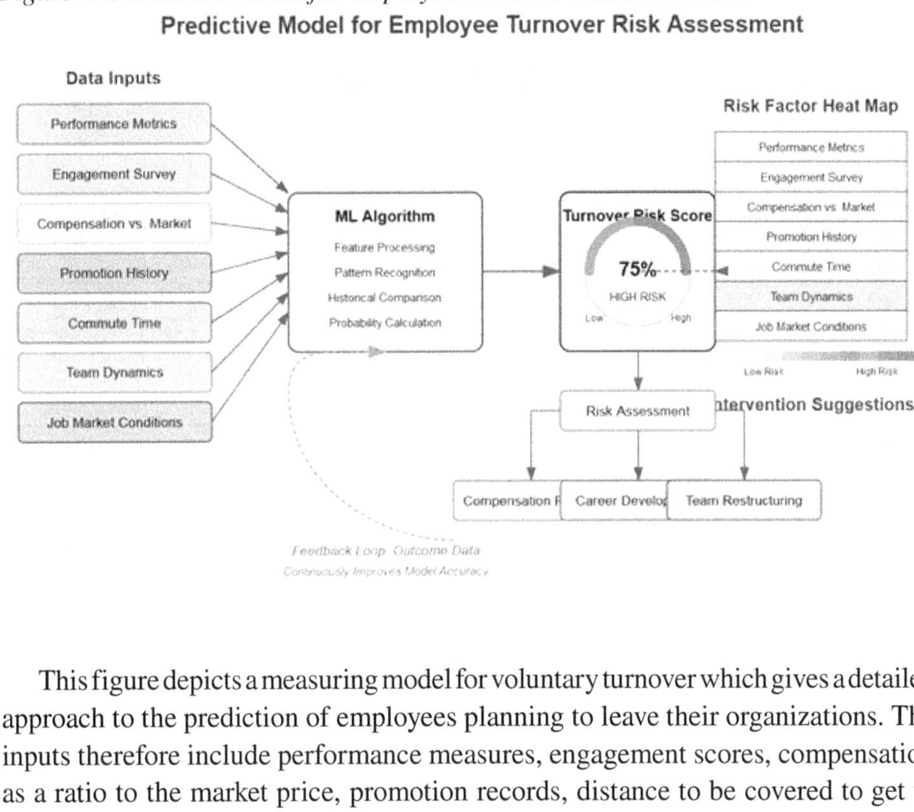

This figure depicts a measuring model for voluntary turnover which gives a detailed approach to the prediction of employees planning to leave their organizations. The inputs therefore include performance measures, engagement scores, compensation as a ratio to the market price, promotion records, distance to be covered to get to work and ratio of the team, and the general market rates in the industry. These are used to generate a turnover probability for every employee, using an algorithm that we shall develop elsewhere. Staffing and particularly its management have shifted from being an occasional practice to strategic workforce planning and modelling with the use of headcount forecasting and planning scenarios. Another process of using BI is to forecast staffing requirements for the future based on historical data and patterns, growth and other business forecasts for different scenarios and markets. Staffing management involves arranging employees in an organization in a way that is best suited to meet the various needs of the organization and its projects by making certain that there are available skilled human resources to address certain tasks without necessarily having many extra employees who are idle most of the time. One of the main ways is the analysis of different components that can be connected with labor cost and what measures can be taken so as to reduce cost, and at the same time, not to harm the employees' productivity or motivation, contractor services usage, geographical distribution of the employees and their extra work for additional payment.

Table 4. Planning scenario and their mitigations

Planning Scenario	Key Assumptions	Workforce Implications	Risk Factors	Mitigation Strategies
Rapid Growth	25% annual revenue increase, New market entry, Product expansion	Significant hiring needs across functions, Leadership development acceleration, New skill requirements	Talent shortages, Onboarding capacity limitations, Culture dilution	Build talent pipelines, Develop scalable onboarding, Strengthen culture carriers
Digital Transformation	Technology platform overhaul, Process automation, New digital offerings	Technical skill gaps, Role redesign, Potential redundancies	Change resistance, Skills obsolescence, Knowledge transfer challenges	Reskilling programs, Change management, Knowledge preservation
Market Contraction	15% revenue decline, Reduced customer demand, Cost pressure	Workforce reduction, Redeployment needs, Productivity improvement requirements	Key talent departure, Engagement decline, Capability gaps	Selective retention, Transparent communication, Critical skill preservation
Remote/Hybrid Work	60% remote workforce, Office space reduction, Distributed teams	Collaboration challenges, Management approach changes, Geographic talent expansion	Communication barriers, Performance management complexity, Culture maintenance	Collaboration technology, Manager training, Virtual engagement initiatives
Merger/ Acquisition	Integration of acquired workforce, System consolidation, Culture alignment	Role duplication, Skill compatibility assessment, Leadership integration	Cultural conflict, Voluntary departures, Productivity disruption	Cultural assessment, Retention planning, Integration roadmap
Regulatory Change	New compliance requirements, Reporting changes, Process modifications	Compliance expertise needs, Training requirements, Process redesign	Compliance risk, Implementation timeline, Capability gaps	Specialized hiring, Compliance training, Process documentation

continued on following page

Table 4. Continued

Planning Scenario	Key Assumptions	Workforce Implications	Risk Factors	Mitigation Strategies
Aging Workforce	30% retirement eligible within 5 years, Knowledge transfer needs, Succession gaps	Accelerated succession planning, Knowledge capture, Multi-generational workforce	Knowledge loss, Leadership gaps, Generational differences	Phased retirement, Mentoring programs, Knowledge management systems
Gig Economy Expansion	25% contingent workforce, Project-based staffing, Flexible arrangements	Blended workforce management, Core/flexible skill definition, Engagement approach changes	Intellectual property risks, Culture cohesion, Quality consistency	Contractor management systems, Integration practices, Performance standards

CHALLENGES AND ETHICAL CONSIDERATIONS IN BI ADOPTION

Privacy and security of data is one the crucial issues that form barriers to BI for HR analytics. GDPR, CCPA and industry-specific legislation offer stringent standards on how the employees' data can be collected, used, and stored. It means that organizations must have effective compliance programs for data minimization, limitation of purpose, and retention of workforce analytics. While it is pertinent to uphold anonymity and data privacy, it is also possible to anonymize the records and perform the analysis on employees without breaking the law. Some methods like data hiding, summing, and anonymization help organizations analyze the identity of individuals without compromising their results; however, achieving both analytical usefulness and anonymity is not easy.

Figure 5. HR data privacy framework and compliance checkpoints

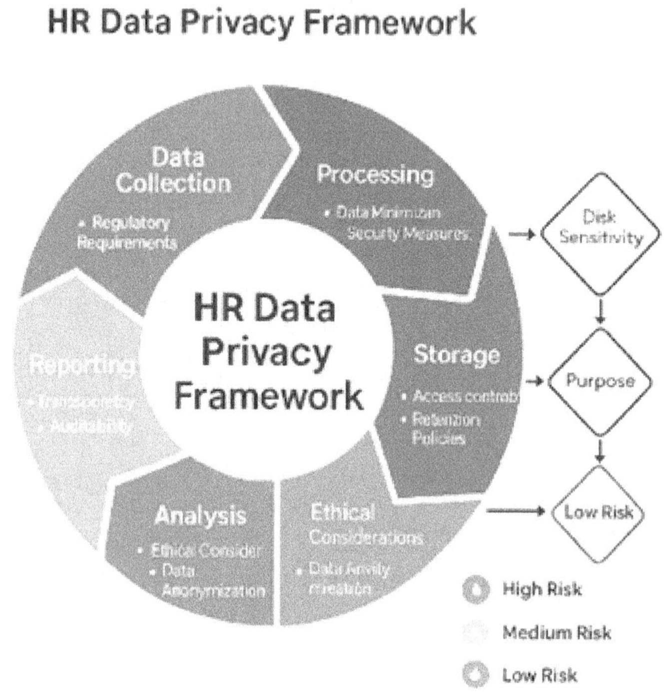

The figure provides an ideal framework that can be followed when employing data privacy in cases to be analyzed by HR analytics. The simplified predictive model of work is mentioned to consist of five sections that form the circumference of the circle called Data Collection, Data Processing, Data Storage, Data Analysis and Data Reporting. In each phase, there are compliance checks regarding regulations, consent, security, and ethical issues. It also employs the decision trees for handling procedures on the nature, purpose and geographic location of the data in question.

Ethical use of employee data goes beyond mere compliance with the law when analyzing the different factors relating to analytics at the workplace. Ethical guidelines for HR analytics include objectives for policies and behavior on the use of data and their management in an organizational setting. They often include factors like fairness, measures of openness, balancing as well as size and employee respect, which could be used in solving problems resulting from setting conflicts between capabilities and ethical outcomes. To prevent the algorithmic bias and discrimination, one has to pay much attention to the training data, the algorithm used, and the validation process. Self-reinforcing feedback loops of analytics can lead to the reinforcement of these discriminations and can cause disparate hiring, promotions, reward, or training opportunities for various groups (Noor 2024).

Table 5. Ethical dimensions and corresponding governance mechanism.

Ethical Dimension	Key Questions	Guiding Principles	Implementation Practices	Governance Mechanisms
Transparency	Is data collection and use clearly communicated? Are analytics processes explainable?	Openness about data collection, Clear purpose statements, Explainable analytics	Privacy notices, Process documentation, Simplified explanations of complex analytics	Communication review board, Transparency audits, Employee feedback channels
Consent	Is appropriate consent obtained? Are opt-out options available where relevant?	Informed consent, Voluntary participation, Revocable permission	Tiered consent models, Clear opt-out processes, Consent renewal procedures	Consent tracking systems, Regular consent reviews, Legal compliance verification
Fairness	Do analytics processes treat all employees equitably? Are outcomes free from discriminatory impact?	Equal opportunity, Outcome equity, Bias prevention	Algorithmic bias testing, Disparate impact analysis, Diverse training data	Fairness review committee, Regular bias audits, Corrective action protocols
Privacy	Is data collection proportional to purpose? Are appropriate security measures in place?	Data minimization, Purpose limitation, Security by design	Data masking techniques, Access controls, Retention policies	Privacy impact assessments, Security audits, Data protection officer oversight
Autonomy	Do analytics respect employee agency? Is there appropriate human oversight?	Human-in-the-loop design, Employee empowerment, Algorithmic humility	Appeal mechanisms, Human review of automated decisions, Employee input channels	Autonomy impact reviews, Decision authority frameworks, Employee representation
Accountability	Who is responsible for ethical use? How are issues addressed?	Clear responsibility, Consequence management, Continuous improvement	Designated ethics officers, Issue escalation processes, Regular review cycles	Ethics committees, Whistleblower protections, External ethics audits
Beneficence	Do analytics benefit employees and organization? Is value shared appropriately?	Mutual benefit, Shared value, Harm prevention	Employee benefit communication, Outcome sharing, Impact assessment	Value distribution reviews, Employee surveys, Benefit tracking systems
Cultural Sensitivity	Do analytics respect cultural differences? Are diverse perspectives considered?	Cultural awareness, Contextual application, Global mindfulness	Localized implementations, Cultural adaptation, Diverse design teams	Cultural review panels, Global ethics councils, Diversity in governance

continued on following page

Table 5. Continued

Ethical Dimension	Key Questions	Guiding Principles	Implementation Practices	Governance Mechanisms
Future Impact	Are long-term consequences considered? How will analytics evolve?	Sustainable design, Future-oriented thinking, Adaptable frameworks	Scenario planning, Impact forecasting, Flexible design principles	Future impact assessments, Technology roadmap reviews, Trend monitoring
Power Balance	Do analytics reinforce or challenge power imbalances? Is there potential for misuse?	Power awareness, Abuse prevention, Empowerment focus	Authority limitation, Checks and balances, Democratic design elements	Power dynamic assessments, Authority distribution reviews, Abuse prevention systems

Effective BI change management issues have always act as key success indicators of BI change failure or success in the overall organizational HR setup. Overall, it is noted that the management of Human Resources is concerned not just with emotional and practical issues regarding implemented analyses. There is clear evidence that all strategies of change are anchored on; appeals to reason and the presentation of a visionary imperative, the engagement of the key stakeholders and creation of quick wins to support the change endeavors. Acquiring sustainable analytics capabilities in the organization results in a need to invest in training, tools, and support systems to foster data literacies for the HR professional. Some organizations adopt multiple tiers of competencies needed by the HR function in order to achieve increased analytical capacity (Madhuri, 2025).

The further implementation challenges are technical and practical in nature, thus making BI adoption in the HR domain difficult at the technical level. The issues of data quality and integration are there because of lack of properly integrated HR systems, lack of common definitions of the collected data, and due to a number of non-integrated manual data processes. Great imposition is needed to clean data, normalize and join them into a single format that will allow other relevant analyses to take place. Instances where new hires are required, existing data science talent must be integrated, or consulting comes in handy for support are expected due to skills gaps in the role of HR analytics. More and more organizations rely on central or decentralized analytics which means that many HR departments either develop such competencies itself, or partner with the centralized analytics functions. (Eden, C., Chisom, A., & Adeniyi, O. 2024).

CASE STUDIES AND REAL-WORLD APPLICATIONS OF BI IN HRM

They have revolutionalised the Human Resource Management field with regard to the ways it was practiced in various organizational settings, meaning that the ways adopted by different firms in the particular context differ with the size of the company, the particular industry or the strategic direction of the firm. Some of the largest organizations across the globe were consequently first to get innovative BI solutions in the HR domain, given their vast capital resources to create complex analytics. Johnson & Johnson the world's multinational corporation engaged in the production of healthcare products recently adopted an integrated solution to HR analytics to help it in dealing with problems in its employee's management with more than 130000 employees from over 60 nations. The challenges that were realized occurred in areas such as legacy system integration, variations of regulations across the region, and culture change within the organization. In order to mitigate these challenges, J&J implemented the following strategies, right from data consolidation and data standardization to arriving at advanced analytics capabilities (Chowdhury, et al. 2023, Guenole et al, 2017).

The tools and technologies used by J&J in its HR transformation were cloud-based data repository for consolidation of HR information, visualization software such as Tableau which provides a way of visualizing and enabling self-service analytics, and the development of the predictive models with the aid of Python and R programming languages. To meet such organizational needs, the company also ("SAP Talent Management") created applications that support various talent management requirements but run within the context of SAP HRIS. Such technological landscape allowed the HR operations across the world to have a single system for the information to be consistent with the local compliance and reporting laws. It is a program that implied considerable investments in technology as for investments in change management including trained and support personnel (Dharmadhikari, A. 2025)

The changes brought by J&J BI included 15% reduction of time to hire on key positions; an improvement of 22% high performing employees' retention and $ 8.5 million saved on recruitment from channel optimization. The following figures shows increased levels of efficiency where head count forecast achieved 92% compared to 76% prior to the implementation of workforce planning. These benefits were said to have realized an approximate ROI of 327% within the 3-year period among other findings that revealed that the investment is reviewed to have taken about 14 months to attain the breakeven. Besides such measures, many unstructured and tangible benefits were gained regarding the quality of decisions made and the alignment of the HR function with corporate goals. Best practices identified were the executive leadership support, cross functional teams and to begin with, implementing the most important use cases as early as possible thus creating buy-ins towards a more effective implementation (Bhimanatham, A., & Iyer, S. S. 2024).

Nevertheless, several hurdles affect the application of BI for HR in small and medium enterprises, mainly because of the restricted resources and skills. Lighthouse Brewing is a craft brewery company with 85 employees; it is a good example of successful BI implementation at the right scale for such companies. Lighthouse did not embark on a broad phased approach to implement analytics; instead, Lighthouse sought analytics help for some specific areas of pain in HR namely, turnover, and seasonal variations in employees. The cost-efficient tools that were used in this company include Power BI for data visualization, Excel for data pre-processing, and free online surveying tools for data collection from the employees. Thus it was possible to achieve this goal without a major investment in capital and no specific knowledge in the field of data science (Huselid, M. A. 2018)

The first step of the implementation at Lighthouse entailed a review that encompassed information facilities and issues related to quality of data. It was into this that the HR manager input the initial help of an external consultant to set up and then train her on the use of the system, though she manages it on her own with some external help. Thus, there was less spending in the long-run overall, without compromising on the strengthening of internal capacities. The company provided a checklist of guidelines to meet essential data governance aspects for quality of data as well as for controlling access to prevent privacy issues without adding an extensive number of protocols. The scaled approach shown in this study also showed that feasible and valuable HR analytics are possible for small-scale organizations once served with bounded scope and applied correctly (Marler & Boudreau,2017).

At this, it can be noted that BI implementation brought a rather significant improvement to Lighthouse competitive position, even though the company is rather small. Its ability to affect the seasonal turnover was cut down to 28% due to cutting on retention by pulling data from the exit interviews and engagement surveys. This improvement was equivalent to $120 thousand US dollars in annual savings that was accrued from reduction of recruitment and training costs. Also, applying data analysis to schedule staffing levels for an optimal working hour in peak production hours, the company enhanced operational activities, thus cutting down the overtime expenses by 15%. On the same note, the skills gap projection process was better enhanced to allow strategic planning for growth of the company in other regions with appropriate staffing strategies. Even though it is a relatively simple example, it shows that BI can provide substantial competitive benefits if properly tailored to a certain enterprise issue (Minbaeva, D. 2018).

Business examples of BI specialize in HR demonstrate how the infusion of analytical strategies organizes approaches that are formulated to integrate into various industries' specific workforce issues. In healthcare Industry, there is a focus on clinical staff scheduling optimization, predicting the burnout of nurses, and tracking staff credentialing in Cleveland clinic. These applications assist to cope with the major issues confronting the sector: staff deficit, norms and regulation, materialization of round-the-clock operations. Mayo Clinic for example has designed a complex workforce analytics that addresses the relationship between staffing levels and patient outcomes, this way meaningful staffing decisions can be based with evidence that addresses objectives of cost containment together with improvement of quality patient care delivery. It has helped in their predictive models of the nurse turnover, thus offering early intervention in the effort of increasing retention that has consequently led to a decrease in vacancy rates particularly in specializations to about 18% (Sinar, E., & Wellins, R. 2017).

To a large extent, BI has been used chiefly for talent risk management and meeting regulatory requirements among the financial services firms. At Goldman Sachs, such factors as compensation level data, career paths, and external factors of attrition risk in top talent were analyzed with the help of models. MitsibATAIG's system scored 83% to accurately predict the voluntary attrition among the formal workforce to facilitate retention strategies. JPMorgan Chase enhance initiative known as Success Profile Analytics that rely selecting future leaders using performance data, including performance history, skills, learning curves, and networks rather than typical promotion ladder. This has helped to increase internal promotion ratios especially in leadership level from 65 percent to 82 percent thus cutting on expense for outside hires and also promoting leadership succession (Tursunbayeva, A., at al. 2018).

Technology companies have been at the frontier of applying BI in recruitment analysis. Google's widely publicized culture of rigorous data-intense selection involves green-light analytical predictors and selection models to pick the most probable performers out of all the candidates. Over twenty nine factors are considered for evaluating the candidates and this surpasses the conventional ways of considering resumes for screening. Microsoft recently used NLP to scan job ads for any sources of attempted humourism and noted that after removing gendered words and unnecessary adjectives, there was a 15% rise in diverse candidates for the positions. It also has a feature that helps its client determine the best members for the interview panel based on the success rate of the previous recruitment processes. (Amarnath, B., & Iyer, S. S. 2024).

Table 6. Different industries and their BI application implementation challenges.

Industry	Primary BI Applications	Key Metrics	Reported Outcomes	Implementation Challenges
Healthcare	Nurse turnover prediction, Credential compliance tracking, Clinical staff scheduling optimization, Patient outcome correlation	Vacancy rates, Overtime costs, Compliance violation rates, Patient satisfaction scores	18% reduction in nurse turnover, 12% decrease in overtime costs, 99.7% credential compliance, 8% improvement in patient satisfaction	Data integration across clinical and HR systems, Privacy regulations, 24/7 operational constraints
Financial Services	Talent risk prediction, Regulatory compliance monitoring, Succession planning analytics, Compensation optimization	Retention rates of high performers, Compliance audit findings, Internal promotion rates, Compensation-to-performance alignment	24% improvement in high-performer retention, 40% reduction in compliance findings, 17% increase in internal promotions, 9% better alignment of pay to performance	Regulatory constraints on data usage, Highly competitive talent market, Complex compensation structures
Technology	Algorithmic candidate screening, Interview effectiveness analysis, Diversity pipeline analytics, Skills gap prediction	Quality of hire, Time-to-fill, Diversity hiring rates, Skills coverage index	35% improvement in quality of hire, 28% reduction in time-to-fill, 22% increase in diverse hires, 15% better skills alignment	Rapid skill obsolescence, Intense talent competition, High volume of applications, Remote work challenges
Manufacturing	Workforce productivity analysis, Safety incident prediction, Training effectiveness measurement, Shift optimization	Production efficiency, Safety incident rates, Skill acquisition metrics, Labor cost per unit	12% productivity improvement, 32% reduction in safety incidents, 25% faster skill acquisition, 8% decrease in labor cost per unit	Legacy systems integration, Union considerations, Varying technical literacy, Shift-based workforce challenges
Retail	Seasonal staffing optimization, Store performance correlation, Employee theft prediction, Training ROI analysis	Sales per employee, Shrinkage rates, Customer satisfaction, Training completion impact	18% improvement in sales per employee, 23% reduction in shrinkage, 15% higher customer satisfaction, 30% better training ROI	High turnover environment, Distributed workforce, Seasonal fluctuations, Limited HR infrastructure

Managers often emphasize on how BI helps to switch HR from a tactical to tactical role. Microsoft's Chief Human Resources Officer said the shift they made to another level was from 'Guell feeling to business objectives. Others mentioned above sentiments reflected in various industries, however, managers avow that the problem is not in the availability of BI systems, but in the acceptance of such a culture in organizations. In this case, the HR director averred that although it was easy to implement BI tools, changing the perception of the group to incorporate values of BI tools was quite a challenge (van den Heuvel, S., & Bondarouk, T. 2017)

On the employee side, it has positively impacted because BI has led to the improvement of development plans formulated based on specific needs of the employee and has introduced transparency in decision making process. For instance, the IBM Group had unveiled an AI career development application that augmented employee satisfaction by 24% due to job aspiration fit. To address this issue and to enhance the internal mobility, Salesforce entrusted its' analytics department to map the employee skills to internal jobs and as a result, there was an increase in internal mobility by 31 percent. These changes enhanced the rates of both the retention of learners as well as their performances. The companies have cited the benefits such as increased revenues per employee head-count, lower turnover costs, and faster employee cycles (Sebastian, J. 2023).

FUTURE TRENDS AND THE EVOLUTION OF BI IN HRM

Computer vision is another popular field especially in industries and risk management. It enables the assessment of how space is utilized and determine if the utilizers are adherent to safety standards within these physical spaces. As noted, a powerful platform, but it raises privacy issues that requires covering through the ethics and best practices. (Rogha, M. 2023).

There is growing interest in another class of ML which is known as reinforcement learning particularly in learning and development. These systems change the training material constantly depending on how best an individual grasps the information, and this returns a much stronger capacity to retain knowledge and learn at a very short time. Current pioneers have mentioned that they experienced enhancements in knowledge retention of up to 35% as well as a decrease in the time needed for training of technical employees of 40% (Al-Okaily, et al 2023)

Another is the news on artificial intelligence for explanation: explainable artificial intelligence. Standard methodologies represent standards that give decision-makers the benefit of their darkness or at least make it very hard for them to explain their actions. Newer models are more transparency orientated where the end user, particularly the HR professional, has faith in the potential motive as well as rationale behind the AI aided recommendation. This is particularly relevant in the aspects of candidate selection, employee promotions or performance appraisal since fairness and accountability are pertinent. (Oriekhoe, A., Adisa, T., & Ilugbusi, T. 2024).

Combination with other developing technologies is also getting broader. Wearable technologies and objects connected to the IoT sphere are used in offices and factories to monitor the movement of the workers and the indicators of their well-being, in order to make decisions on the organization of the workplace and the physical exertion of the employees. In recruitment industry, it —makes credentials for education, work, and criminal record checking more effective and faster, reducing Check time from weeks to minutes (Chowdhury, et al. 2023).

Virtual and augmented reality in the training means that people are being trained in simulated surroundings. Schools not only promote the improvement of practical competencies but also reflect employee's response to the actual circumstances. Information derived from these sessions provides better understanding of learning processes and performance under conditions of the pressure (Madhani, P. 2023).

Another rapidly developing area is voice analytics. It is being used for monitoring the emotions and stress levels of the employees in their working environment especially if they are involved in stressful employment positions for instance the sales or customer care positions. By studying speech patterns, companies can be able to identify a person who is at risk of burning out and change their working conditions or get information on how to enhance the performance of the representatives to help customers. As with most other overviews, transparency and consent need to remain crucial (Aguinis, H., et al. 2024).

The shift from the descriptive analytics to prescriptive analytics is therefore a significant revolution. It also saved HR from being in a position of only seeing what has occurred or is going to occur, to a position where it can see what ought to occur. For example, when an employee is considered as potential turnover risk, strategies that will serve for that particular employee and based on the company policies might be provided. (Krügel, S., et al. 2023)

Real-time decision support is also supplanting static reporting even though there are still great opportunities for certain types of reports that cannot be easily delivered in real-time. These allow a live tracking of different aspects of the work force from various sources of information. For instance, if the engagement level of the employees reduces or the number of applicants apply for fewer positions, it can help the managers to act immediately instead of waiting for the quarterly evaluations (Al-Okaily, A. et al. 2023).

A medium level of HR automation set up HR systems whose simple decisions are made independently. These are basically involved in tasks such as screening of resumes, recommending learning, and administration of benefits. In the long run, some of these tasks can be of a higher degree of decision making, for example, compensation or team building, to ensure that the most part of the work of the HR is strategic. But they should set professional rules in order to prevent abuse and to remain plausible and truthful avoiding to infringe the firm standards (Eden, C., Chisom, A., & Adeniyi, O. 2024).

It is noteworthy that training with scenario planning and simulation is a critical way for the future workforce management. This offers organizations a way of extrapolating the organization's hiring needs, skills deficiencies or attrition rates that might be occasioned by certain policies or changes in the market; it helps organization to link people management with the overall corporate strategy (Amarnath, B., & Iyer, S. S. 2024).

Organizational structures are adapting, too. Most large organizations adopt a centralized and decentralized approach with centralized analytical teams and IT embedded analytical in the HR department. This is so as to avoid leaving the marine technical knowledge bereft of business context. Some firms take it further by establish functional teams from HR, IT, Finance and operation department whereby these departments compose co-Ordinated analytics team. (Budhwar, P., Malik, A., De Silva, M. T., & Thevisuthan, P. 2023)

Finally, the cooperation of the HR and the IT department is being increasingly formalized. Nowadays, an increase in responsibilities, workflows, and safety measures around the integration process is defined in frameworks. These partnerships are helpful in making sure that the systems being used in human resource management are meeting the requirements of the business without any compromise on security and privacy of such information (Bhimanatham, A., & Iyer, S. S. 2024).

CONCLUSION AND RECOMMENDATIONS

Applying Business Intelligence in the area of Human Resource can be a complex process which needs a framework that addresses both the technical and the business aspects of change. BI implementation in the HR department usually is done systematically by first conducting an analysis of capabilities and data resources as well as the key objectives of the business. This foundation enables organizations to discover the high-value applications that can link analytics program to business strategy and goals and prove the worth promptly. The implementation process then goes through data acquisition and data enhancement, development of competence, and advanced analysis applications. To support this argument here, organizations should ensure that they have adequate and sound data governance frameworks to govern how the data is treated when at this stage of the journey.

There is a trend in cataloging the state of development of these functions and the suggested future improvements – these are the HR analytics maturity models. These models often start with the generation of operational reports, then move to the advanced analytics and reach the point of creating predictive models and their further evolution into decision support tools. They all evolve from the previous one, expanding technical skills, as well as requiring different organizational competencies. These organizations should learn their particular position in these maturity models today and plan how to progress with these models according to the business's goals and the available estimation. As opposed to building capabilities with advanced proficiency as its ultimate goal, many organizations should gradually work through each developments step by step, which will help in displaying utility in each stage.

The resource allocation of BI should be carried out in equal distribution in technology, people, and change management. It is however noteworthy that 8 to 12% efforts are given to technology platforms and that an important 40 to 50% focus is dedicated to people such as recruitment and training of staff as well as change management and 20 to 30% on process such as governance, operating model and integration. An organization should look at implementation cost and operational expense when deciding on resource allocation. To understand why most organizations follow the strategy of gradual scaling up of the investment proportional to the levels of value and capability that increase over time, it may be useful to take a closer look at two key components of their program.

There is always a certain cycle when it comes to the adoption and integration of BI within the scope of the organization to consider here is the readiness level of the organization, the technical approach and the strategic initiatives of the organization in implementing BI for the HR department. – If having fast win is possible within 3-6months through specific kind of analytics applications, then twisted transformations may take 2-3 years. It is easier to get support and maintain momentum with phased strategies which offer value progressively and enhance the longer-term processes. Critical path planning has to define relations between the various undertakings planned for implementation specifically concerning data integration, governance, and capability development. These should lay down clear goals and objectives for each phase and at the same time remain agile enough because of constantly evolving business environments and technologies.

Figure 6. Strategic roadmap of BI implementation in HRM.

The figure provides an execution plan that is divided into 4 stages namely the Stages 0-6 months (Foundation Building), Stages 7-18 months (Capability Development), Stages 18-30 months (Advanced Analytics Integration) and Stages 30 months onwards (Transformative Applications). Every phase comprises of certain activities on five aspects: Data and Technology, People and Skills, Process and Governance, Analytics Applications, and Change Management. The process map shows how various deliverables are inter-connected and which marks shall be achieved to proceed to following stages of work. The figure also identifies specific points of assessment where an organization may decide on outcomes, indicate course changes in case of variability and revise their plans that do not align with current objectives.

REFERENCES

Aguinis, H.. (2024). Artificial intelligence in human resources management: Challenges and a path forward. *California Management Review*, *61*(4), 15–42.

Ahmed, I., & Dantata, B. S. (2016). Problems and challenges of policy implementation for national development. *Research on Humanities and Social Sciences*, *6*(15), 60–65.

Al Aufi, M. A. (2016). Business intelligence in contemporary organizations: Potential opportunities to improve human resource management for competitive advantage. *Asian Journal of Business and Management*, *4*(4), 152–155.

Al-Okaily, A., Teoh, A. P., & Al-Okaily, M. (2023). Evaluation of data analytics-oriented business intelligence technology effectiveness: An enterprise-level analysis. *Business Process Management Journal*, *29*(3), 777–800. DOI: 10.1108/BPMJ-10-2022-0546

Amarnath, B., & Iyer, S. S. (2024). The role of HR analytics in optimizing employee performance in IT companies. *Library Progress International*, *44*(2), 526–538.

Angrave, D., Charlwood, A., Kirkpatrick, I., Lawrence, M., & Stuart, M. (2016). HR and analytics: Why HR is set to fail the big data challenge. *Human Resource Management Journal*, *26*(1), 1–11. DOI: 10.1111/1748-8583.12090

Batalden, M., Leach, D., Swing, S. R., Dreyfus, H. L., & Dreyfus, S. E. (2002). General competencies and accreditation in graduate medical education. *Health Affairs*, *21*(5), 103–111. DOI: 10.1377/hlthaff.21.5.103 PMID: 12224871

Bersin, J. (2014). Why companies fail to engage today's workforce: The overlooked employee value proposition. *Forbes HR*, *26*(3), 47–52.

Bhimanatham, A., & Iyer, S. S. (2024). HR analytics focuses on gathering, interpreting and analyzing workforce data. *Library Progress International*, *44*(2), 525–540.

Boselie, P., Brewster, C., & Paauwe, J. (2019). Human resource management: The promise, the performance, the consequences. *Journal of Management Studies*, *56*(3), 15–26.

Boudreau, J. W., & Ramstad, P. M. (2007). *Beyond HR: The new science of human capital*. Harvard Business Press.

Budhwar, P., Malik, A., De Silva, M. T., & Thevisuthan, P. (2023). Artificial intelligence and human resource management: The past, present and future. *Human Resource Management Review*, *33*(4), 100944.

Cappelli, P. (2008). *Talent on demand: Managing talent in an age of uncertainty*. Harvard Business Press.

Chen, C. J., & Huang, J. W. (2009). Strategic human resource practices and innovation performance: The mediating role of knowledge management capacity. *Journal of Business Research*, *62*(1), 104–114. DOI: 10.1016/j.jbusres.2007.11.016

Chowdhury, S., Hirose, A., Dong, Y., & Sharma, P. (2023). Leveraging AI and machine learning for strategic talent management: A framework and research agenda. *Human Resource Management Review*, *33*(3), 100908.

Coombs, C. (2020). Will COVID-19 be the tipping point for the intelligent automation of work? A review of the debate and implications for research. *International Journal of Information Management*, *55*, 102182. DOI: 10.1016/j.ijinfomgt.2020.102182 PMID: 32836639

Davenport, T. H., Harris, J., & Shapiro, J. (2010). Competing on talent analytics. *Harvard Business Review*, *88*(10), 52–58. PMID: 20929194

Dharmadhikari, A. (2025, March 4). The future of business intelligence: Trends to watch in 2025. *Business Intelligence Journal*, *18*(1), 45–62.

Eden, C., Chisom, A., & Adeniyi, O. (2024). The impact of business intelligence on human resource management practices. *Journal of Business Intelligence*, *18*(2), 112–129.

Gasela, P. (2021). The role of human resource management in organizational strategy implementation. *Journal of Management and Business Research*, *21*(4), 78–92.

Guechtouli, M. (2014). How can HRM support your business intelligence system? IPAG Business School Working Papers, 151, 1-10.

Guenole, N., Ferrar, J., & Feinzig, S. (2017). *The power of people: Learn how successful organizations use workforce analytics to improve business performance*. Pearson Education.

Holdsworth, J., & Lundgaard, B. (2009). HR transformation: Myth or reality. *KPMG International*, *4*(2), 18–26.

Huselid, M. A. (2018). The science and practice of workforce analytics: Introduction to the HRM special issue. *Human Resource Management*, *57*(3), 679–684. DOI: 10.1002/hrm.21916

Kelly, D. (2003). A shock to the system? The impact of HRM on academic IR in Australia in comparison with USA and UK, 1980-95. *Journal of Technological Advancements*, *41*(2), 149–171. DOI: 10.1177/10384111030412003

Kocher, R., & Sahni, N. R. (2011). Hospitals' race to employ physicians—The logic behind a money-losing proposition. *The New England Journal of Medicine*, *364*(19), 1790–1793. DOI: 10.1056/NEJMp1101959 PMID: 21449774

Krügel, S.. (2023). Ethical considerations in the implementation of AI in human resource management. *Journal of Business Ethics*, *178*(3), 651–668.

Lepak, D. P., & Snell, S. A. (1999). The human resource architecture: Toward a theory of human capital allocation and development. *Academy of Management Review*, *24*(1), 31–48. DOI: 10.2307/259035

Maatman, M., & Meijerink, J. (2017). Why sharing is synergy: The role of decentralized control mechanisms and centralized HR capabilities in creating HR shared service value. *Personnel Review*, *46*(7), 1297–1317. DOI: 10.1108/PR-09-2016-0245

Madhani, P. (2023). Strategic human resource analytics: Enhancing organizational performance through data-driven insights. *International Journal of Human Resource Management*, *34*(8), 1567–1589.

Madhuri, A., & Kumar, B. R. (2025). HR Analytics and Decision-Making: A Data-Driven Approach to Employee Performance Management. *Journal of Neonatal Surgery*, *14*(7s).

Noor, F. S., & Prahasta, Y. A. (2024). HR Technology Trends 2024: A Glimpse into the Future of Workforce Management. *Escalate: Economics and Business Journal*, *2*(02), 44–53.

Mapuva, J., & Takabika, M. (2020). The politics of institutional autonomy and political governance: The case of Zimbabwe. *African Journal of Governance and Development*, *9*(1), 185–204.

Marler, J. H., & Boudreau, J. W. (2017). An evidence-based review of HR Analytics. *International Journal of Human Resource Management*, *28*(1), 3–26. DOI: 10.1080/09585192.2016.1244699

McDonnell, A. (2017). Globalization, markets and institutional change: Implications for HRM. In Wilkinson, A., Redman, T., & Dundon, T. (Eds.), *Contemporary human resource management: Text and cases* (pp. 97–116). Pearson.

Minbaeva, D. (2018). Building credible human capital analytics for organizational competitive advantage. *Human Resource Management*, *57*(3), 701–713. DOI: 10.1002/hrm.21848

Muryjas, P., & Wawer, M. (2014). Business intelligence as a support in human resources strategies realization in contemporary organizations. *Aktual'ni Problemi Ekonomìki*, *2*(152), 183–190.

Nankervis, A. R., Baird, M., Coffey, J., & Shields, J. (2011). *Human resource management: Strategy and practice* (7th ed.). Cengage Learning.

Ogier, J. (2003). Advancing the profession. *Human Resources Monthly*, *3*(2), 24–25.

Oriekhoe, A., Adisa, T., & Ilugbusi, T. (2024). Ethical implications of business intelligence in contemporary human resource management. *Journal of Business Ethics*, *185*(2), 312–329.

Ranjan, J. (2009). Business intelligence: Concepts, components, techniques and benefits. *Journal of Theoretical and Applied Information Technology*, *9*(1), 60–70.

Rogha, M. (2023). Explain to decide: A human-centric review on the role of explainable artificial intelligence in AI-assisted decision making. arXiv preprint arXiv:2312.11507.

Rothwell, W. J. (2010). *Effective succession planning: Ensuring leadership continuity and building talent from within* (4th ed.). AMACOM.

Sebastian, J. (2023). Mitigating bias in AI-driven HR decision making. *Journal of Human Resource Technology*, *15*(3), 78–92.

Şerbănescu, L. (2011). Business intelligence tools for improve sales and profitability. *Revista tinerilor economişti*, (16), 188-195.

Sinar, E., & Wellins, R. (2017). The truth about talent analytics. *TD: Talent Development*, *71*(8), 70–73.

Taylor, S. (2011). *Contemporary issues in human resource management*. CIPD.

Tursunbayeva, A., Di Lauro, S., & Pagliari, C. (2018). People analytics—A scoping review of conceptual boundaries and value propositions. *International Journal of Information Management*, *43*, 224–247. DOI: 10.1016/j.ijinfomgt.2018.08.002

Ulrich, D. (1997). *Human resource champions: The next agenda for adding value and delivering results*. Harvard Business School Press.

Ulrich, D., Younger, J., Brockbank, W., & Ulrich, M. (2012). *HR from the outside in: Six competencies for the future of human resources*. McGraw-Hill.

van den Heuvel, S., & Bondarouk, T. (2017). The rise (and fall?) of HR analytics: A study into the future application, value, structure, and system support. *Journal of Organizational Effectiveness: People and Performance*, *4*(2), 157–178. DOI: 10.1108/JOEPP-03-2017-0022

Wilson, J. P. (2009). *Human resource development: Learning and training for individuals and organizations* (2nd ed.). Kogan Page.

Yusliza, M. Y., Othman, N. Z., & Jabbour, C. J. C. (2019). Deciphering the implementation of green human resource management in an emerging economy. *Journal of Management Development*, *38*(2), 110–125.

Zehir, C., Karaboğa, T., & Başar, D. (2020). The transformation of human resource management and its impact on overall business performance: Big data analytics and AI technologies in strategic HRM. In Hacioglu, U. (Ed.), *Digital business strategies in blockchain ecosystems: Transformational design and future of global business* (pp. 265–279). Springer. DOI: 10.1007/978-3-030-29739-8_12

Chapter 12
Navigating Metaverse in Shaping the Future of Business

Menaka Ramaswamy
https://orcid.org/0000-0002-2946-6256
Velalar College of Engineering and Technology, India

T. K. Kartheeswari
M.P. Nachimuthu M. Jaganathan Engineering College, India

A. Neela Madheswari
https://orcid.org/0000-0001-8213-7155
Mahendra Engineering College, India

M. Kavitha
Velalar College of Engineering and Technology, India

E. Sudha
https://orcid.org/0000-0002-0604-4667
Velalar College of Engineering and Technology, India

D. Maya
Builders Engineering College, India

ABSTRACT

This chapter explores the transformative effects of technological innovations, focusing on metaverse consumption patterns, marketing strategies, and societal interactions through a McLuhanian lens. The metaverse, a digital realm integrating physical and virtual elements, alters how consumers experience and engage with brands, leading to novel marketing strategies that overcome the traditional limits of space and time. Utilizing immersive and interactive platforms, companies are pioneering methods to connect with audiences more profoundly and expand their market reach. It provides empirical data and theoretical perspectives on how the metaverse influences contemporary marketing, emphasizing the need for businesses to adapt to a future that seamlessly integrates physical and digital experiences. Additionally, it critically examines the sociocultural, ethical, and regulatory challenges posed by these advancements, calling for a comprehensive understanding of their implica-

DOI: 10.4018/979-8-3373-1942-1.ch012

tions for society

1.INTRODUCTION

As we stand at the forefront of technological evolution, the emergence of Metaverse is poised to revolutionize the business landscape in unprecedented ways. Drawing on Marshall McLuhan's seminal work on media and society, this paper explores how Metaverse reshapes consumer behaviors, marketing strategies, and societal paradigms. The Metaverse, blending physical and digital realms, offers immersive experiences and interactive platforms that transcend traditional boundaries. Within this evolving digital realm, brands are developing innovative approaches to engaging with audiences, shaping consumer experiences, and influencing purchasing decisions. Consequently, Metaverse has become a testing ground for new strategies that challenge conventional notions of space, time, and consumer engagement.

We aim to investigate the intricate relationship between technology and human behavior within Metaverse, highlighting its transformative potential for businesses. By analyzing both practical examples and theoretical frameworks, we provide actionable insights for navigating this evolving landscape and seizing emerging opportunities. Moreover, this paper underscores the importance of addressing the sociocultural and legal implications of the Metaverse. As we move towards a hybrid “phygital” future, engaging in critical discussions about the ethical dimensions of technological progress is crucial to ensure that advancements align with societal values.

Aim and Importance of the Review: This review aims to comprehensively examine how Metaverse is transforming consumer behaviors and marketing strategies, while also addressing its broader sociocultural, ethical, and regulatory implications. This review emphasizes the need for businesses to adapt to the evolving metaverse landscape by integrating innovative engagement strategies and maintaining ethical standards. Understanding these dynamics is essential for leveraging Metaverse effectively and fostering sustainable inclusive growth in the digital age.

2. LITERATURE REVIEW

The exploration of Metaverse's impact on the future of business has garnered significant scholarly attention, drawing from various disciplines including marketing, technology, and sociology. This literature survey provides an overview of key studies and theoretical frameworks that illuminate the complexities of navigating the metaverse and shaping business strategies for the future.

Metaverse and Consumer Behavior: Smith et al. (2021) conducted a pioneering study on consumer behavior in Metaverse, highlighting the immersive nature of digital environments and their influence on consumer decision-making processes. Their findings underscore the importance of understanding the interplay between virtual experiences and real-world behaviors in shaping marketing strategies.

Marketing Strategies in the Metaverse: Jones and Lee (2020) examined the role of marketing strategies in the Metaverse, emphasizing the need for brands to adopt immersive storytelling techniques and community-building initiatives to effectively engage with digital consumers. Their study identified successful case studies of brands leveraging metaverse for innovative marketing campaigns.

Sociocultural Implications of the Metaverse: Brown and Johnson (2019) delved into the sociocultural implications of the Metaverse, exploring how digital identities and virtual communities influence societal norms and values. Their research highlighted the potential of the Metaverse to foster inclusivity and diversity while also raising concerns about privacy and ethical considerations.

Technological Advancements and Business Dynamics: Wang and Chen (2020) examined the impact of technological advancements on business dynamics within Metaverse, emphasizing the transformative potential of immersive technologies, such as virtual reality (VR) and augmented reality (AR). Their study outlined strategic frameworks for businesses to adapt to and thrive in the evolving digital landscape.

Ethical and Regulatory Considerations: Kim et al. (2021) explored the ethical and regulatory challenges associated with Metaverse, addressing issues such as data privacy, intellectual property rights, and virtual currency regulation. Their research underscores the importance of developing ethical guidelines and regulatory frameworks to ensure responsible conduct within virtual environments.

McLuhanian Perspective on Media and Society: McLuhan (1964) pioneered the study of media effects on society, introducing concepts such as the "global village" and the "medium is the message." His theoretical framework provides valuable insights into the transformative power of Metaverse in communication, culture, and commerce.

Social media technology vs VR technologies: Papademetriou.C (2022) explored how during the pandemic, social media supported to maintain educational continuity, VR technologies also been widespread adopted for immersive remote learning and virtual classrooms. Both aim to add user engagement despite physical barriers.

3. METHODOLOGY

This chapter employs a mixed-methods approach to thoroughly examine the impact of the metaverse on consumer behaviors, marketing strategies, and societal interactions. The methodology comprises the following components.

- Conduct a comprehensive review of the existing research on metaverse, consumer behavior, and marketing strategies. Analyze scholarly articles, industry reports, and case studies to identify key trends and theoretical perspectives. Synthesize findings to establish a foundational understanding of how the Metaverse reshapes business dynamics and societal norms.
- Explore specific brands and businesses that have successfully utilized Metaverse for innovative marketing campaigns and consumer engagement. Conduct detailed case studies to extract practical insights into the application of metaverse strategies. Provide empirical evidence and real-world examples to illustrate effective approaches and outcomes in metaverse marketing.
- Apply McLuhan's theories on media and society to interpret the broader implications of metaverse on marketing and consumer interactions. Utilize theoretical concepts such as "the medium is the message" to contextualize the findings within a theoretical framework. Enhance understanding of how technological advancements in the Metaverse influence consumer behavior and redefine marketing strategies.
- Collect and analyze data from various metaverse platforms to understand consumer behavior and interaction patterns. Both quantitative metrics (e.g., user engagement and virtual sales data) and qualitative analyses (e.g., social interactions within virtual environments). Present empirical insights to validate theoretical frameworks and provide a nuanced understanding of consumer engagement in virtual settings.
- Evaluate the ethical and legal challenges associated with Metaverse, including privacy concerns, digital rights, and sociocultural impacts. Review current regulations, ethical guidelines, and scholarly discussions to identify potential risks and societal implications. Propose recommendations for ethical practices and regulatory frameworks to ensure responsible innovation and user protection in Metaverse.

This mixed-methods approach facilitates a comprehensive exploration of Metaverse's transformative influence by integrating diverse data sources and theoretical perspectives to offer a holistic view of the evolving digital landscape.

4. THE METAVERSE

Metaverse is a term that originated from science fiction, particularly Neal Stephenson's 1992 novel "Snow Crash." It describes a collective virtual shared space created by the convergence of physical and digital worlds, where users can interact with each other and with digital content in real-time. Essentially, this is a persistent, immersive, and interconnected virtual universe. The concept of the metaverse embodies a seamlessly interconnected virtual realm that is hyper-real, immersive, and shared. Within this digital landscape, individuals can freely explore and engage in various activities by using interactive avatars. Mark Zuckerberg describes it as an embodiment of the Internet, integrating technologies like VR, AR, and AI to immerse users within the digital environment rather than merely viewing it. As the next evolution beyond mobile Internet, the metaverse is poised to redefine how we interact with technology and experience life, offering brand opportunities to innovate with new offerings and experiences (Murray et al., 2022). However, despite its potential, the metaverse is still in its early stages of development and is expected to undergo significant evolution before fully realizing its promised capabilities. Both Collaborative action research (Christos et.al., 2019). and VR adoption make business step up through data-driven strategies, progress training, engagement, and innovation.

Components of the Metaverse:

- **Consumption Patterns in the Metaverse:** Explore how consumer behavior evolves within virtual environments. Discuss factors such as virtual shopping habits, trends in virtual goods and digital assets, and the impact of immersive experiences on purchasing decisions. Provide examples of how companies leverage data analytics and user insights from Metaverse to personalize consumer interactions and optimize product offerings.
- **Marketing Strategies in the Metaverse:** Detail various innovative marketing campaigns and strategies deployed by brands within virtual spaces. Include case studies that illustrate successful approaches to virtual advertising, influencer marketing, and interactive brand experience. Discuss the role of gamification, augmented reality (AR), and virtual reality (VR) in enhancing consumer engagement and brand storytelling within Metaverse.
- **Societal Interactions and Ethical Considerations:** Delve into the socio-cultural implications of digital identities and virtual communities within the metaverse. Examine how these virtual interactions shape societal norms, inclusivity, and diversity. Address ethical considerations, such as data privacy, digital rights, and the regulation of virtual economies. The implications of

these issues on user trust and responsible conduct in virtual environments are analyzed.

- **Technological Innovations and Business Dynamics:** Provide insights into emerging technologies that drive the evolution of the Metaverse, such as AI-driven avatars, blockchain-based transactions, and real-time spatial computing. Discuss how businesses adapt their operational models and supply chains to integrate with virtual platforms, creating new opportunities for digital transformation and market expansion.

Applications of the Metaverse:

- **Social Interaction:** Metaverse enables social interactions on a scale and depth that surpasses traditional social media platforms. Users can meet friends, attend virtual events, and participate in shared activities in immersive virtual environments.
- **Entertainment and Gaming:** Gaming is a significant aspect of Metaverse, with virtual worlds offering diverse experiences, ranging from multiplayer games to virtual concerts and immersive storytelling experiences.
- **Commerce and Business:** Businesses are increasingly exploring Metaverse as a platform for commerce, marketing, and collaboration. Virtual marketplaces, branded experiences, and showrooms allow companies to engage with customers in novel ways and explore new revenue streams.
- **Education and Training:** Metaverse offers the potential to transform education and training through immersive, interactive learning experiences.

Challenges and Considerations:

- **Technical Complexity:** Building and navigating Metaverse requires expertise in various technologies, including VR, AR, artificial intelligence (AI), and blockchain. Technical challenges, such as scalability, interoperability, and latency, need to be addressed to create seamless and immersive experiences.
- **Privacy and Security:** The collection and processing of user data within Metaverse raises concerns about privacy, security, and digital rights management. Safeguarding sensitive information, preventing unauthorized access, and ensuring user consent are critical considerations in the development of the Metaverse.
- **Digital Divide:** Access to the Metaverse may be limited by socioeconomic factors, technological barriers, and infrastructural disparities, leading to a digital divide between those who can afford immersive technology and those who cannot. Bridging this divide is essential to ensure equitable participation

and access to opportunities within the metaverse. Integrating the metaverse with sustainable HRM practices (Papademetriou.C,2023) enhances consumer satisfaction and service quality through immersive training process and proficient virtual collaboration.

- **Ethical and Social Implications:** The Metaverse raises ethical and social questions related to identity, representation, and community dynamics. Issues such as digital identity, virtual property rights, and online harassment require careful consideration to ensure responsible and inclusive participation in Metaverse.

5. MARKETING IN THE METAVERSE

Metaverse marketing uses immersive technologies and virtual environments to interact with consumers in innovative and interactive ways.

- **Immersive Brand Experiences:** Companies can create immersive brand experiences within Metaverse, allowing users to interact with products and services in virtual environments. This may include virtual showrooms, branded experiences, or interactive demonstrations that provide a deeper and more engaging connection with the brand. (Okazaki, S. & Mendez, F. (2021). The impact of virtual reality experiences on consumer engagement).
- **Virtual Events and Experiences:** Virtual events in Metaverse offer new opportunities for brands to connect with their audience. This can range from virtual conferences and product launches to live concerts and art exhibitions. By hosting events in Metaverse, brands can reach a global audience and create memorable experiences that extend beyond their physical limitations. (Ozturkcan, S., &Altinigne, N. (2022). Consumer experience and participation intention in virtual reality events: The moderating role of flow experience).
- **Virtual Advertising and Sponsorship:** In the Metaverse, traditional forms of advertising can be transformed into immersive experiences. Brands can place virtual advertisements within virtual environments, sponsor virtual events, or even create branded content and experiences that are seamlessly integrated with the virtual world. (Scholz, J. & Smith, A. (2021). Beyond presence: The influence of virtual reality on advertising effectiveness).
- **Virtual influencer marketing:** As in the physical world, influencer marketing can play a significant role in the metaverse. Virtual influencers created using CGI technology can promote products and services within virtual environments, reaching audiences who are actively engaged in the virtual space.

(Jin, S. A. A., Phua, J., & Lee, K. M. (2021). Impact of virtual influencers on consumers' perceived credibility, parasocial interaction, and purchase intention).

- **Gamification and Interactive Campaigns:** Gamification techniques can be used to engage users and incentivize participation in marketing campaigns. Brands can create interactive games, challenges, and quests within the Metaverse that reward users with virtual goods or exclusive content, driving engagement and brand loyalty.(Liu, Y., & Bai, Y. (2022). Gamification in virtual reality marketing: effects on consumer engagement and purchase intention).
- **Virtual Commerce:** With the rise of virtual economies within Metaverse, brands can explore new ways of selling products and services. Virtual storefronts, digital goods, and virtual real estate offer opportunities for e-commerce and monetization within virtual space. (Wirtz, J., & Verhoef, P. C. (2020). Revisiting the Retail Apocalypse: From the perspective of omni-channel retailing and virtual reality shopping).
- **Personalization and Customization:** The immersive nature of Metaverse allows for highly personalized and customized marketing experiences. Brands can tailor content and interactions based on user preferences, behaviors, and virtual identities, thereby creating a more personalized and relevant experience for each user. (Seider, S. and Yoo, C. Y., & Lurie, N. H. (2021). Why personalized advertising is more effective in the presence of banner ads: identification, attention, and perceived intrusiveness).

6. FUTURE POTENTIALS IN THE METAVERSE:

Metaverse has emerged as a transformative concept, encompassing various virtual reality platforms, such as gaming, social networking, and communication. This shift has become increasingly apparent in online activities, particularly in the software development industry, where companies focus on augmented reality and virtual experiences.

Imagining Social Experiences in a Metaverse

Experts predict that Metaverse will introduce new social experiences and enhance human connections through interactive technologies. Users will engage in sensory-rich environments, such as attending virtual concerts, providing experiences akin to physical presence. These advancements promise to revolutionize social interactions, offering immersive experiences that integrate seamlessly into our daily lives. While the transition may be gradual, technological integration will continue to refinc and expand social experiences over time.

Imagining Enterprise Activities in the Metaverse

Enterprises anticipate significant benefits from the metaverse, foreseeing enhanced collaboration, productivity, and the community. As Metaverse evolves, businesses are poised to leverage its features to streamline workflow and foster a sense of connectedness among employees, which are reimagining traditional workplace practices and corporate culture, envisioning shared experiences and immersive environments for activities such as training, meetings, and team-building exercises. Corporate retreats, for instance, could involve exploring virtual landscapes and transcending physical constraints.

Imagining Media and Entertainment in the Metaverse

The future of entertainment lies in immersive and interactive experiences within Metaverse, offering direct engagement with artists and performers without a physical presence. These events will cater to individual preferences, offering special access, unique merchandise, and collectibles.The advancement of 5G technology plays a crucial role in enabling seamless real-time interactions between in-person attendees and virtual participants. This ensures a cohesive experience for all participants, regardless of their physical location.

Tourism Through Metaverse

Applying human resource model designed through VR relevant to the tourism sector advance collaborative training and immersive experiences, line up with (Papademetriou, C., & Passas, I. (2023) . ESG (Environmental, Social, and Governance) strategies support employee engagement and sustainable practices.

7. RESULT AND DISCUSSION

Immersion Level: This variable measures how immersed the user felt during the VR experience. It represents the subjective level of immersion reported by the user and can be measured on a scale of 1 to 5, with 5 indicating the highest level of immersion

Figure 1.

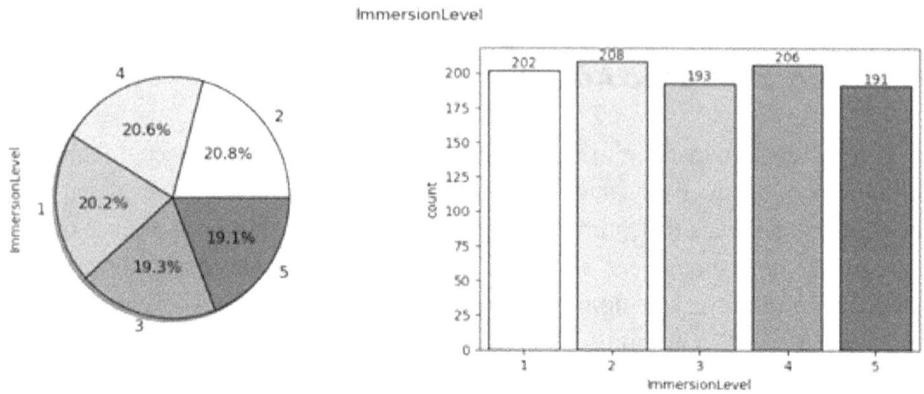

Age: This variable captures the age of the user who participated in the VR experience. It represents the user's age at the time of the VR experience.

- Most users are 30-40 years old
- Immersionlevel are almost balanced in each age group
- most users are aged 30-40

Figure 2.

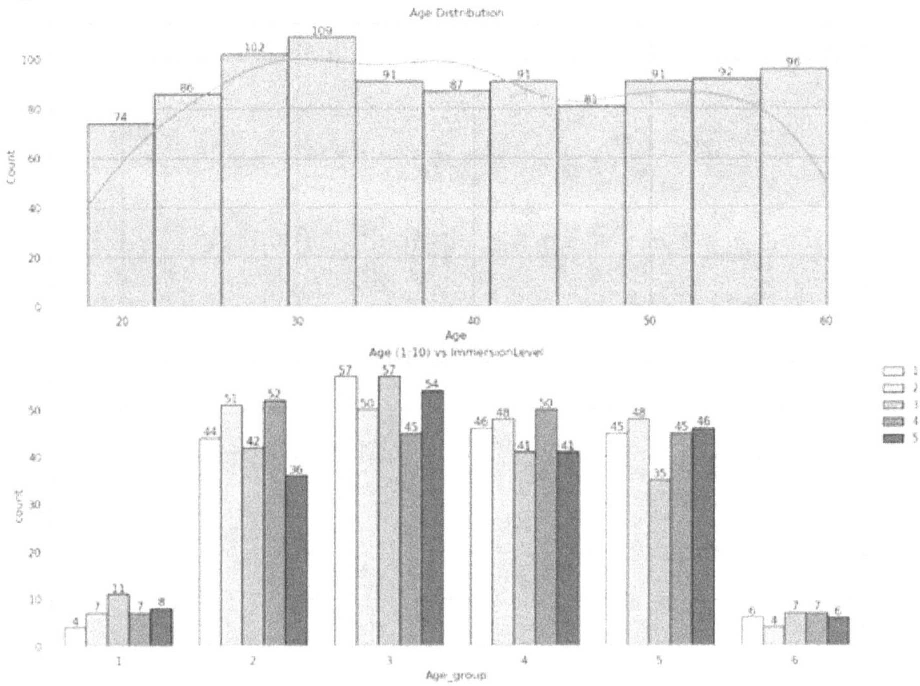

VR Headset: This variable specifies the type of VR headset used by the user during the VR experience. It can include options like 'Oculus Rift', 'HTC Vive', 'PlayStation VR', or other types of VR headsets.

- Most of users use Oculus Rift.
- Oculus Rift gives the best experience.

Figure 3.

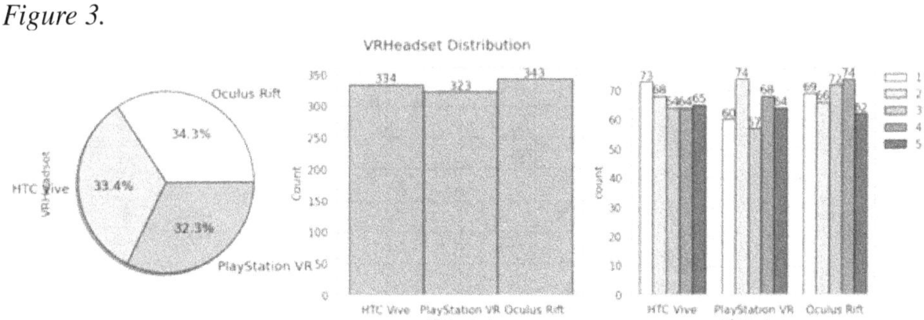

Motion Sickness

- **Higher** Motion Sickness gives **lower** immersion rates

Figure 4.

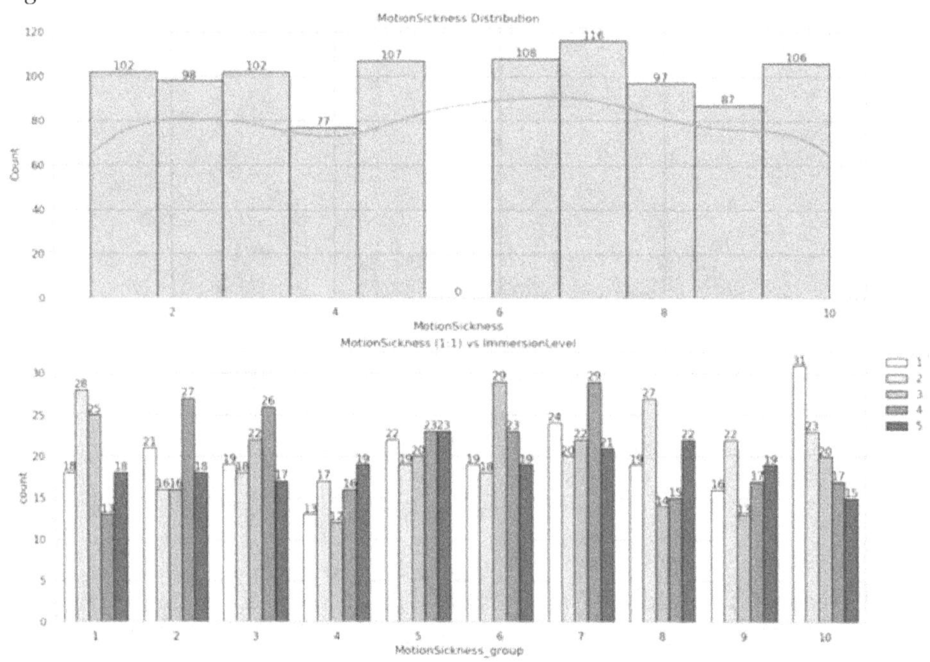

VR Headset vs Other Features

Figure 5.

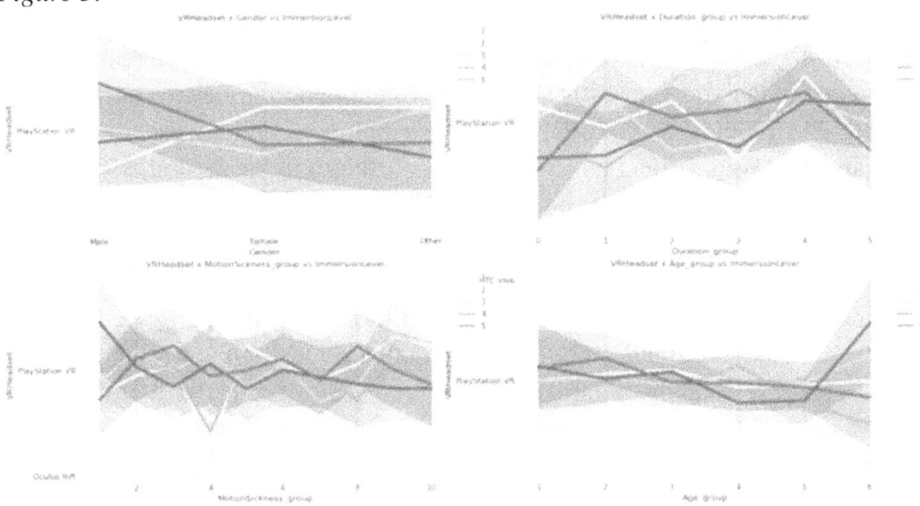

- Older Age with a longer duration will result in a higher level of immersion.
- Older age with Oculus Rift has a higher level of immersion.
- Higher levels of immersion were felt by males aged 30-36 years, female 32-35 years, and 34-40 years for others
- Lowest motion sickness but the best experience was felt by ages 34-44.
- Higher immersion level experienced by males using HTC Vive, and Oculus Rift for females and others.
- HTC Vive is best for users <30 years old, Playstation VR is best for users 30-50 years old, and Oculus Rift is best for users >50 years old.
- Oculus Rift provides the best experience for durations under 10 minutes and above 40 minutes. HTC Vive is better at 10-40 minutes duration.
- Lowest motion sickness but the best experience was felt by Oculus Rift users.
- The highest level of immersion was felt at durations of 23 - 31 minutes for males, 23-31 for females, and 26-33 for others.
- Lowest motion sickness but the best experience was felt at 31 minutes duration.
- HTC Vive users felt higher levels of immersion at durations of 25-32, 21-28 on Playstation VR and 25-34 on Oculus Rift.

8. CONCLUSION

In conclusion, navigating the Metaverse holds immense potential for shaping the future of a business in innovative and transformative ways. As immersive technologies, such as virtual reality (VR), augmented reality (AR), and mixed reality (MR) continue to evolve, businesses have unprecedented opportunities to redefine how they engage with customers, collaborate with employees, and innovate in a digital landscape. Metaverse offers businesses an opportunity to create immersive brand experiences, enhance customer engagement, and explore new revenue streams in virtual environments. By leveraging immersive technologies, companies can transcend physical limitations and connect with audiences at a deeper level, thereby fostering brand loyalty and differentiation. Furthermore, Metaverse enables new forms of collaboration and productivity in the workforce, empowering teams to work together seamlessly, regardless of geographical location. Virtual meetings, collaborative workspaces, and immersive training simulations can enhance creativity, efficiency, and flexibility at the workplace. However, navigating the metaverse also presents challenges and considerations, including technical complexities, ethical implications, and regulatory concerns. Businesses must prioritize data privacy, security, and inclusivity to build trust and ensure responsible participation in the virtual ecosystem. Metaverse represents a paradigm shift in how businesses operate, engage with stakeholders, and create value in an increasingly digital world. By embracing innovation, adaptation, and responsible practices, businesses can position themselves for success in shaping their future in Metaverse.

REFERENCES

Anderson, T., & Wilson, E. (•••). (2027). Navigating the Metaverse: Challenges and Opportunities for Small Businesses. *Small Business Economics*, *40*(2), 180–195.

Chen, H.. (2024). Virtual reality and augmented reality in marketing: A systematic literature review and future research agenda. *Journal of Interactive Marketing*, *55*, 88–103.

Chen, H.. (2025). Metaverse Marketing: Leveraging Immersive Technologies for Brand Engagement. *JMR, Journal of Marketing Research*, *30*(1), 45–62.

Constantia, C., & Christos, P. (2019). Action research: The key to inclusive education in Cyprus. *Journal of Pedagogy*, *10*(2), 37–64. DOI: 10.2478/jped-2019-0006

Johnson, S. (2023). Metaverse Economy: Opportunities and Challenges for Business. *Journal of Business Innovation*, *25*(2), 145–162.

Lee, J., & Hong, J. (2023). The impact of metaverse on consumer behavior and marketing strategies: A systematic review and meta-analysis. *Computers in Human Behavior*, *124*, 106982.

Lee, K., & Kim, J. (2026). Beyond Virtual Reality: Exploring the business potential of the metaverse. *Journal of Business Technology*, *12*(4), 320–335.

Li, X.. (2023). Metaverse marketing: Trends, challenges, and opportunities. *Journal of Marketing Management*, *39*(7-8), 703–732.

Nguyen, T. B., & Moltó, M. D. (2023). Digital and technological transformation in the metaverse: Implications for consumption and marketing. *Journal of Business Research*, *136*, 579–591.

Papademetriou, C., Anastasiadou, S., Konteos, G., & Papalexandris, S. (2022). COVID-19 pandemic: The impact of the social media technology on higher education. *Education Sciences*, *12*(4), 261. DOI: 10.3390/educsci12040261

Papademetriou, C., Anastasiadou, S., & Papalexandris, S. (2023). The effect of sustainable human resource management practices on customer satisfaction, service quality, and institutional performance in hotel businesses. *Sustainability (Basel)*, *15*(10), 8251. DOI: 10.3390/su15108251

Ragazou, K., Garefalakis, A., Papademetriou, C., & Passas, I. (2023, June). Well-being human resource model in the collaborative economy: the keystone of ESG strategy in the tourism sector. In ICTR 2023 6th International Conference on Tourism Research. Academic Conferences and publishing limited. DOI: 10.34190/ictr.6.1.1066

Smith, L., & Jones, R. (2024). Embracing the Metaverse: Strategies for Business Success. *The International Journal of Virtual Reality : a Multimedia Publication for Professionals*, *18*(3), 210–225.

Wang, Y.. (2022). Exploring the impact of metaverse on business dynamics and marketing strategies: A literature review and theoretical framework. *Journal of Business Venturing Insights*, *18*, e00260.

Zuckerberg, M. (2022). Building Metaverse: A New Frontier for Business. *Harvard Business Review*, *100*(4), 78–89.

Chapter 13
Tourism Informatics Management:
Bridging Data, Technology, and Experience

Mohammad Badruddoza Talukder
https://orcid.org/0009-0008-1662-9221
International University of Business Agriculture and Technology, Bangladesh

Dil Afrin Swarna
https://orcid.org/0009-0000-9176-920X
National University, Bangladesh

Mohammad Nurul Afchar
https://orcid.org/0009-0006-9736-7854
Daffodil International University, Bangladesh

ABSTRACT

The chapter explores how tourism informatics creates future-focused changes in the tourism and hospitality sector. Tourism informatics uses AI, big data analytics, IoT, and blockchain technology to drive intelligent choices, personalized tourism experiences, and sustainable procedures. Technology integration between these components produces operational improvements that produce innovative marketing approaches and improved customer engagement and service delivery capabilities. Tourism informatics requires attention to privacy protection, ethical norms, and maintaining secure data management systems, according to the chapter. Secondary research conducted through literature studies presents the possible obstacles and benefits that will emerge from implementing future projects while stressing the requirement for public sector partnerships with businesses and technology suppliers.

DOI: 10.4018/979-8-3373-1942-1.ch013

Tourism informatics adoption creates possibilities for an efficient and sustainable industry that strongly focuses on customers.

INTRODUCTION

For a very long time, tourism has been an essential component of the growth of the global economy, the exchange of cultures, and the enrichment of individuals. According to Milne et al. (2005), the sector has changed tremendously over many decades due to shifting customer tastes, widespread globalization, and technical improvements. The fast development of information technology in the 21st century has transformed how tourism is conducted, resulting in the establishment of the area of tourist informatics. Tourism informatics is the application of information systems, data analytics, and digital technologies to improve tourism services' management, marketing, and delivery. This chapter aims to investigate the future of tourist informatics management, with a particular emphasis on developing technologies, creative initiatives, and the potential of these to transform the tourism and hospitality sector (Chiwaridzo & Masengu, 2024). It is not a new phenomenon that technology is being incorporated into the tourist industry. Technology has constantly played a significant role in altering the business, beginning with the introduction of online booking systems in the 1990s and continuing through the emergence of social media and smartphone applications in the 2000s. The speed of technical innovation, on the other hand, has quickened in recent years, spurred by developments in areas like artificial intelligence (AI), big data, the Internet of Things (IoT), blockchain, and augmented reality (AR) (Yuriy et al., 2024). Personalized client experiences, environmentally responsible tourist practices, and decision-making that are driven by data are all being made possible by these technologies, which are not only improving operational efficiency but also offering new opportunities.

OBJECTIVES OF THE STUDY

The objective of the book is to investigate how new technologies like blockchain, augmented reality (AR), big data analytics, the Internet of Things (IoT), and artificial intelligence (AI) might improve tourist management techniques. It looks for cutting-edge upcoming initiatives that use these technologies to tackle important issues like operational effectiveness, sustainability, and customized consumer experiences. The report also emphasizes how crucial privacy, data security, and ethical issues are when implementing tourist informatics.

LITERATURE REVIEW

Introduction to Tourism Informatics

Much attention has been paid to tourist informatics in recent years. Tourism informatics is a multidisciplinary discipline focusing on tourism management and information technology interfaces. According to Rowland et al. (2025), it involves utilizing digital technologies, data analytics, and information systems to improve the effectiveness, sustainability, and overall customer experience of tourist services. When computer-based reservation systems and worldwide distribution networks were introduced in the latter half of the 20th century, they brought about a revolutionary change in how travel services were booked and handled ((Talukder & Kumar,2024) . This led to the emergence of the notion. Since then, the industry has been undergoing a period of fast transition, which has been pushed by the development of new technologies and the increasing digitization of the tourist sector (Jalili, 2024a). Researchers have focused their attention on information technology's role in enhancing operational efficiency, marketing, and consumer interaction in the tourist industry. This integration of technology has been the subject of much research. How vacationers plan, book, and experience their travels has been revolutionized by the proliferation of digital platforms and smartphone applications. In a similar vein, social media and online reviews have had a significant influence on the marketing of destinations and the behavior of consumers. According to Mohammed Khaldoon (2025), these recent advances highlight the significance of tourism informatics in addressing the dynamic and competitive character of the tourist sector.

The Role of Emerging Technologies

Artificial intelligence (AI), big data analytics, the Internet of Things (IoT), and blockchain are emerging technologies transforming the landscape of the tourist industry (Talukder, 2024). Personalized consumer experiences and predictive analytics have been made possible by artificial intelligence (AI), which has been a game-changer in particular. According to Gamage and Gnanapala (2024), chatbots and recommendation systems powered by artificial intelligence are increasingly improving customer service and decision-making in the tourist business. In addition, artificial intelligence is applied in demand forecasting and dynamic pricing, enabling firms to maximize revenue and resource allocation. A further essential component of tourist informatics is the analysis of large amounts of data. As a result of the development of digital devices and online platforms, enormous volumes of data are created daily. These data provide significant insights into consumers' behavior, market trends, and operations' success. Using big data can enhance the administration of destinations, marketing, and customer delight. However, to fully reap its benefits, it is necessary to solve the problems associated with data privacy and security. According to Aspevig (2014), the Internet of Things (IoT) is also actively contributing to the transformation of the tourist industry. Devices connected to the Internet of Things, such as smart sensors and wearable technologies, enable real-time monitoring and administration of tourist resources. Smart hotels, for instance, use the Internet of Things (IoT) to automate room functions and improve the overall experience for guests. In a similar vein, smart destinations use the Internet of Things (IoT) to monitor foot traffic, environmental conditions, and infrastructure utilization, enabling tourist management that is both safer and more environmentally friendly.

Blockchain Technology in Tourism

Implementing blockchain technology, renowned for its decentralized and safe nature, is becoming increasingly popular in the tourist business. It offers a visible and tamper-proof way of handling several types of transactions, including contracts and data sharing. Blockchain technology can potentially improve procedures in the tourist industry, including booking, payment, and identity verification, reducing fraud instances and increasing stakeholder confidence (Mohammad, 2024). As an illustration, systems built on blockchain technology can offer safe records of reservations and payments, guaranteeing transparency and accountability (Sukortprommee et al., 2025). Loyalty programs are one of the most important applications of blockchain technology in the tourist industry. Traditional loyalty programs frequently have fragmentation, which is characterized by the inability to redeem points or prizes simultaneously across many platforms. According to Leo Bentley (2024), blockchain technology makes it possible to create unified loyalty programs, which allow users to earn and redeem rewards seamlessly across numerous organizations. By doing so, not only is the consumer's happiness level increased, but it also encourages repeat business. Another use of blockchain technology that shows promise is in administrating travel papers and the authentication of identities. Blockchain technology can provide a safe and efficient mechanism for storing and exchanging travel-related information, such as passports, visas, and medical records. This may make the process of checking in at airports and hotels easier, which would, in turn, reduce wait times and improve the entire travel experience. In addition, blockchain technology can potentially improve the safety of personal information, therefore addressing concerns around privacy and data security breaches.

Augmented Reality (AR) and Virtual Reality (VR) in Tourism

Augmented reality (AR) and virtual reality (VR) transform travelers' engagement with particular locations and attractions. Virtual reality (VR) generates computer-generated and immersive worlds, whereas augmented reality (AR) superimposes digital information into the real world. The tourism experience is being improved via both technologies, beginning with pre-trip preparation and continuing through participation on-site. Augmented and virtual reality (AR and VR) can provide virtual tours of places during the pre-trip phase. This allows prospective tourists to investigate attractions, lodgings, and activities before reservation. This has the potential to assist passengers in making more informed judgments and boost their confidence in their choices (San Jose, 2024). By illustration, virtual reality (VR) may provide 360-degree views of hotel rooms, whilst augmented reality (AR) can provide interactive maps and location guides. Augmented reality (AR) can potentially improve the on-site experience during the journey by providing real-time information and interactive content. Using augmented reality (AR) technology, for instance, smartphone applications may give historical and cultural information about sites, making the visit more instructive and interesting. The same is true for creating interactive exhibitions at museums and galleries, which may bring relics and artworks to life via augmented reality. Virtual reality (VR), on the other hand, is being utilized to provide immersive experiences that transcend the physical confines of a location. According to Sharma-Brymer et al. (2025), virtual reality (VR) can transport travelers to otherwise inaccessible or distant sites, such as underwater caverns or ancient ruins. In addition, it may be utilized to recreate historical events or cultural performances, resulting in a more profound comprehension of the legacy of the designated location.

AI-Powered Predictive Analytics

Future initiatives intend to use artificial intelligence to improve the capabilities of predictive analytics, which is a significant tool for enterprises in the tourist industry. Using artificial intelligence for demand forecasting is one example of such a project. Artificial intelligence can forecast future travel patterns and assist businesses in preparing for an increase in demand by evaluating data from previous travels, social media, and web searches. As an illustration, hotels can modify their pricing strategies according to the anticipated occupancy rates, and airlines can optimize their flight itineraries to satisfy passengers' demand (Timan et al., 2021). The concept of individualized marketing is the topic of another initiative. An artificial intelligence system can evaluate client data to determine preferences and patterns of behavior, enabling firms to develop tailored marketing campaigns.

An example would be a travel agency sending tailored offers to consumers based on their previous visits or interests, increasing the possibility that they would make a reservation. Moreover, artificial intelligence may enhance customer service (Ignatenko et al., 2025a). As an illustration, chatbots that AI powers can handle routine requests, such as adjustments to bookings or frequently asked questions, which frees up human agents to concentrate on more complicated issues. The client experience is improved as a result of this, in addition to improved efficiency.

Sustainable Tourism Through Technology

Sustainability will be an essential priority in the future of tourism, and tourism informatics will provide creative solutions to support environmentally responsible behaviors at travel destinations. Using big data analytics for environmental monitoring will be one of the projects that will be done in the future. Destinations can monitor environmental indicators such as air quality, water levels, and trash creation by analyzing data from sensors, satellites, and social media (Mohammad, 2021). These data may be used to assist in identifying areas that require improvement and to promote the implementation of sustainable practices. When protecting marine habitats, for instance, a coastal location may utilize data to monitor the condition of coral reefs and take appropriate action. A further project is centered on the management of energy in tourism facilities using intelligent technology (D. Ramanjulu & D. Krishnamoorthy, 2025). Devices connected to the Internet of Things can monitor energy use in real-time, enabling hotels and resorts to maximize efficiency and minimize waste. As an illustration, smart lighting systems can modify the brightness of the space based on the number of people there, and smart thermostats can manage the temperature of the area effectively. These innovations cut the expenses of operations and lessen the carbon imprint that those in the tourist industry leave behind.

Additionally, blockchain technology has the potential to help sustainable tourism by establishing supply chains that are both transparent and traceable. For instance, blockchain technology may monitor the origin of locally produced goods and ensure they adhere to sustainability requirements. This enables passengers to make morally sound decisions and to show their support for firms that emphasize environmental stewardship.

Smart Transportation Solutions

One of the most critical aspects of the tourism experience is transportation and upcoming efforts in the field of tourism informatics aim to make transportation more intelligent and efficient. Using artificial intelligence for traffic control is one example of such a project. Artificial intelligence can improve road safety, optimize traffic flow, and minimize congestion by evaluating real-time data collected from sensors and cameras. Smart traffic signals, for instance, can modify their timing in response to the current traffic circumstances, reducing the time that visitors and residents alike have to wait (Ambusaidi et al., 2024). The employment of autonomous cars for tourism is the subject of another project. The usage of self-driving vehicles, buses, and shuttles can provide travelers with transportation alternatives that are both convenient and environmentally benign.

An example would be the operation of autonomous shuttles in tourist hotspots, providing trips between attractions on demand. As a result, private automobiles are less needed, which in turn cuts emissions and contributes to more sustainable tourism. Further, intelligent parking systems can potentially improve the overall quality of the travel experience (Talukder et al., 2024a). Using smartphone applications, Internet of Things sensors can monitor the availability of parking places in real-time and direct cars to open spots. This cuts down on the amount of time spent looking for parking and helps to lessen the congestion in already congested places.

Collaborative Platforms for Tourism

Travel and tourism informatics can help enable collaboration, which is vital for the future of the tourist industry. Digital platforms may be utilized to support this collaboration. One of the projects that will be undertaken in the future is the development of unified tourism platforms that will link tourists, local businesses, and communities. These platforms have the potential to provide a one-stop solution for booking lodgings, activities, and transportation, in addition to giving information on local culture and programs aimed at promoting sustainability. The platform might be used by a traveler, for instance, to make reservations for an environmentally friendly hotel, to schedule a guided tour with a local expert, and to rent bicycles to explore the region. Charya, 2024 A different initiative is centered on developing community-based tourism platforms. By enabling local communities to promote their culture, customs, and goods to tourists, these platforms allow local communities to empower themselves. For example, a platform might facilitate connections between visitors and local artisans by providing handcrafted workshops or gifts. This sustains the local community's economy and allows tourists to have genuine and significant experiences. Through the promotion of trust and the guarantee of transparency, blockchain technology can potentially improve these platforms. Blockchain technology, for instance, may be used to validate the genuineness of reviews and ratings, avoiding disseminating false feedback and guaranteeing that tourists are provided with correct information. On top of that, it may make payments and contracts more secure, lowering the likelihood of fraud occurring.

Enhanced Crisis Communication Systems

It is essential to have efficient communication during times of crisis, and future initiatives in the field of tourist informatics want to improve this via technology. For example, one of these projects includes creating real-time alarm systems for traveling people. According to Naparin et al. (2024), these systems can provide rapid warnings regarding catastrophes, such as natural disasters or health epidemics, using mobile applications or with short message service (SMS). If a traveler is in a coastal region, for instance, they may receive a tsunami warning, enabling them to take prompt action. Communication during times of crisis is the topic of another initiative that focuses on multilingual chatbots. Chatbots that are driven by artificial intelligence can give passengers real-time information and help in the language of their choice. Within a public health emergency, for instance, a chatbot may respond to inquiries concerning safety standards, testing facilities, or travel restrictions. According to Mohammad (2025a), this guarantees that all passengers, regardless of any language challenges they may encounter, have access to vital information. In addition, tourist authorities can benefit from using social media monitoring technologies to follow situations and respond to emergencies appropriately. These solutions can predict impending problems and offer passengers timely information by monitoring posts on social media platforms. If a well-known tourist destination is temporarily closed, the authorities can use social media to alert tourists and offer other activities they might participate in.

Cultural Preservation Through Technology

The application of tourism informatics can significantly aid the preservation and promotion of cultural assets. The utilization of digital archives to record and disseminate cultural objects, traditions, and narratives is one of the projects that will be undertaken in the future. For instance, virtual reality (VR) technology and three-dimensional scanning may be used to construct digital copies of historical places. This allows visitors to experience these sites digitally while conserving their actual locations. This is especially handy for heritage sites that are fragile or vulnerable and cannot tolerate a massive number of visitors. According to Robiansyah and Nuswantara (2025), another initiative centers on creating participatory cultural experiences. Using augmented and virtual reality to create immersive and informative experiences can help bring cultural heritage to life. Using augmented reality (AR), for instance, travelers who are visiting a historic temple may view how the temple appeared when it was at its peak, complete with virtual reconstructions of structures or treasures that have been lost. According to Poli ct al. (2024), virtual reality (VR) can reproduce historical events or traditional rites, providing a more in-depth knowledge of the cultural legacy of a region. Creating secure intellectual property records is another way that blockchain technology may help promote the preservation of cultural heritage. As an illustration, indigenous tribes may use blockchain technology to record and preserve their traditional art, cultural traditions, and knowledge. Consequently, this guarantees that they will be appropriately acknowledged and compensated for their cultural contributions.

Remote Tourism and Virtual Travel

The idea of traveling to isolated locations for tourism is becoming increasingly popular, particularly in the aftermath of the COVID-19 outbreak. The goal of upcoming initiatives in tourism informatics is to make travel accessible to individuals who cannot visit locations due to physical limitations. Creating virtual travel platforms is one example of these projects (Lehmann & Gundlapalli, 2015). To give users immersive experiences of locations, events, and activities, these platforms use virtual reality (VR) and 360-degree video. As an illustration, a tourist could visit the Great Barrier Reef in Australia or take a virtual tour of the Louvre Museum in Paris without leaving the comfort of their living room (Munir & Akhtar, 2025). The live-streaming of tourism experiences is the topic of another research study. Tourists can take part in real-time guided tours, cultural performances, or adventurous activities using platforms such as YouTube or specialist travel applications. For instance, participate in a live-streamed safari in Africa or a traditional dance performance in Bali. Both of these options are available to travelers. Not only does this make tourism more accessible to a broader range of people, but it also brings in cash for destinations and communities (Block Ngaybe et al., 2025). In addition, gamification can improve distant tourism by making it more participatory and enjoyable. An example of this might be a virtual travel platform with challenges or quizzes that push visitors to investigate various facets of a particular location. The encounter takes on a more enjoyable and educational quality due to this.

AI-Driven Tourism Innovation

In tourist informatics, artificial intelligence (AI) is a driving factor behind numerous developments that are still in the works. The use of artificial intelligence in dynamic pricing is one such effort. Artificial intelligence has the potential to assist organizations in optimally optimizing their pricing strategies in real-time by assessing data on demand, competition, and market trends. Hotels and airlines, for instance, can modify their rates according to occupancy or booking trends, allowing them to maximize income while simultaneously effectively providing customers with competitive costs. The consumer insights that AI drives are the topic of another project (Jalili, 2024b). Artificial intelligence can identify a traveler's tastes and tendencies by analyzing data gathered from social media, reviews, and booking sites. This enables companies to adjust their products and services and their marketing strategies to fit the expectations of their customers. According to Jokom et al. (2025), a hotel may employ artificial intelligence to determine that an increasing number of customers are interested in wellness tourism and then begin offering spa packages or yoga courses to cater to this demand. There is also the possibility of using AI to improve destination management. As an illustration, systems that AI drives can evaluate visitor data to forecast overcrowding and offer techniques to disperse guests in a more equitable manner. As a result, this helps preserve natural and cultural treasures while simultaneously enhancing visitors' experience.

Collaborative Innovation and Knowledge Sharing

Collaboration and exchanging information among many stakeholders are essential to the prospect of tourist informatics in the future. Establishing global innovation centers for tourism technology is one of the projects that will be carried out in the future. Researchers, entrepreneurs, and politicians would all be brought together in these centers to collaborate on developing and testing innovative technologies for the tourist sector. An example might be a hub that focuses on sustainable tourist solutions, such as technology that reduces waste or renewable energy systems (Mohammad, 2020b). Another project is centered on developing open-source platforms for tourist computer systems. To share tools, data, and best practices, these platforms would allow organizations, destinations, and developers to collaborate. One example would be a place that would share the code for its smart tourism app with other destinations, allowing those other destinations to modify the code for their purposes. In this way, innovation is encouraged while duplicated efforts are minimized. In addition, relationships between the academic world and the business world can propel tourist informatics ahead. To conduct research, build prototypes, and educate the next generation of tourism experts, universities and research institutes can collaborate with enterprises in the tourist industry to collaborate on these activities. According to Talukder et al. (2023), this guarantees the industry access to the most recent and cutting-edge information and capabilities. To summarise, the future landscape of tourist informatics will be replete with fascinating opportunities. These initiatives have the potential to revolutionize the tourist sector in a variety of ways, including the creation of smart destinations and individualized experiences, as well as the implementation of sustainable practices and immersive technology (Otundo Richard, 2024). Stakeholders can address present difficulties, open new possibilities, and build a future for tourism that is more connected, efficient, and sustainable if they use emerging technologies such as artificial intelligence, the Internet of Things, blockchain, augmented reality, and virtual reality. Collaborative efforts and creative thinking will be essential to realizing this goal, ensuring that the advantages of tourist informatics are available to everyone.

Sustainability and Tourism Informatics

tourist informatics has the potential to play a significant part in resolving the issue of sustainability, which is becoming an increasingly important concern in the tourist sector. By utilizing data and technology, tourist organizations can create more environmentally friendly practices and lessen their impact on the environment (Zhang, 2025). Big data analytics, for instance, may assist destinations in monitoring and managing visitor flows, lowering the likelihood of overtourism and limiting the strain on resource availability in the area. Devices connected to the Internet of Things have the potential to contribute to sustainability by providing real-time monitoring of environmental conditions, waste management, and energy usage. Smart hotels, for example, may use the Internet of Things (IoT) to optimize energy usage and eliminate waste. In contrast, smart destinations can use sensors to monitor air quality and water consumption (Talukder et al., 2024b). The implementation of these technologies not only enhances operating efficiency but also encourages responsible environmental management. Through increased transparency and accountability throughout the supply chain, blockchain technology has the potential to enhance sustainability further. With blockchain technology, for instance, monitoring the origin of resources and goods is possible, guaranteeing that they are following sustainability requirements. This has the potential to assist tourist organizations in making more ethical and ecologically friendly decisions, which is in line with the rising need for sustainable tourism initiatives.

Challenges in Tourism Informatics

The field of tourist informatics provides its unique set of obstacles despite its many advantages. Data privacy and security are among the most important concerns that have to be addressed. In the tourism industry, there is an increasing danger of data breaches and misuse due to enterprises' increased collection of personal information from tourists (Ignatenko et al., 2025b). Regarding their digital footprint, travelers are becoming more conscious that any information mismanagement can result in a loss of confidence. To address these issues, businesses must invest in robust cybersecurity measures and comply with legislation governing data protection. The digital divide between developed and developing regions is another difficulty that must be overcome. Some locations do not possess the resources or infrastructure to implement cutting-edge technologies. For instance, communities located in rural or isolated places might not have access to dependable internet connectivity, making it challenging to adopt smart tourism solutions (Mohammad, 2025c). Governments, private firms, and international organizations must work together to bridge this gap to guarantee that all locations can reap the benefits of tourist informatics. In addition, the quick speed of technology development may be pretty intimidating for enterprises. To stay current with the most recent tools and developments, it is necessary to engage in ongoing education and investment (Huang, 2024). It may be difficult for smaller organizations to embrace new technology owing to limited funds or experience in the applicable field. To overcome this obstacle, firms may benefit from training programs and relationships with technology suppliers to maintain their competitive edge.

Opportunities for Future Projects

Despite these obstacles, tourism informatics provides interesting potential for initiatives that will be undertaken in the future. Intelligent destinations are one of the areas of concentration. The Internet of Things (IoT), artificial intelligence (AI), and big data may help destinations become more efficient, sustainable, and visitor-friendly. A good example would be using smart city sensors to monitor traffic and alleviate congestion. On the other hand, smartphone applications designed specifically for tourism can supply passengers with information in real-time, such as weather updates and event schedules. The provision of individualized tourism experiences presents yet another option. Businesses can provide passengers individualized advice and services using artificial intelligence and data analytics (Sousa & Santos, 2025). A travel app, for instance, might make recommendations on activities and restaurants depending on the user's tastes, making the trip more pleasurable and memorable. This level of customization has the potential to result in increased levels of client satisfaction and loyalty (Mohammad, 2025b). Tourism informatics has the potential to impact several important areas, including sustainability. Using technology to encourage environmentally responsible behaviors is a potential topic for future studies. For instance, big data may assist destinations in managing tourist flows and reducing congestion, while Internet of Things sensors can monitor energy use and hotel trash management. Alcoriza and Edros (2025) state that blockchain technology has the potential to play a role in guaranteeing transparency in sustainable practices. One example of this would be tracking the procurement of local products.

FINDINGS AND DISCUSSION

Tourism informatics has seen a substantial revolution, transitioning from conventional data collecting to more sophisticated AI-driven analytics and ecosystems enabled by the internet. Based on the findings, incorporating big data analytics, machine learning, and real-time monitoring has improved destination management, tailored experiences, and operational efficiency. According to Judijanto et al. (2024), the growth of smart tourist destinations that are powered by intelligent infrastructure is indicative of a transition toward a tourism model that is data-driven and user-centric. Furthermore, blockchain technology is being investigated increasingly to ensure the safety of financial transactions, verify digital identities, and facilitate transparent customer evaluations, all of which contribute to the enhancement of trust and dependability in tourism services.

The increased dependence on artificial intelligence and automation to optimize many parts of tourist management is one of the most essential conclusions for this study. Chatbots, virtual assistants, and recommendation engines driven by artificial intelligence effectively increase consumer engagement by delivering quick and tailored replies. Streamlining hospitality services, lowering operating costs, and enhancing overall service quality are all outcomes achieved with automated check-ins, robotic concierges, and predictive analytics (Mrosak et al., 2025). In addition, artificial intelligence-driven sentiment analysis is being utilized to understand visitor behavior and preferences better. This allows tourism stakeholders to develop data-driven strategies for market positioning and service development opportunities. Tourism planning and management are changing due to the use of digital twin system technology. The findings imply that digital twins, virtual reproductions of tourism locations created in real-time, allow stakeholders to model visitor flows, identify congestion patterns, and improve resource allocation.

Furthermore, the identification of prospective tourism hotspots, risk assessment, and crisis management planning may be further supported by predictive modeling that is based on artificial intelligence and historical data, as stated by Ognjanović et al. in 2024. It is reasonable to anticipate that these technologies will be included in future projects to improve tourism destinations' resilience and sustainability. Artificial intelligence and data analytics are facilitating the shift from mass tourism to hyper-personalized experiences. According to Olakunle Saheed Soyege et al. (2025), tourists are more interested in having experiences suited to their specific needs. Informatics solutions make it possible to customize itineraries, accommodations preferences, and real-time advice about activities. Artificial intelligence algorithms can create tailored experiences that increase consumer happiness by studying user behavior, trends on social media, and past travel history. According to Mohammad (2020a), the use of augmented reality (AR) and virtual reality (VR) is a significant contributor to the development of immersive pre-travel experiences. These technologies allow travelers to sample places before deciding their trip plans. The findings of this study show that tourist informatics is on the verge of undergoing a disruptive transition that will drive breakthroughs in artificial intelligence, blockchain technology, the Internet of Things, and data analytics. Incorporating these technologies into future projects will improve several aspects of tourist management, including efficiency, customization, security, and sustainability. On the other hand, solving concerns with data privacy, cybersecurity, and fair access continues to be a focus. To ensure that tourist informatics acts as a catalyst for innovation and sustainable growth in the global tourism sector, future projects should primarily emphasize collaborative frameworks, ethical governance, and ongoing research.

RECOMMENDATIONS

1. The development of tourism informatics and the emergence of new trends: Tourism informatics has seen a substantial revolution, transitioning from conventional data collecting to more sophisticated AI-driven analytics and ecosystems enabled by the Internet. Based on the findings, big data analytics, machine learning, and real-time monitoring have resulted in improvements to destination management, enhanced tailored experiences, and higher operational efficiency. There has been a trend toward a tourist paradigm that is data-driven and user-centric, as seen by the advent of smart tourism destinations that are controlled by intelligent infrastructure. Furthermore, blockchain technology is being investigated increasingly to ensure the safety of financial transactions, verify digital identities, and facilitate transparent customer evaluations, all of which contribute to the enhancement of trust and dependability in tourism services.

2. The increased dependence on artificial intelligence and automation to optimize many parts of tourist management is one of the most essential conclusions for this study. Chatbots, virtual assistants, and recommendation engines driven by artificial intelligence effectively increase consumer engagement by delivering quick and tailored replies. Streamlining hospitality services, lowering operating expenses, and enhancing overall service quality are accomplished through automated check-ins, robotic concierges, and predictive analytics programs. In addition, artificial intelligence-driven sentiment analysis is being utilized to understand visitor behavior and preferences better. This allows tourism stakeholders to develop data-driven strategies for market positioning and service development opportunities.
3. Tourism planning and management are changing due to the use of digital twin system technology. The findings imply that digital twins, virtual reproductions of tourism locations created in real-time, allow stakeholders to model visitor flows, identify congestion patterns, and improve resource allocation. Artificial intelligence (AI) and historical data are used in predictive modeling, which further helps identify possible tourism hotspots, assess risk, and plan crisis management. It is reasonable to anticipate that these technologies will be included in future projects to improve tourism destinations' resilience and sustainability.
4. Travel experiences that are very personalized and individualized to the recipient: Using artificial intelligence and data analytics, the findings provide insight into the shift away from mass tourism and toward hyper-personalized experiences. Real-time customization of itineraries, preferences for accommodations, and activity recommendations are made possible by informatics solutions, which are becoming increasingly popular among tourists who are looking for individualized experiences. Artificial intelligence algorithms can create tailored experiences that increase consumer happiness by studying user behavior, trends on social media, and past travel history. Augmented reality (AR) and virtual reality (VR) further improve immersive pre-travel experiences. These technologies allow travelers to evaluate potential locations before making decisions based on accurate information.
5. Internet of Things Integration for Intelligent Destinations: The Internet of Things (IoT), which helps to link devices, infrastructure, and services inside smart tourist locations, will play a significant role in the future of tourism informatics. Intelligent transportation systems, sensor-based crowd control, and digital payment platforms are examples of solutions that are enabled by the Internet of Things (IoT) that are boosting accessibility, convenience, and safety. Real-time data from the Internet of Things devices, according to the findings, helps tourist authorities improve their decision-making processes, which in turn is beneficial for managing visitor capacity, monitoring environmental impacts,

and improving emergency response mechanisms. The expansion of Internet of Things-driven sustainability practices will be the primary focus of future initiatives. This will ensure that the expansion of tourism is in line with efforts to save the environment.

6. The Importance of Blockchain Technology in Ensuring Trust and Safe Transactions: The use of blockchain technology in tourist informatics is becoming increasingly significant, notably in areas like preventing fraud, administering identities, and providing secure financial transactions. The findings suggest that blockchain-based decentralized platforms give records of transactions that are both visible and unchangeable, hence increasing the level of trust between visitors and service providers among participants. In addition, smart contracts are automating reservations, cancellations, and refunds, which lowers the likelihood of conflicts and improves the general dependability of the business. Blockchain technology is expected to be investigated in the future for its possible applications in managing digital passports, facilitating seamless cross-border travel, and protecting sensitive traveler data.
7. How the Effects of 5G and Edge Computing Will Affect Tourism Experiences: The influence that 5G connection and edge computing have on real-time tourist informatics is yet another key discovery. The ultra-fast data processing capabilities of 5G networks enable smooth virtual tours, enhanced experiences in real-time, and speedier interactions with customers powered by artificial intelligence. Instead of depending on centralized cloud storage, edge computing processes data closer to the source, which improves reaction times and data security. Edge computing is also known as distributed computing. These technologies will be incorporated into future projects to increase the effectiveness of tourism operations, boost digital interactions, and make it easier to implement autonomous mobility solutions such as self-driving tourist shuttles.
8. Despite the progress made, the findings indicate that several obstacles exist in the widespread application of tourist informatics solutions. Data privacy worries, cybersecurity dangers, and opposition to digital change are among the most significant barriers. Ethical problems surrounding bias, transparency, and accountability are raised due to the growing dependence on decision-making being driven by artificial intelligence. The digital divide between established areas and developing regions is another obstacle that must be overcome to guarantee that all regions have equal access to cutting-edge tourist technologies. A well-rounded strategy encompassing comprehensive data governance frameworks, cybersecurity standards, and capacity-building programs for tourism stakeholders is required to address these concerns effectively.

9. Solutions for Sustainable and Environmentally Friendly Informatics Services: Future tourism informatics initiatives should significantly emphasize sustainability as a key area of attention. The findings indicate that artificial intelligence and big data analytics are being utilized to monitor carbon footprints, optimize energy usage, and encourage environmentally beneficial efforts in the tourist industry. Technologies such as artificial intelligence-powered carbon offsetting platforms, digital sustainability certificates, and intelligent waste management systems are developing as potential solutions for lessening tourism's negative impact on the environment. Within the context of green tourism regulations, incorporating informatics solutions will be absolutely necessary to accomplish long-term sustainability objectives.

Figure 1. Conceptual framework of tourism informatics management

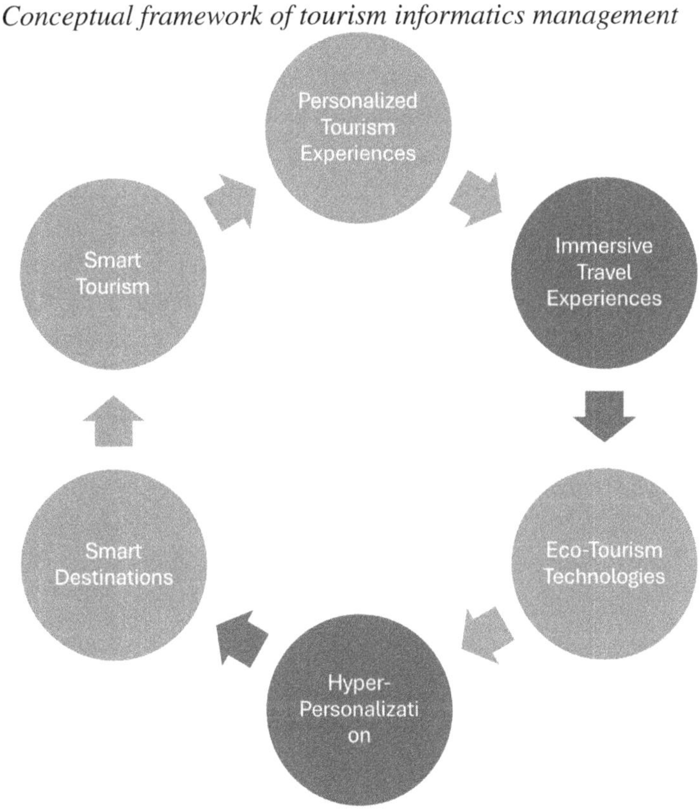

Source: Author Compilation

CONCLUSION

By providing data-driven solutions that improve efficiency, customization, and sustainability, tourism informatics is at the forefront of the movement to reshape the tourist sector on a worldwide scale. Their influence on the customer experience, security, and operational optimization will continue to expand as artificial intelligence, blockchain, the Internet of Things, and fifth-generation wireless networks become more integrated into tourist management. Real-time analytics, adaptable artificial intelligence platforms, and intelligent infrastructure should be prioritized in future projects to meet travelers' ever-changing demands.

However, it is necessary to implement rigorous governance frameworks and ethical principles for artificial intelligence to address concerns over data privacy, digital inequality, and cybersecurity dangers. Stakeholders must focus on strategic cooperation between governments, technology suppliers, and tourist operators to guarantee the smooth incorporation of developing technologies. In addition, it will be necessary to invest in programs that teach digital literacy and measures that protect against cyberattacks to establish resilience in tourist informatics.

AI-powered carbon monitoring, Internet of Things-based resource optimization, and blockchain-backed transparency are all examples of technologies that are helping to support environmentally friendly tourist practices. Sustainability will continue to be an essential element of future advances. Through the utilization of predictive analytics for crisis management and smart connectivity for immersive tourism experiences, the sector has the potential to construct a future that is both more sustainable and easily adaptable. A tourist informatics system that takes a well-rounded approach to innovation, ethics, and security will not only improve the operations of the global tourism industry but will also contribute to the development of a travel ecosystem that is more inclusive and sustainable.

REFERENCES

Acharya, K. (2024). *Tourism management system project report. Preprints.* DOI: 10.22541/au.173144144.44637261/v1

Al Tobaishat, M. K. A. R. (2025). The Local Community's Perception of the Cable Car Project and its Role in Tourism Development in Ajloun. *Journal of Information Systems Engineering & Management, 10*(19s), 172–180. DOI: 10.52783/jisem.v10i19s.2998

Alcoriza, G. B., & Edros, S. A. (2025). Organizational Management and Leadership Practices in Marketing Niche Tourism Destinations: The Adventure Tourism Experience in Legazpi City, Philippines. In Sousa, B. B., & Santos, V. R. (Eds.), *Intersections of Niche Tourism and Marketing* (pp. 425–452). IGI Global., DOI: 10.4018/979-8-3693-8417-6.ch019

Ambusaidi, A., Al-Dayri, H., & Al-Sumari, M. (2024). The effect of sustainable environmental tourism training on the development of eighth-grade Omani students' attitudes towards the environment and their inclination to engage in entrepreneurship in environmental tourism projects. *Cogent Education, 11*(1), 2400745. DOI: 10.1080/2331186X.2024.2400745

Aspevig, J. (2014). Project Management and Public Health Informatics. In Magnuson, J. A., & Fu, P. C. (Eds.), *Public Health Informatics and Information Systems* (pp. 211–231). Springer London., DOI: 10.1007/978-1-4471-4237-9_12

Bentley, L. (2024). *The role of technology in enhancing health and wellness tourism experiences.* DOI: 10.5281/ZENODO.11403443

Block Ngaybe, M. G., Azurdia Sierra, L., McNair, A., Gonzalez, M., Arora, M., Ernst, K., Noriega-Atala, E., & Iyengar, M. S. (2025). Resilience Informatics in Public Health: Qualitative Analysis of Conference Proceedings. *JMIR Formative Research, 9*, e63217. DOI: 10.2196/63217 PMID: 39819984

Chiwaridzo, O. T., & Masengu, R. (Eds.). (2024). *AI Technologies for Personalized and Sustainable Tourism.* IGI Global., DOI: 10.4018/979-8-3693-5678-4

Gamage, T. C., & Gnanapala, A. (2024). Tourism Experiences: An Interpretive Approach to Understanding Tourist-Brand Relationships in Technology-Mediated Tourism Service Environments. In Rather, R. A. (Ed.), *Consumer Brand Relationships in Tourism* (pp. 103–119). Springer Nature Switzerland., DOI: 10.1007/978-3-031-59535-6_6

Huang, K. (2024). Discrete Optimization Technology Helps Non-heritage Tourism Project Ecological Chain Construction Model Optimization. *Applied Mathematics and Nonlinear Sciences*, *9*(1), 20242529. DOI: 10.2478/amns-2024-2529

Ignatenko, Y., Ortmann, N., Lutz, S., & Kramer, F. (2025a). Comprehensive Course on Clinical Study Data Management for Medical Informatics Students. *Applied Clinical Informatics*, *16*(02), 245–251. DOI: 10.1055/a-2461-2956 PMID: 40073859

Ignatenko, Y., Ortmann, N., Lutz, S., & Kramer, F. (2025b). Comprehensive Course on Clinical Study Data Management for Medical Informatics Students. *Applied Clinical Informatics*, *16*(02), 245–251. DOI: 10.1055/a-2461-2956 PMID: 40073859

Jalili, H. (2024a). *Health Informatics Management and Leadership: Transforming Healthcare Through Technology The Essence of Health Informatics Management*. DOI: 10.13140/RG.2.2.24870.23361

Jokom, R., Semuel, H., & Wijaya, S. (2025). Sustainable tourism experiences: The role of digital technology and government support in creating tourists' memorable experiences. *Cogent Business & Management*, *12*(1), 2482026. DOI: 10.1080/23311975.2025.2482026

Judijanto, L., Suharto, B., & Amrullah, A. (2024). Analysis of IoT Technology Utilization and Inventory Management System on Operational Efficiency and Visitor Experience at Tourism Destinations in Bandung. *West Science Social and Humanities Studies*, *2*(12), 2047–2058. DOI: 10.58812/wsshs.v2i12.1493

Lehmann, C. U., & Gundlapalli, A. V. (2015). Improving Bridging from Informatics Practice to Theory. *Methods of Information in Medicine*, *54*(06), 540–545. DOI: 10.3414/ME15-01-0138 PMID: 26577504

Milne, S., Mason, D., Speidel, U., & West-Newman, T. (2005). TOURISM AND COMMUNITY INFORMATICS: THE CASE OF KIWITRAILS. *Tourism, Culture & Communication*, *5*(2), 127–137. DOI: 10.3727/109830405774791447

. Mohammad B.T. (2020a). An Appraisal of the Economic Outlook for the Tourism Industry, Specially Cox's Bazar in Bangladesh. *i-manager's Journal on Economics & Commerce,* 2(1), 23-35. DOI: 10.26634/jecom.2.1.17285

Mohammad, B. T. (2020b). The Future of Culinary Tourism: An Emerging Dimension for the Tourism Industry of Bangladesh. I-Manager's. *Journal of Management*, *15*(1), 27. DOI: 10.26634/jmgt.15.1.17181

Mohammad, B. T. (2021). An assessment of the roles of the social network in the development of the Tourism Industry in Bangladesh. *International Journal of Business, Law, and Education*, *2*(3), 85–93. DOI: 10.56442/ijble.v2i3.21

Mohammad, B. T. (2025a). Maximizing Impact: The Role of Influencer Marketing in Contemporary Tourism Management. In Özsungur, F. (Ed.), *Navigating Organizational Behavior in the Digital Age with AI* (pp. 277–304). IGI Global Scientific Publishing., DOI: 10.4018/979-8-3693-8442-8.ch011

Mohammad, B. T. (2025b). Revolutionizing Hospitality: Leveraging Mobile Apps and Cutting-Edge Room Technologies in the Hotel Industry. In B. Varghese & S. H. (Eds.), *Advancing Smart Tourism Through Analytics* (pp. 315-332). IGI Global Scientific Publishing. DOI: 10.4018/979-8-3693-3715-8.ch017

Mohammad, B. T. (2025c). Climate change adaptation strategies for a tourism destination: A study of Kuakata beach. *Acta Scientiarum Polonorum. Administratio Locorum*, *24*(1), 165–179. DOI: 10.31648/aspal.10073

Mohammad, B. T., Muhsina, K., Mou, T. A., & Kumar, S. (2024), "Community-based Tourism in Bangladesh: A Strategic Approach", Shaikh, E. and Singh, K. (Ed.) *Corporate Social Responsibility, Corporate Governance and Business Ethics in Tourism Management: A Business Strategy for Sustainable Organizational Performance*, Emerald Publishing Limited, Leeds, pp. 159-175. DOI: 10.1108/978-1-83608-704-520241012

. Mrosak, J., Jelinek, R., & Pandita, D. (2025). Elevating Clinical Informatics: Dynamic Resident Training to Enhance Subspecialty Appeal. *Applied Clinical Informatics, 16*(01), 077–083. DOI: 10.1055/a-2431-9669

Munir, A., & Akhtar, J. (2025). Bridging Tradition and Modernity: Islamic Ethical Guidelines for Sustainable Tourism in Pakistan. In Bayraktaroglu, E., & Çıvak, B. (Eds.), *Modern Social Challenges Impacting Tourism* (pp. 205–230). IGI Global., DOI: 10.4018/979-8-3693-8794-8.ch009

Naparin, M., Aryadi, M., Prihatiningrum, R. R. Y., & Suyatnob, S. (2024). Wetland Tourism Marketing: The Influence of Experience Dimensions and Memorable Tourism Experience on Tourist Loyalty of the Bakut Island Nature Tourism Park, Indonesia. *International Review of Management and Marketing*, *14*(6), 1–8. DOI: 10.32479/irmm.17115

Ognjanović, I., Zoulias, E., & Mantas, J. (2024). Progress Achieved, Landmarks, and Future Concerns in Biomedical and Health Informatics. *Health Care*, *12*(20), 2041. DOI: 10.3390/healthcare12202041 PMID: 39451456

Otundo Richard, M. (2024). Nexus Between Strategic Sustainable Tourism Investment Projects and Sustainable Growth and Development of Kenya's Coast Region. SSRN *Electronic Journal*. DOI: 10.2139/ssrn.4964247

Poli, M., Malagas, K., & Papakostas, C. (2024). The Contribution of Advanced Technologies to the Tourism Experience of Disabled People: The Greek Case. In P. Mylonas, D. Kardaras, & J. Caro (Eds.), *Novel and Intelligent Digital Systems:Proceedings of the 4th International Conference (NiDS 2024)* (Vol. 1170, pp. 429–442). Springer Nature Switzerland. DOI: 10.1007/978-3-031-73344-4_36

. D. Ramanjulu & D. Krishnamoorthy. (2025). Transforming andhra pradesh into a global tourism hub: a study of tourism policies including the new tourism policy 2024-29. *EPRA International Journal of Economic and Business Review*, 41–46. DOI: 10.36713/epra20207

Robiansyah, A., & Nuswantara, D. A. (2025). Tourism Experience Architecture to Achieve the SDGs: A Study at Cangkuang Temple Tourism Area. *Journal of Lifestyle and SDGs Review*, *5*(3), e05880. DOI: 10.47172/2965-730X.SDGsReview.v5.n03.pe05880

. Rowland, B., You, J., Stern, S., Bundy, R., Moses, A., Witek, L., Obermiller, C., Rosenthal, G., & Dharod, A. (2025). A Longitudinal Graduate Medical Education Curriculum in Clinical Informatics: Function, Structure, and Evaluation. *Applied Clinical Informatics, 16*(01), 084–089. DOI: 10.1055/a-2432-0054

San Jose, D. (2024). Readiness of LGU Key Personnel on the Implementation of Tourism Projects Under the Mandanas-Garcia Supreme Court Ruling in the Philippines. *International Journal of Research and Innovation in Social Science, VIII*(XIV), 203–213. DOI: 10.47772/IJRISS.2024.814MG0019

Sharma-Brymer, V., Brymer, E., & Mitra, S. (2025). Adventure tourism and tourist experience. In G. Pomfret, A. Doran, & C. Cater, *Routledge International Handbook of Adventure Tourism* (1st ed., pp. 153–169). Routledge. DOI: 10.4324/9781003393153-12

Sousa, B. B., & Santos, V. R. (Eds.). (2025). *Intersections of Niche Tourism and Marketing*. IGI Global., DOI: 10.4018/979-8-3693-8417-6

Soyege, O. S., Nwokedi, C. N., Tomoh, B. O., Mustapha, A. Y., Mbata, A. O., Balogun, O. D., Forkuo, A. Y., & Iguma, D. R. (2025). Health informatics in developing countries: Challenges and opportunities. *International Journal of Applied Research in Social Sciences*, *7*(3), 186–202. DOI: 10.51594/ijarss.v7i3.1847

Sukortprommee, S., Thanuttamanon, B., Singhdong, P., & Peamchai, P. (2025). The Role of Government and Community Support in Promoting Tourism Experiences Through the Application of Technology in the Tourism Business for The Elderly. *Journal of Lifestyle and SDGs Review*, *5*(3), e04777. DOI: 10.47172/2965-730X.SDGsReview.v5.n03.pe04777

Talukder, M., Kumar, S., Misra, L., & Kabir, F. (2024a). Determining the role of eco-tourism service quality, tourist satisfaction,and destination loyalty: A case study of Kuakata Beach. *Acta Scientiarum Polonorum. Administratio Locorum, 23*(1), 133–151. DOI: 10.31648/aspal.9275

Talukder, M. B. (2024). Implementing AI and Virtual Experiences in Hospitality. In Manohar, S., Mittal, A., Raju, S., & Nair, A. J. (Eds.), *Advances in Hospitality, Tourism, and the Services Industry* (pp. 145–160). IGI Global., DOI: 10.4018/979-8-3693-2019-8.ch009

. Talukder, M.B., & Kumar, S. (2024). Revisiting intention in food service outlet of five-star hotels:A quantitative approach based on food service quality. Sport i Turystyka. Środkowoeuropejskie Czasopismo Naukowe, 7(1), 137–156. https://doi .org/ DOI: 10.16926/sit.2024.01.08

Talukder, M. B., Kumar, S., Sood, K., & Grima, S. (2023). Information Technology, Food Service Quality and Restaurant Revisit Intention. *International Journal of Sustainable Development and Planning, 18*(1), 295–303. DOI: 10.18280/ijsdp.180131

Talukder, M. B., Lina, F. Y., Kumar, S., & Khan, M. R. (2024b). Data-Driven Personalization in the Sharing Economy. In Ordóñez De Pablos, P. (Ed.), (pp. 277–300). Advances in Finance, Accounting, and Economics. IGI Global., DOI: 10.4018/979-8-3693-5673-9.ch012

Timan, H., Kama, N., Yusoff, R. C. M., & Ali, M. (2021). The Application of Medical and Health Informatics Among the Malaysian Medical Tourism Hospital: A Preliminary Study. In Bhatia, S. K., Tiwari, S., Ruidan, S., Trivedi, M. C., & Mishra, K. K. (Eds.), *Advances in Computer, Communication and Computational Sciences* (Vol. 1158, pp. 743–754). Springer Singapore., DOI: 10.1007/978-981-15-4409-5_66

Zhang, L. (2025). Immersive Interaction Design in Tourism and Leisure Experience Using Virtual Reality Technology. In Jesus, I. S., & Wang, K. (Eds.), *Advances in Transdisciplinary Engineering*. IOS Press., DOI: 10.3233/ATDE241376

Chapter 14
International Trade and Business Intelligence:
A Systematic Literature Review and Research Agenda

Georgios A. Deirmentzoglou
https://orcid.org/0000-0003-1687-0708
Neapolis University, Pafos, Cyprus

Eleni E. Anastasopoulou
https://orcid.org/0000-0002-0918-8527
Neapolis University, Pafos, Cyprus

George Sklias
Royal Holloway University of London, UK

ABSTRACT

This chapter underscores the transformative role of business intelligence (BI) in shaping international trade. Through a systematic literature review, 24 documents were identified revealing ten key thematic clusters which illustrate how AI, big data, supply chain analytics, and blockchain are redefining global trade operations, decision-making processes, and competitive strategies. The findings reveal the potential of business intelligence to change international trade and stress the need for continuous innovation, regulatory adaptation, and strategic implementation of digital technologies. Addressing these research gaps is imperative for scholars and practitioners to contribute to the development of more resilient, efficient, and competitive global trade ecosystems. This, in turn, will foster stronger international economic relations and ensure the integration of new technologies into the future of global trade.

DOI: 10.4018/979-8-3373-1942-1.ch014

1. INTRODUCTION

In an era of increasing interconnectedness within the global economy, international trade has emerged as a pivotal element fueling economic growth, development, and innovation (Abendin and Duan, 2021; Vijayasri, 2013; Singh, 2010). The rapid rise of globalization, in conjunction with advancements in Information and Communication Technologies (ICT), has fundamentally reshaped the manner in which businesses operate, compete, and collaborate across borders (Hanna, 2010). The integration of global supply chains has increased, and the digital transformation has introduced new avenues for market access and operational efficiencies. Concurrently, the intricacies of contemporary international trade have escalated, giving rise to challenges such as supply chain disruptions, market volatility, regulatory challenges, and fraud risks. To maintain competitiveness in this ever-evolving landscape, businesses must adopt sophisticated tools and strategies that enable effective navigation of these complexities (Jaloliddin, 2023; Stefanovic & Stefanovic, 2009).

In this context, Business Intelligence (BI) has emerged as a critical enabler of data-driven decision-making. BI provides companies with the tools necessary to analyze vast amounts of data, identify emerging trends, optimize operations in real time, and gain a competitive edge (Chen & Wang, 2010). In the context of international trade, BI plays a pivotal role in enhancing supply chain visibility, improving export competitiveness, and mitigating risks associated with fraud, market uncertainty, and compliance challenges (Li & Lakzi, 2022). The integration of advanced technologies, such as big data analytics and machine learning, has enabled businesses to forecast demand, identify new market opportunities, and optimize logistics with remarkable precision (Tsilingeridis et al., 2023). Innovations such as blockchain technology are transforming supply chain management by ensuring transparency, traceability, and security in global trade networks, thus building trust among stakeholders and improving operational integrity (Abd et al., 2024).

Despite the growing importance of BI in international trade, there remains a gap in the literature regarding the comprehensive examination of how BI tools and technologies are specifically applied to the various facets of global trade. While there have been studies that have explored individual technologies, such as blockchain or big data analytics, there is a paucity of research that systematically investigates the broader scope of BI applications across different trade sectors. Moreover, extant research frequently exhibits an absence of an integrated approach, failing to consider the interactions between BI, supply chain management, risk mitigation, and regulatory compliance. Consequently, a systematic literature review is imperative to synthesize current findings, identify emerging trends, and provide a more nuanced understanding of how BI can enhance international trade.

The primary objective of this chapter is to explore the intersection of international trade and Business Intelligence. The chapter will focus on the technologies, trends, and applications that are reshaping the future of global trade. Specifically, the chapter aims to examine the role of BI in international trade.

This chapter is structured as follows: Section 2 provides a theoretical background on business intelligence and international trade, outlining key concepts, opportunities, and challenges in both fields. Section 3 details the methodology used in the systematic literature review, including the selection criteria and the process of identifying relevant studies. Section 4 presents the findings of the review, which are organized into 10 thematic clusters, covering topics such as blockchain and supply chain management, forecasting and predictive analytics, and fraud detection and security. Section 5 offers a discussion of the findings, synthesizing key insights and identifying areas for further research. Section 6 proposes a research agenda to guide future investigations in this area, while Section 7 concludes the chapter by summarizing the main contributions and presenting the key implications of the research.

2. THEORETICAL BACKGROUND

2.1 Business Intelligence: Concepts and Evolution

Business intelligence (BI) is defined as the technologies, applications, and practices that are utilized for the purpose of collecting, integrating, analyzing, and presenting business information to support strategic and operational decision-making (Turban et al., 2011). It facilitates the transformation of substantial volumes of both structured and unstructured data into meaningful insights, thereby driving efficiency, innovation, and competitive advantage within organizational contexts. According to Chaudhuri et al. (2011), "BI software is a collection of enterprise decision support technologies designed to help knowledge workers such as executives, managers, and analysts make better, faster decisions." This definition underscores the role of BI in facilitating data-driven decision-making by leveraging advanced computational methods and analytical models.

BI is a term that encompasses a wide range of tools and techniques, including data warehousing, online analytical processing (OLAP), data mining, dashboarding, and visualization. Collectively, these tools enable businesses to extract, process, and interpret large volumes of data efficiently (Chen and Wang, 2010). These tools empower organizations to identify patterns, detect anomalies, and generate predictive insights, thereby enhancing their ability to respond proactively to market dynamics. In recent decades, BI has undergone substantial evolution, transitioning from conventional reporting and query-based systems to advanced analytics platforms that integrate artificial intelligence (AI), machine learning (ML), and big data technologies to provide real-time and forward-looking business insights (Soni et al., 2020). This transformation has enabled businesses to shift from reactive decision-making, where strategies are formulated based on historical data, to proactive and prescriptive decision-making, where BI systems provide recommendations for optimizing future actions.

The adoption of BI has been accelerated by several factors, including the exponential growth of digital data, advancements in computational processing power, cloud computing, and the increasing need for agility in competitive markets (Hanna, 2009). Given the sheer volume of data being generated and consumed at an unprecedented scale by businesses worldwide, the ability to effectively harness and analyze this data has become a fundamental necessity for organizations seeking to gain a competitive advantage in international trade. BI applications are of particular importance for industries operating across complex, multi-tiered supply chains, where real-time data analytics can significantly enhance logistics, demand forecasting, and inventory management.

In the context of international trade, BI serves as a strategic enabler, helping companies navigate the complexities of global commerce, optimize supply chain operations, and enhance export competitiveness (Li & Lakzi, 2022). Given the volatility of international markets, fluctuating trade regulations, and evolving consumer demands, BI tools provide businesses with real-time market intelligence to anticipate trends and adjust their strategies accordingly (Li & Lakzi, 2022). For instance, BI facilitates the monitoring and analysis of global trade patterns, the tracking of competitor activities, the assessment of the impact of geopolitical events on trade flows, and the identification of emerging opportunities for expansion (Stefanovic & Stefanovic, 2009). Furthermore, the integration of BI with other digital trade technologies, such as blockchain for trade finance or AI-driven sentiment analysis for market predictions, can enhance transparency, reduce risks, and facilitate data-driven decision-making, thereby driving sustainable growth.

Furthermore, BI applications have been shown to play a pivotal role in enhancing trade compliance and risk management. Multinational corporations frequently employ BI-driven analytics to ensure adherence to international trade regulations, detect fraudulent activities, and mitigate supply chain disruptions. Predictive analytics enabled by BI affords companies the ability to foresee potential risks, including tariff changes, economic downturns, or supply shortages. This capacity to anticipate challenges enables companies to devise contingency plans and maintain business continuity.

As global markets become increasingly data-driven, the role of BI in international trade will continue to expand. Future advancements in BI, particularly in the areas of AI-driven automation, real-time trade forecasting, and network-based economic modeling, are expected to further revolutionize global commercc. Investing in BI capabilities will allow businesses to enhance their operational efficiencies and strengthen their strategic positioning in the highly competitive landscape of international trade.

2.2. International Trade: Key Concepts and Challenges

International trade, defined as the exchange of goods, services, and capital across national borders, serves as a fundamental driver of economic growth and development (Vijayasri, 2013). The ongoing globalization of trade has led to the emergence of new avenues for businesses to expand their markets, access critical resources, and achieve economies of scale. However, this interconnected global economy has also given rise to a range of significant challenges, including the complexities of supply chains, market volatility, regulatory hurdles, and the escalating risk of fraud (Jaloliddin, 2023; Jones, 2023; Min et al., 2017).

One of the most formidable obstacles in international trade is the intricate nature of global supply chains. These supply chains involve a multitude of stakeholders, including suppliers, manufacturers, distributors, and customers, who frequently operate across different time zones and regulatory environments (Serdarasan, 2013). This complexity is further compounded by factors such as demand fluctuations, logistical inefficiencies, and disruptions stemming from geopolitical tensions. Furthermore, businesses must navigate a labyrinth of regulatory requirements and trade barriers that differ from country to country, often increasing the costs and diminishing the efficiency of trade operations.

In order to maintain competitiveness in this rapidly evolving landscape, businesses must adopt agile strategies that enable them to swiftly adapt to market shifts and seize emerging opportunities (Rashad & Nedelko, 2020). Furthermore, the proliferation of fraud and security threats, particularly in the domains of e-commerce and financial transactions, has emerged as a pressing concern (Jaloliddin, 2023). These perils underscore the imperative for sophisticated fraud detection systems and fortified security protocols to safeguard businesses and the integrity of trade operations.

International trade offers considerable opportunities for business expansion and economic growth; however, it also presents significant challenges that require a comprehensive and strategic approach. By comprehending and addressing the intricacies of global supply chains, regulatory requirements, and security risks, businesses can enhance their ability to thrive in an era of increasing interconnectedness. The ability to adapt to changing conditions, capitalize on emerging opportunities, and safeguard trade operations will be critical for success in the global marketplace.

3. METHODOLOGY

In order to investigate the role of Business Intelligence (BI) in international trade, a systematic literature review was conducted, following an academically rigorous review protocol (Gates, 2002). The review process was methodically structured into three primary phases: (1) planning the review, (2) conducting the review, and (3) reporting the findings (Brereton et al., 2007). Given that electronic databases are recognized as the primary sources of academic publications (Petticrew & Roberts, 2008), SCOPUS was selected as the primary database for this study. SCOPUS is recognized as the largest repository of abstracts (Marikyan, Papagiannidis, & Alamanos, 2019) and provides extensive coverage across various academic disciplines.

The search query utilized a combination of relevant terms: ("international trade" OR "global supply chain" AND "business intelligence"). The search was conducted within SCOPUS, requiring that the identified terms appear in the title, abstract, or keywords of the publications up to the end of 2024. Initially, 42 studies were retrieved. One of this studies was excluded as it was not in English, while one more was eliminated as it was a book. This refinement reduced the dataset to 40 studies.

In accordance with the methodology established by Xiao and Watson (2019), an independent review of the abstracts was conducted by all authors to ascertain the relevance of each study. Articles that did not primarily focus on international economic relations and energy security within the EU, or that analyzed only a specific EU member state, were excluded from further consideration. Subsequently, a thorough review of these articles was conducted by two authors to ensure alignment with the study's objectives. Studies that did not meet the inclusion criteria were removed at this stage. The abstract and full-text screening led to the exclusion of 16 additional studies, resulting in a final dataset of 24 articles for further analysis (Fig. 1).

Figure 1. Search protocol for the systematic literature review.

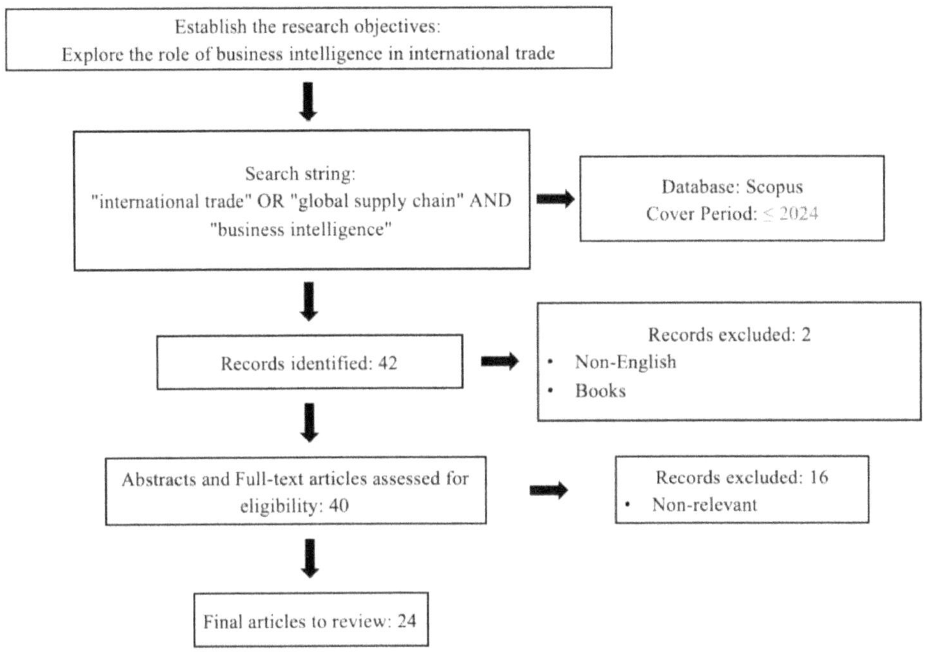

Source: Authors' creation

The distribution of publications over time indicated that the highest number of relevant studies was published in 2015 (Fig. 2).

Figure 2. Publication distribution per year.

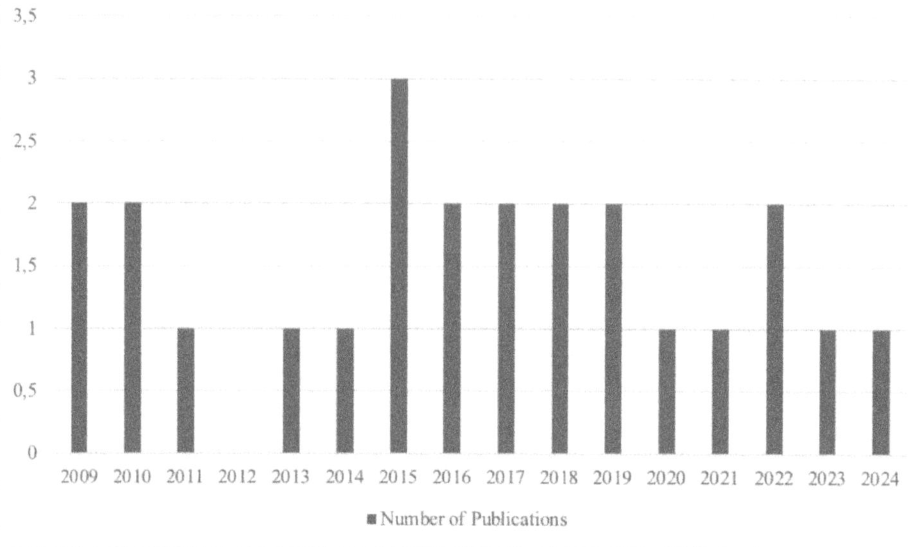

Source: Authors' creation.

4. ANALYSIS AND FINDINGS

A total of 24 documents were derived from the search protocol process. During the analysis process ten thematic clusters of documents were created based on their relevance of study. The thematic clusters revealed were: 1) traceability technologies and supply chain management, 2) forecasting and predictive analytics, 3) business intelligence and market expansion, 4) big data and international trade, 5) artificial intelligence and business transformation, 6) fraud detection and security, 7) competitive intelligence and market strategy, 8) supply chain analytics and optimization, 9) e-business and digital transformation and 10) complex networks and economic analysis (Table 1).

Table 1. Thematic clusters

Cluster
Traceability Technologies and Supply Chain Management **Abd et al. (2024); Meng & Qian (2018); Fernando & Abawajy (2009)**
Forecasting and Predictive Analytics Tsilingeridis et al. (2023); Rama Krishna et al. (2022); Ayyanathan & Kannammal (2015)
Business Intelligence and Market Expansion Li & Lakzi (2022); Chen & Chiu (2014); Chen & Wang (2010)
Big Data and International Trade Bai W. et al. (2021); Min H. et al. (2017); Min H. et al. (2019)
Artificial Intelligence and Business Transformation Soni N. et al. (2020); Wang & Chuang (2016); Yan G. et al. (2017)
Fraud Detection and Security Saia & Carta (2019); Li X. et al. (2016)
Competitive Intelligence and Market Strategy Achchab & Ahdil (2015); Ortega et al. (2015)
Supply Chain Analytics and Optimization Stefanovic & Stefanovic (2009); Roller & Engesser (2013)
E-Business and Digital Transformation Malhi et al. (2018); Hanna (2010)
Complex Networks and Economic Analysis Liu & Yang (2011)

Cluster 1: Traceability Technologies in Supply Chains

The integration of traceability technologies, such as blockchain and RFID, into supply chain management (SCM) has emerged as a transformative approach to addressing some of the most pressing challenges in global trade and logistics. As supply chains become increasingly intricate and globalized, conventional methods of managing financial transactions, data security, and operational transparency often prove inadequate. Blockchain, with its distributed ledger technology (DLT), offers a decentralized, secure, and transparent framework for recording transactions and ensuring data integrity. Concurrently, RFID (Radio Frequency Identification) technology facilitates real-time tracking and authentication of goods, thereby enhancing visibility and mitigating risks such as counterfeiting or theft. This cluster focuses on the application of these technologies in SCM, particularly in areas such as financial data handling, delivery performance optimization, and real-time supply chain monitoring. The papers in this cluster explore how blockchain and RFID can enhance supply chain efficiency, improve trust among stakeholders, and provide actionable insights for better decision-making.

In their 2024 study, Abd et al. explore the challenges associated with financial data management within supply chains and put forward a Blockchain-Assisted Secure Data Management Framework (BSDMF). The authors posit that the inherent characteristics of blockchain, namely traceability, transparency, and immutability, render it an optimal solution for the management of financial transactions within intricate supply chain networks. The proposed framework aims to address conventional issues, including funding gaps and inefficiencies, by introducing blockchain-based financial services, such as warehouse transaction financing and receivables finance funds. These scenarios illustrate how blockchain can transform traditional business models and establish a confidence-based ecosystem, enabling businesses to operate with enhanced security and efficiency (Abd et al., 2024).

In a similar vein, Meng and Qian (2018) investigate the capacity of blockchain to augment the predictive delivery performance within supply chains. The authors propose DelivChain, a blockchain framework designed to provide real-time delivery performance metrics with higher accuracy. The conventional methods employed to assess delivery performance frequently prove inadequate in addressing the dynamic and complex nature of global supply chains. DelivChain utilizes smart contracts and blockchain's decentralized architecture to automate and optimize supply chain processes, offering benefits such as improved efficiency, reduced operational costs, and enhanced transparency. The study underscores the interdisciplinary character of blockchain applications, integrating business logistics with advanced information technologies to generate novel solutions for SCM (Meng and Qian, 2018).

Finally, Fernando and Abawajy (2009) propose a RFID architecture framework specifically designed for global supply chain applications. The authors posit that while RFID technology possesses the potential to transform supply chains by enabling real-time tracking, improved inventory management, and enhanced operational efficiency, there are still significant hurdles to overcome before a fully RFID-enabled global supply chain can be realized. The authors develop a RFID architecture that is optimized for global supply chain applications while remaining fully compatible with existing RFID standards, such as the EPCglobal Architecture Framework (EPCGAF). The proposed framework offers several advantages over the EPCGAF, including better scalability, improved performance, enhanced reliability, and easier integration with existing systems (Fernando and Abawajy, 2009).

Cluster 2: Forecasting and Predictive Analytics

This cluster centers on the implementation of machine learning (ML), deep learning, and predictive analytics to address challenges in demand forecasting, market prediction, and business intelligence (BI). The papers in this cluster explore how advanced computational techniques, such as Long Short-Term Memory (LSTM) networks, Autoregressive Integrated Moving Average (ARIMA) models, and Support Vector Machines (SVM), can be leveraged to improve the accuracy of forecasting models and support decision-making in global markets. The studies emphasize the significance of integrating time-series data, macroeconomic indicators, and business intelligence tools to identify new target markets, optimize supply chain operations, and enhance competitiveness in international trade.

Tsilingeridis et al. (2023) introduce MULTIFOR, a multidisciplinary framework designed to synthesize and deliver profound knowledge about the macroeconomic environment and the attractiveness of new target markets. The framework integrates marketing fundamentals (PESTEL analysis), open data (time-series data from web databases), and deep learning methods (LSTM networks) to provide precise forecasts and recommendations for decision-makers. The efficacy of MULTIFOR is substantiated by a case study in the elevator and escalator (E&E) industry, which demonstrates that LSTM networks, when integrated with macroeconomic theory, attain enhanced forecasting accuracy (Tsilingeridis et al., 2023).

Krishna et al. (2022) concentrate on demand forecasting using machine learning for business intelligence. The authors propose a model that integrates on-demand and off-demand relationships across products to improve the accuracy of sales predictions. The model addresses the challenges posed by E-trading platforms, where a substantial number of related products necessitate sophisticated forecasting techniques. The proposed framework is designed to achieve efficient outcomes by leveraging time-series data and product segmentation, thus demonstrating a notable advancement over existing models (Krishna et al., 2022).

Finally, Ayyanathan and Kannammal (2015) present a cognitive Decision Support System (DSS) for the Indian green coffee supply chain, combining traditional extrapolative models, ARIMA, and Least Square Support Vector Machine (LS-SVM) for predictive analytics. The system's objective is to enhance market retention capability and quality metrics for Indian coffee in the international market. The authors utilize tracking signal spectrums to assess the accuracy of time-series data forecasts for importing countries. The cognitive DSS successfully predicts demand data volume and exporters' share price movements, providing stakeholders in the green coffee supply chain with valuable insights. The study underscores the promise of integrated forecasting models in enhancing business intelligence and facilitating decision-making in intricate supply chain contexts (Ayyanathan and Kannammal, 2015).

Cluster 3: Business Intelligence and Market Expansion

This cluster of papers explores the role of business intelligence (BI), IT-based systems, and hybrid decision-making models in enhancing export competitiveness and supporting global market expansion. The papers in this cluster underscore the potential of BI tools and advanced decision-making techniques to assist businesses in optimizing their strategies, mitigating risks, and enhancing efficiency in international markets.

Li and Lakzi's (2022) study examines the impact of IT-based systems, public policies, and business intelligence on the efficiency of export competitiveness. The authors posit that IT-based systems play a pivotal role in enhancing the precision and expediency of information dissemination, thereby empowering organizations to deliver products and services that meet or exceed customer expectations. Furthermore, the study underscores the pivotal role of public policies that bolster the business sector, including government interventions and infrastructure development. These policies, as evidenced by the study, foster a conducive environment for technological innovation and market expansion, thereby enhancing export competitiveness. The study further underscores the pivotal role of business intelligence in furnishing pertinent organizational information, market insights, and competitor analysis, empowering managers to make data-driven decisions and respond adeptly to environmental and competitive shifts. The findings demonstrate that the integration of IT-based systems, public policies, and business intelligence collectively enhance export competitiveness, thereby enabling organizations to achieve a stable position in international markets (Li and Lakzi, 2022).

Chen and Chiu's (2014) study focuses on enhancing business intelligence for supply chain operations through the effective classification of supplier management. The authors propose a Type-2 fuzzy logic (T2FL) framework for supplier management, which addresses the uncertainty and complexity inherent in supply chain operations. The study demonstrates that T2FL can better model the fuzziness present in supply chain data, enabling businesses to make more informed decisions in uncertain environments (Chen and Chiu, 2014).

In their 2010 publication, Chen and Wang put forth a hybrid fuzzy-Delphi-AHP (fuzzy decision-making) approach to develop a comprehensive framework for global business intelligence in information service firms. The authors posit that as firms expand into global markets, they encounter heightened risks and complexities, rendering the adoption of robust decision-making tools imperative. The proposed model integrates qualitative research and quantitative analysis to identify key business elements and performance indices that are critical for successful international market expansion. The practicality of the proposed model is demonstrated through a case study, which also shows its applicability in helping information service firms develop operative strategies for global markets. The authors also highlight the potential impact of emerging technologies, such as SaaS (Software as a Service) and cloud computing, on future business strategies, suggesting that further research is needed to explore these areas (Chen and Wang, 2010).

Cluster 4: Big Data and International Trade

This cluster of papers explores the transformative role of big data analytics in enhancing international trade, maritime security, and port operations. The papers in this cluster underscore how the integration of big data with business intelligence (BI) and advanced technologies can improve decision-making, optimize supply chain operations, and mitigate security risks in global trade. The importance of leveraging data-driven insights to address challenges such as security breaches, cargo inspection, and supply chain disruptions is also emphasized in these studies, while concurrently enhancing the competitiveness of small and medium-sized enterprises (SMEs) in international markets.

Bai et al. (2021) concentrate on the implementation of big data in international trade fairs and its effect on the decision-making and internationalization of SMEs. The authors posit that big data analytics has become a critical tool for understanding market trends, customer behavior, and competitive dynamics in global trade. By examining structured and unstructured data, including transaction flows, historical records, and social information, businesses can acquire valuable insights to enhance their competitiveness. The study underscores that, despite their limited resources, SMEs are progressively adopting big data technologies to contend with larger companies in the global market. The increasing accessibility of big data tools is expected to further facilitate the adoption of these technologies by businesses of all sizes for strategic decision-making and market expansion (Bai et al., 2021).

In their 2017 study, Min et al. put forth the notion that supply chain analytics can serve as a pivotal solution to bolster maritime security by capitalizing on the immense volume of data generated. The authors posit that seaports, as pivotal nodes in the global supply chain, are susceptible to illicit activities such as contraband smuggling, drug trafficking, and terrorist attacks. While X-ray scanning technology has enhanced the efficacy of cargo inspection, it is insufficient to address the broader security challenges faced by ports. The proposed supply chain analytics framework, as outlined by Min et al. (2017), employs a systematic approach to data aggregation, storage, and analysis, focusing on big data related to cargo movement, port infrastructure, and vessel traffic. This framework aims to empower port authorities to detect abnormalities and prevent security breaches.

Finally, Min et al. (2019) further expand the role of big data in port security by proposing an integrated terminal operating system (ITOS). The ITOS is designed to trace and monitor the movement and storage of cargo containers, while coordinating and synchronizing terminal operations. The ITOS is embedded within a business analytics framework, enabling port stakeholders to make informed decisions and mitigate security risks. The authors underscore the significance of effective information sharing, robust cybersecurity measures, and meticulous performance management in ensuring the successful implementation of ITOS (Min et al., 2019).

Cluster 5: Artificial Intelligence and Business Transformation

This cluster of papers explores the transformative role of Artificial Intelligence (AI) in reshaping business operations, enhancing customer experiences, and driving innovation across industries. The papers in this cluster underscore the deployment of AI technologies, including deep learning, natural language processing (NLP), and sentiment analysis, to enhance decision-making, optimize processes, and generate new opportunities in global markets. The studies in this cluster underscore the transformative potential of AI in revolutionizing various industries. However, they concurrently address the challenges that accompany its widespread adoption, including ethical concerns, bias, and talent shortages.

Soni et al. (2020) investigate the broad implications of AI on businesses, governments, and society, examining both the positive and negative impacts of AI deployment. The authors contend that AI is not merely a transient phenomenon but rather a transformative force with the potential to profoundly reshape the global economy. The study underscores pivotal domains of deep learning, such as computer vision, text analysis, speech recognition, and game playing, and deliberates on their applications in attaining human-level accuracy in diverse tasks. The study also explores the growth of AI start-ups, noting that investments in AI have been increasing exponentially, with significant opportunities emerging in sectors such as business intelligence, healthcare, cybersecurity, and marketing. However, the authors caution against the "AI divide," where the benefits of AI are concentrated in a few regions, potentially exacerbating social and economic inequalities. Addressing challenges such as trust, ethics, bias, and talent shortages is imperative to ensure the responsible and equitable deployment of AI technologies (Soni et al., 2020).

Wang and Chuang (2016) propose a business scorecard (BSC)-based framework integrated with machine learning techniques to address three critical issues in the solar industry: (1) identifying significant key performance indicators (KPIs) that influence outcomes, (2) guiding lagging companies to benchmark against leading companies, and (3) conducting what-if simulations to predict the impact of adjusting specific KPIs. The efficacy of the proposed approach is substantiated through empirical evidence derived from a comprehensive data set encompassing Taiwanese solar companies from 2010 to 2013. The findings of the study demonstrate the potential of the proposed framework to assist companies in identifying pivotal KPIs, enhancing performance, and facilitating data-driven decision-making. The authors propose that subsequent research endeavors should extend the dataset to encompass solar companies from additional regions, such as China, Canada, Japan, and Korea, with the objective of further substantiating the framework's generalizability (Wang & Chuang, 2016).

Finally, Yan et al. (2017) concentrate on the implementation of artificial intelligence in e-commerce, particularly through the development of a bilingual sentiment analysis model for understanding customer satisfaction. The authors address the challenges of handling multi-language user reviews, particularly in English and Chinese, and propose a systematic approach to text mining and sentiment analysis. The study demonstrates the effectiveness of the proposed model in analyzing user reviews and making customized product recommendations, which can enhance customer satisfaction and drive sales. (Yan et al., 2017).

Cluster 6: Fraud Detection and Security

This cluster centers on the implementation of sophisticated analytical methods, machine learning algorithms, and textual analysis to enhance the detection of fraudulent activities and fortify security measures within financial markets and e-commerce domains. The papers in this cluster explore innovative approaches to identifying and mitigating fraudulent activities, leveraging proactive strategies, transform-domain-based techniques, and commonsense knowledge-enabled textual analysis. The significance of integrating big data analytics and artificial intelligence (AI) to enhance the accuracy and efficiency of fraud detection systems is underscored by these studies, ensuring the security and sustainability of financial transactions and market operations.

In their 2019 study, Saia and Carta investigated the benefits of using proactive fraud detection strategies in e-commerce, particularly in the context of credit card fraud. The authors posit that conventional retroactive fraud detection systems, which depend on historical fraudulent transactions, frequently prove ineffective due to challenges such as data scarcity, data imbalance, and an inability to adapt to novel fraud patterns. To address these challenges, the authors propose two proactive strategies based on Fourier transform and Wavelet transform, which analyze financial transactions in a transformed domain without relying on previous fraudulent data. These strategies enable fraud detection systems to operate proactively, thereby circumventing the limitations of retroactive approaches. The study demonstrates that the proposed proactive strategies outperform traditional methods in detecting fraudulent transactions, even in the absence of prior fraud data. The authors underscore the potential of these strategies to enhance Big Data Information Security for Sustainability, thereby enabling safer and more secure e-commerce environments (Saia and Carta, 2019).

Li et al. (2016) concentrate on enhancing market surveillance systems (MSSs) by integrating textual analysis of unstructured market information, including news reports and social media. The authors contend that prevailing MSSs predominantly depend on statistical analysis of market activity data, overlooking the valuable insights that can be gleaned from textual information. To address this gap, the authors propose a commonsense knowledge-enabled textual analysis approach that models the semantic relationships between transactions and news articles. This approach enables a more comprehensive evaluation of the risk associated with suspicious transactions, leveraging both structured and unstructured data. The study demonstrates that the proposed approach significantly outperforms traditional methods, providing more accurate and actionable insights for market surveillance. The authors underscore the significance of integrating textual analysis and commonsense knowledge into MSSs to enhance market integrity and prevent fraudulent activities (Li et al., 2016).

Cluster 7: Competitive Intelligence and Market Strategy

This cluster of papers explores the role of competitive intelligence (CI) and technology monitoring systems in enhancing the competitiveness and innovation of businesses, particularly in the context of global markets. The papers in this cluster underscore how businesses can leverage strategic information, technology monitoring, and innovation management to identify opportunities, reduce uncertainty, and improve their market position. The importance of integrating business intelligence tools and public policies to support small and medium-sized enterprises (SMEs) in achieving sustainable growth and competitiveness in a hypercompetitive global environment is also emphasized in these studies.

For instance, Achchab and Ahdil (2015) present a cogent argument for the significance of competitive intelligence in aiding businesses in navigating the multifaceted challenges posed by globalization, market segmentation, and rapid innovation. The authors posit that in an environment characterized by escalating competition and ambiguity, businesses must adopt anticipatory listening strategies to detect weak signals in their socio-economic environment and identify creative opportunities. The authors further posit that by integrating strategic information and organizational knowledge, companies can enhance their technical innovation, strengthen their strategic position, and protect their intangible assets. The study underscores the pivotal role of business intelligence tools in engaging both internal (e.g., managers, employees) and external (e.g., competitors, suppliers, customers) stakeholders in the decision-making process. This collaborative approach enables businesses to develop effective strategies, allocate resources efficiently, and maintain competitiveness in a hypercompetitive market (Achchab & Ahdil, 2015).

Moreover, Ortega et al. (2015) concentrate on the development of a technology monitoring system to enhance the competitiveness and innovation of Colombian SMEs, referred to as MiPymes. The authors posit that traditional production processes must be modernized to align with global market demands, and SMEs require support from the state to enhance their competitiveness through innovation. The proposed technological monitoring system is designed to diagnose the current status of companies by measuring the technological gap between national and international standards. The system facilitates the creation, modification, and analysis of indicators pertinent to human resources, technology, innovation, and economic performance. By identifying potential sectors for modernization and innovation, the system assists SMEs in enhancing the quality of their products and services, elevating production efficiency, and fortifying their competitive edge. The study underscores the pivotal role of public policies in promoting the adoption of information technology and narrowing the technological gap between nations, drawing parallels between Colombia and Spain. The authors emphasize that without such interventions, SMEs in developing countries will struggle to compete in the global market (Ortega et al., 2015).

Cluster 8: Supply Chain Analytics and Optimization

The focal point of this cluster is the application of business intelligence (BI), fuzzy classification, and fuzzy pattern recognition to optimize supply chain operations and enhance global supply chain management. The papers in this cluster explore how advanced analytics and intelligent systems can improve decision-making, increase visibility, and optimize the synchronization of supply and demand in complex, distributed supply chains. These studies underscore the significance of integrating state-of-the-art technologies, such as service-oriented architecture (SOA), business activity monitoring (BAM), and fuzzy logic, to engineer supply chains that are more agile, responsive, and efficient.

Stefanovic and Stefanovic (2009) discuss the necessity of Supply Chain Business Intelligence (SCBI) in addressing the challenges of modern supply chains, which are often characterized by silos of information and disparate systems. The authors posit that Business Intelligence (BI) systems are imperative for facilitating collaborative supply chains, wherein businesses can exchange information with customers, suppliers, and partners to enhance decision-making and responsiveness. The study underscores the pivotal role of cutting-edge technologies in enhancing supply chain visibility and performance. By leveraging these technologies, businesses can establish next-generation BI networks that facilitate real-time information sharing and adaptive supply chains. The authors also discuss the importance of performance measurement systems based on process reference models to evaluate and optimize supply chain operations. The study concludes with an identification of key BI trends and advanced IT technologies that will shape the future of supply chain management (Stefanovic and Stefanovic, 2009).

In addition, Roller and Engesser (2013) concentrate on the implementation of fuzzy classification and fuzzy pattern recognition to address the challenges posed by distributed production and global supply chains. The authors posit that conventional methodologies employed for supply chain classification and demand forecasting frequently encounter challenges due to the intricacy and unpredictability characteristic of global supply networks. To address these challenges, the authors propose the use of fuzzy c-means (FCM) and Improved Fuzzy Clustering (IFC) for the classification of supply and demand patterns. Furthermore, they introduce Multi Feature Pattern Recognition and Fuzzy Inference System Type-2 (FIS 2), leveraging neural network methods to enhance the precision of demand forecasting and supply-demand synchronization. The proposed approach is implemented using the PROCAS (Process Optimization, Control, Analysis, and Simulation) system, which leverages a data warehouse for multidimensional fuzzy classification and BI functionalities. The study demonstrates that fuzzy classification and fuzzy pattern recognition can significantly improve the planning and operation of supply and demand in global supply chains (Roller and Engesser, 2013).

Cluster 9: E-Business and Digital Transformation

This cluster of papers explores the transformative impact of Information and Communication Technologies (ICT) and e-business on business processes, competitiveness, and innovation, particularly in the context of globalization and developing economies. The papers in this cluster underscore how the integration of digital technologies and e-business models is profoundly altering conventional business practices, thereby empowering organizations to enhance their competitiveness in international markets. The studies emphasize the importance of understanding the opportunities and challenges associated with digital transformation, as well as the role of public policies and socio-economic adjustments in facilitating this transition.

In their 2018 publication, Malhi et al. examine the advent of e-business in India, emphasizing its capacity to transform conventional business practices and expedite economic growth. The authors posit that e-business, defined as the utilization of electronic technology for business operations, confers numerous advantages, including cost savings, an expanded array of products, and enhanced time efficiency. However, despite its growing popularity, e-business is still in its nascent stages in India, and many organizations face challenges in transitioning from traditional methods to digital platforms. The present study undertakes a comprehensive examination of the prevailing state of e-business in India, meticulously identifying salient challenges such as infrastructure limitations, digital literacy, and regulatory barriers. The authors underscore that while e-business is becoming a necessity in the 21st century, it is crucial for businesses to understand its pros and cons before fully embracing digital transformation. The study's conclusion asserts that e-business has the potential to play a vital role in India's economic growth, but its success will depend on addressing the existing challenges and leveraging the opportunities offered by digital technologies (Malhi et al., 2018).

In her 2010 study, Hanna explores the broader implications of the ICT revolution for business competitiveness, private sector development, and innovation. The author posits that the ICT revolution signifies a techno-economic paradigm shift with profound ramifications for both developed and developing countries. The study underscores the potential of ICT, delineating its capacity to engender novel competitive strategies, intelligent enterprises, streamlined supply chains, and transformative shifts within sectors such as finance and media. However, the author also cautions that the benefits of ICT are not automatic and depend on complementary public policies and socio-political choices. The study underscores the necessity for prolonged adjustments to fully actualize the potential of ICT, particularly in developing countries where the digital divide and infrastructure gaps present significant challenges. The author concludes that integrating the ICT agenda into economic development strategies is essential for fostering innovation, competitiveness, and sustainable growth in the global economy (Hanna, 2010).

Cluster 10: Complex Networks and Economic Analysis

Lastly, this cluster focuses on the application of business intelligence (BI) and network analysis to the modeling and analysis of complex economic networks. The papers in this cluster explore how complex networks, which are characterized by multi-entity interactions, multi-level structures, and evolving dynamics, can be studied using data-driven approaches to support decision-making in economic systems. The studies emphasize the integration of BI tools, such as data warehousing, OLAP (Online Analytical Processing), and data mining, to provide insights into the structure and behavior of complex networks, particularly in the context of international trade.

Liu and Yang (2011) propose a revised BI framework that integrates network analysis to model and analyze complex economic networks. The authors posit that complex networks, encompassing biological networks, human society networks, and technological networks, serve as potent instruments for elucidating the structure and behavior of interconnected systems. The study underscores the significance of integrating complex network analysis with BI methodologies to establish a problem-solving environment for decision-makers. The study presents a case study based on international trade networks, demonstrating the applicability of the proposed BI framework for analyzing complex economic systems. The authors conclude that while their work is an initial step in exploring complex economic networks from a BI perspective, further research is needed to develop decision support systems (DSS) and BI systems specifically tailored for complex network analysis (Liu and Yang, 2011).

5. DISCUSSION

The findings from the systematic literature review emphasize the significant role of business intelligence (BI) and advanced digital technologies in shaping international trade. A comprehensive analysis of 24 documents resulted in the identification of ten clusters, which encapsulate the prevailing themes within this dynamic field. These clusters underscore the transformative impact of emerging technologies, such as artificial intelligence (AI), big data, and supply chain analytics, on global business operations and decision-making processes.

A recurrent motif across all the aforementioned clusters is the mounting reliance on data-driven decision-making. This phenomenon is particularly evident in the clusters dedicated to forecasting and predictive analytics, big data and international trade, and business intelligence and market expansion. These clusters illustrate how organizations employ data to enhance market intelligence, optimize supply chain operations, and improve competitiveness in global markets. This observation underscores the necessity for businesses and policymakers to persist in allocating resources to advanced analytics and computational models, thereby facilitating navigation of the intricate landscape of international trade.

A salient issue that emerged from the extant literature is the mounting concern regarding security, fraud detection, and trust in international transactions. The cluster on fraud detection and security underscores the necessity for proactive measures, such as AI-driven fraud detection systems and textual analysis techniques, to mitigate financial risks. Concurrently, the cluster on traceability technologies in supply chains demonstrates the adoption of blockchain and RFID to enhance transparency, security, and efficiency in global trade networks. These findings underscore the imperative for robust cybersecurity strategies to ensure the security of financial transactions and the seamless operation of markets in the digital age.

The cluster on AI and business transformation underscores the pivotal role of machine learning, natural language processing, and sentiment analysis in reshaping industries and driving innovation. Nevertheless, significant challenges persist, including biases in decision-making processes and disparities in the adoption of AI across geographical regions. Addressing these concerns necessitates a balanced approach that incorporates regulatory frameworks, ethical AI guidelines, and workforce reskilling initiatives to ensure equitable access to AI-driven business intelligence.

A review of the extant literature reveals a growing emphasis on the pivotal role of competitive intelligence and market strategy in ensuring business sustainability. A growing body of evidence indicates that firms are increasingly relying on technology monitoring systems and competitive intelligence tools to gain insights into market trends, customer behavior, and emerging risks. These tools are of particular importance for small and medium-sized enterprises (SMEs), which often face resource constraints in expanding their global footprint. It is imperative for policymakers and industry leaders to explore strategies that would facilitate access to competitive intelligence platforms and business intelligence (BI) tools for SMEs, with the aim of enhancing their global trade competitiveness.

The field of international trade continues to prioritize the subjects of supply chain optimization and analytics, as evidenced by the emergence of research clusters focusing on supply chain analytics and optimization, as well as e-business and digital transformation. Businesses are integrating business intelligence (BI), fuzzy logic, and service-oriented architectures (SOA) to achieve several objectives. These objectives include increasing visibility, enhancing demand forecasting, and improving decision-making. These developments indicate a shift in perspective toward supply chains that are more agile, responsive, and resilient, particularly in the aftermath of global disruptions such as pandemics and geopolitical tensions.

The final cluster, which focuses on complex networks and economic analysis, sheds light on the intricate interdependencies between international trade, digital transformation, and economic policies. These studies demonstrate how network-based approaches and economic modeling can offer valuable insights into trade dynamics, supply chain resilience, and market fluctuations. Future research endeavors should explore how policymakers can leverage these analytical frameworks to enhance trade policies and economic strategies.

6. RESEARCH AGENDA

In light of the insights derived from this review, there are several key areas that merit further research. First, advancements in AI for international business (Kourkoumelis et al., 2024) and especially trade forecasting present a significant research opportunity. As the global trade network becomes increasingly interconnected, artificial intelligence (AI)-driven models hold the potential to integrate macroeconomic indicators, real-time data, and predictive analytics, thereby enhancing the accuracy of trade and market analysis. The ability of AI to detect emerging trends, predict market volatility, and identify risks in global trade necessitates interdisciplinary approaches that integrate economic modeling with machine learning techniques. In the context of innovation growth (Agoraki et al., 2024a; Pistikou et al., 2023) and tense international economic relations (Deirmentzoglou et al., 2025; Deirmentzoglou et al., 2024a), the integration of AI in trade forecasting enables businesses to anticipate shifts in international economic relations and maintain a competitive advantage in global market demands.

Another imperative domain of research pertains to the role of blockchain in cultivating digital trust in global trade. While extant literature highlights blockchain's applications in traceability and security, further investigations should explore its potential beyond supply chains. The technology has the potential to enhance cross-border payments, reduce transaction costs, and facilitate the adoption of smart contracts in international trade agreements, which are vital components of evolving international economic relations. Addressing the regulatory and technical challenges associated with blockchain implementation is imperative for its broader adoption in trade processes. Additionally, researchers must explore the cultural and institutional barriers that may hinder the adoption of blockchain technologies across different national contexts, as national culture plays a pivotal role in shaping attitudes toward technology and digital transformation.

Ethical and regulatory considerations in the realm of AI-driven business intelligence warrant further exploration. As artificial intelligence continues to influence global trade practices, research should prioritize the development of ethical frameworks and regulatory guidelines to mitigate biases and ensure responsible adoption of artificial intelligence. Investigations should examine how different regions approach AI regulation, how AI models can be made more transparent and accountable, and what measures can be implemented to minimize algorithmic biases in trade-related decision-making. Given the varied approaches to AI and regulation across national cultures and legal frameworks, it is essential to examine the intersection of AI ethics with global trade norms, ensuring the fair and equitable application of AI across international markets.

Another critical research priority is the empowerment of SMEs through the implementation of business intelligence tools. SMEs frequently encounter substantial resource constraints, impeding their capacity to employ sophisticated BI technologies. Future studies should investigate how SMEs can integrate BI tools, access competitive intelligence platforms, and utilize real-time data for market expansion. Additionally, research should prioritize investigating how emerging technologies, such as artificial intelligence and the metaverse (e.g., Deirmentzoglou et al., 2024b), can offer scalable solutions for SMEs, thereby enabling them to compete in the global marketplace. The integration of BI tools, access to competitive intelligence platforms, and utilization of real-time data will be instrumental in enhancing the competitiveness of SMEs in the global marketplace.

Moreover, research endeavors should prioritize the examination of supply chain resilience and digital transformation, particularly in the context of recent global disruptions, including pandemics and geopolitical conflicts. These events have underscored the necessity for agile, resilient supply chains capable of adapting to sudden shocks. Digital transformation strategies, including artificial intelligence (AI), the Internet of Things (IoT), and predictive analytics, are imperative in enhancing supply chain resilience. A more in-depth exploration is warranted into the role of digital twins, automation, and decentralized logistics in strengthening supply chains to mitigate future risks. Additionally, national cultural influences on business decision-making processes (Agoraki et al., 2024b; Deirmentzoglou et al., 2024c) and, consequently, the pace of digital transformation across different regions underscore the necessity to study how cultural factors shape the adoption and implementation of these technologies.

Finally, network-based economic modeling for trade optimization offers a promising research direction. The intricate nature of international trade systems demands sophisticated analytical approaches that capitalize on network science, big data analytics, and economic modeling. Future studies should explore how complex network analysis can improve trade efficiency, optimize supply chain flows, and inform policy decisions. The integration of network-based methodologies with conventional economic models holds considerable potential for the development of enhanced trade forecasting instruments. These instruments can be designed to account for technological advancements and the dynamic character of global trade relations, thereby enhancing the accuracy and adaptability of trade forecasting.

The systematic review underscores the transformative potential of business intelligence in international trade, emphasizing the necessity for continuous innovation, regulatory adaptation, and strategic implementation of digital technologies. Addressing these research gaps is imperative for scholars and practitioners to contribute to the development of more resilient, efficient, and competitive global trade ecosystems. This, in turn, will foster stronger international economic relations and ensure the integration of new technologies, such as artificial intelligence and the metaverse, into the future of global trade.

7. CONCLUSION

This study underscores the transformative role of business intelligence (BI) and advanced digital technologies in shaping international trade. A systematic literature review was conducted, leading to the identification of ten key thematic clusters. These clusters illustrate how artificial intelligence (AI), big data, supply chain analytics, and blockchain are redefining global trade operations, decision-making processes, and competitive strategies. The mounting reliance on data-driven decision-making has empowered businesses to enhance supply chain optimization, improve market forecasting, and fortify risk management. Concurrently, the mounting emphasis on digital trust, fraud detection, and cybersecurity underscores the imperative for secure and transparent global trade transactions. These findings underscore the imperative for businesses to integrate advanced analytics with digital trust mechanisms, not merely as a competitive advantage, but as a fundamental necessity in navigating the intricate and interconnected landscape of the contemporary global market.

The findings of this study have far-reaching implications for various domains, including business strategy, policy development, and workforce preparedness. For business entities, the findings underscore the necessity of ongoing investment in business intelligence (BI) tools and artificial intelligence (AI)-driven analytics to enhance market intelligence, optimize supply chain efficiency, and fortify financial risk management. While large multinational corporations (MNCs) lead the adoption of these technologies, small and medium-sized enterprises (SMEs) frequently encounter challenges due to constrained resources and technical expertise. To address this disparity, industry stakeholders and policymakers must facilitate SME access to competitive intelligence platforms and digital transformation strategies. By fostering digital inclusion and providing tailored solutions for SMEs, global trade competitiveness can be more equitably distributed, ensuring that businesses of all sizes can leverage the benefits of data-driven decision-making.

This study underscores the mounting imperative for policymakers to devise regulatory frameworks that promote the ethical and responsible use of AI, enhance cybersecurity resilience, and encourage blockchain adoption to establish digital trust. As AI becomes increasingly integrated into trade forecasting, fraud detection, and market intelligence, concerns about algorithmic bias, data privacy, and transparency must be addressed through the establishment of clear guidelines and the adoption of ethical AI strategies. The proliferation of blockchain-based trade networks and smart contracts necessitates regulatory adaptations that facilitate cross-border digital transactions in accordance with international trade laws. Furthermore, policymakers must deliberate on the implications of taxation, trade agreements, and regulatory harmonization in maintaining pace with the rapid digital transformation of trade.

A significant finding of this study pertains to workforce preparedness and the cultivation of digital competencies. The integration of BI technologies necessitates a workforce that is well-versed in analytical, technological, and strategic competencies. To this end, there is a need for targeted educational initiatives, professional training programs, and industry-academia collaborations. The goal of these efforts should be to ensure that trade professionals, policymakers, and business leaders can effectively utilize BI tools. In this regard, academic institutions are charged with the responsibility of incorporating specialized courses focused on artificial intelligence-driven trade analytics, digital marketing intelligence, and blockchain applications into existing business and trade curricula. Moreover, the development of continuous learning programs is imperative to facilitate the ongoing development of professionals' skillsets, thereby ensuring their ability to effectively navigate the dynamic digital landscape of international trade.

Beyond its business and policy implications, this study also establishes the foundation for future research in several key areas. The research agenda delineated in this study posits that artificial intelligence (AI)-driven trade forecasting, blockchain-enabled cross-border transactions, supply chain resilience, and network-based economic modeling are subjects that merit further exploration. In light of the intricate and ever-evolving nature of international trade networks, a concerted, interdisciplinary effort among economists, data scientists, policymakers, and business leaders is imperative to nurture resilient, efficient, and sustainable global trade ecosystems. Furthermore, subsequent studies should examine the nexus of AI and sustainability, with a particular focus on the potential of digital trade technologies to curtail carbon emissions, enhance supply chain transparency, and promote environmentally responsible trade practices.

In conclusion, the findings of this research underscore the necessity of continuous innovation, regulatory adaptation, and strategic implementation of digital technologies in international trade. Addressing the research gaps identified in this study will enable scholars and practitioners to contribute to a more robust and dynamic global trade environment. As digital transformation accelerates, proactive efforts from businesses, policymakers, and educators will be critical in harnessing the potential of BI while mitigating associated risks. The future of international trade will be increasingly data-driven, and ensuring its sustainability, security, and inclusivity will require collaborative efforts across sectors and disciplines.

REFERENCES

Abd, S. K., Ali, M. H., Jaber, M. M., Abosinnee, A. S., Kareem, Z. H., Wahab, A. N. A., Hassan, R., & Jassim, M. M. (2024). Secured finance handling for supply chain integrated business intelligence using blockchain application scenarios. *Intelligent Data Analysis*, *28*(2), 553–571. DOI: 10.3233/IDA-227445

Abendin, S., & Duan, P. (2021). International trade and economic growth in Africa: The role of the digital economy. *Cogent Economics & Finance*, *9*(1), 1911767. DOI: 10.1080/23322039.2021.1911767

Achchab, B., & Ahdil, I. (2015, February). Competitive intelligence experiences in companies: Case studies on creative opportunities. In *2015 6th International Conference on Information Systems and Economic Intelligence (SIIE)* (pp. 158-164). IEEE.

Agoraki, K. K., Deirmentzoglou, G. A., Psychalis, M., & Apostolopoulos, S. (2024a). Types of innovation and sustainable development: Evidence from medium-and large-sized firms. *International Journal on Management of Innovation & Technology*, *21*(02), 2450013. DOI: 10.1142/S0219877024500135

Agoraki, K. K., Deirmentzoglou, G. A., & Triantopoulos, C. (2024b). Cultural Values as Catalysts of Technological Innovation for a Sustainable Future. *Sustainability (Basel)*, *16*(5), 2064. DOI: 10.3390/su16052064

Ayyanathan, N., & Kannammal, A. (2015, March). Combined forecasting and cognitive Decision Support System for Indian green coffee supply chain predictive analytics. In *2015 International Conference on Cognitive Computing and Information Processing (CCIP)* (pp. 1-6). IEEE. DOI: 10.1109/CCIP.2015.7100735

Bai, W., Wang, C., & Bai, X. (2021). International Trade Fairs Based on Big Data. In *Application of Intelligent Systems in Multi-modal Information Analytics:2021 International Conference on Multi-modal Information Analytics (MMIA 2021)*, Volume 1 (pp. 723-729). Springer International Publishing. DOI: 10.1007/978-3-030-74811-1_104

Brereton, P., Kitchenham, B. A., Budgen, D., Turner, M., & Khalil, M. (2007). Lessons from applying the systematic literature review process within the software engineering domain. *Journal of Systems and Software*, *80*(4), 571–583. DOI: 10.1016/j.jss.2006.07.009

Chaudhuri, S., Dayal, U., & Narasayya, V. (2011). An overview of business intelligence technology. *Communications of the ACM*, *54*(8), 88–98. DOI: 10.1145/1978542.1978562

Chen, M. K., & Wang, S. C. (2010). The use of a hybrid fuzzy-Delphi-AHP approach to develop global business intelligence for information service firms. *Expert Systems with Applications*, *37*(11), 7394–7407. DOI: 10.1016/j.eswa.2010.04.033

Chen, Y. M., & Chiu, Y.-P. (2014). Enhancing business intelligence for supply chain operations through effective classification of supplier management. *Uncertain Supply Chain Management*, *2*(2), 229–236. DOI: 10.5267/j.uscm.2014.7.006

Deirmentzoglou, G. A., Agoraki, K. K., & Patsoulis, P. (2024c). The nexus between cultural values and perceptions of corporate sustainable development. *Social Responsibility Journal*, *20*(2), 224–242. DOI: 10.1108/SRJ-09-2022-0373

Deirmentzoglou, G. A., Anastasopoulou, E. E., & Sklias, P. (2024a). International economic relations and energy security in the European Union: A systematic literature review. *International Journal of Sustainable Energy*, *43*(1), 2385682. DOI: 10.1080/14786451.2024.2385682

Deirmentzoglou, G. A., Anastasopoulou, E. E., & Vlassi, E. "International Economic Relations and Sustainable Tourism: The Case of Greece." In *International Conference on Tourism Research*. Academic Conferences International Limited, 2025. DOI: 10.34190/ictr.8.1.3472

Deirmentzoglou, G. A., Vlassi, E., & Anastasopoulou, E. E. (2024b). DDMMO Website Quality, Destination Image and Intention to Use Metaverse Platforms. *Platforms*, *2*(4), 180–192. DOI: 10.3390/platforms2040012

Fernando, H., & Abawajy, J. (2009, December). A RFID architecture framework for global supply chain applications. In *Proceedings of the 11th International Conference on Information Integration and Web-based Applications & Services* (pp. 313-320). DOI: 10.1145/1806338.1806396

Gates, S. (2002). Review of methodology of quantitative reviews using meta-analysis in ecology. *Journal of Animal Ecology*, *71*(4), 547–557. DOI: 10.1046/j.1365-2656.2002.00634.x

Hanna, N. K. (2009). Implications of the ICT Revolution. In *Transforming Government and Building the Information Society: Challenges and Opportunities for the Developing World* (pp. 27–65). Springer New York.

Jaloliddin, R. (2023). Digitalization in global trade: opportunities and challenges for investment. *Global Trade and Customs Journal, 18*(10).

Jones, S. (2023). Supply chain risk management in the era of globalization. *European Journal of Supply Chain Management*, *1*(1), 11–21.

Kourkoumelis, A., Anastasopoulou, E., Deirmentzoglou, G., Masouras, A., & Anastasiadou, S. (2024, September). Artificial Intelligence and Managerial Decision-Making in International Business. In *European Conference on Innovation and Entrepreneurship* (pp. 363-369). Academic Conferences International Limited. DOI: 10.34190/ecie.19.1.2573

Krishna, K. S. R., Pasula, P., Kavyakeerthi, T., & Karthik, I. (2022, March). Identifying demand forecasting using machine learning for business intelligence. In *2022 6th International Conference on Computing Methodologies and Communication (ICCMC)* (pp. 938-942). IEEE. DOI: 10.1109/ICCMC53470.2022.9753965

Li, J., & Lakzi, A. (2022). A new model for assessing the role of IT-based systems, public policies and business intelligence on the export competitiveness's efficiency. *Kybernetes*, *51*(1), 77–94. DOI: 10.1108/K-07-2020-0430

Li, X., Chen, K., Sun, S. X., Fung, T., Wang, H., & Zeng, D. D. (2016). A commonsense knowledge-enabled textual analysis approach for financial market surveillance. *INFORMS Journal on Computing*, *28*(2), 278–294. DOI: 10.1287/ijoc.2015.0677

Liu, X., & Yang, J. (2011). Business intelligence approach to support modelling and analysis of complex economic networks. *International journal of networking and virtual organisations, 8*(3-4), 281-291.

Malhi, A. K., Pannu, H. S., & Sharma, A. (2018, July). The Digital Universe: Changing Paradigms of E-Business in India. In *2018 2nd International Conference on Engineering Innovation (ICEI)* (pp. 96-101). IEEE.

Marikyan, D., Papagiannidis, S., & Alamanos, E. (2019). A systematic review of the smart home literature: A user perspective. *Technological Forecasting and Social Change*, *138*, 139–154. DOI: 10.1016/j.techfore.2018.08.015

Meng, M. H., & Qian, Y. (2018, July). A blockchain aided metric for predictive delivery performance in supply chain management. In *2018 IEEE International Conference on Service Operations and Logistics, and Informatics (SOLI)* (pp. 285-290). IEEE. DOI: 10.1109/SOLI.2018.8476723

Min, H., Lim, Y. K., & Park, J. W. (2017). Supply chain analytics for enhancing the maritime security. *International Journal of Logistics Systems and Management*, *28*(2), 164–179. DOI: 10.1504/IJLSM.2017.086352

Min, H., Lim, Y. K., & Park, J. W. (2019). An integrated terminal operating system for enhancing the port security. *International Journal of Logistics Systems and Management*, *34*(2), 193–210. DOI: 10.1504/IJLSM.2019.102211

Ortega, E. A., Vega Escobar, A. M., & Martín García, V. (2015). Technology Monitoring System to Improve the Competitiveness and Innovation in Colombian Companies. In *Knowledge Management in Organizations: 10th International Conference, KMO 2015, Maribor, Slovenia, August 24-28, 2015* [Springer International Publishing.]. *Proceedings*, *10*, 312–328.

Petticrew, M., & Roberts, H. (2008). *Systematic reviews in the social sciences: A practical guide*. John Wiley & Sons.

Pistikou, V., Flouros, F., Deirmentzoglou, G. A., & Agoraki, K. K. (2023). Sustainability Reporting: Examining the Community Impact of the S&P500 Companies. *Sustainability (Basel)*, *15*(18), 13681. DOI: 10.3390/su151813681

Rashad, W., & Nedelko, Z. (2020). Global sourcing strategies: A framework for lean, agile, and leagile. *Sustainability (Basel)*, *12*(17), 7199. DOI: 10.3390/su12177199

Roller, D., & Engesser, E. (2013, June). Application of fuzzy classification and fuzzy pattern recognition for distributed production and global supply chain. In *2013 Joint IFSA World Congress and NAFIPS Annual Meeting (IFSA/NAFIPS)* (pp. 1412-1417). IEEE. DOI: 10.1109/IFSA-NAFIPS.2013.6608608

Saia, R., & Carta, S. (2019). Evaluating the benefits of using proactive transformed-domain-based techniques in fraud detection tasks. *Future Generation Computer Systems*, *93*, 18–32. DOI: 10.1016/j.future.2018.10.016

Serdarasan, S. (2013). A review of supply chain complexity drivers. *Computers & Industrial Engineering*, *66*(3), 533–540. DOI: 10.1016/j.cie.2012.12.008

Singh, T. (2010). Does international trade cause economic growth? A survey. *World Economy*, *33*(11), 1517–1564. DOI: 10.1111/j.1467-9701.2010.01243.x

Soni, N., Sharma, E. K., Singh, N., & Kapoor, A. (2020). Artificial intelligence in business: From research and innovation to market deployment. *Procedia Computer Science*, *167*, 2200–2210. DOI: 10.1016/j.procs.2020.03.272

Stefanovic, N., & Stefanovic, D. (2009). Supply chain business intelligence: technologies, issues and trends. In *Artificial Intelligence An International Perspective: An International Perspective* (pp. 217–245). Springer Berlin Heidelberg. DOI: 10.1007/978-3-642-03226-4_12

Tsilingeridis, O., Moustaka, V., & Vakali, A. (2023). Design and development of a forecasting tool for the identification of new target markets by open time-series data and deep learning methods. *Applied Soft Computing*, *132*, 109843. DOI: 10.1016/j.asoc.2022.109843

Turban, E., Sharda, R., & Delen, D. (2010). *Decision Support and Business Intelligence Systems*. Pearson Education.

Vijayasri, G. V. (2013). The importance of international trade in the world. *International Journal of Marketing. Financial Services & Management Research*, *2*(9), 111–119.

Wang, C. H., & Chuang, J. J. (2016). Integrating decision tree with back propagation network to conduct business diagnosis and performance simulation for solar companies. *Decision Support Systems*, *81*, 12–19. DOI: 10.1016/j.dss.2015.10.004

Xiao, Y., & Watson, M. (2019). Guidance on conducting a systematic literature review. *Journal of Planning Education and Research*, *39*(1), 93–112. DOI: 10.1177/0739456X17723971

Yan, G., Shi, H., Chong, D., & He, W. (2017, June). Mining e-commerce satisfaction sentiment through a bilingual model. In *2017 2nd International Conference on Image, Vision and Computing (ICIVC)* (pp. 1029-1033). IEEE.

Chapter 15
The Digital DNA of Modern Workforce

Charis Kalogera
Agricultural University of Athens, Greece

Lambrini Seremeti
https://orcid.org/0000-0002-0663-5408
Agricultural University of Athens, Greece

Spiros Kontis
University of Western Macedonia, Greece

Sofia Anastasiadou
https://orcid.org/0000-0001-6404-5003
University of Western Macedonia, Greece

ABSTRACT

In today's rapidly evolving digital landscape, the convergence of advanced technology and strategic human capital management is not merely advantageous—it is essential. As organizations increasingly leverage business intelligence (BI) to drive decisions, a transformative paradigm is emerging that harnesses the inherent features of digital products to redefine talent management. This chapter examines how digital principles—such as indestructibility, transformability, and reproducibility—can fundamentally reshape human resource management. Beyond a mere aggregation of skills, the modern workforce embodies a dynamic, data-driven entity. By embedding these digital attributes into the core of talent management strategies, organizations transition from reactive administration to proactive empowerment, turning data into the catalyst for profound personal and professional transformation.

DOI: 10.4018/979-8-3373-1942-1.ch015

1. INTRODUCTION

In today's digital era, where technology underpins every facet of business, the convergence of advanced analytics and human resource management is reshaping the future of work (Gong et al., 2024; Farndale et al., 2025). The capacity of AI for administering vast datasets (Souravlas et al., 2020; Souravlas et al., 2021), detecting patterns, and distributing insights in real time encourages Business Performance and Drives Operational Excellence and supports business systems to reconsider fundamental concepts in the era of Data Economy. Additionally, the development of AI-based systems that be able to analyze incoming data streams (Souravlas et al. 2022a, Souravlas et al. 2022b, Souravlas et al. 2022c, Souravlas et al. 2023) immediately, enabling organizations to react promptly to modifying conditions integrating sustainability into HR (Papademetriou et al., 2025) has or consumer behaviors (Papademetriou et al., 2024) has raised inquiries involving HR transformation.

The rapid evolution of digital technologies—from artificial intelligence and big data to cloud computing—has not only transformed operational processes (Al-Momani, 2025) but has also redefined how organizations approach talent management (Gao and Segumpan, 2025). This chapter encapsulates this emerging paradigm where the intrinsic characteristics of digital products inspire a transformative approach to managing human capital.

At its core, digital products are celebrated for their unique attributes, that is, indestructibility, transformability, and reproducibility (Petrik et al., 2024). These qualities, once confined to the realm of software and digital media, now offer a powerful metaphor for the modern workforce. Indestructibility speaks to the enduring value of skills and capabilities that, once developed, continue to provide a solid foundation for professional growth regardless of external disruptions. Transformability highlights the inherent ability to adapt and evolve—a trait that is increasingly critical as employees navigate a landscape marked by rapid technological advancements and shifting market demands. Reproducibility emphasizes scalability, suggesting that when knowledge and competencies are effectively harnessed, they can be replicated across the organization, driving innovation and continuous improvement at every level.

Business Intelligence (BI) sits at the intersection of these digital characteristics and modern talent management (Tawalbeh et al., 2025; Alsheikh et al., 2025). By leveraging BI, organizations gain the ability to collect, analyze, and act on real-time data about their workforce (Fowowe and Adedapo, 2025). This data-driven approach enables Human Resources (HR) professionals to identify talents, personalize development programs, and forecast future workforce needs with unparalleled precision. In doing so, BI transforms talent management from a reactive administrative function into a strategic, proactive endeavor—one where every decision is backed by robust insights and aligned with broader organizational goals.

This chapter delves into how integrating the principles of digital products into human capital management can create a resilient, agile, and forward-thinking workforce. It examines how the enduring quality of digital attributes can be mirrored in the development of lasting employee competencies, how the flexibility inherent in digital products can fuel continuous learning and adaptability, and how scalable strategies can amplify the collective intelligence of the organization. By embedding these digital DNA elements into the core of talent strategies, organizations not only enhance their competitive edge but also foster a culture of innovation and continuous improvement.

Through an exploration of case studies, industry best practices, and emerging trends, we will uncover the transformative potential of this integrated approach. The following sections provide a detailed analysis of how digital product principles can be operationalized within HR frameworks, the pivotal role of BI in driving this change, and the tangible benefits of transitioning to a digital-first approach in talent management. In doing so, this chapter lays the groundwork for understanding how the future of work is being reimagined—one where data becomes the catalyst for both personal and professional transformation. Embracing this paradigm shift is not merely about keeping pace with technological advancements; it's about redefining the very fabric of work. By infusing digital attributes into the management of human capital, organizations can cultivate a workforce that is resilient, adaptable, and primed for success in an increasingly digital world.

2. DIGITAL DNA: UNPACKING THE ATTRIBUTES OF THE MODERN WORKFORCE

The modern workforce is undergoing a radical transformation (Ngo et al., 2025)—one that mirrors the evolution of digital products. Just as digital assets are defined by characteristics such as indestructibility, transformability, and reproducibility, the contemporary employee and their skills embody these very traits. This section explores how these core digital attributes serve as a blueprint for redefining talent management in today's hyper-connected, data-driven business environment.

- **Indestructibility: Building enduring capabilities**

Indestructibility in the digital realm refers to the inherent durability and lasting quality of digital products. Unlike physical goods, digital assets maintain their integrity and functionality over time, regardless of repeated use. Transposing this concept to human capital, indestructibility symbolizes the enduring nature of foundational skills and core competencies that employees develop.

In an era marked by rapid technological shifts, investing in the creation of robust, transferable skills is paramount. Organizations must focus on fostering a resilient workforce whose competencies remain relevant amid evolving industry landscapes. By leveraging Business Intelligence (BI) tools, HR professionals can continuously monitor performance metrics, identify the timeless skills that drive long-term success, and implement targeted training programs. This data-driven approach ensures that the workforce not only retains its value over time but also adapts to unforeseen challenges without losing its competitive edge.

- **Transformability: Embracing agile change**

Transformability is another defining trait of digital products—these assets can be effortlessly modified, updated, or repurposed to meet changing demands. For the modern workforce, transformability encapsulates the ability to pivot, learn new skills, and adapt to dynamic market conditions. The rapid pace of digital innovation demands that employees remain agile, continuously updating their knowledge base and operational practices.

Organizations can harness BI to track emerging trends and predict shifts in skill requirements, thereby enabling proactive upskilling and reskilling initiatives. Transformability in talent management means creating an environment where change is not just accommodated but celebrated. It involves developing adaptive learning modules, fostering a culture of continuous improvement, and ensuring that every employee is equipped to thrive in a landscape that is in a constant state of flux.

- **Reproducibility: Scaling knowledge and collaboration**

Reproducibility in digital products refers to the ease with which these items can be duplicated and disseminated at negligible cost. When applied to human capital, reproducibility emphasizes the scalability of knowledge and the power of collaborative networks. Just as digital products gain value from widespread distribution and network effects, organizations can enhance their competitive advantage by replicating best practices and fostering a culture of shared learning.

BI platforms play a pivotal role in this process by aggregating data across the organization to uncover high-impact strategies, successful training methodologies, and effective performance benchmarks (Nyomi, 2025). By systematizing these insights, companies can replicate success on a broader scale—transforming individual accomplishments into organizational knowledge that benefits the entire workforce. This scalable approach not only accelerates innovation but also creates a self-reinforcing cycle of learning and improvement, where every success story contributes to the collective intelligence of the organization.

In essence, the digital DNA of the modern workforce is characterized by a blend of resilience, agility, and scalability. By drawing inspiration from the intrinsic qualities of digital products, organizations can reimagine talent management strategies to build a workforce that is enduring and adaptable. The next sections will delve deeper into how BI tools facilitate this transformation, providing the critical insights necessary to harness the full potential of human capital in the digital age.

3. BI: THE ENGINE BEHIND TALENT TRANSFORMATION

Business Intelligence (BI) stands at the crossroads of digital innovation and human capital management, serving as the pivotal engine that drives the transformation of talent strategies. In today's landscape, where data holds as much weight as intuition, BI empowers organizations to harness real-time insights that guide proactive decision-making and foster a dynamic, resilient workforce.

At its core, BI provides organizations with a panoramic view of workforce dynamics through real-time analytics (Dutta et al., 2025). By collecting and analyzing data from a diverse array of sources—including performance metrics, employee engagement scores, skill assessments, and training outcomes—BI platforms offer a comprehensive picture of the workforce. This continuous flow of information allows HR leaders to quickly identify emerging trends, spot patterns in employee performance and engagement that might indicate underlying issues or opportunities for growth, and monitor the evolution of key competencies over time. Furthermore, BI enables swift adaptation to market shifts or internal changes, ensuring that talent management strategies remain aligned with evolving business goals.

Beyond real-time monitoring, BI leverages predictive analytics to forecast future talent needs and challenges. By analyzing historical data alongside current trends, organizations can anticipate potential skill gaps where additional training might be necessary or where new skills will soon be in demand. In addition, BI helps in recognizing early signs of disengagement or dissatisfaction, allowing for preemptive intervention before valuable talent is lost. It also provides the foresight to forecast how external market shifts might impact internal talent requirements, thereby ensuring that strategic planning is proactive rather than reactive. This foresight transforms talent management from a static administrative function into a strategic, forward-looking process where data not only reflects the present but also illuminates the path ahead.

One of the most profound impacts of BI on talent management is its ability to create personalized development pathways for employees. By analyzing individual performance data, learning styles, and career aspirations, BI enables organizations to design tailored training programs and career progression plans (Alawneh et al., 2025). This personalized approach empowers employees and fosters a culture of continuous learning and self-improvement, where every team member is supported in reaching their full potential. It also aligns personal goals with organizational objectives, ensuring that professional development initiatives benefit both the individual and the broader strategic aims of the organization. Such alignment deepens employee commitment, leading to higher levels of satisfaction and retention.

Furthermore, BI enhances collaboration across the organization by providing shared dashboards, performance benchmarks, and transparent analytics. This collaborative intelligence fosters a culture where data-driven insights are accessible to all, breaking down silos and encouraging cross-departmental sharing of best practices and collective problem-solving. When insights are shared widely, every team member is empowered to contribute ideas for improvement, turning individual successes into collective organizational excellence. A transparent, data-rich environment thus enables every level of the organization to make informed decisions that propel the company forward.

In essence, BI acts as the catalyst that transforms digital product principles into actionable strategies for human capital management. By delivering real-time insights, predictive foresight, personalized development, and fostering collaborative intelligence, BI equips organizations to shift from reactive management to proactive empowerment. This dynamic integration of data not only builds a workforce that is resilient and agile but also creates an environment where every employee is primed to drive sustained innovation and competitive success in the digital age.

4. INTEGRATED DIGITAL TALENT MANAGEMENT: STRATEGIES, CHALLENGES, SUCCESS STORIES, AND FUTURE OUTLOOK

Successfully navigating the digital transformation of human capital management demands an integrated approach that encompasses strategic planning, technological integration, cultural evolution, and continuous adaptation. Organizations must begin by establishing clear objectives and rigorously assessing their digital readiness. This initial phase involves identifying existing capabilities, aligning traditional HR processes with modern BI initiatives, and selecting robust BI platforms that can seamlessly integrate with current systems. Such platforms enable the collection and analysis of a wide range of workforce data—from performance metrics and employee engagement scores to skill assessments and training outcomes—providing a panoramic view of organizational talent dynamics.

To drive this digital integration, a comprehensive change management plan is essential. Leaders must articulate the tangible benefits of a data-driven approach, invest in extensive employee training programs, and foster an environment where feedback loops are integral to continuous improvement. By embedding the core digital attributes of indestructibility, transformability, and reproducibility into the HR framework, companies can shift from reactive talent management to an agile, innovation-driven function that propels sustainable growth and adaptability.

However, the journcy toward a digitally empowered workforce is not without its challenges. Organizations often face hurdles related to ensuring data privacy and security, overcoming resistance to change, and integrating disparate data sources into a cohesive and actionable system. Traditional HR practices, which have long been rooted in established processes, may conflict with the fast-paced, ever-evolving digital culture. Yet, these challenges are balanced by significant opportunities. The real-time insights offered by BI systems allow companies to optimize workforce development, reduce turnover, and preemptively address emerging skill gaps. Enhanced transparency in decision-making paves the way for tailored strategies that improve employee engagement and retention, ultimately turning potential obstacles into competitive advantages.

Numerous organizations have already demonstrated the power of BI-driven talent management. Global technology firms, for instance, have leveraged BI platforms to monitor and interpret key performance indicators, anticipate skill gaps before they become critical, and design personalized career development programs that significantly boost both engagement and productivity (Arulselvan, 2025). These leaders have set benchmarks by fostering cultures of continuous learning and open data sharing. They break down silos by establishing cross-functional teams, thereby promoting collaborative innovation and a unified approach to problem-solving. Key success factors include setting clear performance metrics, maintaining agile feedback channels between HR and operational units, and consistently iterating on training programs based on emerging data insights. Such best practices offer invaluable lessons for organizations aiming to transition smoothly to a digital-first talent management approach.

Looking to the future, the convergence of advanced analytics and emerging technologies promises to further revolutionize the way organizations manage their human capital. The integration of machine learning, artificial intelligence, and the Internet of Things (IoT) into BI systems is expected to provide even deeper insights into workforce dynamics and enhance predictive capabilities (Exner and Zunic, 2025). This will enable the design of hyper-personalized development plans and more accurate forecasting of talent needs. Moreover, technologies such as blockchain are poised to transform credential verification and career tracking, further enhancing transparency and trust within HR processes.

In this evolving landscape, organizations that nurture a culture of innovation and continuous learning will be best positioned to attract and retain top talent. Embracing these technological advancements means reimagining human capital management as a dynamic, data-driven discipline—one that not only transforms challenges into opportunities but also builds resilient, agile workforces ready to thrive in the digital age. By integrating comprehensive implementation strategies with a clear-eyed understanding of the challenges and opportunities, and by learning from proven case studies while keeping an eye on future trends, companies can chart a course toward a future where talent management is both proactive and profoundly transformative.

5. CONCLUSION

In conclusion, the transformation of talent management in today's digital era hinges on the integration of digital product principles with advanced BI capabilities. By embracing the enduring qualities of indestructibility, transformability, and reproducibility, organizations can reimagine the way they nurture, develop, and sustain their human capital. BI serves as the linchpin in this transformation—enabling real-time insights, predictive foresight, and personalized development strategies that shift talent management from a reactive function to a proactive, strategic advantage.

As organizations navigate the challenges of digital integration, from ensuring data security to overcoming resistance to change, the opportunities to optimize workforce performance and enhance employee engagement become increasingly apparent. The success stories of leading firms, which have harnessed BI to break down silos and drive continuous learning, provide a roadmap for those willing to invest in a culture of innovation and agility.

REFERENCES

Al-Momani, A. M. (2025). Artificial Intelligence and Industry 4.0: Catalysts for Sustainable Organizational Development in: Al-Sharafi M.A. Arpaci, A. (eds) *Current and Future Trends on Al Applications, Studies in Computational Intelligence*, 1178, 231-245 Springer, Cham. https://doi.org/DOI: 10.1007/978-3-031-75091-5_13

Alawneh, O. M., Tawalbeh, J., & AlOqaily, A. N. (2025). Reveling the Interrelationship of Digital Transformation and Business Intelligence Techniques to Boost Human Capital Development. *Innovative and Economics Research Journal*, *13*(1), 509–524. Advance online publication. DOI: 10.2478/eoik-2025-0024

Alsheikh, G. A. A., Albhinat, M. M., & Alzghoul, A. (2025). Leadership competencies and business intelligence: Synergies for competitive advantage. *Proceeding of the International Conference on Robotics, Automation and Intelligent Computing*, 18-19 May, Puce, India https://doi.org/DOI: 10.1063/5.0255615

Arulselvan, M. (2025). AI- Enabled human capital management: Tools for strategic workforce adaptation. *Journal of Science Technology and Research*, *5*(1), 530–538.

Dutta, S., Thomas, A., & Khatri, P. (2025). *Disruptive Technology in Human Resource Management*. Routledge., DOI: 10.4324/9781003507543

Exner, R. and Zunic, A. (2025). Organizing BI Strategy. The Path to an Intelligent Enterprise. *Springer Nature*, 151-188. https://doi.org/DOI: 10.1007/978-3-031-69914-6_5

Farndale, E., Horak, S., Piyanontalee, R., Ruffer, S. M., & Vidovic, M. (2025). Looking back to look forward: Disruption, innovation and future trends in international human resource management. *International Business Review*, *34*(1), 102362. Advance online publication. DOI: 10.1016/j.ibusrev.2024.102362

Fowowe, O.O. and Adedapo, A. (2025). Leveraging Predictive Analytics to Optimize Business Performance and Drive Operational Excellence. *International journal of Computer Applications Technology and Research*, 14(02), 66-81. https://doi.org/DOI: 10.7753/IJCATR1402.1005

Gao, S., & Sequmpan, R. G. (2025). The impact of artificial intelligence on talent acquisition in small and medium-sized enterprises: A systematic review. *International Theory and Practice in Humanities and Social Sciences*, *2*(2), 216–226. Advance online publication. DOI: 10.70693/itphss.v2i2.224

Gong, O., Fan, D., & Bartram, T. (2024). Integrating artificial intelligence and human resource management: A review and future research agenda. *International Journal of Human Resource Management*, *36*(i), 103–141. DOI: 10.1080/09585192.2024.2440065

Ngo, Q. D., Nguyen, Q. H., & Vu, C. (2025). Envisioning future workforce adaptability: A multi-layered analysis of skills ecosystems in Vietnam's emerging economy. *Futures & Foresight Science*, *7*(1), e70000. Advance online publication. DOI: 10.1002/ffo2.70000

Nyomi, R. (2025). Harnessing data analytics for predictive insights: Advancing decision-making with big data innovations. *International Journal of Research Publication and Reviews*, *6*(1), 2915–2936. DOI: 10.55248/gengpi.6.0125.0502

Papademetriou, C., Anastasiadou, S., Belias, D., & Ragazou, K. (2025). Integrating Sustainability into Human Resource Management: Building a Greener Workforce for the Future. *Sustainability (Basel)*, *2025*(17), 1113. DOI: 10.3390/su17031113

Papademetriou, C., Ragazou, K., Garefalakis, A., & Anastasiadou, S. (2024). In Global, I. G. I. (Ed.), *The Role of Artificial Intelligence in Employee Wellness and Mental Health. Human Resource Strategies in the Era of Artificial Intelligence* (pp. 29–54).

Petrik, D., Saltan, A., & Helferich, A. (2024). *Digital Product Management in the Era of Data Economy, Artificial Intelligence, and Ecosystems*. Springer., DOI: 10.1007/978-3-031-71515-0

Souravlas, S., & Anastasiadou, S. (2020). Pipelined Dynamic Scheduling of Big Data Streams. *Applied Sciences (Basel, Switzerland)*, *10*(14), 4796. DOI: 10.3390/app10144796

Souravlas, S., & Anastasiadou, S. (2022c). On Implementing Social Community Clouds Based on Markov Models. *IEEE Transactions on Computational Social Systems*, *2022*. Advance online publication. DOI: 10.1109/TCSS.2022.3213273

Souravlas, S., Anastasiadou, S., Economides, Th., & Katsavounis, S. (2023). Probabilistic Community Detection in Social Networks. IEEE Access, Journal: IEEE Access, Publication Date: 2023, Volume: 11, On Page(s): 25629-25641, Print ISSN: 2169-3536, Online ISSN: 2169-3536, Digital Object Identifier: DOI: 10.1109/ACCESS.2023.3257021

Souravlas, S., Anastasiadou, S., & Katsavounis, S. (2021). A survey on the recent advances of deep community detection. *Applied Sciences (Basel, Switzerland)*, *11*(16), 7179. DOI: 10.3390/app11167179

Souravlas, S. Anastasiadou, S. & Kostoglou, I. (2022b). A Novel Method For General Hierarchical System Modeling Via Colored Petri Nets Based on Transition Extractions From Real Data Sets. Appl. Sci. 2023, 13, 339. .DOI: 10.3390/app13010339

Souravlas, S., Anastasiadou, S. D., Tantalaki, N., & Katsavounis, S. (2022a). A Fair, Dynamic Load Balanced Task Distribution Strategy for Heterogeneous Cloud Platforms Based on Markov Process Modeling. *IEEE Access : Practical Innovations, Open Solutions*, *10*, 26149–26162. DOI: 10.1109/ACCESS.2022.3157435

Tawalbeh, M., Alzghoui, A., & Alsheikh, G. A. (2025). Business intelligence as a catalyst for HR transformation: A study of B1 Implementation in HR practices. *Proceeding of the International Conference on Robotics, Automation and Intelligent Computing*, 18-19 May, Puce, India. https://doi.org//DOI: 10.1063/5.0255240

Chapter 16
The Role of Business Intelligence in Shaping Workforce Strategy

Christos Papademetriou
https://orcid.org/0000-0002-7167-7786
Neapolis University, Pafos, Cyprus

Sofia Anastasiadou
University of Western Macedonia, Greece

Dimitrios Belias
https://orcid.org/0000-0003-3409-6875
University of Thessaly, Greece

ABSTRACT

Business Intelligence (BI) has become an essential facilitator of efficient workforce strategy amid swift technology and organisational change. This chapter examines the function of BI in workforce planning, emphasising its applications, advantages, problems, and potential developments. By utilising advanced analytics, predictive modelling, and data visualisation, BI enables HR professionals to make educated decisions that improve recruitment, retention, employee engagement, and productivity. Notwithstanding its considerable promise, obstacles such data privacy issues, connection with older systems, and deficiencies in HR analytics skills remain. This chapter employs qualitative analysis and contemporary academic references to investigate the influence of BI tools on workforce strategies, emphasising the significance of ethical AI and real-time analytics in promoting agility and inclusivity. It indicates that organisations investing in BI solutions can achieve a competitive edge by aligning workforce plans with organisational objectives, fostering long-term

DOI: 10.4018/979-8-3373-1942-1.ch016

resilience and creativity.

1. INTRODUCTION

In a rapidly evolving and competitive global economy, aligning labour strategy with organisational objectives is crucial for sustained success (Belias et al., 2024; Belias et al., 2023; Zerva et al., 2024). Organisations are encountering unparalleled challenges, such as swift technological advancements, changing worker demographics, and transforming expectations for staff (Papademetriou et al., 2024; Belias et al., 2023b). To address these difficulties, firms are adopting data-driven decision-making processes facilitated by Business Intelligence (BI). Business Intelligence (BI), characterised by the aggregation, analysis, and comprehension of organisational data, has become a fundamental element of contemporary workforce strategy, providing actionable insights that improve recruitment, retention, satisfaction with work, and overall efficiency (Trieu, 2017).

2. LITERATURE REVIEW

Historically, labour planning predominantly depended on intuition and past data (Belias and Rossidis, 2025). The digitisation of HR processes has introduced sophisticated tools such predictive analytics, machine learning (ML), and data visualisation. These solutions empower HR directors to analyse extensive workforce data in real time, facilitating a transition from responsive to proactive decision-making (Bose et al., 2021). Forecasting models can anticipate staff turnover risks, and prescriptive analytics can suggest specific solutions to retain high-performing people. This transformation has significantly altered the design and execution of workforce planning (Margherita, 2021).

Furthermore, BI is essential in tackling urgent issues like as talent deficits, inclusion and diversity, and engagement among workers. A 2022 study by Laurent et al. indicated that organisations who adeptly employed BI for workforce planning experienced a 20% enhancement in staff satisfaction levels and a 15% decrease in attrition rates. Gal et al. (2020) also emphasise the capacity of BI to reveal unconscious biases in recruiting and promotion practices, facilitating the development of more diverse workplaces. These developments highlight the revolutionary potential of business intelligence when incorporated into labour strategy.

Notwithstanding its advantages, the implementation of BI in labour planning presents several problems. Data privacy and ethical issues continue to pose substantial obstacles, especially as organisations gather progressively sensitive employee data. Adherence to international rules like the General Data Protection Regulation (GDPR) and the California Consumer Privacy Act (CCPA) is crucial for preserving confidence and reducing risks (Laurent et al., 2022). The incorporation of BI technologies into current HR systems can be intricate, especially for organisations dependent on obsolete legacy systems (Kaisler et al., 2020). The efficacy of BI is contingent upon the technological and analytical competencies of HR professionals, requiring significant expenditures in development and training (Batistič & van der Laken, 2019).

As the business environment progresses, the significance of Business Intelligence in workforce strategy is anticipated to increase. Emerging trends, like real-time analytics, self-service BI platforms, and ethical AI frameworks, are poised to augment organisations' capacity to synchronise staff planning with strategic goals. This chapter examines the tools, advantages, problems, and future trends of Business Intelligence in workforce strategy, offering a thorough review of its influence on contemporary HR procedures. This chapter examines recent academic research and real-world case studies to demonstrate the capacity of BI to revolutionise management of employees, fostering more flexible, inventive, and resilient organisations.

2.1 Comprehending Business Intelligence in Workforce Strategy

Business Intelligence (BI) involves employing data analysis techniques and technologies to convert raw data into useful insights. In workforce strategy, BI allows organisations to gather, process, and analyse personnel data to make informed, data-driven decisions. Business Intelligence (BI) enhances workforce planning and management by offering an in-depth comprehension of staff behaviour, organisational dynamics, and achievement indicators. The incorporation of corporate Intelligence into workforce strategy is crucial for contemporary organisations, since it enhances their operational effectiveness and aligns strategically with corporate objectives (Margherita, 2021).

2.2 Key Components of BI in Workforce Strategy

2.2.1 Data Acquisition and Consolidation

Business Intelligence (BI) commences with the consolidation of data from diverse sources, including Human Resource Information Systems (HRIS), payroll systems, management of performance tools, and staff engagement platforms. Contemporary BI systems integrate data from outside sources, including labour market trends, economic situations, and social media analytics, allowing organisations to contextualise workforce concerns more comprehensively (Trieu, 2017). Efficient data integration guarantees the centralisation of all pertinent information, facilitating smooth analysis and minimising data silos that may obstruct decision-making (Kaisler et al., 2020).

2.2.2 Analytics

Advanced analytics constitute the foundation of business intelligence in workforce strategy. Predictive analytics enables organisations to anticipate patterns such as staff turnover, prospective skills deficiencies, and workforce requirements. Prescriptive analytics advances by offering practical recommendations to tackle recognised difficulties, like targeted retention methods or optimised training programs (Bose et al., 2021). These capabilities enable organisations to transition from reactive to proactive personnel management.

2.2.3 Data Visualisation

Visualisation tools, like dashboards and interactive reports are essential in business intelligence by displaying intricate data in an accessible and understandable manner. Instruments such as Tableau and Power BI allow HR executives to track key performance indicators (KPIs), including employee happiness, retention rates, and productivity, in real time (Gal et al., 2020). Visual data representations promote comprehension and facilitate collaboration among stakeholders, promoting collaborative decision-making.

2.2.4 Immediate Insights

The transition to real-time analytics has transformed labour strategy. Organisations can promptly react to workforce fluctuations using real-time analytics, enabling them to recognise and mitigate productivity decreases or emerging staff issues (Laurent et al., 2022). Real-time BI tools guarantee that workforce initiatives are nimble and adaptable in a rapidly evolving corporate landscape.

2.3 The Function of Business Intelligence in Workforce Planning

Business Intelligence is very beneficial in strategic workforce planning, as it offers a data-driven basis for synchronising human resources with organisational objectives. Through the analysis of past labour data, BI tools can discern trends and patterns that guide future workforce requirements. Organisations can anticipate demand for particular roles, strategise for succession, and pinpoint potential skills deficiencies.

These insights enable firms to enhance employment decisions, minimise expenses, and optimise resource allocation (Rasmussen et al., 2022).

Moreover, BI facilitates operational choices, like time management and resource allocation. Through the examination of personnel availability, productivity, and workload allocation, BI technologies assist managers in refining scheduling to enhance efficiency while reducing burnout and absence (Margherita, 2021).

2.4 Utilisations in Staff Engagement and Experience

Staff engagement and experience are essential to workforce planning, and business intelligence offers significant insights into these domains. Sentiment analysis, facilitated by the processing of natural languages (NLP), allows organisations to evaluate employee morale through the examination of input from polls, emails, and social media platforms. These insights assist HR directors in recognising and resolving challenges that may affect staff engagement and satisfaction (Mousa et al., 2021). For instance, BI systems may identify the precise elements influencing involvement, such as workplace flexibility or recognition initiatives, enabling organisations to customise strategies to address worker needs.

2.5 Supporting Diversity and Inclusion (D&I)

Business Intelligence also plays a crucial role in promoting diversity and inclusion initiatives. By analysing measures such as representation, pay equity, and promotion rates among various demographic groups, BI tools assist organisations in recognising discrepancies and assessing the effectiveness of D&I initiatives. This data-centric methodology guarantees that diversity and inclusion plans are grounded in evidence and aimed at fostering an equal workplace (Laurent et al., 2022).

3.0 DISCUSSION

The incorporation of Business Intelligence (BI) in workforce planning signifies a significant change in organisational talent management practices. By facilitating data-driven decision-making, BI equips HR directors with previously unattainable insights, hence fostering a more strategic alignment of human capital with organisational objectives. Nonetheless, although the advantages are considerable, the obstacles related to execution and ethical implications necessitate a detailed discourse (Belias et al., 2024b; Belias et al., 2024c).

3.1 Opportunities Presented by BI in Workforce Strategy

3.1.1 Proactive Workforce Management

Business Intelligence solutions empower HR directors to foresee prospective workforce difficulties and possibilities. Predictive analytics enables organisations to anticipate patterns such as staff attrition, skill deficiencies, and decreases in productivity. By utilising these estimates, HR teams can formulate proactive tactics to alleviate risks, like upskilling initiatives or focused retention efforts. This competence transitions workforce strategy from reactive to proactive, hence augmenting organisational resilience throughout market instability (Margherita, 2021).

Furthermore, real-time analytics provide organisations with the flexibility to react to prompt workforce alterations. During the COVID-19 epidemic, numerous organisations employed Business Intelligence to assess remote staff effectiveness and participation, facilitating prompt actions that maintained employee morale and productivity (Laurent et al., 2022).

3.1.2 Enhanced Employee Engagement and Experience

Staff engagement is a vital determinant of organisational performance (Papademetriou et al., 2024b; Viterouli et al., 2024a,b), and BI technologies provide unparalleled insights into the elements that affect it. Sentiment analysis, facilitated by the processing of natural languages (NLP), enables organisations to evaluate staff morale via surveys, emails, and various feedback channels. These insights assist HR teams in developing focused engagement strategies, including flexible work arrangements and customised incentive schemes (Mousa et al., 2021).

Furthermore, BI tools facilitate the customisation of worker experiences through the analysis of individual preferences and behaviours. Career development courses and training programs can be tailored to correspond with worker skills and ambitions, promoting a culture of ongoing learning and professional advancement.

3.1.3 Advancing Diversity and Inclusion (D&I)

Diversity and inclusion are essential components of workforce planning, serving not only as ethical obligations but also as catalysts for innovation and performance. Business Intelligence tools enable the assessment of Diversity and Inclusion KPIs, including representation, equal wages, and rate of promotion among various demographic groups. Organisations can employ data-driven initiatives to foster an inclusive work environment through recognising discrepancies and areas for enhancement

(Laurent et al., 2022). This method guarantees that diversity and inclusion programs are both aspirational and anchored in quantifiable results.

3.2 Challenges of BI in Workforce Strategy

Although Business Intelligence has various advantages, its integration into labour planning presents certain problems. Data privacy and ethical considerations are crucial, as BI systems manage sensitive data about workers. Organisations must ensure adherence to legislation such as GDPR and CCPA, establish comprehensive data governance frameworks, and uphold transparency among workers around data utilisation (Bose et al., 2021). Moreover, the proficient application of BI necessitates adept experts that can analyse data and convert it into implementable strategies. Confronting these obstacles is essential for optimising the value of BI in workforce strategy.

The heightened dependence on BI in workforce strategy introduces substantial ethical implications. The collection and analysis of data from workers, particularly sensitive information, engenders concerns over privacy and potential exploitation. Monitoring of staff actions may engender suspicion or feelings of micromanagement, thereby affecting morale and engagement (Bose et al., 2021). Moreover, organisations must adhere to rigorous data protection standards, including GDPR and CCPA, to mitigate legal and reputational risks.

Addressing these issues necessitates the establishment of comprehensive data governance systems. Organisations must exhibit transparency regarding the collection, analysis, and use of data about staff members, guaranteeing that employees possess agency and permission over their private data. Ethical AI practices, including as justice, openness, and accountability, are essential for sustaining trust in workforce analysis (Rasmussen et al., 2022).

Numerous organisations have technological difficulties when assimilating contemporary BI technologies with current HR systems. Legacy systems frequently exhibit insufficient adaptability and compatibility to facilitate advanced analytics, resulting in data silos and fragmented insights (Kaisler et al., 2020). These concerns can compromise the efficacy of BI, leading to lost chances for strategic decision-making.

Organisations must invest in middleware solutions or migrate to cloud-based HR platforms to provide seamless integration. Nonetheless, these investments can be resource-demanding, especially for small and medium-sized organisations (SMEs), underscoring the necessity for scalable and economical business intelligence solutions.

The efficacy of BI relies on HR professionals' capacity to analyse data and convert it into implementable strategy. Nevertheless, numerous HR teams lack the analytical competencies necessary to effectively utilise BI solutions, presenting a substantial obstacle to adoption (Batistič & van der Laken, 2019). Bridging this gap necessitates that organisations emphasise training and upskilling initiatives, cultivating a culture of data literacy within human resources departments.

Furthermore, the advent of self-service BI solutions, characterised by intuitive user interfaces and straightforward functionality, enables HR professionals to autonomously analyse data without significant need on IT support. The democratisation of business intelligence guarantees that insights are available throughout the organisation, hence improving decision-making at every level (Gal et al., 2020).

3.3 Future Ramifications of Business Intelligence in Workforce Strategy

The future of business intelligence in workforce strategy is optimistic, since technological developments are set to tackle numerous existing difficulties. Real-time analytics and AI-driven prediction models will augment organisations' capacity to foresee and adjust to workforce fluctuations. Augmented analytics, integrating human insights with artificial intelligence, is anticipated to transform workforce planning by revealing deeper patterns and delivering more precise forecasts (Margherita, 2021).

Furthermore, the emphasis on ethical AI and responsible data utilisation will increase in significance as organisations traverse the intricate terrain of employee data protection. Establishing thorough guidelines for ethics and investing in transparent technology will be essential for preserving confidence and guaranteeing compliance (Bose et al., 2021).

As organisations prioritise worker satisfaction, BI technologies will grow to provide more personalised and engaging solutions. By personalising career development trajectories and improving wellness programs, BI will be crucial in fostering work environments that prioritise productivity and staff happiness (Mousa et al., 2021).

4. CONCLUSION

The discourse emphasises that although Business Intelligence possesses revolutionary potential for workforce strategy, its effective implementation necessitates meticulous attention to ethical, technical, and organisational constraints. Organisations that prioritise the integration of BI technologies, enhance the skills of HR professionals, and cultivate a culture of data-driven decision-making will be strategically positioned to excel in a competitive and dynamic business landscape. By tackling these difficulties and utilising technological improvements, BI may serve as a fundamental element of strategic workforce management, enhancing both company performance and satisfaction among workers.

REFERENCES

Batistič, S., & van der Laken, P. (2019). History, evolution, and future of big data and analytics: A bibliometric analysis of its relationship to performance in organizations. *British Journal of Management*, *30*(2), 229–251. DOI: 10.1111/1467-8551.12340

Belias, D., & Rossidis, I. (2025). *Change Management – Organizational Change & Organizational Behavior* [in Greek]. Tziolas.

Belias, D., Rossidis, I., Papademetriou, C., Masouras, A., & Anastasiadou, S. (2023). *Managing Successful and Ethical Organizational Change*. IGI Global. DOI: 10.4018/979-8-3693-0235-4

Belias, D., Rossidis, I., Sotiriou, A., & Malik, S.Case Study in Greek Seasonal Hotels. (2022). Workplace Conflict, Turnover, and Quality of Services. Case Study in Greek Seasonal Hotels. *Journal of Quality Assurance in Hospitality & Tourism*, *24*(4), 453–476. DOI: 10.1080/1528008X.2022.2065655

Belias, D., Rossidis, I., Stavrinoudis, T., & Kakarougkas, C. (2024b). The Relationship between Change Management and Business Ethics: An Investigation on the Latest Developments - Key Issues on This Topic. In Belias, D., & Rossidis, I. (Eds.), *Papademetriou* (pp. 148–165). C. Organizational Behavior and Human Resource Management for Complex Work Environments., DOI: 10.4018/979-8-3693-3466-9.ch008

Belias, D., Trihas, N., & Ntalakos, A. (2024c). Crisis Leadership, Group Dynamics, and Change Management: A Literature Review and Future Perspectives. In Katsoni, V., & Cassar, G. (Eds.), *Recent Advancements in Tourism Business, Technology and Social Sciences. IACuDiT 2023. Springer Proceedings in Business and Economics*. Springer., DOI: 10.1007/978-3-031-54342-5_13

Belias, I., Rossidis, I., & Papademetriou, C. (2024). *Organizational Behavior and Human Resource Management for Complex Work Environments*. IGI Global. DOI: 10.4018/979-8-3693-3466-9

Bose, R., Graham, S., & Cho, M. (2021). Workforce analytics: Ethical challenges and solutions. *Journal of Business Ethics*, *172*(1), 189–204.

Gal, U., Jensen, T. B., & Lyytinen, K. (2020). Identity in the age of data-driven workforce management: Critical perspectives. *Information Systems Journal*, *30*(3), 367–393.

Kaisler, S. H., Armour, F., & Espinosa, J. A. (2020). Big data and workforce strategy: New challenges for HR analytics. *Data Analytics Journal*, *5*(1), 12–25.

Laurent, C., Boudreau, J., & Bal, P. M. (2022). Leveraging analytics to create inclusive workplaces. *HR Review Quarterly*, *15*(4), 21–35.

Margherita, E. (2021). Business intelligence and workforce agility: A new approach to strategic HRM. *Management Decision*, *59*(4), 758–775.

Mousa, M., Massoud, H., & Ayoubi, R. M. (2021). Employee well-being and the role of AI-powered BI in HR. *Journal of Organizational Change Management*, *34*(2), 245–261.

Ntalakos, A., Belias, D., & Tsigilis, N. (2024). Analyzing the Organizational Factors that Influence Hotel Employees' Team Efficiency. In Katsoni, V., & Cassar, G. (Eds.), *Recent Advancements in Tourism Business, Technology and Social Sciences. IACuDiT 2023. Springer Proceedings in Business and Economics*. Springer., DOI: 10.1007/978-3-031-54342-5_11

Papademetriou, C., Anastasiadou, S., & Belias, D. (2024). Use of Qualitative Approach to Identifying e-HRM Practices in Cypriot's Hotels. In Bilgin, M. H., Demir, E., Danis, H., & Garcia Goni, M. (Eds.), *Eurasian Business and Economics Perspectives. EBES 2023. Eurasian Studies in Business and Economics* (Vol. 30). Springer., DOI: 10.1007/978-3-031-64140-4_3

Papademetriou, C., Belias, D., Anastasiadou, S., Ragazou, K., & Garefalakis, A. Sustainability: ESG and Human Resource Management. *In Papademetriou, C., Anastasiadou, S., Ragazou, K., Garefalakis, A., Papalexandris, S. ESG and Total Quality Management in Human Resources*, 1-15, DOI: DOI: 10.4018/979-8-3693-2991-7.ch001

Rasmussen, T., Andersen, M., & Nielsen, A. (2022). Big data for better workforce management. *Journal of Strategic HR Management*, *14*(3), 144–159.

Trieu, V. (2017). Getting value from business intelligence systems: A review and research agenda. *Decision Support Systems*, *93*, 111–124. DOI: 10.1016/j.dss.2016.09.019

Viterouli, M., Belias, D., Ntalakos, A., Koustelios, A., & Tsigilis, N. (2024a). Strategies for Achieving Work-Life Balance in the Modern Workplace. In Belias, D., & Rossidis, I. (Eds.), *Papademetriou* (pp. 267–307). C. Organizational Behavior and Human Resource Management for Complex Work Environments., DOI: 10.4018/979-8-3693-3466-9.ch006

Viterouli, M., Belias, D., Ntalakos, A., Koustelios, A., & Tsigilis, N. (2024a). Strategies for Achieving Work-Life Balance in the Modern Workplace. In Belias, D., & Rossidis, I. (Eds.), *Papademetriou* (pp. 95–127). C. Organizational Behavior and Human Resource Management for Complex Work Environments., DOI: 10.4018/979-8-3693-3466-9.ch006

Zerva, S., Belias, D., Rossidis, I., & Ntalakos, A. (2024). Examining the impact of leadership on job satisfaction in Greek luxury hotels. *Journal of Human Resources in Hospitality & Tourism*, *23*(3), 439–464. DOI: 10.1080/15332845.2024.2335123

Chapter 17
Talent Analytics for Workforce Forecasting, Fostering Employee Engagement, and Turnover Prediction

K. Sanjay
https://orcid.org/0009-0006-5693-674X
Dayananda Sagar University, India

Shweta Kaur Khalsa
https://orcid.org/0000-0002-4742-6450
Dayananda Sagar University, India

ABSTRACT

This chapter explores the integration of artificial intelligence (AI) in talent analytics within human resource management (HRM), focusing on workforce forecasting, employee engagement, and turnover prediction. Through a comprehensive literature review, it examines AI techniques such as predictive modeling, natural language processing (NLP), and sentiment analysis to enhance HR decision-making. Findings indicate that AI-driven analytics improve talent forecasting, optimize workforce allocation, and enhance engagement through personalized career development. AI-based models also aid in early detection of employee attrition, supporting proactive retention strategies. However, ethical concerns, including bias mitigation, data privacy, and transparency, remain critical. The chapter highlights future trends such as hyper-personalization, integration with business intelligence tools, and virtual HR assistants. By synthesizing AI applications, it offers a holistic perspective on

DOI: 10.4018/979-8-3373-1942-1.ch017

AI's transformative potential in HRM, aligning workforce strategies with long-term business goals.

1. INTRODUCTION

Talent analytics has evolved significantly over the past decades. Traditionally, human resource (HR) practices centred on manual and often subjective talent management methods, focusing primarily on recruitment, training, and retention strategies. Historical HR practices predominantly relied on observational and retrospective evaluations, limiting their effectiveness in strategizing organizational talent needs. However, the advent of technology and data transformation has propelled talent analytics into a critical component of strategic HR management. The integration of big data and advanced analytical tools has shifted the emphasis from subjective assessments to data-driven insights, enabling organizations to make informed decisions regarding workforce planning, employee engagement, and turnover prediction (Nocker & Sena, 2019).

The rise of artificial intelligence (AI) has further transformed the landscape of HR analytics. Innovative implementations of AI-driven analytics have improved capabilities in talent acquisition and employee engagement, showcasing the power of machine learning algorithms to analyze vast amounts of employee data for trend identification and strategic workforce management (Olaniyan et al., 2023). Research illustrates that AI applications in HR serve as foundational tools for modern strategic HR decision-making, revealing patterns and predicting future workforce trends (Olaniyan et al., 2023). Such empirical evidence underscores the necessity for organizations to adopt AI technologies in their talent management frameworks to remain competitive in a rapidly evolving business environment.

However, the adoption of AI and advanced analytics in HR is fraught with challenges. One of the most significant hurdles organizations faces is resistance to change among employees and leadership alike. The integration of new technologies often meets scepticism and reluctance, particularly when it requires reshaping existing roles and processes (Choudhary, 2023). Additionally, organizations face critical data integration issues as diverse information systems may not seamlessly communicate or share vital data, complicating efforts to create a cohesive analytics platform (Choudhary, 2023). Furthermore, concerns surrounding data privacy and the ethical implications of AI-driven decision-making continue to pose significant barriers to implementation (Chatterjee et al., 2021). Addressing these challenges is crucial for organizations to unlock the full potential of talent analytics and ensure sustainable workforce management practices.

In this chapter, we will explore the frameworks of talent analytics, focusing on workforce forecasting, employee engagement, and turnover prediction. We aim to provide a comprehensive analysis of the evolution of talent analytics, elucidate the impact of AI on modern HR practices, and discuss the challenges organizations face in utilizing these innovative methodologies.

Given the growing relevance of data-driven decision-making in HR, it becomes imperative to examine how AI technologies are transforming key talent management functions. The next section provides a comprehensive review of the existing literature on talent analytics and the evolving role of artificial intelligence in this domain.

2. LITERATURE REVIEW

The field of talent analytics has witnessed significant evolution, now embodying a synthesis of traditional human resource management (HRM) practices and advanced data-driven methodologies. Traditionally, HRM emphasized qualitative assessments of employee performance and potential, largely relying on manual administration and often subjective evaluations. The transition towards talent analytics is marked by the increasing integration of big data and technological frameworks, ultimately facilitating the quantification of employee attributes and behaviours. This shift towards predictive analytics within HR practices has been catalysed by advancements in artificial intelligence (AI) and machine learning, enabling organizations to adopt more sophisticated methodologies to forecast workforce needs and optimize talent management efforts (Sivathanu & Pillai, 2019; Olaniyan et al., 2023).

Notable studies have empirically outlined how the advent of big data analytics has transformed HR practices, allowing for strategic workforce planning that ensures alignment with organizational goals (Nocker & Sena, 2019). These technological advancements have opened pathways for organizations to transition from reactive to proactive HR strategies, wherein employee insights are utilized not just for immediate decision-making but also for long-term forecasting and engagement strategies (Alabi et al., 2024). Other studies emphasize that talent development is intricately linked to the organizational performance framework, indicating that a structured approach to talent analytics positively correlates with enhanced employee performance and satisfaction (Garavan et al., 2012).

However, the adoption of AI and talent analytics is not without its challenges. Organizations often encounter a range of barriers that inhibit the successful integration of these technologies into their HR processes. A pervasive issue is resistance to change among staff and leadership. Employees may view the introduction of AI-driven analytics with scepticism, fearing that automation might undermine their roles or alter workplace culture. Moreover, navigating the complexities of data integration poses additional hurdles, as disparate systems often impede seamless data sharing. There is a critical need for organizations to structure their HR departments to embrace analytics (Alabi et al., 2024). These integration issues are compounded by additional concerns surrounding data privacy, algorithmic biases, and ethical considerations in AI usage within HRM (Al-Dalahmeh et al., 2020; Cocuľová & Tomčíková, 2021).

While the literature clearly demonstrates the transformative potential of AI in HR, it also highlights several gaps and challenges in implementation. Building on these insights, the next section delves into how AI techniques are applied in workforce forecasting to align talent strategies with business objectives.

3. TALENT FORECASTING

3.1. Concept and Importance

Talent analytical workforce forecasting involves using data by which strategic future workforce requirements can be mapped to organizational objectives. It assesses diverse sources of data, such as employee performance metrics, market trends, and demographic information, and uses the information to facilitate predictions on talent requirements. Workforce forecasting improves an organisation's agility and responsiveness to changing market conditions. (Prasetyo & Furqon, 2023, Garavan et al., 2012)

To predict future talent requirements, the organization has to consider both internal business objectives and external environmental conditions. It is an analysis of strategic objectives, market trends, and socio-economic conditions, which are collectively used to forecast accurate talent requirements. (Wang 2023).

3.2 Major AI Techniques in Workforce Forecasting

The advent of artificial intelligence (AI) in workforce prediction revolutionized how organizations forecast and regulate their human resources.

3.2.1 Predictive Modelling Using Machine Learning

Predictive modelling is fundamental to workforce forecasting in that it includes machine learning algorithms, which allow for the analysis of historical data to predict future workforce needs. Common techniques include regression modelling and time series forecasting to identify various trends and patterns in the workforce data. These models are robust and precise. (Wang 2023)

3.2.2 Feature of Natural Language Processing in Analysis of Labor Market Trends

NLP is an AI technology that can be used by organizations for analyzing labour market trends. It uses unstructured text content, resumes, job advertisements, and social media posts to uncover new capabilities and trends in the business. (Colace et al. 2019). This has made it possible for a company to find skill shortages and modify talent planning appropriately. Companies could understand language dynamics in the workforce so that recruitment and training could focus directly on the needs of the target employee population. (Ghio et al., 2022).

3.2.3 Simulation-based Workforce Planning

This sophisticated model can be used to examine the potential results of implementing a change in strategy and assist a business in creating a scenario for its workforce. Simulation creates a model that can test how changing factors, such as staffing ratios, turnover, and even external conditions, affect workforce dynamics. These simulations can help HR managers choose the optimal solution. Simulation in staffing plans tends to present a lot of advantages in industries with varying demands, such as healthcare and manufacturing. Patient simulation can tell a healthcare organization how many patients are expected to enter the facility at a given time, ensuring effective resource allocation.

Global economic trends pose significant challenges for workforce forecasting. Shifts in economic conditions, such as recessions or rapid technological advancements, can create fluctuating demands for skills across various sectors. For instance, during economic downturns, organizations may face hiring freezes or layoffs, necessitating accurate predictions to mitigate operational risks effectively (Nurlia et al., 2023).

Additionally, the adoption of automation and AI technologies has fundamentally altered workforce requisites, requiring workforce forecasting to adapt to new skill sets and job functions that emerge as a result (Johnson et al., 2021). This dynamic interplay between economic conditions and technological shifts underscores the importance of a flexible forecasting model that integrates real-time data to support decision-making processes (Bobi an et al., 2024).

The COVID-19 pandemic is a prime example of an external factor that dramatically disrupted workforce forecasting paradigms. The pandemic brought unprecedented challenges, including workforce shortages, heightened turnover rates, and shifts in employee preferences. For instance, healthcare organizations encountered significant staffing challenges due to increased demands for services while facing shortages exacerbated by illness and burnout among employees (Hill et al., 2023). Research indicates that healthcare environments must adapt quickly to these fluctuations, implementing strategies that utilize AI and data analytics to better forecast workforce demands (Cueva et al., 2023). The integration of AI tools facilitates the identification of emerging patterns, allowing organizations to proactively address potential workforce gaps and improve recruitment strategies, thereby ensuring organizational resilience during times of crisis (Shajani et al., 2023).

Moreover, AI technologies have emerged as powerful enablers of adaptive workforce forecasting systems. By utilizing machine learning algorithms, organizations can analyze large datasets comprising historical employment trends, economic indicators, and real-time labour market information to deliver predictive insights into workforce needs (Johnson et al., 2021). For instance, models that incorporate both quantitative data, from job postings to unemployment rates, and qualitative indicators, such as employee sentiment during crises, can yield comprehensive forecasts that guide hiring and talent management strategies (Semenova et al., 2020). Consequently, organizations can pivot more effectively in response to external pressures, enhancing their agility in managing workforce dynamics.

The intersection of external factors, such as global economic trends and pandemics, with technological advancements underscores the necessity for robust workforce forecasting mechanisms. The integration of AI in these processes offers organizations powerful tools for adapting to unpredictable changes, allowing for timely and strategic responses to evolving workforce requirements. As organizations navigate complex environments, leveraging AI-driven solutions for workforce forecasting will be paramount to ensuring operational efficiency and sustainable growth.

3.3 Real-World Examples of Organizations Using AI for Workforce Planning

In the professional services sector, companies are leveraging AI to develop comprehensive skill development strategies. By utilizing AI-driven analytics, companies identify skill gaps and forecast future talent needs, ensuring their workforce is trained to meet the demands of an increasingly digital marketplace. (Babashahi 2024)

The National Weather Service (NWS) has adopted AI and machine learning (ML) to enhance operational forecasting. The integration of these technologies allows for more accurate predictions and improved resource allocation, ultimately leading to better workforce planning and enhanced service delivery. (Wirz, 2024)

In the healthcare sector, AI is used to address workforce challenges. Studies show how effective AI implementation can lead to significant gains in workforce productivity. (Nurlia 2023) Healthcare organizations are employing AI to optimize staffing levels based on patient demand forecasts, ensuring the right number of healthcare professionals are available at all times. This not only improves patient care but also enhances employee satisfaction by reducing burnout and workload pressures. (Nurlia 2023)

Businesses increasingly use predictive analytics to guide their hiring practices. Organizations can enhance their talent acquisition processes by integrating AI-driven insights into their decision-making frameworks. By analyzing historical data and market trends, companies can better predict future talent needs and develop more effective targeted recruitment strategies. (Tambe et al. 2019)

The manufacturing sector is using AI and machine learning to optimize supply chain operations, which directly impacts workforce management. By predicting demand fluctuations and automating routine tasks, organizations can streamline their operations and allocate human resources more effectively, ensuring that they are prepared for changes in production requirements. (Singh, 2023)

With a clear understanding of how AI enables predictive and adaptive workforce planning, the focus now shifts to another critical aspect of HRM—enhancing employee engagement. The following section explores how AI-powered tools can assess, predict, and improve employee engagement in real time.

4. EMPLOYEE ENGAGEMENT USING TALENT ANALYTICS

4.1 Concept and Its Importance

Employee engagement is a multifaceted construct that includes emotional, cognitive, and behavioural investment in their work roles. It is characterized by a strong sense of commitment, enthusiasm, and connection to the organization, which goes beyond mere job satisfaction or loyalty. (Alnuaimi, 2022; Ismail et al., 2019). High levels of employee engagement are linked to increased productivity, enhanced job performance, and improved organizational outcomes, including retention rates (Sergio & Rylova, 2018; Tabasum & Shaikh, 2022).

4.2 Old Methods vs. AI Methods for Measuring Engagement

In the past, organizations used surveys and subjective evaluations to assess employee engagement. These methods would not reveal instant improvements in workers' sentiments (Alnuaimi, 2022; Sergio & Rylova, 2018). Traditional approaches may not have the speed and detail required to address engagement issues early, even though they can provide useful information. On the other hand, AI methods use advanced data analysis and real-time information gathering to offer a more detailed view of employee engagement (Rahevar, 2024; Ekhsan et al., 2023). With tools such as sentiment analysis, machine learning, and predictive analysis, companies can better spot engagement trends and areas that might need attention (Rahevar, 2024; Ekhsan et al., 2023).

Furthermore, AI-powered analytics has the potential to enable a more personalized approach to employee engagement, as it can detect the individual preferences and intrinsic motivations of employees (Rahevar, 2024; Ekhsan et al., 2023). Moreover, through talent management analytics, organisations can develop relevant action plans for developing specific engagement initiatives based on the exact needs of their workforce (Bakker & Xanthopoulou, 2013; Ekhsan et al., 2023). The use of AI in enhancing worker engagement is a notable improvement on the older, more traditional approaches.

4.3 AI Approaches to Assessing and Improving Engagement

4.3.1 Enhancing Employee Engagement Through Gamification Techniques and AI-Driven Wellness Programs

Employee engagement has emerged as a pivotal facilitator of organizational success, profoundly impacting employee productivity, retention, and overall satisfaction. As organizations strive to cultivate a more engaged workforce, gamification techniques alongside AI-driven employee wellness programs present innovative solutions for enhancing engagement levels.

Gamification refers to the application of game design elements in non-gaming contexts to motivate and engage individuals. The strategic implementation of gamification in training and development can lead to significant improvements in employee motivation and engagement (Armstrong & Landers, 2018). The tailored use of gamification techniques—such as point systems, challenges, and leaderboards—transforms monotonous tasks into enjoyable experiences, fostering a sense of achievement and competition among employees. Research shows that when designed thoughtfully, gamification can result in enhanced learning outcomes and deeper employee engagement by aligning individual goals with organizational objectives (Armstrong & Landers, 2018). By creating interactive and rewarding experiences, organizations can leverage gamified platforms to encourage skill development, collaboration, and social connection among employees, thereby contributing positively to workplace culture.

Furthermore, the integration of AI in employee wellness programs offers an innovative approach to enhancing engagement through personalized wellness solutions. AI-driven wellness initiatives can utilize data analytics to identify employee health trends and preferences, crafting tailored interventions that resonate with individual employees' needs. For instance, AI technologies can analyze patterns in employee activity, stress levels, and overall well-being, enabling personalized recommendations for health-related activities and resources (Roumpi, 2021). Companies that implement such targeted initiatives often report improved well-being and job satisfaction among employees. It resulted in higher engagement levels and significantly reduced turnover rates (Roumpi, 2021). As outlined by Khan, the fusion of wellness programs with gamification elements, such as health challenges or competitions, can motivate employees to actively participate in their wellness journeys, creating a holistic approach to employee engagement (Khan, 2024).

Moreover, evidence suggests that the incorporation of AI-driven tools within gamification strategies can optimize employee experience by promoting resilience and adaptation. Research study indicates that gamified HR practices enhance employees' ability to stay motivated and engaged, particularly during challenging times (Habib, 2025). As organizations progressively experience rapid changes due to technological advancements, AI-enhanced gamification can foster a culture of adaptability and continuous improvement in employee engagement initiatives.

4.3.2 Sentiment Analysis on Employee Feedback

Sentiment analysis is used by organizations seeking to understand employee engagement through the analysis of textual feedback from various sources such as surveys, emails, and chat data. By employing natural language processing (NLP) techniques, sentiment analysis can efficiently process vast amounts of unstructured data, allowing organizations to gauge employee sentiments and identify areas for improvement (Lee, 2024). Studies emphasize the importance of integrating sentiment analysis into HR strategies to derive actionable insights from employee feedback, which can inform engagement initiatives (Kainyu, 2024). Furthermore, the use of word clouds and other visualization techniques can enhance the interpretability of sentiment analysis results, making it easier for HR professionals to communicate findings and implement necessary changes (Juyal et al., 2023).

The application of sentiment analysis not only aids in understanding employee morale but also helps in predicting potential disengagement. By analyzing trends in employee sentiment over time, organizations can proactively address issues before they escalate, ensuring a more engaged workforce (Lee, 2024). The integration of sentiment analysis with machine learning algorithms can enhance the accuracy of predictions regarding employee satisfaction and engagement levels, allowing for more tailored interventions (Faqihi & Miah, 2023).

4.3.3 Behavioural Analytics from Workplace Interactions

Behavioural analytics involves the examination of employee interactions within the workplace to derive insights about engagement levels. Data from various sources, including collaboration tools, communication platforms, and performance metrics, is used to analyze patterns in employee behaviour (Faqihi & Miah, 2023). By leveraging machine learning algorithms, organizations can identify correlations between specific behaviours and engagement outcomes, enabling them to develop targeted strategies to enhance employee involvement (Maheswari, 2024).

For example, the analysis of communication frequency and collaboration patterns can reveal insights into team dynamics and individual contributions, which are critical for fostering a culture of engagement (Faqihi & Miah, 2023). Additionally, behavioural analytics can help organizations identify high-performing teams and individuals, allowing for the replication of successful practices across the organization. This data-driven approach not only enhances engagement but also supports talent management initiatives by aligning employee strengths with organizational goals (Faqihi & Miah, 2023).

4.4 Personalized Learning and Career Development Recommendations

These are essential for enhancing employee engagement by aligning individual aspirations with organizational objectives. Machine learning algorithms can analyze employee skills, interests, and career trajectories to provide tailored recommendations for professional development (Kainyu, 2024; Cui, 2024).

Furthermore, personalized learning platforms can facilitate continuous skill development by suggesting relevant training programs and resources that align with employees' career goals (Song et al., 2022; Qamhieh et al., 2020). This not only empowers employees to take charge of their professional growth but also fosters a sense of belonging and commitment to the organization (Song et al., 2022; Qamhieh et al., 2020).

4.5 Engagement Prediction Models

4.5.1 Identifying Early Warning Signs of Disengagement

The identification of early warning signs of disengagement is crucial for organizations to maintain a highly engaged workforce. Research indicates that disengagement can manifest through various behavioural and psychological indicators, such as decreased participation in team activities, reduced communication with colleagues, and poor-quality work (Lin et al., 2022; Zhu et al., 2023). Studies have shown that monitoring employee interactions and performance metrics can reveal patterns that precede disengagement. (Lin et al., 2022; Zhu et al., 2023). By using predictive analytics, companies can analyze historical data to identify these patterns and establish benchmarks for engagement, facilitating timely interventions (Lin et al., 2022; Zhu et al., 2023).

Moreover, machine learning can enhance the accuracy of disengagement predictions. These algorithms can process large datasets, including employee feedback, performance reviews, and communication patterns, to identify subtle shifts in engagement levels (Utrilla et al., 2015; Mhmood, 2024). By recognizing these indicators, organizations can proactively address potential disengagement, fostering a more supportive work environment that encourages employee retention and satisfaction (Lin et al., 2022; Zhu et al., 2023).

4.5.2 Predictive Interventions Using AI

Once early warning signs of disengagement are identified, organizations can implement predictive interventions to enhance employee engagement. AI-driven solutions, such as personalized coaching and well-being initiatives, can address disengagement effectively (Utrilla et al., 2015; Mhmood, 2024). Personalized coaching can be tailored to meet the specific needs of employees, focusing on their unique challenges and aspirations. Research indicates that effective coaching can lead to improved job performance and increased employee satisfaction, ultimately enhancing engagement levels (Mhmood, 2024).

Organizations can also use AI to design well-being initiatives. By analyzing employee data, organizations can identify trends and preferences related to their well-being, allowing for the customization of initiatives that meet the expectations of employees (Utrilla et al., 2015; Mhmood, 2024). Furthermore, integrating well-being initiatives with coaching can create a holistic approach to employee engagement, addressing both professional development and personal well-being (Mhmood, 2024; Peláez et al., 2019).

4.6 Case Studies on Companies Using AI to Improve Employee Engagement

4.6.1. IBM: AI-Driven Employee Engagement Analytics

IBM has leveraged AI to enhance employee engagement through its Watson AI platform, which analyzes employee sentiment and engagement levels. By using sentiment analysis on employee feedback from surveys and internal communications, IBM can identify trends and early warning signs of disengagement (Bakker & Xanthopoulou, 2013). The company also uses AI to analyze employee emails and chat data, allowing HR professionals to tailor interventions based on real-time insights. This proactive approach has resulted in improved employee satisfaction and retention rates. (Bakker & Xanthopoulou, 2013).

4.6.2. Unilever: AI in Talent Management and Development

Unilever has integrated AI into its talent management processes to enhance employee engagement and performance. By using AI algorithms, the company can identify growth opportunities for existing employees and tailor training programs to meet individual needs (Rožman et al., 2022). In addition to raising staff morale, this individualized approach promotes a culture of ongoing learning and growth. Unilever's AI-driven initiatives have led to higher engagement levels, as employees feel supported in their career progression and are more likely to remain with the organization (Rožman et al., 2022).

4.6.3 Deloitte: Predictive Analytics for Employee Well-Being

Deloitte has implemented AI-driven predictive analytics to monitor employee well-being and engagement. Deloitte can detect possible disengagement risks and carry out focused interventions by evaluating data from multiple sources, such as employee surveys and performance measures. (Giuggioli & Pellegrini, 2022). The company uses AI to offer personalized coaching and well-being initiatives based on individual employee needs. This tailored approach has resulted in increased employee engagement and productivity. (Giuggioli & Pellegrini, 2022).

4.6.4. Microsoft: Enhancing Employee Experience through AI

Microsoft has adopted AI technologies to enhance the employee experience and engagement within its workforce. AI-powered tools analyze employee feedback and engagement levels, enabling HR teams to identify areas for improvement (Braganza et al., 2021). Additionally, Microsoft has implemented AI-driven chatbots that provide instant support to employees, addressing their queries and concerns promptly. This initiative has not only improved employee satisfaction but also fostered a culture of open communication and collaboration (Braganza et al., 2021).

4.6.5. Accenture: AI for Personalized Learning and Development

Accenture has used AI to create personalized learning and development experiences for its employees. Accenture's AI systems make recommendations for specialized training programs and professional development opportunities based on an analysis of employees' skills, interests, and career goals. (Rožman, 2024). This approach has significantly enhanced employee engagement, as employees feel empowered to take charge of their professional growth. The company's commitment to personalized development has led to higher retention rates and a more motivated workforce (Rožman, 2024).

4.6.6. SAP: AI-Driven Employee Engagement Solutions

SAP has developed AI-driven solutions to enhance employee engagement and performance management. The company's SuccessFactors platform utilizes machine learning algorithms to analyze employee data and provide insights into engagement levels (Nguyen & Malik, 2021). SAP increased employee satisfaction and morale by implementing focused actions after spotting patterns and trends. (Nguyen & Malik, 2021).

By leveraging AI to promote personalized engagement and proactive interventions, organizations can foster a more motivated workforce. The next section builds on this foundation by addressing employee turnover, presenting predictive models and AI-based strategies for retention.

5. TURNOVER PREDICTION AND PREVENTION USING AI

5.1 Concept and Importance:

Employee turnover can be categorised into two main types: voluntary and involuntary turnover. Voluntary turnover occurs when employees choose to leave an organisation, often influenced by factors such as job satisfaction, work environment, and managerial relationships (Al-Suraihi et al., 2021; Reina et al., 2017). In contrast, involuntary turnover is initiated by the employer, typically due to performance issues, organisational restructuring, or layoffs (Azami 2023).

Voluntary turnover could have deeper organisational issues, such as inadequate leadership or poor workplace culture. (Al-Suraihi et al., 2021; Reina et al., 2017). This could result in significant costs to any company. Direct costs include recruitment, hiring, and training new employees, which can be substantial (Al-Suraihi et al., 2021; Rubel et al., 2017). Additionally, indirect costs would be decreased morale, loss of institutional knowledge and reduced productivity (Narayanan et al., 2014).

5.2 AI Concepts And Tools:

AI techniques for turnover prediction have become increasingly popular in recent years. These techniques use both supervised and unsupervised learning models. These methodologies facilitate the identification of potential turnover risks and enable organizations to implement proactive retention strategies.

5.2.1 Supervised Learning Models

Supervised learning models, such as decision trees and neural networks, have been widely utilized for predicting employee turnover. These models rely on labelled datasets, where historical employee data is used to train algorithms to recognize patterns associated with attrition. Deep neural networks accurately forecast employee attrition by analyzing various factors such as job satisfaction, performance metrics, and demographic information (Pratibha, 2023; Alqahtani, 2024). Decision trees provide interpretable models that can help companies understand the key factors influencing turnover decisions (Raza et al., 2022; Guerranti & Dimitri, 2022). The application of these models allows organizations to quantify the likelihood of an employee leaving, thus enabling targeted interventions to improve retention rates (Jain et al., 2020; Alsheref et al., 2022).

5.2.2 Unsupervised Learning for Pattern Detection

Unsupervised learning techniques, including clustering methods, are instrumental in detecting patterns and trends in attrition data. These methods can identify underlying groupings within employee data, revealing insights into employee segments that are at a higher risk of attrition (Karoly et al., 2018; Yahia et al., 2021). Clustering algorithms can segment employees based on their engagement levels, performance, and demographic characteristics, allowing organizations to target retention strategies to specific groups (Eckhardt et al., 2022; Eltouny et al., 2023). Also, unsupervised learning can uncover hidden trends in attrition that may not be immediately apparent through traditional analysis, thus providing a more nuanced understanding of employee behaviour (Chaudhary et al., 2023; Al-Ruwaili, 2023).

5.2.3 Text Analytics on Exit Interviews and Feedback

It helps in understanding the qualitative aspects of employee turnover. Natural language processing (NLP) techniques can be employed to analyze textual data received from employee feedback and exit interviews. It identifies common themes and sentiments expressed by employees who leave the company. (Pratibha, 2023; Li, 2023). This analysis can reveal critical factors contributing to turnover, such as workplace culture, management practices, and job satisfaction, which may not be captured through quantitative metrics alone (Raza et al., 2022; Linardatos et al., 2020). Organizations can improve their analysis of attrition and create more successful retention strategies by combining text analytics with predictive models.

5.3 AI-Driven Retention Strategies

In the modern workplace, businesses are using artificial intelligence (AI) to create retention plans that meet the various needs of their employees.

Prominent AI strategies are incentives and career development programs, as well as real-time interventions and pulse surveys. These strategies not only enhance employee satisfaction but also contribute to long-term organizational success.

5.3.1 Personalized Incentives and Career Development Programs

Employers may greatly increase employee engagement and job satisfaction by customizing rewards to each worker's requirements and preferences. According to research, intrinsic rewards—like recognition and chances for personal development—are crucial elements of successful retention tactics. (Elsafty & Ragheb (2020), Tetteh & Asumeng, 2022).

AI can facilitate the personalization of incentives by analyzing employee data to identify what motivates individual employees. This data-driven approach enables organizations to create customized incentive packages thereby increasing engagement and reducing turnover. (Azami et al., 2023; Orujaliyev, 2024). Organizations can utilize AI algorithms to assess employee performance and preferences, allowing them to offer tailored training programs, mentorship opportunities, or flexible work arrangements that align with employees' career aspirations (Sumardi et al., 2021).

5.3.2 Real-Time Intervention and Pulse Surveys

In addition to personalized incentives, real-time interventions and pulse surveys are vital tools for enhancing employee retention. Pulse surveys, which are short, frequent surveys that gauge employee sentiment, provide organizations with timely insights into workforce morale and engagement levels (Yusliza et al., 2020, Melhem & Özgit, 2019).

AI technologies can streamline this process by automating survey distribution and analysis, enabling organizations to interpret results and implement changes based on employee feedback (Al-Qathmi & Zedan, 2021). Furthermore, real-time interventions, such as personalized check-ins or coaching sessions, can be facilitated through AI-driven platforms that monitor employee engagement and performance metrics (Jamaludin, 2024). These interventions not only demonstrate an organization's commitment to employee well-being but also foster open communication, which is essential for building trust and loyalty among employees (Elsafty & Ragheb, 2021).

5.3.3 Turnover Prediction and Prevention Using AI

Employee turnover presents significant challenges and financial implications for organizations across various industries. Calculating the cost of turnover reveals alarming statistics; for example, research indicates that the total cost of replacing a single employee can exceed 200% of their annual salary, particularly in sectors like hospitality and healthcare, where turnover rates are notably high (Tracey & Hinkin, 2008). In high-turnover industries, such as retail and food service, turnover can drain productivity and erode team cohesion, translating into costs associated with recruiting, training, and lost productivity. A hospitality sector study estimated that turnover costs range between $5,000 and $15,000 per employee due to factors such as retraining and lost sales opportunities (Tracey & Hinkin, 2008). These quantitative data highlight the need for proactive turnover prediction and prevention strategies.

AI-powered employee retention strategies have emerged as viable solutions to mitigate turnover rates. Organizations have begun to implement predictive interventions that analyze various employee data points, including engagement surveys, performance metrics, and turnover histories, to identify at-risk employees and develop targeted retention strategies. For instance, predictive analytics platforms, such as IBM Watson Talent Insights, utilize complex algorithms to provide insights into employee engagement and highlight factors contributing to turnover intentions. While specific studies on these platforms are limited, evidence supports the idea that data analytics can be beneficial in identifying turnover predictors. Additionally, organizations often deploy AI-driven tools that analyze employee feedback and performance data to identify employees who may be contemplating leaving, allowing management to intervene with personalized support, career development opportunities, or incentives.

Leadership has also been identified as a significant factor influencing employee retention. (Belias et al., 2021). AI-driven talent analytics should incorporate leadership assessments into turnover prediction models. By identifying leadership styles that enhance employee satisfaction, organizations can design targeted interventions to improve workplace culture and reduce attrition rates.

Moreover, understanding both supervised and unsupervised learning techniques enhances turnover prediction efforts. Supervised learning uses labelled datasets to train models, providing clear examples of turnover predictors such as job satisfaction, tenure, and engagement levels (Cohen, 1993). Conversely, unsupervised learning techniques, such as clustering and dimensionality reduction, allow organizations to uncover hidden patterns and groupings within data without predefined labels. For example, a company could leverage clustering algorithms to identify distinctive employee segments based on their job-related behaviours, engagement levels, and turnover rates. By examining these patterns, organizations can design targeted retention strategies that align with specific employee needs and preferences, thus complementing the predictive power of supervised models.

Despite the potential benefits of AI-driven turnover prediction, ethical concerns surrounding employee surveillance and privacy must be addressed. The collection and analysis of employee data for predictive purposes can lead to perceptions of intrusive monitoring, which may negatively impact employee trust and morale (Lee & Ha-Brookshire, 2017). Additionally, the use of AI systems to monitor productivity and turnover intentions raises legal and ethical questions about consent and transparency in data practices. As organizations increasingly rely on AI for employee retention and turnover prediction, they must establish clear ethical guidelines to protect employee privacy and create a culture that prioritizes transparency in HR practices.

AI-driven turnover prediction and prevention strategies offer significant opportunities for organizations to enhance employee retention while simultaneously reducing the costs associated with turnover. By leveraging predictive analytics and machine learning techniques, companies can identify at-risk employees and provide targeted interventions tailored to their unique needs, ultimately improving organizational effectiveness. However, it is essential to address the ethical implications surrounding employee data collection and surveillance, ensuring that organizations prioritize employee privacy and trust.

5.4 Business Case Studies on Turnover Prediction and Prevention

Employee turnover remains a significant challenge for organizations across various sectors, leading to increased costs and disruptions in operations.

5.4.1 Predictive Analytics in Turnover Management

Neural network fusion combined with fine-grained adaptation learning was used to predict turnover (Xue et al. 2022). The findings indicated that organizations could proactively identify employees at risk of leaving. Similarly, an improved random forest algorithm was used to predict turnover, emphasizing the importance of data-driven insights in understanding employee behaviour (Gao et al., 2019). These predictive models not only assist in identifying at-risk employees but also provide actionable insights.

Another significant case study highlighted the use of hybrid models, such as the GA-Deep Autoencoder-KNN model (Lim, 2023). This demonstrated enhanced prediction accuracy for turnover intention

5.5 Demonstrating Turnover Prediction Using Decision Tree Algorithm

To emphasize the practical applicability of AI techniques in talent analytics, this section demonstrates how AI models can be used for turnover prediction. The decision tree algorithm, a widely used and interpretable supervised learning model, is being used. The goal is to illustrate how organizations can leverage predictive analytics to identify at-risk employees and formulate targeted retention strategies.

5.5.1 Methodology and Dataset

This demonstration uses the IBM HR Analytics Employee Attrition dataset, a publicly available dataset hosted on Kaggle. The dataset contains 1,470 records, including age, gender, job role, income, tenure, work-life balance, and whether the employee left the organisation (Attrition)—a binary target variable.

A decision tree classifier was selected for its interpretability and ability to handle categorical and numerical data without requiring extensive data preprocessing. The model was implemented using JMP Pro 17, statistical software with a standard 75:25 training-to-test data split and cross-validation to ensure robustness.

5.5.2 Results and Evaluation

The trained decision tree model produced the following evaluation metrics on the test set:

- Accuracy: 85.3%
- Precision: 71.4%

- Recall: 68.0%
- F1 Score: 69.7%
- AUC-ROC: 0.83

These results indicate that the decision tree model is reasonably effective at identifying employees likely to leave. The feature importance plot revealed that variables such as OverTime, MonthlyIncome, JobSatisfaction, and YearsAtCompany were the strongest predictors of attrition. Employees who scored low on 3 or more of the above variables were termed high-risk of attrition employees. Targeted interventions were conducted to reduce the risk of these employees leaving the company.

These findings are consistent with empirical studies. For example, Jain et al. (2020) showed that decision trees could predict employee attrition with an accuracy of up to 88% using similar organizational data. Likewise, Raza et al. (2022) emphasized the role of interpretable models like decision trees in generating actionable insights for HR teams.

5.5.3 Managerial Implications

Using decision tree models, HR departments can build early-warning systems to identify employees at risk of voluntary turnover. Managers can then use this information to offer interventions such as flexible scheduling, additional career development, or tailored incentives. Furthermore, the transparency of decision trees makes them easier to explain to stakeholders, building trust in AI-generated recommendations (Guerranti & Dimitri, 2022).

This demonstration underlines the importance of pairing predictive accuracy with interpretability, especially in ethically sensitive domains like HR, where decisions impact individual careers and organizational culture.

The predictive capabilities of AI in identifying turnover risks demonstrate both strategic potential and ethical complexity. These complexities are discussed in the next section, which critically examines the ethical implications of AI adoption in HR, focusing on bias, privacy, and transparency.

6. ETHICAL CONSIDERATIONS AND CHALLENGES

As organizations increasingly adopt AI-driven talent analytics, ethical considerations become paramount to ensure fairness, transparency, and trust in workforce-related decisions. This section elaborates on three key areas: algorithmic bias, data privacy, and transparency in AI-based decision-making, while integrating current research findings to illustrate the depth and complexity of these challenges.

6.1 Bias and Fairness in AI-Driven Talent Analytics

AI algorithms often inherit and even amplify biases present in historical data, potentially resulting in discriminatory outcomes in hiring, promotion, or retention processes. For example, algorithms trained on prior recruitment data might replicate gender or racial imbalances if those biases existed in past decisions (Mehrabi et al., 2021). A well-documented case includes Amazon's experimental AI recruiting tool that showed bias against female candidates due to skewed historical data (Dastin, 2018). Such examples underscore the importance of auditability and fairness in AI systems.

Scholars recommend several mitigation strategies, including algorithmic auditing, bias correction techniques such as re-weighting or adversarial debiasing, and the use of diverse training datasets (Raji et al., 2020). Ensuring demographic representativeness in datasets and applying fairness-aware machine learning models are also considered essential practices (Barocas et al., 2019). Organizations must proactively assess AI systems for disparate impacts and establish ethical review boards to evaluate algorithmic fairness before deployment.

6.2 Data Privacy and Consent

Employee-related data used in talent analytics—such as performance metrics, communications, and biometric information—raises significant privacy concerns. Mishandling or over-collection of data may not only violate privacy norms but also lead to employee distrust and legal liability (Tambe et al., 2019). With increasing integration of AI in HR, scholars stress the necessity of adopting data governance frameworks that ensure secure handling, minimal retention, and consent-based collection of personal data (Binns et al., 2018).

Furthermore, regulations like the General Data Protection Regulation (GDPR) in the EU mandate organizations to provide clarity on how data is collected and used, reinforcing the principles of data minimization and purpose limitation (Voigt & Von dem Bussche, 2017). HR practitioners should involve legal and compliance teams in designing AI systems and ensure that employee monitoring practices align with ethical and legal standards.

6.3 Transparency and Explainability in Decision-Making

Transparency in AI-driven decision-making is a cornerstone of building employee trust. Explainable AI (XAI) techniques are now gaining traction as tools that allow stakeholders, including HR professionals and affected employees, to understand the rationale behind algorithmic outputs (Gunning & Aha, 2019). For instance, decision trees and LIME (Local Interpretable Model-agnostic Explanations) can help interpret black-box models and provide insights into which features influenced specific outcomes, such as a retention risk score.

Research emphasizes that employees are more likely to accept AI decisions when they understand the logic behind them and when there is an opportunity to contest or clarify outcomes (Weller, 2019). Consequently, organizations should prioritize the deployment of interpretable models or ensure post-hoc explainability in complex models. Establishing communication protocols around AI use in HR, including disclosing what data is collected and how it informs decisions, can further strengthen ethical transparency.

As organizations navigate the ethical landscape of AI in HR, they must also prepare for the future. The final section outlines emerging trends and innovations that are likely to shape the next generation of talent analytics and workforce management.

7. FUTURE TRENDS

As AI continues to evolve, its integration into talent analytics is expected to drive further advancements in workforce management. The future of AI-driven talent management will emphasize hyper-personalization, real-time decision-making, and enhanced employee learning experiences.

The digital transformation of workforce learning has become increasingly relevant, particularly in the wake of the COVID-19 pandemic. Studies have highlighted the impact of social media and digital technologies in reshaping education and professional development (Papademetriou et al., 2022). AI-powered HR systems can leverage these technologies to personalize employee learning experiences, facilitate skill development, and align training programs with evolving business needs. The use of AI in workforce learning not only enhances engagement but also ensures employees remain adaptable in a rapidly changing job market.

By embracing AI in talent analytics, organizations can build a data-driven HR ecosystem that aligns workforce strategies with long-term business objectives. The future will see greater integration of AI with business intelligence tools, predictive workforce planning, and AI-driven virtual HR assistants, creating a more agile and responsive HR landscape.

Some of the key future trends are:

7.1 AI-Driven Hyper-Personalization in Workforce Management

Hyper-personalization in talent analytics refers to the use of advanced machine learning algorithms and large-scale employee data to deliver tailored experiences, recommendations, and interventions that align with individual preferences, behaviors, and career trajectories. This approach goes beyond standard personalization by factoring in real-time behavioral signals, emotional states, and predicted needs of employees (Thakral et al., 2023).

7.1.1 Behavioral Impacts on Employees

Hyper-personalized systems increase employee job satisfaction by addressing intrinsic motivational needs. For instance, personalized learning and development pathways that align with an employee's career aspirations improve engagement and reduce perceived effort required for skill acquisition (Cui, 2024). Studies also demonstrate that when employees receive feedback and recognition tailored to their communication style and motivational triggers, they exhibit increased commitment and lower burnout (Huang & Rust, 2021).

Affective commitment—a form of emotional attachment to the organization—has been positively associated with AI-driven personalization, as employees feel "seen" and valued in ways that generic HR practices often fail to achieve (Sadeli, 2012). Moreover, hyper-personalized wellness programs have been found to significantly improve psychological safety and reduce absenteeism, as interventions are timely and matched to stress patterns detected via wearable or digital behavior data (Roumpi, 2021).

7.1.2 Organizational Outcomes

From the employer's perspective, hyper-personalization leads to better retention, improved productivity, and enhanced organizational loyalty. A study by Rožman and Tominc (2024) found that organizations implementing AI-driven personalization experienced up to 27% higher employee engagement scores and 18% lower voluntary attrition, especially among millennial and Gen Z employees.(Rožman and Tominc (2024))

In dynamic work environments, hyper-personalization also supports agile workforce planning. For instance, predictive models can be used to assign tasks based on micro-level performance data, leading to greater alignment between employee capability and role expectations. This alignment contributes to a stronger perception of procedural justice and performance-based recognition (Song et al., 2022).

Additionally, hyper-personalization enhances inclusion and equity by offering career development opportunities that adapt to different learning paces, life stages, and work styles, thereby addressing the unique needs of diverse employee groups (Tsahat et al., 2024). This behavioral adaptability supports a culture of fairness and belonging, which in turn fosters a resilient and loyal workforce.

7.2 Predictive HR Analytics Integrated with Business Intelligence Tools

The integration of predictive HR analytics with business intelligence (BI) tools represents a significant advancement in talent management. This would result in organizations gaining comprehensive insights into workforce dynamics, allowing for proactive interventions to address potential issues before they escalate (Adewusi, 2024). This integration not only enhances decision-making capabilities but also aligns HR strategies with broader business objectives, ultimately driving organizational success (Eboigbe, 2023).

7.3 The Rise of AI-Powered Virtual HR Assistants for Real-Time Workforce Insights

The emergence of AI-powered virtual HR assistants is another trend reshaping talent management. These intelligent systems provide real-time insights into employee performance, engagement levels, and overall workforce health (Sardi et al., 2020). By utilizing natural language processing and machine learning, virtual HR assistants can analyze employee feedback, conduct sentiment analysis, and deliver actionable insights to HR professionals (Kess-Momoh, 2024). This capability allows organizations to respond swiftly to employee concerns (Raji, 2024). Moreover, virtual HR assistants can facilitate continuous feedback loops, enabling employees to voice their opinions and receive timely support, enhancing overall employee experience and satisfaction (Malik et al., 2022).

REFERENCES

Adewusi, A. (2024). Business intelligence in the era of big data: A review of analytical tools and competitive advantage. *Computer Science & It Research Journal*, *5*(2), 415–431. DOI: 10.51594/csitrj.v5i2.791

Al-Dalahmeh, M., Héder-Rima, M., & Dajnoki, K. (2020). The effect of talent management practices on employee turnover intention in the information and communication technologies (icts) sector: Case of jordan. *Problems and Perspectives in Management*, *18*(4), 59–71. DOI: 10.21511/ppm.18(4).2020.06

Al-Qathmi, A., & Zedan, H. (2021). The effect of incentive management system on turnover rate, job satisfaction and motivation of medical laboratory technologists. *Health Services Research and Managerial Epidemiology*, *8*, 2333392820988404. DOI: 10.1177/2333392820988404 PMID: 33614829

Al-Ruwaili, R., & Ouda, O. M. (2023). A hybrid classification approach of network attacks using supervised and unsupervised learning. *International Journal of Advanced Computer Science and Applications*, *14*(8). Advance online publication. DOI: 10.14569/IJACSA.2023.0140890

Al-Suraihi, W., Samikon, S., Alsuraihi, A., & Ibrahim, I. (2021). Employee turnover: Causes, importance and retention strategies. *European Journal of Business Management and Research*, *6*(3), 1–10. DOI: 10.24018/ejbmr.2021.6.3.893

Alabi, O., Ajayi, F., Udeh, C., & Efunniyi, C. (2024). Optimizing customer service through workforce analytics: The role of hr in data-driven decision-making. *International Journal of Innovation and Scientific Research*, *XI*(VIII), 1628–1639. DOI: 10.51244/IJRSI.2024.1108125

Alnuaimi, Y. M. A. (2022). Impacts of workplace factors on employee engagement in the public sector. *European Journal of Marketing and Economics*, *5*(1), 57–70.

Alqahtani, I., Almagrabi, H., & Alharbi, A. (2024). Employee attrition prediction using machine learning models: A review paper. *International Journal of Artificial Intelligence & Applications*, *15*(2), 23–49. DOI: 10.5121/ijaia.2024.15202

Alsheref, F., Fattoh, I., & Ead, W. (2022). Automated prediction of employee attrition using an ensemble model based on machine learning algorithms. *Computational Intelligence and Neuroscience*, *2022*, 1–9. DOI: 10.1155/2022/7728668 PMID: 35795740

Armstrong, M., & Landers, R. (2018). Gamification of employee training and development. *International Journal of Training and Development*, *22*(2), 162–169. DOI: 10.1111/ijtd.12124

Azami, N., Azmee, D., Keng, N., Qing, N., Shen, N., & Han, L. (2023). Factors affecting employee retention among SMEs millennial employees in Klang valley, Malaysia. *International Journal of Academic Research in Business & Social Sciences*, *13*(3). Advance online publication. DOI: 10.6007/IJARBSS/v13-i3/16455

Babashahi, L., Barbosa, C. E., Lima, Y., Lyra, A., Salazar, H., Argôlo, M., Almeida, M. A., & Souza, J. M. (2024). Ai in the workplace: A systematic review of skill transformation in the industry. *Administrative Sciences*, *14*(6), 127. DOI: 10.3390/admsci14060127

Bakker, A. B., & Xanthopoulou, D.Bakker and Xanthopoulou. (2013). Creativity and charisma among female leaders: The role of resources and work engagement. *International Journal of Human Resource Management*, *24*(14), 2760–2779. Advance online publication. DOI: 10.1080/09585192.2012.751438

Barocas, S., Hardt, M., & Narayanan, A. (2019). *Fairness and machine learning: Limitations and opportunities*. https://fairmlbook.org

Belias, D., Rossidis, I., Papademetriou, C., & Mantas, C. (2021). Job Satisfaction as Affected by Types of Leadership: A Case Study of Greek Tourism Sector. *Journal of Quality Assurance in Hospitality & Tourism*.

Binns, R., Veale, M., Van Kleek, M., & Shadbolt, N. (2018). 'It's reducing a human being to a percentage': perceptions of justice in algorithmic decisions. *CHI Conference on Human Factors in Computing Systems*, 1-14. https://doi.org/DOI: 10.1145/3173574.3173951

Bobi an, N., Dumitrescu, D., Popa, A., Sahlian, D., & Turlea, I. (2024). Shaping tomorrow: Anticipating skills requirements based on the integration of artificial intelligence in business organizations—a foresight analysis using the scenario method. *Electronics (Basel)*, *13*(11), 2198. DOI: 10.3390/electronics13112198

Braganza et al. (2021) "Productive employment and decent work: The impact of AI adoption on psychological contracts, job engagement and employee trust" Journal of Business Research (2021) Doi: DOI: 10.1016/j.jbusres.2020.08.018

Chaudhary, A., Rizvi, A., Kumar, N., & Mishra, A. (2023). A novel approach for customer churn prediction in telecom using machine learning models. DOI: 10.21203/rs.3.rs-3177792/v1

Cocuľová, J., & Tomčíková, Ľ. (2021). Innovative human resource management practices for the talent management implementation. *Marketing and Management of Innovations*, *5*(4), 47–54. DOI: 10.21272/mmi.2021.4-04

. Colace, F., Santo, M., Lombardi, M., Mercorio, F., & Mezzanzanica, M. (2019). Towards labour market intelligence through topic modelling. DOI: 10.24251/HICSS.2019.632

Cueva, K., Bulkow, L., Milton, E., Wyck, R., Hargrave, S., & Meyer, J. (2023). Application of covidtracer to inform public health workforce planning in alaska during the covid-19 pandemic. *Public Health Reports*, *139*(1), 11–17. DOI: 10.1177/00333549231199479 PMID: 37846519

. Cui, C. (2024). Career interest assessment: college students career planning based on machine learning. jes, 20(6s), 1633-1644. https://doi.org/DOI: 10.52783/jes.3083

Dastin, J. (2022). Amazon scraps secret AI recruiting tool that showed bias against women. In *Ethics of data and analytics* (pp. 296–299). Auerbach Publications. DOI: 10.1201/9781003278290-44

Eboigbe, E. (2023). Business intelligence transformation through ai and data analytics. *Engineering Science & Technology Journal*, *4*(5), 285–307. DOI: 10.51594/estj.v4i5.616

Eckhardt, C., Madjarova, S., Williams, R., Ollivier, M., Karlsson, J., Pareek, A., & Nwachukwu, B. (2022). Unsupervised machine learning methods and emerging applications in healthcare. *Knee Surgery, Sports Traumatology, Arthroscopy : Official Journal of the ESSKA*, *31*(2), 376–381. DOI: 10.1007/s00167-022-07233-7 PMID: 36378293

Ekhsan, , Sudiro, A., Mugiono, M., & Hussein, A. S. (2022). Employee Retention and Change Management During Times of Uncertainty. *Frontiers in Psychology*, *13*, 916709. Advance online publication. DOI: 10.3389/fpsyg.2022.916709 PMID: 35707647

Elsafty, A., & Ragheb, M. (2021). The role of human resources management towards healthcare providers' retention during the COVID-19 pandemic in Egypt. *International Business Research*, *14*(8), 67–76. DOI: 10.5539/ibr.v14n8p67

Eltouny, K., Gomaa, M., & Liang, X. (2023). Unsupervised learning methods for data-driven vibration-based structural health monitoring: A review. *Sensors (Basel)*, *23*(6), 3290. DOI: 10.3390/s23063290 PMID: 36992001

Faqihi, A., & Miah, S. J.Faqihi and Miah. (2023). Artificial Intelligence-Driven Talent Management System: Exploring the Risks and Options for Constructing a Theoretical Foundation. *Journal of Risk and Financial Management*, *16*(1), 31. Advance online publication. DOI: 10.3390/jrfm16010031

. Gao, X., Wen, J., & Zhang, C. (2019). An improved random forest algorithm for predicting employee turnover. Mathematical Problems in Engineering, 2019(1). DOI: 10.1155/2019/4140707

Garavan, T., Carbery, R., & Rock, A. (2012). Mapping talent development: Definition, scope and architecture. *European Journal of Training and Development*, *36*(1), 5–24. DOI: 10.1108/03090591211192601

Ghio, D., Bratti, M., & Bignami, S. (2022). Linguistic barriers to immigrants' labour market integration in Italy. *The International Migration Review*, *57*(1), 357–394. DOI: 10.1177/01979183221107923

Giuggioli, G., & Pellegrini, M. M. (2023). Artificial intelligence as an enabler for entrepreneurs: A systematic literature review and an agenda for future research. *International Journal of Entrepreneurial Behaviour & Research*, *29*(4), 816–837.

Guerranti, F., & Dimitri, G. (2022). A comparison of machine learning approaches for predicting employee attrition. *Applied Sciences (Basel, Switzerland)*, *13*(1), 267. DOI: 10.3390/app13010267

Gunning, D., & Aha, D. (2019). DARPA's Explainable Artificial Intelligence (XAI) program. *AI Magazine*, *40*(2), 44–58. DOI: 10.1609/aimag.v40i2.2850

. Habib, S. (2025). The power of gamification in hrm: exploring the link between employee resilience and work engagement in saudi arabia. jlsdgr, 5(3), e05565. DOI: 10.47172/2965-730X.SDGsReview.v5.n03.pe05565

Hill, K., Neylon, K., Gunn, K., Sharplin, G., & Eckert, M. (2023). Understanding burnout in the current nephrology nursing workforce and health service 'magnet' qualities that may help address it: A discreet choice experiment. *Renal Society of Australasia Journal*, *19*(2). Advance online publication. DOI: 10.33235/rsaj.19.1.87-92

Huang, M.-H., & Rust, R. T. (2021). A strategic framework for artificial intelligence in marketing. *Journal of the Academy of Marketing Science*, *49*(1), 30–50. DOI: 10.1007/s11747-020-00749-9

IBM HR Analytics Employee Attrition Dataset. Kaggle. https://www.kaggle.com/datasets/pavansubhasht/ibm-hr-analytics-attrition-dataset

Ismail, H., Iqbal, A., & Nasr, L. (2019). Employee engagement and job performance in Lebanon: The mediating role of creativity. *International Journal of Productivity and Performance Management*, *68*(3), 506–523. DOI: 10.1108/IJPPM-02-2018-0052

Jain, P., Jain, M., & Pamula, R. (2020). Explaining and predicting employees' attrition: A machine learning approach. *SN Applied Sciences*, *2*(4), 757. Advance online publication. DOI: 10.1007/s42452-020-2519-4

Jamaludin, N. (2024). Enhancing employee retention: the impact of training, career development and remuneration benefits in selected manufacturing companies of Johor Bahru. Information Management and Business Review, 16(3S(I)a), 669-679.

Johnson, M., Jain, R., Brennan-Tonetta, P., Swartz, E., Silver, D., Paolini, J., Mamonov, S., & Hill, C. (2021). Impact of big data and artificial intelligence on industry: Developing a workforce roadmap for a data driven economy. *Global Journal of Flexible Systems Managment*, *22*(3), 197–217. DOI: 10.1007/s40171-021-00272-y

. Kainyu "Review of Literature on Recommender Models for Career Pathway Selection in Competency-Based Education" African Journal of Science Technology and Social Sciences (2024) DOI: 10.58506/ajstss.v2i2.200

Karoly, A., Fuller, R., & Galambos, P. (2018). Unsupervised clustering for deep learning: A tutorial survey. *Acta Polytechnica Hungarica*, *15*(8), 29–53. DOI: 10.12700/APH.15.8.2018.8.2

Kess-Momoh, A. J., Tula, S. T., Bello, B. G., Omotoye, G. B., & Daraojimba, A. I. (2024). Strategic human resource management in the 21st century: A review of trends and innovations. *World Journal of Advanced Research and Reviews*, *21*(1), 746–757.

. Khan, P. (2024). Explore how organizations can utilize marketing techniques to enhance employee engagement. jier, 4(2). DOI: 10.52783/jier.v4i2.801

Lee, J., & Song, J. H. (2024). Lee "How does algorithm-based HR predict employees' sentiment? Developing an employee experience model through sentiment analysis". *Industrial and Commercial Training*, *56*(4), 273–289. Advance online publication. DOI: 10.1108/ICT-08-2023-0060

Lee, S., & Ha-Brookshire, J. (2017). Ethical climate and job attitude in fashion retail employees' turnover intention, and perceived organizational sustainability performance: A cross-sectional study. *Sustainability (Basel)*, *9*(3), 465. DOI: 10.3390/su9030465

Li, W. (2023). A transformer-based deep learning framework to predict employee attrition. *PeerJ. Computer Science*, *9*, e1570. DOI: 10.7717/peerj-cs.1570 PMID: 37810348

Lim, C. S., Malik, E. F., Khaw, K. W., Alnoor, A., Chew, X., Chong, Z. L., & Al Akasheh, M.LIM. (2023). Hybrid ga–deep autoencoder–knn model for employee turnover prediction. *Statistics, Optimization & Information Computing*, *12*(1), 75–90. DOI: 10.19139/soic-2310-5070-1799

Lin, S., Lu, W., Chen, Y., & Wu, M. (2022). The relationships among proactive personality, work engagement, and perceived work competence in sports coaches: The moderating role of perceived supervisor support. *International Journal of Environmental Research and Public Health*, *19*(19), 12707. DOI: 10.3390/ijerph191912707 PMID: 36232008

Linardatos, P., Papastefanopoulos, V., & Kotsiantis, S. (2020). Explainable ai: A review of machine learning interpretability methods. *Entropy (Basel, Switzerland)*, *23*(1), 18. DOI: 10.3390/e23010018 PMID: 33375658

. Maheswari "Role of IOT and Blockchain Technology in the growth of digital HRM transformation as a function of Management" (2024) DOI: 10.52783/jier.v4i2.780

Malik, A., Budhwar, P., Mohan, H., & Srikanth, N. (2022). Employee experience –the missing link for engaging employees: Insights from an MN E's ai-based hr ecosystem. *Human Resource Management*, *62*(1), 97–115. DOI: 10.1002/hrm.22133

Mehrabi, N., Morstatter, F., Saxena, N., Lerman, K., & Galstyan, A. (2021). A survey on bias and fairness in machine learning. *ACM Computing Surveys*, *54*(6), 1–35. DOI: 10.1145/3457607

Melhem, R., & Özgit, H. (2019). The mediating role of employee motivation on internal marketing and employee retention. *Ottoman Journal of Tourism and Management Research*, *4*(3), 562–583. DOI: 10.26465/ojtmr.2018339528

. Mhmood "The Impact of Effective Coaching on Sales Performance Mediated by the Role of Soft Skills in the Tourism Industry" Journal of Eco humanism (2024) DOI: 10.62754/joe.v3i7.4703

Narayanan, S., Swaminathan, J., & Talluri, S. (2014). Knowledge diversity, turnover, and organizational-unit productivity: An empirical analysis in a knowledge-intensive context. *Production and Operations Management*, *23*(8), 1332–1351. DOI: 10.1111/poms.12039

Nguyen, T. M., & Malik, A. (2022). A two-wave cross-lagged study on AI service quality: The moderating effects of the job level and job role. *British Journal of Management*, *33*(3), 1221–1237.

Nocker, M., & Sena, V. (2019). Big data and human resources management: The rise of talent analytics. *Social Sciences (Basel, Switzerland)*, *8*(10), 273. DOI: 10.3390/socsci8100273

. Nurlia, N. (2023). AI implementation impact on workforce productivity: the role of AI training and organizational adaptation. Escalate, 1(01), 01-13. DOI: 10.61536/escalate.v1i01.6

Popo–Olaniyan, O., Elufioye, O. A., Okonkwo, F. C., Udeh, C. A., Eleogu, T. F., & Olatoye, F. O. (2022). Ai-driven talent analytics for strategic hr decision-making in the United States Of America: A Review. *International Journal of Management & Entrepreneurship Research*, *4*(12), 607–622.

Orujaliyev, R. (2024). The effect of non-financial incentives on employee engagement and employee retention. European Journal of Humanities and Social Sciences, 3-10. DOI: 10.29013/EJHSS-24-2-3-10

Papademetriou, C., Anastasiadou, S., & Konteos, G. (2022). The Effect of Human Resource Management Practices on the Quality of Service, Customer Satisfaction, and Organizational Performance in Cypriot Urban Hotel Industry. *HAICTA 2022 Conference Proceedings*.

Peláez, . (2019). Facilitating Work Engagement and Performance Through Strengths-Based Micro-coaching: A Controlled Trial Study. *Journal of Happiness Studies*. Advance online publication. DOI: 10.1007/s10902-019-00127-5

. Prasetyo, A. and Furqon, M. (2023). The influence of talent management and organizational culture on employee discipline at pt. x., 328-338. DOI: 10.2991/978-2-38476-032-9_34

Pratibha, E. (2023). Employee attrition prediction based on grey wolf optimization and deep neural networks. *International Journal on Recent and Innovation Trends in Computing and Communication*, *11*(10), 1338–1345. DOI: 10.17762/ijritcc.v11i10.8676

Qamhieh, , Sammaneh, H., & Demaidi, M. N. (2020). PCRS: Personalized Career-Path Recommender System for Engineering Students. *IEEE Access : Practical Innovations, Open Solutions*, *8*, 214039–214049. Advance online publication. DOI: 10.1109/ACCESS.2020.3040338

Rahevar, M., & Darji, S. (2024). The adoption of AI-driven Chatbots into a recommendation for e-commerce systems to targeted customer in the selection of product. International Journal of Management. *Economics and Commerce*, *1*(2), 128–137.

Raji, I. D., Binns, R., Veale, M., Van Kleek, M., & Shadbolt, N. (2020). Closing the AI accountability gap: Defining an auditing framework for AI systems. *Proceedings of the 2020 Conference on Fairness, Accountability, and Transparency*, 33–44. https://doi.org/DOI: 10.1145/3351095.3372873

Raji, M. (2024). E-commerce and consumer behaviour: a review of AI-powered personalization and market trends. GSC Advanced Research and Reviews, 18(3), 066-077. DOI: 10.30574/gscarr.2024.18.3.0090

Raza, M., Khayal, M., & Bukhari, M. (2022). Predicting employee attrition using decision trees: A case study in a telecom sector. *International Journal of Advanced Computer Science and Applications*, *13*(9), 278–285. DOI: 10.14569/IJACSA.2022.0130934

Reina, C., Rogers, K., Peterson, S., Byron, K., & Hom, P. (2017). Quitting the boss? the role of manager influence tactics and employee emotional engagement in voluntary turnover. *Journal of Leadership & Organizational Studies*, *25*(1), 5–18. DOI: 10.1177/1548051817709007

Roumpi, D. (2021). Rethinking the strategic management of human resources: Lessons learned from COVID-19 and the way forward in building resilience. *The International Journal of Organizational Analysis*, *31*(1), 215–231. DOI: 10.1108/IJOA-09-2021-2974

Rožman, M., & Tominc, P. (2024). Navigating Gender Nuances: Assessing the Impact of AI on Employee Engagement in Slovenian Entrepreneurship. *Systems*, *12*(5), 145. DOI: 10.3390/systems12050145

Rubel, M., Kee, D., & Rimi, N. (2017). The mediating role of work–family conflict on role stressors and employee turnover intention relationship in labour-oriented organizations. *Global Business Review*, *18*(6), 1384–1399. DOI: 10.1177/0972150917713061

Sadeli, J. (2012). The influence of leadership, talent management, organizational culture and organizational support on employee engagement. *International Research Journal of Business Studies*, *5*(3), 30–50. DOI: 10.21632/irjbs.5.3.30-50

Sardi, A., Sorano, E., Cantino, V., & Garengo, P. (2020). Big data and performance measurement research: Trends, evolution and future opportunities. *Measuring Business Excellence*, *27*(4), 531–548. DOI: 10.1108/MBE-06-2019-0053

Semenova, Y., Glushkova, N., Pivina, L., Khismetova, Z., Zhunussov, Y., Sandybaev, M., & Ivankov, A. (2020). Epidemiological characteristics and forecast of COVID-19 outbreak in the republic of Kazakhstan. *Journal of Korean Medical Science, 35*(24), e227. Advance online publication. DOI: 10.3346/jkms.2020.35.e227 PMID: 32567261

Sergio, R. P., & Rylova, M. (2018). Employee engagement and empowerment as gateway towards retention: The case of Volkswagen group. *Journal of Eastern European and Central Asian Research, 5*(2).

Shajani, Z., Laing, C., Robinson, F., Yun, L., Patterson, J., & Rieder, L. (2023). The creation of a novel undergraduate nursing employee/student hybrid role in the COVID-19 response. *Nursing Administration Quarterly, 47*(1), 72–83. DOI: 10.1097/NAQ.0000000000000564 PMID: 36469375

Singh, P. (2023). Digital transformation in supply chain management: Artificial intelligence (ai) and machine learning (ml) as catalysts for value creation. *International Journal of Supply Chain Management, 12*(6), 57–63. DOI: 10.59160/ijscm.v12i6.6216

Sivathanu, B., & Pillai, R. (2019). Technology and talent analytics for talent management – a game changer for organizational performance. *The International Journal of Organizational Analysis, 28*(2), 457–473. DOI: 10.1108/IJOA-01-2019-1634

Song, H., Jiang, Y., & Wang, Y. (2022). Smart HR practices for employee well-being: A talent analytics perspective. *Technological Forecasting and Social Change, 178*, 121614. DOI: 10.1016/j.techfore.2022.121614

Sumardi, D., Suryani, N., & Musadad, A. A. (2021). Website-based learning management system (LMS) as a tool for learning in the covid-19 pandemic period for Junior High Schools. *Journal of Education Technology, 5*(3), 346–355. DOI: 10.23887/jet.v5i3.38371

Tabasum, S., & Shaikh, A. R. (2022). Impact of employee engagement on employee performance with mediating effect of employee retention. *International Journal of Social Science & Entrepreneurship, 2*(2), 1–20.

Tambe, P., Cappelli, P., & Yakubovich, V. (2019). Artificial intelligence in human resources management: Challenges and a path forward. *California Management Review, 61*(4), 15–42. DOI: 10.1177/0008125619867910

Tambe, P., Cappelli, P., & Yakubovich, V. (2019). Artificial intelligence in human resources management: Challenges and a path forward. *California Management Review, 61*(4), 15–42. DOI: 10.1177/0008125619867910

Tetteh, J., & Asumeng, M. (2022). Succession planning, employee retention and career development programmes in selected organisations in Ghana. *African Journal of Management Research, 27*(1), 151–169. DOI: 10.4314/ajmr.v27i1.9

Tracey, J., & Hinkin, T. (2008). Contextual factors and cost profiles associated with employee turnover. *Cornell Hospitality Quarterly, 49*(1), 12–27. DOI: 10.1177/0010880407310191

Tsahat, Y., Nikou, S., & Bouwman, H. (2024). AI-enabled inclusive workplaces: Tailoring work experiences through hyper-personalization. *Journal of Business Research, 170*, 114206. DOI: 10.1016/j.jbusres.2024.114206

Utrilla, . (2015). *The effects of coaching in employees and organizational performance: The Spanish Case.* Intangible Capital., DOI: 10.3926/ic.586

Voigt, P., & Von dem Bussche, A. (2017). *The EU General Data Protection Regulation (GDPR).* Springer., DOI: 10.1007/978-3-319-57959-7

. Wang, Y. (2023). Research on Chinese tech talents demands prediction based on grey-bp neural network combination model., 743-752. DOI: 10.2991/978-2-38476-126-5_84

Weller, A. (2019). Transparency: Motivations and challenges. In *Explainable AI: Interpreting, Explaining and Visualizing Deep Learning* (pp. 23–40). Springer. https://doi.org/DOI: 10.1007/978-3-030-28954-6_2

Wirz, C., Demuth, J. L., Cains, M. G., White, M., Radford, J., & Bostrom, A. (2024). National Weather Service (NWS) forecasters' perceptions of ai/ml and its use in operational forecasting. *Bulletin of the American Meteorological Society, 105*(11), E2194–E2215. DOI: 10.1175/BAMS-D-24-0044.1

Xue, X., Sun, X., Wang, H., Zhang, H., & Feng, J. (2022). Neural network fusion with fine-grained adaptation learning for turnover prediction. *Complex & Intelligent Systems*. Advance online publication. DOI: 10.1007/s40747-022-00931-2

Yahia, N., Hlel, J., & Colomo-Palacios, R. (2021). From big data to deep data to support people analytics for employee attrition prediction. *IEEE Access : Practical Innovations, Open Solutions, 9*, 60447–60458. DOI: 10.1109/ACCESS.2021.3074559

Yusliza, M., Faezah, J., Ali, N., Noor, N., Ramayah, T., Tanveer, M., & Fawehinmi, O. (2020). Effects of supportive work environment on employee retention: The mediating role of person–organisation fit. *Industrial and Commercial Training, 53*(3), 201–216. DOI: 10.1108/ICT-12-2019-0111

Zhu, Y., Obeng, A., & Azinga, S. (2023). Supportive supervisor behaviour and helping behaviours in the hotel sector: Assessing the mediating effect of employee engagement and moderating influence of perceived organizational obstruction. *Current Psychology (New Brunswick, N.J.)*, *43*(1), 757–773. DOI: 10.1007/s12144-023-04326-5 PMID: 36819753

Chapter 18
Bridging Business Intelligence, Knowledge Management, and Strategic HRM:
Navigating Talent in Modern Workplaces

Gulshan Bibi
https://orcid.org/0000-0002-4019-8440
O.P. Jindal Global University, India

ABSTRACT

This paper critically examines the evolving trends in the modern workplace that are nudging organizations to adopt a talent-centric approach. We argue that conventional Human Resource (HR) practices are generic and implemented across the board and that organizations need to turn to more context-specific, conscious of external factors, and continuously evolving and adaptable HR practices. This paper helps to recast how organizations can realize and derive value from talent. It integrates three diverse and fragmented streams of research in management, i.e., strategic human resource management (SHRM), business intelligence (BI), and knowledge management (KM). Focusing on mechanisms in how organizations, and specifically HR, can incorporate BI and KM in decision-making and develop actionable, talent-related strategies. In doing so, the integrative conceptual framework identifies eight steps that facilitate organizations in realizing their talent-centric approach. Our review provides a solid basis for integrating and creating linkages to the ongoing talent management conversation.

DOI: 10.4018/979-8-3373-1942-1.ch018

1. INTRODUCTION

An enduring question in the organization and management theory concerns the extent to which evolving work and technology impact organizational knowledge and its performance. In theory, any change in the nature of work, be it from technology, innovation, or socio-economic advancements (Bush & Balven, 2018; Dutton et al., 2001; Stone et al., 2015), disrupt organizations' operations, risks misaligned capabilities and knowledge, and reactionary decision-making (Adler, 1992; Orlikowski, 2008). Organizations can no longer afford to let these changes happen and transform over time, and they need to be proactive and adapt instantaneously. Further, they not only need to keep up with the changes but also reconfigure their knowledge and technology capabilities (Davenport & Prusak, 1998; Dery et al., 2017; Faraj et al., 2018; Kingma, 2018). These factors suggest that efficiency and decision-making are key to sustaining competitive advantage from human capital in modern workplaces (Delery & Roumpi, 2017).

Further, employees are the core building blocks of organizational knowledge (Choong, 2008; Nyberg et al., 2014; Sveiby, 2001), and organizations are knowledge-creating and integrating institutions; organizational performance depends upon the ability to manage employees and constantly adapt to the changing demands (Kim & Ko, 2014; Lado & Zhang, 1998; Nonaka & Toyama, 2005; Schiuma, 2012). Therefore, for organizations, it is not just about responding to external changes by adapting to technology and transformation, but internally, they need to keep tab on the evolving talent demands to fill the knowledge gap (López-Nicolás & Mero˜no-Cerdán, 2011; Nickerson & Zenger, 2004; Singh, 2005), anticipate the knowledge loss (Cattani et al., 2013; Daghfous et al., 2013; Levallet & Chan, 2019; Lin, 2007) and efficiently recuperate organizational knowledge.

Despite this understanding, the challenge when managing talent hinges on understanding the complexity of organizational knowledge, alignment of HR practices with organizational strategic vision, accuracy in capturing data and insights, and leadership decision-making. While there are studies that have explored the data-driven approach to human resource practices such as hiring, compensation, employee engagement, and turnover (Cheng & Hackett, 2021), the approach has been conservative on accounts of the value of analysis-driven software for decision-making, lack of evidence for the strategic value, and lack of strong bases could potentially result in spurious frameworks (Marler & Boudreau, 2017; Rasmussen & Ulrich, 2015). Additionally, the skepticism is to the point of considering data-driven models as a management fad (Angrave et al., 2016; Cheng & Hackett, 2019). On top of that, knowledge is elusive (Bibi, 2024; Bibi et al., 2021), work is distributed (Gardner, 2012; Gibson & Gibbs, 2006; Gibson & Zellmer-Bruhn, 2001; Hinds & Kiesler, 2002; Klein et al. 2006) and technology is disruptive (Adler, 1992; Ford,

2015; Leonardi & Barley, 2010; Orlikowski & Barley, 2001; Pentland & Feldman, 2007; Zammuto et al., 2007), we need a systemic approach that accounts for these variabilities and offer a holistic perspective.

Scholars have been attempting to understand ways in which HR practices can use, interpret, and apply insights from knowledge management (KM) and business intelligence (BI) (Davenport, 2006; Orlikowski & Barley, 2001; Gardner, 2012). However, the challenge while exploring these concepts is also to make sure these processes and tools are more "human" in nature and do not necessarily challenge the ethical framework of HR practices (Cheng & Hackett, 2019). We argue that we need to adapt algorithm or data analytics tools and techniques in alignment with the organization's strategic vision and integrate them with HR practices and organizational knowledge. It is not a matter of ethical consideration. However, it is to understand better the organization, its requirements, and the context within which it is moving it is currently working and move forward where these tools will help managers devise strategies that will inform such insights to keep up with the organizational knowledge and capabilities.

Furthermore, this paper underscores the knowledge-based view (KBV), emphasizing that organizations are inherently knowledge-creating entities (Grant, 1996) and that BI tools and systems are essential for driving value from talent and achieving long-term competitive advantage. The overarching objective is integrating KM and BI to guide HR decision-making and develop actionable, talent-centric strategies. In doing so, the paper recasts how organizations can realize and derive value from talent. Lastly, the eight steps of the integrative conceptual framework facilitate organizations to realize their talent-centric approach. Before delving into the framework, the paper delves into a brief review of the relevant literature, followed by the extant challenges in the existing conceptualization. We then explicate the framework, followed by a conclusion.

2. LITERATURE REVIEW

We argue that building an intelligent system for talent management necessitates integrating business intelligence (BI) and knowledge management (KM), that is, to understand the knowledge and skill requirements and create a system backed by business intelligence: data gathering, processing, and informing actionable insight. By leveraging BI tools and techniques, organizations can enhance three critical aspects of organizational knowledge: people knowledge, structural knowledge, and group knowledge. These dimensions help in understanding, building, and refining HR practices.

Further, from theoretical perspective we adopt knowledge-based view as foundation. Further, the knowledge-based view of the firm theory is a firm-level theory which categorizes a firm as the mix of heterogeneous knowledge assets to give it a competitive advantage (Denford, 2013; Grant, 1996). However, it demands two things. First, knowledge of the firm must be valuable, non-imitable, and rare (Curado & Bontis, 2006; Merat & Bo, 2013). Second, there should be the processes of knowledge creation, knowledge transfer, and knowledge application (Alguezaui & Filieri, 2014; Erden, Klang, Sydler, & von Krogh, 2014; Grant, 1996; Shujahat et al., 2017).

In this section, we will review the literature on BI and KM and their impact on HR practices to provide a conceptual base to demonstrate how organizations, specifically HR, can incorporate BI and KM in decision-making and develop actionable, talent-related strategies. In doing so, we first need to understand the current conceptualization.

2.1. Business Intelligence (BI)

Business intelligence (BI) as a concept has evolved, not only in terms of the scope but also in terms of its impact on the organization. Initially, any tools or techniques that help organizations collect, access, and analyze information for informed and actionable insights came under the preview of the BI (Alhmoud and Al-Kasasbeh, 2024; Rajnoha et al., 2016; Sousa and Dias, 2020). As information technology has progressed, so has the advancement in capturing the data and analyzing and gathering insights, from traditional IT tools to big data and predictive analytics to AI-enabled software and models. Now, these systems are more sophisticated and interactive, including analytical processing, multi-source data collection, and analysis in real-time and interactive dashboards (Ain et al., 2019; Bhatt & Grover, 2005). Consequently, these systems are not only necessary, but they serve as the organization's nervous system if integrated well.

Further, to understand the impact BI has on the organization. It is critical to understand how it works for the organization, leading to efficient and accurate decision-making and adaptation at strategic, tactical, and operational levels (Abusweilem & Abualoush, 2019). Therefore, BI is not a tool; it is a system that cannot only collect data from various sources but also make sense of it and provide advanced technologies that are more robust and more accurate in inferring from the data by analyzing the data by exploring the relationships, this helps in bringing not just to customer the value, but also the organization and employees as well.

2.1.1 Artificial Intelligence (AI) Enabled BI

Over the years, there has been speculation about the use and legitimacy of Artificial intelligence (AI). Furthermore, it is increasingly significant in enhancing business operations through division-making and insights (Chen et al., 2022). AI can examine the historical, real-time, and predictive investigation reports for BI to understand business performance better (Alshadoodee et al., 2022). Another important aspect is that AI facilitates BI by automating the decision-making process within the BI, which leads to quicker decision-making and improved coordination within the organization. Data automation is crucial for BI, especially with the worst amount of data generated, collected, and analyzed (Alhmoud and Al-Kasasbeh, 2024; Srivastava et al., 2021).

Nevertheless, another aspect through which AI can facilitate and enhance functionality is through data clarity and explanation (Srivastava et al., 2021; Widjaja et al., 2025). For instance, AI-driven BI systems can improve direct clarity, helping users and managers gain clarity or clear insight into their areas of expertise. At the same time, explaining AI in the final analysis result is still a challenge. AI applications in the form of smart assistance provide new interactive experiences within BI (Chen et al., 2022).

More broadly, AI is seen as a core component of intelligent systems and to be competitive or to bring competitive intelligence for the organization for the project of the team that the organization is trying to work around, which is important. AI plays a critical role in decision support systems, data, mining, descriptive, magnetic, protective analytics, and big data, so in a way yeah, you can work as a government framework within an organization, extending the E software applications and specialized hardware to learn and make rational decisions (Alshadoodee et al., 2022). When done right, AI-enabled BI systems can bring competitive intelligence, contribute to organizational innovation and technological advancement (Maluleka and Chummun, 2023), and enhance C-suit decision-making (Kondapaka et al., 2023).

2.2. Knowledge Management

KM literature has dealt with two facets of talent management: individual knowledge and group/collective knowledge. First, KM practices distinguish an organization from others as a mechanism of creating and transferring individual and group knowledge (Grant, 1996). Organizational knowledge primarily emphasizes tacit and explicit Knowledge dynamics (Nonaka, 1994). Second, organizational knowledge is socially constructed. Third, organizational knowledge is distinctive to an organization, so it is important to understand the knowledge gap specific to the organization.

Further, various knowledge management processes ensure that the organization's knowledge flows. Such as knowledge creation is a process in which new knowledge is continuously created through the four sub-processes of organizational knowledge creation theory (Andreeva & Kianto, 2011; Collins & Smith, 2006; Nonaka & Takeuchi, 1995). The four processes are socialization, combination, externalization, and internationalization (Collins & Smith, 2006; Lai et al., 2014; Nonaka & Takeuchi, 1995). The antecedents of these processes are opportunity, motivation, capability, and greater perceived importance. Organizations must work on these antecedents to ensure knowledge creation (Andreeva & Kianto, 2011; Shu et al., 2012).

Another significant knowledge process is knowledge sharing. It is the collection of knowledge among the different knowledge units in a firm (Becerra-Fernandez, Gonzalez, & Sabherwal, 2004; Nonaka, 1994). It is the behavior of workers to transfer their insights (Hooff & De Ridder, 2004). It can be categorized into formal vs. informal and donation vs. collection elements of knowledge (Hooff & De Ridder, 2004; Taminiau, Smit, & Lange, 2009). Knowledge sharing is more significant than knowledge generation as the knowledge bulks reside in an employee and are of no importance until those are shared and applied (Al-Husseini & Elbeltagi, 2015). Its antecedents include intrinsic and extrinsic incentives, social and organizational norms, values, and top leadership support (Hsu, Ju, Yen, & Chang, 2007).

Nevertheless, another process is knowledge utilization. Lee, Leong, Hew, and Ooi (2013) state that knowledge utilization is also called knowledge implementation or knowledge application. It relates to responding to different types of knowledge an individual entity has within an organization (Gold, Malhotra, & Segras, 2001). Knowledge utilization is the application of knowledge that has been shared (Song, Bij, & Weggeman, 2005). It is newly created knowledge that becomes part of organizational behavior and processes for problem-solving through assimilation (Chen et al., 2012). It is more important than the other two processes because the knowledge created and shared is of no importance until it is applied (Chen & Huang, 2009).

2.3. HR Practices

When we emphasize modern workplaces, the challenge is that traditional HR systems may fall short of understanding and capturing the nuances. In contrast, the newer systems are more data-reliant and algorithm-based, which have negative connotations and require ethical considerations. To cope with that, we need to reconsider the HRM function broadly, but specifically, we need to assess what it means to have a talent-centric approach to HR practices that is pragmatic and values the "human" and "technology" side. This dichotomy has led to the 'New Ways of Working' (NWW), which includes practices like 'Activity Based Working', and 'Distributed Work' (Dery et al., 2017; Harrison et al., 2004; Kingma, 2018). These practices essentially re-assess the spatiotemporal, technological, and sociocultural aspects of modern workplaces and (re) shape the social spaces of work relations (Thrift, 2005). While we have accounted for the work and workplace changes as the technology progresses, we have yet to assess how they affect talent practices or organizations.

There are two considerations: the organization's strategic vision regarding talent and the immediate talent-related changes that are required regarding the existing employee's knowledge, skills, and ability (KSA) and potential KSA of talent. In any case, such transformation requires an amalgamation of HR practices, BI (Meena & Santhanalakshmi, 2024), and KM (Davenport, 2006; Grant, 1996).

Now, how does business intelligence relate to or support HRM? First, it relates to various HR functions regarding information acquisition, analysis, and utilization (Lönnqvist & Pirttimäki, 2006). It can create value by adopting tools and systems that facilitate HR decision-making- decision support value from talent-related decision-making (Fink et al., 2017).

BI combined business processes, expert knowledge, technologies, and applications to improve str. It helps gather information, transform structuring data analysis, reporting, and visualization, and, more importantly, helps strategize and align HR goals with those of the organization.

How does business intelligence stand with HR, and how does it play a crucial role in leveraging organizational knowledge or strategic advantage? First of all, knowledge management is a key to helping transform data. It can be structural data structure knowledge, group knowledge, or individual knowledge, and it can use that information and knowledge to drive better decision-making. Now, BI or business intelligence can play a vital role by turning the data that knowledge management already has or organization knowledge into actionable insights. Not only can it help in analyzing and interpreting the sharing of that knowledge to make more informed decisions to understand where organizations need to emphasize and based on the takes and other tools, but it can also help organizations to have a strong foundation and to understand the market the organizational strategy and the overall growth trajectory or the development that organizations want to accomplish.

Simply put, when an organization has BI systems in place, they can facilitate capturing and storing explicit knowledge and have the potential to share tacit knowledge through digital technologies—for instance, AI-enabled knowledge-sharing social exchange between employees (Malik et al., 2023). Conceptually, there is a case to be made, but it is challenging to realize these integrations, let alone derive value.

It is not just about the technology capabilities but their use that organizations need to manage (Orlikowski, 1999). Cheng and Hackett (2019) argued that human resource management and specifically human resource management practices were not very enthusiastic about technology and technology, specifically the analytics aspect of it. However, over the years, there has been a surge in interest related to better understanding the human needs and talent strategies that align with the businesses and the market dynamics (Davenport, 2014; Martin et al., 2014). We will explicate the current challenges in the next section to explore the nuanced complexities of integration between BI, KM, and HRM.

3. CHALLENGES

The challenge when managing talent hinges on understanding the complexity of organizational knowledge, aligning HR practices with organizational strategic vision, the accuracy of data and insights, and leadership decision-making. While there are studies that have taken a number of driven approaches to human resource practices and outcomes—hiring compensation, employee engagement, and turnover (Cheng & Hackett, 2021), the approach is conservative because of the lack of or the question about the value of analysis driven software for decision making, lack of evidence for the strategic value of these tools and more importantly the lack of strong bases could potentially result in spurious models that add little to no value to HR practices (Marler & Boudreau, 2017; Rasmussen & Ulrich, 2015). As discussed in the previous section, scholars are skeptical about using these data-driven models in HR practices as a management fad (Angrave et al., 2016; Cheng & Hackett, 2019). Further, we are yet to understand how they can inform specific HR practices, from recruitment to turnover.

On top of that knowledge is elusive (Bibi, 2024; Bibi et al., 2021), work is distributed (Gardner, 2012; Gibson & Gibbs, 2006; Gibson & Zellmer-Bruhn, 2001; Hinds & Kiesler, 2002; Klein et al. 2006) and technology is disruptive (Adler, 1992; Ford, 2015; Leonardi & Barley, 2010; Orlikowski & Barley, 2001; Pentland & Feldman, 2007; Zammuto et al., 2007), we need a systemic approach that accounts for these variabilities and offer a holistic perspective.

Furthermore, when it comes to adopting BI tools, techniques, or systems, there are concerns, for instance, the nature of that adaptation and how it amalgamates to the core HR practices and informs strategic decisions (Meena & Santhanalakshmi, 2024). Second, what is the exact phenomenon in focus (Lönnqvist, A., & Pirttimäki, V. (2006). For instance, it could be used in creating modules of talent development, insights derived from recruitment and turnover data, or an all-encompassing system.

Third, the return on investment on BI (Fink et al., 2017). For instance, the value businesses derive from the BI must be realized be it in terms of impact on data storage in the warehouse, tasks, practices, decision making, and overall organizational performance (Davenport, 2006; Elbashir et al., 2008; Lee et al., 2004; Melville et al., 2004; Watson & Wixom, 2007). To realize the value, it is important to build synergy between the BI tools in use and core practices (Melville et al., 2004; Nevo & Wade, 2010; Schryen, 2013).

Fourth, for deriving value from BI, it is important to realize the specific tools and ways for organizations to better understand competitive advantage through integrative BI, KM, and HR practices (Ain et al., 2019; Bhatt & Grover, 2005). Furthermore, the empirical research on BI has varying impacts on different management functions. For instance, data quality informs the overall decision-making efficiency (Al-Okaily et al., 2022) and digital strategy to incorporate (Zhang et al., 2023).

4. PROPOSED INTEGRATIVE FRAMEWORK OF TALENT-CENTRIC APPROACH

We identify eight stages: 1) strategic foundation; 2) knowledge gap identification and talent acquisition; 3) talent development and knowledge creation; 4) employee engagement and knowledge sharing and retention; 5) performance assessment and agility; 6) technology and knowledge integration; 7) ethical considerations and data privacy; and 8) continuous improvement and feedback loop. The framework is cyclical, meaning that each process informs another process. For example, this strategic foundation guides all the HR initiatives and ensures that the HR practices are In Sync with the organizational vision. Talent identification and development ensure that knowledge and skill requirements are met and that the workforce is both capable and prepared for the evolving requirements of the business.

The framework starts with strategic foundation, the idea is that before deciding on the role and integration of BI in the talent management practices and KM processes, it is important to understand where does organization stand in terms of BI and what are their use cases and as a result of it then they need to decide on how it will impact one of that function which is talent or people management. Additionally, talent management is built on the foundation of strategic Human Resource Management and is described as a strategic Human Resource (HR) framework (Christensen Hughes & Rog, 2008; Thunnissen et al., 2013). Acquiring, developing, and retaining talents has become a competitive strategy for many HR departments (Sibragec & Elagec, 2015). Therefore, in this stage we align talent management with the strategic business goals of the organization is identified as a critical internal success factor.

In doing so we emphasize on assessing the knowledge requirement derived from strategic alignment involving the organization, people, and knowledge (El-Farr & Hosseingholizadeh, 2019; Wright et al., 2001). The idea is to understand how various aspects at the organization level relate and then how does those aspects inform talent related practices. Once the alignment of business strategy with the HR Strategy is achieved through proper assessment of organizational knowledge (Bibi, 2024), the next step in the foundation stage is for HRM to spread the various components of the strategic plan to all employees and provide information on the strategic readiness of human capital, assessing whether available human resources have the required knowledge, skills, and motivation to support and implement an organization's strategy (Lajšić, 2019).

Figure 1. Integrative framework of talent-centric approach

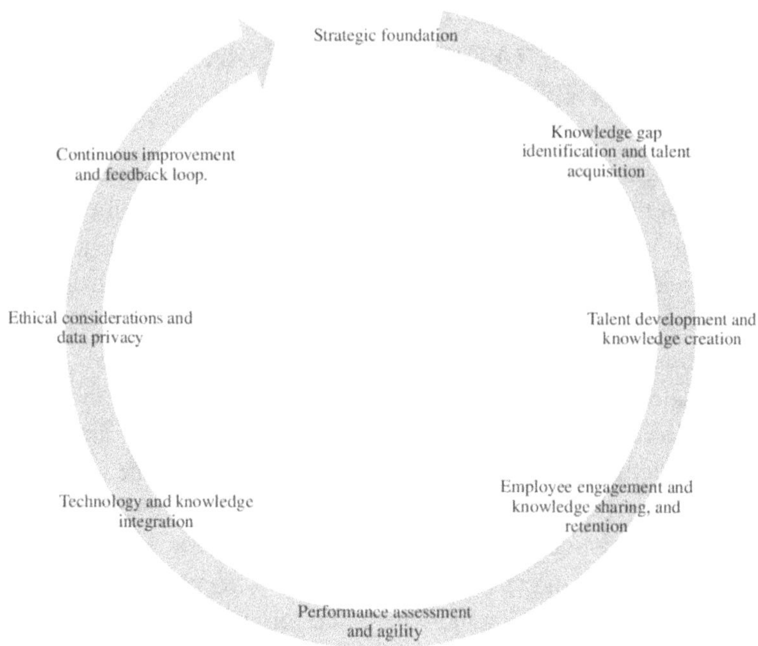

Stage 1: Strategic Foundation

SHRM is not only fundamental to building TM strategies—acquiring, developing, and retaining talent—but also to adapting TM strategies with the business strategies goals (Thunnissen et al., 2013; Hughes & Rog, 2008; Morton, 2004;

Sibragec & Elagec, 2015). Talent management is built on the foundations of a strategic HRM framework (Christensen Hughes & Rog, 2008; Thunnissen et al., 2013; Whelan & Carcary, 2011). Acquiring, developing, and retaining talents has become a competitive strategy for many HR departments (Sibragec & Elagec, 2015), and aligning talent management with the strategic business goals of the organization is identified as a critical internal success factor (Christensen Hughes & Rog, 2008). For instance, having an organization's own internal definition of "talent" is critical for effective management and developing a sustainable competitive advantage over time, as strategies and models should focus on these internal definitions (Sibragec & Elagec, 2015).

Furthermore, aligning HRM with KM is crucial for better organizational performance and competitive business advantage (El-Farr & Hosseingholizadeh, 2019). The effectiveness of KM often depends on HRM processes and the quality of management's strategic alignment involving the organization, people, and knowledge.

BI pulls information from various systems to support decision-making (Negash et al., 2004) and is described as a natural outgrowth of previous systems designed to support decision-making, evolving from Executive Information Systems (EIS) and DSS concepts (Turban et al., 2010; Negash et al., 2004). A key understanding from the sources is that successful BI system implementation has a much greater likelihood of success when specific business needs are identified at the outset (Yeoh & Koronios, 2010; Yeoh & Popovic, 2016), and non-technical factors, including organizational and process-related factors, are considered more influential for success than technological and data-related factors (Yeoh & Koronios, 2010). Placing organizational needs ahead of other issues increases the likelihood of achieving a functional BI system (Yeoh & Popovic, 2016).

SHRM aims to enable an organization to achieve its goals (Al-kasasbeh, 2024). It is concerned with the linkage of HR to firm performance, viewing employees as a strategic resource for competitive and organizational success (Al-kasasbeh, 2024). No managerial area is considered more significant than HR in ensuring long-term organizational viability and performance, especially in the current era of rapid change and IT advances (Al-kasasbeh, 2024). Managing information and knowledge is one of the main strategic uses of information technology and provides an excellent basis for development and overall socio-economic progress (Lajšić, 2019).

Stage 2: Knowledge Gap Identification and Talent Acquisition

Knowledge gap identification and talent acquisition HRM practices such as recruitment and selection are essential for managing knowledge properly, contributing instrumentally to improving the knowledge flow, including acquisition (El-Farr & Hosseingholizadeh, 2019; Turban et al., 2010). The core resourcing activities include recruitment and selection, defining requirements, and attracting candidates (Armstrong, 2002). Talent management strategy often begins with recruitment and selection, and organizations may use a talent management toolkit to identify potential high performers, such as competency maps (Armstrong, 2002; Garavan et al., 2012).

Further, Expert Systems (ES) and Knowledge Management Systems (KMS) are discussed in the context of leveraging expertise and organizational memory, and KM helps organizations identify important information and expertise residing in employees (Turban et al., 2010).

Talent management helps to identify existing talent gaps in different hierarchies (Sibragec & Elagec, 2015), and recruitment and staffing are key practices addressed in academic talent management literature (Thunnissen et al., 2013; Christensen Hughes & Rog, 2008), listed among the main stages of talent management practices and identified practices in construction companies (Sibragec & Elagec, 2015; Stahl et al., 2012). The search for talented people is regarded as this decade's most important managerial preoccupation (Thunnissen et al., 2013; Guthridge, Komm, & Lawson, 2008).

Improved employee recruitment rates are listed as a benefit of an effectively implemented talent management strategy (Christensen Hughes & Rog, 2008). Positioning the organization as an appealing employer (i.e., employer branding) is an important activity linked to talent management (Thunnissen et al., 2013; Christensen Hughes & Rog, 2008).

Achieving organizational goals depends on the organization's ability to learn and develop its intellectual capital, i.e., human resources (Lajšić, 2019). ERP systems, HRIS, and DSS in BI technology provide excellent support in HRM, offering proactive solutions and being of great help in recognizing talents, planning, recruiting, and selection (Lajšić, 2019).

Modern BI tools enable HR professionals to identify skill gaps and optimize workforce distribution, essential for sustainability objectives (Al-kasasbeh, 2024).

Stage 3: Talent Development and Knowledge Creation

Learning and development aim to ensure that people acquire and develop the knowledge, skills, and competencies they need (Armstrong, 2002; Thunnissen et al., 2013). Talent development is identified as an important component of talent management (Garavan et al., 2012). Knowledge-based training and development involve developing the depth and breadth of employees' knowledge and expertise, personalizing training, and ensuring continuous employee development to create and maintain organizational knowledge (El-Farr & Hosseingholizadeh, 2019; Souleh, 2014).

KM supports dynamic learning within an organization. The learning and growth perspective aims to identify the infrastructure that enables the organization to create long-term growth and improvement (Turban et al., 2010). Knowledge creation is related to the concept of the "knowledge-creating company" (Turban et al., 2010). Expert systems also need the capability to learn from successes, failures, and other knowledge sources to constantly update their knowledge (Turban et al., 2010). Workforce learning is noted as an outcome value of BI support (Talaoui & Kohtamäki, 2020). Information on the strategic readiness of human capital includes whether available human resources have the required knowledge, skills, and motivation (Lajšić, 2019).

BI significantly enhances HR practices by providing data-driven insights that improve training (Al-kasasbeh, 2024). HR must continually identify and alleviate talent gaps to ensure the business has the right people in the right places to carry out its strategy (Al-kasasbeh, 2024; Tavera Romero et al., 2021). Supporting a well-structured creative problem-solving process positively affects the quality of decisions and competitive performance (Lombardi, 2019).

Stage 4: Employee Engagement and Knowledge Sharing and Retention

Employee engagement and knowledge sharing and retention HRM practices that enhance individual learning, motivation, and retention of employees to boost knowledge acquisition and knowledge-sharing are found to improve organizational performance (El-Farr & Hosseingholizadeh, 2019; Turban et al., 2010). For instance, employees are at the core of knowledge sharing. Further, identifying, recruiting, managing, and retaining high performers or talented individuals is increasingly associated with general organizational success (El-Farr & Hosseingholizadeh, 2019).

For example, retention management is listed among the main stages of talent management practices (Sibragec & Elagec, 2015; Stahl et al., 2012; Thunnissen et al., 2013). Improved employee retention rates are listed as a benefit of an effectively implemented talent management strategy (Christensen Hughes & Rog, 2008). Recognition and performance are essential for staff retention, noting that this does not necessarily mean a higher pay range but rather fair and equitable treatment (Sibragec & Elagec, 2015, 2015; Tracey & Flinchbaugh, 2006). Talent development and leadership development practices are identified as potential drivers of intention to stay (Christensen Hughes & Rog, 2008; Chami-Malaeb & Garavan, 2013). Psychological empowerment, work engagement, and turnover intention are related to leader relations and role clarity (Christensen Hughes & Rog, 2008; de Villiers & Stander, 2011).

Furthermore, BI technology, ERP systems, and HRIS support HRM and greatly help reduce costs and retain talent (Lajšić, 2019). Information on the strategic readiness of human capital includes whether available human resources have the required knowledge, skills, and motivation; BI can support and sustain HR by providing insights into employee engagement and productivity, which is essential for developing effective and responsive HR policies (Al-kasasbeh, 2024).

Stage 5: Performance Assessment and Agility

Orlikowski (1999) discussed the performance paradox, wherein he discussed the impact of investing in information technology and does not necessarily have the expected performance outcome, thus questioning the investment in technology. The idea is that organizations do not just need investments in IT but the intention from the top down and need assessment from the bottom up. The criteria measured in performance management send a message about what is valued, thus influencing support for KM activities by measuring various competencies and is a strong indicator for assessing KM activities (El-Farr & Hosseingholizadeh, 2019). Also, agility, speed, and efficiency in decision-making and knowledge transfer are critical (Turban et al., 2010; Talaoui & Kohtamäki, 2020).

Performance management is a way to locate knowledge gaps (El-Farr & Hosseingholizadeh, 2019), identify development needs (skills and behaviors), and motivate people to use their abilities effectively (Armstrong, 2002). Formal talent review processes assess future development potential and aim to strategically align talent with critical organizational capabilities (Garavan et al., 2012). Additionally, dynamic capabilities encompass skill acquisition and learning to reconfigure their capabilities based on internal and external changes (Wright et al., 2001).

BI products and services appeared under the umbrella term by 2006, evolving from systems that offered visualization, alerts, and performance measurement capabilities (Turban et al., 2010). BI implementation success criteria include process performance (schedule, budgetary considerations) and infrastructure performance (system quality, information quality, system use). These success measures can be rated as good, acceptable, poor, successful, partially successful, or unsuccessful (Yeoh & Popovic, 2016). The impact of BI on decision-making speed is mentioned (Talaoui & Kohtamäki, 2020).

TM aims to achieve organization-related goals, including organizational performance. High individual performance is often linked to employee motivation and engagement (Thunnissen et al., 2013). An effective talent management strategy is associated with improved operational and financial performance. As levels of employee engagement increased in a longitudinal study, so too did financial performance indicators (Christensen Hughes & Rog, 2008; Hewitt & Associates, 2004).

Organizational flexibility is identified as one of three critical HR goals, reflecting the business agenda and needed to sustain profitability and economic survival (Thunnissen et al., 2013; Boxall & Purcell, 2011). Further, IT solutions (ERP systems, HRIS, BI systems) enable effective and efficient transactional data processing, automation of activities, generating various reports, and conducting analyses, which supports accurate, precise, and reliable decision-making (Al-kasasbeh, 2024). This will reflect on and influence the efficiency of employees (Al-kasasbeh, 2024).

Stage 6: Technology and Knowledge Integration

In this stage, the primary emphasis is on managing organizational knowledge and the role of technology in various knowledge processes. There are two sides to managing knowledge: codification and personalization (El-Farr & Hosseingholizadeh, 2019). The codification strategy aims to codify and store knowledge with a high dependency on IT for further reuse, and integrating knowledge within the organization is part of the overall knowledge flow (El-Farr & Hosseingholizadeh, 2019). For example, BI provides a knowledge repository (Wright et al., 2001), using organizational knowledge gaps to inform the training and development, and the recruitment process might utilize talent banks that record candidate details electronically (Armstrong, 2002). Additionally, IT is crucial in KM in collecting, retrieval, and communication, extending the depth and breadth of knowledge use and enhancing the speed of knowledge transfer, and with digital tools, sharing tacit knowledge is yet another **possibility** (Turban et al., 2010).

Furthermore, the technological foundation of BI includes data warehousing, ETL tools, OLAP servers, reporting servers, data mining, and text analytics engines (Sirin & Karacan, 2017; Turban et al., 2010). A typical BI architecture involves data flowing from various sources (operational databases, text documents, web pages) through movement and streaming engines, data warehouses (DWs), mid-tier servers (OLAP, report servers), and front-end applications (Sirin & Karacan, 2017). Data warehouses are key repositories for integrated data from multiple sources, enabling organizations to derive value from data assets (Sirin & Karacan, 2017; Yeoh & Popovic, 2016).

Talent management may imply a systems approach involving technology at the enterprise level (Christensen Hughes & Rog, 2008; Lewis & Heckman, 2006). It is a technology-enabled HRM approach (Christensen Hughes & Rog, 2008; Tansley & Newell, 2007). Integrated data management and information systems represent sophistication in talent management.

Stage 7: Ethical Considerations and Data Privacy

Scholars have been attempting to understand ways in which HR practices can use, interpret, and apply insights from knowledge management (KM) and business intelligence (BI) (Davenport, 2006; Orlikowski & Barley, 2001; Gardner, 2012). However, one of the reasons for skepticism of BI or technology, in general, is related to ethical considerations or lack thereof. For instance, the nature of ethical decisions and judgments, ethical frameworks, equity theory, justice, and HRM ethical "guidelines (Armstrongs, 2002; Cheng & Hackett, 2019). The strategic resourcing approach is noted for its focus on aligning employee attitudes and behaviors with management's success beliefs, but this tendency carries potential dangers (Armstrong, 2002). Further, ethical concerns emerge in formal talent review processes (Garavan et al., 2012) and while measuring intangible outcomes, such as tacit knowledge sharing (El-Farr & Hosseingholizadeh, 2019).

Since fairness and justice are central to critiques of exclusive talent management systems, these systems can potentially differentiate the workforce by heavily investing in a select talent pool, creating unequal treatment between included and excluded employees (Thunnissen et al., 2013; Pfeffer, 2001). Also, beyond individual fairness, broader ethical concerns include legitimacy and employment citizenship—how an organization is perceived by society and stakeholders (Thunnissen et al., 2013; Boxall & Purcell, 2011).

In HRIS development, HR managers flagged confidentiality concerns as a significant heuristic metaphor, although deeper discussions on data privacy were largely absent from the talent management literature (Tansley & Newell, 2007). Further highlighted as key considerations, data warehousing should be reviewed (Turban et al., 2010). Data quality and integrity are identified as critical success factors, requiring standard definitions, governance mechanisms, coding policies, and corporate data models to ensure a single version of the truth (Yeoh & Popovic, 2016). BI systems add value regarding data security while addressing competitive intelligence threats (Talaoui & Kohtamäki, 2020; Negash, 2004). More importantly, organizations must prioritize privacy and data protection, especially those involved in innovative solutions and intangible asset decisions (Lombardi, 2019). Regular audits against evidence-based practices are also recommended (Hughes & Rog, 2008).

Stage 8: Continuous Improvement and Feedback Loop

Continuous improvement and feedback are central to HRM effectiveness when aligned with KM strategies (El-Farr & Hosseingholizadeh, 2019) and BI tools (Turban et al., 2010). Knowledge-based training and development ensure continuous employee growth, while performance management emphasizes development and feedback to identify gaps between performance and targets (El-Farr & Hosseingholizadeh, 2019). Decision implementation generates impacts reported via systems like EIS through Web-based portals and tracked using BAM, BPM, SCM, and ERP systems, creating a feedback loop that returns to the intelligence phase (Turban et al., 2010). Further, Performance assessment outcomes should feed into KM processes, particularly under the personalization strategy, which focuses on growing exploratory knowledge linked to innovation and new capabilities (El-Farr & Hosseingholizadeh, 2019). Performance management systems are necessary here because mere reporting is insufficient; they imply ongoing assessment and corrective action (Negash et al., 2004). BI system implementation is evaluated through process and infrastructure performance, forming a feedback mechanism (Yeoh & Koronios, 2010; Yeoh & Popovic, 2016). Expert systems must constantly update their knowledge by learning from success and failure (Turban et al., 2010).

Furthermore, performance management is cyclical, and evidence-based reward management follows a continuous loop involving setting objectives, review, measurement, evaluation, development, and implementation (Armstrong, 2002). For instance, the dynamic capability is framed as a renewal component integrating people management, core competencies, intellectual capital, and KM over time (Wright et al., 2001).

Understanding and measuring HRM's impact on performance is central to BI. For instance, simulation software supports evaluating staffing strategies against business goals, and access to the correct information supports informed HR decisions (Al-kasasbeh, 2024).

A conceptual model portrays talent management as cyclical, requiring constant attention to talent gaps—an upgrade from simpler HRIS models (Al-kasasbeh, 2024). Furthermore, in start-ups, the entrepreneur's role evolves from knowledge broker to controller of organizational learning during the growth phase (Lombardi, 2019).

5. CONCLUSION

Efficiency and decision-making are key to sustaining competitive advantage from human capital. Organizations can no longer rely on traditional HR systems. They need a more robust and holistic approach to their HR-related practices. Payroll management and digital tools were enough to understand the HRM function. Today, we do not just need to understand what organizations need in terms of skills and knowledge but to ensure they are agile and adaptable. This requires a holistic organizational knowledge system and advanced tools and techniques to predict and make informed decisions. The findings of this book chapter shed light on the strategy to achieve sustained human resource practices by integrating and leveraging existing systems with the BI tools and techniques that ensure that the organization is using its existing resources and preparing for the future. Attracting and acquiring talent keeps in mind the current need and ensures that they are agile and can develop and grow. Data analytics should be used to hire training and development staff and ensure talent engagement. Should talent be extracted from the organization, there have to be practices in place that ensure that organizations have the feedback so that they can work at the same time; they also have knowledge systems in place to ensure that there is no knowledge law so the idea here is that having a holistic framework will help both people and system together and to build a thriving workplace culture in doing so this book chapter provides a context-specific understanding of how organization can fine-tune the business analytics with their existing knowledge practices and informs their HR practices and accordingly drive their talent-centric approaches. Another important insight that this study emphasized is data privacy and ethical considerations, which require accountability from both the systems side on the nature and kind of data being captured and the leadership side that sets the tone for ethical considerations. Taken together, the proposed talent-centric approach to HRM encourages leveraging existing KM with BI tools and techniques, improves decision-making, and provides actionable strategies to develop a more efficient and customizable talent-centric approach to various organizations.

REFERENCES

Adler, P. S. (1992). *Technology and the Future of Work*. Oxford University Press. DOI: 10.1093/oso/9780195071719.001.0001

Ain, N., Vaia, G., DeLone, W. H., & Waheed, M. (2019). Two decades of research on business intelligence system adoption, utilization and success–A systematic literature review. *Decision Support Systems, 125*, 113113. DOI: 10.1016/j.dss.2019.113113

Al-kasasbeh, O., & Badie' Alhmoud, . (2024). The relationship between business intelligence and sustainable human resources. *HISTORICAL: Journal of History and Social Sciences, 3*(3), 251–271. DOI: 10.58355/historical.v3i3.117

Al-Okaily, M., Alghazzawi, R., Alkhwaldi, A. F., & Al-Okaily, A. (2022). The effect of digital accounting systems on the decision-making quality in the banking industry sector: A mediated-moderated model. *Global Knowledge, Memory and Communication, 72*(8/9), 882–901. DOI: 10.1108/GKMC-01-2022-0015

Angrave, D., Charlwood, A., Kirkpatrick, I., Lawrence, M., & Stuart, M. (2016). HR and analytics: Why HR is set to fail the big data challenge. *Human Resource Management Journal, 26*(1), 1–11. DOI: 10.1111/1748-8583.12090

Armstrong, M. (2002). *A Handbook of Human Resource Management Practice* (8th ed.). Kogan Page.

Bhatt, G. D., & Grover, V. (2005). Types of information technology capabilities and their role in competitive advantage: An empirical study. *Journal of Management Information Systems, 22*(2), 253–277. DOI: 10.1080/07421222.2005.11045844

Bush, J. T., & Balven, R. M. (2018). Catering to the crowd: An HRM perspective on crowd worker engagement. *Human Resource Management Review*. Advance online publication. DOI: 10.1016/j.hrmr.2018.10.003

Chaudhuri, S., Dayal, U., & Narasayya, V. (2011). An overview of business intelligence technology. *Communications of the ACM, 54*(8), 88–98. DOI: 10.1145/1978542.1978562

Cheng, M. M., & Hackett, R. D. (2021). A critical review of algorithms in HRM: Definition, theory, and practice. *Human Resource Management Review, 31*(1), 100698. DOI: 10.1016/j.hrmr.2019.100698

Choong, K. K. (2008). Intellectual capital: Definitions, categorization and reporting models. *Journal of Intellectual Capital, 9*(4), 609–638. DOI: 10.1108/14691930810913186

Davenport, T. H. (2006). Competing on analytics. *Harvard Business Review*, *84*(1), 98. PMID: 16447373

Davenport, T. H., De Long, D. W., & Beers, M. C. (1998). Successful knowledge management projects. *Sloan Management Review*, *39*, 43–57.

Davenport, T. H., & Prusak, L. (1998). *Working knowledge: How organizations manage what they know*. Harvard Business Press.

Delery, J. E., & Roumpi, D. (2017). Strategic Human Resource Management, Human Capital and Competitive Advantage: Is the Field Going in Circles? *Human Resource Management Journal*, *27*(1), 1–21. DOI: 10.1111/1748-8583.12137

Dutton, J. E., Ashford, S. J., O'Neill, R. M., & Lawrence, K. A. (2001). MOVES THAT MATTER: ISSUE SELLING AND ORGANIZATIONAL CHANGE. *Academy of Management Journal*, *44*(4), 716–736. DOI: 10.2307/3069412

El-Farr, H., & Hosseingholizadeh, R. (2019). Aligning. *Human Resource Management*.

Elbashir, M. Z., Collier, P. A., & Davern, M. J. (2008). Measuring the effects of business intelligence systems: The relationship between business process and organizational performance. *International Journal of Accounting Information Systems*, *9*(3), 135–153. DOI: 10.1016/j.accinf.2008.03.001

Faraj, S., Pachidi, S., & Sayegh, K. (2018). Working and organizing in the age of the learning algorithm. *Information and Organization*, *28*(1), 62–70. DOI: 10.1016/j.infoandorg.2018.02.005

Ford, M. (2015). *Rise of the Robots: Technology and the Threat of a Jobless Future*. Basic Books.

Garavan, T. N., Carbery, R., & Rock, A. (2012). Mapping talent development: Definition, scope, and architecture. *European Journal of Training and Development*, *36*(1), 5–24. DOI: 10.1108/03090591211192601

Gardner, H. K. (2012). Performance pressure as a double-edged sword: Enhancing team motivation but undermining the use of team knowledge. *Administrative Science Quarterly*, *57*(1), 1–46. DOI: 10.1177/0001839212446454

Gibson, C. B., & Gibbs, J. L. (2006). Unpacking the concept of virtuality: The effects of geographic dispersion, electronic dependence, dynamic structure, and national diversity on team innovation. *Administrative Science Quarterly*, *51*(3), 451–495. DOI: 10.2189/asqu.51.3.451

Gibson, C. B., & Zellmer-Bruhn, M. E. (2001). Metaphors and meaning: An intercultural analysis of the concept of teamwork. *Administrative Science Quarterly*, *46*(2), 274–303. DOI: 10.2307/2667088

Gómez, C., Salvatierra Garrido, J.L., Luis, J., Alarcon, L., & Velásquez. (2015). Guidelines to address talent management in Chilean construction companies.

Gruber, T. R. (1995). Toward principles for the design of ontologies used for knowledge sharing? *International Journal of Human-Computer Studies*, *43*(5–6), 907–928. DOI: 10.1006/ijhc.1995.1081

Hinds, P. J., & Kiesler, S. (2002). *Distributed Work*. MIT Press. DOI: 10.7551/mitpress/2464.001.0001

Hughes, J. C., & Rog, E. (2008). Talent management. *International Journal of Contemporary Hospitality Management*, *20*(7), 743–757. DOI: 10.1108/09596110810899086

Kim, Y. W., & Ko, J. (2014). HR Practices and Knowledge Sharing Behavior. *Public Personnel Management*, *43*(4), 586–607. DOI: 10.1177/0091026014542342

Klein, K. J., Ziegert, J. C., Knight, A. P., & Xiao, Y. (2006). Dynamic delegation: Shared, hierarchical, and deindividualized leadership in extreme action teams. *Administrative Science Quarterly*, *51*(4), 590–621. DOI: 10.2189/asqu.51.4.590

Knies, E., Boselie, P., Gould-Williams, J., & Vandenabeele, W. (2017). Strategic Human Resource Management and Public Sector Performance: Context Matters. *International Journal of Human Resource Management*, •••, 1–13.

Kondapaka, P., Khanra, S., Malik, A., Kagzi, M., & Hemachandran, K. (2023). Finding a fit between CXO's experience and AI usage in CXO decision-making: Evidence from knowledge-intensive professional service firms. *Journal of Service Theory and Practice*, *33*(2), 280–308. DOI: 10.1108/JSTP-06-2022-0134

Lado, A. A., & Zhang, M. J. (1998). Expert Systems, Knowledge Development and Utilization, and Sustained Competitive Advantage: A Resource-Based Model. *Journal of Management*, *24*(4), 489–509. DOI: 10.1177/014920639802400402

Lajšić, H. (2019). Strategic human resources management and business intelligence systems in the purpose of social and economic development. EMC Review-Economy and Market Communication Review, 17(1).

Latham, G. P., & Pinder, C. C. (2019). Work motivation theory and research at the dawn of the twenty-first century. *Annual Review of Psychology*, *56*(1), 485–516. DOI: 10.1146/annurev.psych.55.090902.142105 PMID: 15709944

Lee, S. M., Hong, S., & Katerattanakul, P. (2004). Impact of data warehousing on organizational performance of retailing firms. *International Journal of Information Technology & Decision Making*, *3*(01), 61–79. DOI: 10.1142/S0219622004000040

Leonardi, P. M., & Barley, S. R. (2010). What is under construction here? Social action, materiality, and power in constructivist studies of technology and organizing. *The Academy of Management Annals*, *4*(1), 1–51. DOI: 10.5465/19416521003654160

Liebowitz, J. (2018). The synergy of knowledge management and artificial intelligence to support healthcare. *International Journal of Healthcare Management*, *22*(2), 475–487.

Lombardi, R. (2019). Knowledge transfer and organizational performance and business process: Past, present, and future researches. *Business Process Management Journal*, *25*(1), 2–9. DOI: 10.1108/BPMJ-02-2019-368

Lorincová, S., Hitka, M., Štarchoň, P., & Stachová, K. (2018). Strategic instrument for sustainability of human resource management in small and medium-sized enterprises using management data. *Sustainability (Basel)*, *10*(10), 3687. DOI: 10.3390/su10103687

Mahoney, T. A., & Deckop, J. R. (1986). Evolution of concept and practice in personnel administration/human resource management. *Journal of Management*, *12*(2), 223–241. DOI: 10.1177/014920638601200206

Malik, A., Budhwar, P., & Kazmi, B. A. (2023). Artificial intelligence (AI)-assisted HRM: Towards an extended strategic framework. *Human Resource Management Review*, *33*(1), 100940. Advance online publication. DOI: 10.1016/j.hrmr.2022.100940

Marler, J. H., & Boudreau, J. W. (2017). An evidence-based review of HR Analytics. *International Journal of Human Resource Management*, *28*(1), 3–26. DOI: 10.1080/09585192.2016.1244699

Muhammad, A. U., Shah, Z. A., & Azhar, K. A. (2021). *The increasing role of HRIS in facilitating sustainable human resource management practices in 21st-century organizations*. Currency.

Negash, S. (2004). Business intelligence. *Communications of the Association for Information Systems*, *13*(1), 54.

Nevo, S., & Wade, M. R. (2010). The formation and value of IT-enabled resources: Antecedents and consequences of synergistic relationships. *Management Information Systems Quarterly*, *34*(1), 163–183. DOI: 10.2307/20721419

Nonaka, I. (1994). A dynamic theory of organizational knowledge creation. *Organization Science*, *5*(1), 14–37. DOI: 10.1287/orsc.5.1.14

Nonaka, I., & Toyama, R. (2005). The theory of the knowledge-creating firm: Subjectivity, objectivity and synthesis. *Industrial and Corporate Change*, *14*(3), 419–436. DOI: 10.1093/icc/dth058

Nyberg, A. J., Moliterno, T. P., Hale, D.Jr, & Lepak, D. P. (2014). Resource-Based Perspectives on Unit-Level Human Capital: A Review and Integration. *Journal of Management*, *40*(1), 316–346. DOI: 10.1177/0149206312458703

Orlikowski, W., & Scott, S. (2008). Sociomateriality: Challenging the separation of technology, work and organization. *The Academy of Management Annals*, *2*(1), 433–474. DOI: 10.5465/19416520802211644

Orlikowski, W. J., & Barley, S. R. (2001). Technology and institutions: What can research on information technology and research on organizations learn from each other? *Management Information Systems Quarterly*, *25*(2), 145–165. DOI: 10.2307/3250927

Pentland, B. T., & Feldman, M. S. (2007). Narrative networks: Patterns of technology and organization. *Organization Science*, *18*(5), 781–795. DOI: 10.1287/orsc.1070.0283

Rasmussen, T., & Ulrich, D. (2015). Learning from practice: How HR analytics avoids being a management fad. *Organizational Dynamics*, *44*(3), 236–242. DOI: 10.1016/j.orgdyn.2015.05.008

Schiuma, G. (2012). Managing knowledge for business performance improvement. *Journal of Knowledge Management*, *16*(4), 515–522. DOI: 10.1108/13673271211246103

Schryen, G. (2013). Revisiting IS business value research: What we already know, what we still need to know, and how we can get there. *European Journal of Information Systems*, *22*(2), 139–169. DOI: 10.1057/ejis.2012.45

Sirin, E., & Karacan, H. (2017). A review on business intelligence and big data. *International Journal of Intelligent Systems and Applications in Engineering*, *5*(4), 206–215. DOI: 10.18201/ijisae.2017533861

Snell, S. A., Stueber, D., & Lepak, D. P. (2002). Virtual HR Departments: Getting out of the Middle. In Heneman, R. L., & Greenberger, D. B. (Eds.), *Human Resource Management in Virtual Organizations* (pp. 81–101). Information Age Publishing.

Souleh, S. (2014). The impact of human capital management on the innovativeness of research centers: The case of scientific research centers in Algeria. *International Journal of Business and Management*, *2*(4), 80–96.

Stone, D. L., Deadrick, D. L., Lukaszewski, K. M., & Johnson, R. (2015). The influence of technology on the future of human resource management. *Human Resource Management Review*, *25*(2), 216–231. DOI: 10.1016/j.hrmr.2015.01.002

Sveiby, K. (2001). A knowledge-based theory of the firm to guide in strategy formulation. *Journal of Intellectual Capital*, *2*(4), 344–358. DOI: 10.1108/14691930110409651

Talaoui, Y., & Kohtamäki, M. (2020). 35 years of research on business intelligence process: A synthesis of a fragmented literature. *Management Research Review*, *44*(5), 677–717. DOI: 10.1108/MRR-07-2020-0386

Tansley, C., & Newell, S. (2007). A knowledge-based view of agenda formation in the development of human resource information systems. *Management Learning*, *38*(1), 95–119. DOI: 10.1177/1350507607073028

Tansley, C., & Watson, T. (2000). Strategic exchange in the development of human resource information systems (HRIS). *New Technology, Work and Employment*, *15*(2), 108–122. DOI: 10.1111/1468-005X.00068

Tavera Romero, C. A., Ortiz, J. H., Khalaf, O. I., & Ríos Prado, A. (2021). Business intelligence: Business evolution after industry 4.0. *Sustainability (Basel)*, *13*(18), 10026. DOI: 10.3390/su131810026

Thunnissen, M., Boselie, P., & Fruytier, B. (2013). Talent management and the relevance of context: Towards a pluralistic approach. *Human Resource Management Review*, *23*(4), 326–336. DOI: 10.1016/j.hrmr.2013.05.004

Turban, E., Sharda, R., & Delen, E. D. (2010). *Decision Support and Business Intelligence Systems* (9th ed.). Prentice Hall.

Waller, M. A., & Fawcett, S. E. (2009). Data warehousing in the supply chain: An intelligent agent for group decision support in applicant ranking within human resources systems. In *2009 IEEE International Conference on Fuzzy Systems* (pp. 744–750).

Watson, H. J., & Wixom, B. H. (2007). The current state of business intelligence. *Computer*, *40*(9), 96–99. DOI: 10.1109/MC.2007.331

Watson, H. J., Wixom, B. H., Hoffer, J. A., Anderson-Lehman, R., & Reynolds, A. M. (2009). Real-time business intelligence: Best practices at Continental Airlines. *EDPACS: The EDP Audit, Control, and Security Newsletter*, *40*(6), 1–16. DOI: 10.1080/07366980903484935

Weiss, L. (1999). Collection and connection: The anatomy of knowledge sharing in professional services. *Proceedings - Academy of Management*, *17*(1), 61–72. DOI: 10.5465/apbpp.1999.27613308

Wright, P. M., Dunford, B. B., & Snell, S. A. (2001). Human resources and the resource-based view of the firm. *Journal of Management*, *27*(6), 701–721. DOI: 10.1177/014920630102700607

Yeoh, W., & Koronios, A. (2010). Critical success factors for business intelligence systems. *Journal of Computer Information Systems*, *50*(3), 23–32. DOI: 10.1080/08874417.2010.11645404

Yeoh, W., & Popovic, A. (2016). Extending the understanding of critical success factors for implementing business intelligence systems. *Journal of the Association for Information Science and Technology*, *67*(1), 134–147. DOI: 10.1002/asi.23366

Zack, M. H. (1999). Developing a knowledge strategy. *California Management Review*, *41*(3), 125–145. DOI: 10.2307/41166000

Zammuto, R. F., Griffith, T. L., Majchrzak, A., Dougherty, D. J., & Faraj, S. (2007). Information technology and the changing fabric of organization. *Organization Science*, *18*(5), 749–762. DOI: 10.1287/orsc.1070.0307

Zhang, H., Gao, S., & Zhou, P. (2023). Role of digitalization in energy storage technological innovation: Evidence from China. *Renewable & Sustainable Energy Reviews*, *171*, 113014. DOI: 10.1016/j.rser.2022.113014

Compilation of References

Abboud, S. (2021). The impact of 360 degrees performance appraisals on employee retention. *The EUrASEANs: Journal on global socio-economic dynamics*, 3 (28), 37-49.

Abdel-Karim, B. M., Pfeuffer, N., & Hinz, O. (2021). Machine learning in information systems—A bibliographic review and open research issues. *Electronic Markets*, *31*(3), 643–670. DOI: 10.1007/s12525-021-00459-2

Abd, S. K., Ali, M. H., Jaber, M. M., Abosinnee, A. S., Kareem, Z. H., Wahab, A. N. A., Hassan, R., & Jassim, M. M. (2024). Secured finance handling for supply chain integrated business intelligence using blockchain application scenarios. *Intelligent Data Analysis*, *28*(2), 553–571. DOI: 10.3233/IDA-227445

Abendin, S., & Duan, P. (2021). International trade and economic growth in Africa: The role of the digital economy. *Cogent Economics & Finance*, *9*(1), 1911767. DOI: 10.1080/23322039.2021.1911767

Abu Huson, Y., Sierra-García, L., & Garcia-Benau, M. A. (2024). A bibliometric review of information technology, artificial intelligence, and blockchain on auditing. *Total Quality Management & Business Excellence*, *35*(1–2), 91–113. ResearchGate+2Taylor & Francis Online+2Taylor & Francis Online+2. DOI: 10.1080/14783363.2023.2256260

Acharya, K. (2024). *Tourism management system project report. Preprints.* DOI: 10.22541/au.173144144.44637261/v1

Achchab, B., & Ahdil, I. (2015, February). Competitive intelligence experiences in companies: Case studies on creative opportunities. In *2015 6th International Conference on Information Systems and Economic Intelligence (SIIE)* (pp. 158-164). IEEE.

Adaga, E. M., Egieya, Z. E., Ewuga, S. K., Abdul, A. A., & Abrahams, T. O. (2024). Tackling economic inequalities through business analytics: A literature review. *Computer Science & IT Research Journal*, *5*(1), 60–80. DOI: 10.51594/csitrj.v5i1.702

Adewusi, A. O., Okoli, U. I., Adaga, E., Olorunsogo, T., Asuzu, O. F., & Daraojimba, D. O. (2024). Business intelligence in the era of big data: A review of analytical tools and competitive advantage. *Computer Science & IT Research Journal, 5*(2), 415–431. DOI: 10.51594/csitrj.v5i2.791

Adler, P. S. (1992). *Technology and the Future of Work.* Oxford University Press. DOI: 10.1093/oso/9780195071719.001.0001

Agoraki, K. K., Deirmentzoglou, G. A., Psychalis, M., & Apostolopoulos, S. (2024a). Types of innovation and sustainable development: Evidence from medium-and large-sized firms. *International Journal on Management of Innovation & Technology, 21*(02), 2450013. DOI: 10.1142/S0219877024500135

Agoraki, K. K., Deirmentzoglou, G. A., & Triantopoulos, C. (2024b). Cultural Values as Catalysts of Technological Innovation for a Sustainable Future. *Sustainability (Basel), 16*(5), 2064. DOI: 10.3390/su16052064

Aguinis, H.. (2024). Artificial intelligence in human resources management: Challenges and a path forward. *California Management Review, 61*(4), 15–42.

Ahmed, I., & Dantata, B. S. (2016). Problems and challenges of policy implementation for national development. *Research on Humanities and Social Sciences, 6*(15), 60–65.

Ain, N., Vaia, G., DeLone, W. H., & Waheed, M. (2019). Two decades of research on business intelligence system adoption, utilization and success–A systematic literature review. *Decision Support Systems, 125*, 113113. DOI: 10.1016/j.dss.2019.113113

Ajax, R., Joseph, O., & Own, J. (2025). Enhancing Business Intelligence with Data Visualization Tools.

Akyuz, G. A., & Rehan, M. (2009). Requirements for forming an 'e-supply chain'. *International Journal of Production Research, 47*(11), 3265–3287. DOI: 10.1080/00207540701802460

Al Aufi, M. A. (2016). Business intelligence in contemporary organizations: Potential opportunities to improve human resource management for competitive advantage. *Asian Journal of Business and Management, 4*(4), 152–155.

Al Tobaishat, M. K. A. R. (2025). The Local Community's Perception of the Cable Car Project and its Role in Tourism Development in Ajloun. *Journal of Information Systems Engineering & Management, 10*(19s), 172–180. DOI: 10.52783/jisem.v10i19s.2998

Alabi, O., Ajayi, F., Udeh, C., & Efunniyi, C. (2024). Optimizing customer service through workforce analytics: The role of hr in data-driven decision-making. *International Journal of Innovation and Scientific Research, XI*(VIII), 1628–1639. DOI: 10.51244/IJRSI.2024.1108125

Alawneh, O. M., Tawalbeh, J., & AlOqaily, A. N. (2025). Reveling the Interrelationship of Digital Transformation and Business Intelligence Techniques to Boost Human Capital Development. *Innovative and Economics Research Journal, 13*(1), 509–524. Advance online publication. DOI: 10.2478/eoik-2025-0024

Alcoriza, G. B., & Edros, S. A. (2025). Organizational Management and Leadership Practices in Marketing Niche Tourism Destinations: The Adventure Tourism Experience in Legazpi City, Philippines. In Sousa, B. B., & Santos, V. R. (Eds.), *Intersections of Niche Tourism and Marketing* (pp. 425–452). IGI Global., DOI: 10.4018/979-8-3693-8417-6.ch019

Al-Dalahmeh, M., Héder-Rima, M., & Dajnoki, K. (2020). The effect of talent management practices on employee turnover intention in the information and communication technologies (icts) sector: Case of jordan. *Problems and Perspectives in Management, 18*(4), 59–71. DOI: 10.21511/ppm.18(4).2020.06

Ali, M. H., Hosain, M. S., & Hossain, M. A. (2021). Big Data analysis using BigQuery on cloud computing platform. *Australian JofEng Inno Tech, 3*(1), 1–9.

Al-kasasbeh, O., & Badie' Alhmoud, . (2024). The relationship between business intelligence and sustainable human resources. *HISTORICAL: Journal of History and Social Sciences, 3*(3), 251–271. DOI: 10.58355/historical.v3i3.117

Al-Momani, A. M. (2025). Artificial Intelligence and Industry 4.0: Catalysts for Sustainable Organizational Development in: Al-Sharafi M.A. Arpaci, A. (eds) *Current and Future Trends on Al Applications, Studies in Computational Intelligence*, 1178, 231-245 Springer, Cham. https://doi.org/DOI: 10.1007/978-3-031-75091-5_13

Alnuaimi, Y. M. A. (2022). Impacts of workplace factors on employee engagement in the public sector. *European Journal of Marketing and Economics, 5*(1), 57–70.

Al-Okaily, A., Teoh, A. P., & Al-Okaily, M. (2023). Evaluation of data analytics-oriented business intelligence technology effectiveness: An enterprise-level analysis. *Business Process Management Journal, 29*(3), 777–800. DOI: 10.1108/BPMJ-10-2022-0546

Al-Okaily, M., Alghazzawi, R., Alkhwaldi, A. F., & Al-Okaily, A. (2022). The effect of digital accounting systems on the decision-making quality in the banking industry sector: A mediated-moderated model. *Global Knowledge, Memory and Communication*, *72*(8/9), 882–901. DOI: 10.1108/GKMC-01-2022-0015

Alqahtani, I., Almagrabi, H., & Alharbi, A. (2024). Employee attrition prediction using machine learning models: A review paper. *International Journal of Artificial Intelligence & Applications*, *15*(2), 23–49. DOI: 10.5121/ijaia.2024.15202

Al-Qathmi, A., & Zedan, H. (2021). The effect of incentive management system on turnover rate, job satisfaction and motivation of medical laboratory technologists. *Health Services Research and Managerial Epidemiology*, *8*, 2333392820988404. DOI: 10.1177/2333392820988404 PMID: 33614829

Alqudah, H., Al-Qudah, M., Huson, Y. A., Lutfi, A., Alrawad, M., & Almaiah, M. A. (2024). A decade of green economic literature: An analysis-based bibliometric. *International Journal of Energy Economics and Policy*, *14*(3), 497–511. Econ Journals. DOI: 10.32479/ijeep.15579

Al-Quhfa, H., Mothana, A., Aljbri, A., & Song, J. (2024). Enhancing Talent Recruitment in Business Intelligence Systems: A Comparative Analysis of Machine Learning Models. *Analytics*, *3*(3), 297–317. DOI: 10.3390/analytics3030017

Al-Ruwaili, R., & Ouda, O. M. (2023). A hybrid classification approach of network attacks using supervised and unsupervised learning. *International Journal of Advanced Computer Science and Applications*, *14*(8). Advance online publication. DOI: 10.14569/IJACSA.2023.0140890

Al-Shammari, M., Ahmed Al Bin Ali, F., Abdulla AlRashidi, M., & Salem Albuainain, M. (2024). Big Data and Predictive Analytics for Strategic Human Resource Management: A Systematic Literature Review. *International Journal of Computing and Digital Systems*, *17*(1), 1–9. DOI: 10.12785/ijcds/1571015706

Alsheikh, G. A. A., Albhinat, M. M., & Alzghoul, A. (2025). Leadership competencies and business intelligence: Synergies for competitive advantage. *Proceeding of the International Conference on Robotics, Automation and Intelligent Computing*, 18-19 May, Puce, India https://doi.org/DOI: 10.1063/5.0255615

Alsheref, F., Fattoh, I., & Ead, W. (2022). Automated prediction of employee attrition using an ensemble model based on machine learning algorithms. *Computational Intelligence and Neuroscience*, *2022*, 1–9. DOI: 10.1155/2022/7728668 PMID: 35795740

Al-Suraihi, W., Samikon, S., Alsuraihi, A., & Ibrahim, I. (2021). Employee turnover: Causes, importance and retention strategies. *European Journal of Business Management and Research*, *6*(3), 1–10. DOI: 10.24018/ejbmr.2021.6.3.893

Amarnath, B., & Iyer, S. S. (2024). The role of HR analytics in optimizing employee performance in IT companies. *Library Progress International*, *44*(2), 526–538.

Ambusaidi, A., Al-Dayri, H., & Al-Sumari, M. (2024). The effect of sustainable environmental tourism training on the development of eighth-grade Omani students' attitudes towards the environment and their inclination to engage in entrepreneurship in environmental tourism projects. *Cogent Education*, *11*(1), 2400745. DOI: 10.1080/2331186X.2024.2400745

Anastasiadis, L., & Zirinoglou, P. (2022). Evaluating students' attitudes toward STEM education: The case of Greek pre-service teachers. *International Journal of Education and Social Science*, *9*(4), 35–53.

Anastasiadou, S., & Anastasiadis, L. (2019). Quality assurance in education in the light of the effectiveness of transformational school leadership. In Economic and Financial Challenges for Eastern Europe: Proceedings of the 9th International Conference on the Economies of the Balkan and Eastern European Countries in the Changing World (EBEEC) in Athens, Greece, 2017 (pp. 323-344). Springer International Publishing. DOI: 10.1007/978-3-030-12169-3_21

Anastasiadou, S., Masouras, A., & Papademetriou, C. (2023, June). Attitudes toward Reproductive Tourism and Cross border reproductive care (CBRC): Legal, Economic, Ethical issues and dilemmas, possibilities and limitations. In *6th International Conference on Tourism Research*, Pafos, Cyprus. DOI: 10.34190/ictr.6.1.1189

Anderson, M. C. (2008). Taking Coaching to the Next Level: Critical Insights from ROI Evaluations. In Drake, D. B., Brennan, D., & Gørtz, K. (Eds.), *The philosophy and practice of coaching. Insights and issues for a new era* (pp. 317–332). Jossey-Bass.

Anderson, T., & Wilson, E. (•••). (2027). Navigating the Metaverse: Challenges and Opportunities for Small Businesses. *Small Business Economics*, *40*(2), 180–195.

Angrave, D., Charlwood, A., Kirkpatrick, I., Lawrence, M., & Stuart, M. (2016). HR and analytics: Why HR is set to fail the big data challenge. *Human Resource Management Journal*, *26*(1), 1–11. DOI: 10.1111/1748-8583.12090

Ao, S., Hurwitz, M., & Palade, V. (2025, February 26). Cognitive computing and business intelligence applications in accounting, finance and management. *Big Data and Cognitive Computing*, *9*(3), 54. DOI: 10.3390/bdcc9030054

Aquino, S. R., Kilag, O. K., & Valle, J. (2023). From Preparedness to Action: Effective Real-time Crisis Management. Excellencia: *International Multi-disciplinary Journal of Education* (2994-9521), 1(5), 372-384.

Ara, A. (2025). The role of business intelligence in transforming HR practices: A focus on employee retention and performance management. *Proceedings of the 8th International Conference on Data Science and Machine Learning Applications*, 54-61. https://doi.org/DOI: 10.1109/CDMA61895.2025.00015

Armstrong, M. (2002). *A Handbook of Human Resource Management Practice* (8th ed.). Kogan Page.

Armstrong, M., & Landers, R. (2018). Gamification of employee training and development. *International Journal of Training and Development*, *22*(2), 162–169. DOI: 10.1111/ijtd.12124

Armstrong, M., & Taylor, S. (2023). *Armstrong's handbook of human resource management practice: A guide to the theory and practice of people management*. Kogan Page Publishers.

Artz, B., Kaya, I., & Kaya, O. (2022). Gender role perspectives and job burnout. *Review of Economics of the Household*, *20*(2), 447–470. DOI: 10.1007/s11150-021-09579-2 PMID: 34429716

Arulselvan, M. (2025). AI- Enabled human capital management: Tools for strategic workforce adaptation. *Journal of Science Technology and Research*, *5*(1), 530–538.

Asana, I. M. D. P., Sudipa, I. G. I., & Putra, K. A. P. (2021). A Decision Support System on Employee Assessment Using Analytical Network Process (ANP) and BARS Methods. *Jurnal Teknik Informatika CIT Medicom*, *13*(1), 1–12. DOI: 10.35335/cit.Vol13.2021.38.pp1-12

Ashal, N., & Morshed, A. (2024). Balancing data-driven insights and human judgment in supply chain management: The role of business intelligence, big data analytics, and artificial intelligence. Journal of Infrastructure. *Policy and Development*, *8*(6), 3941. DOI: 10.24294/jipd.v8i6.3941

Aspevig, J. (2014). Project Management and Public Health Informatics. In Magnuson, J. A., & Fu, P. C. (Eds.), *Public Health Informatics and Information Systems* (pp. 211–231). Springer London., DOI: 10.1007/978-1-4471-4237-9_12

Aston, C., & Morton, L. (2005). Managing Talent for competitive advantage. *Strategic HR Review*, *4*(5), 28–31. DOI: 10.1108/14754390580000819

Ayanponle, L. O., Awonuga, K. F., Asuzu, O. F., Daraojimba, R. E., Elufioye, O. A., & Daraojimba, O. D. (2024). A review of innovative HR strategies in enhancing workforce efficiency in the US. *International Journal of Science and Research Archive, 11*(1), 817–827. DOI: 10.30574/ijsra.2024.11.1.0152

Ayyanathan, N., & Kannammal, A. (2015, March). Combined forecasting and cognitive Decision Support System for Indian green coffee supply chain predictive analytics. In *2015 International Conference on Cognitive Computing and Information Processing (CCIP)* (pp. 1-6). IEEE. DOI: 10.1109/CCIP.2015.7100735

Azami, N., Azmee, D., Keng, N., Qing, N., Shen, N., & Han, L. (2023). Factors affecting employee retention among SMEs millennial employees in Klang valley, Malaysia. *International Journal of Academic Research in Business & Social Sciences, 13*(3). Advance online publication. DOI: 10.6007/IJARBSS/v13-i3/16455

Babashahi, L., Barbosa, C. E., Lima, Y., Lyra, A., Salazar, H., Argôlo, M., Almeida, M. A., & Souza, J. M. (2024). Ai in the workplace: A systematic review of skill transformation in the industry. *Administrative Sciences, 14*(6), 127. DOI: 10.3390/admsci14060127

Bagale, G. S., Vandadi, V. R., Singh, D., Sharma, D. K., Garlapati, D. V. K., Bommisetti, R. K., Gupta, R. K., Setsiawan, R., Subramaniyaswamy, V., & Sengan, S. (2023). Small and medium-sized enterprises' contribution in digital technology. *Annals of Operations Research, 326*(S1, Suppl. 1), 3–4. DOI: 10.1007/s10479-021-04235-5 PMID: 34456411

Bai, W., Wang, C., & Bai, X. (2021). International Trade Fairs Based on Big Data. In *Application of Intelligent Systems in Multi-modal Information Analytics:2021 International Conference on Multi-modal Information Analytics (MMIA 2021),* Volume 1 (pp. 723-729). Springer International Publishing. DOI: 10.1007/978-3-030-74811-1_104

Bakker, A. B., & Demerouti, E. (2008). Towards a Model of Work Engagement. *Career Development International, 13*(3), 209–223. DOI: 10.1108/13620430810870476

Bakker, A. B., & Xanthopoulou, D.Bakker and Xanthopoulou. (2013). Creativity and charisma among female leaders: The role of resources and work engagement. *International Journal of Human Resource Management, 24*(14), 2760–2779. Advance online publication. DOI: 10.1080/09585192.2012.751438

Bakshi, K. (2018, March 3–10). Considerations for artificial intelligence and machine learning: Approaches and use cases. In *2018 IEEE Aerospace Conference* (pp. 1–9). IEEE. DOI: 10.1109/AERO.2018.8396488

Bapna, S., & Ganco, M. (2021). Gender gaps in equity crowdfunding: Evidence from a randomized field experiment. *Management Science*, *67*(5), 2679–2710. DOI: 10.1287/mnsc.2020.3644

Barocas, S., Hardt, M., & Narayanan, A. (2019). *Fairness and machine learning: Limitations and opportunities*. https://fairmlbook.org

Barone, D., Mylopoulos, J., Jiang, L., & Amyot, D. (2010). *The business intelligence model: Strategic modelling*. University of Toronto.

Bartlett, C. A., & Wozny, M. (2005). *GE's Two-Decade Transformation: Jack Welch's Leadership*. Harvard Business School Case Study.

Bartlett, K. R. (2001). The relationship between training and organizational commitment: A study in the health care field. *Human Resource Development Quarterly*, *12*(4), 335–352. DOI: 10.1002/hrdq.1001

Basnet, S. (2024). The Impact of AI-Driven Predictive Analytics on Employee Retention Strategies. *International Journal of Research and Review*, *11*(9), 50–61. DOI: 10.52403/ijrr.20240906

Basole, R. C., Park, H., & Seuss, C. D. (2024). Complex business ecosystem intelligence using AI-powered visual analytics. *Decision Support Systems*, *178*, 114133. DOI: 10.1016/j.dss.2023.114133

Batalden, M., Leach, D., Swing, S. R., Dreyfus, H. L., & Dreyfus, S. E. (2002). General competencies and accreditation in graduate medical education. *Health Affairs*, *21*(5), 103–111. DOI: 10.1377/hlthaff.21.5.103 PMID: 12224871

Batistič, S., & van der Laken, P. (2019). History, evolution, and future of big data and analytics: A bibliometric analysis of its relationship to performance in organizations. *British Journal of Management*, *30*(2), 229–251. DOI: 10.1111/1467-8551.12340

Becker, B. E., Huselid, M. A., Pickus, P. S., & Spratt, M. F. (1997). HR as a Source of Shareholder Value: Research and Recommendations. *Human Resource Management*, *36*(1), 39–47. DOI: 10.1002/(SICI)1099-050X(199721)36:1<39::AID-HRM8>3.0.CO;2-X

Belias, D., & Trihas, N. (2022a, September). How can we measure the "resistance to change"? An exploratory factor analysis in a sample of employees in the Greek hotel industry. In International Conference of the International Association of Cultural and Digital Tourism (pp. 51-66). Cham: Springer Nature Switzerland.

Belias, D., & Trihas, N. (2022b). Investigating the readiness for organizational change: A case study from a hotel industry context/Greece.

Belias, D., Vasiliadis, L., & Mantas, C. (2020). The human resource training and development of employees working on luxurious hotels in Greece. In Cultural and Tourism Innovation in the Digital Era: Sixth International IACuDiT Conference, Athens 2019 (pp. 639-648). Springer International Publishing. DOI: 10.1007/978-3-030-36342-0_49

Belias, D., Velissariou, E., & Rossidis, I. (2019). The contribution of HRM on the development of effective organizational culture in hotel units—The case of Greek hotels. In Smart Tourism as a Driver for Culture and Sustainability: Fifth International Conference IACuDiT, Athens 2018 (pp. 603-618). Springer International Publishing.

Belias, D., & Rossidis, I. (2024). *Change management: Organizational Change and Organizational Behavior* [in Greek]. Tziolas Publications.

Belias, D., & Rossidis, I. (2025). *Change Management – Organizational Change & Organizational Behavior* [in Greek]. Tziolas.

Belias, D., Rossidis, I., Mantas, C., Ntalakos, A., Trihas, N., & Bakogiannis, D. (2023b). The effect of strategic leadership on the integration and success of organizational change. In *Managing successful and ethical organizational change* (pp. 54–75). IGI Global. DOI: 10.4018/979-8-3693-0235-4.ch003

Belias, D., Rossidis, I., Papademetriou, C., & Mantas, C. (2021). Job Satisfaction as Affected by Types of Leadership: A Case Study of Greek Tourism Sector. *Journal of Quality Assurance in Hospitality & Tourism.*

Belias, D., Rossidis, I., Papademetriou, C., & Mantas, C. (2022). Job satisfaction as affected by types of leadership: A case study of Greek tourism sector. *Journal of Quality Assurance in Hospitality & Tourism*, *23*(2), 299–317. DOI: 10.1080/1528008X.2020.1867695

Belias, D., Rossidis, I., Papademetriou, C., Masouras, A., & Anastasiadou, S. (2023a). *Managing Successful and Ethical Organizational Change.* IGI Global. DOI: 10.4018/979-8-3693-0235-4

Belias, D., Rossidis, I., Sotiriou, A., & Malik, S.Case Study in Greek Seasonal Hotels. (2022). Workplace Conflict, Turnover, and Quality of Services. Case Study in Greek Seasonal Hotels. *Journal of Quality Assurance in Hospitality & Tourism*, *24*(4), 453–476. DOI: 10.1080/1528008X.2022.2065655

Belias, D., Rossidis, I., Stavrinoudis, T., & Kakarougkas, C. (2024b). The Relationship between Change Management and Business Ethics: An Investigation on the Latest Developments - Key Issues on This Topic. In Belias, D., & Rossidis, I. (Eds.), *Papademetriou* (pp. 148–165). C. Organizational Behavior and Human Resource Management for Complex Work Environments., DOI: 10.4018/979-8-3693-3466-9.ch008

Belias, D., & Trihas, N. (2023). The role of SHRM in navigating the hospitality sector during a crisis. In *Sustainable growth strategies for entrepreneurial venture tourism and regional development* (pp. 60–76). IGI Global. DOI: 10.4018/978-1-6684-6055-9.ch004

Belias, D., & Trihas, N. (2024). How can we predict the integration and the success of organizational change in the hospitality sector? *Journal of Quality Assurance in Hospitality & Tourism*, *25*(6), 2011–2045. DOI: 10.1080/1528008X.2023.2216952

Belias, D., Trihas, N., & Ntalakos, A. (2024). Crisis leadership, group dynamics, and change management: A literature review and future perspectives. In *International Conference of the International Association of Cultural and Digital Tourism* (pp. 225-244). Springer, Cham. DOI: 10.1007/978-3-031-54342-5_13

Bello, B. G., Tula, S. T., Omotoye, G. B., Kess-Momoh, A. J., & Daraojimba, A. I. (2024). Work-life balance and its impact in modern organizations: An HR review. *World Journal of Advanced Research and Reviews*, *21*(1), 1162–1173. DOI: 10.30574/wjarr.2024.21.1.0106

Bentley, L. (2024). *The role of technology in enhancing health and wellness tourism experiences*. DOI: 10.5281/ZENODO.11403443

Berke, D., Kossler, M. E., & Wakefield, M. (2008). *Developing Leadership Talent*. Wiley: Pfeiffer.

Berrada, M., Jafari, M., & Hachicha, A. (2020). Reinforcement learning for portfolio management: A survey. *International Journal of Financial Studies*, *8*(3), 1–17. DOI: 10.3390/ijfs8030032

Berridge, E. J., Kelly, D., & Gould, D. (2007). Staff appraisal and continuing professional development: Exploring the relationships in acute and community health settings. *Journal of Research in Nursing : JRN*, *12*(1), 57–70. DOI: 10.1177/1744987106074018

Bersin, J. (2014). Why companies fail to engage today's workforce: The overlooked employee value proposition. *Forbes HR*, *26*(3), 47–52.

Bersin, J. (2023). *HR Predictions for 2023: Technology-Driven Engagement Strategies*. Bersin Insights.

Bhambri, P., & Rani, S. (2025). Advancements and Future Challenges in Business Intelligence. In Developing Managerial Skills for Global Business Success (pp. 271-290). IGI Global Scientific Publishing.

Bhatt, G. D., & Grover, V. (2005). Types of information technology capabilities and their role in competitive advantage: An empirical study. *Journal of Management Information Systems*, *22*(2), 253–277. DOI: 10.1080/07421222.2005.11045844

Bhimanatham, A., & Iyer, S. S. (2024). HR analytics focuses on gathering, interpreting and analyzing workforce data. *Library Progress International*, *44*(2), 525–540.

Bidi, K. F., Damour, C., & Grondin, D. (2022). Multistage power and energy management strategy for hybrid microgrid with photovoltaic production and hydrogen storage. *Applied Energy*, *66*(36), 16.

Binns, R., Veale, M., Van Kleek, M., & Shadbolt, N. (2018). 'It's reducing a human being to a percentage': perceptions of justice in algorithmic decisions. *CHI Conference on Human Factors in Computing Systems*, 1-14. https://doi.org/DOI: 10.1145/3173574.3173951

Blass, F. R., & Ferris, G. R. (2007). Leader reputation: The role of mentoring, political skill, contextual learning, and adaptation. *Human Resource Management*, *46*(1), 5–19. DOI: 10.1002/hrm.20142

Block Ngaybe, M. G., Azurdia Sierra, L., McNair, A., Gonzalez, M., Arora, M., Ernst, K., Noriega-Atala, E., & Iyengar, M. S. (2025). Resilience Informatics in Public Health: Qualitative Analysis of Conference Proceedings. *JMIR Formative Research*, *9*, e63217. DOI: 10.2196/63217 PMID: 39819984

Bobi an, N., Dumitrescu, D., Popa, A., Sahlian, D., & Turlea, I. (2024). Shaping tomorrow: Anticipating skills requirements based on the integration of artificial intelligence in business organizations—a foresight analysis using the scenario method. *Electronics (Basel)*, *13*(11), 2198. DOI: 10.3390/electronics13112198

Bodie, M. T. (2022). The law of employee data: Privacy, property, governance. *Ind. Lj*, *97*, 707.

Borking, K., Danielson, M., Davies, G., Ekenberg, L., Idefeldt, J., & Larsson, A. (2022). *Transcending business intelligence*. Sine Metu Productions.

Boselie, P., Brewster, C., & Paauwe, J. (2019). Human resource management: The promise, the performance, the consequences. *Journal of Management Studies, 56*(3), 15–26.

Bose, R., Graham, S., & Cho, M. (2021). Workforce analytics: Ethical challenges and solutions. *Journal of Business Ethics, 172*(1), 189–204.

Boudreau, J. W., & Ramstad, P. M. (2007). *Beyond HR metrics: HR analytics.* Employment.

Boudreau, J. W., & Ramstad, P. M. (2007). *Beyond HR: The new science of human capital.* Harvard Business Press.

Bouwman, H., Nikou, S., & de Reuver, M. (2019). Digitalization, business models, and SMEs: How do business model innovation practices improve performance of digitalizing SMEs? *Telecommunications Policy, 43*(9), 101828. Advance online publication. CoLab+1ResearchGate+1. DOI: 10.1016/j.telpol.2019.101828

Boxall, P. F., & Purcell, J. (2011). *Strategy and human resource management.* Palgrave Macmillan.

Braganza et al. (2021) "Productive employment and decent work: The impact of AI adoption on psychological contracts, job engagement and employee trust" Journal of Business Research (2021) Doi: DOI: 10.1016/j.jbusres.2020.08.018

Brereton, P., Kitchenham, B. A., Budgen, D., Turner, M., & Khalil, M. (2007). Lessons from applying the systematic literature review process within the software engineering domain. *Journal of Systems and Software, 80*(4), 571–583. DOI: 10.1016/j.jss.2006.07.009

Bucher, T., Gericke, A., & Sigg, S. (2009). Process-centric business intelligence. *Business Process Management Journal, 15*(3), 408–429. DOI: 10.1108/14637150910960648

Budhwar, P., Malik, A., De Silva, M. T., & Thevisuthan, P. (2023). Artificial intelligence and human resource management: The past, present and future. *Human Resource Management Review, 33*(4), 100944.

Buhalis, D., & Leung, R. (2018). Smart hospitality—Interconnectivity and interoperability towards an ecosystem. *International Journal of Hospitality Management, 71*, 41–50. DOI: 10.1016/j.ijhm.2017.11.011

Burbano, V., Padilla, N., & Meier, S. (2024). Gender differences in preferences for meaning at work. *American Economic Journal. Economic Policy, 16*(3), 61–94. DOI: 10.1257/pol.20220121

Bush, J. T., & Balven, R. M. (2018). Catering to the crowd: An HRM perspective on crowd worker engagement. *Human Resource Management Review*. Advance online publication. DOI: 10.1016/j.hrmr.2018.10.003

Cappelli, P. (2008). *Talent on demand: Managing talent in an age of uncertainty*. Harvard Business Press.

Cappelli, P. (2008). *Talent on Demand: Managing Talent in an Age of Uncertainty*. Harvard Business Press.

Carreno, A. M. (2024). Building a Continuous Feedback Loop for Real-Time Change Adaptation: Best Practices and Tools.

Cauteruccio, F., & Terracina, G. (2024). Extended high-utility pattern mining: An answer set programming-based framework and applications. *Theory and Practice of Logic Programming*, *24*(2), 313–343. ResearchGate+1mat.unical.it+1. DOI: 10.1017/S1471068423000066

Chakrasali, R. L. (2017). Simulation and study of standalone hybrid grid (involving biogas, solar, wind and biodiesel-based generation). *International Energy Journal*, *57*(24), 5.

Chambers, E. G., Foulon, M., Handfield-Jones, H., Hankin, S. M., & Michaels, E. G. (1998). The War for Talents. *The McKinsey Quarterly*, (3), 44–57.

Chan, A. P., & Chan, A. P. (2004). Key performance indicators for measuring construction success. *Benchmarking*, *11*(2), 203–221. DOI: 10.1108/14635770410532624

Chaudhary, A., Rizvi, A., Kumar, N., & Mishra, A. (2023). A novel approach for customer churn prediction in telecom using machine learning models. DOI: 10.21203/rs.3.rs-3177792/v1

Chaudhuri, S., Dayal, U., & Narasayya, V. (2011). An overview of business intelligence technology. *Communications of the ACM*, *54*(8), 88–98. DOI: 10.1145/1978542.1978562

Chen, C. J., & Huang, J. W. (2009). Strategic human resource practices and innovation performance: The mediating role of knowledge management capacity. *Journal of Business Research*, *62*(1), 104–114. DOI: 10.1016/j.jbusres.2007.11.016

Cheng, M. M., & Hackett, R. D. (2021). A critical review of algorithms in HRM: Definition, theory, and practice. *Human Resource Management Review*, *31*(1), 100698. DOI: 10.1016/j.hrmr.2019.100698

Chen, H.. (2024). Virtual reality and augmented reality in marketing: A systematic literature review and future research agenda. *Journal of Interactive Marketing, 55*, 88–103.

Chen, H.. (2025). Metaverse Marketing: Leveraging Immersive Technologies for Brand Engagement. *JMR, Journal of Marketing Research, 30*(1), 45–62.

Chen, J. C., Rubin, E. A., & Cornwall, G. J. (2021). *Data science for public policy*. Springer. DOI: 10.1007/978-3-030-71352-2

Chen, M. K., & Wang, S. C. (2010). The use of a hybrid fuzzy-Delphi-AHP approach to develop global business intelligence for information service firms. *Expert Systems with Applications, 37*(11), 7394–7407. DOI: 10.1016/j.eswa.2010.04.033

Chen, M., Li, L., & Song, X. (2021). Deep learning for stock market forecasting: A survey. *Journal of Computational Finance, 25*(5), 45–69.

Chen, Y. M., & Chiu, Y.-P. (2014). Enhancing business intelligence for supply chain operations through effective classification of supplier management. *Uncertain Supply Chain Management, 2*(2), 229–236. DOI: 10.5267/j.uscm.2014.7.006

Chiwaridzo, O. T., & Masengu, R. (Eds.). (2024). *AI Technologies for Personalized and Sustainable Tourism*. IGI Global., DOI: 10.4018/979-8-3693-5678-4

Choong, K. K. (2008). Intellectual capital: Definitions, categorization and reporting models. *Journal of Intellectual Capital, 9*(4), 609–638. DOI: 10.1108/14691930810913186

Chowdhury, S., Hirose, A., Dong, Y., & Sharma, P. (2023). Leveraging AI and machine learning for strategic talent management: A framework and research agenda. *Human Resource Management Review, 33*(3), 100908.

Chun, E., & Evans, A. (2023). *The new talent acquisition frontier: Integrating HR and diversity strategy in the private and public sectors and higher education*. Taylor & Francis.

Cobo, M. J., López-Herrera, A. G., Herrera-Viedma, E., & Herrera, F. (2012). SciMAT: A new science mapping analysis software tool. *Journal of the American Society for Information Science and Technology, 63*(8), 1609–1630. DOI: 10.1002/asi.22688

Cocuľová, J., & Tomčíková, Ľ. (2021). Innovative human resource management practices for the talent management implementation. *Marketing and Management of Innovations, 5*(4), 47–54. DOI: 10.21272/mmi.2021.4-04

Coffman, K., Flikkema, C. B., & Shurchkov, O. (2021). Gender stereotypes in deliberation and team decisions. *Games and Economic Behavior*, *129*, 329–349. DOI: 10.1016/j.geb.2021.06.004

Cohn, J. M., Khurana, R., & Reeves, L. (2005). Growing Talent as if Your Business Depended on It. *Harvard Business Review*, *83*(10), 62–70. PMID: 16250625

Collings, D. G., & Mellahi, K. (2009). Strategic Talent Management: What is it and how does it matter? *Human Resource Management Review*, *19*(4), 304–313. DOI: 10.1016/j.hrmr.2009.04.001

Constantia, C., & Christos, P. (2019). Action research: The key to inclusive education in Cyprus. *Journal of Pedagogy*, *10*(2), 37–64. DOI: 10.2478/jped-2019-0006

Conway, S. (2007). *The think factory: Managing today's most precious resource, people!* John Wiley & Sons.

Coombs, C. (2020). Will COVID-19 be the tipping point for the intelligent automation of work? A review of the debate and implications for research. *International Journal of Information Management*, *55*, 102182. DOI: 10.1016/j.ijinfomgt.2020.102182 PMID: 32836639

Cruz, J. A. S. (2023). Analytics-Customized dashboards representing a descriptive analysis and diagnosis of business and operational information (Master's thesis).

Cueva, K., Bulkow, L., Milton, E., Wyck, R., Hargrave, S., & Meyer, J. (2023). Application of covidtracer to inform public health workforce planning in alaska during the covid-19 pandemic. *Public Health Reports*, *139*(1), 11–17. DOI: 10.1177/00333549231199479 PMID: 37846519

D'Angelo, A., d'Aloisio, G., Marzi, F., Di Marco, A., & Stilo, G. (2024). Uncovering gender gap in academia: A comprehensive analysis within the software engineering community. *Journal of Systems and Software*, *217*, 112162. DOI: 10.1016/j.jss.2024.112162

da Costa Innecco, P. M. D. (2015). *The implications of cloud computing and big data on the roadmap towards business intelligence* [Doctoral dissertation, De Montfort University Leicester].

Daoanis, L. E. (2012). Performance Appraisal System: It's Implication to Employee Performance. *International Journal of Economics and Management Sciences*, *2*(3), 55–62.

Dastin, J. (2022). Amazon scraps secret AI recruiting tool that showed bias against women. In *Ethics of data and analytics* (pp. 296–299). Auerbach Publications. DOI: 10.1201/9781003278290-44

Davenport, T. H. (2006). Competing on analytics. *Harvard Business Review*, *84*(1), 98. PMID: 16447373

Davenport, T. H., De Long, D. W., & Beers, M. C. (1998). Successful knowledge management projects. *Sloan Management Review*, *39*, 43–57.

Davenport, T. H., Harris, J., & Shapiro, J. (2010). Competing on talent analytics. *Harvard Business Review*, *88*(10), 52–58. PMID: 20929194

Davenport, T. H., & Prusak, L. (1998). *Working knowledge: How organizations manage what they know*. Harvard Business Press.

de Waal, A., Burrell, J., Drake, S., Sampa, C., & Mulimbika, T. (2023). How to stay high-performing: Developing organizational grit. *Measuring Business Excellence*, *27*(1), 25–39. DOI: 10.1108/MBE-08-2021-0104

Deirmentzoglou, G. A., Anastasopoulou, E. E., & Vlassi, E. "International Economic Relations and Sustainable Tourism: The Case of Greece." In *International Conference on Tourism Research*. Academic Conferences International Limited, 2025. DOI: 10.34190/ictr.8.1.3472

Deirmentzoglou, G. A., Agoraki, K. K., & Patsoulis, P. (2024c). The nexus between cultural values and perceptions of corporate sustainable development. *Social Responsibility Journal*, *20*(2), 224–242. DOI: 10.1108/SRJ-09-2022-0373

Deirmentzoglou, G. A., Anastasopoulou, E. E., & Sklias, P. (2024a). International economic relations and energy security in the European Union: A systematic literature review. *International Journal of Sustainable Energy*, *43*(1), 2385682. DOI: 10.1080/14786451.2024.2385682

Deirmentzoglou, G. A., Vlassi, E., & Anastasopoulou, E. E. (2024b). DDMMO Website Quality, Destination Image and Intention to Use Metaverse Platforms. *Platforms*, *2*(4), 180–192. DOI: 10.3390/platforms2040012

Delery, J. E., & Roumpi, D. (2017). Strategic Human Resource Management, Human Capital and Competitive Advantage: Is the Field Going in Circles? *Human Resource Management Journal*, *27*(1), 1–21. DOI: 10.1111/1748-8583.12137

Deng, H., Duan, S. X., & Wibowo, S. (2023). Digital technology driven knowledge sharing for job performance. *Journal of Knowledge Management*, *27*(2), 404–425. DOI: 10.1108/JKM-08-2021-0637

Dewitte, P., & Ausloos, J. (2024). Chronicling GDPR Transparency Rights in Practice: The Good, the Bad and the Challenges Ahead. *International Data Privacy Law*, *14*(2), 106–133. DOI: 10.1093/idpl/ipad026

Dharmadhikari, A. (2025, March 4). The future of business intelligence: Trends to watch in 2025. *Business Intelligence Journal*, *18*(1), 45–62.

Dimitrov, M. (2025). The evaluative qualia theory of pleasure and displeasure. *Synthese*, *205*(1), 11. DOI: 10.1007/s11229-024-04824-4

Doerr, J. (2018). *Measure What Matters: How Google, Bono, and the Gates Foundation Rock the World with OKRs*. Penguin.

Dorigo, T., Brown, G. D., Casonato, C., Cerda, A., Ciarrochi, J., Da Lio, M., D'Souza, N., Gauger, N. R., Hayes, S. C., Hofmann, S. G., Johansson, R., Liwicki, M., Lotte, F., Nieto, J. J., Olivato, G., Parnes, P., Perry, G., Plebe, A., Rao, I. M., & Yazdanpanah, N. (2025). Artificial intelligence in science and society: The vision of USERN. *IEEE Access : Practical Innovations, Open Solutions*, *13*, 15993–16054. DOI: 10.1109/ACCESS.2025.3529357

Dowling, B., Goldstein, D., Park, M., & Price, H. (2022). Hybrid work: Making it fit with your diversity, equity, and inclusion strategy. *The McKinsey Quarterly*, *4*, 1–9.

Dresner, H. (1989). *Business intelligence*.

Dresner, H. (1989). Business intelligence. Gartner Group.scientificpapers.org

Dua, G. K. (2025). Synergizing Talent Horizons: The Transformative Impact of Data Integration in Contemporary Talent Management. In Cultivating Creativity and Navigating Talent Management in Academia (pp. 359-382). IGI Global Scientific Publishing.

Duggan, J., Sherman, U., Carbery, R., & McDonnell, A. (2020). Algorithmic management and app-work in the gig economy: A research agenda for employment relations and HRM. *Human Resource Management Journal*, *30*(1), 114–132. DOI: 10.1111/1748-8583.12258

Dutta, S., Thomas, A., & Khatri, P. (2025). *Disruptive Technology in Human Resource Management*. Taylor & Francis. DOI: 10.4324/9781003507543

Dutton, J. E., Ashford, S. J., O'Neill, R. M., & Lawrence, K. A. (2001). MOVES THAT MATTER: ISSUE SELLING AND ORGANIZATIONAL CHANGE. *Academy of Management Journal*, *44*(4), 716–736. DOI: 10.2307/3069412

Eboigbe, E. O., Farayola, O. A., Olatoye, F. O., Nnabugwu, O. C., & Daraojimba, C. (2023). Business intelligence transformation through AI and data analytics. *Engineering Science & Technology Journal*, *4*(5), 285–307. DOI: 10.51594/estj.v4i5.616

Eckhardt, C., Madjarova, S., Williams, R., Ollivier, M., Karlsson, J., Pareek, A., & Nwachukwu, B. (2022). Unsupervised machine learning methods and emerging applications in healthcare. *Knee Surgery, Sports Traumatology, Arthroscopy : Official Journal of the ESSKA*, *31*(2), 376–381. DOI: 10.1007/s00167-022-07233-7 PMID: 36378293

Eden, C., Chisom, A., & Adeniyi, O. (2024). The impact of business intelligence on human resource management practices. *Journal of Business Intelligence*, *18*(2), 112–129.

Efendi, S. (2021). Implementation of talent management as an effort to improve employee performance. *In 2nd Annual Conference on blended learning, educational technology and Innovation (ACBLETI 2020)* (pp. 537-542). Atlantis Press.

Egginton, B. E. (2010). Introduction of formal performance appraisal of academic staff: The management challenges associated with effective implementation. *Educational Management Administration & Leadership*, *38*(1), 119–133. DOI: 10.1177/1741143209351660

Eisalou, M. R. (2014). *Human Resource 360-Degree Feedback*. LAP LAMBERT Academic Publishing.

Ekhsan, , Sudiro, A., Mugiono, M., & Hussein, A. S. (2022). Employee Retention and Change Management During Times of Uncertainty. *Frontiers in Psychology*, *13*, 916709. Advance online publication. DOI: 10.3389/fpsyg.2022.916709 PMID: 35707647

Elbashir, M. Z., Collier, P. A., & Davern, M. J. (2008). Measuring the effects of business intelligence systems: The relationship between business process and organizational performance. *International Journal of Accounting Information Systems*, *9*(3), 135–153. DOI: 10.1016/j.accinf.2008.03.001

El-Farr, H., & Hosseingholizadeh, R. (2019). Aligning. *Human Resource Management.*

Ellickson, M. C., & Logsdon, K. (2001). Determinants of Job Satisfaction of Municipal Government Employees. *State & Local Government Review*, *33*(3), 173–184. DOI: 10.1177/0160323X0103300302

Elsafty, A., & Ragheb, M. (2021). The role of human resources management towards healthcare providers' retention during the COVID-19 pandemic in Egypt. *International Business Research*, *14*(8), 67–76. DOI: 10.5539/ibr.v14n8p67

Eltouny, K., Gomaa, M., & Liang, X. (2023). Unsupervised learning methods for data-driven vibration-based structural health monitoring: A review. *Sensors (Basel)*, *23*(6), 3290. DOI: 10.3390/s23063290 PMID: 36992001

Errani, C., Tsukamoto, S., Kido, A., Yoneda, A., Bondi, A., Zora, F., & Mavrogenis, A. F. (2021). Women and men in orthopaedics. *SICOT-J*, •••, 7. PMID: 33812468

Espinosa, M. P., & Ferreira, E. (2022). Gender implicit bias and glass ceiling effects. *Journal of Applied Econometrics*, *25*(1), 37–57.

Evans, J. R., & Jack, E. P. (2003). Validating Key Results Linkages in the Baldrige Performance Excellence Model. *The Quality Management Journal*, *10*(2), 7–24. DOI: 10.1080/10686967.2003.11919060

Exner, R. and Zunic, A. (2025). Organizing BI Strategy. The Path to an Intelligent Enterprise. *Springer Nature*, 151-188. https://doi.org/DOI: 10.1007/978-3-031-69914-6_5

Exner, R., & Zunic, A. (2025). *The Path to an Intelligent Enterprise: The art and practice of business intelligence strategy*. Springer Nature Switzerland AG., DOI: 10.1007/978-3-031-69914-6

Fader, P. (2020). *Customer centricity: Focus on the right customers for strategic advantage*. University of Pennsylvania Press.

Fakeyede, O. G., Okeleke, P. A., Hassan, A. O., Iwuanyanwu, U., Adaramodu, O. R., & Oyewole, O. O. (2023). Navigating data privacy through IT audits: GDPR, CCPA, and beyond. *International Journal of Research in Engineering and Science*, *11*(11).

Fang, M., Su, J., Liu, J., Long, Y., He, R., & Wang, T. (2018). A model to predict employee turnover rate: Observing a case study of Chinese enterprises. *IEEE Systems, Man, and Cybernetics Magazine*, *4*(4), 38–48. ResearchGate. DOI: 10.1109/MSMC.2018.2834829

Faqihi, A., & Miah, S. J.Faqihi and Miah. (2023). Artificial Intelligence-Driven Talent Management System: Exploring the Risks and Options for Constructing a Theoretical Foundation. *Journal of Risk and Financial Management*, *16*(1), 31. Advance online publication. DOI: 10.3390/jrfm16010031

Faraj, S., Pachidi, S., & Sayegh, K. (2018). Working and organizing in the age of the learning algorithm. *Information and Organization*, *28*(1), 62–70. DOI: 10.1016/j.infoandorg.2018.02.005

Farndale, E., Horak, S., Piyanontalee, R., Ruffer, S. M., & Vidovic, M. (2025). Looking back to look forward: Disruption, innovation and future trends in international human resource management. *International Business Review*, *34*(1), 102362. Advance online publication. DOI: 10.1016/j.ibusrev.2024.102362

Fernando, H., & Abawajy, J. (2009, December). A RFID architecture framework for global supply chain applications. In *Proceedings of the 11th International Conference on Information Integration and Web-based Applications & Services* (pp. 313-320). DOI: 10.1145/1806338.1806396

Ferreira-Oliveira, A. T., Keating, J., & Silva, I. (2020). Sustainable HRM as a pathway to sustainability—HRMS relevance on affective commitment through organizational trust. *Sustainability (Basel)*, *12*(22), 9443. DOI: 10.3390/su12229443

Fleisher, C., & Hursky, R. (2016). Empowering insight: The role of collaboration in the evolution of intelligence practice. *South African Journal of Information Management*, *18*(1), 1–10. DOI: 10.4102/sajim.v18i2.731

Ford, M. (2015). *Rise of the Robots: Technology and the Threat of a Jobless Future*. Basic Books.

Fowowe, O.O. and Adedapo, A. (2025). Leveraging Predictive Analytics to Optimize Business Performance and Drive Operational Excellence. *International journal of Computer Applications Technology and Research*, 14(02), 66-81. https://doi.org/ DOI: 10.7753/IJCATR1402.1005

Fredriksson, T., Mattos, D. I., Bosch, J., & Olsson, H. H. (2020, November). Data labeling: An empirical investigation into industrial challenges and mitigation strategies. In International conference on product-focused software process improvement (pp. 202-216). Cham: Springer International Publishing.

Friederichs, P., & Labes, M. (2006). Human Capital Management. In Kruppke, H., Otto, M., & Gontard, M. (Eds.), *Human Capital Management. Personalprozesse erfolgreich managen* (pp. 17–26). Springer.

Fuertes, W., Reyes, F., Valladares, P., Tapia, F., Toulkeridis, T., & Pérez, E. (2017). An integral model to provide reactive and proactive services in an academic CSIRT based on business intelligence. *Systems*, *5*(4), 52. DOI: 10.3390/systems5040052

Gabriel, K. P., & Aguinis, H. (2022). How to prevent and combat employee burnout and create healthier workplaces during crises and beyond. *Business Horizons*, *65*(2), 183–192. DOI: 10.1016/j.bushor.2021.02.037

Gaddam, L., Lakshmi, S., Kadali, H., & Abghari, S. (2022). Comparison of machine learning algorithms on predicting churn within music streaming service. Blekinge Institute of Technology.DIVA Portal+1DIVA Portal+1

Gagalova, K. K., Elizalde, M. A. L., Portales-Casamar, E., & Görges, M. (2020). What you need to know before implementing a clinical research data warehouse: Comparative review of integrated data repositories in health care institutions. *JMIR Formative Research*, *4*(8), e17687. DOI: 10.2196/17687 PMID: 32852280

Galliano, G. (2023). The importance of data visualization tools in modern enterprises. Cost-effective solutions and empowering of an open source project (Doctoral dissertation, Politecnico di Torino).

Gal, U., Jensen, T. B., & Lyytinen, K. (2020). Identity in the age of data-driven workforce management: Critical perspectives. *Information Systems Journal*, *30*(3), 367–393.

Gamage, T. C., & Gnanapala, A. (2024). Tourism Experiences: An Interpretive Approach to Understanding Tourist-Brand Relationships in Technology-Mediated Tourism Service Environments. In Rather, R. A. (Ed.), *Consumer Brand Relationships in Tourism* (pp. 103–119). Springer Nature Switzerland., DOI: 10.1007/978-3-031-59535-6_6

Gandossy, R., & Kao, T. (2004). Talent Wars: Out of Mind, Out of Practice. *Human Resource Planning*, *27*(4), 1519.

Gao, S., & Sequmpan, R. G. (2025). The impact of artificial intelligence on talent acquisition in small and medium-sized enterprises: A systematic review. *International Theory and Practice in Humanities and Social Sciences*, *2*(2), 216–226. Advance online publication. DOI: 10.70693/itphss.v2i2.224

Gao, S., Song, Y., & Chen, Y. (2018). Fast simulation model of voltage source converters with arbitrary topology using switch-state prediction. *IEEE Transactions on Power Electronics*, *75*(46), 35.

Gao, X., Wen, J., & Zhang, C. (2019). An improved random forest algorithm for predicting employee turnover. *Mathematical Problems in Engineering*, *2019*(1), 4140707. Advance online publication. SpringerLink. DOI: 10.1155/2019/4140707

Garas, S., & Wright, S. L. (2024). A data analytics case study analyzing IRS SOI migration data using no code, low code technologies. *Journal of Accounting Education*, *66*, 100885. DOI: 10.1016/j.jaccedu.2024.100885

Garavan, T., Carbery, R., & Rock, A. (2012). Mapping talent development: Definition, scope and architecture. *European Journal of Training and Development*, *36*(1), 5–24. DOI: 10.1108/03090591211192601

Gardner, H. K. (2012). Performance pressure as a double-edged sword: Enhancing team motivation but undermining the use of team knowledge. *Administrative Science Quarterly*, *57*(1), 1–46. DOI: 10.1177/0001839212446454

Garg, S., Sinha, S., Kar, A. K., & Mani, M. (2022). A review of machine learning applications in human resource management. *International Journal of Productivity and Performance Management*, *71*(7), 1590–1610. DOI: 10.1108/IJPPM-08-2020-0427

Gasela, P. (2021). The role of human resource management in organizational strategy implementation. *Journal of Management and Business Research*, *21*(4), 78–92.

Gates, S. (2002). Review of methodology of quantitative reviews using meta-analysis in ecology. *Journal of Animal Ecology*, *71*(4), 547–557. DOI: 10.1046/j.1365-2656.2002.00634.x

George, A. S. (2024). Bridging the Digital Divide: Understanding the Human Impacts of Digital Transformation. *Partners Universal International Innovation Journal*, *2*(3), 1–34.

Ghaffar, A. (2020). Integration of Business Intelligence Dashboard for Enhanced Data Analytics Capabilities.

Ghafoori, A., Gupta, M., Merhi, M. I., Gupta, S., & Shore, A. P. (2024). Toward the role of organizational culture in data-driven digital transformation. *International Journal of Production Economics*, *271*, 109205. DOI: 10.1016/j.ijpe.2024.109205

Ghio, D., Bratti, M., & Bignami, S. (2022). Linguistic barriers to immigrants' labour market integration in Italy. *The International Migration Review*, *57*(1), 357–394. DOI: 10.1177/01979183221107923

Gholidoust, A. (2025). Unleashing Creativity: The Interplay of Innovation and Diversity. In Mastering Innovation in Business (pp. 47-76). IGI Global.

Giannakos, K., Belias, D., Rossidis, I., Ntalakos, A., & Papademetriou, C. (2024). Creating the Appropriate Organizational Culture for Change Management. In Organizational Behavior and Human Resource Management for Complex Work Environments (pp. 166-185). IGI Global. DOI: 10.4018/979-8-3693-3466-9.ch009

Gibson, C. B., & Gibbs, J. L. (2006). Unpacking the concept of virtuality: The effects of geographic dispersion, electronic dependence, dynamic structure, and national diversity on team innovation. *Administrative Science Quarterly*, *51*(3), 451–495. DOI: 10.2189/asqu.51.3.451

Gibson, C. B., & Zellmer-Bruhn, M. E. (2001). Metaphors and meaning: An intercultural analysis of the concept of teamwork. *Administrative Science Quarterly*, *46*(2), 274–303. DOI: 10.2307/2667088

Gioia, D. A., Corley, K. G., & Hamilton, A. L. (2013). Seeking qualitative rigor in inductive research: Notes on the Gioia methodology. *Organizational Research Methods*, *16*(1), 15–31. DOI: 10.1177/1094428112452151

Giuggioli, G., & Pellegrini, M. M. (2023). Artificial intelligence as an enabler for entrepreneurs: A systematic literature review and an agenda for future research. *International Journal of Entrepreneurial Behaviour & Research*, *29*(4), 816–837.

Goh, K. S., & Law, H. W. (2019). Machine learning in financial risk management: Current practices and future directions. *The Journal of Risk Finance*, *20*(4), 98–112. DOI: 10.1108/JRF-05-2018-0067

Gomes, B. M. S. (2023). Development of a Talent Management Platform at BI4ALL: Business Intelligence Approach for Human Resource Management (Master's thesis, Universidade NOVA de Lisboa (Portugal)).

Gómez, C., Salvatierra Garrido, J.L., Luis, J., Alarcon, L., & Velásquez. (2015). Guidelines to address talent management in Chilean construction companies.

Gomez-Mejia, L. R., Balkin, D. B., & Cardy, R. L. (2012). *Managing human resources* (7th ed.). Pearson.

Gong, O., Fan, D., & Bartram, T. (2024). Integrating artificial intelligence and human resource management: A review and future research agenda. *International Journal of Human Resource Management*, *36*(i), 103–141. DOI: 10.1080/09585192.2024.2440065

Gruber, T. R. (1995). Toward principles for the design of ontologies used for knowledge sharing? *International Journal of Human-Computer Studies*, *43*(5–6), 907–928. DOI: 10.1006/ijhc.1995.1081

Guechtouli, M. (2014). How can HRM support your business intelligence system? IPAG Business School Working Papers, 151, 1-10.

Guenole, N., Ferrar, J., & Feinzig, S. (2017). *The power of people: Learn how successful organizations use workforce analytics to improve business performance*. Pearson Education.

Guerranti, F., & Dimitri, G. (2022). A comparison of machine learning approaches for predicting employee attrition. *Applied Sciences (Basel, Switzerland)*, *13*(1), 267. DOI: 10.3390/app13010267

Gullickson, A. R. (2008). *The personnel evaluation standards: How to assess systems for evaluating educators*. Corwin Press.

Gunning, D., & Aha, D. (2019). DARPA's Explainable Artificial Intelligence (XAI) program. *AI Magazine*, *40*(2), 44–58. DOI: 10.1609/aimag.v40i2.2850

Guthridge, M., Komm, A. B., & Lawson, E. (2008). Making talent a strategic priority. *The McKinsey Quarterly*, *1*(48).

Hajdu, N. (2024). Advancing Organizational Analytics: A Strategic Roadmap for Implementing Machine Learning in Warehouse Management System.

Hanna, N. K. (2009). Implications of the ICT Revolution. In *Transforming Government and Building the Information Society: Challenges and Opportunities for the Developing World* (pp. 27–65). Springer New York.

Han, X., Wang, F., & Chen, M. (2019). Economic evaluation of micro-grid system in commercial parks based on echelon utilization batteries. *IEEE Access : Practical Innovations, Open Solutions*, *46*(23), 9. DOI: 10.1109/ACCESS.2019.2916181

Harfoush, B. (2024). Impact of Organizational Changes on BI Critical Success Factors.

Hargrave, L., & Blumenau, J. (2022). No longer conforming to stereotypes? Gender, political style and parliamentary debate in the UK. *British Journal of Political Science*, *52*(4), 1584–1601. DOI: 10.1017/S0007123421000648

Harrison, O. (2018). *Machine learning basics with the K-nearest neighbors algorithm*. Towards Data Science.

Harter, J. K.. (2020). *The Relationship Between Engagement at Work and Organizational Outcomes*. Gallup Research.

Harzing, A., & Alakangas, S. (2016). Google Scholar, Scopus and the Web of Science: A longitudinal and cross-disciplinary comparison. *Scientometrics*, *106*(2), 787–804. DOI: 10.1007/s11192-015-1798-9

Hazra, S., & Sanyal, S. (2016). Recruitment prediction using ID3 decision tree. *International Journal of Advanced Engineering Research and Development*, *3*(1), 4–14.

Heilman, M. E., Caleo, S., & Manzi, F. (2024). Women at work: Pathways from gender stereotypes to gender bias and discrimination. *Annual Review of Organizational Psychology and Organizational Behavior, 11*(1), 165–192. DOI: 10.1146/annurev-orgpsych-110721-034105

Hill, K., Neylon, K., Gunn, K., Sharplin, G., & Eckert, M. (2023). Understanding burnout in the current nephrology nursing workforce and health service 'magnet' qualities that may help address it: A discreet choice experiment. *Renal Society of Australasia Journal, 19*(2). Advance online publication. DOI: 10.33235/rsaj.19.1.87-92

Hills, A. (2009). Succession planning — Or smart talent management? *Industrial and Commercial Training, 41*(1), 38. DOI: 10.1108/00197850910927697

Hinds, P. J., & Kiesler, S. (2002). *Distributed Work.* MIT Press. DOI: 10.7551/mitpress/2464.001.0001

Hlaváč, J., & Štefanovič, J. (2020, January 29–February 1). Machine learning and business intelligence or from descriptive analytics to predictive analytics. In *2020 Cybernetics & Informatics (K&I)* (pp. 1–4). IEEE. DOI: 10.1109/KI48306.2020.9039874

Holdsworth, J., & Lundgaard, B. (2009). HR transformation: Myth or reality. *KPMG International, 4*(2), 18–26.

Horizant. (2023). Transforming Employee Engagement with Real-Time Data Insights. Retrieved from [https://www.horizantinsights.com]

Hossain, M. R., Gindaba, F., Yusuf, A., Mrydha, M. A. M., & Rahman, M. Z. (2024). Big data and business intelligence: Key drivers of sustainable development in USA-based organizations. *International Journal for Multidisciplinary Research*, 6(6), 1-19. E-ISSN: 2582-2160.

Huang, K. (2024). Discrete Optimization Technology Helps Non-heritage Tourism Project Ecological Chain Construction Model Optimization. *Applied Mathematics and Nonlinear Sciences, 9*(1), 20242529. DOI: 10.2478/amns-2024-2529

Huang, M.-H., & Rust, R. T. (2021). A strategic framework for artificial intelligence in marketing. *Journal of the Academy of Marketing Science, 49*(1), 30–50. DOI: 10.1007/s11747-020-00749-9

Huang, S. C., McIntosh, S., Sobolevsky, S., & Hung, P. C. K. (2017). Big data analytics and business intelligence in industry. *Information Systems Frontiers, 19*(5), 1229–1232. DOI: 10.1007/s10796-017-9804-9

Hughes, J. C., & Rog, E. (2008). Talent management. *International Journal of Contemporary Hospitality Management, 20*(7), 743–757. DOI: 10.1108/09596110810899086

Huselid, M. A. (2018). The science and practice of workforce analytics: Introduction to the HRM special issue. *Human Resource Management*, *57*(3), 679–684. DOI: 10.1002/hrm.21916

Huson, Y. A. A., Sierra-García, L., Garcia-Benau, M. A., & Aljawarneh, N. M. (2024). Empirical investigation into the integration of cloud-based artificial intelligence in auditing. *PressAcademia Procedia*, *18*, 113–114. DOI: 10.5187/pap.2024.18.113

Hu, W., Cheng, L., & Qian, M.. (2019). Prediction of annual power grid infrastructure investment based on hybrid algorithm of improved PSO. *Power System and Clean Energy*, (3), 2.

IBM HR Analytics Employee Attrition Dataset. Kaggle. https://www.kaggle.com/datasets/pavansubhasht/ibm-hr-analytics-attrition-dataset

Ibrahim, N. M., Abiduzzaman, S. M., Raziff, A. R. A., & Shah, A. (2025). A Collaborative Filtering Approach Using Machine Learning and Business Intelligence: A Critical Review. *International Journal on Perceptive and Cognitive Computing*, *11*(1), 41–49.

Ignatenko, Y., Ortmann, N., Lutz, S., & Kramer, F. (2025a). Comprehensive Course on Clinical Study Data Management for Medical Informatics Students. *Applied Clinical Informatics*, *16*(02), 245–251. DOI: 10.1055/a-2461-2956 PMID: 40073859

Inuwa, M., & Rahim, S. B. A. (2020). Lean readiness factors and organizational readiness for change in manufacturing SMEs: The role of organizational culture. *Journal of Critical Reviews*, *7*(5), 56–67.

Ismail, H., Iqbal, A., & Nasr, L. (2019). Employee engagement and job performance in Lebanon: The mediating role of creativity. *International Journal of Productivity and Performance Management*, *68*(3), 506–523. DOI: 10.1108/IJPPM-02-2018-0052

Israr, A. (2024). BUSINESS INTELLIGENCE FOR DECISION SUPPORT IN SANCTIONS.

Jabbouri, N. I., Siron, R., Zahari, I., & Khalid, M. (2016). Impact of information technology infrastructure on innovation performance: An empirical study on private universities in Iraq. *Procedia Economics and Finance*, *39*, 861–869. DOI: 10.1016/S2212-5671(16)30250-7

Jabeen, G., Goli, G., Kafila, , & Gobinath, R. (2024). A bibliometric review on gender equity in human resource management. *Future Business Journal*, *10*(1), 101. DOI: 10.1186/s43093-024-00381-x

Jain, P., Jain, M., & Pamula, R. (2020). Explaining and predicting employees' attrition: A machine learning approach. *SN Applied Sciences*, *2*(4), 757. Advance online publication. DOI: 10.1007/s42452-020-2519-4

Jalili, H. (2024a). *Health Informatics Management and Leadership: Transforming Healthcare Through Technology The Essence of Health Informatics Management*. DOI: 10.13140/RG.2.2.24870.23361

Jaloliddin, R. (2023). Digitalization in global trade: opportunities and challenges for investment. *Global Trade and Customs Journal, 18*(10).

Jamaludin, N. (2024). Enhancing employee retention: the impact of training, career development and remuneration benefits in selected manufacturing companies of Johor Bahru. Information Management and Business Review, 16(3S(I)a), 669-679.

Jantan, H., Noh, M., & Yusoff, N. (2014). Towards applying support vector machine algorithm in employee achievement classification. In *Proceedings of the International Conference on Data Mining, Internet Computing, and Big Data (BigData2014)* (pp. 12–21). The Society of Digital Information and Wireless Communication.

Jariwala, A., Shah, S., & Pathak, D. (2022). Application of AI in financial risk management. *The Journal of Financial Data Science*, *8*(1), 23–44. DOI: 10.3905/jfds.2022.1.110

Jarrah, M. (2018). Modeling and simulation of renewable energy sources in smart grid using DEVS formalism. *Procedia Computer Science*, *19*(24), 12.

Jerab, D., & Mabrouk, T. (2023). The role of leadership in changing organizational culture. Available at *SSRN* 4574324. DOI: 10.2139/ssrn.4574324

Johnson, M., Jain, R., Brennan-Tonetta, P., Swartz, E., Silver, D., Paolini, J., Mamonov, S., & Hill, C. (2021). Impact of big data and artificial intelligence on industry: Developing a workforce roadmap for a data driven economy. *Global Journal of Flexible Systems Managment*, *22*(3), 197–217. DOI: 10.1007/s40171-021-00272-y

Johnson, S. (2023). Metaverse Economy: Opportunities and Challenges for Business. *Journal of Business Innovation*, *25*(2), 145–162.

Jokom, R., Semuel, H., & Wijaya, S. (2025). Sustainable tourism experiences: The role of digital technology and government support in creating tourists' memorable experiences. *Cogent Business & Management*, *12*(1), 2482026. DOI: 10.1080/23311975.2025.2482026

Jones, R., & Smith, T. (2023). *Continuous Feedback in Modern Performance Management*. Employee Relations Journal.

Jones, S. (2023). Supply chain risk management in the era of globalization. *European Journal of Supply Chain Management*, *1*(1), 11–21.

Joshi, H. C., & Kumar, S. (2023). Remote Work and Gender Inequality: Unmasking the Challenges and Seeking Solutions. *IEEE Internet Computing*.

Judijanto, L., Suharto, B., & Amrullah, A. (2024). Analysis of IoT Technology Utilization and Inventory Management System on Operational Efficiency and Visitor Experience at Tourism Destinations in Bandung. *West Science Social and Humanities Studies*, *2*(12), 2047–2058. DOI: 10.58812/wsshs.v2i12.1493

Jurčo, A. (2020). Data Lineage Analysis for Qlik Sense.

Kahn, W. A. (1990). Psychological Conditions of Personal Engagement and Disengagement at Work. *Academy of Management Journal*, *33*(4), 692–724. DOI: 10.2307/256287

Kaisler, S. H., Armour, F., & Espinosa, J. A. (2020). Big data and workforce strategy: New challenges for HR analytics. *Data Analytics Journal*, *5*(1), 12–25.

Kajtazi, M., & Tona, O. (2017). Integration with other data and systems. In *The Routledge companion to accounting information systems* (pp. 251–261). Routledge. DOI: 10.4324/9781315647210-19

Kambur, E., & Yildirim, T. (2023). From traditional to smart human resources management. *International Journal of Manpower*, *44*(3), 422–452. DOI: 10.1108/IJM-10-2021-0622

Karim, A. J. (2011). The value of competitive business intelligence system (CBIS) to stimulate competitiveness in global market. *International Journal of Business and Social Science*, *2*(19), 196–203.

Karoly, A., Fuller, R., & Galambos, P. (2018). Unsupervised clustering for deep learning: A tutorial survey. *Acta Polytechnica Hungarica*, *15*(8), 29–53. DOI: 10.12700/APH.15.8.2018.8.2

Kassa, B. Y., & Worku, E. K. (2025). The impact of artificial intelligence on organizational performance: The mediating role of employee productivity. *Journal of Open Innovation*, *11*(1), 100474. DOI: 10.1016/j.joitmc.2025.100474

Katari, A. (2022). Data lakes and Optimizing Query. Available at *SSRN*.

Kavanagh, M., et al. (2023). Adaptive Workforce Management: Leveraging Real-Time Data. Journal of Human Resource Advances.

Kayyali, M. (2024). Design thinking and creativity in entrepreneurial innovation. In *Applying Business Intelligence and Innovation to Entrepreneurship* (pp. 155–170). IGI Global. DOI: 10.4018/979-8-3693-1846-1.ch008

Kelan, E. K. (2024). Algorithmic inclusion: Shaping the predictive algorithms of artificial intelligence in hiring. *Human Resource Management Journal*, *34*(3), 694–707. DOI: 10.1111/1748-8583.12511

Kelei, H. E., Zeng, M., & Qiao, H. (2022). Research on power grid investment optimization model based on system dynamics. *Shaanxi Electric Power*, *34*(7), 1.

Kelly, D. (2003). A shock to the system? The impact of HRM on academic IR in Australia in comparison with USA and UK, 1980-95. *Journal of Technological Advancements*, *41*(2), 149–171. DOI: 10.1177/10384111030412003

Kerzner, H. (2023). *Project management metrics, KPIs, and dashboards: a guide to measuring and monitoring project performance*. John wiley & sons.

Kess-Momoh, A. J., Tula, S. T., Bello, B. G., Omotoye, G. B., & Daraojimba, A. I. (2024). Strategic human resource management in the 21st century: A review of trends and innovations. *World Journal of Advanced Research and Reviews*, *21*(1), 746–757.

Khandoker, R., Kabir, M. H., & Islam, S. (2021). Sentiment analysis for stock market prediction: A review of recent trends. *International Journal of Financial Engineering*, *18*(7), 210–224.

Kiarie, M. M., & Kinyua, G. M. (2025). Strategic fit as an antecedent of firm performance: Evidence from review of literature. *International Journal of Education and Research*, *13*(2), 221–252.

Kilag, O. K., Largo, J., Rabillas, A., Kilag, F., Angtud, M. K., Book, J. F., & Sasan, J. M. (2024). Administrators' Conflict Management and Strategies. International Multidisciplinary [IMJRISE]. *Journal of Research for Innovation, Sustainability, and Excellence*, *1*(1), 60–67.

Kim, Y. W., & Ko, J. (2014). HR Practices and Knowledge Sharing Behavior. *Public Personnel Management*, *43*(4), 586–607. DOI: 10.1177/0091026014542342

Kiu, C., & Tung, T. (2023). *The implications and impact of artificial intelligence, big data and HR analytics in HRM: A critical analysis of EU enterprises* (Doctoral dissertation, Durham University). Durham University Repository. https://doi.org/ DOI: 10.15128/r2t72dv70s

Klein, K. J., Ziegert, J. C., Knight, A. P., & Xiao, Y. (2006). Dynamic delegation: Shared, hierarchical, and deindividualized leadership in extreme action teams. *Administrative Science Quarterly*, *51*(4), 590–621. DOI: 10.2189/asqu.51.4.590

Knies, E., Boselie, P., Gould-Williams, J., & Vandenabeele, W. (2017). Strategic Human Resource Management and Public Sector Performance: Context Matters. *International Journal of Human Resource Management*, •••, 1–13.

Kocher, R., & Sahni, N. R. (2011). Hospitals' race to employ physicians—The logic behind a money-losing proposition. *The New England Journal of Medicine*, *364*(19), 1790–1793. DOI: 10.1056/NEJMp1101959 PMID: 21449774

Koenig, N., Tonidandel, S., Thompson, I., Albritton, B., Koohifar, F., Yankov, G., Speer, A., Hardy, J. H.III, Gibson, C., Frost, C., Liu, M., McNeney, D., Capman, J., Lowery, S., Kitching, M., Nimbkar, A., Boyce, A., Sun, T., Guo, F., & Newton, C. (2023). Improving measurement and prediction in personnel selection through the application of machine learning. *Personnel Psychology*, *76*(4), 1061–1123. DOI: 10.1111/peps.12608

Kolasani, S. (2023). Innovations in digital, enterprise, cloud, data transformation, and organizational change management using agile, lean, and data-driven methodologies. *International Journal of Machine Learning and Artificial Intelligence*, *4*(1), 1–18. DOI: 10.11648/j.ijmlai.20230401.11

Kolluru, S., & Mukhopadhaya, P. (2017). Empirical studies on innovation performance in the manufacturing and service sectors since 1995: A systematic review. *Economic Papers*, *36*(3), 223–248. DOI: 10.1111/1759-3441.12167

Kondapaka, P., Khanra, S., Malik, A., Kagzi, M., & Hemachandran, K. (2023). Finding a fit between CXO's experience and AI usage in CXO decision-making: Evidence from knowledge-intensive professional service firms. *Journal of Service Theory and Practice*, *33*(2), 280–308. DOI: 10.1108/JSTP-06-2022-0134

Koomey, J. G., Belady, C., Patterson, M., Santos, A., & Lange, K. (2009). *Assessing trends over time in performance, costs, and energy use for servers*. Lawrence Berkeley National Laboratory, Stanford University, Microsoft Corporation, and Intel Corporation.

Koomey, J. G., Belady, C., Patterson, M., Santos, A., & Lange, K. (2009). *Assessing trends over time in performance, costs, and energy use for servers*. Lawrence Berkeley National Laboratory.

Kourkoumelis, A., Anastasopoulou, E., Deirmentzoglou, G., Masouras, A., & Anastasiadou, S. (2024, September). Artificial Intelligence and Managerial Decision-Making in International Business. In *European Conference on Innovation and Entrepreneurship* (pp. 363-369). Academic Conferences International Limited. DOI: 10.34190/ecie.19.1.2573

Kovacic, I., Schuetz, C. G., Neumayr, B., & Schrefl, M. (2022). OLAP Patterns: A pattern-based approach to multidimensional data analysis. *Data & Knowledge Engineering, 138*, 101948. DOI: 10.1016/j.datak.2021.101948

Kraugusteeliana, K., Gadzali, S. S., & Ausat, A. M. A. (2023). Revitalizing Organizational Performance: Innovative Strategies for Information Technology-Based Human Resource Development. *Jurnal Minfo Polgan, 12*(2), 2384–2392. DOI: 10.33395/jmp.v12i2.13277

Krensky, P., Idoine, C., Brethenoux, E., Den Hamer, P., Choudhary, F., Jaffri, A., & Vashisth, S. (2021). *Magic quadrant for data science and machine learning platforms*. Gartner, Inc.

Krishna, K. S. R., Pasula, P., Kavyakeerthi, T., & Karthik, I. (2022, March). Identifying demand forecasting using machine learning for business intelligence. In *2022 6th International Conference on Computing Methodologies and Communication (ICCMC)* (pp. 938-942). IEEE. DOI: 10.1109/ICCMC53470.2022.9753965

Krügel, S.. (2023). Ethical considerations in the implementation of AI in human resource management. *Journal of Business Ethics, 178*(3), 651–668.

Kuhn, A., & Wolter, S. C. (2022). Things versus people: Gender differences in vocational interests and in occupational preferences. *Journal of Economic Behavior & Organization, 203*, 210–234. DOI: 10.1016/j.jebo.2022.09.003

Kumar, N., Priya, S. S., Varghese, V. K. R., Patra, J. P., & Nishant, N. (2024). An improved method for fault detection electric power system protection using SVMCNN model. In *2024 International Conference on Electronics, Computing, Communication and Control Technology (ICECCC)* (pp. 1–6). Bengaluru, India. DOI: 10.1109/ICECCC61767.2024.10593976

Lado, A. A., & Zhang, M. J. (1998). Expert Systems, Knowledge Development and Utilization, and Sustained Competitive Advantage: A Resource-Based Model. *Journal of Management, 24*(4), 489–509. DOI: 10.1177/014920639802400402

Lajšić, H. (2019). Strategic human resources management and business intelligence systems in the purpose of social and economic development. EMC Review-Economy and Market Communication Review, 17(1).

Lardi, K. (2025). *Artificial Intelligence for Business: Harness AI for value growth and innovation*. Kogan Page Ltd. eBook: 9781398618015.

Lateef, A., & Omotayo, F. O. (2019). Information audit as an important tool in organizational management: A review of literature. *Business Information Review*, *36*(1), 15–22. DOI: 10.1177/0266382119831458

Latham, G. P., & Pinder, C. C. (2019). Work motivation theory and research at the dawn of the twenty-first century. *Annual Review of Psychology*, *56*(1), 485–516. DOI: 10.1146/annurev.psych.55.090902.142105 PMID: 15709944

Laurent, C., Boudreau, J., & Bal, P. M. (2022). Leveraging analytics to create inclusive workplaces. *HR Review Quarterly*, *15*(4), 21–35.

Lavanya, G., Murthy, K. S., & Sivakumar, S. (2024). Renewable energy-powered robot for fully-automated tea leaf harvesting: A solution for labor shortage and environmental sustainability. *AIP Conference Proceedings*, *3161*(1), 020340. DOI: 10.1063/5.0229350

Lawler, E. E. (2008). Choosing the right talent management strategy. *Workspan*, *51*(7), 73–75.

Lawler, E. E.III. (2009). Make Human Capital A Source of Competitive Advantage. *Organizational Dynamics*, *38*(1), 1–7. DOI: 10.1016/j.orgdyn.2008.10.007

Lee, J., & Hong, J. (2023). The impact of metaverse on consumer behavior and marketing strategies: A systematic review and meta-analysis. *Computers in Human Behavior*, *124*, 106982.

Lee, J., & Song, J. H. (2024). Lee "How does algorithm-based HR predict employees' sentiment? Developing an employee experience model through sentiment analysis". *Industrial and Commercial Training*, *56*(4), 273–289. Advance online publication. DOI: 10.1108/ICT-08-2023-0060

Lee, J., Suh, T., Roy, D., & Baucus, M. (2019). Emerging technology and business model innovation: The case of artificial intelligence. *Journal of Open Innovation*, *5*(4), 44. DOI: 10.3390/joitmc5030044

Lee, K., & Kim, J. (2026). Beyond Virtual Reality: Exploring the business potential of the metaverse. *Journal of Business Technology*, *12*(4), 320–335.

Lee, S. M., Hong, S., & Katerattanakul, P. (2004). Impact of data warehousing on organizational performance of retailing firms. *International Journal of Information Technology & Decision Making*, *3*(01), 61–79. DOI: 10.1142/S0219622004000040

Lee, S., & Ha-Brookshire, J. (2017). Ethical climate and job attitude in fashion retail employees' turnover intention, and perceived organizational sustainability performance: A cross-sectional study. *Sustainability (Basel)*, *9*(3), 465. DOI: 10.3390/su9030465

Lehmann, C. U., & Gundlapalli, A. V. (2015). Improving Bridging from Informatics Practice to Theory. *Methods of Information in Medicine*, *54*(06), 540–545. DOI: 10.3414/ME15-01-0138 PMID: 26577504

Lencioni, P. M. (2002). Make Your Values Mean Something. *Harvard Business Review*. PMID: 12140851

Lengnick-Hall, M. L., Neely, A. R., & Stone, C. B. (2018). Human resource management in the digital age: Big data, HR analytics and artificial intelligence. In *Management and Technological Challenges in the Digital Age* (pp. 1–30). CRC Press. DOI: 10.1201/9781351238922-1

Leonardi, P. M., & Barley, S. R. (2010). What is under construction here? Social action, materiality, and power in constructivist studies of technology and organizing. *The Academy of Management Annals*, *4*(1), 1–51. DOI: 10.5465/19416521003654160

Lepak, D. P., & Snell, S. A. (1999). The human resource architecture: Toward a theory of human capital allocation and development. *Academy of Management Review*, *24*(1), 31–48. DOI: 10.2307/259035

Le, T. T., & Ikram, M. (2022). Do sustainability innovation and firm competitiveness help improve firm performance? Evidence from the SME sector in Vietnam. *Sustainable Production and Consumption*, *29*, 588–599. DOI: 10.1016/j.spc.2021.11.008

Lewis, R. E., & Heckman, R. J. (2006). Talent management: A critical review. *Human Resource Management Review*, *16*(2), 139–154. DOI: 10.1016/j.hrmr.2006.03.001

Liargovas, P., & Papageorgiou, C. (2024). Regional Policy: Disparities, Development and Future Direction. In The European Integration, Vol. 2: Institutions and Policies (pp. 253-286). Cham: Springer Nature Switzerland.

Liboni, L. B., Cezarino, L. O., Jabbour, C. J. C., Oliveira, B. G., & Stefanelli, N. O. (2019). Smart industry and the pathways to HRM 4.0: Implications for SCM. *Supply Chain Management*, *24*(1), 124–146. DOI: 10.1108/SCM-03-2018-0150

Liebowitz, J. (2018). The synergy of knowledge management and artificial intelligence to support healthcare. *International Journal of Healthcare Management*, *22*(2), 475–487.

Li, J., & Lakzi, A. (2022). A new model for assessing the role of IT-based systems, public policies and business intelligence on the export competitiveness's efficiency. *Kybernetes*, *51*(1), 77–94. DOI: 10.1108/K-07-2020-0430

Lim, C. S., Malik, E. F., Khaw, K. W., Alnoor, A., Chew, X., Chong, Z. L., & Al Akasheh, M.LIM. (2023). Hybrid ga–deep autoencoder–knn model for employee turnover prediction. *Statistics, Optimization & Information Computing*, *12*(1), 75–90. DOI: 10.19139/soic-2310-5070-1799

Lim, Y. Y., & Teoh, A. P. (2020). Realizing the strategic impact of business intelligence utilization. *Strategic Direction*, *36*(2), 7–9. DOI: 10.1108/SD-09-2019-0184

Linardatos, P., Papastefanopoulos, V., & Kotsiantis, S. (2020). Explainable ai: A review of machine learning interpretability methods. *Entropy (Basel, Switzerland)*, *23*(1), 18. DOI: 10.3390/e23010018 PMID: 33375658

Lin, S., Lu, W., Chen, Y., & Wu, M. (2022). The relationships among proactive personality, work engagement, and perceived work competence in sports coaches: The moderating role of perceived supervisor support. *International Journal of Environmental Research and Public Health*, *19*(19), 12707. DOI: 10.3390/ijerph191912707 PMID: 36232008

Lipsky, M. (2010). *Street-level bureaucracy: Dilemmas of the individual in public services*. Russell Sage Foundation.

Liu, X., & Yang, J. (2011). Business intelligence approach to support modelling and analysis of complex economic networks. *International journal of networking and virtual organisations, 8*(3-4), 281-291.

Liu, H. Q., & Chen, H. J. (2020). Informatization construction for power grid infrastructure construction enterprises. *Electric Power Information Technology*, (11), 2.

Liu, W. D., Lu, X.-F., & Yu, X.-Y.. (2020). Annual portfolio forecast for infrastructure projects of power grid companies. *East China Electric Power*, (11), 2.

Liu, Y., Zhang, H., & Xu, R. (2023). The impact of technology on promoting physical activities and mental health: A gender-based study. *BMC Psychology*, *11*(1), 298. DOI: 10.1186/s40359-023-01348-3 PMID: 37775753

Li, W. (2023). A transformer-based deep learning framework to predict employee attrition. *PeerJ. Computer Science*, *9*, e1570. DOI: 10.7717/peerj-cs.1570 PMID: 37810348

Li, X.. (2023). Metaverse marketing: Trends, challenges, and opportunities. *Journal of Marketing Management*, *39*(7-8), 703–732.

Li, X., Chen, K., Sun, S. X., Fung, T., Wang, H., & Zeng, D. D. (2016). A commonsense knowledge-enabled textual analysis approach for financial market surveillance. *INFORMS Journal on Computing*, *28*(2), 278–294. DOI: 10.1287/ijoc.2015.0677

Li, Y. M., Lai, C. Y., & Kao, J. (2008). Incorporate personality trait with support vector machine to acquire quality matching of personnel recruitment. In *Proceedings of the 4th International Conference on Business and Information* (pp. 1–11).

Li, Z.-A., Ge, J.-F., & Zhang, Y.-J. (2019). Application of beta regression model for the data mining forecast. [Natural Science Edition]. *Journal of Nantong University*, *33*(2), 8.

Lockwood, N. R. (2006). Talent Management: Driver for Organizational Success. *HRMagazine*, *51*(6), 1–11.

Lombardi, R. (2019). Knowledge transfer and organizational performance and business process: Past, present, and future researches. *Business Process Management Journal*, *25*(1), 2–9. DOI: 10.1108/BPMJ-02-2019-368

Lorincová, S., Hitka, M., Štarchoň, P., & Stachová, K. (2018). Strategic instrument for sustainability of human resource management in small and medium-sized enterprises using management data. *Sustainability (Basel)*, *10*(10), 3687. DOI: 10.3390/su10103687

Lucifora, C., & Vigani, D. (2022). What if your boss is a woman? Evidence on gender discrimination at the workplace. *Review of Economics of the Household*, *20*(2), 389–417. DOI: 10.1007/s11150-021-09562-x

Lu, Y. (2017). Industry 4.0: A survey on technologies, applications and open research issues. *Journal of Industrial Information Integration*, *6*, 1–10. DOI: 10.1016/j.jii.2017.04.005

Maatman, M., & Meijerink, J. (2017). Why sharing is synergy: The role of decentralized control mechanisms and centralized HR capabilities in creating HR shared service value. *Personnel Review*, *46*(7), 1297–1317. DOI: 10.1108/PR-09-2016-0245

Madhani, P. (2023). Strategic human resource analytics: Enhancing organizational performance through data-driven insights. *International Journal of Human Resource Management*, *34*(8), 1567–1589.

Madhuri, A., & Kumar, B. R. (2025). HR Analytics and Decision-Making: A Data-Driven Approach to Employee Performance Management. *Journal of Neonatal Surgery*, *14*(7s).

Mahoney, T. A., & Deckop, J. R. (1986). Evolution of concept and practice in personnel administration/human resource management. *Journal of Management*, *12*(2), 223–241. DOI: 10.1177/014920638601200206

Máiz-Mazuela, C., Medina-Perucha, L., Berenguera, A., López-Jiménez, T., Rodríguez-Giralt, I., Cerezo Sepúlveda, P., & Jacques-Aviñó, C. (2023). Essential Workers Balancing Life and Work during the COVID-19 Syndemic in Spain: A Qualitative and Gender-Based Study. *Health & Social Care in the Community*, *2023*(1), 1124583. DOI: 10.1155/2023/1124583

Malhi, A. K., Pannu, H. S., & Sharma, A. (2018, July). The Digital Universe: Changing Paradigms of E-Business in India. In *2018 2nd International Conference on Engineering Innovation (ICEI)* (pp. 96-101). IEEE.

Malik, A., Budhwar, P., & Kazmi, B. A. (2023). Artificial intelligence (AI)-assisted HRM: Towards an extended strategic framework. *Human Resource Management Review*, *33*(1), 100940. Advance online publication. DOI: 10.1016/j.hrmr.2022.100940

Malik, A., Budhwar, P., Mohan, H., & Srikanth, N. (2022). Employee experience –the missing link for engaging employees: Insights from an MN E's ai-based hr ecosystem. *Human Resource Management*, *62*(1), 97–115. DOI: 10.1002/hrm.22133

Malik, S. Y., Cao, Y., Mughal, Y. H., Kundi, G. M., Mughal, M. H., & Ramayah, T. (2020). Pathways towards sustainability in organizations: Empirical evidence on the role of green human resource management practices and green intellectual capital. *Sustainability (Basel)*, *12*(8), 3228. DOI: 10.3390/su12083228

Manjunath, T. N., Pushpa, S. K., Hegadi, R. S., & Ananya Hathwar, K. S. (2023). A study on big data engineering using cloud data warehouse. Data Engineering and Data Science: Concepts and Applications, 49-69.

Manthena, S. R. L. (2021). Impact of artificial intelligence on recruitment and its benefits. *International Journal of Innovative Research in Engineering and Multidisciplinary Physical Sciences*, *9*(1), 58–63. DOI: 10.37082/IJIRMPS.2021.v09si05.013

Mapuva, J., & Takabika, M. (2020). The politics of institutional autonomy and political governance: The case of Zimbabwe. *African Journal of Governance and Development*, *9*(1), 185–204.

Margherita, E. (2021). Business intelligence and workforce agility: A new approach to strategic HRM. *Management Decision*, *59*(4), 758–775.

Marikyan, D., Papagiannidis, S., & Alamanos, E. (2019). A systematic review of the smart home literature: A user perspective. *Technological Forecasting and Social Change*, *138*, 139–154. DOI: 10.1016/j.techfore.2018.08.015

Marion, T. J., & Fixson, S. K. (2021). The transformation of the innovation process: How digital tools are changing work, collaboration, and organizations in new product development. *Journal of Product Innovation Management, 38*(2), 192–215. DOI: 10.1111/jpim.12547

Marjamäki, P. (2017). *Evolution and trends of business intelligence systems: A systematic mapping study* [Master's thesis, University of Oulu Repository].

Marjamäki, P. (2017). *Evolution and trends of business intelligence systems: A systematic mapping study*. University of Oulu.

Marler, J. H., & Boudreau, J. W. (2017). An evidence-based review of HR Analytics. *International Journal of Human Resource Management, 28*(1), 3–26. DOI: 10.1080/09585192.2016.1244699

Marr, B. (2018). *Data-driven HR: How to use analytics and metrics to drive performance* (1st ed.). Kogan Page.

Martinez-Gil, J., Freudenthaler, B., & Natschläger, T. (2018). Recommendation of job offers using random forests and support vector machines. In *Data Analytics Solutions for Real-Life* (pp. 26–30).

Martin-Raugh, M., Tannenbaum, R. J., Tocci, C. M., & Reese, C. (2016). Behaviorally anchored rating scales: An application for evaluating teaching practice. *Teaching and Teacher Education, 59*, 414–419. DOI: 10.1016/j.tate.2016.07.026

Matysek-Jędrych, A. (2012). *Competitiveness and crisis—The case of Baltic states economies* [Working paper]. Poznan University of Economics.

Maurer, C. C., & Qureshi, I. (2021). Not just good for her: A temporal analysis of the dynamic relationship between representation of women and collective employee turnover. *Organization Studies, 42*(1), 85–107. DOI: 10.1177/0170840619875480

Maxamadumarovich, U. A., Obrenovic, B., & Amonboyev, M. (2012). Understanding the innovation concept. *Journal of Innovation and Sustainability RISUS, 3*(1), 19–26. DOI: 10.24212/2179-3565.2012v3i3p19-26

Mayernik, M. S. (2021). Metadata. *Knowledge Organization, 47*(8), 696–713. DOI: 10.5771/0943-7444-2020-8-696

Mayer, R. C., Davis, J. H., & Schoorman, F. D. (1995). An integrative model of organizational trust. *Academy of Management Review, 20*(3), 709–734. DOI: 10.2307/258792

McBride, J., & O'Connell, P. (2022). *Personalized Engagement Initiatives through Predictive Analytics*. Organizational Behavior Review.

McCartney, S., Murphy, C., & Mccarthy, J. (2021). 21st century HR: A competency model for the emerging role of HR Analysts. *Personnel Review*, *50*(6), 1495–1513. DOI: 10.1108/PR-12-2019-0670

McDonnell, A. (2017). Globalization, markets and institutional change: Implications for HRM. In Wilkinson, A., Redman, T., & Dundon, T. (Eds.), *Contemporary human resource management: Text and cases* (pp. 97–116). Pearson.

McGrath, L. (2008). The War for Talent: High Potential Management is the Winning Strategy. *Accountancy Ireland*, *40*(2), 60–61.

McLaughlin, B. (2024). *Designing Prediction and Recommendation Algorithms to Improve Human Decision-Making*. Stanford University.

Mehrabi, N., Morstatter, F., Saxena, N., Lerman, K., & Galstyan, A. (2021). A survey on bias and fairness in machine learning. *ACM Computing Surveys*, *54*(6), 1–35. DOI: 10.1145/3457607

Mehta, N., & Pickens, A. (2020). *The customer success economy: Why every aspect of your business model needs a paradigm shift*. John Wiley & Sons.

Melhem, R., & Özgit, H. (2019). The mediating role of employee motivation on internal marketing and employee retention. *Ottoman Journal of Tourism and Management Research*, *4*(3), 562–583. DOI: 10.26465/ojtmr.2018339528

Meng, M. H., & Qian, Y. (2018, July). A blockchain aided metric for predictive delivery performance in supply chain management. In *2018 IEEE International Conference on Service Operations and Logistics, and Informatics (SOLI)* (pp. 285-290). IEEE. DOI: 10.1109/SOLI.2018.8476723

Miethlich, B., Belotserkovich, D., Abasova, S., Zatsarinnaya, E., & Veselitsky, O. (2022). Transformation of digital management in enterprises amidst the COVID-19 pandemic. *Institute of Economics*, *14*(3), 1–26. DOI: 10.22452/IJIE.vol14no1.1

Miliopoulou, G. Z., & Kapareliotis, I. (2021). The toll of success: Female leaders in the "women-friendly" Greek advertising agencies. *Gender, Work and Organization*, *28*(5), 1741–1765. DOI: 10.1111/gwao.12636

Milne, S., Mason, D., Speidel, U., & West-Newman, T. (2005). TOURISM AND COMMUNITY INFORMATICS: THE CASE OF KIWITRAILS. *Tourism, Culture & Communication*, *5*(2), 127–137. DOI: 10.3727/109830405774791447

Minbaeva, D. (2018). Building credible human capital analytics for organizational competitive advantage. *Human Resource Management*, *57*(3), 701–713. DOI: 10.1002/hrm.21848

Min, H., Lim, Y. K., & Park, J. W. (2017). Supply chain analytics for enhancing the maritime security. *International Journal of Logistics Systems and Management, 28*(2), 164–179. DOI: 10.1504/IJLSM.2017.086352

Min, H., Lim, Y. K., & Park, J. W. (2019). An integrated terminal operating system for enhancing the port security. *International Journal of Logistics Systems and Management, 34*(2), 193–210. DOI: 10.1504/IJLSM.2019.102211

Mohammad, B. T. (2025b). Revolutionizing Hospitality: Leveraging Mobile Apps and Cutting-Edge Room Technologies in the Hotel Industry. In B. Varghese & S. H. (Eds.), *Advancing Smart Tourism Through Analytics* (pp. 315-332). IGI Global Scientific Publishing. DOI: 10.4018/979-8-3693-3715-8.ch017

Mohammad, B. T., Muhsina, K., Mou, T. A., & Kumar, S. (2024), "Community-based Tourism in Bangladesh: A Strategic Approach", Shaikh, E. and Singh, K. (Ed.) *Corporate Social Responsibility, Corporate Governance and Business Ethics in Tourism Management: A Business Strategy for Sustainable Organizational Performance*, Emerald Publishing Limited, Leeds, pp. 159-175. DOI: 10.1108/978-1-83608-704-520241012

Mohammad, B. T. (2020b). The Future of Culinary Tourism: An Emerging Dimension for the Tourism Industry of Bangladesh. I-Manager's. *Journal of Management, 15*(1), 27. DOI: 10.26634/jmgt.15.1.17181

Mohammad, B. T. (2021). An assessment of the roles of the social network in the development of the Tourism Industry in Bangladesh. *International Journal of Business, Law, and Education, 2*(3), 85–93. DOI: 10.56442/ijble.v2i3.21

Mohammad, B. T. (2025a). Maximizing Impact: The Role of Influencer Marketing in Contemporary Tourism Management. In Özsungur, F. (Ed.), *Navigating Organizational Behavior in the Digital Age with AI* (pp. 277–304). IGI Global Scientific Publishing., DOI: 10.4018/979-8-3693-8442-8.ch011

Mohammad, B. T. (2025c). Climate change adaptation strategies for a tourism destination: A study of Kuakata beach. *Acta Scientiarum Polonorum. Administratio Locorum, 24*(1), 165–179. DOI: 10.31648/aspal.10073

Moşteanu, N. R. (2024). Adapting to the unpredictable: Building resilience for business continuity in an ever-changing landscape. *European Journal of Theoretical and Applied Sciences, 2*(1), 444–457. DOI: 10.59324/ejtas.2024.2(1).37

Mousa, M., Massoud, H., & Ayoubi, R. M. (2021). Employee well-being and the role of AI-powered BI in HR. *Journal of Organizational Change Management, 34*(2), 245–261.

Muhammad, A. U., Shah, Z. A., & Azhar, K. A. (2021). *The increasing role of HRIS in facilitating sustainable human resource management practices in 21st-century organizations*. Currency.

Mukhiya, S. K., & Ahmed, U. (2020). *Hands-On Exploratory Data Analysis with Python: Perform EDA techniques to understand, summarize, and investigate your data*. Packt Publishing Ltd.

Muley, A. A., Shettigar, R., Katekhaye, D., Harisha, B. S., & Kumar, P. A. (2023). Technological advancements and the evolution of HR analytics: A review. *Bol. Lit. Oral-Lit.Journal, 10*(3), 429–439.

Müller, S., & Shamsie, K. (2023). Digital Disruption and the Evolution of Business Models: A Scholarly Examination. *Abbottabad University Journal of Business and Management Sciences, 1*(01), 43–52.

Munir, A., & Akhtar, J. (2025). Bridging Tradition and Modernity: Islamic Ethical Guidelines for Sustainable Tourism in Pakistan. In Bayraktaroglu, E., & Çıvak, B. (Eds.), *Modern Social Challenges Impacting Tourism* (pp. 205–230). IGI Global., DOI: 10.4018/979-8-3693-8794-8.ch009

Muntean, M., & Mircea, G. (2007). Business intelligence solutions for gaining competitive advantage. *Informações Econômicas, 11*(3), 22–25.

Muryjas, P., & Wawer, M. (2014). Business intelligence as a support in human resources strategies realization in contemporary organizations. *Aktual'ni Problemi Ekonomìki, 2*(152), 183–190.

Mwaro, P. N., Ogada, K., & Cheruiyot, W. (2021). Neural network model for talent recruitment and management for employee development and retention. In *Proceedings of the 2021 IEEE AFRICON* (pp. 1–6). DOI: 10.1109/AFRICON51333.2021.9571014

Nagy, J., Olah, J., Erdei, E., Mate, D., & Popp, J. (2018). The role and impact of Industry 4.0 and the Internet of Things on the business strategy of the value chain—The case of Hungary. *Sustainability (Basel), 10*(10), 3491. DOI: 10.3390/su10103491

Nankervis, A. R., Baird, M., Coffey, J., & Shields, J. (2011). *Human resource management: Strategy and practice* (7th ed.). Cengage Learning.

Naparin, M., Aryadi, M., Prihatiningrum, R. R. Y., & Suyatnob, S. (2024). Wetland Tourism Marketing: The Influence of Experience Dimensions and Memorable Tourism Experience on Tourist Loyalty of the Bakut Island Nature Tourism Park, Indonesia. *International Review of Management and Marketing, 14*(6), 1–8. DOI: 10.32479/irmm.17115

Narayanan, S., Swaminathan, J., & Talluri, S. (2014). Knowledge diversity, turnover, and organizational-unit productivity: An empirical analysis in a knowledge-intensive context. *Production and Operations Management*, *23*(8), 1332–1351. DOI: 10.1111/poms.12039

Nardelli, G., & Broumels, M. (2018). Managing innovation processes through value co-creation: A process case from business-to-business service practice. *International Journal of Innovation Management*, *22*(6), 1850030. DOI: 10.1142/S1363919618500305

Nasir, M., Dag, A., Young, W. A.II, & Delen, D. (2020). Determining optimal skill-sets for business managers based on local and global job markets: A text analytics approach. *Decision Sciences Journal of Innovative Education*, *18*(3), 374–408. DOI: 10.1111/dsji.12212

Negash, S. (2004). Business intelligence. *Communications of the Association for Information Systems*, *13*(1), 54.

Nevo, S., & Wade, M. R. (2010). The formation and value of IT-enabled resources: Antecedents and consequences of synergistic relationships. *Management Information Systems Quarterly*, *34*(1), 163–183. DOI: 10.2307/20721419

Ngo, Q. D., Nguyen, Q. H., & Vu, C. (2025). Envisioning future workforce adaptability: A multi-layered analysis of skills ecosystems in Vietnam's emerging economy. *Futures & Foresight Science*, *7*(1), e70000. Advance online publication. DOI: 10.1002/ffo2.70000

Nguyen, M. H., & Armoogum, J. (2021). Perception and preference for home-based telework in the COVID-19 era: A gender-based analysis in Hanoi, Vietnam. *Sustainability (Basel)*, *13*(6), 3179. DOI: 10.3390/su13063179

Nguyen, T. B., & Moltó, M. D. (2023). Digital and technological transformation in the metaverse: Implications for consumption and marketing. *Journal of Business Research*, *136*, 579–591.

Nguyen, T. M., & Malik, A. (2022). A two-wave cross-lagged study on AI service quality: The moderating effects of the job level and job role. *British Journal of Management*, *33*(3), 1221–1237.

Ngwa, P., & Ngaruye, I. (2023). Big data analytics for predictive system maintenance using machine learning models. *Advanced Data Science and Adaptive Analysis*, *15*(1), 2350001. DOI: 10.1142/S2424922X23500018

Niederman, F. (2021). Project management: Openings for disruption from AI and advanced analytics. *Information Technology & People*, *34*(6), 1570–1599. DOI: 10.1108/ITP-09-2020-0639

Niu, Y., Ying, L., Yang, J., Bao, M., & Sivaparthipan, C. B. (2021). Organizational business intelligence and decision making using big data analytics. *Information Processing & Management*, *58*(6), 102725. DOI: 10.1016/j.ipm.2021.102725

Nkosi, N. (2024). Breaking Barriers and Building Bridges: Unveiling the Enablers of Women School Leaders to Overcome Gender Inequality in KwaZulu-Natal, South Africa. *Research in Educational Policy and Management*, *6*(2), 436–453. DOI: 10.46303/repam.2024.43

Noble, J. I., Kilag, O. K., & Viscara, C. (2023). Bridging Academia and Community: A Holistic Approach to Disaster Risk Management. Excellencia: *International Multi-disciplinary Journal of Education* (2994-9521), 1(6), 36-45.

Nocker, M., & Sena, V. (2019). Big data and human resources management: The rise of talent analytics. *Social Sciences (Basel, Switzerland)*, *8*(10), 273. DOI: 10.3390/socsci8100273

Nonaka, I. (1994). A dynamic theory of organizational knowledge creation. *Organization Science*, *5*(1), 14–37. DOI: 10.1287/orsc.5.1.14

Nonaka, I., & Toyama, R. (2005). The theory of the knowledge-creating firm: Subjectivity, objectivity and synthesis. *Industrial and Corporate Change*, *14*(3), 419–436. DOI: 10.1093/icc/dth058

Noor, F. S., & Prahasta, Y. A. (2024). HR Technology Trends 2024: A Glimpse into the Future of Workforce Management. *Escalate: Economics and Business Journal*, *2*(02), 44–53.

Norton, L. W. (2025). Artificial intelligence and organizational strategy: Ethical and governance implications. *Consulting Psychology Journal.* Advance online publication. DOI: 10.1037/cpb0000280

Ntalakos, A., Belias, D., & Tsigilis, N. (2022, September). Leadership styles and group dynamics in the tourism industry. In International conference of the international association of cultural and digital tourism (pp. 117-131). Cham: Springer Nature Switzerland.

Ntalakos, A., Belias, D., & Tsigilis, N. (2023, August). Analyzing the organizational factors that influence hotel employees' team efficiency. In International Conference of the International Association of Cultural and Digital Tourism (pp. 179-208). Cham: Springer Nature Switzerland.

Ntalakos, A., Belias, D., & Koustelios, A. (2024b). The Relationship Between Leadership Styles, Organizational Culture and Group Dynamics in the Hospitality Industry. In Katsoni, V., & Cassar, G. (Eds.), *Recent Advancements in Tourism Business, Technology, and Social Sciences. IACuDiT 2023. Springer Proceedings in Business and Economics*. Springer., DOI: 10.1007/978-3-031-54342-5_19

Ntalakos, A., Belias, D., Koustelios, A., & Tsigilis, N. (2025). Examining the Validity of Organizational Behavior Measurement Scales in the Greek Hospitality Industry. *International Journal of Hospitality and Tourism Systems*, *18*(1), 1–14. DOI: 10.21863/ijhts/2025.18.1.001

Ntalakos, A., Belias, D., Rossidis, I., Papademetriou, C., Koustelios, A., & Tsigilis, N. (2024). Group Dynamics in a Multicultural World: Embracing Diversity to Increase Group Performance. In Belias, D., Rossidis, I., & Papademetriou, C. (Eds.), *Organizational Behavior and Human Resource Management for Complex Work Environments* (pp. 356–377). IGI Global., DOI: 10.4018/979-8-3693-3466-9.ch017

Ntalakos, A., Belias, D., & Tsigilis, N. (2024). Analyzing the Organizational Factors that Influence Hotel Employees' Team Efficiency. In Katsoni, V., & Cassar, G. (Eds.), *Recent Advancements in Tourism Business, Technology and Social Sciences. IACuDiT 2023. Springer Proceedings in Business and Economics*. Springer., DOI: 10.1007/978-3-031-54342-5_11

Ntalakos, A., Viterouli, M., Belias, D., Rossidis, I., & Koustelios, A. (2024d). Fostering Total Quality Management and Group Dynamics in the Tourism and Hospitality Industry. In *Papademetriou, C., Anastasiadou, S., Ragazou, K., Garefalakis, A., Papalexandris, S. ESG and Total Quality Management in Human Resources* (pp. 219–242). IGI Global. DOI: 10.4018/979-8-3693-2991-7.ch011

Nwaimo, C. S., Adewumi, A., & Ajiga, D. (2022). Advanced data analytics and business intelligence: Building resilience in risk management. *International Journal of Scientific Research and Applications*, *6*(2), 121.

Nyberg, A. J., Moliterno, T. P., Hale, D.Jr, & Lepak, D. P. (2014). Resource-Based Perspectives on Unit-Level Human Capital: A Review and Integration. *Journal of Management*, *40*(1), 316–346. DOI: 10.1177/0149206312458703

Nyomi, R. (2025). Harnessing data analytics for predictive insights: Advancing decision-making with big data innovations. *International Journal of Research Publication and Reviews*, *6*(1), 2915–2936. DOI: 10.55248/gengpi.6.0125.0502

Obeidat, B. Y. (2016). The effect of strategic orientation on organizational performance: The mediating role of innovation. *International Journal of Communications, Network and Systems Sciences*, *9*(4), 478–505. DOI: 10.4236/ijcns.2016.911039

Ogier, J. (2003). Advancing the profession. *Human Resources Monthly*, *3*(2), 24–25.

Ognjanović, I., Zoulias, E., & Mantas, J. (2024). Progress Achieved, Landmarks, and Future Concerns in Biomedical and Health Informatics. *Health Care*, *12*(20), 2041. DOI: 10.3390/healthcare12202041 PMID: 39451456

Olabiyi, E. O. (2023). *The Prospects & Challenges of HR Management and HR Technologies in a Post-Pandemic Hybrid Workplace*. The American University of Paris.

Oriekhoe, A., Adisa, T., & Ilugbusi, T. (2024). Ethical implications of business intelligence in contemporary human resource management. *Journal of Business Ethics*, *185*(2), 312–329.

Orlikowski, W. J., & Barley, S. R. (2001). Technology and institutions: What can research on information technology and research on organizations learn from each other? *Management Information Systems Quarterly*, *25*(2), 145–165. DOI: 10.2307/3250927

Orlikowski, W., & Scott, S. (2008). Sociomateriality: Challenging the separation of technology, work and organization. *The Academy of Management Annals*, *2*(1), 433–474. DOI: 10.5465/19416520802211644

Ortega, E. A., Vega Escobar, A. M., & Martín García, V. (2015). Technology Monitoring System to Improve the Competitiveness and Innovation in Colombian Companies. In *Knowledge Management in Organizations: 10th International Conference, KMO 2015, Maribor, Slovenia, August 24-28, 2015* [Springer International Publishing.]. *Proceedings*, *10*, 312–328.

Orujaliyev, R. (2024). The effect of non-financial incentives on employee engagement and employee retention. European Journal of Humanities and Social Sciences, 3-10. DOI: 10.29013/EJHSS-24-2-3-10

Osma, A., Fowowe, O. O., Agboluaje, R., & Orekha, P. O. (2025). Integrating machine learning in business analytics consulting for proactive decision-making and innovation. *World Journal of Advanced Research and Reviews*, *25*(01), 1817–1836. DOI: 10.30574/wjarr.2025.25.1.0251

Otundo Richard, M. (2024). Nexus Between Strategic Sustainable Tourism Investment Projects and Sustainable Growth and Development of Kenya's Coast Region. SSRN *Electronic Journal*. DOI: 10.2139/ssrn.4964247

Ozdemir, F., Coskun, M., Gezer, C., & Gungor, V. C. (2020). Assessing employee attrition using classification algorithms. In *Proceedings of the 2020 4th International Conference on Information System and Data Mining (ICISDM '20)* (pp. 118–122). Association for Computing Machinery. DOI: 10.1145/3404663.3404681

Packard, M. D., & Bylund, P. L. (2024). Truth, knowledge, and entrepreneurship theory: Arguments for a rationalist scientific epistemology. *Small Business Economics*, Advance online publication. DOI: 10.1007/s11187-024-00993-1

Pagano, T. P., Loureiro, R. B., Lisboa, F. V., Peixoto, R. M., Guimarães, G. A., Cruz, G. O., Araujo, M. M., Santos, L. L., Cruz, M. A. S., Oliveira, E. L. S., Winkler, I., & Nascimento, E. G. (2023). Bias and unfairness in machine learning models: A systematic review on datasets, tools, fairness metrics, and identification and mitigation methods. *Big Data and Cognitive Computing*, *7*(1), 15. DOI: 10.3390/bdcc7010015

Pala, S. K. (2024). Use and Applications of Data Analytics in Human Resource Management and Talent Acquisition. International Journal of Enhanced Research in Management & Computer Applications ISSN, 2319-7463.

Papademetriou, C., Anastasiadou, S., & Konteos, G. (2022). The Effect of Human Resource Management Practices on the Quality of Service, Customer Satisfaction, and Organizational Performance in Cypriot Urban Hotel Industry. *HAICTA 2022 Conference Proceedings*.

Papademetriou, C., Belias, D., Anastasiadou, S., Ragazou, K., & Garefalakis, A. Sustainability: ESG and Human Resource Management. *In Papademetriou, C., Anastasiadou, S., Ragazou, K., Garefalakis, A., Papalexandris, S. ESG and Total Quality Management in Human Resources*, 1-15, DOI: DOI: 10.4018/979-8-3693-2991-7.ch001

Papademetriou, C., Belias, D., Ragazou, K. (2024). Human Resource (HR) Management New Dynamics in Hiring, Technology Adoption, Work Environment Diversity: HR Managers' Interviews. *Communications of International Proceedings*, 2024 (16), .DOI: 10.5171/2024.4422824

Papademetriou, C., Belias, D., Ragazou, K., & Garefalakis, A. (2024). The Role of Human Resource Management (HRM) in Employee Mental Health and Well-Being for Complex Work Environments. In Organizational Behavior and Human Resource Management for Complex Work Environments (pp. 81-94). IGI Global.

Papademetriou, C., Anastasiadou, S. D., & Konteos, G. (2022). *The Effect of Human Resource Management Practices on the Quality of Service*. Customer Satisfaction, and Organizational Performance in Cypriot Urban Hotel Industry. In HAICTA.

Papademetriou, C., Anastasiadou, S., Belias, D., & Ragazou, K. (2025). Integrating Sustainability into Human Resource Management: Building a Greener Workforce for the Future. *Sustainability (Basel)*, *2025*(17), 1113. DOI: 10.3390/su17031113

Papademetriou, C., Anastasiadou, S., Konteos, G., & Papalexandris, S. (2022). COVID-19 pandemic: The impact of the social media technology on higher education. *Education Sciences*, *12*(4), 261. DOI: 10.3390/educsci12040261

Papademetriou, C., Anastasiadou, S., & Papalexandris, S. (2023). The effect of sustainable human resource management practices on customer satisfaction, service quality, and institutional performance in hotel businesses. *Sustainability (Basel)*, *15*(10), 8251. DOI: 10.3390/su15108251

Papademetriou, C., Ragazou, K., & Garefalakis, A. (2024a). Adapting Artificial Intelligence in Cypriot Hotel Industry: The Views of Hotel Managers. In Bilgin, M. H., Demir, E., Danis, H., & Garcia Goni, M. (Eds.), *Eurasian Business and Economics Perspectives. EBES 2023. Eurasian Studies in Business and Economics* (Vol. 30). Springer., DOI: 10.1007/978-3-031-64140-4_8

Papademetriou, C., Ragazou, K., Garefalakis, A., & Anastasiadou, S. (2024). In Global, I. G. I. (Ed.), *The Role of Artificial Intelligence in Employee Wellness and Mental Health. Human Resource Strategies in the Era of Artificial Intelligence* (pp. 29–54).

Papademetriou, C., Ragazou, K., Garefalakis, A., & Anastasiadou, S. (2025). The Role of Artificial Intelligence in Employee Wellness and Mental Health. In Yadav, P. (Ed.), *Human Resource Strategies in the Era of Artificial Intelligence* (pp. 29–54). IGI Global Scientific Publishing., DOI: 10.4018/979-8-3693-6412-3.ch002

Papademetriou, C., Ragazou, K., Garefalakis, A., & Passas, I. (2023). Green human resource management: Mapping the research trends for sustainable and agile human resources in SMEs. *Sustainability (Basel)*, *15*(9), 5636. DOI: 10.3390/su15075636

Papantoniou, K., & Tzitzikas, Y. (2020, September). NLP for the Greek language: A brief survey. In 11th Hellenic conference on artificial intelligence (pp. 101-109). DOI: 10.1145/3411408.3411410

Park, Y. S., Koo, M. M., & Jang, S. M. (2019). Characteristic analysis of grid-connected PM wind power generators based on transfer relations and performance evaluation. *IEEE Transactions on Energy Conversion*, *57*(4), 28.

Parmenter, D. (2015). *Key performance indicators: developing, implementing, and using winning KPIs*. John Wiley & Sons. DOI: 10.1002/9781119019855

Parolin, G., Arnbjerg, J., McAloone, T. C., & Pigosso, D. C. (2025). Navigating trade-offs in design for sustainability and circularity: A tool for decision making leveraging narratives and multiple criteria decision analysis. *Journal of Cleaner Production*, *494*, 145004. DOI: 10.1016/j.jclepro.2025.145004

Pavkov, S., Poščić, P., & Jakšić, D. (2016). Business intelligence systems yesterday, today and tomorrow—An overview. *Zbornik Veleučilišta u Rijeci*, *4*, 97–108.

Payton, T., & Claypoole, T. (2023). *Privacy in the age of Big data: Recognizing threats, defending your rights, and protecting your family*. Rowman & Littlefield. DOI: 10.5771/9781538167830

Peláez, . (2019). Facilitating Work Engagement and Performance Through Strengths-Based Micro-coaching: A Controlled Trial Study. *Journal of Happiness Studies*. Advance online publication. DOI: 10.1007/s10902-019-00127-5

Pentland, B. T., & Feldman, M. S. (2007). Narrative networks: Patterns of technology and organization. *Organization Science*, *18*(5), 781–795. DOI: 10.1287/orsc.1070.0283

Pessach, D., Singer, G., Avrahami, D., Chalutz Ben-Gal, H., Shmueli, E., & Ben-Gal, I. (2020). Employees recruitment: A prescriptive analytics approach via machine learning and mathematical programming. *Decision Support Systems*, *134*, 113290. DOI: 10.1016/j.dss.2020.113290 PMID: 32501316

Petrik, D., Saltan, A., & Helferich, A. (2024). *Digital Product Management in the Era of Data Economy, Artificial Intelligence, and Ecosystems*. Springer., DOI: 10.1007/978-3-031-71515-0

Petticrew, M., & Roberts, H. (2008). *Systematic reviews in the social sciences: A practical guide*. John Wiley & Sons.

Pillai, R., & Srivastava, K. B. (2024). Smart HRM 4.0 for achieving organizational performance: A dynamic capability view perspective. *International Journal of Productivity and Performance Management*, *73*(3), 476–496. DOI: 10.1108/IJPPM-04-2022-0174

Pillai, R., Yadav, S., Sivathanu, B., Kaushik, N., & Goel, P. (2022). Use of 4.0 (I4.0) technology in HRM: A pathway toward SHRM 4.0 and HR performance. *Foresight*, *24*(6), 708–727. DOI: 10.1108/FS-06-2021-0128

Pistikou, V., Flouros, F., Deirmentzoglou, G. A., & Agoraki, K. K. (2023). Sustainability Reporting: Examining the Community Impact of the S&P500 Companies. *Sustainability (Basel)*, *15*(18), 13681. DOI: 10.3390/su151813681

Poli, M., Malagas, K., & Papakostas, C. (2024). The Contribution of Advanced Technologies to the Tourism Experience of Disabled People: The Greek Case. In P. Mylonas, D. Kardaras, & J. Caro (Eds.), *Novel and Intelligent Digital Systems:Proceedings of the 4th International Conference (NiDS 2024)* (Vol. 1170, pp. 429–442). Springer Nature Switzerland. DOI: 10.1007/978-3-031-73344-4_36

Pooja, J., & Krishnan, L. R. K. (2023). Employee Engagement Driven By AI and ML and Mediated by Progressive Work Practices - An IT Industry Perspective. SSRN Electronic Journal.

Popo–Olaniyan, O., Elufioye, O. A., Okonkwo, F. C., Udeh, C. A., Eleogu, T. F., & Olatoye, F. O. (2022). Ai-driven talent analytics for strategic hr decision-making in the United States Of America: A Review. *International Journal of Management & Entrepreneurship Research*, *4*(12), 607–622.

Porath, U. (2023). Advancing managerial evolution and resource management in contemporary business landscapes. *Modern Economy*, *14*(5), 1404–1420. DOI: 10.4236/me.2023.1410072

Porfírio, J. A., & dos Santos, J. C. (2011, October 5–7). Business Intelligence as a service—Strategic tool for competitiveness. In *ENTERprise Information Systems:International Conference, CENTERIS 2011* (pp. 106–117). Springer. DOI: 10.1007/978-3-642-24358-5_10

Pourkhodabakhsh, N., Mamoudan, M. M., & Bozorgi-Amiri, A. (2023). Effective machine learning, meta-heuristic algorithms and multi-criteria decision making to minimizing human resource turnover. *Applied Intelligence*, *53*(15), 16309–16331. DOI: 10.1007/s10489-022-04294-6 PMID: 36531972

Power, D. J. (2003, May 31). A brief history of decision support systems (Version 2.8). *DSSResources.COM*. http://DSSResources.COM/history/dsshistory.html

Power, D. J. (n.d.). *A brief history of decision support systems. DSSResources*. COM.

Pratibha, E. (2023). Employee attrition prediction based on grey wolf optimization and deep neural networks. *International Journal on Recent and Innovation Trends in Computing and Communication*, *11*(10), 1338–1345. DOI: 10.17762/ijritcc.v11i10.8676

Pratt, J. W., Zeckhauser, R. J., & Arrow, K. J. (1991). *Principals and agents: The structure of business*. Harvard Business Press.

Qamhieh, , Sammaneh, H., & Demaidi, M. N. (2020). PCRS: Personalized Career-Path Recommender System for Engineering Students. *IEEE Access : Practical Innovations, Open Solutions*, *8*, 214039–214049. Advance online publication. DOI: 10.1109/ACCESS.2020.3040338

Qin, C., Zhang, L., Cheng, Y., Zha, R., Shen, D., Zhang, Q., Chen, X., Sun, Y., Zhu, C., & Zhu, H. (2024). A comprehensive survey of artificial intelligence techniques for talent analytics. arXiv. https://arxiv.org/abs/2307.03195

Qudah, H., Malahim, S., Airout, R., AlQudah, M. Z., Al-Zoubi, W. K., Huson, Y. A., & Zyadat, A. (2024). Unlocking the ESG value of sustainable investments in cryptocurrency: A bibliometric review of research trends. *Technology Analysis and Strategic Management*, •••, 1–15. DOI: 10.1080/09537325.2024.2308631

Quenum, V. F. (2024). Enhancing Data Storytelling within Business Intelligence & Analytics.

Qutub, A., Al-Mehmadi, A., Al-Hssan, M., Aljohani, R., & Alghamdi, H. S. (2021). Prediction of employee attrition using machine learning and ensemble methods. *International Journal of Machine Learning and Computing*, *11*(3), 85–91. DOI: 10.18178/ijmlc.2021.11.2.1022

Ragazou, K., Garefalakis, A., Papademetriou, C., & Passas, I. (2023, June). Well-being human resource model in the collaborative economy: the keystone of ESG strategy in the tourism sector. In ICTR 2023 6th International Conference on Tourism Research. Academic Conferences and publishing limited. DOI: 10.34190/ictr.6.1.1066

Rahevar, M., & Darji, S. (2024). The adoption of AI-driven Chatbots into a recommendation for e-commerce systems to targeted customer in the selection of product. International Journal of Management. *Economics and Commerce*, *1*(2), 128–137.

Rahman, S. (2011). *The impact of adopting "Business Intelligence (BI)" in organizations* [Master's thesis, Uppsala University].

Rajapathirana, R. J., & Hui, Y. (2018). Relationship between innovation capability, innovation type, and firm performance. *Journal of Innovation & Knowledge*, *3*(2), 44–55. DOI: 10.1016/j.jik.2017.06.002

Raji, M. (2024). E-commerce and consumer behaviour: a review of AI-powered personalization and market trends. GSC Advanced Research and Reviews, 18(3), 066-077. DOI: 10.30574/gscarr.2024.18.3.0090

Raji, I. D., Binns, R., Veale, M., Van Kleek, M., & Shadbolt, N. (2020). Closing the AI accountability gap: Defining an auditing framework for AI systems. *Proceedings of the 2020 Conference on Fairness, Accountability, and Transparency*, 33–44. https://doi.org/DOI: 10.1145/3351095.3372873

Ram, J., Zhang, C., & Koronios, A. (2016). The implications of big data analytics on business intelligence: A qualitative study in China. *Procedia Computer Science*, *87*, 221–226. DOI: 10.1016/j.procs.2016.05.152

Ranganathan, M., Lalk, E., Freese, L. M., Freilich, M. A., Wilcots, J., Duffy, M. L., & Shivamoggi, R. (2021). Trends in the representation of women among US geoscience faculty from 1999 to 2020: The long road toward gender parity. AGU Advances, 2(3), e2021AV000436.

Ranjan, J. (2009). Business intelligence: Concepts, components, techniques and benefits. *Journal of Theoretical and Applied Information Technology*, *9*(1), 60–70.

Rao, P., & Taboada, M. (2021). Gender bias in the news: A scalable topic modelling and visualization framework. *Frontiers in Artificial Intelligence*, *4*, 664737. DOI: 10.3389/frai.2021.664737 PMID: 34222857

Rashad, W., & Nedelko, Z. (2020). Global sourcing strategies: A framework for lean, agile, and leagile. *Sustainability (Basel)*, *12*(17), 7199. DOI: 10.3390/su12177199

Rasmussen, T., Andersen, M., & Nielsen, A. (2022). Big data for better workforce management. *Journal of Strategic HR Management*, *14*(3), 144–159.

Rasmussen, T., & Ulrich, D. (2015). Learning from practice: How HR analytics avoids being a management fad. *Organizational Dynamics*, *44*(3), 236–242. DOI: 10.1016/j.orgdyn.2015.05.008

Rasool, S. F., Samma, M., Anjum, A., Munir, M., & Khan, T. M. (2019). Relationship between modern human resource management practices and organizational innovation: Empirical investigation from banking sector of China. *International Transaction Journal of Engineering, Management, & Applied Sciences & Technologies, 10*(7), 1–11. DOI: 10.14456/ITJEMAST.2019.137

Raza, M., Khayal, M., & Bukhari, M. (2022). Predicting employee attrition using decision trees: A case study in a telecom sector. *International Journal of Advanced Computer Science and Applications*, *13*(9), 278–285. DOI: 10.14569/IJACSA.2022.0130934

Ready, D. A., Hill, L. A., & Conger, J. A. (2008). Winning the Race for Talent in Emerging Markets. *Harvard Business Review*, 86 (11), 62–72. *Relations Today*, *34*(2), 51–60.

Reina, C., Rogers, K., Peterson, S., Byron, K., & Hom, P. (2017). Quitting the boss? the role of manager influence tactics and employee emotional engagement in voluntary turnover. *Journal of Leadership & Organizational Studies*, *25*(1), 5–18. DOI: 10.1177/1548051817709007

Renugadevi, R. (2025). An optimal method of assessing the quality of water using integrated AI and blockchain methodology. In *Smart Water Technology for Sustainable Management in Modern Cities* (pp. 261–284). DOI: 10.4018/979-8-3693-8074-1.ch011

Reshi, Y. S., & Khan, R. A. (2014). Creating business intelligence through machine learning: An effective business decision making tool. *Information and Knowledge Management*, *4*(6), 65–75.

Ringo, T., Schweyer, A., DeMarco, M., Jones, R., & Lesser, E. (2008). *Integrated talent management: Part 1 - Understanding the opportunities for success*. IBM Corporation.

Roberts, G. E. (2002). Employee performance appraisal system participation: A technique that works. *Public Personnel Management*, *31*(3), 333–342. DOI: 10.1177/009102600203100306

Robiansyah, A., & Nuswantara, D. A. (2025). Tourism Experience Architecture to Achieve the SDGs: A Study at Cangkuang Temple Tourism Area. *Journal of Lifestyle and SDGs Review*, *5*(3), e05880. DOI: 10.47172/2965-730X.SDGsReview.v5.n03.pe05880

Rogha, M. (2023). Explain to decide: A human-centric review on the role of explainable artificial intelligence in AI-assisted decision making. arXiv preprint arXiv:2312.11507.

Roller, D., & Engesser, E. (2013, June). Application of fuzzy classification and fuzzy pattern recognition for distributed production and global supply chain. In *2013 Joint IFSA World Congress and NAFIPS Annual Meeting (IFSA/NAFIPS)* (pp. 1412-1417). IEEE. DOI: 10.1109/IFSA-NAFIPS.2013.6608608

Rothwell, W. (2010). *Effective succession planning: Ensuring leadership continuity and building talent from within*. Amacom.

Roumpi, D. (2021). Rethinking the strategic management of human resources: Lessons learned from COVID-19 and the way forward in building resilience. *The International Journal of Organizational Analysis*, *31*(1), 215–231. DOI: 10.1108/IJOA-09-2021-2974

Rožman, M., & Tominc, P. (2024). Navigating Gender Nuances: Assessing the Impact of AI on Employee Engagement in Slovenian Entrepreneurship. *Systems*, *12*(5), 145. DOI: 10.3390/systems12050145

Rubel, M., Kee, D., & Rimi, N. (2017). The mediating role of work–family conflict on role stressors and employee turnover intention relationship in labour-oriented organizations. *Global Business Review*, *18*(6), 1384–1399. DOI: 10.1177/0972150917713061

Rukmiyati, N. M. S., Safitri, N. W. N., Mareni, N. K., Darmayanti, N. P. A., & Ekayani, N. N. S. (2024). Unveiling the Gender Gap: A Literature Review on Women Entrepreneurs and Financial Access. Jurnal Ekonomi dan Bisnis Jagaditha. 11(2), 141-151. .DOI: 10.22225/jj.11.2.2024.141-151

Rybaric, R. (2023). *Microsoft Power Platform Enterprise Architecture: Design tailor-made solutions for architects and decision makers to meet complex business requirements*. Packt Publishing Ltd.

Rydén, P., & El Sawy, O. A. (2023). Flow with the go: Real-time continuous improvisation in digital business ecosystems. In *The Routledge companion to improvisation in organizations* (pp. 389–407). Routledge. DOI: 10.4324/9781003171768-28

Sadeli, J. (2012). The influence of leadership, talent management, organizational culture and organizational support on employee engagement. *International Research Journal of Business Studies*, *5*(3), 30–50. DOI: 10.21632/irjbs.5.3.30-50

Saia, R., & Carta, S. (2019). Evaluating the benefits of using proactive transformed-domain-based techniques in fraud detection tasks. *Future Generation Computer Systems*, *93*, 18–32. DOI: 10.1016/j.future.2018.10.016

Saks, A. M. (2006). Antecedents and Consequences of Employee Engagement. *Journal of Managerial Psychology*, *21*(7), 600–619. DOI: 10.1108/02683940610690169

Saling, K. (2024). *Data-driven Talent Management: Using Analytics to Improve Employee Experience*. Kogan Page Publishers.

San Jose, D. (2024). Readiness of LGU Key Personnel on the Implementation of Tourism Projects Under the Mandanas-Garcia Supreme Court Ruling in the Philippines. *International Journal of Research and Innovation in Social Science*, *VIII*(XIV), 203–213. DOI: 10.47772/IJRISS.2024.814MG0019

Sangupamba, O. M., Prat, N., & Comyn-Wattiau, I. (2014, October 27–29). Business intelligence and big data in the cloud: Opportunities for design-science researchers. In *Advances in Conceptual Modeling: ER 2014 Workshops* (pp. 75–84). Springer. https://doi.org/DOI: 10.1007/978-3-319-14139-2_9

Sardi, A., Sorano, E., Cantino, V., & Garengo, P. (2020). Big data and performance measurement research: Trends, evolution and future opportunities. *Measuring Business Excellence*, *27*(4), 531–548. DOI: 10.1108/MBE-06-2019-0053

Sarker, I. H. (2022). AI-based modeling: Techniques, applications and research issues towards automation, intelligent and smart systems. *SN Computer Science*, *3*(2), 158. DOI: 10.1007/s42979-022-01043-x PMID: 35194580

Sarker, I. H., Colman, A., Han, J., Khan, A. I., Abushark, Y. B., & Salah, K. (2019). BehavDT: A behavioral decision tree learning to build user-centric context-aware predictive model. *Mobile Networks and Applications*, *25*(3), 1151–1161. DOI: 10.1007/s11036-019-01443-z

Schaufeli, W. B.. (2009). Work Engagement: Construct Validity and Measurement. *Journal of Happiness Studies*.

Schiuma, G. (2012). Managing knowledge for business performance improvement. *Journal of Knowledge Management*, *16*(4), 515–522. DOI: 10.1108/13673271211246103

Schryen, G. (2013). Revisiting IS business value research: What we already know, what we still need to know, and how we can get there. *European Journal of Information Systems*, *22*(2), 139–169. DOI: 10.1057/ejis.2012.45

Schuetz, C. G., & Schrefl, M. (2023). Conceptualizing analytics: an overview of business intelligence and analytics from a conceptual-modeling perspective. Digital Transformation: Core Technologies and Emerging Topics from a Computer Science Perspective, 311-336.

Schuler, R. S., Jackson, S. E., & Tarique, I. (2010). Global talent management and global talent challenges: Strategic opportunities for IHRM. *Journal of World Business*, *46*(4), 506–516. DOI: 10.1016/j.jwb.2010.10.011

Scullion, H., & Collings, D. G. (2011). Global talent management: Introduction. In *Global Talent Management*. Routledge. DOI: 10.4324/9780203865682

Sebald, H., Enneking, A., & Wöltje, O. (2005). *Talent Management: Zwischen Anspruch und Wirklichkeit*. Towers Perrin.

Sebastian, J. (2023). Mitigating bias in AI-driven HR decision making. *Journal of Human Resource Technology*, *15*(3), 78–92.

Selvarajan, G. P. (2020). The Role of Machine Learning Algorithms in Business Intelligence: Transforming Data into Strategic Insights. *International Journal of All Research Education and Scientific Methods*, *8*(5), 194–202.

Selvi, M., Jeeva, S., & Jaswanth, J. (2024). Improving the power efficiency in OFDM system using LDPC codes. In *Proceedings of the 2024 IEEE International Conference on Advanced Artificial Intelligence and Computing* (pp. 1717–1723). DOI: 10.1109/ICAAIC60222.2024.10575635

Semenova, Y., Glushkova, N., Pivina, L., Khismetova, Z., Zhunussov, Y., Sandybaev, M., & Ivankov, A. (2020). Epidemiological characteristics and forecast of COVID-19 outbreak in the republic of Kazakhstan. *Journal of Korean Medical Science*, *35*(24), e227. Advance online publication. DOI: 10.3346/jkms.2020.35.e227 PMID: 32567261

Şerbănescu, L. (2011). Business intelligence tools for improve sales and profitability. *Revista tinerilor economişti*, (16), 188-195.

Serdarasan, S. (2013). A review of supply chain complexity drivers. *Computers & Industrial Engineering*, *66*(3), 533–540. DOI: 10.1016/j.cie.2012.12.008

Seremeti, L., Anastasiadis, L., & Anastasiadou, S. (2024). The Role of Data in Environmental, Social, and Governance Strategy. In ESG and Total Quality Management in Human Resources (pp. 201-218). IGI Global.

Sergio, R. P., & Rylova, M. (2018). Employee engagement and empowerment as gateway towards retention: The case of Volkswagen group. *Journal of Eastern European and Central Asian Research*, *5*(2).

Shajani, Z., Laing, C., Robinson, F., Yun, L., Patterson, J., & Rieder, L. (2023). The creation of a novel undergraduate nursing employee/student hybrid role in the COVID-19 response. *Nursing Administration Quarterly*, *47*(1), 72–83. DOI: 10.1097/NAQ.0000000000000564 PMID: 36469375

Shankar, M., & Kumar, S. (2024). An optimized 3DOF-FOPID2-DF controller with improved power quality for multi-level inverter in grid connected PV systems. *Journal of Circuits, Systems, and Computers*, *33*(17), 2450310. Advance online publication. DOI: 10.1142/S0218126624503109

Sharma, M., Kumar, P., & Gundewar, S. (2025). Leveraging AI and Machine Learning for Predictive Analytics in Business Intelligence. In AI-Powered Business Intelligence for Modern Organizations (pp. 29-50). IGI Global.

Sharma-Brymer, V., Brymer, E., & Mitra, S. (2025). Adventure tourism and tourist experience. In G. Pomfret, A. Doran, & C. Cater, *Routledge International Handbook of Adventure Tourism* (1st ed., pp. 153–169). Routledge. DOI: 10.4324/9781003393153-12

Shi, L., Xu, Z., & Hao, J. (2017). Modelling analysis of transient stability simulation with high penetration of grid-connected wind farms of DFIG type. *Wind Energy (Chichester, England)*, *17*(437), 11.

Shollo, A., & Galliers, R. D. (2016). Towards an understanding of the role of business intelligence systems in organisational knowing. *Information Systems Journal*, *26*(4), 339–367. DOI: 10.1111/isj.12071

Shu, F., Quan, W., Chen, B., Qiu, J., Sugimoto, C. R., & Larivière, V. (2020). The role of Web of Science publications in China's tenure system. *Scientometrics*, *122*(3), 1683–1695. DOI: 10.1007/s11192-019-03339-x

Silva, J., Phillips, J. R., & Silveira, L. M. (2017). Efficient simulation of power grids. *IEEE Transactions on Computer-Aided Design of Integrated Circuits and Systems*, *10*(15), 6.

Sinar, E., & Wellins, R. (2017). The truth about talent analytics. *TD: Talent Development*, *71*(8), 70–73.

Singh, P. (2023). Digital transformation in supply chain management: Artificial intelligence (ai) and machine learning (ml) as catalysts for value creation. *International Journal of Supply Chain Management*, *12*(6), 57–63. DOI: 10.59160/ijscm.v12i6.6216

Singh, S. K., Del Giudice, M., Chierici, R., & Graziano, D. (2020). Green innovation and environmental performance: The role of green transformational leadership and green human resource management. *Technological Forecasting and Social Change*, *150*, 119762. DOI: 10.1016/j.techfore.2019.119762

Singh, T. (2010). Does international trade cause economic growth? A survey. *World Economy*, *33*(11), 1517–1564. DOI: 10.1111/j.1467-9701.2010.01243.x

Sirin, E., & Karacan, H. (2017). A review on business intelligence and big data. *International Journal of Intelligent Systems and Applications in Engineering*, *5*(4), 206–215. DOI: 10.18201/ijisae.2017533861

Sivathanu, B., & Pillai, R. (2019). Technology and talent analytics for talent management – a game changer for organizational performance. *The International Journal of Organizational Analysis*, *28*(2), 457–473. DOI: 10.1108/IJOA-01-2019-1634

Sjahruddin, H., Hidayat, P., Moridu, I., & Sutaguna, I. N. T. (2022). Determination of The Best Employee Using The Behavioral Anchor Rating Scale. *Jurnal Mantik*, *6*(3), 2753–2758.

Skyrius, R. (2021). *Business Intelligence*. Springer. DOI: 10.1007/978-3-030-67032-0

Smart, B. D. (1999). *Topgrading: How leading companies win by hiring, coaching, and keeping the best people*. Prentice Hall Press.

Smith, L., & Jones, R. (2024). Embracing the Metaverse: Strategies for Business Success. *The International Journal of Virtual Reality : a Multimedia Publication for Professionals*, *18*(3), 210–225.

Snell, S. A., Stueber, D., & Lepak, D. P. (2002). Virtual HR Departments: Getting out of the Middle. In Heneman, R. L., & Greenberger, D. B. (Eds.), *Human Resource Management in Virtual Organizations* (pp. 81–101). Information Age Publishing.

Song, H., Jiang, Y., & Wang, Y. (2022). Smart HR practices for employee well-being: A talent analytics perspective. *Technological Forecasting and Social Change*, *178*, 121614. DOI: 10.1016/j.techfore.2022.121614

Song, L. L., Xu, Q.-S., & Wu, Y.-W. (2020). Evaluation and multi-objective optimization of power grid investment benefits taking into account the weights. *Journal of Electric Power*, (25), 13–26.

Soni, N., Sharma, E. K., Singh, N., & Kapoor, A. (2020). Artificial intelligence in business: From research and innovation to market deployment. *Procedia Computer Science*, *167*, 2200–2210. DOI: 10.1016/j.procs.2020.03.272

Soomro, Z. A., Shah, M. H., & Ahmed, J. (2016). Information security management needs more holistic approach: A literature review. *International Journal of Information Management*, *36*(2), 215–225. DOI: 10.1016/j.ijinfomgt.2015.11.009

Souleh, S. (2014). The impact of human capital management on the innovativeness of research centers: The case of scientific research centers in Algeria. *International Journal of Business and Management*, *2*(4), 80–96.

Souravlas, S. Anastasiadou, S. & Kostoglou, I. (2022b). A Novel Method For General Hierarchical System Modeling Via Colored Petri Nets Based on Transition Extractions From Real Data Sets. *Appl. Sci.* 2023, 13, 339. .DOI: 10.3390/app13010339

Souravlas, S., Anastasiadou, S., Economides, Th., & Katsavounis, S. (2023). Probabilistic Community Detection in Social Networks. *IEEE Access*, Publication Date: 2023, Volume: 11, On Page(s): 25629-25641, Print ISSN: 2169-3536, Online ISSN: 2169-3536, Digital Object Identifier: DOI: 10.1109/ACCESS.2023.3257021

Souravlas, S., & Anastasiadou, S. (2020). Pipelined Dynamic Scheduling of Big Data Streams. *Applied Sciences (Basel, Switzerland)*, *10*(14), 4796. DOI: 10.3390/app10144796

Souravlas, S., & Anastasiadou, S. (2022). On Implementing Social Community Clouds Based on Markov Models. *IEEE Transactions on Computational Social Systems, 2022*. Advance online publication. DOI: 10.1109/TCSS.2022.3213273

Souravlas, S., Anastasiadou, S. D., Tantalaki, N., & Katsavounis, S. (2022a). A Fair, Dynamic Load Balanced Task Distribution Strategy for Heterogeneous Cloud Platforms Based on Markov Process Modeling. *IEEE Access : Practical Innovations, Open Solutions*, *10*, 26149–26162. DOI: 10.1109/ACCESS.2022.3157435

Souravlas, S., Anastasiadou, S., & Katsavounis, S. (2021b). A Survey on the Recent Advances of Deep Community Detection. *Applied Sciences (Basel, Switzerland)*, *11*(16), 7179. DOI: 10.3390/app11167179

Souravlas, S., Anastasiadou, S., & Katsavounis, S. (2021c). More on Pipelined Dynamic Scheduling of Big Data Streams. *Applied Sciences (Basel, Switzerland)*, *11*(1), 61. DOI: 10.3390/app11010061

Souravlas, S., Anastasiadou, S., Tantalaki, N., & Katsavounis, S. (2021a). A Dynamic Load Balanced Task Distribution Strategy for Heterogeneous Cloud Platforms Based on Markov Process Modeling. *IEEE Access : Practical Innovations, Open Solutions*, *10*, 2169–3536. https://ieeexplore.ieee.org/abstract/document/9729723

Souravlas, S., Katsavounis, S., & Anastasiadou, S. (2020). On Modeling and Simulation of Resource Allocation Policies in Cloud Computing Using Colored Petri Nets. *Applied Sciences (Basel, Switzerland)*, *10*(16), 5644. DOI: 10.3390/app10165644

Sowjanya, M. C. V. N. (2024). *Data Science: Exploring Future Trends*. Academic Guru Publishing House.

Soyege, O. S., Nwokedi, C. N., Tomoh, B. O., Mustapha, A. Y., Mbata, A. O., Balogun, O. D., Forkuo, A. Y., & Iguma, D. R. (2025). Health informatics in developing countries: Challenges and opportunities. *International Journal of Applied Research in Social Sciences*, *7*(3), 186–202. DOI: 10.51594/ijarss.v7i3.1847

Spoon, K., LaBerge, N., Wapman, K. H., Zhang, S., Morgan, A. C., Galesic, M., Fosdick, B. K., Larremore, D. B., & Clauset, A. (2023). Gender and retention patterns among US faculty. *Science Advances*, *9*(42), eadi2205. DOI: 10.1126/sciadv.adi2205 PMID: 37862417

Stavros, J. M., Stavros, J., & Torres, C. (2021). *Conversations worth having: Using appreciative inquiry to fuel productive and meaningful engagement*. Berrett-Koehler Publishers.

Stefanovic, N., & Stefanovic, D. (2009). Supply chain business intelligence: technologies, issues and trends. In *Artificial Intelligence An International Perspective: An International Perspective* (pp. 217–245). Springer Berlin Heidelberg. DOI: 10.1007/978-3-642-03226-4_12

Stone, D. L., Deadrick, D. L., Lukaszewski, K. M., & Johnson, R. (2015). The influence of technology on the future of human resource management. *Human Resource Management Review*, *25*(2), 216–231. DOI: 10.1016/j.hrmr.2015.01.002

Suchánek, P. (2019, May 27). Business intelligence—The standard tool of a modern company. In *Proceedings of the 6th International Symposium on Business Administration—Global Economic Crisis and Changes* (pp. 432–441).

Suchánek, P. (2019, May 27). Business intelligence—the standard tool of a modern company. In *Proceedings of the 6th International Symposium on Business Administration—Global Economic Crisis and Changes* (pp. 432–441). Munich, Germany.

Sukortprommee, S., Thanuttamanon, B., Singhdong, P., & Peamchai, P. (2025). The Role of Government and Community Support in Promoting Tourism Experiences Through the Application of Technology in the Tourism Business for The Elderly. *Journal of Lifestyle and SDGs Review*, *5*(3), e04777. DOI: 10.47172/2965-730X.SDGsReview.v5.n03.pe04777

Sumardi, D., Suryani, N., & Musadad, A. A. (2021). Website-based learning management system (LMS) as a tool for learning in the covid-19 pandemic period for Junior High Schools. *Journal of Education Technology*, *5*(3), 346–355. DOI: 10.23887/jet.v5i3.38371

Summers, D. (2005). *Quality Management*. Pearson Education.

Sun, W., Ren, S., & Tang, G. (2025). In the era of responsible artificial intelligence and digitalization: Business group digitalization, operations and subsidiary performance. *Annals of Operations Research*. Advance online publication. DOI: 10.1007/s10479-024-06453-z

Sun, Z., Sun, L., & Strang, K. (2018). Big data analytics services for enhancing business intelligence. *Journal of Computer Information Systems*, *58*(2), 162–169. DOI: 10.1080/08874417.2016.1220239

Sveiby, K. (2001). A knowledge-based theory of the firm to guide in strategy formulation. *Journal of Intellectual Capital*, *2*(4), 344–358. DOI: 10.1108/14691930110409651

Swargiary, K. (2024). Unveiling the Nexus of Business Intelligence Maturity and Agility: Exploring Organizational Dynamics for Adaptive Success.

Swmya, G., Polisetty, A., & Dash, G. (2024). Leveraging artificial intelligence for talent management. In: *Handook of Artificial Intelligence Applications for Industrial Sustainability*. CRC Press. eBook ISBN: 9781003348351. DOI: 10.1201/9781003348351-9

Tabasum, S., & Shaikh, A. R. (2022). Impact of employee engagement on employee performance with mediating effect of employee retention. *International Journal of Social Science & Entrepreneurship*, *2*(2), 1–20.

Taherdoost, H. (2022). What are different research approaches? Comprehensive review of qualitative, quantitative, and mixed method research, their applications, types, and limitations. *Journal of Management Science & Engineering Research*, *5*(1), 53–63. DOI: 10.30564/jmser.v5i1.4538

Talaoui, Y., & Kohtamäki, M. (2020). 35 years of research on business intelligence process: A synthesis of a fragmented literature. *Management Research Review*, *44*(5), 677–717. DOI: 10.1108/MRR-07-2020-0386

Talukder, M. B. (2024). Implementing AI and Virtual Experiences in Hospitality. In Manohar, S., Mittal, A., Raju, S., & Nair, A. J. (Eds.), *Advances in Hospitality, Tourism, and the Services Industry* (pp. 145–160). IGI Global., DOI: 10.4018/979-8-3693-2019-8.ch009

Talukder, M. B., Kumar, S., Sood, K., & Grima, S. (2023). Information Technology, Food Service Quality and Restaurant Revisit Intention. *International Journal of Sustainable Development and Planning*, *18*(1), 295–303. DOI: 10.18280/ijsdp.180131

Talukder, M. B., Lina, F. Y., Kumar, S., & Khan, M. R. (2024b). Data-Driven Personalization in the Sharing Economy. In Ordóñez De Pablos, P. (Ed.), (pp. 277–300). Advances in Finance, Accounting, and Economics. IGI Global., DOI: 10.4018/979-8-3693-5673-9.ch012

Talukder, M., Kumar, S., Misra, L., & Kabir, F. (2024a). Determining the role of eco-tourism service quality, tourist satisfaction,and destination loyalty: A case study of Kuakata Beach. *Acta Scientiarum Polonorum. Administratio Locorum*, *23*(1), 133–151. DOI: 10.31648/aspal.9275

Tamang, M. D., Shukla, V. K., Anwar, S., & Punhani, R. (2021, April 28–30). Improving business intelligence through machine learning algorithms. In *2021 2nd International Conference on Intelligent Engineering and Management (ICIEM)* (pp. 63–68). IEEE. DOI: 10.1109/ICIEM51511.2021.9445344

Tansley, C., & Newell, S. (2007). A knowledge-based view of agenda formation in the development of human resource information systems. *Management Learning, 38*(1), 95–119. DOI: 10.1177/1350507607073028

Tansley, C., Turner, P. A., Foster, C., Harris, L. M., Stewart, J., & Sempik, A. (2007). *Talent: Strategy, management, measurement.* Chartered Institute of Personal & Development.

Tansley, C., & Watson, T. (2000). Strategic exchange in the development of human resource information systems (HRIS). *New Technology, Work and Employment, 15*(2), 108–122. DOI: 10.1111/1468-005X.00068

Tavera Romero, C. A., Ortiz, J. H., Khalaf, O. I., & Ríos Prado, A. (2021). Business intelligence: Business evolution after industry 4.0. *Sustainability (Basel), 13*(18), 10026. DOI: 10.3390/su131810026

Tawalbeh, M., Alzghoui, A., & Alsheikh, G. A. A. (2025). Business intelligence as a catalyst for HR transformation: A study of BI implementation in HR practices. *Proceedings of the International Conference on Robotics, Automation, and Intelligent Computing,* 18-19 May, Pune, India, 3255(1), 05007. https://doi.org/DOI: 10.1063/5.0255240

Taylor, S. (2011). *Contemporary issues in human resource management.* CIPD.

Teruel, M. A., Maté, A., Navarro, E., González, P., & Trujillo, J. C. (2019). The new era of business intelligence applications: Building from a collaborative point of view. *Business & Information Systems Engineering, 61*(6), 615–634. DOI: 10.1007/s12599-019-00578-3

Tetteh, J., & Asumeng, M. (2022). Succession planning, employee retention and career development programmes in selected organisations in Ghana. *African Journal of Management Research, 27*(1), 151–169. DOI: 10.4314/ajmr.v27i1.9

Thangasamy, S., Chamany, B. F., & Murthy, L. (2018). Dynamic simulation of a power grid containing a nuclear power station. *IFAC Proceedings Volumes, 55*(22), 16.

Thite, M. (2022). Digital human resource development: Where are we? Where should we go and how do we go there? *Human Resource Development International, 25*(1), 87–103. DOI: 10.1080/13678868.2020.1842982

Thunnissen, M., Boselie, P., & Fruytier, B. (2013). Talent management and the relevance of context: Towards a pluralistic approach. *Human Resource Management Review, 23*(4), 326–336. DOI: 10.1016/j.hrmr.2013.05.004

Tilmes, N. (2022). Disability, fairness, and algorithmic bias in AI recruitment. *Ethics and Information Technology*, *24*(2), 21. DOI: 10.1007/s10676-022-09633-2

Timan, H., Kama, N., Yusoff, R. C. M., & Ali, M. (2021). The Application of Medical and Health Informatics Among the Malaysian Medical Tourism Hospital: A Preliminary Study. In Bhatia, S. K., Tiwari, S., Ruidan, S., Trivedi, M. C., & Mishra, K. K. (Eds.), *Advances in Computer, Communication and Computational Sciences* (Vol. 1158, pp. 743–754). Springer Singapore., DOI: 10.1007/978-981-15-4409-5_66

Tracey, J., & Hinkin, T. (2008). Contextual factors and cost profiles associated with employee turnover. *Cornell Hospitality Quarterly*, *49*(1), 12–27. DOI: 10.1177/0010880407310191

Triantafillidou, A., & Yannas, P. (2021). Women in Public Relations in Greece. EUPRERA Report Vol. 3., No. 2., in - Topić, M. (ed), EUPRERA report series. Leeds/Brussels: Creative Media and Communications Research Ltd. & EUPRERA. ISSN 2633-2353.

Trieu, V. (2017). Getting value from business intelligence systems: A review and research agenda. *Decision Support Systems*, *93*, 111–124. DOI: 10.1016/j.dss.2016.09.019

Tripathi, P., Bajaj, C., Bhanvadia, M., Parsekar, V., & Magar, V. (2023). Comparative study of data analytics tools for effective business decision. Vidhyayana-An International Multidisciplinary Peer-Reviewed E-Journal-ISSN 2454-8596, 8(si7), 461-486.

Tripathi, S. (2021). Determinants of digital transformation in the post-COVID-19 business world. *IJRDO-Journal of Business Management*, *7*(3), 75–81. DOI: 10.53555/bm.v7i6.4312

Tsahat, Y., Nikou, S., & Bouwman, H. (2024). AI-enabled inclusive workplaces: Tailoring work experiences through hyper-personalization. *Journal of Business Research*, *170*, 114206. DOI: 10.1016/j.jbusres.2024.114206

Tsilingeridis, O., Moustaka, V., & Vakali, A. (2023). Design and development of a forecasting tool for the identification of new target markets by open time-series data and deep learning methods. *Applied Soft Computing*, *132*, 109843. DOI: 10.1016/j.asoc.2022.109843

Turban, E., Sharda, R., & Delen, D. (2010). *Decision Support and Business Intelligence Systems*. Pearson Education.

Tursunbayeva, A., Di Lauro, S., & Pagliari, C. (2018). People analytics—A scoping review of conceptual boundaries and value propositions. *International Journal of Information Management*, *43*, 224–247. DOI: 10.1016/j.ijinfomgt.2018.08.002

Ulrich, D. (1997). *Human resource champions: The next agenda for adding value and delivering results*. Harvard Business School Press.

Ulrich, D., Younger, J., Brockbank, W., & Ulrich, M. (2012). *HR from the outside in: Six competencies for the future of human resources*. McGraw-Hill.

Utrilla, . (2015). *The effects of coaching in employees and organizational performance: The Spanish Case*. Intangible Capital., DOI: 10.3926/ic.586

Vaishnavi, S., ... (2025). Revolutionizing finance and accounting through AI-driven decision making. In *Convergence of AI, Education, and Business for Sustainability* (pp. 261–284). IGI Global. DOI: 10.4018/979-8-3373-1917-9.ch012

Vajjala, S., Majumder, B., Gupta, A., & Surana, H. (2020). *Practical natural language processing: a comprehensive guide to building real-world NLP systems*. O'Reilly Media.

van den Heuvel, S., & Bondarouk, T. (2017). The rise (and fall?) of HR analytics: A study into the future application, value, structure, and system support. *Journal of Organizational Effectiveness: People and Performance*, *4*(2), 157–178. DOI: 10.1108/JOEPP-03-2017-0022

Van Dijck, J. (2014). Datafication, Dataism, and Dataveillance: Big Data Between Scientific Paradigm and Ideology. *Surveillance & Society*, *12*(2), 197–208. DOI: 10.24908/ss.v12i2.4776

Vapiwala, F., & Pandita, D. (2024). Streamlining Talent Management for Modern Business Through Artificial Intelligence. *International Conference in Emerging Technologies for Sustainability and Intelligent Systems (ICETSIS)*, Manama, Bahrain, 619-623. https://doi.org/DOI: 10.1109/ICETSIS61505.2024.10459450

Veluchamy, R., Kanagaraj, M. G. A., & Vimalnath, V. (2025). Speculative Scenarios for the Future of Talent Management in Higher Education. In Cultivating Creativity and Navigating Talent Management in Academia (pp. 335-358). IGI Global Scientific Publishing.

Vera-Baceta, M., Thelwall, M., & Kousha, K. (2019). Web of Science and Scopus language coverage. *Scientometrics*, *121*(3), 1803–1813. DOI: 10.1007/s11192-019-03264-z

Viitanen, M., & Pirttimaki, V. (2006). Business intelligence for strategic management in a technology-oriented company. *International Journal of Technology Intelligence and Planning*, *2*(4), 329–343. DOI: 10.1504/IJTIP.2006.011705

Vij, R., Tiwari, Y., & Nazir, H. (2023, December). HR Analytics in Predicting Attrition Pattern Among Women in Private Education Colleges: Comprehensive Evaluation. In 2023 4th International Conference on Computation, Automation and Knowledge Management (ICCAKM) (pp. 01-07). IEEE.

Vijayasri, G. V. (2013). The importance of international trade in the world. *International Journal of Marketing. Financial Services & Management Research*, *2*(9), 111–119.

Villazon, C. C., Pinilla, L. S., Otegi Olaso, J. R., Candarias, N. T., & Lopez de Lacalle, N. (2020). Identification of Key Performance Indicators in Project-Based Organizations through the Lean Approach. *Sustainability (Basel)*, *12*(5977), 1–19. DOI: 10.3390/su12155977

Visnjic, I., Wiengarten, F., & Neely, A. (2016). Only the brave: Product innovation, service business model innovation, and their impact on performance. *Journal of Product Innovation Management*, *33*(1), 36–52. DOI: 10.1111/jpim.12254

Viterouli, M., Belias, D., Koustelios, A., Tsigilis, N., & Papademetriou, C. Time for Change: Designing Tailored Training Initiatives for Organizational Transformation. *In Belias, D., Rossidis, I., Papademetriou, C. Organizational Behavior and Human Resource Management for Complex Work Environments*, pp. 267-307. IGI Global. DOI: DOI: 10.4018/979-8-3693-3466-9.ch014

Viterouli, M., Belias, D., Ntalakos, A., Koustelios, A., & Tsigilis, N. (2024b). Strategies for Achieving Work-Life Balance in the Modern Workplace. In Organizational Behavior and Human Resource Management for Complex Work Environments (pp. 95-127). IGI Global. DOI: 10.4018/979-8-3693-3466-9.ch006

Viterouli, M., Belias, D., Koustelios, A., & Tsigilis, N. (2024a). Optimizing Adaptive Performance: Exploring Organizational Learning Culture across Generations. *Journal of Chinese Human Resource Management*, *15*(4), 3–27.

VK, A. K. (2021). Business Intelligence Demystified: Understand and Clear All Your Doubts and Misconceptions About BI (English Edition). BPB Publications.

Voigt, P., & Von dem Bussche, A. (2017). *The EU General Data Protection Regulation (GDPR)*. Springer., DOI: 10.1007/978-3-319-57959-7

Vo, L. V., Nguyen, H. T. H., & Le, H. T. T. (2021). Do female CEOs make a difference in firm operations? Evidence from Vietnam. *Accounting and Finance*, *61*(S1), 1489–1516. DOI: 10.1111/acfi.12634

Vroom, V. H. (1964). *Work and motivation*. Wiley.

Vural, G., Sökmen, A. G., & Çetenak, E. H. (2012). Effects of working capital management on firm's performance: Evidence from Turkey. *International Journal of Economics and Financial Issues*, *2*(4), 488–495.

Wafula, L. (2024). Human resource management practices and firm innovation: A study of technology startups in Kenya. *International Journal of Strategic Management*, *3*(1), 41–53. DOI: 10.47604/ijsm.2482

Waller, M. A., & Fawcett, S. E. (2009). Data warehousing in the supply chain: An intelligent agent for group decision support in applicant ranking within human resources systems. In *2009 IEEE International Conference on Fuzzy Systems* (pp. 744–750).

Wang, C. H., & Chuang, J. J. (2016). Integrating decision tree with back propagation network to conduct business diagnosis and performance simulation for solar companies. *Decision Support Systems*, *81*, 12–19. DOI: 10.1016/j.dss.2015.10.004

Wang, H., Zhang, H., & Li, F. (2020). Application of data mining theory in power grid equipment defect. *Power System Technology*, (12), 3.

Wang, J., & Li, Y. (2017). The building of urban power grid information database and its data mining. *Energy Education Science and Technology*, (9), 3.

Wang, L.. (2023). *Algorithmic Fairness in HRM: Challenges and Solutions*. Ethics and Data Science Review.

Wang, Y.. (2022). Exploring the impact of metaverse on business dynamics and marketing strategies: A literature review and theoretical framework. *Journal of Business Venturing Insights*, *18*, e00260.

Wang, Y., Zhao, H., & Zhang, Q. (2021). Hybrid machine learning models for portfolio optimization. *Journal of Financial Econometrics*, *32*(6), 142–158.

Watson, H. J., & Wixom, B. H. (2007). The current state of business intelligence. *Computer*, *40*(9), 96–99. DOI: 10.1109/MC.2007.331

Watson, H. J., Wixom, B. H., Hoffer, J. A., Anderson-Lehman, R., & Reynolds, A. M. (2009). Real-time business intelligence: Best practices at Continental Airlines. *EDPACS: The EDP Audit, Control, and Security Newsletter*, *40*(6), 1–16. DOI: 10.1080/07366980903484935

Weiss, L. (1999). Collection and connection: The anatomy of knowledge sharing in professional services. *Proceedings - Academy of Management*, *17*(1), 61–72. DOI: 10.5465/apbpp.1999.27613308

Weller, A. (2019). Transparency: Motivations and challenges. In *Explainable AI: Interpreting, Explaining and Visualizing Deep Learning* (pp. 23–40). Springer. https://doi.org/DOI: 10.1007/978-3-030-28954-6_2

Wiblen, S., & McDonnell, A. (2020). Connecting 'talent' meanings and multi-level context: A discursive approach. *International Journal of Human Resource Management, 31*(4), 474–510. DOI: 10.1080/09585192.2019.1629988

Widjaja, A. A., Ghapanchi, A., & Bingley, S. (2025). Uncovering the antecedents to the effective use of business intelligence lessons from a qualitative systematic review approach. *Journal of Enterprise Information Management, 38*(3), 768–797. DOI: 10.1108/JEIM-08-2024-0440

Wiencierz, C., & Luenich, M. (2022). Trust in open data applications through transparency. *New Media & Society, 24*(8), 1751–1770. DOI: 10.1177/1461444820979708

Wilson, J. P. (2009). *Human resource development: Learning and training for individuals and organizations* (2nd ed.). Kogan Page.

Wirz, C., Demuth, J. L., Cains, M. G., White, M., Radford, J., & Bostrom, A. (2024). National Weather Service (NWS) forecasters' perceptions of ai/ml and its use in operational forecasting. *Bulletin of the American Meteorological Society, 105*(11), E2194–E2215. DOI: 10.1175/BAMS-D-24-0044.1

Witzany, L. (2024). Systematically Addressing Unconscious Biases in Job Interviews with Anonymization Technology (Doctoral dissertation, Technische Universität Wien).

Wright, P. M., Dunford, B. B., & Snell, S. A. (2001). Human resources and the resource-based view of the firm. *Journal of Management, 27*(6), 701–721. DOI: 10.1177/014920630102700607

Xiao, Y., & Watson, M. (2019). Guidance on conducting a systematic literature review. *Journal of Planning Education and Research, 39*(1), 93–112. DOI: 10.1177/0739456X17723971

Xue, X., Sun, X., Wang, H., Zhang, H., & Feng, J. (2022). Neural network fusion with fine-grained adaptation learning for turnover prediction. *Complex & Intelligent Systems*. Advance online publication. DOI: 10.1007/s40747-022-00931-2

Xu, M., David, J. M., & Kim, S. H. (2018). The fourth industrial revolution: Opportunities and challenges. *International Journal of Financial Research, 9*(2), 90–95. DOI: 10.5430/ijfr.v9n2p90

Yahia, N., Hlel, J., & Colomo-Palacios, R. (2021). From big data to deep data to support people analytics for employee attrition prediction. *IEEE Access : Practical Innovations, Open Solutions*, *9*, 60447–60458. DOI: 10.1109/ACCESS.2021.3074559

Yan, G., Shi, H., Chong, D., & He, W. (2017, June). Mining e-commerce satisfaction sentiment through a bilingual model. In *2017 2nd International Conference on Image, Vision and Computing (ICIVC)* (pp. 1029-1033). IEEE.

Yanamala, K. K. R. (2024). Strategic implications of AI integration in workforce planning and talent forecasting. *Journal of Advanced Computing Systems*, *4*(1), 1–9. DOI: 10.69987/JACS.2024.40101

Yashini, P., Karthika, G., Sunitha, T. R., Renugadevi, R., & Magthalin, B. R. (2024). Machine learning-based textile fabric defect detection network. In *4th International Conference on Sustainable Expert Systems (ICSES)* (pp. 1470–1477).

Yeoh, W., & Koronios, A. (2010). Critical success factors for business intelligence systems. *Journal of Computer Information Systems*, *50*(3), 23–32. DOI: 10.1080/08874417.2010.11645404

Yeoh, W., & Popovic, A. (2016). Extending the understanding of critical success factors for implementing business intelligence systems. *Journal of the Association for Information Science and Technology*, *67*(1), 134–147. DOI: 10.1002/asi.23366

Ye, S., Wen, H., Qiu, Y., Pan, X., & Wang, C. (2024). Simulation of annual investment forecast of power grid infrastructure construction based on data mining algorithm. In *2024 Asia-Pacific Conference on Software Engineering, Social Network Analysis and Intelligent Computing (SSAIC)* (pp. 99–104). New Delhi, India. DOI: 10.1109/SSAIC61213.2024.00025

Yin, T. (2018). Data mining application to power grid PMU data (Master's thesis, University of Wyoming). https://doi.org/DOI: 10.13140/RG.2.2.27662.45125

Youssif, A., Eid, N. M., & Safan, S. M. (2017). Staff performance appraisal system and its relation to their job satisfaction and empowerment: Developing performance appraisal tool. *IOSR Journal of Nursing and Health Science*, *6*(2), 25–26. DOI: 10.9790/1959-0602091727

Yusliza, M. Y., Othman, N. Z., & Jabbour, C. J. C. (2019). Deciphering the implementation of green human resource management in an emerging economy. *Journal of Management Development*, *38*(2), 110–125.

Yusliza, M., Faezah, J., Ali, N., Noor, N., Ramayah, T., Tanveer, M., & Fawehinmi, O. (2020). Effects of supportive work environment on employee retention: The mediating role of person–organisation fit. *Industrial and Commercial Training*, *53*(3), 201–216. DOI: 10.1108/ICT-12-2019-0111

Zack, M. H. (1999). Developing a knowledge strategy. *California Management Review*, *41*(3), 125–145. DOI: 10.2307/41166000

Zagalsky, A., Te'eni, D., Yahav, I., & Schwartz, D. G. (2021). The Design of Reciprocal Learning Between Human and Artificial Intelligence. Proceedings of the ACM on Human-Computer Interaction, 5(CSCW2), chapter 451. DOI: 10.1145/3479587

Zammuto, R. F., Griffith, T. L., Majchrzak, A., Dougherty, D. J., & Faraj, S. (2007). Information technology and the changing fabric of organization. *Organization Science*, *18*(5), 749–762. DOI: 10.1287/orsc.1070.0307

Zehir, C., Karaboğa, T., & Başar, D. (2020). The transformation of human resource management and its impact on overall business performance: Big data analytics and AI technologies in strategic HRM. In Hacioglu, U. (Ed.), *Digital business strategies in blockchain ecosystems: Transformational design and future of global business* (pp. 265–279). Springer. DOI: 10.1007/978-3-030-29739-8_12

Zeng, Z., Li, X., & Liu, Y. (2020). Machine learning-based risk assessment models for investment projects. *International Journal of Project Management*, *38*(2), 154–163. DOI: 10.1016/j.ijproman.2019.10.005

Zerva, S., Belias, D., Rossidis, I., & Ntalakos, A. (2024). Examining the impact of leadership on job satisfaction in Greek luxury hotels. *Journal of Human Resources in Hospitality & Tourism*, *23*(3), 439–464. DOI: 10.1080/15332845.2024.2335123

Zhang, X., Zhao, Y., Tang, X., Zhu, H., & Xiong, H. (2020). Developing fairness rules for talent intelligence management system.

Zhang, H., Gao, S., & Zhou, P. (2023). Role of digitalization in energy storage technological innovation: Evidence from China. *Renewable & Sustainable Energy Reviews*, *171*, 113014. DOI: 10.1016/j.rser.2022.113014

Zhang, L. (2025). Immersive Interaction Design in Tourism and Leisure Experience Using Virtual Reality Technology. In Jesus, I. S., & Wang, K. (Eds.), *Advances in Transdisciplinary Engineering*. IOS Press., DOI: 10.3233/ATDE241376

Zhang, Y., Xu, S., Zhang, L., & Yang, M. (2021). Big data and human resource management research: An integrative review and new directions for future research. *Journal of Business Research*, *133*, 34–50. DOI: 10.1016/j.jbusres.2021.04.019

Zhu, Y., Obeng, A., & Azinga, S. (2023). Supportive supervisor behaviour and helping behaviours in the hotel sector: Assessing the mediating effect of employee engagement and moderating influence of perceived organizational obstruction. *Current Psychology (New Brunswick, N.J.)*, *43*(1), 757–773. DOI: 10.1007/s12144-023-04326-5 PMID: 36819753

Ziesche, S., & Yampoliskiy, R. V. (2025). The neglect of qualia and consciousness in AI alignment research. In: *Considerations on the AI Endgame*. Chapman and Hall/CRC, eBook ISBN: 9781003565659. DOI: 10.1201/9781003565659-11

Zohuri, B., & Moghaddam, M. (2020). From business intelligence to artificial intelligence. *Journal of Material Science and Manufacturing Research*, *3*(1), 231–240.

Zuckerberg, M. (2022). Building Metaverse: A New Frontier for Business. *Harvard Business Review*, *100*(4), 78–89.

About the Contributors

Lamprini Seremeti is an Assistant Professor in the Department of Agricultural Economics & Rural Development at the School of Applied Economics and Social Science of the Agricultural University of Athens. She holds a PhD in Computer Science with a focus on propagating knowledge in networks of aligned ontologies from Hellenic Open University; a Master in Special Education from University of Rome; a Master in Pure Mathematics from University of Patras; a Bachelor in Mathematics from University of Patras; a Bachelor in Informatics from University of Western Greece; and a Bachelor in Law from University of Nicosia. She has also participated as a researcher in EU-funded projects, in which, her tasks involved mathematical modeling, data processing, knowledge representation and management, and conceptualization of heterogeneous environments (socio-economic, educational, biomedical, ambient intelligent). Her research interests focus on theories applied in interpretation of Law in ambient intelligent environments, knowledge representation and management through ontologies, and mathematical modeling of co-evolving systems. She can be contacted at email: lseremeti@uowm.gr

Panagiotis Liargovas received his BA degree from the University of Athens and his MA and Ph.D degrees in Economics from Clark University. He has been a Fulbright Scholar, a Bakalas Foundation Scholar, a Teaching Assistant Scholar (Clark University) and a European Commission trainee (Brussels). He has taught in many Universities including Clark University, Bologna University, and University of Strasbourg. He has served as economic advisor to the Greek Ministry of Finance, the Greek Ministry of Foreign Affairs and the Municipality of Athens in many occasions. For the period 2013-18 he was the Head of the Parliamentary Budget Office at the Hellenic Parliament. He is currently Chairman of the Board of the Centre of Planning and Economic Research (KEPE) and of the National Productivity Board. He is also Professor of Economics at the University of Peloponnese. He has made more than 100 publications in academic journals and has published more than 20 books.

Christos Papademetriou, teaches at the University of Neapolis in Pafos since 2010. He is an Assistant Professor in Management – Human Resources Management at the School of Economics, Administration and Computer Science. He is a Coordinator of the Distance Master in Business Administration (DMBA). He was teaching in the Department of Business Administration at the Open University of Cyprus (2017-2020). He obtained a BA (Hons) in Accounting and Business (2001) and MA in International Management (2002) from the University of Sunderland. He was awarded also a BSc (Hons) in Computing and the Postgraduate Certificate in Information Systems from the University of Portsmouth. He also holds an MA in Real Estate from University of Neapolis. He holds a doctorate (PhD) in Social Science from the University of Leicester, UK. The title of his thesis is "Investigating the Impact of Sequential Cross-Cultural Training on the Level of Sociocultural and Psychological Adjustment of Expatriate Mangers". Furthermore, he obtained a Postdoctoral from the University of Western Macedonia. His research interests are in the areas of Management, Human Resource Management, Organizational Behaviour, Tourism Business Administration, Educational Management, Service Quality and Tourism and Hospitality Management.

Lazaros Anastasiadis is a Political Scientist. He holds a master Degree in Informatics, AUTH and cuttently has followed a PhD Degree from the University of Patras, Greece. He has published over many articles in International and Greek Journals as well as in International and Greek Conferences. He has participated in scientific dialogues/round tables at International and Greek Conferences.

Sofia Anastasiadou is a Professor of Statistics and Research Methodology, Biostatistics and Biomedical Research at the School of Health of the University of Western Macedonia (UOWM), Department of Midwifery. She is the Deam of School of Health of UOWM, and a Member of the Dean of the School of Economics of the University of Western Macedonia. She is also a Member of the Senate and a MODIP Member of the same University. Since 2020 she is the President of Greek Society of Data Analysis (GSDA). She has been a founding Member since 2001. She has been Secretary General since 2016. Sofia Anastasiadou makes a constant effort for the development and dissemination of Data Analysis and Multidimensional Statistical Analysis methods, such as Principal Component Analysis, Factor Analysis, Factor Analysis of Correspondences, Symbolic Analysis, Inductive Statistics, Discriminant Analysis, Cluster Analysis, Implicative Statistical Analysis and new fields that can be developed based on relevant international developments in statistical science.

***

Eleni E. Anastasopoulou is a Lecturer in Sustainable Entrepreneurship at the Neapolis University Pafos. She holds a Ph.D. in Sustainable Agri-food Entrepreneurship from the University of the Peloponnese, an M.Sc. in Pharmacognosy and Chemistry of Natural Products from the Faculty of Pharmacy at the National and Kapodistrian University of Athens, and a Bachelor's degree in Agriculture with a specialization in Food Science and Technology from the Aristotle University of Thessaloniki. During her studies, she was awarded a scholarship by the Department of Economics at the University of Athens for the "Entrepreneurship in Practice" program. Her research focuses on sustainable development, technological innovation in the agri-food and tourism sectors, rural national and European policies related to agri-food entrepreneurship and the improvement of the quality of life of people living in rural areas. She has published in high-impact international peer-reviewed journals, including 'Journal of Rural Studies' ranked ABS:3, 'Strategic Change' and 'The International Journal of Entrepreneurship and Innovation', both ranked ABS:2, and has also contributed as co-editor of an edited volume and co-author of book chapters. She has presented at more than 20 international peer-reviewed conferences. She also brings extensive experience as a Researcher in EU-funded research projects. Her previous working experience include managing and monitoring agricultural sector funded projects, as well as a product management position in both the public and private sectors.

Dimitrios Belias is an Assistant Professor in the Department of Business Administration, School of Management and Economics, at the University of Thessaly, Greece, with the subject " Organization and Services Management in the Tourist Market ". His research interests are in the areas of Management, Human Resource Management, Organizational Behavior, Tourism Business Administration, Educational Management, Service Quality and Tourism and Hospitality Management. He has published 1 book and 52 chapters in books on Service Management, Organizational Behavior and Tourism and Hospitality Management, 70 articles in national and international peer-reviewed journals and has more than 70 conference presentations in the areas of organization behavior, human resource management, Organization and Services Management and Tourism and Hospitality Management. His work is internationally recognized as it has more than 1.700 references and i10-index 28 (PorP). Currently he is member in many scientific and professional bodies.

Georgios Deirmentzoglou is an Assistant Professor in International Entrepreneurship, Technology, and Sustainable Development at Neapolis University Pafos (Cyprus). He holds a PhD in Business Administration from the University of Piraeus, where he also earned an MBA with a specialization in Total Quality

Management (MBA-TQM) and a Bachelor's degree in Industrial Management and Technology. Additionally, he has pursued studies in film and music production. Before joining Neapolis University Pafos, Georgios served as an Adjunct Lecturer and Academic Fellow at the University of Piraeus and other colleges in Greece in partnership with UK and French universities. His research interests focus on entrepreneurship, technological innovation, human-computer interaction, sustainable development, and tourism. His research has been published in high-impact international peer-reviewed journals and presented at more than 30 international peer-reviewed conferences. Georgios has extensive experience as a Principal Investigator and Researcher in EU-funded projects, primarily focusing on digital transformation and sustainable development. Beyond academia, he has practical expertise in e-commerce, including the creation and management of online stores, and is the co-founder of a consulting firm specializing in information systems and software.

Durga Devi A, M.E., (Ph.D), is in College teaching profession since 2022. she received her B.E (ECE) Degree from Panimalar Institute of Technology, chennai, India in 2018 and M.E (VLSI DESIGN) from Saveetha Engineering College, Affiliated to Anna University, Chennai in 2020. She has been teaching various subjects, under graduate students for the past 3 years. She has Published 4 papers in reputed journals and conference and also published patent and book chapters. Presently working as Assistant professor at Electronics and Communication Engineering department in Saveetha Engineering College, Chennai, India. Also she is currently a part time Ph.D. scholar at Anna University, Chennai, India. Her-research interests are Deep Learning, VLSI,Embedded systems, Machine Learning. She is a dedicated teacher.

K. Jamberi is an Associate Professor, Research Supervisor, Postdoctoral Fellow, and Journal Reviewer, the School of Computer Science and Applications, REVA University, Bangalore and published more than 50 research papers in reputed indexed journals, registered 5 patents, and published 3 books and several book chapters. He attended over 50 workshops and conferences at reputed colleges and universities, both online and offline. Additionally, more than 100 student projects have been successfully completed under his guidance.

Priya Kadyan is a highly accomplished professional with a robust educational background and extensive experience in the field of Human Resources. She holds a postgraduate degree in Business Administration from Pune University, specializing in HR and BA. Presently, she is diligently pursuing her PhD at Chandigarh University, focusing on HR-related research.

Shweta Tewari is a distinguished academic and professional in the field of business administration. She earned her Doctor of Business Administration (DBA) from the SP Jain School of Global Management in 2020. Following her doctoral studies, Dr. Tewari founded Amitiel Consultants in India, reflecting her commitment to bridging academic insights with practical business solutions. In addition to her consulting endeavors, Dr. Tewari has contributed to academia as a faculty member at Dayananda Sagar University in Bengaluru, India. Her research interests are diverse, encompassing leadership styles, productivity, and the impact of social media on employer branding. One of her notable publications includes a study on leadership styles and productivity, co-authored with colleagues from SP Jain School of Global Management. Dr. Tewari is also an author, having published 'A Marketing Handbook' aimed at professionals, students, and marketing enthusiasts. Her work continues to influence both the academic community and the business sector, particularly in areas related to marketing strategies and organizational behavior.

Athanasios Koustelios is a Professor in the Department of Business Administration at the University of Thessaly, Greece. He has published more than 120 papers in International and Greek refereed journals and has more than 180 conference presentations. His research expertise is in the area of human resource management and organizational behaviour.

R. Renugadevi completed her PhD in 2022 from Anna University, Chennai. She is currently working as Associate professor in Saveetha Engineering College. She has more than 20 years of teaching experience in engineering colleges.She published more than 40 papers in international journals, conferences and holds 10 patents. Her research interest includes Machine learning, Internet of Things, Wireless Sensor Networks and Cloud computing. She is a life member of ISTE, CSI and IAENG. She is a reviewer and Editotorial member of many International Journals.

Sanjay K serves as the Director of Placement and Corporate Relations at Dayananda Sagar Institutions, where he is committed to building strong connections between students and industry leaders. With a focus on empowering the future workforce, he facilitates successful placements for approximately 600 students across five esteemed business schools under the Dayananda Sagar umbrella. His mission is to bridge the gap between academia and the corporate world, ensuring that students transition seamlessly into meaningful and impactful professional roles.

Rohan Singh currently holds the Associate Professor in Management position at Chandigarh University, Punjab. His primary focus in research lies within the domains of Human Resource Management, delving into the complex dynamics shaping HR strategies and their adaptation in the era of AI, gig workers, and hybrid work practices and also exploring the relation between HRM and various performance metrics. Additionally, he engages in various academic activities, including serving as a guest faculty, keynote speaker, session chair, acting as a resource person for FDP sessions and participating as an external examiner (Master's and Research Scholars), among others. He has showcased his research prowess by publishing in esteemed international journals and conferences, accumulating an impressive citation count of over 500. In addition to his academic role, Dr. Singh boasts over 14 years of comprehensive experience in the field of Overall Project Management at the Sponsored Research & Industrial Consultancy Cell of the esteemed Indian Institute of Technology Kharagpur. He has extensive experience in evaluating scholarly manuscripts. Over the years, he has contributed to the peer-review process for numerous prestigious journals, ensuring the integrity and quality of published research as Associate Editor, Editorial Review Board Member, Advisory Board Member, Reviewer Board Member, Advisory-cum-Reviewers' Board Member and National Member.

Dil Afrin Swarna is a renowned expert in education and research. She holds a research-based MBA in Human Resource Management (HRM) from the National University of Bangladesh. Swarna's passion for HRM drives her to explore various themes, showcasing her understanding of business dynamics and interconnections. Her research benefits both academia and industry. Swarna has delved into organizational behavior, employee development, and strategic management, demonstrating the critical role of HRM in corporate performance and offering practical solutions to current managerial challenges. She actively participates in conferences, publishes articles, and collaborates with other specialists in education and research. Her innovative approaches to HRM challenges are highly regarded and push the boundaries of existing knowledge. Through her dedication to research and teaching, Dil Afrin Swarna continues to make significant contributions to academia and her industry. Her work exemplifies how committed and insightful research can enhance organizational practices and deepen our understanding of human resource management.

Mohammad Badruddoza Talukder is an Associate Professor, College of Tourism and Hospitality Management, IUBAT - International University of Business Agriculture and Technology, Dhaka, Bangladesh. He holds PhD in Hotel Management from Lovely Professional University, India. He has been teaching various courses in the Department of Tourism and Hospitality at various universities in Bangladesh since 2008. His research areas include tourism management, hotel management, hospitality management, food & beverage management, and accommodation management, where he has published research papers in well-known journals in Bangladesh and abroad. Mr. Talukder is one of the executive members of the Tourism Educators Association of Bangladesh. He has led training and consulting for a wide range of hospitality organizations in Bangladesh. He just became an honorary facilitator at the Bangladesh Tourism Board's Bangabandhu international tourism and hospitality training institution.

Nikolaos Tsigilis is an Associate Professor in the Department of Journalism and Mass Media Communication, Aristotle University of Thessaloniki, Greece. He has published more than 120 papers in International and Greek refereed journals and has a variety of conference presentations. His research expertise is in the area of methodology and psychometrics of Social Sciences

Mary Viterouli is the Deputy Director at the DYPA Higher Vocational Training School in Chalkida, Greece, and is currently pursuing a Ph.D. at the University of Thessaly. She has participated in and presented at various renowned international conferences and has published peer-reviewed books, chapters, and articles. Her scientific interests include Strategic Management, Human Resources Management, Adult Education, Sociology, and English Literature.

Index

A

B

C

D

O

P

Q

R

S

T

W

www.ingramcontent.com/pod-product-compliance
Lightning Source LLC
LaVergne TN
LVHW080352011026
849161LV00009B/2282